THE DOUBLE ELEPHANT FOLIO

THE STORY OF
AUDUBON'S *BIRDS OF AMERICA*

Shown on the cover is the wing tip of an American Magpie. Plate 357, the Audubon print of that bird, appears as the frontispiece. The endpapers are printed with the pictures of the Chinese wallpaper at Temple Newsam House to which had been affixed a number of birds cut out of the first volume of Audubon's *Birds of America*.

Plate 357, "American Magpie." Courtesy of the Library, Field Museum of Natural History.

THE DOUBLE ELEPHANT FOLIO

THE STORY OF
AUDUBON'S
BIRDS
OF AMERICA

WALDEMAR H. FRIES

AMERICAN LIBRARY ASSOCIATION
CHICAGO 1973

LIBRARY OF CONGRESS CATALOGING IN PUBLICATION DATA

Fries, Waldemar H   1889–
    The double elephant folio.

    Includes bibliographical references.
    1. Audubon, John James, 1785-1851. The birds of America. 2. Audubon, John James, 1785-1851.
I. Title.
QL674.A953F74   598.2'973   73-12101
ISBN 0-8389-0103-4

JAN 6 '75

Copyright © 1973 by the American Library Association.
All rights reserved. No part of this publication
may be reproduced in any form without permission
in writing from the publisher, except by
a reviewer who may quote brief
passages in a review.

Printed in the United States of America

To
Elizabeth

without whose encouragement
and help
this work would not have reached fruition

CONTENTS

Illustrations xi
Acknowledgments xiii
Apologia xxi

I
CREATION OF THE DOUBLE ELEPHANT FOLIO OF *BIRDS OF AMERICA*

1	Search for an Engraver, 1823–1826	3
2	Edinburgh and Lizars, 1826–1827	12
3	First Visit to London, 1827	17
4	From Lizars to Havell, 1827	23
5	London and Paris, 1828	27
6	First Return to America, 1829–1830	35
7	Supervising the Work in England, 1830	42
8	The Letterpress, 1830–1831	47
9	Second Return to America, 1831–1832	56
10	Boston and the Labrador Journey, 1832	67
11	Winter at Charleston, 1833–1834	77
12	In London Again, 1834–1836	86
13	Third Return to America, 1836–1837	97
14	Completion of the "Great Work," 1837–1839	107

CONTENTS

15	Sale of the Remaining Folios	115
16	Audubon, Artist and Scientist	126

II

SUBSCRIBERS, SETS, AND COSTS

17	Subscribers	137
18	Original Subscription List	141
19	Final Lists of Subscribers	151
20	Complete and Incomplete Sets	172
21	Sets Broken Up or Destroyed	181
22	Sets Recorded but Present Locations Not Known	187
23	Distribution of the Sets and Statistical Summary	193
24	Original Cost and Subsequent Prices	197

III

CENSUS AND SURVEY OF EXTANT COMPLETE SETS

25	Questions of Internal Evidence: Legends and Watermarks of Prints of the First Ten Plates	209
26	Provenances of Sets in the United States and Canada	225
27	Provenances of Sets in England and Scotland	325
28	Provenances of Sets in Other Countries	343

APPENDIXES

A	Octavo Edition	353
B	The Bien Chromolithograph Edition	355
C	Joseph Bartholomew Kidd and the Oil Paintings of Audubon's *Birds of America*	360
D	Reproductions of Audubon's *Birds of America*	368
E	Uncolored Prints of the *Birds of America*	383
F	Editions of Audubon's Prospectus	385
G	The Copper Plates	390
H	Chronology of the Engraving of the Plates	399

Contents

I	Bay's Alphabetical Index to the *Birds of America*	401
J	Woodward's List	416
K	Additional Variants Found in Plate Legends and Watermarks	421
L	Subscribers Whose Names Audubon Published	440
M	Subscribers Who Discontinued and Amounts Paid	452
	Abbreviations of Works Cited	453
	Notes	455
	Index	485

ILLUSTRATIONS

Frontispiece
American Magpie, Plate 357

Audubon's Ledger "B"	*following page* 58
Shipping box, 2 views	
Page from an Audubon exhibition catalogue	
Announcement of an Audubon exhibition	
Audubon's 1834 announcement of publication of *Birds of America*	102
Audubon's 1837 announcement of publication of *Birds of America*	
Dialogue mentioning Audubon in a popular 19th-century magazine	
Columbia Jays from Plate 96 mounted on Chinese wallpaper	
The Flicker (pl.37) and the Florida Jay (pl.67) mounted on Chinese wallpaper	
Audubon's handwritten invitation to an exhibition	
Audubon's folder of subscribers' names	176
A portion of the list of subscribers	
Detail, showing the Duke of Orleans' signature	
Detail, showing the signature of Edward Everett	
Prospectus for the Octavo edition	
Display of individual prints at the Shelburne Museum	
Display of individual prints at Manoir Richelieu	
1931 prices of Audubon prints	
The New York State Library's Double Elephant folio saved from a fire	

ILLUSTRATIONS

Two representations of legends of Plate 3	*following page* 222
Two representations of legends of Plate 4	
Two representations of legends of Plate 5	
Two representations of legends of Plate 9	
Plate 110 of the Field Museum set	268
Plate 9 of the Field Museum set	
Composite Plate 110 of the Field Museum set	
Ottoman built to house the Euphemia Gifford set, 2 views	
J. Whatman watermark	
Legend of Plate 2, showing erasures and watermark	
The Field Museum's Double Elephant folio	334
One volume of the Trinity College Library set	
One volume of the set belonging to the Public Library of Cincinnati and Hamilton County	
Two volumes of the Duke University set	
One volume of the Audubon Shrine and Wildlife Sanctuary set	
One volume of the Lord Hesketh set	
Kidd's (?) oil painting of Audubon's "Song Sparrow"	436
Damascene plate depicting Audubon's "Red-shouldered Hawk"	
Damascene plate depicting Audubon's "Stilt Sandpiper"	
Prospectus to *Birds of America*, first and second sheets	
Plate 34, showing Audubon's instructions to Havell	
Plate 230, two states	
Plate 6, two states	

ACKNOWLEDGMENTS

It was at the Free Library of Philadelphia that I first saw, carefully protected by a glass case, the opened volumes of the Double Elephant Folio of Audubon's *Birds of America*. The label stated that these had been the Naturalist's own set and that the volumes contained 13 more than the usual 435 prints. When I retired from business in the mid-1950s, I began to look for other sets of the folio. However, at that time I did not contemplate entering upon an Audubon research project, that of tracking down the extant sets and preparing for publication a complete story of Audubon's remarkable accomplishment. As I began to locate additional sets, the one at the Houghton Library at Harvard University was the first to be examined carefully. This set had been brought out for me by the assistant librarian, G. W. Cottrell. As we were examining the prints, questions arose, not only about the prints but about the work in general, the answers to which neither of us seemed to know. It was then that Mr. Cottrell turned to me and said, "You have retired from business and have the time. Why don't you do something about it?" Thus the "Elephant Hunt" (so designated by my artist friend, Edward Shenton of Philadelphia) began in earnest.

However, as this Audubon project continued, it was to develop into more than just the search for the extant sets and the provenance of these. The ramifications of the work is established by the table of contents. Much of what has been accomplished in the fifteen years of research was made possible only with the cooperation of many individuals, personally or in their professional capacities as librarians, curators, and the like.

It is with a sense of deep appreciation and with renewed thanks, that I record the names of those helpful persons. As the scope of the research broadened, additional visits were made to the Houghton Library for here there is a very large collection of Auduboniana, including Audubon family correspondence, original journals of the Naturalist, early drawings, and other material. On these many visits there was the unstinted help of Carolyn Jakeman and her associates and, on

ACKNOWLEDGMENTS

occasion, that of Roger Stoddard. In connection with the folio in the Widener Library, Robert H. Haynes offered his assistance. In Boston, Stephen T. Riley, Director, and the library staff at the Massachusetts Historical Society helped locate information concerning the New England subscribers to the *Birds of America*.

Since the writing of the manuscript was done in Providence, R. I., I was extremely fortunate that there were available the resources of the libraries of Brown University. Here the librarian, David Jonah, took a personal interest, often passing along Audubon material which came to his attention. In the circulation department Paul Richards and Mary Vandersea were ever ready to help locate needed material. When reproductions of illustrations were required, George Henderson and his staff in the Photographic Laboratory were close at hand. Finally, Thomas Adams of the John Carter Brown Library furnished the letters of introduction to members of the staff of the British Museum which were to aid me in obtaining access to various departments of that institution.

It was fortunate for me that in Providence there were two sets of the folio, one originally subscribed for by the Providence Athenaeum, and the other in the possession of Albert E. Lownes (which he recently presented to Brown University). On numerous occasions when it was necessary to make comparisons of prints, the permission to examine the folios was generously granted by Mr. Lownes and Mrs. Annie C. Cook of the Athenaeum. While visits to the Providence Public Library were not frequent, Stuart Sherman and his staff did supply some much-needed information. Finally, in the library of the Rhode Island School of Design were found references to exhibitions of Audubon prints.

Frequent requests were made of rare book dealers for information relating to provenance. I am indebted to the following for their help: the late Harry S. Newman, Mable Zahn, Warren R. Howell, George Goodspeed, and J. N. Bartfield.

Over the years my wife and I visited many libraries, universities, and other public institutions. Always, when the purpose of our research became known, the most cordial and helpful cooperation was forthcoming. Let me now recall briefly those who extended their help: Amherst College, Newton McKeon; Bowdoin College, Richard Harwell, Kenneth Carpenter; The City College in the City of New York, Miss Isbenderian; Columbia University, Halsey Thomas. When I examined the folio at Columbia University I was told that Laurence Gomme, at one time manager of Brentano's Rare Book Department and for many years an appraiser of rare books and libraries, had begun making a record of those Audubon folios which had appeared in auction sales and in dealers' catalogs. When he was informed of my Audubon research he graciously shared this information with me.

Assistance was also given by: Cornell University, Michael Jasenas; Duke University, Evelyn Harrison (at the Woman's College Library); University of Illinois, E. B. Downes; Indiana University, the Lilly Library, David Randall (who also helped with the provenance of several sets); Johns Hopkins University (Evergreen House), Elizabeth Baer; Université Laval (Quebec), Antonio Drolet;

Acknowledgments

Lehigh University, James D. Mack; Louisiana State University, Mrs. Kenneth Kahao; McGill University (Wood Library of Ornithology), Margaret E. Hubbard; University of Michigan, Russell E. Bidlack (whose research on the folio at the university contributed much to the story of the provenance of the set); University of Minnesota, John Parker; Northwestern University, Jens Nyholm; University of Southern California, Hancock Library of Biology and Oceanography, Dorothy M. Halmos; Syracuse University, Lester G. Wells; Trinity College, Donald B. Engley; Union College, Helmer L. Webb, Edwin K. Tolan, Ruth Anne Evans; Vassar College, Dorothy A. Plum; Williams College (Chapin Library), Rex Dennis Parady; University of Wisconsin, Samuel A. Ives; Yale University, Marjorie G. Wynne.

Certain of the library visits were especially fruitful. At the Legislative Library of New Brunswick, Canada, there was kept a complete file of Auduboniana collected by the librarian, Maurice P. Boone. Among the papers was a newspaper clipping which helped to locate the Audubon family folio, the one I had seen at the Free Library of Philadelphia and which is presently in Texas. During the visit to the Grosvenor Reference Library, Buffalo, the librarian, Jane D. Van Arsdale, brought to my attention the copy of "A Brief Record of the Elephant folio edition of Audubon's Birds of America, to Whom They Belong and Where They Can Be Found." This had been prepared many years previously by Anthony Woodward, the first librarian of the American Museum of Natural History. I have never located another copy of this list, and how it came into possession of the donor of the set at the library is not known.

Other libraries follow: Boston Public Library, John Alden, Harriet Swift; also in Boston, The Athenaeum, Walter Muir Whitehill, Ebenezer Gray, David McKibben; another Athenaeum, that in Minneapolis, Betty L. Engebretson; Charleston Library Society, Virginia Rugheimer; Peabody Institute Library (now a branch of the Enoch Pratt Library of Baltimore), Frank N. Jones; Free Library of New Bedford, James S. Healey, Frances Ann Bold; John Crerar Library, Herman H. Henkle, William S. Buddington. It was my good fortune to visit with Jens Christian Bay at his home, shortly before his death. It was he who, while librarian at the Crerar, had prepared an "Alphabetical Index to the Birds of America." James Jerome Hill Reference Library, Russell F. Barnes; Library Association of Portland, Oregon, James H. Burghardt, Mrs. Annette Bartholomae, Bernhard Van Horne; Library of Congress, Fred R. Goff, J. Melvin Edelstein; National War College Library, C. J. Stansfield; Library of Parliament, Ottawa, Francis A. Hardy, A. Pamela Hardisty; Milwaukee Public Library, Wilbert B. Beck; New York Public Library, Karl Kup, Joseph T. Rankin; New York Society Library, Sylvia C. Hilton; the Pierpont Morgan Library, F. B. Adams, Jr.; The Public Library of Cincinnati and Hamilton County, Yeatman Anderson III; St. Louis Mercantile Library Association, Clarence E. Miller, Elizabeth Tindall; The Toronto Public Library, Jean MacMillan (also providing assistance in the provenance of this folio was James L. Baillie, Department of Ornithology, Royal Ontario Museum); The Free Library of Philadelphia, Emerson Greenaway

ACKNOWLEDGMENTS

(whose inquiries regarding two folios during a visit to Russia were to be of considerable help), Howell J. Heaney; California State Library, Eugene Pike; the Commonwealth of Massachusetts, State House Library, Ruth G. Hedden; State Library, Annapolis, Maryland, Nelson J. Molter; McKissick Memorial Library, University of South Carolina, Alfred Rawlinson, Mrs. Mary Shipps; North Carolina State Library, Mrs. Georgia R. Faison.

Art Galleries: Delaware Art Museum, Bruce St. John; Henry E. Huntington Library and Art Gallery, Robert O. Schad, Leonard Gregory; Museum of Fine Arts of Boston, Francis Dolloff; National Academy of Fine Arts, Katharine Shepard; The R. W. Norton Art Gallery, Richard W. Norton, Jr.

Academies: American Philosophical Society—not only was the folio examined but the large collection of Audubon letters was to be especially helpful. During the many visits courteous assistance was received from Mrs. Gertrude Hess and her associates, Mrs. Duncan and Messrs Smith and Spawn; Academy of Natural Sciences of Philadelphia, Mrs. Maurice Phillips; California Academy of Sciences, whose folio, which was donated to the Academy by Edward E. Hills, has not been examined; however, considerable correspondence concerning the set has been carried on with Ray Brian, present librarian, and his predecessor, Veronica J. Sexton.

Institutions: Peabody Institute, Eban Dale Sutton Reference Library, Miss Dorothy Cooper; Louisiana State Museum, C. E. Frampton; Smithsonian Institution, H. G. Deignan, Thomas Montague Beggs. Here I would like to interject my thanks to Roger Pineau, managing editor of the Smithsonian Press, for his thoughtfulness in bringing my manuscript to the attention of the American Library Association.

Audubon Societies: National Audubon Society (N.Y.C.), Amy Clampitt; Audubon Shrine and Wildlife Sanctuary (Pa.), J. D'Arcy Northwood. The folio now held here was originally shown to me by Frederic Church at the home of his sister-in-law, in Locust Valley, New York. It was Mr. Church who made available the correspondence through which it became possible to determine the provenance of the set. The folio at the Audubon State Park Museum, Henderson, Kentucky, was first examined at the home of Mrs. Carll Tucker. At the Audubon Museum I also received the help and cooperation of Mrs. Thomas E. Lett and her associate, Mrs. Oscar Hurst, when I checked the large collection of Auduboniana which the museum contains and which was leased by the State of Kentucky from Miss Matilda Tyler and Mrs. Charles E. Winters, descendants of the Naturalist, who had given me permission to make the examination. I am also grateful to another Audubon descendant, Morris Tyler of New Haven, for the opportunity to examine certain Audubon material in his possession.

Foundations: Mitchell Wolfson Foundation, Inc., Key West, Florida, Mrs. Lillian Stone (this folio was examined while it was still on loan to the National Audubon Society in New York City); H. J. Lutcher Stark Foundation, Orange, Texas. In addition to the examination of the folio, my visits to the office of Mr. Stark were for the purpose of obtaining a complete description of the 13 extra

Acknowledgments

prints which the set contained. In this endeavor, many helpful facilities were made available to me, including the services of his secretary, Mrs. Willie Lee DeLane.

Historical Societies: Indiana Historical Society, Caroline Dunn; New-York Historical Society, Carolyn Scoon.

Museums: American Museum of Natural History, Hazel Gay. As the Audubon research progressed, I received encouragement in my efforts from the following members of the museum staff—Robert Cushman Murphy, Dean Amadon, and E. Thomas Gilliard. Other museums were: Buffalo Museum of Science, Ruth A. Sparrow; Carnegie Museum, Anna R. Tauber; Charleston Museum, E. Milby Burton; Cleveland Museum of Natural Science, William Scheele, James R. Skelley; The Cooper Union for Advancement of Science, Gerd Muehsam, Fred H. Graves; Field Museum of Natural History, Meta P. Howell, E. Leland Webber, W. Peyton Fawcett; Peabody Museum, Salem, Massachusetts, Dorothy E. Snyder (whose continued interest in the Audubon research has been stimulating), Paul Blanchette.

Schools: Oliver Wendell Holmes Library, Phillips Academy, Andover, Massachusetts, Elizabeth Eades; The Groton School, Groton, Massachusetts, Henry H. Richards, Betty Gash.

There is now the opportunity to renew my thanks to those who granted to my wife and me the privilege of visiting their homes to examine an Audubon folio: John Henry Dick, Mr. and Mrs. Daniel W. Evans, Mrs. Grace Phillips, Mr. and Mrs. H. Bradley Martin, Mr. and Mrs. Paul Mellon (and their curator, Willis VanDevanter), Mr. and Mrs. Joseph Verner Reed, Mrs. Carll Tucker, and Mr. and Mrs. Edwin Vare.

When my wife and I decided to journey abroad to search for and examine folios, our work in England and Scotland was made easier by a stroke of good fortune. In the late 1950s Katharine Tousey, a member of the staff of the Massachusetts Audubon Society, had spent many months in those countries, lecturing on Audubon and exhibiting a film depicting various sections of the United States in which the Naturalist had travelled. While engaged in this endeavor, she also began a search for the Audubon folios and did locate several. Before we left on our trip, this information was made available to me, a kind and thoughtful favor for which I was most grateful and which simplified my own work.

In London, our first visit was to the Reading Room at the British Museum where the folios were examined with the help and under the supervision of Harold Nixon and Ian R. Williams; this was followed by the examination of the set at the British Museum (Natural History) on Cornwell Road where our guides and helpers were M. J. Rowland, Gavin Bridson, and Frederick C. Sawyer; at the Victoria and Albert Museum J. P. Fuller did the honors.

While in London I learned that the set originally subscribed for by the Society of Writers to Her Majesty's Signet in Edinburgh and purchased a short time previously was temporarily at the establishment of H. Sotheran, Ltd. Mr. L. J. Simpson of that firm very kindly notified Mr. Stanley Smith, the father of the present owner, of our presence in London. Not only was permission obtained to examine the set, but Mr. Smith joined us in this activity. During our London visit, we also had occasion to thank Edmund M. Dring, Managing Director of Bernard Quaritch, Ltd., for having helped us with the provenance of certain sets which had passed through the hands of that firm. While in London I had hoped that I might personally thank Lionel Robinson who had sent me helpful information concerning those folios which he had sold. However, my visit to 16 Pall Mall was in vain, for he was not at home.

Audubon had recorded a subscription with the "London Institution." A visit to the University of London, with the aid of Miss P. M. Baker, produced considerable information concerning the provenance of this set.

Prior to the trip abroad I had discovered that there were also a number of folios in other countries besides England and Scotland. In determining the provenance of the French subscribers, I was aided by the information provided me through the help of Joseph Verner Reed who, in 1958, while assistant to the American Ambassador, Amory Houghton, had arranged for certain preliminary research on my behalf.

Thus there was now undertaken an extended journey to visit the locations where the folios could be examined. A listing of the libraries, museums, and other institutions visited follows, together with the names of those persons who graciously gave their time to help us in our work.

Academies and Museums: Academy of Sciences, Zoological Institute, Leningrad, Professor A. I. Ivanov, C. B. Yuriev; Darwin Museum, Moscow, Madam Ignatieva Vera; Zoological Museum, Moscow, Professor C. P. Dement'ev, who, with Professor Ivanov, helped me in the location of the Russian sets. The Polish Academy of Science, Institute of Zoology, Warsaw, Professor Nast, Joseph Miecyzslaw, Curator of Birds, who showed us the beautiful collection of South American hummingbirds, and Jan Pinowski; Staatliche Museen, Meiningen (Thuringia), Deutsche Demokratische Republik (This folio was not examined. I was advised of it by Dr. Claus Nissen of Mainz and detailed information concerning the prints was sent to me by Ludwig Baege, Erfurt, D.D.R.).

Libraries: Edinburgh Public Library, C. S. Minto; Biblioteca Naçional de Lisbõa, Dr. Carlotta Gil Pereira; Bibliothèque de l'Institut de France, Mme. Hautecoeur, Le Conservateur en Chef; Muséum National d'Histoire Naturelle, Bibliothèque Centrale, Mme. G. Duprat, Le Conservateur en Chef; Bibliothèque Nationale, Mlle. Françoise Gardey, Conservateur au Cabinet des Estampes; Birmingham Reference Library, Miss I. A. Wilson; The Picton Reference Library, Liverpool, G. Chandler, L. G. Hipperson, R. Bioletti, E. H. Seagroatt; Chetham's Library, Manchester, Misses Hilda Lofthouse and P. M. Leech; The John Rylands Library, Manchester, Ronald Hall, K. Fermery; Great Hall Library, Manchester, Hilda M. McGill; The Mitchell Library, Glasgow, W. A. G. Alison; Paisley Public Library, Alice A. Brown; Sandeman Library, Perth, A. J. Tait, who, through correspondence, provided the story of the Coates visit to Audubon at Minniesland; State Library, Leningrad, Fanny Davidovra; Teyler's Stichting,

Acknowledgments

Haarlem, J. H. van Borssum Buisman (and H. P. Baard, Directeur of the Frans Hals Museum, who located Mr. Buisman for us); Windsor Castle, The Royal Library, Robert Mackworth Young.

Universities: Cambridge University Library, J. C. Oates, James Claydon, Miss Mary E. Riven, University Archives; Cambridge University, Fitzwilliam Museum, Phyllis M. Giles; Oxford University, Radcliffe Science Library, W. H. Beyer, H. Stocker; The Library of Christ Church, J. F. A. Mason, H. J. R. Wing; Queen's College, R. L. M. Drummond-Hay; University Library, Scientific and Medical Department, Copenhagen, B. Lippenthin; Edinburgh University Library, C. P. Finlayson, Stanley M. Simpson; Glasgow University Library, R. C. McKenna, Clifford Dobb; University of Newcastle upon Tyne, W. S. Mitchell, C. J. Hunt, M. B. Line. I am grateful to Christopher Gilbert, for his assistance in helping to identify the "cut out" birds from the prints of *Birds of America* which were pasted on the Chinese wallpaper in Temple Newsam House, Leeds.

During our visit abroad my wife and I were most cordially welcomed in our visits to the private homes of the Duke and Duchess of Portland, Welbeck Abbey; the Duke and Duchess of Bedford, Woburn Abbey; and Lady Christian Hesketh, Easton Neston. Our thanks also to T. S. Wragg, keeper of the Devonshire Collections, who arranged for the examination of the folio at Chatsworth, and to the Honourable Lord Fitzwilliam, of Milton, who gave permission to examine the set at Wentworth Woodhouse. Since it had not been possible to examine the folio purchased by John Galvin of Loughlinstown House, county Dublin, Ireland, detailed information regarding this folio as well as photographs were sent to me by Mr. Galvin and his son, Shean.

My appreciation also is gladly and warmly extended to Howard C. Rice, former assistant librarian of Princeton University Library, for his continued encouragement during the research; to Joseph Ewan, of Tulane University, for the many pertinent references he sent to me; to Edward Dwight, of the Munson-Williams-Proctor Institute in Utica, New York, whose extensive knowledge of the Audubon paintings was freely shared; and finally to Dr. G. Edmund Gifford, Jr., for the information on the Baltimore subscribers and those in the medical profession.

Special thanks are also due to those ladies who combined in that arduous task of deciphering and transcribing the author's manuscript: Mrs. Avery Bates, while a student at Pembroke College, Mrs. Margaret Cranmer, and Mrs. Madeline Gross, who carried on the bulk of the work.

The following members of the Editorial staff of ALA—Pauline Cianciolo, Richard A. Gray, and Sylvia Royt—have provided invaluable services in the preparation of the manuscript for publication. For this cooperation the author is grateful.

APOLOGIA

> That Subscribers should die, is a thing we cannot help, that such fellows as Vigors should mortify us, cannot again be countermanded.—but depend on it our *Industry*, our truth and the regular manner in which we publish our Work—this will always prove to the World & to our Subscribers, that nothing more can be done than what we do, nay that I doubt if any other *Family* with our pecuniary means ever will raise for themselves such a *Monument* as "the Birds of America" is over their tomb! —from Audubon's letter of 21 December 1833 to his son Victor, the original of which is at the American Philosophical Society, Philadelphia, Pa.

Here is yet another book about Audubon. One may perhaps wonder why, considering the many works that have been written about the Naturalist since his death in 1851.

Books about the Naturalist began to appear within five years after he died. The first was *Audubon the Naturalist*, based for the most part on excerpts from the *Ornithological Biography*, published in 1856 in England by Mrs. Horace St. John. The author was the granddaughter of William Roscoe (1753-1831), a writer mainly of historical and botanical works, who had befriended the Naturalist when he first arrived in Liverpool in 1826.

In 1868, again published in England, came the story of Audubon's life, edited by Robert Buchanan* from materials sent to him by Lucy Audubon and consisting mostly of excerpts from the many journals Audubon had written during the periods he was away from his family. The following year an American edition

---

* *The Life and Adventures of John James Audubon, the Naturalist.* Edited from materials supplied by his widow by Robert Buchanan (London: Sampson Low, Son, and Marston, 1868; 2d ed., 1869). Róbert Williams Buchanan (1841-1901), a writer and poet in his own right, was hired by the publisher to "cut down what was prolix and unnecessary, and to connect the whole in some sort of a running narrative...." For biographical details, see John Foster Kirk, *A Supplement to Allibone's Critical Dictionary of English Literature* ... (Philadelphia: Lippincott, 1891), v.1, p.240; British Museum, *Catalogue of Printed Books*, v.28, col. 1109; *Dictionary of National Biography*, Suppl. 2 (1901-11), p.245-48.

that differed but slightly from the English edition was published. Both the English and American works were republished with frequency. From time to time other books about the Naturalist appeared, including one in 1902 with John Burroughs as the author. It was not until 1917 that a definitive biography, in two volumes, by Professor Francis Hobart Herrick, of Western Reserve University, was published.

Following Herrick's biography a spate of books about the Naturalist came along, two published as late as 1966 and 1967. Yet, how much would have been written had Audubon not produced what in 1826 Baron Cuvier described as the "most magnificent monument which has yet been raised to ornithology"? To this the English critic, Sacheverell Sitwell, added, "The *Birds of America* is a heroic undertaking; and that one man should have endured the hardships and ardours of so many long and lonely journeys, painted the pictures, written the text, and contrived the publication upon so gigantic a scale, puts his name among the immortals."

The dramatic escalation in the cost of the Double Elephant folio offers another index to the magnitude of Audubon's achievement. As Sitwell stated in 1953, "There are 435 plates in the first edition of Audubon's *Birds of America;* a reproduction of just one of them in its actual size, were there an aquatinter alive who could undertake it, would cost something approaching a thousand pounds in money at its present value." Audubon left a record of the cost of the publication from the year 1827 to its completion. This amounted to $115,640. A subscriber originally paid approximately $1,000 for a set of the folio. In November 1969 a set sold at auction for £90,000, or $216,000, the highest price to be paid for the four volumes of Audubon's "Great Work" to date.

There are, of course, references to Audubon's activities relating to the *Birds of America* scattered through many of the books written about him, but in every instance that information is merely incidental to the story of his life. The purpose of this work is to set down in detail the complete story of the Double Elephant folio, recorded from the time the Naturalist envisioned the engraving of his drawings to the present time, with the census of the extant sets of the two hundred copies which it is believed were sold and came into the possession of the public.

The table of contents indicates the extent to which the ramifications of the work of publishing *Birds of America* was pursued during fifteen years of research. A considerable portion of the information unearthed and herein included has never before been recorded.

I

CREATION
OF THE DOUBLE ELEPHANT
FOLIO OF
BIRDS OF AMERICA

1

SEARCH FOR AN ENGRAVER
1823-1826

It was on 17 May 1826 that John James Audubon, determined to find an engraver for his drawings of birds native to America, sailed from New Orleans on the ship *Delos*, under command of Captain Joseph Hatch of Kennebunk, Maine, bound for Liverpool.[1] Three years earlier, the Naturalist, then in his thirty-ninth year, had written in his journal:

> I have finally determined to break through all bonds and pursue my ornithological pursuits. My best friends regarded me as a madman, and my wife and family alone gave me encouragement. My wife determined that my genius should prevail, and that my final success as an ornithologist should be triumphant.[2]

Audubon, in his determination to "pursue his ornithological pursuits," had gone to Philadelphia in the spring of 1824. There he hoped to find help that would enable him to complete his ornithological work by arranging for the publication of his drawings. It is possible that the drawings had been sent to Philadelphia previously, for in his journal there is an entry dated 8 September 1823 reading, "I sent my drawings to Philadelphia and resolved to visit that city. . . ."[3]

At the time there were living in Philadelphia such famous and outstanding artists as Thomas Sully, Robert Rembrandt Peale, and Titian Peale. The scientists Lesueur, Thomas Say, Richard Harlan, and Charles Lucien Bonaparte were also Philadelphia residents. Bonaparte was then a young man of twenty-one but, within two years, he was to begin the publication of *American Ornithology; or the Natural History of Birds of the United States, not given by Wilson*. Also, located there were the Academy of Natural Sciences and the American Philosophical Society. Finally, it was in Philadelphia that in 1806 Alexander Wilson had begun his publication, the *American Ornithology; or The Natural History of the Birds of the United States*, which work was completed by George Ord after Wilson's death in 1814.

But Audubon's visit to Philadelphia was disappointing. He met the artists and the scientists, including Charles Lucien Bonaparte, who took him to Thomas

3

Lawson, the engraver of Wilson's *American Ornithology*. But Lawson, after seeing Audubon's drawings, had not been agreeable to engraving them. According to Audubon, Lawson found the drawings "too soft, too much like oil paintings."[4] Lawson was, however, shortly to engrave the plates for Bonaparte's work.

A journal entry indicates that Audubon had met George Ord, Alexander Wilson's friend and editor of the posthumous volumes of his *American Ornithology*, at a meeting of the "Philosophical Academy." Ord, when shown the drawings, strongly objected to the depiction of birds and plants together; however, he "spoke highly of them otherwise." At the time Ord was engaged in that edition of Wilson's work which was published in three volumes, in 1828–1829, with a folio atlas and 76 plates. This endeavor could have accounted for his antagonism toward Audubon.[5]

Fortunately, while in Philadelphia Audubon met another engraver, Gideon Fairman, who was favorably impressed and who, in appreciation of the excellence of the drawings, advised Audubon to seek an engraver in England.[6] At the time Fairman was a member of the firm of Fairman, Draper and Company. He had been a successful engraver for many years and had recently returned from a three-year residence in England. (It is possible that Fairman had suggested to Audubon the name of William Home Lizars who, in the autumn of 1826, was to begin engraving the *Birds of America*.)

Following his unsuccessful attempt in Philadelphia to arrange for the publication of his drawings, Audubon had visited New York, Niagara Falls, and Pittsburgh with a stopover in Louisville, after which he returned to Bayou Sara in Louisiana where, on one of the plantations, his wife was teaching a class of girls. Although he had made some of his finest drawings during this period in Bayou Sara, a stay which lasted until April of 1826, much of his time was spent in giving dancing and fencing lessons. As Audubon himself related, "the dancing speculation fetched two thousand dollars and with this capital and my wife's savings I was now able to foresee a successful issue to my great ornithological work."[7]

Thus it was that in April of 1826 the Naturalist packed up his drawings, said to have been "over four hundred in number,"[8] and set out for New Orleans, whence on 17 May he sailed for Liverpool. The time between leaving his wife at Bayou Sara and the departure of his ship Audubon spent in New Orleans, the sailing of the *Delos* having been delayed. The day before sailing Audubon had obtained from his old friend Vincent Nolte, a merchant in New Orleans, a letter of introduction to Richard Rathbone of Liverpool.[9] Audubon and Nolte had met first in 1811 while Audubon was returning to Henderson, Kentucky, from a visit to Mill Grove in Pennsylvania. Nolte, who had just arrived in the United States from England, was on his way to New Orleans. The meeting had taken place in a small inn, "close by the Fall of the Juniata River" in Pennsylvania.[10]

Audubon had supplied himself with many letters of introduction, including some from Henry Clay, DeWitt Clinton, Andrew Jackson, and General W. Clark. But the most valuable letter of all he carried with him was to be the one addressed to "Richard Rathbone, Esq., Liverpool," which Nolte had given him.

Search for an Engraver, 1823–1826

The *Delos* arrived in the Mersey River opposite Liverpool at 9:30 on the night of Thursday, 20 July 1826. The next morning Audubon disembarked and promptly called on Alexander Gordon, his wife's brother-in-law, who was married to Lucy Audubon's younger sister, Anne. Gordon was a partner in the counting house of Gordon, Forstall.[11] Another call was to the office of Richard Rathbone who, however, was absent. A day later Audubon received a note from Rathbone inviting him to dinner on the following Wednesday on which occasion another guest was William Roscoe, the historian and botanist. This was followed by visits to the home of William Rathbone, the father of Richard, who lived at Green Bank, three miles from Liverpool. Soon, he was asked to show his drawings not only by the Rathbones but also by other Liverpool families, such as the Traills and the Hodgsons. It was at the home of the Hodgsons that Audubon met Lord Stanley, Earl of Derby, who not only praised the drawings but later became one of the subscribers to *Birds of America*. William Roscoe also complimented him upon his drawings, telling him, "Mr. Audubon, I am filled with surprise and admiration."[12]

Not only did Roscoe extend his praises, but he arranged for Audubon to exhibit his drawings at the Liverpool Royal Institution of which Roscoe had been the first president. There are included among the Roscoe manuscripts in the Liverpool Public Libraries several letters from Audubon to William Roscoe. There is one written a few days after Audubon's arrival in Liverpool wherein he thanked Roscoe for "the draft you had made to announce the exhibition of my Drawings" and asked, "can I beg of you to be present at the Committee this morning? Your influence is such that all difficulties would be levelled before you." With another letter written on 8 September 1826, at Green Bank, the home of William Rathbone, Sr., just prior to his leaving for Manchester, he sent a drawing of a robin to Roscoe, one of the many drawings he made for his benefactors in Liverpool.[13]

The exhibition opened on 1 August with an attendance of 413 persons.[14] The following day Audubon wrote in his journal, "I put up this day two-hundred and twenty-five of my drawings, the *coup d'oeil* was not bad, and the room was crowded."[15]

A detailed account of the interest shown in the exhibition by the inhabitants of Liverpool was given by the Naturalist in a letter written on 7 August 1826 to Nicholas Berthoud, merchant at Shippingport, Kentucky, husband of Mrs. Audubon's sister, Eliza Bakewell:

> To give you an idea of the crowd that rushed to the Institution during the six hours (two hours each day for three days) that my drawings were in view (about half of the 450), at one sight hung on a purple cloth ground for the purpose of exhibiting paintings of greater merits, I will tell you that 413 persons entered the hall in two hours. And I had to stand on view and listen to the plaudits of each individual. At the request of very many of my acquaintances here, I suffered the exhibition to be general, and (to be) opened from 10 o'clock until dusk; and it has been kept crowded.[16]

This was the reception received by a total stranger who had arrived in England less than two weeks previously. The newspapers, too, were full of flattering accounts in praise of Audubon's drawings.[17] He sent a bundle of these papers to his wife in Bayou Sara.[18]

Audubon realized full well that it was the help of the Rathbone family and their friends which had been responsible, in no small way, for the splendid reception which the exhibition of his drawings was receiving. In his journal on 17 September he said, "I have been thinking over my stay in Liverpool, surely I can never express my indebtedness to my many friends there, especially the Roscoes, the families Rathbone and Dr. Thomas S. Traill."[19]

The drawings were exhibited in Liverpool for four weeks without a cent of expenses and brought in a hundred pounds. When the exhibition had first opened, it was suggested to Audubon that he be remunerated for exhibiting his pictures, but he did not think this should be done since the room was given to him gratis. However, a week later the committee of the Royal Institution met and requested him to exhibit his drawings by tickets of admission.

During the weeks his drawings were being exhibited at the Royal Institution, Audubon began the oil paintings, the "Otter in a Trap" and the "Wild Turkey Cock." The painting of the otter was finished by 4 August and presented to Mrs. William Rathbone. Before the exhibition closed, the painting of the turkey cock was completed and sent to the Royal Institution where it was to remain as a permanent gift.[20]

Meanwhile Audubon was laying his plans for the future. He decided that he would first go to Manchester, then to Derbyshire to visit Lord Stanley whom he had met in Liverpool,[21] then to Birmingham, from thence to France to see his venerable stepmother at Nantes, with perhaps a stop at Brussels, and back again to London.[22] During his stay in Liverpool he had obtained many letters of introduction to be used on his future travels. These included letters to Baron Humboldt, General Lafayette, Sir Walter Scott, Sir Thomas Lawrence, Hannah Moore, Maria Edgeworth, Coenraad Jacob Temminck, and "500 besides."[23]

In accordance with these plans, Audubon left Liverpool for Manchester on 9 September. William Roscoe, who had suggested the visit to Manchester, had also arranged for the exhibition of Audubon's drawings there, with the result that immediately upon his arrival the Naturalist was putting up his drawings in the Exchange Building. He remained in Manchester until 26 September. This exhibition did not meet with the same success as had the one in Liverpool. It was even held in two different locations, but was poorly attended.[24] On one occasion, only twenty persons had come to see his "Birds."[25] As a consequence, Audubon wrote in his journal, "I see plainly that my expenses in Manchester will not be repaid, in which case I must move shortly."[26]

Audubon had not been favorably impressed with the city of Manchester itself, finding it to be "a miserably laid out place and the smokiest I was ever in."[27] As was his custom, he would arise early and walk into the country, but he found the countryside not so verdant, nor the county seats so clean looking as Green Bank, the home of the Rathbones.

From the primary sources available it is not known to what extent, if at all, Audubon had given any thought to the financing of his proposed "Great Work." While in Manchester it was his good fortune to meet the American consul, a Mr. F. S. Brookes, a native of Boston. It was Brookes who first advised Audubon to have a subscription book.[28] Extensively used in England and elsewhere from the seventeenth century, the subscription approach had proved invaluable in the publication of books of limited market potential by providing funds, in advance and at intervals, that could be expended to meet publication costs. Brookes evidently made a persuasive case for his position, for Audubon wrote in his Journal on 23 September 1826: "I have concluded to have a Book of Subscription etc. . . . ."[29] The final argument in favor of the subscription book appears to have been the approval of William Roscoe, to whom Audubon talked late in September after returning to Liverpool from Manchester.[30]

In adopting this approach, Audubon had moved significantly forward. On 22 October 1826 he wrote to Charles Lucien Bonaparte as follows:

> My dear Sir:
>
> Will you permit me to honor my list of subscribers with your name and ask your father-in-law [Joseph Bonaparte, erstwhile King of Spain] if I may also have his? I hope you will not feel offended. I have no wish to call as a mercenary, but positively for the honor of enriching my list with names. I have some hope of forwarding my first Number (size of life, 20 engravings) in about four months. You would oblige me much if you will send me a copy of all your observations on the *Birds* of Wilson, your synopsis, &c., and a copy of your second volume. Should you please to do so, direct the whole to Messrs. Rathbone Brothers & Company, Liverpool.
>
> Pray remember me to *our* friends of Philadelphia, and believe me, my dear Sir,
>
> Your truly obliged, obedient servant,
> [signed]
> J. J. AUDUBON

[*Audubon wrote beneath the above copy:*]

> The same, nearly, to DeWitt Clinton, Henry Clay, General Andrew Jackson, General William Clark.[31]

This surviving letter apparently is one of the first the Naturalist wrote to solicit names for his subscription book.

Audubon was also giving thought at this time to the publication of a prospectus. He was promised aid with this endeavor by both Rathbone and Roscoe. It was, however, realized that nothing could be done about a prospectus without more knowledge of what the cost of the publication would be.[32] Not until 17 March of the following year was Audubon to complete and distribute the first draft of the prospectus.[33]

The letter to Bonaparte stipulated that the engravings will be the "size of life." This apparently had always been Audubon's hope. His original drawings were of life size and as he envisaged the "Large Work," he wanted the engravings to represent faithfully his originals, even to size. However, his hopes encountered temporary opposition and from a formidable adversary. In the Liverpool home of Dr. Traill, Audubon met Henry G. Bohn of London, an antiquarian book dealer. Bohn, in offering advice to Audubon, spoke strongly against the size of the work as contemplated, feeling that a smaller size would be more suitable for the English market. The large size, he believed, would result in a very limited market—only among public institutions and a few noblemen. Even Dr. Traill and William Roscoe, in whose presence the conversation with Bohn had taken place, were convinced that Bohn's plan was the one to follow. Bohn also advised that the work should be printed in Paris and brought to England where it should be bound and the title page printed and from whence it would be issued to the world as an English publication. To these suggestions Audubon made the following reply in his journal: "*This I will not do; no work of mine shall be other than that true metal—if copper, copper, if gold, gold, but not copper gilded.*"[34]

Although the foregoing comment clearly reflects Audubon's honesty, his abhorrence of the fraudulent, it does not address itself to the question of size. Bohn was instrumental in settling this issue, however. Shortly after the initial meeting, Bohn accompanied Audubon to the Academy where the Naturalist's drawings were on exhibit. On viewing them, Bohn at first expressed surprise, then enthusiasm and "finally said they must be published the full size of life and he was sure that they would pay."[35] Like William Roscoe, Bohn too was "filled with surprise and admiration." Apparently from this point on, that the drawings would be engraved full size was never again in doubt.

The Manchester exhibition continued until 23 October when the drawings once again were packed. On the following morning, Audubon was en route to Edinburgh, "leaving Manchester much poorer than I was when I entered."[36]

Upon his arrival in Edinburgh two days later, Audubon took lodgings with a Mrs. Dickie in George Street. No sooner was he settled than he began his calls on those to whom he had been given letters of introduction. Among the first he met was Professor Robert Jameson, an eminent Scottish naturalist, who at this time was engaged in the preparation of an ornithological publication in cooperation with Prideaux John Selby, an English ornithologist. It had been suggested to Audubon by Edward Roscoe that he should connect himself with this project, but the idea did not appeal to him for "if my work deserved the attention of the public, it must stand on its own legs, not on the reputation of men superior in Education and literary acquirements, but possibly not so in the actual observation of Nature at her best, in the Wilds, as I certainly have seen her."[37]

By means of his own efforts, presenting the letters of introduction, and the help of Professor Jameson, who offered every possible assistance, it was not long before Audubon's lodgings in George Street began to be visited by many, both male and female, and his "birds" admired by all.[38] Among these visitors was Dr. Robert Knox, the celebrated anatomist of the Edinburgh College of Surgeons. It was he who characterized the ornithological work upon which Selby and Jameson were engaged as a "Job book."[39]

Throughout his stay in Edinburgh, much of Audubon's time continued to be occupied by a stream of visitors who came to view his drawings. He was entertaining, as he wrote in his journal, "Many noblemen, among whom I especially liked Sir Patrick Walker and his lady; but I welcomed all ladies, gentlemen, artists and I dare say critics."[40] But after 19 November the Naturalist was freed from the burden of displaying the drawings in his lodgings, for on that day a committee of the Royal Institution invited him to exhibit publicly in the rooms of the Institution. Here the exhibition continued until 23 December and was very well attended. Audubon recorded the receipts from the exhibition, which are summarized briefly as follows:

Cash received from 14 Nov. to 23 Dec.	£152-18-0
Catalogues	20-12-6
Total	£173-10-6 ($770)

with expenses around 30 pounds (sterling).[41]

With the removal of the drawings from his lodgings, Audubon resumed his painting in oil. His first endeavor was the "Turkey Cock with Hen and Nine Young," all the "size of life."[42] This painting, as well as others painted during this time, was also exhibited with the drawings at the Royal Institution. The large painting of the "Turkey Cock, Hen and Young," is now at Harvard College.

From the beginning of Audubon's stay in Edinburgh, he had hoped to meet Sir Walter Scott, whom he held in high esteem. He had passed near Scott's home approaching the city. Writing of this in his journal, he said, "who knows if I shall ever see the home of the man to whom I am indebted for so much pleasure?"[43] The Naturalist believed that Professor Jameson might arrange a meeting with Scott but was told that the writer was busy with a novel and the life of Napoleon, and that "probably I should not see him."[44] But on 22 January, Captain Basil Hall took Audubon to Scott's home. On 24 January, Audubon again visited Scott, this time taking along some of his drawings. Noting this visit in his journal, Scott wrote, "Visit from Mr. Audubon who brings some of his birds. The drawings are of the first order—the attitudes of the birds of the most animated character and the situations appropriate. . . ."[45] In March, when the engraving of the first number of five plates was completed, a set was presented to Scott's daughter Anne, whom Audubon had met on several occasions prior to his visit to Scott's home.[46]

That Audubon was penetrating the world of scholarship is evidenced by the fact that on 16 December he was invited to attend a meeting of the Wernerian Society at the University of Edinburgh.

In preparation for the meeting Audubon wrote in his journal, "I purchased a tame Pigeon, killed, packed up all my wires and hammer, and at one o'clock, having a coach, I was put in it with my *position board* to go to the Wernerian Society, at the University." He described that visit as follows:

> We enter the room of the *Wernerian Society of Edinburgh!* What a name it has in America! The room is a plain oblong square, and two tables, one chimney, many long seats, and a chair for the President were all I saw there with the exception of a stuffed Swordfish on the table for examination that day. Several persons were already present. I unrolled my drawing of the Buzzard for them to look at. . . . Professor Russell, &c. P. Neill read my letter on the Buzzard first, not very well. Professor Jameson rose, made quite a eulogy about it, all my work, and lastly about *myself.* I had the Society's thanks.
>
> I then shewed them my manner of putting up my specimens for drawing birds. This they thought inconceivably ingenious.[47]

Audubon was proposed for membership at this meeting and it was decided that his election should take place at the next meeting.[48] Shortly afterwards the Naturalist demonstrated his method of drawing birds to Sir William Jardine (1800–1874) and Prideaux John Selby (1788–1867) when they visited his rooms. In his journal entry he remarked, "They work very well indeed, although I perceived at once that Mr. Selby was more enthusiastic and therefore worked faster than Sir. W."[49]

That the stay in Edinburgh during the closing months of 1826 was productive of results is self-evident. Audubon was broadening his connections among people of power, influence, and prestige. His exhibits were bringing the appreciation of many and the kudos of the knowledgeable. But his first necessity was to find an engraver competent to undertake his exacting commission. Once again a letter of introduction provided the necessary entree. One of the most productive of such letters Audubon ever presented was the one addressed to the printer and horticulturist, Patrick Neill, for it was Neill who, on 30 October, when Audubon called on him to show him his drawings, immediately took the Naturalist to see the engraver, William Home Lizars. At the time, Lizars was engaged in engraving illustrations for Selby's *Birds of England* as well as those for an edition of Wilson's *American Ornithology*, edited by Sir William Jardine, whose first wife, Jane Home, was the niece of Lizars.

Lizars, upon looking in Audubon's portfolio, was immediately impressed by the drawings and exclaimed, "My God, I never saw anything like these before."[50] The following day they met again, Lizars having brought Professor Jameson to call on Audubon in his lodgings. The next evening, Audubon was entertained at dinner by the Lizarses and was presented with a book of superb views of Edinburgh, on the first page of which had been written, "To John J. Audubon, as a very imperfect expression of the regard entertained for his abilities as an artist, and for his worth as a friend, by William H. Lizars, engraver of the 'Views of Edinburgh.' "[51] Also during this visit, Audubon was shown examples of Lizars's work —printing from copper, coloring with watercolors and oil. The next day, Lizars and his wife visited Audubon at his lodgings. They were shown the paintings of the larger birds—the turkey cock, female turkey with brood, and the whooping crane. In writing of this visit on 2 November 1826 in his journal, Audubon stated, "We were too numerous a party to transact business then, and the subject was adjourned."[52]

While Lizars is frequently mentioned in the journal during the following days, the first definite reference to the arrangement for engraving the *Birds of America* is found on 19 November, when Audubon wrote, "it was settled by Mr. Lizars that he would undertake the publication of the first number of the 'Birds of America.' "[53] However, the Naturalist had been so occupied with the large number of visitors desiring to see his drawings, as well as by outside entertainment, that he had made no entries in his journal from 6 November until 19 November. It would, therefore, appear that Audubon and Lizars had arrived at an agreement covering the publication of the *Birds of America* sometime between those two dates. That agreement may have been made as early as 10 November.

When the arrangement for the publication of *Birds of America* had been made, Lizars quickly began his work. On 26 November, when visiting Lizars, Audubon was shown "many useful sketches, and two plates of my birds well advanced."[54] Two days later, on the 28th, he went to observe the engravers at "work on my birds. I was delighted to see how faithfully copied they were, and scarcely able to conceive the 'adroit' required to form all the lines exactly *contrary* to the model before them."[55] A day or two later, when he dined with the Lizarses, he saw the first proof impression of one of the drawings. On 10 December, in Audubon's journal can be found this definite statement about the progress of the work:

> It is now a month since my work was begun by Mr. Lizars; the paper is of unusual size, called "double elephant" and the plates are to be finished in such superb style as to eclipse all of the same kind in existence. The price of each number, which will contain five prints, is to be two guineas, and all individuals have the privilege of subscribing for the whole, or any portion of it. The two plates now finished are truly beautiful. This number consists of the Turkey-cock [this painting has been chosen to prove the necessity of the size of the work],[56] the Cuckoos on the pawpaws, and three small drawings, which in the center of the large sheet have a fine effect, and an air of richness, that I think must ensure success, though I do not yet feel assured that all will go well. Yet on the other hand things bear a better aspect than I expected to see for many months, if ever.[57]

Audubon's intimation of difficulties which would beset him was prophetic, and yet with Lizars actively engaged with the engraving, "things" certainly did bear a promising aspect. That which had impelled the Naturalist to Britain initially, the need to secure the services of an expert engraver, he had at last found in Edinburgh.

2

EDINBURGH AND LIZARS
1826-1827

Once the major hurdle of finding an engraver had been overcome, there followed a period of waiting but certainly not of inaction. Although the exhibition of Audubon's drawings had closed shortly before Christmas 1826, he did not wish to leave Edinburgh before Lizars had completed the engraving and coloring of the first five plates which were to comprise fascicle Number 1 of the originally projected eighty. As the Naturalist said, "altho my Drawings are much admired if the work itself was inferior nothing could be done and until I have it I cannot expect many subscribers. . . ."[1] Lizars had begun his work about 10 November. Audubon did not leave Edinburgh until the following 5 April.

During those many months the Naturalist constantly was working towards obtaining subscriptions. Interestingly enough his first subscription, which was recorded in his diary on 28 November, seems to have been that of Dr. Meikleham of Trinidad,[2] but this was discontinued in January 1828.[3]

On 7 December Audubon received a note from "Dr. Jameson desiring me to put down the University of Edinburgh as a Subscriber,"[4] which was more fortunate as this appears in the final list of European subscribers.

Audubon, with his flowing hair, his continued use of frontier attire, and his magnetic personality, seems never to have lacked for friends in high places. At the mid-December meeting of the Wernerian Society he had met Lady Morton of Dalmahoy and, as a result, spent several days after Christmas 1826 at the home of Lord Morton, a former Chamberlain to Queen Charlotte, wife of George III. With his ornithologist's eye, the Naturalist described Lord Morton as "a small, slender man, tottering on his feet, weaker than a newly hatched Partridge."[5]

At Dalmahoy Audubon was invited to show his drawings and toward the end of his stay, his hostess "asked for my subscription book and wrote with a steel pen 'The Countess of Morton,' she wished to pay for the first number but this I declined."[6] Possibly due to the death of Lord Morton in July 1827, hers was another subscription that was never to be completed.

Edinburgh and Lizars, 1826–1827

Just about the time Audubon had reached Edinburgh in October, another visitor from America arrived there, a Miss Harriet Douglas of New York. She was a wealthy lady of Scottish descent who had come with her two brothers to bring about the settlement of an uncle's estate. Miss Douglas, like Audubon, was much entertained, and they met at a party given by Professor Jameson. There was mention in her diary of visiting Audubon at his lodgings and becoming a subscriber.[7] After her marriage she was listed in Audubon's records as "Mrs. Douglas Cruger, New York." Audubon's journal entry for 21 March noted:

> Called on Miss D———, the fair American. To my surprise I saw the prints she had received the evening before quite abused and tumbled. This, however, was not my concern, and I regretted it only on her account, that so little care should be taken of a book that in fifty years will be sold at immense prices because of its rarity.[8]

What a prophet of the future he was! Miss Douglas, whatever her failings, was his first American subscriber.

At least nineteen names from this period in Edinburgh are on the original subscription list, but of these, only four appear to have completed their sets. In addition to the two described previously, these were the Society of Writers to His Majesty's Signet and Henry Witham, Esq.

While in Edinburgh Audubon met Joseph Bartholomew Kidd (1808–1889), the young Scottish landscape painter—an event with beneficial consequences, for some years later he arranged with Kidd to reproduce in oils many of the *Birds of America* drawings. Also, shortly before the Naturalist left Edinburgh, Dr. David Brewster, an optician, suggested that the camera lucida would save him time and labor in drawing and outlining his birds.[9] This instrument was to be used much later to make the Octavo edition of the *Birds*.

The first three months of 1827 were filled with feverish activity for Audubon. During the daylight hours, he continued his painting in oil, including the canvases of "Pheasants attacked by Fox," "Wild Pigeons," and the "Black Cocks." The painting of the "Black Cocks," for which he was offered 200 guineas,[10] was exhibited at the Royal Institution of Edinburgh. After Audubon visited the exhibition, he described his reaction in his journal on 10 February as follows:

> I visited the Royal Institution this morning and saw my Black Cocks over the first of the firstroom doors. I know well that the birds are drawn as well as any birds ever have been; but what a difference exists between drawing one bird or a dozen and amalgamating them with a sky, a landscape, and a well adapted foreground. Who has not felt a sense of fear while trying to combine all this?[11]

The painting is now in possession of Harvard College.

The dinner invitations continued unabated. On one occasion Audubon had promised to dine at three different houses on the same day. When he discovered his error, he made his apologies to all and went to none.[12] He still found time to write articles on natural history to be read at meetings of the Wernerian Society.

These were published later in scientific magazines. References to the exhibition of his drawings had already appeared in the newspapers. There were also articles about him and his drawings in such scientific magazines as the *Edinburgh Journal of Sciences*, *Blackwood's Magazine*, and the *New Philosophical Magazine*. Audubon estimated the circulation of the three magazines to be upwards of thirty thousand copies.[13]

As always, Audubon wrote fantastic numbers of letters, including long, detailed accounts to "My dearest Friend," his wife Lucy. The letter of 24 March indicates that the engraving and printing of the first five plates must have been concluded shortly before, for he wrote:

> I now send thee a copy of the first number of the *Birds of America* and some Prospectuses. I wish thee to see if the Library of New Orleans and the College Library there also would subscribe, Judge Matthews perhaps might manage this, but remember that I am not anxious to have subscribers that *will not pay well*. . . .[14]

There is an unusual gap in Audubon's journal between 23 March and 5 April, when he departed Edinburgh. "Probably since ten years I have not been so long without recording my deeds or my thoughts." He had been "busily employed copying some of my drawings, from five in the morning till seven at night . . . to improve myself in oil and in perspective. . . . Every day brought me packets of letters of introduction and I called here and there to make my adieux."[15] But at last, at six o'clock in the morning of 5 April, Audubon set forth on his way to London with the first number, plates 1 to 5, in hand. However, he did not arrive in London until 21 May, due to the many intervening stops essential to promoting his "Birds."

The Naturalist's itinerary began with several stops in Northumberland. The first, one which lasted until 11 April, was in Belford, at Twizel House, the home of Prideaux John Selby and his family. This visit must have come as a most welcome change to Audubon. At Twizel House he took long walks and hunted on the moors, but it was a busman's holiday too, for he drew birds for Selby and even made an oil painting for the elder Selby daughter. He later wrote his wife that while at the Selbys three subscribers were added to his list.[16] Not one of these subscriptions seems to have been completed.

The Naturalist left Twizel House with Selby's brother-in-law, a Captain Mitford, who took him to his home near Morpeth for the night. From there Audubon went to Newcastle upon Tyne, a very busy stop indeed. No sooner had he secured lodgings in Collingswood Street than he was presenting his letters of introduction. Even on the first afternoon of his arrival, five people called at his lodgings to view his drawings. In all, at least two hundred persons visited him during the next four days.[17] Toward the end of his visit in Newcastle, he wrote in his journal: "I am tired out holding up drawings, I may say, all day; but have been rewarded by an addition of five subscribers to my work."[18] Thomas Bewick (1753–1828), the wood engraver, was enthusiastic and put down his name on behalf of the Literary and Philosophical Society of Newcastle but Audubon commented that "his enthusiasm misled him, for the learned body . . . did not think proper to ratify the compact."[19] In short, only one of the eight names obtained in Newcastle, that of Armorer Donkin, remained on the final subscription list.

Next Audubon made two stops in Yorkshire. On Sunday morning, 22 April, he left Newcastle and arrived in the city of York that evening, there to spend a week. His journal entry noted that with rain and snow he "had felt dull as a martin surprised by the weather. . . . It will be strange if York gives me no subscribers, when I had eight at Newcastle."[20] But "a great number of visitors"[21] did come, of course. Of the ten subscriptions listed then, three were completed. These were the Yorkshire Philosophical Society, John Clough, and Jos^a S. Crompton. Of these sets, the first two are now in the United States.

How did Audubon travel the exhausting miles of those days? Usually by horse-drawn coach, as his journal entry for 29 April indicates; he breakfasted at five o'clock in the morning, left York at six, and did not arrive in Leeds until half after nine in the evening.[22] The motor-map distance between the two cities is only twenty-four miles. That day he rode on the outside of the coach and was rewarded by the sight of a covey of partridges, which perhaps helped ease his discomfort and tedium.

With Audubon's arrival in Leeds, one full year had elapsed since he had left his family in Louisiana. He referred to this in his journal on 1 May:

> This is the day on which last year I left my Lucy and my boys with intention to sail for Europe. How uncertain my hopes at that time were as to the final results of my voyage,—about to leave a country where most of my life had been devoted to the study of Nature, to enter one wholly unknown to me, without a friend, nay, not an acquaintance in it. Until I reached Edinburgh I despaired of success; the publication of a work of enormous expense, and the length of time it must necessarily take; to accomplish the whole has been sufficient to keep my spirits low, I assure thee. Now I feel like beginning a New Year. My work is about to be known, I have made a number of valuable and kind friends, I have been received by men of science on friendly terms, and now I have a hope of success if I continue to be honest, industrious and consistent. My pecuniary means are slender, but I hope to keep afloat, for my tastes are simple; if only I can succeed in rendering thee and our sons happy, not a moment of sorrow or discomfort shall I regret.[23]

As usual, the following morning Audubon "started with my letters." His hopes were high when he met a "good ornithologist"[24] among others, but when he left Leeds on 6 May he had obtained only five subscriptions, of which three were to be completed. One of the three was the Leeds Philosophical and Literary Society. The others, the folios of Thomas Walker and John Marshall, are now in the United States.

On 6 May Audubon left Yorkshire and travelled to Manchester in Lancashire where he had shown his drawings the previous September. Though he had with him his box containing 250 drawings, this time he exhibited only the first number of the engraved work at Messrs. Jackson. His days were spent in obtaining subscriptions and his evenings in visiting friends and acquaintances. It was a good week, for he added eighteen names to his subscription list.[25]

After the successful visit to Manchester Audubon spent the following week at the home of the elder Rathbones at Green Bank, near Liverpool. He also saw friends and acquaintances in Liverpool, including his wife's brother-in-law, Alexander Gordon. Here he added five new subscriptions bringing the number of subscribers "positively procured" to forty-nine, which is "a number far above my expectations at my start from Edinburgh and that astonishes all my friends here."[26] At this time he received word that his engraver, Lizars, had begun the second number of the engravings and hoped to have it completed in about two months.[27]

While in Liverpool Audubon wrote a long letter to his wife in which he outlined in detail the "manner in which this Great work of mine has been undertaken and the means that are intended to be employed to carry it throughout in all its parts." He then continued,

> In the first place I have been careful not to have had more copies struck than could possibly be helped to try with the least cost the result of the 1st number. This consisted of 50 copies only. Mr Lizars assured me that the filling of that quantity would save and balance the expense and risk. The result has been a fortunate one, not only the first 50 copies engraved, printed & colored have been subscribed for and delivered but more than 50 have been *struck* or *printed since* and I am glad to say I have subscribers enough to take the whole. in this way we follow the demand by printing more & more copies as they are required by the improvement of my list of Subscribers and take good care to have only a very small stock of copies over the demand—Thus now with one hundred Subscribers (who all pay on delivery) hundred Copies of each number that consists of 5 plates averaging in quality and appearance those I have sent thee, leave a benefit of 42 pounds 9 shillings and 4 pence Sterling. and that repeated 5 times during one Year gives—£212.6.8 sterling. When 200 Subscribers will be had the amount will be [———] more than double *because* the plates are paid for by the first 100 copies sold and of course the printing coloring and paper is the only additional expense. Therefore 200 Subscribers gives a profit on each number of £174.18.8 sterling and 5 times that amount £879.7.4 Sterling which makes in Dollars about 3902 per annum—enough to maintain us even in this Country in a style of Elegance and Comfort that I hope to see thee enjoy— Should I be so fortunate to reach the number of 500 Subscribers and my health does not impair in consequence of my great exertions the sum per annum clear of expenses will be £2821 sterling, making in Dollars about ten thousand seven hundred and forty nine!—
>
> "Now my present care is to procure plenty of Subscribers and manage to collect the money closely so as to enable Mr. Lizars to keep his hands at work and *the work* in progress, to meet those callings both very necessary, I will now visit London for which place I leave tomorrow, and where I hope to have a good batch of Subscribers."[28]

Thus was the Naturalist planning for the future.

3

FIRST VISIT TO LONDON
1827

On 20 May Audubon left for London, accompanied by his close friend, Robert Bentley, the publisher, whom he had met soon after he had reached Liverpool the previous year. The Naturalist had been very happy during his week's stay at Green Bank, the home of the senior Rathbones, and in Liverpool where he had visited his friends the Roscoes, Dr. and Mrs. Traill, and others. In his journal he wrote that "with heavy heart I said adieu to those dear Rathbones and will proceed to London lower in spirits than I was in Edinburgh the first three days."[1] Even on 23 May, two days after his arrival in London, he noted in his journal, "Although two full days have been spent in London, not a word have I written, my heart would not bear me up sufficiently. Monday was positively a day of gloom to me. After breakfast Mr. Bentley took a walk with me through the City, he leading, and I following as if an ox to the slaughter."[2]

However, it was not long before Audubon began to call on those individuals for whom he had received letters of introduction. Also within the week he was exhibiting the first number of engraved prints at the Linnaean Society to which he had been taken by John George Children, at the time Secretary of the Royal Society and attached to the Department of Zoology at the British Museum. Audubon expressed the reaction to his work as follows: "All present pronounced the work *unrivalled* and warmly wished me success."[3]

While in London, Audubon's daylight hours were occupied with the solicitation of subscriptions to the *Birds of America* and the production of oil paintings which he sold to help defray his living expenses. At night he was once more entertained at dinners, attended meetings of the learned societies, and, accompanied by Bentley, enjoyed theatrical entertainment. However, Audubon had really arrived in London at the wrong season of the year insofar as his ability to measurably increase his list of subscribers was concerned. Writing to his son on 25 August, he commented:

> At this present moment the Town is called empty. All or almost all, the Nobility, the Gentry of 1st Class and most all travellers are gone either to their Chateaux, Watering Places on the European Continent. . . . Amongst all this bustle I have been, and wearied almost by its constancy during this spring—yet I was much too late, and the Critical Politique State of Affairs here certainly was a great means of deterring many persons of Rank from seeing my Work; therefore I had fewer names in London for the time spent in it than I gathered in one week at Manchester.[4]

It was during the visit to London that the Naturalist hoped to obtain a subscription from His Gracious Majesty, George IV. To obtain an audience with the king he sought the help of Albert Gallatin, the envoy extraordinaire from the United States. Gallatin found Audubon's request naïve, telling him, "It is impossible—My dear Sir, the king sees nobody, he has the gout, is peevish, and spends his time playing whist at a shilling a rubber. I had to wait six weeks before I was presented to him in my position of ambassador, and then I merely saw him six or seven minutes."[5]

Audubon thought that perhaps he could obtain an audience with the king if he were to present him with a painting. With this in view he painted an oil of "English Pheasants Surprised by a Spanish Dog." He had shown the painting to John George Children and to Sir Walthen Waller, the oculist to the king, both of whom had admired the painting. They had prevailed upon Sir Thomas Lawrence, the portrait painter, to come to Audubon's lodgings at 55 Great Russell Street. Audubon had received a letter of introduction to the painter from Thomas Sully which he had presented soon after his arrival in London. Sir Thomas had visited him several times, admiring both his drawings and his oil paintings. More than this, Sir Thomas had brought some of his friends to Audubon's lodgings, and these friends had purchased many of the Naturalist's oil paintings at a time when Audubon was sorely pressed for funds.

> I was a bankrupt, when my work was scarcely begun, and in two days more I should have seen all my hopes of publication blasted; for Mr. Havell [the engraving of the plates had been transferred from the Lizars establishment in Edinburgh to that of Robert Havell in London] had already called to say that on Saturday I must pay him sixty pounds. I was then not only not worth a penny but had actually borrowed five pounds a few days before to purchase materials for my pictures. But these pictures which Sir Thomas sold for me enabled me to pay my borrowed money and to appear full-handed when Mr. Havell called. Thus I passed the Rubicon![6]

It was on one of his visits to Audubon's lodgings that Sir Thomas saw the painting of the "English Pheasants Surprised by a Spanish Dog." When Audubon told Sir Thomas that he was planning to present it to the king, the painter, after examining the picture, remarked, "Mr. Audubon, that picture is too good to be given away; his majesty would accept it, but you never would be benefitted by the gift more than receiving a letter from his private secretary, saying that it had been placed in his collection."[7]

However, before leaving London in September, through the efforts of Sir Walthen Waller and J. G. Children, a subscription from King George IV was obtained. Audubon described the event as follows:

> The King! My dear Book! it was presented to him by Sir Walter [sic], Bart. K.C.H., at the request of my excellent friend J. P. [sic] Children of the British Museum. His Majesty was pleased to call it fine, permitted me to publish it under his particular patronage, approbation, and protection, became a subscriber on the usual terms, not as kings generally do, but as a gentleman, and my friends all spoke as if a mountain of sovereigns had dropped in an ample purse at once, and for me.[8]

At the same time the subscription of the Duchess of Clarence was obtained.

In the prospectus, which was published in May 1828, the following appears on the title page: "Under the Particular Patronage of His Most Gracious Majesty." There is also a list of 131 subscribers which is headed by "His Most Gracious Majesty George IV." This subscription was not completed, as the king died in 1830.

The name of the Duchess of Clarence also appears on the list of subscribers. As the wife of William IV, she became Queen Adelaide upon the death of George IV. Her death did not occur until after the completion of the engraving of the *Birds of America*, but it has not been possible to determine if the subscription was completed.

From Audubon's letter of 6 August to his wife, it is known that to help defray his day-to-day expenses he painted six pictures in oil—"one of Ducks—one of Rabbits—one of Common Fowls, one of Pigeons, one of Partridges, one of an Otter—all measuring 42. Inches by 28." These he had framed at a cost of £22.10.0, earned by "drawing trifles in a Scotch Lady's Album," and sent to the Liverpool exhibition where he hoped to sell all of them at a price of from twenty to thirty guineas each.[9]

The Naturalist's search for subscribers at this time resulted in the addition of but three new names to his subscription list. These were Lord Stanley (1799–1869), the fourteenth Earl of Derby, then President of the Zoological Society; John George Children (1777–1852) of the Zoological Department of the British Museum; and Charles Lucien Bonaparte (1803–1857). Audubon and Children eventually became such close friends that Children supervised the work of the engravers at the Havell establishment during the Naturalist's first return trip to America in 1829–30. As for Bonaparte, Audubon had made his acquaintance in Philadelphia in 1824. On 18 June 1827, while in England for a brief visit, Bonaparte called on Audubon at his London lodgings, at which time the subscription was obtained.

In May, writing to his wife from Liverpool, Audubon advised her that he had procured forty-nine subscribers since leaving Edinburgh.[10] However, he was soon to learn that the problem was not only to obtain subscribers but to collect payment from them for the delivered prints. In September, while still in London, when he learned that there was due him about five hundred and fifty pounds from subscribers, Audubon determined to take what he called a "Grand Tour" and endeavor to collect the funds due him and augment the number of subscribers.[11] In Manchester, the first place the Naturalist visited, he was greeted "à bras ouverts" by his many friends,[12] but, more important, he was able to collect a large portion of the money owed him and obtain nine subscribers. It is possible to trace these new subscriptions, for on the original list of subscribers the following names have noted beside them, "Manchester, Sept. 1827.":

      Thomas Heywood, Manchester
      Edward Holme, M.D., Manchester
      D. Grant, Esq., 4 Moseley St., Manchester
      James Darbyshire, Esq., Manchester
      John Blackwall, Esq., F.L.S., Manchester
      Robert Garnett, Oak Hill, Cheetham, near Manchester
      Lawrence Fort, Birch Hill near Manchester
      Tho. Joseph Trafford, Trafford Park, Manchester
      Thomas Haigh, Esq., Cheetham Hill, near Manchester.

Most of the Manchester subscribers did not complete their subscriptions, for the final list of subscribers included only the names of James Darbyshire and John Blackwall. When Ledger "B" was searched, the names of Thomas Joseph Trafford and Thomas Haigh were not included therein. The others—Messers Heywood, Holme, Grant, Garnett, and Fort—according to Ledger "B," received the first volume of one hundred prints, numbers 21 and 22, and the first volume of the *Ornithological Biography*.

From Manchester the tour took Audubon to Leeds, where he arrived on 20 September. Meeting with no success in obtaining additional subscriptions, he hastened on to York, where the previous May he had obtained the subscription of the York Philosophical Society. The Naturalist, calling at the rooms of the society, found the poorly colored prints which he returned to Havell "for proper treatment."[13] These were prints which had originally been colored in Edinburgh at the establishment of W. H. Lizars.

In York, Audubon had appointed as his agent one M. A. Barclay. He was to learn later that Barclay had done almost nothing to further his interests and had not even delivered all the finished numbers to the subscribers. Audubon remained in York over a week and, although his visit was unfruitful, he continued hopeful. Writing in his journal on 12 October, the Naturalist said, "I have set my heart on having two hundred subscribers on my list by the first of May next, should I succeed I shall feel well satisfied, and able to have thee and our sons all together."[14]

Audubon's next stop was Newcastle upon Tyne where he arrived on 15 October. Immediately after his arrival he obtained the subscription of Charles William Stewart, third Marquis of Londonderry.[15] This name is third on the original subscription list, preceded only by "His Most Gracious Majesty George IV" and "Her Royal Highness the Duchess of Clarence." However, the subscription does not seem to have been completed. Once again, the ledger reads "Vol. 1., 21 & 22, Biog." This would indicate that the first volume of 100 prints, as well as the *Ornithological Biography*, had been sent to the Marquis. Since the death of the

Marquis did not occur until 1854, it would be interesting to know the reasons for the lapse of this subscription.

While in Newcastle, Audubon visited Thomas Bewick but was unable to spend much time with him. Also, having received an invitation to visit the Selbys, he left for Twizel House at Belford on 19 October. During this weekend with Selby, he learned that the third number of the *Birds of America* had not been received by his host and that this seemed to be the case with other subscribers as well.[16]

From Newcastle the Naturalist proceeded to Edinburgh. One reason for his return visit to this city was to settle his account with Lizars, and another was to appoint an agent for Edinburgh.

Audubon recorded his visit with Lizars on 27 October:

> W. H. Lizars saw the plates of No. 3 (plates 11–15) and admired them much; called his workmen, and observed to them that the London artists beat them completely. He brought his account, and I paid him in full. I think he regrets now that he decided to give my work up; for I was glad to hear him say that should I think well to intrust him with a portion of it, it should be done as well as Havell's, and the plates delivered in London at the same price. If he can fall twenty-seven pounds in the engraving of each number, and do them in a superior style to his previous work, how enormous must his profits have been.[17]

For his agent Audubon selected Daniel Lizars, a bookseller and brother of W. H. Lizars. Having discovered that undelivered numbers of *Birds of America* had been lying for some time at the establishment of W. H. Lizars, he urged his new agent to lose no time in forwarding the numbers to the subscribers.

While in Edinburgh the Naturalist learned that Lady Ellen Hall and W. H. Williams were among those who had withdrawn their subscriptions. In his journal, under date of 31 October, is this reference to subscribers: "It is true six of my first subscribers have abandoned the work without ever giving me a reason." He was even discouraged by the engraver Lizars, who "dampened my spirits a good deal by assuring me that I would not find Scotland so ready at paying for my work as England and positively advised me not to seek for more subscribers either here or at Glasgow."[18]

Audubon did, however, go to Glasgow during his stay in Edinburgh. During a visit of four days he was able to obtain but one subscriber. According to the original subscription list, this would appear to have been the "College of Glasgow as Trustees of Hunterian Museum." The University Librarian and Keeper of the Hunterian Books and Manuscripts at the University of Glasgow has stated that there is at the university a set of the folio which he believes to be the one recorded on the final list of European subscribers as set number 38. On the other hand, the record in the ledger shows the subscription to have been uncompleted, only the first volume of the *Birds of America* with Numbers 21 and 22, and the first volume of the *Ornithological Biography* having been sent to this subscriber.

Some interesting observations about Glasgow appear in Audubon's journal.

One subscriber in a city of 150,000 souls, rich handsome and with much learning. Think of 1400 pupils in one college! Glasgow is a fine city; the Clyde is a small stream crossed by three bridges. The shipping consists of about a hundred brigs and schooners, but I counted eighteen steam vessels, black, ugly things as ever were built. One sees few carriages, but *thousands* of carts.[19]

Leaving Glasgow on 8 November, Audubon headed back to Liverpool. En route he met with Sir William Jardine, visited at Twizel House, the home of Prideaux John Selby, and made short stopovers at York and Manchester. No mention was made of additional subscribers obtained on the return trip, either in his journal or in letters written during this time.

Upon the Naturalist's arrival in Liverpool, he contacted old friends, among them the Rathbones, the Traills, and John Chorley. Again he was anxious to procure subscribers and at the suggestion of Dr. Traill, he called on W. W. Currie, President of the Liverpool Athenaeum, from whom he received permission to show his work, and "to have notes of invitation printed to be sent to each of the members, for them to come and inspect the work as far as it goes." That this exhibition met with but little success is evident from Audubon's entry in his journal for 3 December that there were many visitors at the Athenaeum but no subscribers.[20] The following day he recorded having received one subscription.

Soon after returning to Liverpool, Audubon wrote a long letter to his wife in which he described in detail the events of his trip to Edinburgh, mentioning also that since leaving London he had obtained twenty additional subscribers and that "I have now 114 substantial subscribers."[21] It was at this time that he wrote in his journal, "By advice of our consul Mr. Maury, I have presented a copy of my work to the President of the United States and another to the House of Congress through Henry Clay."[22] No evidence has been found that he carried through these intentions.

Meanwhile the work on the *Birds of America* had progressed to the extent that Audubon received from Havell the fifth number as well as "three full sets for my new subscribers here."[23] It has not been possible to identify these subscribers.

4

FROM LIZARS TO HAVELL
1827

Audubon had been in London but a short time when he received disquieting news from Edinburgh concerning the coloring of the prints of the *Birds of America*, as his journal entry of 18 June indicated:

> On Thursday morning I received a long letter from Mr. Lizars informing me that his colorers had struck work, and everything was at a stand-still; he requested me to try to find some persons here who would engage in that portion of the business and he would do his best to bring all right again. This was quite a shock to my nerves.[1]

On 21 June Audubon received a second letter from Lizars which, he noted, "was far from allaying my troubles. I was so struck with the tenure [sic] of it that I cannot help thinking now that he does not wish to continue my work."[2] This journal entry as recorded by Lucy Audubon in her biography of the Naturalist contains this additional sentence, "Have made an engagement with Mr. Havell for coloring, which I hope will relieve my embarrassment."[3]

Does this mean that the "engagement made with Mr. Havell" included the engraving of the plates as well as the coloring of the prints? More detailed information contained in a letter written to his wife from London on 6 August would seem to indicate that the decision to remove the engraving to London as well as the coloring was made sometime after 21 June. There are no further references in Audubon's journal regarding the matter; in fact, there are no entries in the journal from 2 July until September when under the dateline, "Leeds, September 30, 1827," he wrote, "I removed the publication of my work from Edinburgh to London, from the hands of Mr. Lizars into those of Robert Havell, No. 79 Newman St. because the difficulty of finding colorers made it come too slowly, and also because I have it done better and cheaper in London."

The details of Audubon's difficulties with Lizars are contained in the long letter to his wife:

23

> I am still here although London is comparatively speaking deserted; it was my intention to have left about 3 weeks ago to travel again to augment the number of my subscribers, but I was prevented from so doing on account of the tardiness of Mr Lizars my Engraver at Edinburgh who nearly exausted my patience by not supplying the subscribers, for several months after my expectation, of the 1st. Number.—he began engraving the 2nd. number the 1st of May last and I have been anxious to see it out also before my departure but after much delays and perplexities, I was forced last week to write him to forward me the *coppers engraved* here to have the Impressions printed and Colored here. I received the whole yesterday in good order and I am truly glad of it, for London affords all sorts of facilities imaginable or necessary for the Publication of such immense work and hereafter my *Principal* business will be carried on here—I have made arrangements with a Mr Havell an excellent Engraver who has a good establishment containing Printers—Colorers and Engravers So that I can have all under my eye when I am in London and no longer will be stoppd [with] by the want of Paper, or Coppers that Mr Lizars was obliged to order from here; sometimes with risks and at all events with a considerable expense *extra*.[4]

Audubon alluded to the fact that Lizars had not only delayed in supplying subscribers with the first number (plates 1–5) of the *Birds of America*, but also that he had not begun to engrave the second number until May, although the engraving of the first had been completed in March. It is possible, of course, that there may have been another reason—the strike of the colorers—for the delay in providing Audubon's subscribers with prints and the engraving of the second number.

In the autumn of 1826, when the arrangement for engraving the *Birds of America* had been entered upon with Lizars, the latter had been busily engaged since 1825 in engraving the plates for Volume I of the *Illustrations of Ornithology* by Sir William Jardine, Bart. (1800–1874), and Prideaux John Selby (1788–1867). While the plates for the *Illustrations* were smaller than those for the *Birds of America* (21″ × 17″ compared to 39½″ × 26½″), engraving them was nevertheless a formidable undertaking. Audubon had commented on this in a letter written to his wife on 12 December 1826; "He [Lizars] was busily employed sorting Mr. Selby's plates for eleven numbers."[5] There certainly was a conflict of interests.

Under what circumstances were the Naturalist and Robert Havell, Jr., brought together? Neither in the journals nor in Audubon's letters are any details available. However, an account purporting to clear up the mystery has been published by a collateral descendant of the engraver.

George Alfred Williams (1875–1932), whose mother was the great-granddaughter of Luke Havell, the brother of the engraver's father, through his friendship with Amelia Jane Havell Lockwood (1827–1907), the eldest daughter of the engraver, and by means of notebooks, correspondence, and the family Bible, found it possible to fill in many of the gaps and clarify several details which had been obscure.

The story, as recorded by Williams, is as follows:

> Arriving in London with a portfolio of designs demanding almost the impossible for their reproduction, Audubon made further search without success

[Williams overlooks the fact that when Audubon had first arrived in London in May of 1827, his purpose was to obtain subscribers. It was not until after word had been received from Lizars of the strike of the colorists that the search began], and when the quest seemed most hopeless, he was introduced to Robert Havell, Sr. The elder Havell was an engraver of note who ran, in connection with a Zoological Gallery, a studio from which he published works of fine quality. He had practiced the art of engraving under his father, Daniel Havell, and at the time of meeting Audubon was fifty-eight years old, well past the years of his greatest achievements as represented by *Views on the Thames, Gentlemen's Country Seats,* etc. He felt he was too old to undertake so important and extensive a work as Audubon's but he strove to find a younger engraver to work under his instructions to carry out the naturalist's plans. Havell, Sr., at once sought the advice of his friend Colnaghi of Colnaghi and Company, who showed Havell, Sr., an unfinished proof of a landscape as a sample of the work of one of his young engravers. The work so pleased the elder Havell that he asked Colnaghi to let him interview the engraver. "Then," said Colnaghi, "send for your son!"[6]

Robert Havell, Jr., at the time that he met Audubon, was thirty-four years of age and already highly regarded in his own right as a draftsman and aquatint engraver of unusual talent. He had aspired since childhood to follow a career in the arts, contrary to the wishes of his father who had intended instead that the son enter a learned profession. In the spring of 1825, father and son were estranged. Leaving his father's house and London, as well, Young Havell set out on an extended sojourn in Monmouthshire to sketch and paint. The works he produced during this period were acclaimed upon his return to London and secured for him commissions from many of that city's leading publishers, among them the large and prestigious Colnaghi and Company.

The singular incident of the anonymous engraver's proof brought about a reconciliation between father and son, who then entered upon a successful business partnership, henceforth known as Robert Havell and Son. The older Havell was to print and color many of the prints of the *Birds of America* until his death in 1832.[7]

Also at this time there began the enduring friendship between Audubon and Robert Havell, Jr. Although the Naturalist was to complain frequently about the coloring of the plates, he seemed always to be pleased with the engraving. So much so, that on one occasion in response to certain criticism he wrote, "Now it happens that I, the party most concerned about engraving am perfectly confident that the birds were ever so beautifully and softly represented on copper." Again, in appreciation of work being done by the engraver, Audubon presented him with a silver loving cup bearing the inscription, "To Robert Havell from his friend J.J.A., 1834."

Williams also included in his account the following incident which is said to have occurred during the negotiations with Havell:

> Audubon asked Havell to make a trial drawing on copper of the *Prothonotary Warbler*, and the plate No. 3 in Volume 1 of the original folio was completed in two weeks. This date was given to me by Mrs. Lockwood with the following

story concerning it: The naturalist was sent for to inspect the proof. He looked at it intently, then took it up and, dancing about the room, cried, "Ze jig is up, ze jig is up!" At first the Havells thought that this meant he was displeased, but Audubon, throwing his arms around Havell, embraced him in genuine enthusiasm and gave ample evidence that he realized that he had at last found his engraver.[8]

Why Audubon should have asked Havell to engrave the painting of the prothonatory warbler is difficult to explain. In March of 1827, before Audubon had left Edinburgh for London, Lizars had engraved the first number of five plates of *Birds of America*, which included the prothonatory warbler (plate 3). In addition, many extant sets of the folio contain a print of Plate 3, on which is found, "Engraved by W. H. Lizars, Edin." When the Havell plate is included in the folio the inscription reads, "Engraved, Printed & Coloured, by R. Havell Jun.ʳ" Was then the plate of the Prothonatory Warbler engraved twice?

In the letter to his wife of 6 August, wherein Audubon had advised her of the removal of the work to London, he also set down the price he was paying Havell for the engraving, printing, and coloring of each number of five plates as follows:

		Sgs	Pce
consisting of 5 Plates with the lettering and Coppers Included is	£ 42.	0.	0.
the price of coloring 100 sts @ 8/6	42.	10.	9.
Paper for Do. 1 Ream	14.	1.	0.
Printing the 100 sets	11.	5.	0.
100 tin cases to forward the sets to each person	5.	0.	0.
	£114.	16.	0. [9]

Audubon had stated in his prospectus that the cost of each number of five prints was to be two guineas (two pounds and two shillings), so that the proceeds from the sale of a hundred numbers would be £210 against the above cost of £114.16s.0, yielding a profit of nearly £106 or $530 on each hundred sets of five numbers (25 plates).

The Naturalist made another interesting observation in the letter of 6 August to his wife, namely that 1500 copies could be struck off before the copper plates would require repair. In a letter written on 25 August from London to his son in Louisville, Audubon also set forth the cost of publishing the engravings of the *Birds of America* as agreed upon with Havell. There are slight variations in the figures—the cost of printing is stated to be £12 instead of £11.5s., and the paper £14 instead of £14.1s. He told his son that as he now had a hundred subscribers, the income per year from the issuance of five numbers would be 1000 guineas or £1050, "which leaves a benefit of about 500 pounds sterling."[10]

5

LONDON AND PARIS
1828

By 1 January 1828, Audubon was again on the move. After a visit to his friends Robert Bentley and E. W. Sergeant in Manchester, he reached London on the fifth of the month. This time he arrived in better spirits. Writing in his journal on 5 January, he noted: "I am again in London but not dejected and low in spirits and disheartened as I was when I came in May last; no indeed! I have now *friends* in London, and hope to keep them."[1]

Friends indeed the Naturalist did have. Among them at this time were Children, Vigors, Temminck, and Baron Cuvier. After Audubon was settled in his new quarters at 95 Great Russell Street, one of his first tasks was to go over with Havell drawings which were to make up the numbers to be issued in 1828. Some of the new species among the twenty-five birds that were to comprise these numbers, he decided to name in honor of his friends. And so, as the work progressed during the year, included in the numbers were the following: Plate 30, Vigors's Vireo; Plate 35, Children's Warbler; Plate 45, Traill's Fly Catcher; Plate 55, Cuvier's Regulus. No bird, however, was named in honor of Temminck.[2]

Not only did Audubon have friends in London, there he received honors as well. Writing to his wife on 6 February, he stated: "The season is just begun in London and I have invitations to attend the Royal, Linaean & Zoological Societies, and I hope to procure a good number of Subscribers as a copy of my Work will always go with me."[3]

Friendship's course, however, is subject to reversals. Although Audubon in 1828 had named a bird in honor of Nicholas Aylward Vigors (1787–1840), almost three years later he was moved to comment in a letter written to his son Victor, "that Subscribers should die is a thing we cannot help, that such a fellow as Vigors should mortify us, cannot again be countermanded." What the circumstances were that arose in his relationship with Vigors that caused Audubon to refer thus to him have been impossible to determine.

Audubon and Vigors had met in June 1827 when the latter was Secretary of the

Zoological Society of London.[4] Vigors had been assisting Prideaux John Selby with his *Illustrations of British Ornithology* (1825–1829), a project in which Sir William Jardine also was involved. When, in 1828, Vigors had asked Audubon to write some papers for the Zoological Society, the Naturalist refused, as he did all others who asked, for his writing at the time was confined to the *Ornithological Biography*.[5] In the same year, however, Audubon advised Vigors that he wished to name one of his "new birds" after him[6] and did so, as plate 30 in Number 6, "Vigors's Vireo (Sylvia Vigorsii, Male)," proves. The Naturalist's identification of this bird as a new species was, unfortunately, in error, for it had been figured and identified earlier by Alexander Wilson as the male of the "Pine Creeping Warbler (Sylvia Pinus),"[7] now known as the pine warbler (*Dendroica pinus*). The history of Audubon's specimen and the probable reason for his quite honest mistake are to be found in the first volume of his *Ornithological Biography*, in which he explained, "The individual represented . . . I shot upwards of twenty years ago and have never met with another of its kind. It was in the month of May, on a small island of the Perkioming Creek, forming part of my farm of Mill Grove."[8]

It is difficult to trace all the subscriptions Audubon acquired during his stay in London, a stay which was to last until 1 September. One of these appears to have been that of David Lyon, a subscription received through the help of Sir Thomas Lawrence,[9] but one which again does not seem to have been completed. When Robert Bentley, the Naturalist's friend and agent at Manchester, visited London late in January, he brought news of some new subscribers and also "a letter from the Rev. D—— to ask to be excused from continuing the work."[10] This probably was the Reverend Mr. Dunbar of Applegarth, a name which appears on the original subscription list but which is not found on later lists. From his agent in Edinburgh, Daniel Lizars, Audubon learned of the loss of four subscribers, but the names were not disclosed. These cancellations led to his expressing himself in the journal as follows: "Query: how many amongst my now long list of subscribers will continue the work throughout."[11]

In March, Audubon visited both Cambridge and Oxford with the intention of gaining additional subscriptions. At Cambridge he obtained subscriptions from "The University Library; George Thackeray, D.D., Provost of Kings College; The Cambridge Philosophical Society; The Fitzwilliam Museum by M. Davy, Vice-chancellor; Hon'ble W. C. Wentworth Fitzwilliam."[12]

Audubon noted in his journal that he had suggested to Lord Fitzwilliam that he sign his name on the subscription book immediately above that of Countess of Morton.[13] The original subscription list shows that this was done. There is at Cambridge University the following receipt from Audubon for the payment of five numbers:

> Rec*d* of John Lodge, Esq. Ten pounds Ten Shillings the amount for Five Numbers of my Work on the Birds of America
>
> [signed]
> JOHN J. AUDUBON
>
> *Cambridge*
> *March 13*
> *1828*

London and Paris, 1828

Sets of the work were also delivered to other subscribers, so that in all Audubon received 52 guineas at Cambridge.[14]

Before going to Oxford Audubon found it necessary to return to London for some business with Havell whom he found engaged in coloring one hundred sets of Number 6. Included among these was Number 26, the Carolina Paroquet, the engraving of which Audubon expressed his approval with, "I think it is a beautiful piece of work."[15]

On 24 March, having completed his work in London, the Naturalist was in Oxford where he succeeded in obtaining only two subscribers:

> The Anatomical School of Christ College, Dr. Kidd
> The Radcliffe Library, Dr. Williams.[16]

On his quests for subscriptions Audubon usually carried with him a supply of the numbers completed thus far so he could provide a new subscriber with a set, or more, whenever the opportunity presented itself. However, when the Naturalist delivered the set of plates to Dr. Williams, he was chagrined to find the copies of the first number to be poorly finished. Referring to this incident in his journal, he expressed his feelings thus:

> When I saw it, it drew a sigh from my heart. Ah! Mr. Lizars was this the way to use a man who paid you so amply and so punctually? I rolled it up and took it away with me, for it was hardly coloured at all, and have sent a fair new set of five numbers.[17]

Understandably, Audubon was disheartened by his lack of success at Oxford. On 29 March, the night before leaving that city, he wrote in his journal:

> Tomorrow, probably, I leave here and much disappointed. There are here twenty-two colleges intended to promote science in all its branches; I have brought here samples of a work acknowledged to be at least good, and not one of the colleges subscribed. I have been most hospitably treated, but with so little encouragement for my work there is no reason for me to remain.[18]

It was in February, shortly after Audubon had first arrived in London, that he had settled accounts with his engraver Havell for the numbers produced in 1827 and, having done this, the Naturalist concluded that "either through him or Mr. Lizars I have met with a loss of nearly £100, for I am charged for fifty numbers more than can be accounted for by my agents or myself."[19] As a consequence, during the remainder of his stay in London, Audubon kept close watch over the engraving and coloring of the plates, spending many hours at the Havell shop especially to superintend the coloring. His comment, "While I am not a colorist, and Havell is a very superior one, I *know* the birds," indicates his concern for this aspect of his "Great Work."[20] Havell at the time was printing the eighth number (plates 36–40), while the ninth and tenth (plates 41–50) were being engraved.[21]

The extent to which Audubon's time and energies were devoted to advancing his "Large Work" must be considered as almost total. Not only did he apply himself to the augmentation of his list of subscribers and the engraving, printing, and coloring of the plates, he also turned to painting in oils once again. During June and July the Naturalist had eight paintings in progress. One of these, developed from a sketch of an eagle pouncing upon a lamb that had been drawn quite some time previously, is presently at the Audubon Shrine and Wildlife Sanctuary, Mill Grove, Audubon, Pennsylvania.[22] Another of the paintings executed at this time was a copy of the group of black cocks or grouse which Audubon had painted and sold for £100 earlier.[23] Moreover, there were certain of his drawings which the Naturalist wished to redraw and finish in "better style." One he mentioned in particular, the white-headed eagle feeding on a wild goose, which he had drawn originally while he was traveling on the Mississippi, "now I shall make it breakfast on a Catfish."[24] Both drawings of the eagle are included in the collection of Audubon's original drawings at the New-York Historical Society.

Then too, early in August Audubon had met C. R. Parker, the artist, whose acquaintance he had made some years earlier in Natchez, Mississippi. Parker asked that he be permitted to paint a portrait of Audubon dressed as a woodsman. Permission was given and Parker finished the portrait late in August. Audubon considered it a good likeness.[25]

For some months Audubon had hoped to persuade his wife and sons to come to England, but they did not think well of the idea. With no immediate prospect of seeing his family, Audubon became depressed. Although he had returned to London in high spirits, soon after his arrival, he became physically unwell.[26] As time went on, he became more and more dispirited, often wishing he were back in America,[27] so much so that, on 21 April, he wrote in his journal:

> The same feeling still exists this year that I felt last, during my whole stay in London. I hate it, yes I cordially hate London, and yet cannot escape from it. I neither can write my Journal here, nor draw well, and if I walk to the fields around, the very voice of the sweet birds I hear has no longer any charm for me, the pleasure being too much mingled with the idea that in another hour all will again be bustle, filth and smoke.[28]

Even such honors as being elected a member of the Zoological Society of London and a Fellow of the Linnaean Society did little to revive his spirits.[29]

The Naturalist also received tributes as well as honors. William Swainson prepared an extended review of the *Birds of America*, parts of which review Audubon included in a new issue of his prospectus. In appreciation of Loudon's having printed the Swainson review in his *Magazine of Natural History*, Audubon himself wrote an article which appeared in the July number of that magazine.[30] This was the only article Audubon wrote during his London stay. He had refrained from scientific publication, in part on the advice of his friend, J. G. Children. The Naturalist's own attitudes toward independent scientific publication are discussed more fully in chapter 8.

Perhaps Audubon's dejection of spirit also may have been caused by the difficulty he was experiencing in augmenting his subscription list. In a letter to his wife on

8 August, he told her that his subscriptions then totaled 125.[31] In a journal entry dated 9 August, he referred to the matter of subscribers thus:

> I have been at work from four every morning til dark; I have kept up my correspondence, my publication goes well and regularly, and this very day seventy sets have been distributed; yet the number of my subscribers has not increased; on the contrary, I have lost some.[32]

The only new subscription it is possible to trace to this period is that of Lord Milton. In a letter written to William Swainson on 1 July, Audubon told him that, "I received a visit on Saturday last of the whole of Lord Milton's family who after complimenting the author of the 'Birds of America' very kindly subscribed for two copies of the work."[33] While the name "The Right Honourable Viscount Milton" appears on the final lists of subscribers, Ledger "B" indicates there was only one subscription.

Audubon had brought with him to London a letter of introduction to William Swainson which had been given to him by his friend, Dr. Traill, but the Naturalist had not immediately been able to go to Swainson's home near St. Albans to deliver it.[34] However, on 28 May, soon after the appearance of Swainson's review in Loudon's *Magazine*, he visited with Swainson and his family at Highland Hall near Tyttenhanger Green, a small settlement on the highroad two miles southeast of St. Albans, in Hertfordshire. Here he spent four days and, as he wrote in his journal, ". . . my visit was of the most agreeable nature." Also, "whilst there I began a drawing for Mrs. Swainson, and showed Mr. Swainson how to put up birds in my style, which delighted him."[35]

It is possible that Audubon had for some time been contemplating a visit to Paris and that such a visit was discussed with Swainson during that weekend in May, for on 13 August he wrote to Swainson asking that he accompany Audubon to France, reminding him that he "wished to go when we were talking together at Tyttenhanger."[36] On 19 August, when the Naturalist again visited the Swainsons, it was decided that both Mr. and Mrs. Swainson would accompany him to Paris on 1 September. When the three departed on that day, they were also accompanied by the artist Parker.

Arriving in Paris on 4 September 1828, Audubon was to remain in that city for two months before returning to London. While Parker was occupied with painting portraits of both Cuvier and Redouté, and Swainson was working steadily at the Museum of the Jardin des Plantes, Audubon set about searching for subscribers to his *Birds of America*. He at once visited the Baron Cuvier (1769–1832), statesman, author, philosopher, and one of the greatest naturalists of modern times.[37] Audubon learned from Cuvier that his work was unknown in France.[38]

Cuvier not only entertained Audubon, but he also inquired as to the price of the work and was given a copy of the prospectus.[39] On 8 September, Cuvier took Audubon to a meeting of the Academy of Sciences where the prints of *Birds of America* were exhibited. At the same time Cuvier announced his intention to review the work for the "Memoirs of the Académie."[40]

THE DOUBLE ELEPHANT FOLIO

A laudatory review was actually finished and presented to the Royal Academy of Sciences before Audubon completed his visit to Paris. In it Cuvier wrote that the *Birds of America* was "the most magnificent monument which has yet been made to ornithology."* Audubon incorporated both this review and that of Swainson's which had appeared in the May 1828 issue of Loudon's *Magazine of Natural History* in all future printings of his prospectus. Both reviews are also included in the first volume of the *Ornithological Biography*.

Yet when it came to obtaining subscribers, Audubon was beset by difficulties. Among the first persons he called on was a Paris banker who, after reading the letter of introduction presented by Audubon, gave the Naturalist to understand that "as to ornithology, all he knew about it was that large feathers were called *quills* and were useful in posting ledgers."[41] A visit to the Prince of Massena, son of one of Napoleon's marshals, was more fruitful and a subscription was obtained. The prince, who had learned about Audubon's work through Charles Bonaparte,[42] regretfully warned the Naturalist that there were few persons in France able to subscribe to his work and that he should not expect more than six or eight names in Paris.[43]

To obtain the subscription of Charles X, then King of France, Audubon was advised to write to Baron de la Bouillerie, intendant of the king's household.[44] The letter was written on 13 September. It has been preserved and is in the "Archives de France."[45] Bouillerie referred the matter to Petain, Librarian of the Royal Chateau of St. Cloud, who wrote in praise of the work as follows: "Such a collection would be missed by the Library of His Majesty and I have the honour of proposing that you, Sir, subscribe for a copy."[46] On the subscription list, the King of France is entered twice, first as "His Christian Majesty-Charles X" and then as "La Bibliothèque particulière du Roi, Gallerie du Louvre-Paris."

Soon after his arrival in Paris, Audubon called on Pierre Joseph Redouté (1759–1840), the noted French painter of flowers. Through the good offices of Redouté, the Naturalist was invited by the Duc d'Orléans to exhibit his prints at the Palais Royal. The duke, after praising the prints, stated, "This surpasses all I have seen, and I am not astonished now at the eulogisms of M. Redouté."[47] A subscription was promptly forthcoming.[48] The original subscription list bears the actual signature of the duke, "S.A.R.—le Duc d'Orléans" and the inscription "his handwriting" written beside the signature by someone else, probably by Audubon himself. Later, again with the help of Redouté, the subscription of the Duchess of Orléans was received.[49]

Before Audubon left Paris, he entered into an agreement with Redouté whereby they were to exchange works, and he did immediately receive nine numbers of that artist's "Belles Fleurs" and "Les Roses."[50] The Redouté account in Ledger "B" indicates that numbers 1 to 71 (prints 1–335) were delivered to Redouté, with the last entry dated 1837.

---

* On peut le caractériser en peu de mots, en disant que c'est le monument le plus magnifique qui ait encore été élevé à l'ornithologie.

Audubon had not been in Paris long before it was suggested that he should contact the Minister of the Interior who, he was told, had "the power to subscribe to anything, and for as many copies of any work as the farmers of France can well pay for through the enormous levies imposed on them."[51] On 2 October, he was finally able to exhibit the prints to the minister on whom these created a favorable impression. Audubon was instructed to put his terms in writing and advised that he would receive a reply as soon as possible.[52] However, he was left waiting until 26 October before he received word that the Minister of the Interior had subscribed for six sets of *Birds of America*. On the same day, Baron de la Bouillerie advised the Naturalist of the king's subscription for his private library.[53]

By this time Audubon had made up his mind to leave Paris, for in his journal entry of 26 October 1828, he had written: "I have now thirteen subscribers in Paris; I have been here two months, and have expended forty pounds. My adieux will now be made, and I shall be *en route* for London before long."[54] In a letter to his son Victor, written shortly after his return to London, in a reference to his Paris trip the number of subscribers is given as fourteen, listing however only "King Charles Tenth; Duke of Orleans; Duchess of Orleans; Prince Massena; Baron Cuvier; Minister of the Interior, 6 Copies."[55] In addition, the original subscription list also includes these subscribers: M. Pitois of the firm of F. G. Leviault, P. J. Redouté, and La Bibliothèque de l'Institut Royal per M. Feuillet.

Audubon's Ledger "B" indicates that none of these last subscriptions were completed. As to the others, King Charles abdicated and fled to England in August 1830. He was succeeded by the Duke of Orléans as Louis Philippe the First. The ledger shows that the King and the Queen, the former Duchess of Orléans, received sixty-seven numbers or 335 plates. It is possible that the remaining prints were delivered by Audubon's Paris agent, Pitois.

Baron Cuvier died in 1832. Although Cuvier's library was purchased by the French government, there is no record of the subscription having been continued. At the present time there are at the Bibliothèque Nationale 125 prints. It is believed that these are the prints delivered to the baron prior to his death. This seems to be confirmed by the entry in Ledger "B" which shows that number of prints had been delivered to Cuvier.

The library of the Prince of Massena was broken up around 1850, and no details are available as to the distribution of the contents. As for the prints delivered to the Minister of the Interior, no trace has been found of the six sets of the first volume and Number 21, which, according to Audubon's records, were delivered and paid for.

There is a complete four-volume set of the folio at the Bibliothèque Centrale du Muséum National d'Histoire Naturelle, and at the Bibliothèque de l'Institut de France there are two volumes containing 400 prints and a portfolio with the last thirty-five prints unbound.

Baron Cuvier had saluted Audubon's *Birds of America* as "the most magnificent monument which has yet been made to ornithology." To gain an appreciation of the justice of this tribute, one must first of all, of course, examine the 435 plates which compose the "Great Work." Also, one can attend very closely to Audubon's descriptions of his own methods and techniques. In the introduction to Volume I of the *Ornithological Biography*, he wrote:

> Merely to say, that each of my illustrations is of the size of nature, were too vague—for many it might only convey the idea that they are so, more or less, according as the eye of the delineator may have been more or less correct in measurement simply obtained through that medium; and of avoiding error in this respect I am particularly desirous. Not only is every object, as a whole, of the natural size, but also every portion of each object. The compass aided me in its delineation, regulated and corrected each part, even to the very foreshortening which now and then may be seen in the figures. The bill, the feet, the legs, the claws, the very feathers as they project one beyond another, have been accurately measured. The birds, almost all of them, were killed by myself, after I had examined their motions and habits, as much as the case admitted, and were regularly drawn on or near the spot where I procured them. The positions may, perhaps, in some instances, appear outré; but such supposed exaggerations can afford subject of criticism only to persons unacquainted with the feathered tribes; for, believe me, nothing can be more transient or varied than the attitudes or positions of birds. The Heron, warming itself in the sun, will sometimes drop its wings several inches, as if they were dislocated; the Swan may often be seen floating with one foot extended from the body; and some Pigeons, you well know, turn over when playing in the air.[56]

The magnificence of Audubon's monument to ornithology was not, however, to be achieved solely through the fine precision and accuracy of the Naturalist's delineation of his bird figures. The success of the final work presupposed Audubon's close supervision of its production. When one of the colorers brought a number to Audubon, of which the prints were so "shamefully done that I would not think of forwarding it," he insisted that it "be washed, hot pressed, and done over again. Depend upon it, my work will not fail for the want of my own very particular attention." This he wrote in his journal on 17 November, shortly after his return from Paris.[57]

Confirming evidence that his work was not failing he learned from his friend, Richard Harlan of Philadelphia, who late in December advised Audubon that the first number of *Birds of America* had been displayed both at the Academy of Natural Sciences and the American Philosophical Society.[58] These were the prints which Charles Lucien Bonaparte had taken with him to America in the autumn of 1827, upon his return from a short visit to England.[59]

6

FIRST RETURN TO AMERICA
1829-1830

Audubon had not been long in England before he began to express his need for the help and counsel of his wife and his two sons. As early as 21 December 1826, when Lizars had begun the engraving of the plates and when the first subscribers had been obtained, he wrote a long letter to his wife who had remained at Beech Woods, in Bayou Sara, Louisiana, teaching a class of young ladies. In this letter he reviewed his activities since arriving in England, and his future plans in the pursuance of his great undertaking, the publication of the *Birds of America*. He had realized that

> In the event of ultimate success I must have either my son or some other person to travel for me to see about the collection of payments for the work and to procure new subscribers constantly as I conceive my Victor [Victor Audubon was then in his 19th year, having been born 12 June 1809] a well fit man for such business and as it would at once afford him the means of receiving a most complete education and a knowledge of Europe surpassing that of probably any other man—In case I say of success I will write for him immediately when I hope no more constraint or opposition will be made to my will—I am now better aware of the advantages of a family in unison than ever and I am quite satisfied that by acting conjointly and by my advice we can realize a handsome fortune for each of us—it needs but industry & perseverance—going to America is a mere song and I now find that most valuable voyages could be made by procuring such articles as are wanted here and most plentiful there—It is now time to know from thee what thy future intentions are. I wish thee to act according to thy dictates but wish to know what those Dictates are—think that we are far divided and that either sickness or need may throw one into a most shocking situation without either friend or help for as thou sayest thyself "the World is not indulgent." Cannot we move together and feel and enjoy the natural need of each other—Lucy my friend think of all this very seriously—not a portion of the earth exists but will support us amply and we may feel Happiness anywhere if careful.[1]

THE DOUBLE ELEPHANT FOLIO

Early in 1827, when the engraving was well under way, the first subscribers had been obtained, and Audubon was about to leave for London, again he wrote his wife:

> I have a great number of letters for London and some hopes to succeed there in augmenting my list of Subscribers sufficiently to enable me to write to thee, Lucy my Love come to me. Oh my dear Wife how I pray God and hope that this may soon come![2]

In May of the same year, in another letter to Lucy in which he reviewed the progress of his undertaking thus far, he estimated that with a subscription list numbering two hundred it would be possible to "maintain us even in this Country in a style of Elegance and Comfort that I hope to see thee enjoy." He concluded his letter with:

> Thou are quite comfortable I know in Louisiana therefore wait there with a little patience. I hope the end of this year will see me under headway sufficient to have thee with me with comfort here and *thou* I need not tell thee that I long every hour of the time I am absent for thee. I conceive it best to be prudent.[3]

By December of the same year, again writing to his wife, he set forth his financial condition, saying, "Now Dearest Lucy, keep up a good heart and make all arrangements as soon as possible."[4]

No letters from Lucy are available from which to learn her reactions. However, from a letter written by Audubon in February 1828, it would appear that there was a hesitancy on her part to join him. In this letter Audubon had written:

> Now my Lucy let me talk of matters of greater importance.—When at Liverpool, about a month ago, I thought that I would feel sufficiently settled, after balancing my accounts, to write to thee to come directly to England and I hoped so the more, as I am really and truly in want not only of a *wife*, but of a kind & true friend, to consult and to help me by dividing with me a portion of my hard labours—yet thy entire comfort is the only principle that moves me, and fearing that thou might expect more than I can yet afford I refrained from doing it for the present.—however, my Love do thou not be disheartened, depend upon it, I shall not diminish in my exertions, and I certainly have good hopes.—I leave thee from my heart perfectly at liberty to do whatever may be most agreeable to thee, to enable thee to spend thy time in peace and comfort and to know thou art happy & quite well must sufice me until we meet to part no more.[5]

There were, of course, other letters to his wife and his son Victor in which the matter of the family's joining him in Europe was mentioned, but what finally brought matters to a head would seem to have been a letter written to Audubon by Lucy on 8 November 1828. When this letter was acknowledged on 20 January 1829, he wrote that he had been debating what would be the best thing to do:

> as I plainly read in it, the same that has filled every other that has come from thee since I left America i.e. the *uncertainty* of thy *ever* joining me in Europe.—I have

First Return to America, 1829–1830

> therefore come to the following conclusion, which thou mayest take for granted if I have life within me.—I will sail for America (New York) on or about the 1st day of April next and will (God willing) be on American soil once more in all May next.—I had no wish to go there so soon, although as I have often repeated to thee [that] I always intended to go on account of my work; but I have decided in doing so *now* with a hope I can persuade thee to come over here with me and under my care and charge.[6]

He had also written in the same letter:

> I have wrote duplicate letters to Victor on this subject, with strongest injunction to keep it a perfect secret, and I wish thee to do the same. Only 3 or 4 friends in England will know *positively* when I have gone, my Subscribers, and the *World* will think me on the European Continent after more Patronage—this is absolutely necessary for the safe keeping of my present subscribers, most all of which would become alarmed and would expect the work to fall through.[7]

However, before Audubon did leave for America, he was persuaded by J. G. Children of the British Museum to go openly, for "many valuable reasons."[8]

The remaining three months prior to Audubon's sailing for America on 1 April 1829 were set down in detail in a journal which has been destroyed. The granddaughter of the Naturalist, Maria R. Audubon, quotes from this journal in part as follows:

> I have made up my mind to go to America, and with much labor and some trouble have made ready. My business is as well arranged for as possible; I have given the agency of my work to my excellent friend Children, of the British Museum, who kindly offered to see to it during my absence. I have collected some money, paid all my debts, and taken passage in the packet ship 'Columbia' Captain Delano.[9]

So well had Audubon arranged the future work of his engraver that on 21 January he had been able, when writing to Charles Lucien Bonaparte, to list the drawings which were to compose the five numbers to be published in the year 1829.[10]

Arriving in New York in May, Audubon did not tarry there. He did, however, take the opportunity to exhibit his prints at the New York Lyceum, an institution from which he hoped to obtain a subscription to his *Birds of America*.[11] Before leaving New York, he wrote a long letter to his wife in which he outlined his future plans in great detail:

> 1. I have come to America to remain as long as consistent with the *safety* of my publication in London without my personal presence, and according to future circumstances either to return to England on the 1st of October next or if possible not til the 1st of April 1830....
> 2. I wish to employ and devote every moment of my sojourn in America at Drawing such Birds and Plants as I think necessary to enable me to give my publication *throughout* the degree of perfection that *I am told* exists in that portion already published and now before the Public.[12]

He further advised her that he had left in the hands of his engraver, Havell, sufficient drawings to complete "this present year and those necessary to form the 1st number of the next year."

Audubon had stated in the prospectus he issued that five plates were to constitute a number: "one Plate from one of the largest Drawings, one from the second size, and three from smaller Drawings." Before the publication of the *Birds of America* had begun, and while Audubon was drawing birds at Beech Woods, he had written: "Chance, and chance alone, had divided my drawings into three different classes, depending on the magnitude of the objects to be represented."[13] It was a format which at times caused a problem for Audubon, that of providing the large drawing. Nevertheless this arrangement was carried out to the very end.

In the same letter the Naturalist also raised the question of Lucy's returning with him to England: "Thy determination must be prompt either 'yes' or 'no'—if coming thou must settle as quick as prudence will permit...."

Audubon left New York for Philadelphia on 14 May. In accordance with his determination to "employ and devote every moment of my sojourn in America to Drawing such Birds and Plants I think necessary,"[14] he remained only a very few days in that city before removing to Camden. The spring migration was under way, and for three weeks the Naturalist roamed the countryside surrounding Camden. In the middle of June he departed for Great Egg Harbor on the New Jersey coast, where he remained until early in July when he again returned to Philadelphia. On 1 August Audubon departed for the Great Pine Swamp located in Northampton County near Mauch Chunk (now Jim Thorpe), Pennsylvania. His visit to the Great Pine Swamp lasted until 1 October, when he again returned to Philadelphia.[15]

While in Philadelphia, Audubon completed the drawings which he had begun during the visits to New Jersey and the Great Pine Swamp. He even engaged George Lehman to assist him "in finishing the plants."[16] The Naturalist had met Lehman in Pittsburgh some years previously. Three years hence Lehman would again help Audubon during a trip to Florida. On 11 October Audubon informed his wife that he had finished forty-two drawings "in four months, 11 Large, 11 Middle size and 20 Small comprising 95 birds from Eagles downwards, with plants, nests, flowers and 60 different kind of eggs."[17]

A letter to his son Victor at Louisville, written while Audubon was in the Great Pine Swamp, informed him that "My last subscriber is a Dasher—The Right Honorable Lord Viscount Kingsborough! Quite enough to fill a small inn."[18] Although the name is entered on the subscription list, Lord Kingsborough did not complete his subscription. Ledger "B" shows delivery only of Volume I and numbers 21 to 31 of the *Birds* and Volume I of the *Biography*.

In Philadelphia, Audubon received word from his wife that she could settle her affairs in January, so on 11 October he wrote her:

> I do most sincerely hope and wish that thou mayest settle thy business *very early* in Jan.*y* and reach Louisville about the end of that month—we ought to stay with Victor & John the month of February and be underway Eastwardly by

the very first day of March so as to sail from New York or Boston as best may please thee on the 1st of April next.[19]

At the end of October Audubon set out from Philadelphia to join his family in the south. He stopped off at Louisville to visit his two sons. The elder, Victor, was employed as a clerk in the office of his uncle, William G. Bakewell, while the younger, John, was employed by another uncle, Nicholas A. Berthoud. The Naturalist hastened on, reaching Bayou Sara on 17 November to finally join his wife at Beech Grove, the home of William Garret Johnson, located at St. Francisville, near Wakefield in West Feliciana Parish. Here Mrs. Audubon had been a governess and teacher since 1827.[20]

Since it was not possible to leave until the first of the year, Audubon employed his time searching the woods for birds and animals to draw and paint, adding considerably to his collection. The drawings included several exquisite unfinished deer heads, the picture of the "Black Vulture Attacking the Head of Deer," several large hawks, and some beautiful squirrels.[21]

The actual departure and the trip north were described by Audubon in a letter to his sons:

> Our plans were soon arranged. Your mother collected the moneys due her, and on the first of January, eighteen hundred and thirty, we started for New Orleans... We stayed a few days at our friend Mr. Brand's... and on the seventh of January took passage in the splendid steamer Philadelphia for Louisville, paying sixty dollars fare. We were fourteen days getting to Louisville, having had some trouble with the engine. I passed my time there at Mr. Berthoud's and your uncle W. Bakewell's, and amused myself hunting and stuffing birds until the seventh of March, when we took a steamer for Cincinnati, and thence to Wheeling and so on to Washington in the mail-coach. Congress was in session, and I exhibited drawings to the House of Representatives and received their subscription as a body. I saw the President, Andrew Jackson, who received me with great kindness, as he did your mother also afterwards. I became acquainted with the Hon, Edward Everett, Baron Krudener, and other distinguished persons, and we left for Baltimore. There my drawings were exhibited, and I obtained three subscribers, and left for Philadelphia, where we remained one week. I saw my friends Harlan, Mr. McMurtrie, and Sully, and went to New York from whence we sailed in the packet-ship Pacific, Captain R. Crocker, for England.[22]

Although the journal which Audubon kept during his visit to America has disappeared, the *Life of Audubon*, edited by his wife Lucy, contains this excerpt dated 5 May (1829), New York: "A Mr. Benjamin Smith subscribed to my work on the passage. He had his family, eight servants, five dogs, and cloth and twine enough to fly kites the world over—an excellent and benevolent man." Notice of this subscription must have been communicated to his engraver at once, for in a postscript to his letter of 7 July 1829 to Havell, the Naturalist wrote: "I hope you have delivered Mr. Smith's copy." In the final list of subscribers, subscriber number 57 of the European subscribers is: "Benjamin Smith, Esq. M. P. London."[23]

Although nearly ten months intervened between the time Audubon received the Smith subscription and that of the House of Representatives, there is no record of any other subscriptions in that interval.

It is, however, possible to record some details concerning the subscriptions mentioned to his sons. The subscription obtained in Washington was actually that of the "Joint Committee of the Library of Congress." This committee was composed of three senators and three representatives, with Edward Everett, a representative from Massachusetts, the chairman. Another subscriber listed by Audubon as having been obtained in Washington was Baron Krudener, Envoy Extraordinaire for Russia. Since there is no record of this subscription in Ledger "B," it would appear that this subscription was not completed.

During his stay in Washington, Audubon had obtained a letter of introduction from Everett to Robert Gilmor, a wealthy Baltimore merchant. In this letter, which must have been written before the subscription for the Joint Committee of the Library of Congress had been obtained, Everett wrote that Audubon had not received a single subscription in America. With Gilmor's aid, Audubon arranged an exhibition of his original paintings at the Library Company of Baltimore, from 10 to 12 o'clock on 23 March. The exhibition was repeated the following day.[24]

Writing to his sons, Audubon had stated that he had obtained three subscribers in Baltimore.[25] On the original subscription list the following names appear in order:

> Robert Gilmor, Baltimore, Md.
> Nat*l* Potter, Baltimore, Md. Proff. of Med.
> John B. Morris, Baltimore, Md.

All three subscriptions were completed, but the name of Nat*l* Potter does not appear on the list of final subscribers published in the fifth volume of the *Ornithological Biography*. The Potter folio is presently at the New York Public Library (*see* chapter 26).

When Gilmor had received ninety prints, he donated these to the Library Company of Baltimore, of which he was president. He continued to give the additional prints to the Library Company until the set was completed. Eventually the folio was purchased by the Peabody Institute Library, now a branch of the Enoch Pratt Library, for $6,000.[26]

Although Audubon spent a week in Philadelphia after he left Baltimore before sailing from New York to Liverpool on 1 April, he had not secured any additional subscriptions there.

It was while visiting his sons and other relatives in Louisville on his way north from Louisiana with his wife that Audubon set down in a letter to his elder son, Victor, his wishes, "or indeed my *Will* should any accidents befall either me or your Mother." He continued:

> These are as follows—In case of my death and your Mother's surviving it is my desire and *will* that you should immediately proceed to England and France to take arrangement of my affairs in those Countries and to settle by collections

and taking whatever property of any description that I may have there, to balance accounts with my different agents and particularly my Engraver Mr Rob*t* Havell Jun*r* now residing at London 79 Newman Street Oxford Street who holds my Copper Plates, prints &c and who was appointed my agent when I last left England—My friend J. G. Children of the British Museum has my books of business and my original Drawings. I would and do desire you to follow his advises, and he can give you much information—

My excellent friends the Family Rathbone of Liverpool hold money of mine, Books &c and to them I strongly recommend you and desire you should follow their advise.—through Mr. Havell you can find my agents and his own accounts will [enable] assist you in your collections.—Should your Mother survive me it is my Will that you give or pay over to her one entire half of [all] of these collections as well as one full half of whatever other property you may find—the other half I desire you to divide with your Dear Brother John equally, I mean to say the monies and other property. Should you feel enclined with the advise of your Dear Mother to continue the publication of my present Work on "the Birds of America" conjointly with your Mother as administratrix in which case you must divide the profits with her and your Brother John as expressed above —that publication brings me now between six and seven hundred pounds profit per annum and to continue it would be Honorable and agreeable to yourselves and would gratify my present wishes—Should this not meet your views or those of your Mother whom I desire you ever to consult and to treat with that attention and respect due her, make a sale if possible to some one person or persons of the whole on hand and the original Drawings these latter after my death will I think be of value.—In such case the division of moneys and of property is to be made as expressed above—Should we both die on our passage to England or elsewhere (I mean your Mother and myself) I desire you to become my executor and yourself and your Brother John my Heirs and in such case to devide whatever property or moneys &c equally or continue my publication conjointly with or without your Brother as both of you may arrange it between yourselves— with my blessings and the fervent hope that you will act honestly and honorably so as to deserve the Superior blessings of our God.

The above was signed and acknowledged by Lucy's brother, W. G. Bakewell, and also a brother-in-law, Nicholas Berthoud.[27]

While Audubon was in America, word had reached him from different sources that all was not well with the operation of his work in England. There had been a loss of subscribers, failure of payments by others, and finally the belief had arisen among his subscribers that Audubon did not intend to return to England. To allay the fears of his engraver, and to reassure his subscribers, Audubon wrote to Havell: "All will be well when I return—Tell my friend Children to have an *advertist* in the times news paper to contradict what ever may be said about my not returning to England."[28]

7

SUPERVISING THE WORK IN ENGLAND
1830

Upon his return to England early in 1830 Audubon found an array of vexing problems awaiting him. His list of English subscribers had diminished while he had been in America. Some subscribers had feared that he would not return and that, as a consequence, the *Birds of America*, ambitiously projected in eighty numbers, would not be completed. Although such rumors undoubtedly did result in discontinuances, Audubon believed there was another, more compelling, factor responsible for the withdrawal of subscribers. This was the deterioration of the technical quality of Havell's work, particularly with respect to the coloring of the plates. Henceforth, in addition to his work on the *Birds*, the Naturalist not only had to address himself to the pursuit of new subscribers, he also had to make a determined effort to reinstate as many as he could of those subscriptions which had lapsed.

During 1830, Audubon arranged for a series of exhibits of his work in various English provincial cities. From 1 May through the first week of June, he held an exhibition of his new drawings at Manchester. From the point of view of gaining new subscribers, the exhibition was a failure, for attendance was slim. The results of the Manchester exhibit were but one new subscriber plus the reinstatement of three subscriptions which had been abandoned. Audubon noted: "The Races and the very bad weather were all against me."[1] However, from another point of view, that of learning how the technical defects in Havell's work were contributing to the discontinuation of subscriptions, the exhibit was a success.

On 7 June, after his visit to Manchester, he wrote his engraver:

> Do let me urge you more than ever to pay the strickest attention to the Colourers for it is doubtless through their evident carelessness that the Work suffers so much at present—I could have had many new names at Manchester, had not the people there seen different setts in differnt Houses *almost of differnt colours for the same plate*.—I myself saw 2 setts that I scarcely could believe had been

sent from your House.—there is no other complaint, they all agree that the Engraving is better than the first numbers.²

A few days later he wrote again: "I saw this day several plates of the Baltimore Oriole (pl. 12) with the hanging nests no more like my drawing than a chimney sweep is to your beautiful wife."³

From Manchester Audubon proceeded to Birmingham where the plates were exhibited in a room offered him by the Society of Arts. To this exhibition Audubon issued four hundred "Notes of Invitation for Town and Country." As he wrote his wife: "So that if I do not succeed it will not be for lack of Industry."⁴ However, he met with but little success, for when the exhibition closed on 1 July he had been able to add only one name, that of John G. Reeves, to his subscription list.⁵ Furthermore, he found additional reason to complain about the prints which led him during the visit to Birmingham to write his engraver:

> I have examined you may depend at great leisure all the Plates as they hang on the walls around me, and I am surprised myself to see how carelessly *I have past over faults* which no difference of time in the engraving or colouring could not have greatly improved.—Your letter Engraver must be dismissed or become considerably more careful and in fact must now correct his past errors. When I return to London *you & I* must have regular and compleat overhauling of the Coppers, and see what can be done to redeem the character of a work of this Magnitude and one which you cannot but conceive of Importance to your own Standing as a good Engraver and a Good Man—
>
> I have been quite startled at finding that complaints respecting the work had reached this [Birmingham] from Liverpool, Manchester &c Several persons who have expressed a wish to have it say that they dare not do so fearfull of disappointment equal to that of their friends *who have subscribed.*—Should I find the same complaints as I proceed from one large town to another through out England as I am now determined to do—I must candidly tell you that I will abandon the Publication and return to my Own Woods untill I leave this World for a better one.—I have fully made up my mind to that effect and I hope you now know me too well not to believe every word of it as if I were now on my way to America.⁶

From the viewpoint of the modern researcher, perhaps it must be said that Audubon was unduly meticulous and that he found grave faults where they in fact existed only in small degree. It occasionally has been possible for this researcher simultaneously to compare prints struck off from the same plate. On the whole, the variations in colors have been slight. The differences have been noticeable principally in the shades of the blues and the greens; the former color would be too dark, a criticism often made by the Naturalist, while in the latter there would be a slight yellow tinge. On the whole, however, the work of the colorists has shown a remarkable uniformity. This latter finding is a tribute to the indefatigable supervision of Havell's work either by Audubon or by his son, Victor. Nevertheless, the freshness of the colors, revealed by the examination of many sets of the folio, has definitely been affected in certain instances by the manner in which the volumes have been stored. When these had been placed one on top of the other, their sheer weight has helped produce a chemical reaction between the oil and the pigments used and the bleach or chlorine in the Whatman paper, with the result that an impression of the bird of one print appears on the verso of the preceding print. This condition obtains particularly where the so-called earth colors or heavy browns and blacks were used.

Between 27 April, when the Audubons reached Liverpool, and 1 October, when he departed for Edinburgh, the Naturalist spent much of his time traveling the English provinces, ever seeking new subscribers. This quest was an inescapable necessity, for it was currently incoming subscription money that sustained the ongoing publication of the "Great Work," and there is evidence that Audubon's finances were quite precarious at times. Shortly after returning to England, he once again had to resort to painting birds and flowers for which he found a ready sale at satisfactory prices.[7] Although such sideline activities frequently replenished his dwindling treasury, only a growing subscription list would ultimately sustain the enterprise. However, his potential subscribers were for the most part to be found among the English aristocracy, the nobility, and even royalty.

It will be recalled how, in September 1827, Audubon had finally succeeded in securing a subscription from King George IV. To Audubon's dismay, no doubt, this subscription ceased when King George died on 28 June 1830. For this reason the Naturalist was particularly pleased to receive the subscription of the Marchioness of Hertford. Writing to his engraver of this event, he observed: "The Marchioness of Hertford received me with great kindness, desired me to call upon her when in Town and has promised to recommend my Work to her large and valuable Circle of acquaintances."[8] At the time, the marchioness was well along in years, as she had been born in 1760. She was the second wife of the marquess whom she had married when she was twenty, and not only one of England's richest heiresses but of such beauty as is rarely bestowed upon woman. During her husband's lifetime she had been a mistress of George IV.[9] Audubon had good reason to feel that the lady could aid him in his search for subscribers, but whether she was instrumental in obtaining any is not known. Her own subscription was never completed, for she died on 12 April 1834. When Audubon visited Leeds in September of that year he learned that the whole of the first volume had been cut and pasted "on the walls of her Superb rooms" at Temple Newsam.[10] In Leeds, he had the good fortune to obtain one additional subscriber, Benjamin Gott, whose son had previously subscribed.

It was inevitable that the political events of the times would affect Audubon's efforts to obtain new subscribers as well as hold those he had secured previously. A tentative plan to visit Paris had to be canceled when the Bourbon Dynasty in France was overthrown in the Revolution of 1830 and the House of Orléans, in the person of Louis Philippe, placed on the throne. The deposed king, Charles X, who fled to England, had been a subscriber. The new king, the former Duke of Orléans, was also a patron. Neither subscription was destined to be completed.

The proposed trip to France having been canceled, Audubon's travels were confined to the English provinces. In addition to Leeds, he visited Birmingham, Manchester, York, Hull, Scarborough, Whitby, Newcastle-on-Tyne, and Bedford. In Manchester, where subscribers had been lost, Audubon was able to reinstate the subscriptions of Thomas Barker and Joseph C. Dyer. He also obtained two new subscriptions, those of John Kennedy and Jacob Davies, but not one of these subscriptions was completed. Writing to his engraver about his success in Manchester, the Naturalist informed him: "I have 29 names in Manchester."[11]

With his arrival at York on 13 September, Audubon arranged to "exhibit No 17 & 18 and my Drawings at the Philosophical Society—and also the Plain Drawings to prove to a few refractory Gents the difference between those of Lizars & yours."[12] The only subscription traced to this visit is that of his agent, Alexander Barclay, again one that does not seem to have been completed. After York, the Naturalist visited the cities of Hull, Scarborough, and Whitby, arriving in Newcastle on 30 September. He had looked forward to having some success at Hull, for he had been advised that there were in that city "a good Museum and Two Large & rich publick Libraries." However, no new subscriptions were obtained; furthermore, he discontinued relationship with his agent, Rees Davies, and took from him a set of prints on hand "rumpled and sullied shockingly."[13] Audubon, writing about the various cities he had visited, commented:

> all three [Hull, Scarborough, and Whitby] of which are so truly miserable that neither could rise the wind suficiently to subscribe to a single Copy.—at Hull the Philosophical Society made Two grand efforts having called *a committee of the Whole* but it would not do!—however there I, thank God settled with Rees Davies [a bookseller] who gave me a bill at 3 Months for the balance due me then—of course I have done with him.—at Scarbrough they are considerably poorer so that this might almost be ranged under the head of beggars, was it not too often the case that Philosophers are in fact Garret mongers.—Poor Whitby. —I am doubtful if there are any Philosophers there at all rich or poor.—So after much time & money lost I felt truly glad to return to the Main Road and to find ourselves once more in the Land of Sweets.[14]

In November of 1828, when Audubon had returned from Paris, ten numbers (50 plates) of the *Birds of America* had been completed and were being delivered to subscribers. During that month, Havell was supplied with the drawings for the plates of the eleventh number, which was to be the first number of the year 1829. When, in April of that year, Audubon left for America, he had placed his drawings in the custody of his friend, John G. Children of the British Museum, who had agreed to supervise the engraving and to furnish Havell with the necessary drawings. On 20 November 1829, Mrs. Havell, on behalf of her husband, wrote to Audubon that Number 14 (plates 66–70) had been delivered; also that they would deliver Number 15 (plates 71–75) in December, and that Number 16 (plates 76–80) would be finished in February, "and I shall be standing still for work ready to commence your new collection."[15] To this letter Audubon replied from Louisville on 29 January 1830, advising his engraver: "I will be in time (God willing) for the 16 no—& will be on the spot to give you materials for the 17*th*."[16]

During the time Audubon was off to Manchester, Liverpool, and Birmingham, Havell completed the engraving of Number 17 (plates 81–85) and was in the process of engraving Numbers 18 and 19 (plates 86–95). The latter numbers included specimens of a hawk, and Audubon desired that particular pains be taken with the engraving of these birds, so on 1 July he wrote Havell, "not to compleat the Plate of the Hawks . . . until I see you."[17]

Unlike Audubon's earlier years of subscription solicitation in England, in the summer of 1830 his travels were lightened by the fact that his wife Lucy could accompany him. She was not with him during the spring of that year, however, for from April to July she remained in the home of her sister, Mrs. Alexander Gordon, in Liverpool.

That Audubon was an exacting craftsman is obvious and that he placed great demands on Havell is equally obvious. He could, however, be gracious. When Audubon was in Newcastle, Havell had sent him in addition to a supply of prospectuses, the proofs of Number 19 (plates 91–95). Acknowledging these, he wrote Havell, "I am much pleased with them all and I think that you have either improved very much or have been more careful than ever before as I think these the best of your productions."[18]

Soon after 1 October, Audubon left Newcastle for Edinburgh where he turned his attention to a new aspect of his enterprise, the publication of a narrative text, or letterpress, to accompany his *Birds of America*.

8

THE LETTERPRESS
1830-1831

As early as November of 1826, shortly after Lizars had begun the engraving of the *Birds of America*, Audubon had written in his journal: "I shall publish the letterpress in a separate book, at the same time with the illustrations, and shall accompany the descriptions of the birds with many anecdotes and accounts of localities connected with the birds themselves, and with my travels in search of them."[1]

Had Audubon included the letterpress with the engravings, he would have been required, under the British Copyright Act of 1709, to deposit a copy of the work in nine libraries in the United Kingdom. Hence his letterpress appeared separately in the five volumes of the *Ornithological Biography*.

With Havell anticipating the completion of the engraving of the first 100 drawings of *Birds of America* by year's end (1830), the Naturalist realized the necessity for beginning the preparation of the letterpress for the species which had been engraved. In this connection he felt the need of assistance in providing the scientific details.

With this in mind, Audubon wrote from Manchester, on 22 August, to William Swainson:

> If you can have the time to spare & the inclination to *Bear a hand* in the text of my work.—by my furnishing you with the ideas & observations which I have and you to add *the science* which I have not!—If it would suit you and Mrs. Swainson to take us as boarders for a few months when being almost always together I could partake of your observations & you of mine.—I would like to receive here your ideas on this subject & if possible what amount you would expect from us as remuneration.—My first volume will comprise an introduction and *one hundred letters addressed to the Reader* referring to the 100 plates forming the first volume of my illustrations.—I will enter even on local descriptions of the country.—Adventures and anecdotes, speak of the trees & the flowers the reptiles or the fishes or insects as far as I know—I wish if possible to make a *pleasing* book as well as an *instructive* one.

As to the matter of boarding with the Swainsons, he added that: "we will furnish our own wines, porter or ale."[2]

Swainson replied to this letter promptly, advising that the idea of the Audubons boarding at Tyttenhanger Green, the Swainson home, was impractical, that he expected to be remunerated at the rate of "from 5/ to 7/6 sheet," and that "it would be understood that my name stands on the title page as responsible for such portions as concerns me."[3] The proposed literary partnership never materialized, though the two men continued on friendly personal terms. In a letter to Charles Lucien Bonaparte, Audubon wrote that the salary wanted by Swainson, namely 250 pounds sterling per volume, was beyond his financial means and that MacGillivray asked little more than 50 to 60 pounds.[4]

Audubon already had been preparing material for the "biographies" of the first hundred birds when he arrived in Edinburgh early in October. Because he had been unable to arrange with Swainson for assistance with the writing of his letterpress, he immediately began to look for help from other sources. He sought out Professor James Wilson, a naturalist, whose acquaintance he had made in 1826 during his earlier visit to Edinburgh,[5]

> ... to ask if he knew of any person who would undertake to correct my ungrammatical manuscripts, and to assist me in preparing the more scientific part of the "Biography of the Birds." He gave me a card with the address of Mr. W. McGillivray [MacGillivray], spoke well of his talents, and away to Mr. McGillivray I went. He had long known of me as a naturalist. I made known my business, and a bargain was soon struck. He agreed to assist me, and correct my manuscripts for two guineas per sheet of sixteen pages, and I that day began to write the first volume.[6]

The arrangement with William MacGillivray was to last until the five volumes of the letterpress were completed in 1839.

While Audubon was engaged in writing his letterpress for the first volume, he learned that there were soon to be published three editions of Wilson's *Ornithology*. The first of these, edited by Professor Robert Jameson, appeared in 1831; the second, by Sir William Jardine, was published in 1832; and the third, by a Captain Thomas Brown, was published in 1835.[7] Commenting on these forthcoming publications in his journal, Audubon wrote:

> Most persons would probably have been discouraged by this information, but it only had a good effect on me, because since I have been in England I have studied the character of Englishmen as carefully as I studied the birds in America. And I know full well that, in England novelty is always in demand, and that if a thing is well known it will not receive much support. Wilson has had his day, thought I to myself, and now is my time. I will write, and I hope to be read; and not only so, but I will push my publication with such unremitting vigor, that my book shall come before the public. . . . Writing now became the order of the day. I sat at it as soon as I awoke in the morning, and continued the whole long day, and so full was my mind of birds and their habits, that in my sleep I continually dreamed of birds. I found Mr. McGillivray equally industrious, for

although he did not rise so early in the morning as I did, he wrote much later
at night (this I am told is a characteristic of all great writers); and so the manuscripts went on increasing in bulk, like the rising of a stream after abundant
rains, and before three months had passed the first volume was finished. Meanwhile your mother copied it all to send to America, to secure the copyright
there.[8]

Why did Audubon feel it necessary to secure the collaboration of William MacGillivray? Perhaps Audubon himself can supply us with a most succinct answer to
this question. On 1 May 1832 he had written to Charles Lucien Bonaparte, "I am
a plain family man. You know I derive no knowledge from classical education."[9]
In another letter to Bonaparte (January 1832), the Naturalist commented, "I
think I see a smile on your lips of the idea of my presumption but I could not
help writing *Something*, and I am finally convinced that the book will be composed
of nothing but plain truth."[10] In yet an earlier letter to Bonaparte, written 14 July
1830, Audubon stated: "You yourself know better than anyone living, the best
judge, that I am not a learned naturalist, I am only and to a very great extent a
practical one." In that same letter he confessed that he "scarcely ever read a book
on the subject" and also that "with my lack of education, I must content myself
with the simple facts."[11]

It is clear that Audubon always kept uppermost a very realistic view of his own
scientific limitations, and always gave full credit to the contributions of MacGillivray. In his introduction to Volume 1 of the *Ornithological Biography*, the
Naturalist wrote:

> I feel pleasure in here acknowledging the assistance which I have received from
> a friend, Mr William MacGillivray, who being possessed of a liberal education
> and a strong taste for the study of the Natural Sciences, has aided me, not in
> drawing the figures of my Illustrations, nor in writing the book now in your
> hand, although fully competent for both tasks, but in completing the scientific
> details and smoothing down the asperities of my Ornithological Biographies.[12]

As years went on, Audubon's knowledge of the scientific aspects of ornithology
increased, so much so that in the introduction of Volume 5 of the *Ornithological
Biography*, he wrote:

> My friend MacGillivray and myself were up to the elbows among the birds
> which I had brought in spirits with me from America, I acting as secretary, he
> as prime minister. Under his kind tuition, I think I have learned something of
> anatomy which may enable me, at some future period, to produce observations
> that may prove interesting even to you, good Reader, for I promise that no
> sooner shall I have returned to America and procured specimens of any species
> whose digestive and respiratory organs have not been described in this work,
> than I will try to examine them in detail and publish the results in the Journals
> of some of our scientific institutions.[13]

Although Audubon cannot be regarded as a natural scientist, at least not in the
twentieth-century meaning of this term, he did contribute many original and

valuable ornithological facts. That he did excel as a keen observer of birds is attested to by Dr. Robert Cushman Murphy, for many years Lamont Curator of Birds at the American Museum of Natural History. In a pamphlet entitled *John James Audubon, An Evaluation of the Man and His Work* (New-York Historical Society, 1956), Murphy stated,

> To a certain extent the biographies, whether in the original or as a rearrangement of the text in the Royal Octavo editions of the *Birds of America*, have become a half forgotten treasure. They are surely replete with information that compilers of later works have not yet used. Many ornithologists have had the experience of making some new discovery in bird behavior, which has proven unknown to their most erudite colleagues, only to find that keen eyed Audubon had minutely described the same phenomenon a hundred years before. A case in point is the life history of the beautiful Roseate Spoonbill, of Florida Bay and the Gulf Coast, which was exhaustively studied just before World War II by Robert Allen of the National Audubon Society. Mr. Allen found that of all the published accounts of this extraordinary bird, Audubon's was the freshest and soundest as well as one of the most exhaustive.

This recent testimonial amply confirms Audubon's own evaluation of himself as a naturalist. He called himself "a practical scientist" and "a man of plain facts," and so he was. But within the limited theoretical framework of his scientific outlook, he was unexcelled as an observer during his own day, as he remains in our own time.

To carry out the arduous assignment of writing the *Ornithological Biography*, Audubon earlier had apparently decided to forego the writing of scientific journal articles, thereby conserving his energies. His journal entry dated 9 January 1828 has the following comment:

> Had a long letter from John Chorley [a Liverpool acquaintance], and after some talk with my good friend J. G. Children, have decided to write nothing more except the biographies of my birds. It takes too much time to write to this one and to that one, to assure them that what I have written is *fact*. When Nature as it is found in my beloved America is better understood, these things will be known generally, and when I have been dead twenty years, more or less, my statements will be accepted everywhere; till then they may wait.

In January of 1831, Audubon arranged with his friend P. Neill, of Edinburgh, to do the printing of the *Ornithological Biography*.[14] By 29 March, the printing of 750 copies of the book had been completed.[15] The price of the book to the subscribers of the *Birds of America* was to be one guinea, to nonsubscribers, twenty-five shillings.[16] Later he decided against charging his subscribers for the *Ornithological Biography*, for, after delivering a copy to subscriber George H. Head, he wrote his engraver: "Deliver all the continuing subscribers a copy gratis but none to those who have discontinued without receiving 25 shillings."[17] He also arranged for publication of the *Ornithological Biography* in America. By February, through Dr. McMurtry of Philadelphia, arrangements had been completed for the publication of five hundred copies of Volume 1 in that city, to be printed by James Kay, Junior, and Company. The estimated cost of the American edition was $700.[18]

Upon publication of Volume 1 of the *Ornithological Biography* at the end of March, Audubon had not long to wait for the critical reception of his work in the British press. The entry for 15 April in his journal contains the following observation:

> Several reviews of my work have appeared. One in Blackwood's magazine is particularly favorable. The editor, John Wilson is a clever good fellow, and I wrote to thank him. Dr. Took, an Irishman of lively manners, brought the editors of the *Atlas* to see my birds, and they have praised also.[19]

It is evident that critical opinion of his work was not always completely satisfying to Audubon, for occasionally there are indications of asperity in his feelings about his critics. The following are observations Audubon wrote to his engraver after he had examined Number 20 (plates 96–100), the final number of the first volume of *Birds of America*: "I look upon these engravings as the best *I ever saw of birds in any country*—and the *Devil* take the critics say I, and do you go on in the same throughout this mighty work our names will go farther together than any critics of nonsense of the present day."[20]

Busily occupied as he was with the writing of the letterpress, Audubon somehow found time to attend to the many details concerned with the publication of the *Birds of America*. Among others these details involved compliance with the British copyright act and dealing with the complaints of subscribers. Since Audubon was printing his letterpress separately from the engravings of the *Birds of America*, it was not necessary for him to deposit copies of the folio in the nine libraries of Great Britain as required under the British Copyright Act of 1709. He did become concerned lest the inclusion of a "title page" might make him liable, but in the end each subscriber was furnished with such a page for each volume. However, the Naturalist did decide against the "Page of Contents" which he had requested his engraver to prepare for the George Head copy, writing him on 23 March, "do not print any Sheet of content at all."[21]

Very soon after the Naturalist's arrival in Edinburgh, he met one of his early subscribers, Miss Maria Woodruff Smith of Clapham, who had discontinued "it because numbers 1 to 9, which she received were so very bad that she could not think of giving *house room* to any more such *trash* so she called the work. After much talk and her seeing how beautifully engraved the 19th No is & how superfinely coloured she concluded that she would resume. . . ."[22] In November 1830, George H. Head, a banker from Carlisle, visited Audubon and became a subscriber. Audubon, when advising his engraver of this subscription, wrote:

> As I was about stopping my letter George H. Head, Esquire banker of Carlisle came in and *has subscribed*. Now do you do your best and find him a *handsome clean copy well coloured* &c directed as above as soon as you can—of the 20 Numbers with a Sheet of Title, page of Contents & Subscribers names, in a good portfolio, with Silverpaper for the whole and write to me when this is done.[23]

The name of this subscriber is not included in the final list of subscribers. Furthermore the entry in Ledger "B" shows that only Volume 1 and Numbers 21 to 31 (plates 101–10) with the first volume of the *Ornithological Biography* were delivered. However, Banker Head did pay forty guineas when the first volume was delivered.[24] It is possible that the Head subscription may have been completed through one of Audubon's agents, for there is at Amherst College a set of the folio in which the first volume contains a sheet of Whatman paper on which there are engraved a list of subscribers similar to the one published in the prospectus issued shortly after the first volume of the letterpress was completed. No engraved list of subscribers has been found in any set other than the one at Amherst.

Shortly before the end of 1830 Audubon had received another subscription, that of Thomas Walker of Ravenfield, near Doncaster. This subscription was completed. Not long after the first of the new year, Havell advised Audubon that there had been received by him the subscription of the Boston Athenaeum, sent by Thomas H. Perkins.[25] It is possible that this subscription had been obtained with the help of Edward Everett, through whom Audubon had received the subscription of the Library of Congress and who was a prominent member of the Athenaeum.

Just as Audubon frequently received complaints from his subscribers, so he, with even greater frequency, complained to Havell about certain faults in the engraving. This was particularly true of the letter engravings.[26] Examination of the extant sets of the folio has brought to light examples of the same plate on which arabic numerals had been used on one print and roman on another. Also, in some instances the legend would appear within the body of a plate, and on another example of the same plate it would be found at the bottom. While Audubon was still engaged with his letterpress, Mrs. Audubon had written to Havell: "The changes in printing on the plates he hopes to send Monday or Tuesday next."[27]

Audubon wrote the very long and detailed letter containing "the changes in printing" on 2 March 1831. This letter, written on foolscap, 16¼" × 10¼", is now in the Princeton University Library. The Naturalist's requests began thus: "I wish you to set about having the plates reengraved I mean the lettering as soon as possible and to employ such engravers as will do justice to the whole of it." In addition, he set down in complete detail the arrangement which was to be applied generally, using the plates of "Selby's Flycatcher" (pl. 9) and the "Carolina Turtle Dove" (pl. 17) as examples. He specified that titles were to be "Always at the bottom of the plate." The plate numbers were to be in roman letters; the legend for his name was to be, "Drawn from nature by J. J. Audubon, F.R.S., F.L.S."; that of the engraver, "Engraved, printed and coloured by R. Havell, Jun." His other instructions were:

> When the space left at the bottom of the plate is small, let the name run on in a continuous line thus,
> Wild Turkey, Meleagris Gallopavo. Linn. Male. American Cane. Miegia macrosperma. [*Written on one line.*]

The Letterpress, 1830–1831

Let the naming be uniform in all the plates, that is let the English names of the birds be all in one character, the Latin names also in one character, &c

> Carolina Turtle Dove.
> Columba carolinensis. Linn.
> Males, 1.   Females, 2.

The above announcement and lettering to be adopted throughout.
For the largest plates. Let the letters not be larger than those of Plate 46. N. 10.
For the middle-sized plates, let them be the size of those of Plate 47. N. 10.
For the small plates, as in . . . Plate 64 N. 13.
Be sure not to have any at the *top* of the plates, not to make Capital letters where they should be small, and to have the whole uniform—no flourishes
    the dots (.,) to be as in manuscript.

Finally, the Naturalist listed the titles for the first forty-four plates.

It had now become necessary for Audubon to supply his engraver with the drawings for the second volume of the *Birds of America*. Early in December, Lucy Audubon had written Havell: "The drawings for the 21 No. you shall have as soon as the Raven [pl. 101] is painted, say in a week."[28] It would have been out sooner had it not been for the foggy weather.[29] In February of the following year, Audubon sent the engraver fifteen drawings, sufficient for three numbers.[30] As the engraving of the second volume began, it had evidently occurred to Audubon that it might be well were the work speeded up, so he wrote Havell, asking: "if he could not manage to publish 6 Nos. per annum instead of 5."[31]

Audubon had stated in the original prospectus that "There are upwards of 400 Drawings, and it is proposed that they shall comprise Three Volumes, each containing about 130 Plates to which an Index will be given at the end of each, to be bound up with the Volume." As has been related earlier, such an index was not prepared. On the other hand, the number of plates was increased to 435, a total of eighty-seven numbers. At the rate the work had progressed thus far, an additional eleven years would have been required to complete it. However, Havell was able to increase the yearly output, so that the remaining 335 plates were engraved by June of 1838.

With the completion of the letterpress for the first volume of the *Ornithological Biography* and the printing of the manuscript, Audubon was anxious to leave Edinburgh so that he might again visit Newcastle, Leeds, York, Manchester, Chester, Birmingham, and Liverpool where he wished personally to deliver copies of his book to his subscribers. He was delayed in getting started by the tardy delivery of Number 21 (plates 101–5), which did not reach him until 13 April. With their arrival Audubon wrote Mrs. Havell:

> I can only say that I am pleased with all, and hope your good husband's health is restored and that he will live to see his name raised sky high above that of all other Engravers of Birds—give him our best thanks and also tell him the more he works at present the more he will enjoy the older days when Industry herself becomes impotent and drowsy.[32]

In the same letter he also wrote that he hoped by showing his subscribers number 21 "to bring to their sense of duty" those subscribers who had defaulted on their subscriptions.

In April Audubon had received the subscription of Mrs. [Miss] Euphemia Gifford, Duffield Bank, Derby, a relative of his wife Lucy. The elder of Audubon's two sons had been named Victor Gifford after this relative. As early as 1808, when Audubon was living in Louisville, he had sent a number of his drawings to Miss Gifford. At the time these drawings were made they "were simply intended for the gratification of my best friends on earth my beloved wife, as well as myself, and some of her relatives, especially Miss Euphemia Gifford, to whom as good fortune would have it, I sent about thirty before I removed to Henderson." Plate 434, "The Small Headed Flycatcher," figured in London, was derived from a drawing sent to Miss Gifford at that time.[33]

Audubon expressed his appreciation for this subscription in a letter to Miss Gifford as follows:

> I do not only feel grateful to you for your Patronage but proud to be able to add to my List of Subscribers the name of my wife's earliest and best of friends, and in forwarding you a copy of my work will take satisfaction in attending to the coloring and finishing of each separate Plate or engraving.

This subscription was completed.[34]

In the same month Audubon made an arrangement with John Calvert of Leeds to exchange the first volume of the *Birds of America* for the "best Double Barreled Gun, Case, Implements, etc." This was no doubt in anticipation of the forthcoming journey to America. It is known from another letter written to Miss Gifford just prior to his sailing that he had obtained the subscription of her "Royal Highness the Landgravine Hesse Homburg."[35] This subscription was not completed; in fact, in Ledger "B" Audubon had written after the name of this subscriber the word, "Humbug."

In a journal entry the Naturalist summarized his activities prior to his departure from England on his second journey to America and also reviewed the task of publishing the *Birds of America* which he had begun five years previously as follows:

> April 15. We left Edinburgh this day, and proceeded towards London by way of New Castle, York, Leeds, Manchester, and Liverpool. At the latter place we spent a few days, and travelled on that extraordinary road called the railway, at the rate of twenty-four miles an hour. On arriving at London I found it urgent for me to visit Paris, to collect monies due me by my agent [Pitois] there.
>
> We have received letters from America of a cheering kind, and which raised my dull spirits, but in spite of all this I feel dull, rough in temper and long for nothing so much as my dear woods. I have balanced my accounts with the "Birds of America," and the whole business is really wonderful; forty thousand dollars have passed through my hands for the completion of the first volume. Who would believe that a lonely individual, who landed in England without a

friend in the whole country, and with only sufficient pecuniary means to travel through it as a visitor, could have accomplished such a task as this publication? Who would believe that once in London Audubon had only one sovereign left in his pocket, and did not know of a single individual to whom he could apply to borrow another, when he was on the verge of failure in the very beginning of his undertaking; and above all, who would believe that he extricated himself from all his difficulties, not by borrowing money, but by rising at four o'clock in the morning, working hard all day, and disposing of his works at a price which a common laborer would have thought little more than sufficient remuneration for his work? To give you an idea of my actual difficulties during the publication of my first volume, it will be sufficient to say, that in the four years required to bring that volume before the world, no less than fifty of my subscribers, representing the sum of fifty-six thousand dollars, abandoned me! And whenever a few withdrew I was forced to leave London, and go to the provinces to obtain others to supply their places, in order to enable me to raise the money to meet the expenses of engraving, coloring, paper, printing &c; and that with all my constant exertions, fatigues, and vexations, I find myself now having but one hundred and thirty standing names on my list.

England is most wealthy, and among her swarms of inhabitants there are many whom I personally know, and to whom, if I were to open my heart, there would be a readiness to help me for the sake of science; but my heart revolts from asking such a favor, and I will continue to trust in that Providence which has helped me thus far.[36]

9

SECOND RETURN TO AMERICA
1831-1832

Even while Audubon was at sea en route to America during the month of August 1831, he pressed forward on the task which was to preoccupy him for the next year. The work on the folio was now running into its second volume. Since it was planned that the third volume should see the beginning of the water birds, it had become necessary for him to undertake drawings of these species. Taking advantage of calm seas, he obtained a boat with some hands to row him about, with the result that he was able to draw specimens of forked-tailed (Leach's petrels) and fulmar petrels (fulmars). In these endeavors, Audubon was assisted by a taxidermist, Henry Ward, who was to accompany him for most of the forthcoming year.[1]

As always, Audubon's itinerary was methodical. He stopped briefly in New York, then proceeded to Philadelphia[2] where he attended a meeting of the Academy of Natural Sciences on 16 September. However, from the day he arrived, which was 3 September 1831, he intended to proceed "to the Floridas as fast as Steamboats or Coaches will allow."[3] In Philadelphia, the traveling party of the Naturalist, his wife Lucy, his son Victor, and Henry Ward was augmented by a fifth person, George Lehman (?–1870), a Swiss landscape painter whose services Audubon had previously used. Proceeding south, the group went to Baltimore, whence Victor escorted his mother to Louisville while his father, Ward, and Lehman continued en route to the Floridas.

Despite Audubon's determination to reach his destination "as fast as Steamboats or Coaches will allow," he could not neglect either the search for new subscribers or personal service to old ones. While in Philadelphia he obtained the subscriptions of the Philosophical Society (The American Philosophical Society), John P. Wetherill, Dr. Richard Harlan, and the Academy of Natural Sciences.

In a letter written to his engraver on 20 September from Philadelphia, Audubon stated that while in New York he had "delivered Nos 21, 22, & 23 to Major Lang for Mr. Ed*d* Harris."[4] Harris had befriended Audubon during the Naturalist's

Second Return to America, 1831–1832

visit to Philadelphia in 1824. It was undoubtedly the subscription by Harris which Audubon had obtained in New York, for on the original subscription list, Harris's name precedes those of the Philadelphia subscribers. Encouraged by his success in obtaining four subscribers in Philadelphia, Audubon wrote his engraver from that city, "I wish you to forward six more Volumes and following numbers as soon as possible care of Mes*srs* Walker & C*o*, New York—bound as those which are now at Sea."[5] This last was a reference to his instructions, given to Havell before leaving England, that six copies of Volume 1 of *Birds of America* be bound and shipped to America as soon as possible.

As the Naturalist continually searched for new subscribers, he also maintained a continuous supervision of the interests of his old subscribers. While in Baltimore, he called on subscribers Morris, Gilmor, and Dr. Potter, whose subscriptions he had obtained during his first trip to America, and learned that they had not yet received Numbers 19 and 20 (the last parts of Volume 1). Accordingly, Audubon wrote Havell to send these numbers along at once and reported that plate 82, the one of the whippoorwill, when received by Morris, had been cut almost in two.[6] He also delivered sets of Numbers 22 and 23 to those subscribers who had already received the prints for Number 21.

From Baltimore Audubon went to Richmond, Virginia, there seeking a subscription on behalf of the State of Virginia from Governor John Floyd, to whom he had a letter of introduction. The governor promised to propose to the legislature that it subscribe. A similar promise was made by the librarian of the college [probably the University of Virginia].[7] Neither the state nor the college ever subscribed. And on leaving Richmond, Audubon contemplated going to Columbia, South Carolina, in the hope of obtaining the subscription of the University of South Carolina, or, as he called it, "Columbia College."[8] However, it appears that he did not carry out this intention, for the evidence indicates that instead he went directly to Charleston.

During the eleven months that comprised the period of September 1831 through July 1832, Audubon and his two assistants were to execute a journey which took them from the starting point of New York, southward through Charleston, St. Augustine, Florida, Key West, the Tortugas, and then northward through Charleston, Philadelphia, and finally to Boston where he arrived in early August 1832.

That Audubon was able to carry out his ambitious plan of traveling through the Floridas in search of water bird specimens depended in large measure on his ability to secure the active support of the United States government, which was on three occasions to place official Navy schooners at his disposal. Audubon was also to enjoy other favors from the United States government.

In January 1831, Audubon learned from one of his Baltimore subscribers, a Mr. Morris, who was also acting as his agent, that an import duty of 15 percent was being imposed on the prints of *Birds of America* as they arrived at United States ports of entry. Rightly considering this a serious threat to his business prospects, Audubon quickly acted to enlist the aid of Edward Everett, a representative from

Massachusetts whom he had met in Washington on his first return to America. Audubon asked Congressman Everett to seek a congressional remedy for this grievance. On 15 May, Everett wrote to advise the Naturalist that it had not been possible to secure the necessary action in the 1830–31 session of Congress, but that he would continue his efforts. It is known from a letter written from Boston on 5 February 1833 by Audubon to his son Victor, who was then in London supervising the production of the "Large Work," that the duty had been removed.[9] Current research discloses that an 1824 act of Congress had imposed duties on "printing, copperplate, and stainers' paper." This portion of the act was repealed by the 14 July 1832 "Act to Alter and Amend the Several Acts Imposing Duties on Imports." This revised act is to be found in the *Statutes at Large*, Twenty-second Congress, First Session, 1832. It is, of course, conjectural to what extent Audubon's importunities to Edward Everett contributed to this result.

On 16 October Audubon and his party arrived in Charleston,[10] which city was to be their point of embarkation for a sea voyage to St. Augustine aboard the naval schooner *Agnes*. Upon his arrival there, the Naturalist began at once to deliver letters of introduction, among the first of which was one to the Reverend Samuel Gilman (1791–1858), a native of Boston and, at that time, the Unitarian minister in Charleston.[11] Gilman had evidently volunteered to help Audubon find less expensive lodgings, for it was in the course of this search that they met the Reverend John Bachman, to whom Gilman introduced the Naturalist. It is possible that Bachman had heard about Audubon and they may even have corresponded, but they had never before met.[12]

John Bachman (1790–1874), a Lutheran minister in Charleston, had had from his earliest boyhood an irrepressible desire to study natural history. A friendship was formed immediately, and Bachman invited not only Audubon but the two assistants as well to stay at his home. Of this invitation, Audubon wrote to his wife who was in Louisville with her brother, William Bakewell, "Why my Lucy Mr Bachman would have us all stay at his house — he would have us to make free there as if we were at our own encampment at the head of Some unknown Rivers—he would not suffer us to proceed farther South for 3 weeks."[13] This friendship between the two men was to be lifelong. Not only was Bachman to be of invaluable help to Audubon with the *Birds of America*, he was to become co-author of the *Viviparous Quadrupeds of North America*. And Audubon's two sons married two of the clergyman's daughters.

Later in the year when the Naturalist was in Florida, Bachman continued to exert himself on Audubon's behalf by functioning as his agent. Bachman informed Audubon that the legislature of South Carolina had subscribed for the university. The circumstances surrounding his efforts in procuring the subscription Bachman described in his letter of 23 December 1831 to Audubon as follows:

> I arrived in Columbia almost too late, for the "House" had just resolved that the State was too poor to subscribe for Audubon's work. I felt that it would be a disgrace to the State and for the first time in my life I turned to electioneering.

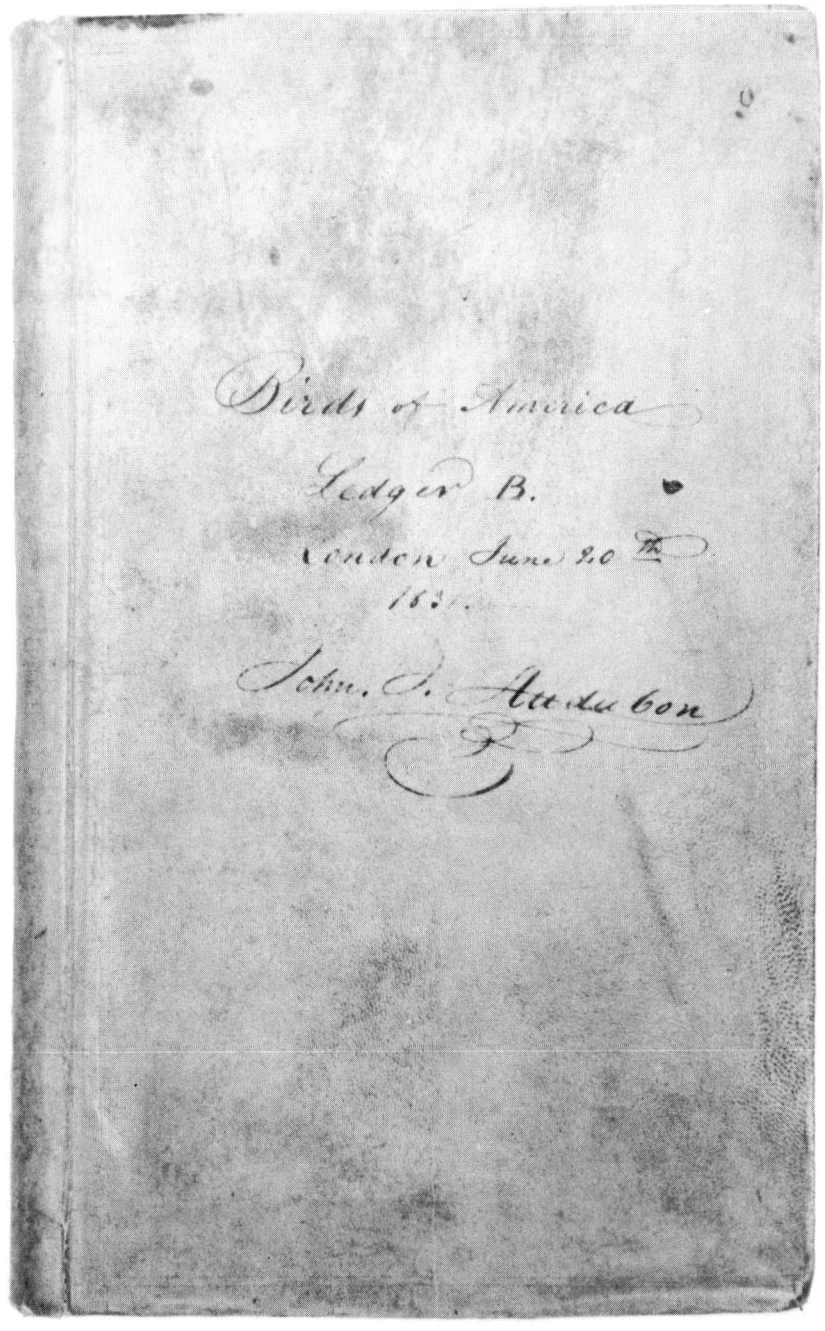

Audubon's Ledger "B." The inscription on the cover reads:
Birds of America
Ledger B
London June 20th
1831
[signed] John J. Audubon
Courtesy of the Audubon State Park Museum, Henderson, Ky.

Shipping box (closed) of the type used by Audubon. Courtesy of the American Museum of Natural History, New York.

The same box open. Courtesy of the American Museum of Natural History, New York.

CATALOGUE

OF

Mr JOHN J. AUDUBON'S

Birds of America,

BEING THAT PORTION OF HIS COLLECTION NOW EXHIBITING

AT THE

EDINBURGH ROYAL INSTITUTION.

Land Birds.

English Names.	Linnæan Names.
1. The Bird of Washington, or Great Sea Eagle,	*Falco washingtoniensis*,—Female.
2. White-Headed Eagle,	*F. leucocephalus*,—Male.
3. Red-Tailed Hawks,	*F. borealis.*
4. Ash-Coloured Hawk,	*F. atricapillus.*
5. Winter Hawk,	*F. hyemalis.*
6. Marsh Hawk,	*F. uliginosus.*
7. Swallow-tailed Hawk,	*F. furcatus.*
8. Mississippi Kite,	*F. mississipiensis.*

Page from the catalogue of an Audubon exhibition held at the Edinburgh Royal Institution, 20 November–24 December 1826. Courtesy of the Edinburgh Royal Institution.

BIRDS OF AMERICA.
THE PROVIDENCE ATHENEUM
Having imported at much expense, Audubon's Ornithology, wherein every BIRD is represented of its ACTUAL SIZE, and splendidly and accurately colored to the life, propose making an exhibition of the Plates. THEY have taken, for that purpose, Rooms Nos. 43 and 45, ARCADE, which will be kept open from 9 o'clock A. M. to noon, and from 1 o'clock P. M. to 4 P. M. for 6 weeks from the 1st of October. Admittance 25 cents. Season tickets 50 cents, to be had at A. S. BECKWITH'S Bookstore, and at the door.
o17 1mdis

Announcement of the Providence Atheneum of an Audubon exhibition held in October and November 1832, which appeared in the *Rhode Island County Journal* for 26 October 1832. Courtesy of James T. Tyson, Providence, R.I.

> And now behold me among the back countrymen, spinning long yarns. The thing, however, took, and your book is subscribed for.

Bachman also wrote in this letter that he had written to William Gaston, a merchant in Savannah, to interest him in procuring subscribers.[14]

Audubon was not ungrateful for his new friend's hospitality, for in a letter, Bachman noted that Audubon had used the expression "a load of gratitude" in a letter of thanks. Bachman's retort was:

> now suppose we say no more about this. Your visit to me gave me new life, induced me to go carefully over my favorite study, and made me and my family happy. We have, therefore, been mutually obliged and gratified.

From this letter of Bachman's it is known that Audubon was presenting the Bachman family with a copy of the first volume of *Birds of America*.[15] Whether or not the family received the other volumes is not known. This first volume is now in the possession of the H. J. Lutcher Stark Memorial Library of Orange, Texas.

Audubon's days while in Charleston were occupied with trips to the surrounding country and adjacent islands in the company of Bachman and other residents of Charleston. Birds were hunted, skinned, and painted. Before leaving, Audubon had figured fifteen birds, which were to make five drawings when finished. Among these were one of two large curlews (plate 231) and one of five ground doves on a wild orange branch (plate 182). The background view of Charleston on plate 231 was the work of Lehman. Also, while in Charleston, Ward had skinned and preserved 220 specimens, comprising sixty species of birds.[16]

During this period, Audubon's efforts to secure additional subscriptions were considerably reinforced by those of Bachman, who had inaugurated a plan to obtain new ones through the distribution among his friends of subscription papers, each to be filled with twelve names at five dollars per annum and nineteen dollars cash to pay for the first volume. In this manner, he expected to be able to procure half a dozen subscribers to the "Great Work." In a letter to his wife describing this plan, Audubon observed, "The Papers here have *blown me up* sky high [and] The Society of Natural Sciences of Philadelphia has *at last* elected me one of their members."[17]

After one interruption, the schooner *Agnes* having been forced to put back to St. Simon's Island off the coast of Georgia because of rough seas, Audubon and his assistants arrived at St. Augustine.[18] Their stay in northern Florida lasted until early March. The first three weeks were spent searching for birds in and around St. Augustine, with Audubon and Lehman busily drawing, but with Ward almost idle due to the scarcity of specimens to skin and preserve. The weather was most changeable, alternatingly hot and sultry followed by cold days.[19] By 5 December, Audubon had drawn seventeen different species and 103 skins as well as two boxes of shells had been collected. Included among these drawings was one of particular interest, that of the Brazilian caracara (plate 161), now known as Audubon's caracara.[20]

It was while visiting the Bulow plantation, some fifty miles from St. Augustine, that Audubon learned that the United States government had placed at his disposal the schooner *Spark* under the command of Lieutenant Piercy. This was the second vessel the United States government was to make available to the Naturalist. On the receipt of this news the party returned to St. Augustine, reaching that city on 15 January. However, the *Spark* was unable to get under way until later in the month.

The journey to the mouth of the St. John's River did not provide Audubon with many new species of birds, but it did furnish many interesting experiences, vividly described in the following "Episodes" which are included in the second volume of the *Ornithological Biography*:

> The Lost One
> The Live-Oakers
> Spring Garden
> St. John's River in Florida.

After the expedition to the mouth of the St. John's River, the return voyage of the *Spark* from St. Augustine to Charleston was marred by rough seas. The vessel was struck by gales and forced to put in at Savannah. This misadventure at sea proved to be a fortunate circumstance for Audubon, for Savannah was the home of William Gaston, a prosperous merchant whose support and assistance were to materially aid the Naturalist in his production of the "Great Work." John Bachman had written to Gaston on Audubon's behalf; Audubon had assigned his baggage trunks in care of the merchant; and he also held in his possession a letter of introduction to Gaston from his friends, the Rathbones of Liverpool.

Audubon's meeting with the "Merchant of Savannah" was described in detail as an episode included in the second volume of the *Ornithological Biography*, from which the following is quoted in part:

> In company of a gentleman, who kindly offered to guide me, I therefore proceeded, and was fortunate enough to meet him on the street. The merchant took my arm under his, and as we proceeded, talked of the many demands of money made on him for charitable purposes, the high price of the "Birds of America," and his inability to subscribe for that work, concluding with telling me, that he much doubted if even a single purchaser could be got in Savannah.
>
> My spirits were sadly depressed, for my voyage to the Floridas had been expensive and unprofitable, not having been undertaken at the proper season; and I confess I thought more of my family than of what the gentleman said to me. However, we reached his counting-house, where I met Major Le Conte, of the United States' army, with whom I was previously acquainted. Our conversation turned on the difficulties which authors have to encounter even in their own country. I observed that the merchant was extremely attentive, and at length seemed uneasy. He rose from his seat, spoke to his clerk, and sat down again. The Major took his leave, and I was about to follow him, when the merchant addressing himself to me, said he could not conceive why the arts and sciences should not be encouraged by men of wealth in our country. The clerk now returned and handed him some papers, which he transferred to me saying, "I

subscribe to your work; here is the price of the first volume; come with me, I know you now, and I will procure you some others; every one of us is bound to you for the knowledge you bring to us of things, which, without your zeal and enterprise, might probably never have reached us. I will now make it my duty to serve you, and will be your agent in this city."[21]

Gaston was as good as his word. Before Audubon left that day (9 March 1832) for Charleston two more subscriptions, those of James Potter and Alexander Telfair, were forthcoming, with payment from each subscriber for the first volume. Two days after Audubon arrived in Charleston, he received a letter from Gaston enclosing $200 with another subscription, that of Daniel Blake.[22]

William Gaston's expressed attitudes toward the support of Audubon's great enterprise indicate that he thought of himself as a patron of the arts and sciences. In this sense, he constitutes an American counterpart of the aristocratic patrons whose support Audubon sought so assiduously in England. When later the Naturalist attempted and failed to procure a subscription from Baron Rothschild, he explicitly compared Rothschild and Gaston in terms of the two men's attitudes toward the duties of the rich to support the arts and sciences. Gaston's contribution to Audubon's work is graphically shown in the memorandum which the Naturalist sent to his wife with the request that it be forwarded to Havell. The list which follows includes fifteen names of subscribers obtained since Audubon's arrival in America the previous September. Four of the Savannah subscriptions were directly or indirectly William Gaston's contributions.[23] The King subscription Audubon had obtained earlier when the *Agnes* had been forced to put back to St. Simon's Island off the Georgia coast.[24]

Miss Douglas and Ed*d* Harris	New York	2
Thomas Perkins	Boston	1
R*d*. Harland M.D. Philo*al* Society Society of Nat*l* Sciences John P. Wetherill	---- Phil*a*	4
Nath*l* Potter M.D. Rob*t* Gilmor John B. Morris	---- Baltimore	3
W*am* Gaston James Potter Alex*r* Telfair Tho*s* Butler King Daniel Blake	---- Savannah	5
Legislature of S. C*a* Soc'y Natural History Charleston 2	South C*a*.	3
Legislature of Louisiana	---- Louisiana	2
Library of Congress	Washington C.y.	1
Mr. Hancock	Louisville Ky.	1 —22.

The foregoing list Audubon sent his wife from Charleston during the month of March 1832. It does not reflect two additional subscriptions procured through the agency of William Gaston in the city of Savannah. These were the subscriptions of David Mongin and Thomas Young.[25]

Encouraged by the gratifying results obtained in Charleston and Savannah, Audubon instructed his wife to have Havell "make a desparate push and have *20 finished* [of the first volume] and bound as soon as possible and shipped to New York in parcels of *5 or 6* as soon as ready. . . ."[26] With the rapid increase in the number of American subscribers and the realization that he would have to prolong his stay in America in order to obtain the specimens for the drawings of the water birds which were required for the third volume which was to contain no land birds, the necessity for sending Victor to London "*to push the Printing Coloring & Delivery* of the work to our Subscribers" became more apparent.[27]

Audubon had been much disappointed with his expedition to northern Florida. While on the schooner *Spark* he had written his wife, "I have been extremely mortified that *not one Drawing* have we made since one whole month detained by winds &c and the scarcity of Specimens." For his assistant Lehman, there had been nothing to do in more than a month.[28] Audubon had hoped that the *Spark* would proceed to Key West after her journey up the St. John's River but the vessel had had to return to Norfolk to be refitted. Audubon applied to his friend Edward Everett in Washington for help. The representative from Massachusetts immediately sent Audubon's letter to Louis McLane, Secretary of the Treasury, who in turn forwarded it to the Secretary of the Navy, Levi Woodbury. When Audubon received the subscription of the Library of Congress in 1830, Woodbury, then a senator from New Hampshire, had been a member of the Committee for the Library of Congress. Woodbury immediately furnished Audubon with credentials to the officers of the Navy "requesting [them] to furnish every aid in the prosecution of [his] scientific researches."[29]

Audubon had to remain in Charleston five weeks before there arrived a government vessel to take him and his "*Lads* to the confines of our Southern Coast." During that period he had made "*9 Beautiful* Drawings and collected an immense deal of information."[30]

Although Audubon had been disappointed that the northern Florida venture had not been more fruitful, the fact that the advance payments for the first volume of the *Birds of America* made by the Savannah subscribers had made it possible for him to send $1333.32 (£300) to his engraver in London on 28 March must have been most encouraging.[31]

The United States Navy schooner *Marion*, designated "The Lady of the Green Mantle" by the wreckers and smugglers, which was to take Audubon and his "lads" to Key West and the Tortugas arrived in Charleston on 13 April. Two days later they set out on a voyage which was to last nearly two months.[32]

The many and varied adventures of this voyage were graphically described by the Naturalist in the *Ornithological Biography* in anecdotes which he called "Episodes." In the second volume were included "Death of a Pirate," "The Florida Keys

Second Return to America, 1831–1832

[No. 1]," "The Florida Keys [No. 2]," and "The Turtlers"; in the third volume, "Wreckers of Florida."

This time Audubon's efforts were marked with success. The many species abounding in the Keys were almost all "new to us; their lovely forms appeared to be arranged in more brilliant apparel than I had ever before seen, and as they gambolled in happy playfulness among the bushes, or glided over the light green waters, we longed to form a more intimate acquaintance with them."[33]

Among the species figured during the voyage were the following:

Plate		Plate	
162	Zenaida Dove	252	Florida Cormorant
167	Key-West Dove	262	Tropic Bird
169	Mangrove Cuckoo	271	Frigate Pelican
170	Gray Tyrant	275	Noddy Tern
177	White-crowned Pigeon	279	Sandwich Tern
207	Booby Gannet	281	Great White Heron
235	Sooty Tern	431	American Flamingo.
238	Great Marbled Godwit		

Audubon's preoccupation with the task of securing drawings of water birds for the forthcoming third volume of the *Birds of America* did not free him from anxiety concerning the continuation of the engraving of the "Large Work" in England. On one occasion, he received disturbing news regarding internal conditions in that country, the result of the conflict concerning the Reform Bill. There had been riots, especially in Bristol, where a large conflagration resulted in loss of life.[34] The continuation of his work in England during his absence concerned him so much that he had written his wife:

> I am constantly fretting about the Continuation of *our* work in England. . . . Should Havell die Victor must go to England and make arrangements for the Continuation of the Engraving & Coloring, &c with Havell's assistant, *Mr. Blake*, from whom I have understood and do know that equally good work may be expected.[35]

Although Audubon himself was by no means uninvolved in the continuous supervision of Havell's work in England, the burden of this duty while the Naturalist was in Florida largely devolved on Lucy and Victor Audubon.

In October of the previous year, prior to leaving Baltimore for Louisville with her son Victor, Mrs. Audubon had written to Havell regarding the subscriptions which had just been obtained in Philadelphia. She had instructed him to be careful with the coloring of the prints and reminded him to send along the six additional copies of the first volume of the *Birds of America*. With her arrival in Louisville she took it upon herself to write the engraver once a week. At times these letters carry postscripts written by Victor Audubon. In view of the uncertainty of her husband's location as he traveled in the South, the supervision of Havell's activities as it concerned the American subscribers was assumed by the wife and son.[36]

In one of Lucy's letters written on 11 October 1831 she instructed Havell not to sell individual numbers, stating this to be unfair to the subscribers.[37] In a postscript, the son, alluding to the same matter wrote:

> I wish you to bear in mind in case application for *one or two* numbers of the Birds of America should be made that it will be to the detriment of the work to sell anyone, a part of it, as the regular subscriber would have reason to complain of such proceeding, as partial and unjust. You will therefore refuse to sell either one or more numbers to *any one*.

It was in this letter that Mrs. Audubon wrote: "I have procured a subscriber here though I have only been here five days, the name you must add to your list is a Mr. Hancock–Locust Grove near Louisville." A short time later Mrs. Audubon notified Havell of an additional subscriber from Louisville, Garnett Duncan.[38]

Both Mrs. Audubon and Victor found reason to complain to the engraver about the prints and the copies of the first volume sent to the subscribers in America. On 22 November 1831, Mrs. Audubon wrote Havell:

> I have heard from Dr. Harlan of the arrival of the six volumes, but I am sorry to say they are in very bad order and will copy for you what the doctor says that if you find any part of the damage is owing to the mismanagement on your part you will in the future avoid it: "I regret to inform you that Nos. for Volume Second that came with the six vols bound up were very much creased, and in instances much soiled, the copy I kept for myself is the worst, has one plate much torn!"[39]

On 16 January 1832, Victor wrote to Havell:

> On examination of the 1st volume of the work recd this day for Mr. Hancock of this place I was grieved to find that several of the plates have been entirely *too highly colored*. Particularly the Passenger Pigeon and the Partridge. Also the Red-tailed Hawk plate No. 51 — the Blue Bird in Plate No. 36 is coloured with bad ultramarine which is now nearly black, the Indigo Birds Plate No. 74 are very badly done and the Humming Birds, are also finished with too bright green [plate 47]. I mention these being the most prominent defects and in fact because almost every person in this country having *seen* the birds, they consequently become a critical observer of all such defects.[40]

The Havell correspondence with Mrs. Audubon is not available, but these strictures must have given umbrage to the engraver, for two months later Mrs. Audubon wrote him:

> I am very sorry any expression of mine should have offended you, that was not our intention but whatever remarks I made were in consequence of the facts which I stated to you respecting the plates and work, and from the authority of my husband repeated in his letters since we parted, to give you notice of any errors that you who are always at the work can not see so clear as those who only occasionally look it over, and I assure you Mr. Audubon will thank me for pointing out those things which I have and on which his success and reputation so much depend, Mr. A. and I are of one mind, we do not doubt your zeal nor

good intentions, but we think ourselves at liberty to state any changes we think
for our benefit and my Son and myself now act for Mr. Audubon, and must feel
very much alive to remarks made that, I have repeated to you, in more than one
letter merely because I cannot tell how many of my letters may reach you, or
if more than one as so very few of yours reach me. I did not write in anger to
you but sorrow in consequence of the complaints from Philadelphia, and allow
me to say from the specimen in the Copy here for Dr. Croghan. . . .[41]

A month later, when word had been received from Havell of the loss of Sir
William Jardine and John Selby as subscribers, Victor again wrote:

> I observe you seem to be ignorant of the cause of their withdrawing their
> names. It is out of my power to say what could have produced this unfortunate
> event, but it is a strong hint for you to use every exertion towards making the
> work as excellent as possible and is an evidence that these gentlemen at least are
> dissatisfied with their copies. You will therefore be at once aware of the *absolute
> necessity* of having every portion of the work *well done*.

Referring to complaints already made concerning prints received in America, he
added:

> So long as such faults are permitted to appear you will be loosing subscribers
> daily. My Father has been very fortunate in procuring subscribers here since his
> arrival and you have to exert yourself to make the colorers and those who print
> the work do it as well as possible and all will go right.[42]

According to the third volume of the *Ornithological Biography*, on 28 May 1832,
Audubon was still in Key West.[43] Shortly afterwards, the *Marion* departed for
Charleston. It was here that his association with Henry Ward and George Lehman
terminated. Ward obtained employment at the Museum of Natural History in
Charleston, and Lehman, after completing his work on the drawings, returned to
his home in Philadelphia. The available documentary evidence does not indicate
how Audubon spent his time during the few days he remained in Charleston, but
there is evidence that the subscription of a "citizen's library" was obtained at
this time.

After leaving Charleston, Audubon journeyed north via Norfolk and reached
Philadelphia in six days. Here he finished the drawings begun in Florida, consulted
ornithological books, and studied the new species collected in Florida. On 17 July,
he attended a meeting of the Academy of Natural Sciences in Philadelphia to
which he presented fourteen species of the Florida birds.

Mrs. Audubon and the two sons arrived in Philadelphia early in July, but the
Audubon family was to be only briefly reunited. As a complete family group, they
did journey together to Boston in late July and early August of 1832. However,
as Victor's letter of 21 July to Havell indicates, he "planned to sail for Europe on
the 1st of October." Preparing to serve as his father's deputy in London, Victor
stated that he wished to be informed when Havell hoped to be finished engraving
the drawings that had been left with him so that he [Victor] might bring over to
England the necessary drawings to continue the work.

Although young Audubon stated that his father was delighted with the new engravings, he was nonetheless constrained to add that "the colorers have used body colors and blotted around the edges. Plate 122, Blue Grosbeak, you have called Fringilla corulea instead of coerulea, also Plate 116, the Ferruginous Thrush is most particularly injured by body colors."[44] At this point, when Havell had completed the engraving of Numbers 26 and 27, plates 126–35, the Double Elephant Folio of the *Birds of America* was becoming more clearly and definitely than ever before an Audubon family enterprise.

10

BOSTON AND
THE LABRADOR JOURNEY
1832

From Philadelphia, with but a one-day stopover in New York, the family went to Boston. On 13 August Audubon wrote his engraver, "I have been in this beautiful city about one week and have obtained 6 new subscribers."[1] These were J. G. Cushing, Samuel Appleton, Dr. George C. Shattuck, Thomas Perkins, G. W. Pratt, and P. J. [T.] Jackson. In this letter Audubon also advised his engraver of the subscription of Gustavus Schmidt of New Orleans.

When Audubon wrote the introduction to the second volume of the *Ornithological Biography*, he had this to say about Boston:

> Boston! Ah! reader, my heart fails me when I think of the estimable friends whose society afforded me so much pleasure in that beautiful city, the Athens of our Western World. Never, I fear, shall I have it in my power to return a tithe of the hospitality which was there shown towards us, or of the benevolence and generosity which we experienced, and which evidently came from the heart, without the slightest mixture of ostentation. Indeed, I must acknowledge that although I have been happy in forming many valuable friendships in various parts of the world, all dearly cherished by me, the outpouring of kindness which I experienced at Boston far exceeded all that I have ever met with.[2]

He continued:

> Think of her Adamses, her Perkins, her Everetts, her Peabodys, Cushings, ... Quincys, Storys, ... Paines, Greens, Tudors, Davises, and Pickerings, whose public and private life presents all that we deem estimable, and let them be bright examples of what the citizens of a free land ought to be. But besides these honourable individuals whom I have taken the liberty of mentioning, many others I could speak of with delight; and one I would point out in particular, as him to whom my deepest gratitude is due, one whom I cannot omit mentioning, because of all the good and the estimable, he it is whose rememberance is most dear to me:—that generous friend is [George Parkman].

George Parkman (1791–1849) had been a professor in the Medical Institute of Harvard College and doubtless introduced Aubudon to Josiah Quincy, the president of Harvard University. Later, he also acted as Audubon's agent in Boston. Parkman, a retired physician, was the possessor of considerable wealth, both inherited and accumulated through successful Boston real estate operations. He was also donor of the land on which the building of the Medical Institute of Harvard College was erected. Parkman was murdered by Dr. John Webster, professor of chemistry at the Medical Institute, on 23 November 1849. Webster was hanged for that crime on 30 August 1850.[3]

In addition to the solicitation of subscriptions, Audubon continued his drawing, figuring the following species: marsh wren (Nuttall's Lesser Marsh Wren, plate 175), flycatcher (Olive-sided, plate 174) and a thrush.[4] There were also excursions into the country, one to the estate of his friend and benefactor Thomas H. Perkins, in the company of Thomas Nuttall, whose ornithological work had just been published.[5] Another trip was to Salem, where Audubon hoped to find a flycatcher which had been described by Nuttall.[6] It is possible that the subscription of Susan Burley of Salem was obtained at this time.

Early in September Audubon together with his wife and sons began a journey which was to take them along the shores of Maine to Eastport, on to New Brunswick, Canada, up the St. John's River to Woodstock, then to Houlton, Maine, south along the Penobscot River to Old Town, thence to Bangor and Boston. This journey and certain incidents occurring on the trip are graphically described by Audubon in two episodes published in the second volume of the *Ornithological Biography*, namely, "Journey in New Brunswick and Maine," and "The Force of the Waters."[7] As the route taken led along the coast, it is likely that while at Portland, Maine, the subscription of John Neal was obtained. Eventually difficulties arose between Audubon and Neal. In April 1834 the Naturalist wrote his son, "John Neal is a scamp and I have written Docr Parkman to take the Work back & hold it to order, or dispose of it should opp'y offer."[8]

One of the drawings which resulted from this expedition was that of the "Spotted or Canada Grous" (plate 176), now called the spruce grouse. This species was found by Audubon at Dennisville, Maine (near Eastport).[9]

The autumn and winter of 1832–33 Audubon, with his wife and son John, spent in Boston, the Naturalist busily engaged in soliciting subscriptions, making frequent excursions into the surrounding country, drawing, and finally, laying plans for the expedition to the coast of Labrador. The older son, Victor, soon after the arrival of the family in Boston, departed for Europe, there to superintend the publication of the *Birds of America*.

When Victor, then twenty-four years of age, left America he carried with him a letter to the engraver in which Audubon wrote,

> ... my son carries with him a set of seven numbers which you have forwarded to this country and upon several of which I have made observations. It is always with sorrow that I find myself forced to remonstrate respecting the faults now

and then existing in the publication and I wish you to listen well to whatever my son tells you on the subject. My work has now reached the pitch of Standing both in America & Europe that calls for the greatest exertion on my part to render quite and entirely true what is said of it . . . and you, My Dear Sir, ought to second me in these efforts with all your Care and exertion. . . . This work connects you with me, and gives you a name that must greatly assist you, even now in augmenting your general business, and should this Immense Work fail for want of attention or good finishing in its execution while in your hands, you must become an equal sufferer with me, if not a greater one in a pecuniary point of view.

In this letter Audubon actually threatened the removal of the work but stated that he hoped never to see such a thing happen. "*Do your best* and all will go well."[10]

Another letter written by Audubon to his son Victor provides some of the details of the operation of the engraving, printing, coloring, and distribution of the prints of the *Birds of America*. When Victor arrived in London and began to supervise the work at the Havell establishment, he found it difficult to understand the accounts which Havell delivered to him. After he had explained his difficulties to his father, the latter wrote him:

In your letter to us you seem not to understand the accounts which Havell has delivered to you, I will try therefore to give you some idea of my mode of proceeding with him when in England. I make Havell [make] a list of the delivery of each Numbers as they go to the subscribers—this he does by putting down the individual's name, his residence &c the day of delivery &c—and this list is given to me for examination. I compare the names with my Original list of Subscribers and can easily judge if any mistakes have taken place or indeed if any of the Subscribers have been omitted; a thing which now & then took place before I followed the plan just mentioned.—as new Subscribers present themselves Havell adds their name to his own list and furnishes them with all the numbers published at that time and with which I am charged if no *stock* of such numbers are on hand.—I think that (140) this amount of delivery is much less than it ought to be, as I am fully persuaded that we have more than 140 subscribers—I therefor advise you to ask for an *Individual* list of delivery and that list must of course agree with the a/c he renders you, or the mistakes must be corrected at once if any exist.—I think it well and indeed necessary to settle accounts with Havell as often as convenient, at least after the compleat delivery of each new numbers,—or setts of numbers for Volumes ordered, including the amount for paper, printing and binding.—Whenever you travel through the towns where Agents are, ask of them to show you also a list of what they receive from Havell, and another of the persons to whom they deliver; *by so doing* you will detect any errors which might take place.[11]

This letter also divulged the fact that Audubon carried the original subscription list with him and that he was reluctant to part with it. He advised his son:

Your Dear Mamma is now at my side copying the Original list of Subscribers for you—it goes with this.—I wish you to be extremely particular in comparing the names of all the Individuals thereon with Havell's list of delivery—and tick such as have died or discontinued their Subscriptions for the Work.—Make *a good* memorandum of the latters, and as you travel call on them and ask the reasons why their Subscription has been redrawn, perhaps you may recall Many.—Copy this list yourself and send back to us the present one with observations attached to such names as need any observations.—It will enable us to judge how the business stands both in Europe and in America.—I think that we now have about 200 standing names.[12]

Although Audubon had always realized the importance of the original subscription list as a help in obtaining additional subscribers, he also believed that when the name of a subscriber was appended to the list, the signer was legally liable. He implied this in an earlier letter to Victor: "It seems to me that every bona fide subscription ought to stand good in Law & Equity.—Ask some worthy friend or Lawyer en passant."[13]

During the fall and winter months Audubon was able to add the following names to his subscription list:

> Frederic Tudor, Boston
> James Brown, Cambridge
> The Library of the General Court of Massachusetts
> The Library of Harvard College, Cambridge
> Providence Athenaeum
> James Arnold, New Bedford, Massachusetts
> William Oakes, Ipswich, Massachusetts
> Boston Natural History Society
> William Sturges (Sturgis), Boston
> John Neal, Portland.[14]

One other subscriber not included among those listed in the foregoing was also obtained during the Boston visit. On the original list of subscribers, following the name of Frederic Tudor, there was written "Gentleman of Boston. One copy by S. E. G[reene]." No reference to the "Gentleman of Boston" has been found in Audubon's letters or in his journals, nor is the name included on the subscriber's lists in the *Ornithological Biography*. However, it is possible that this was Thomas Lindell Winthrop (1760–1841) who, under the circumstances which follow, donated a set of the folio to the Massachusetts Historical Society of which he was elected president in 1835. The Proceedings of the Massachusetts Historical Society indicate that at the monthly meeting, 30 March 1837, "Mr. Isaac P. Davis, the Keeper of the Cabinet, also communicated a present from a gentleman, whose name he had not permission to mention, Audubon's plates."

The four volumes of the *Birds of America* as well as four volumes of the *Ornithological Biography* are listed in the catalog of the Library of the Massachusetts Historical Society, dated "Boston MDCCCLIX." Winthrop also was a subscriber to the Octavo Edition of the *Birds of America*, for his name appears in Volume 2, p.201, on "List of Subscribers since publication of the First Volume.—Hon. Thomas L. Winthrop." The folio which had been donated by Winthrop was sold by the Massachusetts Historical Society in 1905 for $2,000.

Audubon was particularly fortunate when obtaining many of the New England subscribers to receive payment in full for the first volume. With James Brown a special arrangement was made—he was to pay $100 per annum until the completion of the work.[15] These advance payments and others which Audubon was to receive later in New York made it possible for him to send to his son "Three hundred pounds which . . . will assist you much in paying for the 20 Volumes I have asked of you to have ready as soon as possible, and to be shipped to New York per 1st opportunities as you have a certain number of those volumes bound."[16]

Included among the drawings which were completed during the Boston visit are the following, which were actually sent to the engraver on 28 April 1833:

No 37.	Plate	181.	Golden Eagle	Figures 1
	" —	182.	Ground Doves	5
	" —	183.	Golden crested Wren	2
	" —	184.	Mangrove Humming Bird	5
	" —	185.	Bachman's Warbler	2
No 38.	" —	186.	Pinnated Grous	3
	" —	187.	Boat Tail Grackle	2
	" —	188.	Tree Sparrow	2
	" —	189.	Snow Bunting	3
	" —	190.	Yellow bellied Woodpecker	2
				17

Although Audubon included among the foregoing species some which he had probably painted before his arrival in Boston, such as the ground doves, mangrove hummingbird, Bachman's warbler, and boat-tailed grackle, he had also made others as well, for when sending the drawings to London he wrote: "I should have sent you 2 more Numbers had I Two large Plates for them, but hoping that I may meet with something Large & perhaps New I shall not do so, until I return [from Labrador] which will be Still time enough."[18] Audubon's reference to "something Large" is indicative of the problem he always faced in the arrangement of the numbers; namely that, as he had stated in his prospectus, "Five Plates will constitute a Number; one Plate from one of the largest Drawings, one from one of the second size, and three from the smaller Drawings."

Audubon wrote about the drawing of the golden eagle in some detail. Early in February he purchased from E. Greenwood, the proprietor of the New England Museum of Boston, a golden eagle which had been caught in a spring trap set for foxes in the White Mountains of New Hampshire. The bird was kept in a cage for some time so that Audubon could study its movements to determine the position in which he might best represent it. Eventually the bird was killed and Audubon, after working nearly one whole night outlining and then working constantly at drawing it, was suddenly seized with a

> spasmodic affection that much alarmed my family, and completely prostrated me for several days; but thanks to my heavenly Preserver, and the immediate and unremitting attention of my most worthy friends Drs. Parkman, Shattuck (George Cheyne Shattuck, 1783–1854), and Warren (John Collins Warren, 1778–1856), I was restored to health and enabled to pursue my labours.

The drawing of the eagle took fourteen days to complete, "and I had never before laboured so incessantly excepting at that of the Wild Turkey."[19]

Sometime during Audubon's long stay in Boston, probably in the autumn or early winter, there was held at the Athenaeum an exhibition of his original drawings. It will be recalled that the subscription of the Athenaeum to the *Birds of America* had been sent to England in 1830. Invitations reading:

> Sir
>   Yourself, Family, and Friends are respectfully invited to view some of the *Original Drawings* belonging to the Work entitled "the Birds of America" by
>   JOHN J. AUDUBON
>   the Author
> at the Athenaeum between the hours of 11 & 1

addressed to Frederic Tudor and to Dr. George C. Shattuck have been found, but it has not been possible to determine the date of the exhibition which was probably held late in 1832 or early in 1833.

At the end of March Audubon left Boston for a visit to New York and Philadelphia. As soon as he had reached New York he wrote to his son Victor: "The 10 Volumes ½ Bound which I found here are good, and I have reason to hope that ere a fortnight elapses they will be subscribed for and paid for."[20] The same letter contained the following exhortation:

> I advise that on your receipt of this, you have seven Copies prepared and forwarded to *Boston direct* care of Docr George Parkman provided a good ship offers itself.—If not by Packet to New York with directions to Nicholas [Berthoud] to forward the Box to Boston by the way of Steamer to Providence &c.—See that sheets of paper are placed between each volume as without this the beading will be rubbed & injured. . . . I advise also that Ten 1st Volumes ½ Bound each with all successive Numbers be immediately prepared & forwarded to Nicholas.—These to be ready in case of demand in this Country, the Country which after all begins to smile on us, poor Naturalists!

Audubon's hopes turned out to be not unduly optimistic, for on 15 April, writing to his son from New York, he advised him of the following subscriptions: "P. G. Stuyvesant of New York and General Stephen VanRenseller [Van Rensselaer] of Albany."[21] On the 28th he sent these additional subscriptions: "The State of Maryland; Richard F. Carman, New York; L. Reed, New York; The State of New York."[22]

From the original subscription list and payment records in Ledger "B," it is possible to determine that the following additional New York subscriptions were obtained: "Ed*d* Prime, James G. King, W. A. Duer for the Library of Columbia College, C. Low (Cornelius), Rob*t*. Ray, and J. L. Joseph." Once again, many of the subscriptions obtained at New York were accompanied by an advance payment of $220 for the first volume.

Audubon had for some years contemplated making a journey to the coast of Labrador to procure and make drawings of birds, and to study the habits of those which nested in that part of the continent. To make the necessary arrangements for such a trip he went to Eastport, Maine, early in May 1833. There the Naturalist chartered the schooner *Ripley*, out of Baltimore, a staunch new vessel of 106 tons, under the command of one Captain Emery.

Audubon had hoped that his friend Harris from Philadelphia would accompany him to Labrador but Harris was unable to do so. Audubon did however recruit the following young men to join him and his son John: George C. Shattuck, Jr., (1813–1893), the son of Audubon's Boston doctor and subscriber; William Ingalls (1813–1903), also of Boston; Joseph A. Coolidge (1815–1901) of Maine; and Thomas Lincoln (1806–1883), of Dennisville, Maine, whose name ornithologists all will remember, as it was immortalized by Audubon in the name of a new species of sparrow discovered in Labrador. From a letter written by young Shattuck to his father it is known that the *Ripley* was costing Audubon $350 per month, and that the young men were paying three dollars a week for board. Also, that the vessel was "victualled" for five months and that among the articles to be put on board were "potatoes; rice; beans; beef; pork; butter; cheese." These young men proved to be a devoted and energetic group of helpers.

Repeated delays prevented the *Ripley* from getting underway until 6 June. However, during the stay in Eastport, Audubon and some of the party did have the opportunity to visit Grand Manan Island, a favorite habitat for seabirds in the Bay of Fundy.

From Eastport, the *Ripley* passed through the Gut of Canso and headed for the Magdalen Islands, where the party landed and made collections. On 14 June they approached the famous Bird Rock "and thought it covered with snow" but "what we saw was not snow—but Gannets!" On 17 June they passed Anticosti Island, and what appeared to be sails on the horizon proved to be snowdrifts on Labrador.

The following day they landed at the mouth of Natashquan River. Here there were ducks, geese, auks, and guillemots in great multitudes, as well as gulls and terns; many were breeding and all seemed wilder than at points farther south, a circumstance which was explained as soon as they discovered the astounding proportions which the traffic in eggs of seafowl had attained even at that time. It was on 27 June that the new bird (Fringilla lincolnii—now, *Melospiza lincolnii*) was procured and which Audubon named after his young companion, Thomas Lincoln.

The *Ripley* left its anchorage at American Harbor or Natashquan on 28 June and stood out to sea, the usual recourse to avoid the intricacies of the coast. After proceeding fifty miles or more the schooner touched at numerous islands, where guillemots, puffins, and black-backed gulls were breeding in vast numbers, finally anchoring in what has been identified as the harbor of Wapitagun. The party remained here until 14 July when the *Ripley* took the party forty-three miles farther east to Little Maccatina or Hare Harbor. There they stayed until 21 July, when they proceeded to Bai de Portage. Here were met numerous individuals engaged in the sealing industry, all of whom Audubon questioned for information on the country and its products. On 25 July, they started for "Chevalier's Settlement" but were caught in a storm and came in to Bras d'or Bay [Bradore]. It was here that they found the Labrador duck, which in 1875, but forty-two years later, was to become extinct.

Under the date of 10 August, Audubon wrote in his journal:

> I have been drawing so constantly, often seventeen hours a day, that the weariness of my body at night has been unprecedented, by such work at least. . . . But I thank God that I did accomplish my task; my drawings are finished to the best of my ability, the skins well prepared by John.

On 11 August, Audubon and his men departed from Labrador for Newfoundland, landing in St. George's Harbor on the 13th.

After a short stay, the expedition continued to Pictou, Nova Scotia. Here Audubon and his party met Professor Thomas McCullough (1788-1843), a naturalist who, in the following years, was to send Audubon many bird skins. From Pictou they went overland to Truro, Halifax, and on to Windsor where they watched the famous tides of the Bay of Fundy, and thence by steamboat to St. Johns, New Brunswick. Instead of continuing through the woods to Quebec as had been planned, they hastened to Eastport which they reached on 31 August. With the *Ripley* docked and their collections securely packed, all but Coolidge and Lincoln returned to Boston. On 7 September Audubon was again in New York.

The Labrador experience was in a measure disappointing. Although stormy weather is common on this coast, Audubon was certainly unfortunate in experiencing an unusual stormy season. On fifty-four days between 17 June and 11 August that were spent on the Labrador coast, he noted rain, fog, and storm on at least twenty-five, and he had apparently only twenty-five of fine weather. Still another handicap was the "ignorant ass" of a pilot, who, not knowing the region, exposed them to no inconsiderable danger of shipwreck on entering or leaving harbors, and who was obliged to sail for safety on the rough waters of the Gulf of St. Lawrence, rather than in the calm and narrow waterways among the islands.

Audubon did bring back with him twenty-three large drawings of birds, complete or nearly so, and seventy-three bird skins, as well as considerable collections of marine animals and plants. In addition, much valuable information was obtained concerning the birds nesting in the northern regions. The expense of the journey had been heavy, amounting, as he told his son, to "about $2,000."[23]

Awaiting the Naturalist in New York were Numbers 32 and 33 (plates 156–65) of the *Birds of America*. These he found eminently satisfactory, for he wrote his son Victor:

> I have examined Nos 32 and 33 and must say that I look on these 10 plates as the best I ever saw of birds and they do *Havell* and *yourself* my beloved son great Credit everything is better—the birds are Fac Simile of my Drawings—Soft and beautiful the colouring is clear transparent and true to nature—the plants are seriously better—I am delighted—never was a *Crow* for instance represented in print before now.—If Havell goes on in this present style and principle, I will be bound that neither I or you will have a word of Complaint about his Works.—tell him this—the black capt*d* Titmouse is not dark enough on the back and in my Drawing there must be *a white spot at the lower end of the black cap* next [to] the shoulders—this white spot distinguishes our bird from the European of the same name, *which* is a different species. . . .[24]

Before the end of September Audubon was able to send to London the drawings which completed the second volume of the *Birds of America*, namely Numbers 39 and 40, and listed them as follows:

Willow Grous.		2 figures & Youngs
Great American Shrike	4.	" " "
Lincoln's Finch	2.	" " "
Canadian Titmouse	3.	" " "
Ruby crowned Wren	2.	" " "
	13.	Figures adult.—

[*The finch Audubon had named for Thomas Lincoln, the young man from Dennisville, Me., who had accompanied him on the Labrador trip*].

Labrador Falcon	2.
American Cross bill	7.
White winged Cross bill	4.
Winter Wren	3.
Shore Lark	6.
	22. figures

3 Extra Plates (Small).—
    Lesser red Poll
    Little Owl—
    Red bellied Woodpecker.[25]

When Audubon advised his son Victor that these drawings were being sent he wrote: "You must stick a *Cricket* or a *Grass hoper* on a thorn before the bill of the Male Shrike on the wing. It is their habit—but could not procure one yesterday and today it rains hard." He continued: "Have the edges of the little *Grous* (Young) softened in the Engraving—The outer primary of the male bird is pure white, it is dirty in the drawing because the White colour I used happened to be *bad*." These instructions were followed by the engraver. Plate 192, the "Shrike," shows a cricket placed on the branch of the hawthorne, while on the print of the "Willow Grous" (ptarmigan, plate 191), the outer primary of the adult birds is the proper pure white.

When the plates were engraved, the first five, in order, composed Number 39, plates 191 to 195. But in Number 40, a change was made. While the "Labrador Falcon" was used for plate 196, and the "American Crossbill" for plate 197, the "Brown-headed Worm-eating Warbler" was substituted for the "White-winged Crossbill" in plate 198, and, for plate 199, the "Little Owl" was used. Plate 200, the "Shore Lark," completed the last number of Volume 2. The "White-winged Crossbill" is plate 364; the "Winter Wren" is plate 360, birds 1, 2, and 3; and the "Red-bellied Woodpecker" is plate 416, birds 3 and 4.

11

WINTER AT CHARLESTON
1833-1834

In his letter of 9 September in which Audubon had sent his son Victor an account of his Labrador experiences, he had also outlined his plans for the balance of 1833 and for the following year. He also mentioned that he hoped to leave New York within ten days for the express purpose of obtaining additional subscribers. At the time Audubon felt far more sanguine about increasing the number of American subscribers than he did about adding many European names to his list. Letters from his engraver earlier in the year had advised him of the unsettled conditions in England; as a result, the Naturalist had written Havell: "All I regret is the unquiet state of England with Ireland—it seems that this in a very great measure puts a stop to our business in England at least."[1]

Audubon, in his quest for subscribers, planned to visit Philadelphia, Baltimore, and Washington. In the latter city it was his hope to obtain subscriptions from various departments of the government. From Philadelphia he then proposed to continue on to Norfolk, Richmond, Fredericksburg, and Savannah, with a final stop at Charleston where Bachman had invited him together with his wife and son John to spend the winter. The Naturalist's goal was to obtain fifty additional subscribers.[2] The possibility that he might be needed in London also was not overlooked. On 15 September, again writing his son, he asked: "*If you can* possibly do without me in England for another Year acquaint me immediately—do the same should the case prove vice versa."[3]

On 25 September Audubon and his wife left New York for their journey south, arriving at Philadelphia the same day; their son John, however, sailed directly to Charleston. In Philadelphia Audubon called on old friends, visited public places, "but no one stopped me to subscribe for my book." Not only did he receive no subscriptions in Philadelphia,

> ... nay, I was arrested there for debt, [one of the old partnership debts] and was on the point of being taken to prison, had I not met William Norris, Esq., who kindly offered to be my bail. This event brings to my mind many disagree-

able thoughts connected with my former business transactions, in which I was *always* the *single* loser, that I will only add I made the necessary arrangements to have it paid.[4]

However, the visit to Baltimore, the next stop, was rewarding. Here subscriptions were obtained from Joseph E. Walker, Baltimore Museum; John S. Donnell, Evan Poultney, and E. Geddings, M.D.[5] Audubon hoped that he might also obtain the subscription of the Library of Baltimore and of the College of Surgeons at a future date.[6]

While in Baltimore, Audubon also went to Washington to call on Governor Lewis Cass, then Secretary of War, from whom he hoped to obtain permission to join an expedition to the Rocky Mountains. Such permission was not immediately forthcoming. However, the Naturalist was fortunate, while in that city, to meet Washington Irving, with whom he was acquainted, who took him to the office of Roger B. Taney, Secretary of the Treasury. Taney granted Audubon the privilege of the revenue cutters along the coast, south of Delaware Bay.[7] During this Washington visit, Audubon left "one Volume half bound in the hands of the Librarian of Congress, because he told me that he *had no doubt* that Congress would subscribe for a 2nd copy of the Work."[8]

After the visit to Baltimore and Washington, Audubon went to Richmond, calling upon Governor Floyd of Virginia, who again assured the Naturalist that he would try to induce the state to subscribe for the *Birds of America*.[9] Although Audubon tried again at a later date, he was never able to obtain the subscription of the state of Virginia nor that of any institution or individual of that state.

Leaving Richmond on 16 October, the Audubons proceeded to Petersburg via stage, but at that city boarded a car "drawn by a locomotive, which dragged us twelve miles an hour, and sent out sparks of fire enough to keep us constantly busy in extinguishing them on our clothes." At Blakely they boarded a stage, which took them through Halifax, Raleigh, Fayetteville, and thence to Columbia, South Carolina. Here Audubon met Thomas Cooper, president of Columbia College [University of South Carolina], who assured the Naturalist that he had seen a rattlesnake climb a five-rail fence on his land. More importantly, Audubon received from the treasury of the state of South Carolina $420 on account for its subscription of one set of the *Birds of America*.[10]

Although Audubon had intended to visit Savannah before going to Charleston, he changed his plans and, dreading the railway, hired a carriage for forty dollars to take him and his wife to Charleston, arriving in that city four days later. There the Audubons joined their son John and were kindly received by the Reverend Mr. John Bachman.[11]

Immediately Audubon began work on additional drawings. Before leaving New York, he had arranged five numbers of water birds for the beginning of Volume 3 of the *Birds of America*. These were to be sent to London on 20 October, having been kept separate from the drawings of the land birds sent earlier "to devide the chances of loss at Sea."[12] His first compositions in Charleston consisted of "3 New small Birds (Land) which I will forward you in about 10 Days and which I wish you to place in the 2d Volume in lieu of 3 others which I will name to you in my next letter." He also intended to "finish all the unfinished Drawings of Water Birds which I have ere I go to the Floridas and have them arranged and named ready for publication."[13] By the end of December he wrote his son Victor: "I have nearly *one hundred* Drawings of Water Birds ready for Publication and *I* pronounce them equal to any previous ones."[14] On 18 January, five numbers of these were sent to New York to be reshipped to London. When sending these he wrote to his son, "Inclosed is a list of them and 3 more numbers composed of Drawings which you have in England, *and which* should you not receive the present 5 numbers, have published rather than to stop the Work from going on regularly—but I hope the 5 Numbers will reach you safely."[15] This shipment was insured for $4,000.[16]

The work on the drawings of the water birds for the third volume of *Birds of America* had become a family project at the Bachman home. Audubon wrote to Victor that "John, myself and Miss Maria (sister of John Bachman's Wife) are drawing constantly, to finish all the unfinished Drawings now on hand; I think that 30 days hence, that task will be accomplished."[17] Maria Martin's work for Audubon was to continue after the Naturalist had left. It consisted, for the most part, of drawing some backgrounds, though she may actually have made one or two drawings of birds.[18]

During the winter visit of the Audubons with the Bachman family in Charleston, the Reverend Mr. Bachman assisted Audubon in numerous ways, not the least among which were Bachman's efforts to defend Audubon against his critics. Audubon had written two articles, one on the habits of the rattlesnake and the other on the habits of the turkey buzzard.[19] These articles had been attacked in print. In response to these criticisms, Audubon and Bachman carried on a series of experiments on turkey buzzards in order to secure additional evidence in support of the position which Audubon had previously taken. Bachman then wrote an article relating to these experiments which was published in Loudon's *Magazine of Natural History*. It was also read to the Boston Society of Natural History on 5 February 1834.[20] Copies of the report on the experiment were also sent to the American Philosophical Society, Philadelphia; the Lyceum of New York; the Royal Society of London; and the Royal Institute of France.

The *Birds of America* itself was harshly criticized. Among the severest critics of this work were George Ord (1781–1866) of Philadelphia, editor of volumes 8 and 9 of Alexander Wilson's *American Ornithology*, and Charles Waterton (1782–1865), the English naturalist and traveler.[21] The most vicious attacks were those of Waterton's which were published in Loudon's *Magazine of Natural History* in 1833 and 1834.[22]

Victor Audubon replied to Waterton's criticism in June 1833, and sent a copy to his father.[23] Audubon learned about Waterton's attack upon his arrival in Charleston, in a letter from Victor. The Naturalist commented on the matter to his son as follows: "Your Short letter of Sep'r 7th came to hand here a few days ago, but not the Loudon's Journals of which you speak."[24] When a copy of Victor's reply reached Audubon a few weeks later Audubon wrote his son, "Your reply to Mons Waterton is excellent."[25]

> I am sorry that you should trouble yourself about the attacks of Mr. Waterton, and more so that you should answer to any of these attacks.—depend upon it, the World will Judge for itself and I conceive, that the regular publication of our Work, accompanied with well ascertained facts will sooner or later cast aside any such animadversions, and that the true cause of their appearance through such persons as Mr Waterton will very soon be properly understood.—
>
> The World is well aware that it is not necessary for any one inclined to publish falsehoods or form tales of Wonder, to travel as I constantly do, at an (I am sorry to say) enormous expense, keeping a regular Journal of all my actions and the whole of *my* observations connected with the Science which I am studying, when on the contrary I might with ten fold ease settle myself in some corner of London and write nolens volens all such fables as might cross my brains and publish these without caring a Jot about the consequences.— but I feel greatly proud of our Work, I feel greatly proud that I am the happy possessor of a most excellent Wife and Two Sons whom I can view as my dearest and best attached Friends—I am greatly proud that *I* possess the knowledge that every word I have published or shall publish is truth and nothing but the result of my own observations in fields and forests where neither of my enemies have or ever will tread with as firm a foot & step as I have done and still do.—There is another thing of which I am equally very proud, that is that I have firmly attached to me, both in Europe, and in our Country a large sett of excellent & learned Friends.—I have received unprecedented privileges at the hands of our Government, as well as from that of England; I see our Work progress well & steadily, in a word I feel happy within my heart. This is the palm I have always searched for, and it is the truest blessing on Earth![26]

Audubon himself never directly replied to his critics.

Several years earlier, in a letter to Charles Lucien Bonaparte, Audubon had commented on his own lack of scientific education. In the course of these remarks, he had observed that he had "scarcely ever read a book on the subject."[27] The subject in question, of course, was ornithology. That Audubon was by this time well read and familiar with the ornithological literature then current becomes obvious in light of a letter Lucy Audubon wrote for him to his friend Edward Harris, of Moorestown, New Jersey, during the Charleston winter (the Naturalist had been ill and confined to his bed for ten days). This letter is of particular interest since from its contents is available a record of the reference books which Audubon used.[28]

In the letter Harris was advised:

> There are in the upper story of Mr. Berthouds [Audubon's brother-in-law in New York City] Wharehouse several boxes trunks &c containing books, papers, bird skins &c out of which I am in great and immediate want of *Viz*

> *Temmincks Manual* 2 volumes stitched in paper, large octavo size—2 vols Bewicks Birds, and one vol Bewicks Quadrupeds. a pamphlet entitled observations on *Thallassidroma's* [petrels] by Charles Bonaparte and also another by the same author entitled "observations on the Nomenclature of Wilsons Ornithology". I want also Bonaparte's *catalogue*. This I fear I have not but it is to be found at the New York Lyceum and an application to the Secretary thereof in my name would perhaps obtain it as a *gift* or *loan* to me.

Although Harris lived in Moorestown, he frequently was in New York, visiting at the home of a brother-in-law who was connected with the *New York Gazette*. In addition Audubon also requested Harris to call on

> Mr. Peal of the Museum [in Philadelphia] and ask him to send the following Birds, preserved in the Skins which he obligingly promised to have collected for me:
>
> Sylvia Philadelphia, Wilson, No. 130. Bonap. Syn*op*.
> ["Mourning Warbler," fig.1, pl.399]
> Sylvia Maritima——Wilson No. 107   do   do
> ["Cape May Warbler," figs.3 & 4, pl.414]
> Sylvia Tygrina [tigrina], Montana of Wilson No 119. Bonap. Synop.
> ["Blue Mountain Warbler," fig.3, pl.434].

Finally he wished Harris

> to procure a half a dozen of the *Black headed Titmouse (Parus atricapillus)* No. 157. Bonap. ["Black-capped Chickadee," figs.3 & 4, pl.353] *Shot in the State of New York*. Two or three in the Skin and two or three in Spirits.—I look upon this, as a distinct species from the Bird of the same name found in the Southern States but cannot establish its specific characters without specimens [alongside is written: "this between ourselves"].

The Naturalist concluded his request for specimens with

> I want besides a handsome specimen in the skin (Scolopax Grisea) summer plumage with red breast & belly S. Novaboracensis. No 267 Bonap. ["Red-Breasted Snipe" or "dowitcher," pl.335], and a pair of *Fuligula Albola* No 363 Bonap. ["Buffle Head Duck," pl.325] Anas Strepera No 324 Bonap. ["Gadwall Duck," pl.348] in very full plumage.

Immediately upon his recovery Audubon was again at work, arranging the water birds for the third volume, writing to his son, "I have nearly *one hundred* Drawings of Water Birds ready for publication, and I pronounce them equal to any previous ones."[29]

Throughout the Charleston winter, as always during his fourteen-year labor, Audubon was beset by anxieties attendant upon the production of his "Great Work." Apparently no aspect of this enterprise was free from anxiety; and so he had to deal with complaints from subscribers, with worry concerning possible losses at sea, with errors committed by his engraver, with the relationship between

THE DOUBLE ELEPHANT FOLIO

Havell and himself or between Havell and his deputy, Victor Audubon, and always with money matters. It was while visiting his Charleston subscribers that the Naturalist learned that the numbers for the *Birds of America* were not arriving properly. He wrote to Victor:

> ... to my surprise on my arrival here I was told that not a single sett of Nos 26. 27. 28. 29. 30. & 31 had ever been received by J. Bachman or any of the Societies. 3 setts of each of these Numbers are now wanted here to compleat the parts they have received, making in all 18 Numbers. I have written to New York to know if those Nos had been received from England & forwarded to this place, and I wish you in case they have been shipped from England to say to us when, and by what Vessel.—Nos 32 & 33 have come to hand here, and at Columbia College, where to my astonishment I find *they* have been received in regular order.[30]

Difficulties with shipments of numbers were to continue to plague him. There was a shipment which had been sent to New York, the numbers of which "were *Wet and good for nothing*.—These have been sold at auction in New York and have I been vexed enough on that account."[31] Surely this must have been the first auction of prints of the *Birds of America*.

There were also problems with the prints. There arrived in Charleston late in January Numbers 34 and 35 for the local subscribers and for Columbia College. These Audubon considered on the whole "very fine" but discovered that the engraver had made the following errors in nomenclature: "plate [170] instead of Grey Tyrant have Pipiry Fly Catcher—*Muscicapa Matinatus*—[pl.174.] *Muscicapa Cooperi*—also have the *black headed Titmouse* as follows (*for it is a new Species*) The Lesser black headed Titmouse—*Parus Caroliniensis* [pl.160]. My letter press will do the rest.—I write to Havell."[32]

Audubon was also worried about the arrival in London of the drawings needed to complete the second volume, which he had sent in October. Also cause for concern was the relationship between his engraver and his son, Victor, for there were indications that some friction had arisen. However, on 23 December, with the arrival of mail from England, he was able to write his son:

> Last evening we had the pleasure of yours of the 28*th* Oct*r* and one from Havell on the 9*th* Oct*r* also.—As regards Havell, we are glad all with him is amicably arranged, and hope that he will not trouble us about extra prices—not even for the *Water Birds!*
>
> The safe arrival of my last Drawings sent you has relieved me of the great anxiety. I constantly fret about them until the receiving of your letter last night.[33]

In the same letter Audubon expressed himself quite philosophically in response to certain disquieting news regarding individuals and subscribers when he wrote:

> That Subscribers should die, is a thing we can not help, that such fellows as Vigors should mortify us, cannot again be countermanded.—but depend upon it our *Industry*, our *truth*, and the regular manner in which we publish our Work—this will always prove to the World & to our Subscribers, that nothing

more can be done than what we do, nay that I doubt if any other *Family* with our pecuniary means ever will raise for themselves such a *Monument* as "the Birds of America" is, over their tomb!

Another problem facing the Naturalist was that of funds to provide payment to his engraver. To meet this contingency he advised his son that:

> I will exert myself to the very utmost to send you forthwith 2. or 3. or 4 hundred pounds to alleviate the difficulties (if any there are) in your calls for cash. I have already written Docr Parkman to exert himself in trying to have some advances made on a/c of the 2d Volume at Boston & have requested to forward you if successful whatever he may get immediately. I shall in a few days go to Savannah to try with W*am* Gaston to do the same there.—I wish you had made it *a point* to have sent me the 20 Volumes for which I have so often written to you—through these I could have sent you perhaps one thousand pounds—but now this is all over and I must do the best I can without any of them but 2 Copies.—[34]

When the letter of 23 December was written, the expectations were that Audubon's voyage "round the Floridas, Gulph of Mexico &c will begin about the 1*t* of Feby next." But in January the Naturalist advised his son: "The Die is however cast.—I have given up my urgent wishes to revisit the Floridas, and a certain portion of the Western & Northwestern portion of our own beloved Country.—"[35] From the tone of the opening of this letter, in which he wrote: "I have been much tormented for some weeks passed on account of the requisitions which you have made that I should return to England as early in the Spring as possible—" it is evident that either his son or his engraver or both felt that his presence was needed in England.

Having decided to return in June or earlier, if possible, Audubon was confronted by additional financial hazards. On 15 February he wrote his son:

> I will try to settle as much of our affairs ere we depart as may be in my power, but *The Times* appear to be bad just now on account of the U.S. Bank's affairs which if the papers say true, have greatly distressed the Country particularly the Eastern States where it is reported many heavy failures have taken place.[36]

During the year 1833 financial conditions in the United States had become chaotic, in part due to the action President Jackson took in ordering the removal of government deposits from the Bank of the United States. The celebrated diarist, Philip Hone (1780–1851), on 31 December of that year, wrote in his diary as follows: "Public confidence is shaken, and sauve-qui-peut is the maxim of the day. Never in any year did the 31st. of December fail so completely to redeem the pledges of the 1st of January."[37]

Immediately before leaving Charleston Audubon was successful in obtaining considerable funds:

> I collected 200 Dollars for the 2d Volume from the Charleston Library— 200 Do for the 2d of the Natural History Society there.—and but 140 Doll*s* from

> the Citizens private Library and that on a/c of the first Volume 1/2 bound—so that that last Society is in arrears 80 Dollars for the first Volume, and 150 for 15 Nos of the 2d Vol. delivered to them. I received 220 Dolls for the 1st Volume 1/2 bound from Mr Rees—I forwarded you 252£ from Wam Gaston for all the subscribers 2d Vols at Savannah except Mr King of St Simons Island whose amount will be forwarded to the Rathbones for you shortly if not already done by Wam Gaston, who proves to be a man in a million![38]

Audubon's hope of obtaining payments from his Boston subscribers was not fulfilled. Doctor Parkman wrote him that "he did not think it likely for him to Collect money on a/c of the 2nd Volume."[39] Audubon wrote that he would go to Boston and try to collect the money himself. This he did not do. He did, however, obtain one additional subscription from William J. Rees, "Sumpter District, Stateburg." In January Audubon, having received two copies of Volume 1 of the *Birds of America*, sent his son John "to deliver it to Mr. Rees' agent who I expect will pay John."[40]

On 1 March Audubon, his wife, and son John, began their journey back to New York City from whence they would sail to England. They arrived in Baltimore on 8 March, having passed through Washington, but remaining there for only one hour.[41]

Audubon had expected to remain in Baltimore for about a month during which he hoped to make several drawings of ducks. He had, however, found it difficult to obtain the desired specimens.[42] There awaiting him were four letters from his son Victor, the last dated 22 January from which he learned that Number 37 (plates 181–85) had been delivered to European subscribers and was on the way to America. The Naturalist also learned that Havell had hired an additional engraver in order that eight or ten instead of the usual five numbers each year might be produced. He was further advised that were Havell to be provided with the necessary materials, Volume 4 could be completed five, if not four, years hence. Audubon related these developments in a letter to his friend Bachman with the observation that "Havell speaks of retiring from business at the Completion of the Birds of America (which proves clearly that he has lost nothing by that Publication) and remove to America."[43] In that same letter he noted:

> If the work is to proceed so much faster now I will have to work harder than ever and God knows if I shall be able to stand it, not withstanding all my willingness and everlasting anxiety respecting the completion of the work.[44]

The Naturalist found conditions distressingly severe in Baltimore. "Nothing is spoken of here except hard times, no cash. Therefore my chances for an increase of Subscribers is also very dull."[45] He actually lost one Baltimore subscriber, Evan Poultney, president of the Bank of Maryland which had failed. Fortunately, one new subscription was obtained—that of Thomas Edmondson, Jr. Also, while in Baltimore, Audubon learned that the Library of Congress had purchased the extra copy of the first volume of the *Birds of America* which he had left with the library on his way south.[46]

Winter at Charleston, 1833-1834

Before the end of March the Audubons were again on their way. There was a stopover in Philadelphia where the Naturalist had hoped to collect some money. He was able to obtain but $50, payments from three subscribers for individual numbers. When Audubon arrived in New York early in April, he at once arranged passage for himself as well as for his wife and son on the packet *North America* which was scheduled to sail for Liverpool on the 16th of the month.[47]

Despite the unpropitious financial conditions prevailing in the United States, Audubon continued to be the beneficiary of loyal and generous friends. One such friend was Edward Harris, who once again demonstrated his feelings when he sent to Audubon in New York "four hundred and ninety Dollars for all the Numbers of the Work." The Naturalist's brother-in-law, Nicholas Berthoud, also assisted him in collecting two notes due on 1 November. One note was for $200 from Dr. Nathaniel Potter of Baltimore for the second volume of the *Birds of America*, and the second in the amount of $400, paid by Doctor E. Geddings of Baltimore, of which $200 was for the first volume received and $200 for the second volume which, it was expected, he would have received by that time.[48]

Audubon was now in his fiftieth year. The publication of the *Birds of America* had begun eight years before, and the Naturalist was beginning to feel that he was aging. On 24 November 1833, he had written to his engraver to ask:

> Can we not push the work still faster?—Can *you* not publish the 2d Volume, (all Water Birds, and in my opinion easier than those of the Land) at the rate of 10 Numbers per annum?—It would be a great satisfaction to me, as I conceive myself growing old very fast.—So much travelling exposure and fatigue do I undergo, that the Machine me thinks is wearing out; and it would indeed be a pleasure for me to see the last of the present Publication.[49]

That this request Havell had already agreed to is known from Audubon's letter to Bachman of 13 March 1834 in which he observed:

> Havell has added another engraver to his *atelier* and says that he will publish 8 or 10 numbers per annum instead of the usual numbers (5) and that if materials can be given him the 4th Volume will be finished in 5 years from now—if not in 4.

Despite Audubon's success in inducing Havell to expedite the publication of the *Birds of America*, he still felt great anxiety regarding its continuation in the event he himself should not be able to carry on. This feeling is clearly expressed in a letter to his son Victor, sent prior to the sailing of the *North America*, in which he wrote:

> Now my Dear Son, do recollect that it is my most ardent wish that in the case of a total loss on our part, that *you continue* the Publication of *the Birds of America* to the best of your Abilities, and assisted by our most worthy Friends John Bachman & Edd Harris.[50]

12

IN LONDON AGAIN
1834-1836

The voyage to England which began in mid-April lasted but twenty days, so that in early May Audubon, his wife, and son John were in Liverpool. Prior to leaving America the Naturalist had been advised by Victor to proceed to London via Manchester "for the purpose of collecting a pair of hundred pounds." This he did immediately after arrival, not by coach but by rail, as he wrote Bachman, "*36 miles in one hour and 8 minutes*, mark that!" The day of the iron horse had arrived.[1]

After a few days, the family succeeded in procuring good rooms in London at 73 Margaret Street, Cavendish Square, not far from the engraver which was very desirable, "As the Gentlemen are obliged to be inspecting the progress of the work all the day."[2]

An insight to the Audubon family life is obtained from a letter written by the Naturalist to John Bachman:

> Our Dear Sons are studying every day.—My Old Friend [his wife] mends our socks Makes our shirts, Reads to us at Times, but dranks no brandy now a days—she has cast off her purchased sham curls [and] wears her own dear grey locks and looks all the better—John can make a pretty good Portrait in black chalk and Victor a pretty Landscape in Oil.—They are studying music & other matters—on the whole we are Happy and Contented as much as can be whilst absent from our Dear & beloved friends of Charleston.—Tell my Sweet heart [Maria Bachman], that Cruickshank has Improved my Minature[3] very considerably—he has worked over the Hair &c—This picture goes to *Turner* to be engraved in Mezzotints and you shall hear report hereafter."[4]

A year later when the family was residing in Edinburgh, Audubon, again in a letter to Bachman, wrote:

> Our Sons are Improving in their different ways of painting at a surprising rate—John has finished about 50 Portraits for which he has been paid, and he could Maintain *Two* very decently in Edinburgh through his art. he has made excellent copies of beautiful Pictures, from the originals of Sir Henry Raeburn—

2 of Walter Scot—one of Sir H. Raeburn—and 2 beautifull Children.—he is now at the Royal institution copying a beautiful Murillo.—Victor paints Landscapes, Battles, and other subjects and comes on equally well.—They visit the best and most learned Society of Edinburgh, passing their evenings alternately at Professors Wilson, Jameson, Trail, and others.[5]

Finally, the two brothers, working together, copied in oil a picture originally painted by their father. This was sold for "One Hundred Guineas" ($500). Neither the subject of the painting nor the purchaser was mentioned when Audubon wrote to Bachman regarding the matter.[6]

In London, the family generally arose at five, for as Lucy wrote her cousin Euphemia Gifford,

> Mr. A finds two or three hours then so much silent and agreeable that he takes advantage of it for writing all he can, but were it not for his presence being required so constantly at Mr. Havell's the Engraver, we should live a little remote from all this crowd and noise of London.[7]

In the summer the family arose at four o'clock and retired at ten in the evening.[8]

In addition to the supervision of the engraving of the *Birds of America*, completion of the second volume of the *Ornithological Biography* demanded much of the Naturalist's time. During the winter of 1833–34, while living in Charleston with the Bachman family, he had "written as much of the Biography as I could and I am a hundred times better prepared to arrange this for Publication, than I was when I wrote the first Volume."[9]

Before the end of May the Naturalist wrote to MacGillivray in Edinburgh asking him if he would again be willing to revise the material for the *Biography*, as well as what his terms would be for the work involved. MacGillivray was agreeable and, as to the terms, answered, "let them be such as you please with respect to money, but as time is valuable to me, I should like that arrangements be made so as to prevent unnecessary loss of it by letting me have the manuscript, books, &c in due array."[10] Accordingly these were immediately sent to him. When twenty-five descriptions had reached Edinburgh, MacGillivray wrote Audubon,

> This volume will certainly be much richer and more interesting, it will also be larger. You wish to know my opinion as to the improvement of your style. It seems to me to be much the same as before, but the information you give is more diversified and more satisfactory. Your first volume is only beginning to be known. Chambers has reprinted many of the sketches, and Hunt has one in a late number. Had it been of the post 8vo size, in two volumes it would have gone off in style; but your imperial size and regal price do not answer for the radicals, or republicans either. Could you sacrifice the first volume, reprint it of a small size and continue the series to the end? In suggesting this, I firmly believe that my only object is to let the book have fair play. Lizars has sold five or six thousand copies of his ill written compilations; and if you were to

issue yours in similar style—not of writing but of printing—with 20 woodcuts or engravings in each volume, I am certain it would spread over the land like a flock of migratory pigeons. Even without embellishments it would fly but were you to give it those additional wings, it would sweep along in beautiful curves, like the nighthawk or the purple-breasted swallow.[11]

Audubon did not change the format.

All through the summer Audubon kept supplying MacGillivray descriptions of birds for the *Biography*. At the end of August he wrote to Bachman:

> I have written so constantly for two months that I was obliged to leave off after having finished 100 articles of Biography and 13 Episodes.—I became swelled as I was at your house &c and have been Idle these 10 days to assist my recovery.[12]

In the same letter Audubon also informed Bachman about his other activities, and commented on current ornithological works then available in England, advising him,

> Since here I have read, Selby's & Temminck's Works, but they are I am sorry to say *not from Nature*. not a word could I find in them but what was compilation—I could not even be told at what time the Golden Eagle laid her eggs in Europe! Sir W*am* Jardine is published an enormous quantity of trash all compilation and takes the undue liberty of giving *figures* from my Work and those of all others who may best suit his views.—Mr Gould is publishing the Birds of England, of Europe &c &c &c—in all sorts of ways—Swainson has 17 volumes in his head and on papers half finished. . . . Yarrel who is a first rate *Naturalist* and a most excellent man is now publishing a beautiful Work (Wood cuts) on the Fishes of this country—Two Brothers *Meyers* are also publishing the Birds of England—in fact You could not pass a Bookseller's shop from the extreme "West end" to Wapping without seeing New books on Zoology in every window—and "at most reduced prices!"[13]

As to the Gould publication, in the following spring Audubon agreed to exchange a copy of his work "with Mr. Gould, for his publications—and have by me, 13 Numbers of his Birds of Europe—his century of Hymealan Birds—and his monograph of Trogons—I have also purchased a monograph of Parrots from a Mr Lear."[14]

By the first week in October Audubon, on his arrival in Edinburgh, found that MacGillivray had completed his revisions of the material for the second volume of the *Biography*, the pages of which were then sent to Neil and Company, printers in Edinburgh. Sheets of this volume then were forwarded to Dr. Parkman in Boston for the American edition which was published by Hilliard Gray, and Company.[15]

No sooner had the second volume of the *Ornithological Biography* been sent to the printer than Audubon began work on the third volume. In January he wrote to Bachman, asking for his help.

In London Again, 1834–1836

> I am now closely engaged at writing my 3d Vol of Ornithological Biography, one hundred species more of the Birds of America will be in the eye of the students of nature and of the critic by Jan*y* next or before; All water birds too. What a treat for me in this vol to disclose things unknown to all the world before now, except, as we have known our dear selves.—

But to accomplish all this the Naturalist needed Bachman's help.

> I must ask you in the most earnest manner to assist all you can and merely enable me to publish *no trash*. but pure, clean, truths, and nothing but facts—which makes me stand so proud in my own estimation for what I have already done.—My work I feel assured will be a standard one for ages to come. for I feel certain that with the exception of some few errors, the truths & facts contained in my writings and in my figures of Birds will become more apparent to every student of nature *out of his closet!* send me as soon as you can possibly procure them for me (*do not mind the expense*) the eggs of the fresh and salt water marsh hens, distinctly numbered, and the weights of several of each of these birds, how many eggs in the nest Etc*a* the same of the Virginian rail if you can, and of the American bittern the same in respect to the Wood duck, do, of the least bittern, the same of the Frigate pelican, for this apply to the commander of the *cutter* that goes to Key West, tell him of the importance to science &c &c—and all other eggs he might collect on the coast. along with a *few feathers* or wings or legs or even bills of the different species attached to the eggs of each so that I could swear to their identity.—American coot.ditto—Wilsons plover is said in your hand writing in my notes to breed with you, do try to see to that.write all you know of it procure eggs Etc*a*, what of the whooping Crane, Kildeer plover, *Wood Ibis* Ardia Herodias the measurements of and weight—Yellow breasted rail, Great & least Terns. dob chicks grebe I believe breeds with you? solitary sandpipers sandwich tern Rosiate tern, these 3 last I shot in the Floridas and have their eggs, but unfortunately not numbered—*Long billed Curlew*, woodcock all you know about it, pied oyster catcher, send me several skins—Hooded merganser Male female and young from your market—save the tracheas in spirits of every water bird you can get for me and weigh every bird carefully after putting down their measurements. Spotted Sand pipers Eggs Half a bushel of them if you *can for sale*—

It was not only from Bachman that the Naturalist sought help, for he requested the former to "write to many of your friends in the country—spur them up on the sea islands beg of the collector of the custom house to assist you." Audubon continued his letter to Bachman with:

> I am almost mad with the desire of publishing my 3d Vol this year. I am growing old fast and must work at a double quick time now—this will make me postpone my return to America until 1st April 1836 (the hoped for day of my departure for America with John) but it will assure my complete publication of the great work, bear me a hand and all will go on famously well.[16]

By late April one-fourth of the biographies for the third volume were completed, but the pace at which Audubon was writing had affected his health and he became ill:

> ... this rendered me *puffy* I could scarcely breath—my appetite was gone—My digestion bad,—in other Words I was attacked by dispesia [sic] as bad as ever.—Then I thought of a change of Work—for in the changes of Labour, the body and the mind undergo sure and certain relief—I took to Drawing! and what do you think—I have positively *finished* 33 Drawings of American Birds in England—this has enabled me to *swell* my third volume of Illustrations with 57 species not given by Alexr Wilson.[17]

On 31 December Audubon was able to advise Bachman that the third volume of the *Ornithological Biography*, consisting of 639 pages without the introduction, was finished and published.[18]

Although Audubon had expressed doubt of his being able to procure many additional subscribers in England, he nevertheless set out to augment his list very soon after his arrival in London. Shortly before leaving America he had received from the New York banking house of Prime, Ward, King and Company "11 Letters of Solid Introduction to Powerful houses in London & Paris which I hope in God I will be able to remit in due time."[19] One of the letters was for the British banking firm of Baring Brothers. This letter was lost.[20]

Another letter was addressed to the famous London banker, Baron Rothschild (Nathan Mayer, 1778–1836). An account of Audubon's visit with Baron Rothschild is recorded in some detail in *The Life of Audubon*, edited by the Naturalist's wife Lucy, and published in 1869.[21] From that account it is known that when Audubon told the banker he [Audubon] would be honored by his subscription to the *Birds of America*, Rothschild's reply was, "Sir, I never sign my name to any subscription, but you may send your work and I will pay for a copy of it. Gentlemen I am busy, I wish you good morning." The narrative continues:

> A few days afterwards I sent the first volume of my work half bound and all the numbers besides, then published. On seeing them we were told that he ordered the bearer to take them to his house which was done directly. Number after number was sent and delivered to the Baron, and after eight or ten months my son made out his account and sent it by Mr. Havell, my engraver, to his banking-house. The Baron looked at it with amusement, and cried out "What, a hundred pounds for birds! Why sir, I will give you five pounds, and not a farthing more." Representations were made to him of the magnificence and expense of the work, and how pleased the Baroness and wealthy children would be to have a copy; but the great financier was unrelenting. The copy of the work was actually sent back to Mr. Havell's shop, and as I found that instituting legal proceedings against him would cost more than it would come to, I kept that work and afterwards sold it to a man with less money but a nobler heart. What a distance there is between two such men as the Baron Rothschild of London and the merchant of Savannah!

In London Again, 1834–1836

The Rothschild name appears on the original subscription list as "N. M. Rothschild Esq. London." In Volume 2 of the *Ornithological Biography* it is listed as "Baron N. M. Rothschild, London." Furthermore, in Ledger "B" there is recorded the delivery of the first two volumes in 1834 and also a payment in the amount of £93. 13. 0. to Havell in February 1836. However, this must have been received from the man "with less money but a nobler heart," whoever he was. Many years later a member of the Rothschild family, the second baron, Lionel Walter Rothschild (1868–1937), did purchase a set of the Double Elephant folio of the *Birds of America* which is presently in the British Museum (Natural History).

In a letter to Charles Lucien Bonaparte on 20 August, mention was made of two subscriptions obtained at this time, one from the agent of the Duke of Tuscany of Florence and the other from "His Grace the Duke of Buccleuch of Dalkeith Castle."[22] With the delivery of the first two volumes which were completed at that time to the agent of the Duke, Audubon was paid £93. 5. 0. Both of these subscriptions were completed; the folio of the Duke of Tuscany is presently in the Biblioteca Nazionale in Florence, Italy, while that of the Duke of Buccleuch was, a few years ago, purchased by a New York print dealer, broken up, and the individual prints sold.

As Audubon had anticipated, he was finding it difficult to increase the number of English subscribers. Careful examination of the original subscription list indicates that the only additional subscribers added to list during the period from May 1834 to his departure for America in July 1836 were the following:

> Chas. Fox, Perran (Perrair?), near Truro
> John Tobin, Liverpool
> London Institution per Mr. Brayley
> His Grace, the Duke of Northumberland
>   by T. Lindell—May 27, 1836
> Col. Lloyd Phillips, Aberryscivish, Wales
>   by Havell May 28, 1836
> W*am* Warren, Esq. 24 Queen Street, Brompton.

In the summer of 1833 Victor Audubon had visited the Continent and at that time was successful in obtaining the subscription of the Tylerian Library of Haarlem, Holland. In a letter to his friend Edward Harris in America concerning his inability to obtain additional subscribers in England, Audubon noted:

> We receive no new subscribers in Europe. The taste is passing for Birds like a flitting shadow—Insects, reptiles and fishes are now the rage, and these fly, swim or crawl on pages innumerable in every Bookseller's window. When this is also passed, naturalists will have to turn over a new leaf and commence afresh, or go to the antipodes in search of material to please the taste for novelty's sake. However my work will I hope be finished ere I leave this world, and must be appreciated in years to come, when perhaps my children's children will feel proud of their ancestor "The American Woodsman."[23]

During his expeditions to Florida and Labrador in 1832, Audubon had accumulated some 3000 bird skins. These had been shipped to Europe in the autumn of 1833;[24] some of these skins the Naturalist proposed to sell in England, others were to be retained for a particular purpose. In September of the previous year the Naturalist had written his son Victor, "should these [drawings] be lost I can renew them from *the Skins*,"[25] first having made outlines of those sent.

On 14 June Audubon left at the British Museum a list of bird skins which he offered to sell that institution.[26] In August he wrote John Bachman; "I sold 52 pounds sterling of Skins to the British Museum about a month ago—and again 25 £ worth two days ago—& Havell has sold a good number more.—So I shall not be a loser in that way."[27] At the time, the skin of the wild turkey cock brought $100 and that of the female $25.

By the end of August the Naturalist found it necessary to set out on a trip to Manchester and other cities "to see the *Whole* of my Patrons." There was to be a meeting on 8 September of about "500 Philosophers on Zoology" at Edinburgh from all parts of the British Isles, but Audubon was not planning to attend, for he had "other fish to fry."[28]

There was good reason why Audubon should see his patrons in Manchester. He had obtained thirty-eight subscribers in that city and environs. During the interval he had been in America conditions in that large industrial city had been unsettled; even riots had occurred, and, as a result, subscribers had been lost.

Arriving in Manchester on 5 September the Naturalist sought out as many subscribers as he could in the hope that he might persuade them to continue the work. Among the lapsed subscriptions which Audubon endeavored to redeem were those of W. Birch, Robert H. Garnett, D. Grant, George Humphrey, G. W. Wood.[29] His efforts, however, were not successful, for none of these names appear on the final list of subscribers. Of the thirty-eight subscriptions obtained from the residents of Manchester and its environs, only eight were completed.

In the hope that he might obtain some new subscriptions, Audubon had brought with him on this trip a bound volume of his works as well as some of the prints of the water birds. These he displayed on many occasions, but he did not obtain the desired result.

From Manchester Audubon went to Leeds. Here he tried to persuade a Miss Rhodes to continue her subscription. He found the lady unwell and not expected to live; hence he could not see her. Again in Leeds and in Halifax nearby he sought new subscribers but again was unsuccessful. In a letter to his wife describing the trip in detail, he observed: "You see what trouble I have had yet have done so little good. My seeing people is however quite necessary." What he did accomplish was to collect some money from his agents, obtaining from Mrs. Robinson of Leeds a note for £79 9s. 8d. and cash for £8 10s. 6d.[30]

With the completion of the second volume of the *Birds of America* (plates 101–200), work progressed rapidly on the numbers for the third volume so that by 3 August numbers 41, 42, and 43 were completed, with work on Numbers 44, 45, 46 in process, and Number 47 expected to be completed by the end of the year. However the engraving proceeded more quickly than anticipated, for by 1 November Audubon had received prints 271 to 275 for Number 55, and on 22 January of the following year the first number (61) of the last volume (plates 301–5) was under the graver.[31] The rapid pace of the engraving was to continue, so that when Audubon left London in July for New York with his son John, he took with him "Nos. 63, 64, 65 and 66 (being up to Plate 330) for all subscribers in America."[32]

Not only was the engraving of the plates for the *Birds of America* proceeding at an accelerated pace, but the quality of the work was such as to greatly please the Naturalist. Writing to Havell concerning Number 54 (plates 266–70), Audubon thus commended him:

> The Whole is quite beautiful—you have exceeded anything previously done and you may now challenge the world of ornithological Engravers without any fear! . . . The plate of the Parasiticus is splendid and so is that of Wilson's Petrel.—in the latter you have managed the Water surprizingly well, and I am glad to see the fine cutting of Mr Blake [one of Havell's assistants]—The head of the Male Cormorant is equal to Nature. Indeed I have only to say, that I never felt better pleased than whilst gazing on the 5 plates these 20 minutes past.[33]

When Audubon received the prints for Number 55 (plates 271–75), he again considered the work well done both as to engraving and coloring but cautioned the engraver that "the *Legs and feet* of the *Cayenne Tern* [royal tern, plate 273] *which must be coloured as black as possible without interference to the Engraving before delivery.*—I think you have been quite fortunate with the Frigate Pelican!"[34] The Naturalist then mentioned that he was sending Havell the last five drawings for the third volume, adding his admonition to the engraver for "your *most especial care* the plate [281] of the Great White Heron—it is a new bird of my own discovery and I should like to have it treated in your best manner.[35] When he received the print he commented:

> I have examined, and that closely too, the Plates of Ardea occidentalis [great white heron] *the Bird* is perfect! The termination of the darker portions of the sky are too harsh, and I should like you to have these extremities or *outer edges* SCRAPED and the purplish tint about those parts rendered darker by the *Colourers.* If you can subdue the little figures of the Heron in the distance somewhat, it will improve the plate.—but take it "all in all" it is most excellent, and I feel highly gratified that you have met my wishes with it.[36]

At the same time with the increased activity of the engravers, colorists, and the like, the weekly operating costs of the shop now totaled, "one hundred pounds per week, or about $450.[37]

On 5 May 1835 Audubon wrote John Bachman, "recollect, that it is only Twelve Months since we arrived in England, and I venture to say no family, collectively or separately has Worked harder, and produced more Work than the Family Audubon's—." There was to be no letdown, for in addition to his preoccupation with the completion of the third volume of the *Biography*, and the necessity to keep his engraver supplied with drawings (one number a month was now being engraved), Audubon had to obtain information about the birds which were to be described in the fourth volume of the *Biography* and procure specimens of those species needed for the anatomical studies which were henceforth to be included in this work. As he had written Bachman,

> My principal Wish in the finishing of my Letter press, i.e., the fourth Volume of it, is to bring in it a good and close comparative anatomical account of the Type of each of our Ornithological species by which I now think, the least errors committed by my predecessors or by Myself heretofore can at once be detected and *corrected!!*

Many letters were written to Bachman and other friends in America pleading for help,

> To render my *present* publication a Standard Work, I feel extremely desirous to do all in my power, as well as in the power of those who love and esteem me and are able to assist me, to deliver all imaginable *assistance* from all and every One with whom I am now acquainted with, and on whom I think I might look upon with reliance.—You my Dear Bachman are foremost on the list!"[38]

A typical letter (in part) is the following sent to Bachman from Edinburgh on 15 September 1835:

> My dear Bachman.
> Although I have letters of yours to answer, I will write to you in considerable earnest, and this all about the Birds of America, and especially those which will form the 4th Volume of my Work and are about you, or at least in the Carolinas, Georgia and the Floridas.—
>   1. Black-winged Hawk, Falco Dispar, Breeds about the Santee, where Ward Killed 6 and says found their nests.—now can you learn anything more of them and should find the nest and eggs or young describe, measure, weigh &c &c and save Specimen and Eggs! Perhaps Docr Wilson could assist us in this desiderate—
>   2. Red bellied Woodpecker—very precise descriptions of Habits, eggs, migration, *food* &c *Weight* Measurements accurate.
>   3. Hairy Woodpecker, the same thing as above—
>   4. Red cockaded Woodpecker.—DoDoDo.—
>   5. Bank Swallow, This is a most interesting species, try to watch them when digging their holes, nest, Eggs, Incubation of every species of Bird you can procure will be most valuable, I *suspect* that we have two species of this Swallow.—
>   6. Cape May Warbler, 7. Blue Mountain Do., 8. Blue winged Yellow and 9. Golden winged Do (I suspect these 2 last to form only one species.)
>   10. Black-capt Titmouse—Try to find Nests, eggs, &c.— Edd Harris has sent me a specimen of both species from the Jerseys.—11. Scarlet Tanager, all about

him.—12. Black Throated Bunting.—13. Pine Grosbeak.—14. White winged Cross bill—of these 2 last you may probably receive information from some friend down East.—15. Winter Wren.—and whatever other Land Birds not included in My Two published volumes.—

Now for the Water Bird.—
1. Ring Plover.   All the Tringas.—
2. Black bellied D*o*
3. Turn Stone.
4. White Heron.
5. Blue D*o*
6. American Bitern, could you find the nest of this bird about the round O.
7. Green Heron.—
8. Scolopax Courlan
16. Roseate Spoon bill   Where is Doc*r* Strobell? if in the Floridas, he
9. Scarlet Ibis   would I am sure assist us in good observations,
10. Flamingo   and perhaps in procuring eggs &c of these birds.
11. Glossy Ibis
12. Long legged Avoset   Perhaps Breed in the Sea Islands?
13. American Avoset
14. Tell Tale Godwit
15. *Bartram Sandpiper*, I have not a single specimen of this, although a fine Drawing of Two figures.
17. Yellow breasted Rail.—
Breed about you very early in the season, in Feb*y* & March in Louisiana where I procured the female & eggs, but I never saw a Male Bird.—
18. Purple Gallinule, all about it—
19. Black Skimmer—Do Do
20. Marsh Tern   all these are common about you and breed there.—I have
21. Great Tern   no specimen of the first, although I have shot many but it
22. Least Tern   is now years ago.—
23. Gulls of any sort in any kind of plumage, but must be accurately Measured and Weighed—The colour of the eyes, bill and feet Marked down and also the date of their being procured—I am positif in saying that we have undescribed species along the Southern Shores, and probably also some Terns. Memorandums on all the species of Ducks which visit you in Winter, measurements and Weights Wanted—could be done in the Market without purchasing—[39]

The foregoing letter is transcribed only in part. It will be noted that in some instances Audubon had requested that Bachman send the eggs of the species. From the very beginning of the work Audubon had hoped to include drawings of eggs with the *Birds of America*. He had mentioned this in his prospectus, and, in 1829 on his first trip to America, he had written his wife that among his paintings were those of "60 different kinds of Eggs."[40] The Naturalist probably had been deterred from including the illustrations of eggs in the fourth volume by the necessity of adding to this volume the drawings of western birds which he had obtained from Nuttall and Townsend. The large collection of drawings of birds eggs were eventually sent to Dr. James Trudeau in June 1839.[41]

In January 1836 the Audubon family had returned to London, the third volume of the *Biography* having been completed the previous month. By the 26th of the month, the first number (plates 301–5) of the last volume of *Birds of America* came under the graver. At the same time Number 58 (plates 286–90) had been printed and sent to America while Number 59 (plates 291–95) was already engraved. Audubon had been told by his engraver:

> that unless *I* keep him back, the enormous work will be finished and compleat in 22 *Months*, from this date!! how delicious is the Idea, and how comfortable should I feel at this moment were I able fully to say to Havell *you shall not be detained a Moment!* But there are drawbacks in all undertakings and in mine especially numerous ones.[42]

All during the winter and spring of 1836 the engraving of the *Birds of America* proceeded at so rapid a pace that on 1 August when Audubon and his son John sailed for New York aboard the ship *Gladiator*, under the command of Captain T. Briton, they were able to take with them Numbers 63 through 66 (plates 311–30) for the Naturalist's American subscribers.

13

THIRD RETURN TO AMERICA
1836-1837

On 4 September, after a smooth passage of thirty-three days, the *Gladiator* arrived in New York. Audubon and his son John went immediately to the home of Nicholas Berthoud, the brother-in-law of Lucy Audubon.[1] They had planned to proceed south to Charleston without delay, but in a letter from John Bachman awaiting the Naturalist's arrival, he was advised to postpone the trip south until October as there was great anxiety in Charleston of a cholera epidemic which actually did break out in mid-September.[2]

Since Berthoud was of the opinion that Audubon could obtain about ten subscriptions in New York, the Naturalist decided to devote "my time to this desiderata."[3] The first name added to his list was that of a Col. Thorne of Paris who was traveling to England on the *Gladiator*. Although this name is on the original subscription list, no additional information concerning the subscription has been found. The names of Samuel Swartout, James Watson Webb, J. Van Rensselaer, M.D., and Thomas H. Faile on the original list of subscribers were probably added at this time. Also at this time Audubon learned that J. J. Hughes of Manchester, Mississippi, had not only subscribed but had paid in advance for the first three volumes of the *Birds of America*. It is possible that this subscription had been obtained by the Naturalist's New Orleans agent and subscriber, James Grimshaw. The latter had married a daughter of Nicholas Berthoud and at the time of Audubon's arrival in America was visiting the Berthouds.[4]

Audubon's success in obtaining these additional subscribers encouraged him to write to England: "I wish Victor to Send me as soon as possible as many Compleat Setts of 1/2 bound Volumes as he can as I forsee that many will be wanted here."[5]

Before leaving for Boston on 17 September,[6] Audubon sent to Bachman the following consignment:

> One fine Pointer Dog from the Earl of Derby which is intended as a companion to the Bitch sent Friend Bachman, and 4 Cages of Birds, as follows. 4 Pigeons,

3 Jays, 4 Starlings and 4 Larks; the residue of 265 which we had when the Gladiator left London Docks *and* one Box of Bird Skins.[7]

The visit to Boston proved most successful. Here the Naturalist obtained additional subscriptions from Elizabeth Pickman of Salem, Salem Athenaeum, Augustus Thorndike, and Daniel Webster.[8]

It was during Audubon's previous visit to Boston in the winter of 1832–33 that the Boston Natural History Society had subscribed. Now the Naturalist learned that a portion of the funds needed to pay for this subscription had not been fully obtained. However, during the visit the balance was collected through the help of Dr. George C. Shattuck. Audubon noted this event in his journal thus:

> September 27. In the evening Dr. Shattuck finished the subscription list of the society, by presenting me to his lady, who subscribed for one-tenth and the Dr. then put down his son George's name for one-twentieth, making in his own family one-fourth of the whole, or two hundred and twenty dollars, for which he gave me his cheque. Without the assistance of this generous man, it is more than probable that the society never would have had a copy of the "Birds of America."[9]

Dr. Shattuck also had helped Audubon collect payments due from other subscribers. Among the papers in the Shattuck file at the Massachusetts Historical Society are the following copies of receipts dated August 1836:

James Arnold	Vol. 3	Unbound $200.
Wm Oates	" "	Hf Bound $220.
John Brown	" "	Unbound $200.
Harvard University	" "	Hf Bound $220.
E. A. Greenwood	" "	Unbound $200.[10]

Dr. Shattuck, after the Naturalist left Boston, continued to collect payments from subscribers. By the end of the year he had deposited in the Atlas bank $659 to Audubon's credit. In all, Audubon received $2800[11] from his subscribers while in Boston, which sum included $220 from the Commonwealth of Massachusetts.

In 1834 Thomas Nuttall (1786–1859), a botanist, and Dr. John Kirk Townsend (1809–1851), an experienced ornithologist, had set out on a journey to the mouth of the Columbia River, an expedition which, in part, had been financed by the Academy of Natural Sciences of Philadelphia. Audubon had been in New York but a few days when he received a letter from Dr. Harlan saying "that Nuttall & Townsend had forwarded about 100 New Species of Birds from the Pacific Side of the Rocky Mountains."[12] This was followed by a letter from Edward Harris in which he enumerated the new species of birds collected by Nuttall and Townsend.[13] Anxious to see the "rara avis," the Naturalist hastened to Philadelphia, going to the Academy where he had

> a great treat in looking over and handling the rare collection made by Nuttall and Townsend in their excursion on and over the Rocky Mountains. It belongs to the Academy, which assisted the travellers with funds to promote this

journey; it contains about forty new species of birds, and its value cannot be described.[14]

While in Philadelphia Audubon met his friend Edward Harris who, when told about the new species, offered to give him five hundred dollars towards purchasing them.[15] However, during this visit to Philadelphia the Naturalist was unable to obtain any of the specimens.

When Audubon reached Boston on 20 September, he learned that Nuttall had arrived in that city from California a few days previously. On the following day the two men met and Audubon received the promise of duplicates of all the species Nuttall had brought for the Academy in Philadelphia. Before Audubon left Boston, Nuttall did give him five new species of birds.[16]

Late in October Audubon returned to Philadelphia. This time he was successful in obtaining the desired specimens from the Nuttall-Townsend collection. As he wrote Bachman:

> Now Good Friend open your Eyes! aye open them tight!! Nay place specks on your probosis if you chuse! Read aloud!! quite aloud!!! I have purchased *Ninety Three Bird Skins!* Yes 93 Bird Skins!—Well what are they? Why nought less than 93 Bird Skins sent from the Rocky Mountains and the Columbia River by Nuttall and Townsend!—Cheap as Dirt too—only one hundred and Eighty-Four Dollars for the whole of these, and hang me if you do not echo my saying so when *you see them!!* Such beauties! such rarities! Such Novelties! Ah my Worthy Friend how we will laugh and talk over them![17]

The Nuttall-Townsend collection provided about seventy figures for more than a tenth of the 435 plates. As a group, the paintings of the western birds were not among the most admired, as they often did not have the animation that Audubon depicted in the birds with which he was familiar and which he had collected himself. Also the settings in which the western birds were portrayed frequently lacked authenticity and detail, for the Naturalist, unfortunately, had not been supplied with information about the habits and habitats of these birds until after he had completed the plates. Thus he figured many without backgrounds, the birds perching on bare branches, and usually sketched in vague, imaginary scenes of barren plain, or streambank, and distant mountains, with unidentifiable plants and grasses. However, Nuttall did provide the nests of some species as well as some of the western butterflies he had collected. These Audubon introduced to advantage. In several of the most pleasing of these paintings, the western birds are shown nonchalantly perched on eastern plants. The most successful compositions to a naturalist's eye are the two plates in which strictly western plants furnish perches for the birds. One of these, the "Band-tailed Pigeon" (plate 367), shows the striking Northwestern or Pacific dogwood, *Cornus nuttalli* Aud., named for its discoverer, which has six white involuted bracts instead of the four of the well-known eastern species. The other, "Four Western Corvids" (plate 362), shows the California sycamore, *Platanus racemosa* Nutt., as well as a magpie (*Pica nuttalli*) named for Nuttall.[18]

Audubon had to depend on Nuttall and Townsend to provide descriptions of the western birds for the fourth and fifth volumes of the *Ornithological Biography*. For the new species there were no other sources of information, and for those that had been collected by earlier explorers, the published facts were often all too meager.[19] At the end of October 1837, about a year before the fourth volume appeared Audubon wrote urgently to his friend, the dependable Edward Harris, asking the latter to immediately purchase and forward the new birds that had recently arrived in Philadelphia with Townsend. Moreover he charged Harris with the task of obtaining detailed descriptions of the habits, dates, localities, nests, eggs, songs, migrations, and whatever else Townsend knew concerning any and all birds he had seen on his journey.

In December 1836 Audubon wrote his engraver that inclusion of the drawings of the western birds would make it necessary to arrange the plates differently from plate 350 on. However, at that time the Naturalist still believed that he could complete the work with 400 plates,[20] which, however, he was unable to do, even by placing several species together on single plates. Furthermore, some of the specimens of western birds received from Townsend in 1837 could not be included in the Double Elephant Folio, but these did appear in the Octavo edition.

With the purchase of the species of the western birds completed, Audubon began his journey south to Charleston, arriving in Baltimore on 5 November.[21] He obtained no new subscriptions there, but he did collect $380 from his subscribers. When he arrived in Washington the following day, he immediately called on another old friend, Col. John James Abert (1788–1863), who was associated with the Bureau of Topographical Engineers of the United States Army.

Colonel Abert first took Audubon to the office of President Jackson, to whom Audubon had been given a letter of introduction by Samuel Swartout, the Collector of the Port of New York, and himself a subscriber to the *Birds of America*. After the President had read Swartout's letter twice, he said, "Mr. Audubon, I will do all in my power to serve you, but the Seminole War will, I fear, prevent you from having a cutter; however as we shall have a committee at twelve o'clock, we will consider this, and give you an answer to-morrow."[22]

The next visit was to Levi Woodbury, Secretary of the Treasury.[23] Audubon had first met Woodbury in 1830 when the latter, then a senator from New Hampshire, had been a member of the Joint Committee of the Library of Congress from which a subscription to the *Birds of America* had been obtained. Secretary Woodbury received him politely and "promised me the use of a Cutter." Audubon had hoped that he might obtain a subscription to the *Birds of America* from the various government departments and mentioned this to Woodbury, but nothing was decided at the time.

While in New York Audubon had received several letters of introduction from Washington Irving, one being to Benjamin F. Butler, Attorney General of the United States. Butler was the next to be visited. Audubon wrote of this interview as follows:

Third Return to America, 1836-1837

> He read Washington Irving's letter, laid it down, and began a long talk about his talents, and after a while came around to my business; saying, that the government allows so little money to the departments, that he did not think it probable that their subscription could be obtained without a law to that effect from Congress. This opinion was anything but gratifying; but he made many courteous promises to bring the matter before the next Congress, and I bad him adieu, hoping for the best.[24]

That evening Audubon spent at the home of Levi Woodbury and while there he was handed an order for the use of a cutter and was also informed that the Treasury Department "had subscribed for one copy of our Work."[25] The story of this subscription in which other departments of the government shared is related in detail in the provenance of the War Department copy of the *Birds of America* now at the Library of Congress.

The next day, following a visit with the Secretary of the Navy, Mahlen Dickinson, Audubon with his son John dined "en famille" with President Jackson. It is of interest to note that they "dined on a fine young turkey which was shot within twenty miles of Washington."[26]

Leaving Washington early the next morning, father and son proceeded to Charleston, travelling the last part of the way "on one of the most extraordinary rail-roads in the world." They reached their destination on 16 November.[27]

Although the Naturalist had received from the Secretary of the Treasury an order for the use of a revenue cutter, no vessel was made available to him until after the apparent end of the Seminole War in February 1837. In the interval, Audubon was kept busy with various activities. First, there was the drawing of the western birds, which he noted thus in his journal:

> I opened the box containing Dr. Townsend's precious series of birds . . . drew upwards of seventy figures of the species which I had procured in Philadelphia, assisted in the finishing of the plants, branches of trees, and flowers, which accompany those figures, by my friend's sister-in-law Miss M[aria] Martin, to whom I now again offer my most sincere thanks.[28]

In addition, the Naturalist, together with his friend Bachman, made occasional excursions into the country and to the nearby islands in search of birds and to collect information for the *Ornithological Biography*. Undoubtedly he made use of these excursions to obtain the information for which he had asked Bachman in the many letters he had written from England prior to his departure the previous July.

Also Audubon continued to augment his collection of bird skins with the help of McCullough of Pictou, Nova Scotia, Harlan of Philadelphia, Brewer of Boston and others, so that by March he was able to write his son Victor that

> I have collected . . . altogether about 200 Species of Birds in the flesh, many Duplicates of some of the Species, and wish you in case of my death to see to the receiving of every one of the Kegs or Barrels containing them; to place

them into the hands of W*am* MacGillivray, and to have *compleat, minute, anatomical descriptions* of *each Species* (whether already published or not) and to attach these descriptions by Generas or subgeneras to the Descriptions or Biographies forming the *4th* Volume, nearly the whole of which Victor and MacGillivray can manage to publish from my Journals, notes &c and the notes of John Bachman, & Thomas Nuttall, or the assistance of Young Townsend should he return from the Pacific.[29]

In the middle of February, upon learning that the war in Florida had ended, Audubon decided to go to Mobile to ascertain when a revenue cutter would be available, since during the war all vessels of this character had been sent to Florida, and none had remained at Charleston.[30] On 17 February, accompanied by his son John and his friend Edward Harris of Moorestown, New Jersey, who had been visiting the Bachmans since early in the month, the journey was begun. The party went by train to Augusta and from there journeyed by coach across Georgia through Alabama to Montgomery.

Before arriving at Mobile, the travelers witnessed a most pathetic sight which Audubon graphically described as follows:

> ... the next morning we breakfasted at the Village of [———] where 100 Creek Warriors were confined in Irons, preparatory to leaving for ever the Land of their births!—Some miles onward we overtook about two thousands of these once free owners of the Forest, marching towards this place [Mobile] under an escort of Rangers, and militia mounted Men, destined for distant lands, unknown to them, and where alas, their future and latter days must be spent in the deepest of Sorrows, afliction and perhaps even physical want—This view [has] produced on my mind an aflicting series of reflections more powerfully felt than easy of description—the numerous groups of Warriors, of half clad females and of naked babes, trudging through the mire under the residue of their ever scanty stock of Camp furniture, and household utensiles—The evident regret expressed in the[ir] masked countenances of some and the tears of others—the howling of their numerous dogs; and the cool demeanour of the chiefs,—all formed such a Picture as I hope I never will again witness in reality—had Victor been with us, ample indeed would have been his means to paint Indians in sorrow.[31]

When the trio reached Mobile, Audubon's first enquiry was for Judge Henry Hitchcock, one of the subscribers to the *Birds of America*. However, Judge Hitchcock was absent from the city. The visit to Mobile was a short one and, after a trip to Pensacola, Florida, Audubon and his son arrived in New Orleans early in March. Harris remained in Pensacola temporarily.

The stay in New Orleans, which lasted until 23 March, was enlivened by visits not only with old friends but also with many notables of the city, including the former governor André Bienvenue Roman (1795–1866), who had helped procure the subscription of the state of Louisiana to the *Birds of America*. Attempts to obtain new subscribers here were fruitless.[32]

"BIRDS OF AMERICA."

J. J. AUDUBON has returned from the UNITED STATES, and begs to inform his Patrons, that since his arrival, he has made arrangements with Mr. R. HAVELL, his Engraver, that will enable him to complete his Work on the BIRDS OF AMERICA in Four Years, although originally contemplated to require Eight Years from this period.

The Third Volume, now in progress, will consist of WATER BIRDS, and the Fourth, which will be the last, will contain what remain unpublished, of both the Land and Water Birds.

The Water Birds and the remainder of the Land Birds will be found to be equal, if not to surpass, the Two First Volumes, in interest, beauty, and execution.

The Second Volume of Letter-press will soon be published.

It is now certain that the "BIRDS OF AMERICA" will be a very scarce Work; and the Author cannot bind himself to furnish copies to those who may neglect to order them before the Work is finished. He will, therefore, consider it a favor of those persons desirous of possessing it, if they will forward their Orders, as soon as convenient, to *J. J. Audubon*, or to *Mr. Robert Havell, Zoological Gallery, 77, Oxford Street, opposite the Pantheon, London.*

London, June 1834.

Audubon's June 1834 published announcement that *Birds of America* would be completed in four years. Courtesy of The New-York Historical Society.

THE BIRDS OF AMERICA.
By J. J. AUDUBON, F.R.S., &c.

When only a few Numbers of this Work had been published, Mr. Audubon was informed that many Noblemen and Gentlemen, as well as a considerable number of Natural History and other Societies, Libraries, &c. were desirous of possessing it, but that the time to be occupied in the publication (16 years) was so great, the casualties of life so many, and the probability of its ever being finished, therefore, so remote, they determined to await its completion before they subscribed.
With respect to many Societies, moreover, the rules preclude them, for the above reasons, from subscribing to any work of this kind published periodically.
Mr. Audubon, therefore, feels desirous, for the information of such persons or Societies, to announce that seventy-eight Numbers have now appeared, and that with seven more it will be completed. He confidently expects to present the last Number to his Subscribers on the 1st of April or May next.
As a comparatively small number of persons only are acquainted with this work, for the information of others, it may be well to observe that the whole of the Birds (about 470 Species) known to inhabit North America, with the exception of those of Mexico and Texas, are exhibited.
The figures are all of the size of life, after drawings made from nature, during the last thirty-five years; and the Birds are accompanied by a very large number of Botanical Specimens, some of them not figured in any other work.
This Publication was commenced in 1826, and the Prospectus then issued anticipated a period of sixteen years as necessary for its completion; of that term only twelve years have elapsed, and in six months more it will be terminated.
In addition to the fidelity with which every Bird and Plant is represented, this Work has another great attraction, from the circumstance that it forms a complete history of the Birds of America, and will in after times be a point from which to institute a comparison for the purpose of ascertaining what changes civilization produces in the Fauna of that great continent.
It was contemplated that eighty Numbers would finish the Work; but in consequence of new and rare Species having been recently discovered by the Author, and also received from the Prince of Musignano, Thos. Nuttall, Esq., Dr. John Townsend, and others, eighty-five Numbers will be required (in which will be included the Eggs of many of the Species).
The particulars of the plan of the Work may be reduced to the following heads:
The size is whole-sheet double elephant, the paper being of the finest quality.
The Work appears in Numbers—each consisting of five Plates.
The price of each Number is Two Guineas, payable on delivery.
The number of perfect copies at present subscribed for does not exceed 190, of which upwards of 80 are subscribed for in America; and the expense of getting them up is so great, that not more than ten or fifteen copies, above the number subscribed for, will be prepared.
The Establishment necessary for its publication will be broken up when the last Number is coloured; and any application for the Work must be made to the Author, 4, Wimpole-street, London; or Mr. R. Havell, Engraver, 77, Oxford-street, before the 1st of May next, as after that time no subscription can be received.
London, November 1, 1837.

Audubon's 1837 announcement that *Birds of America* would soon be completed appeared in the 6 January 1838 issue of *The Athenaeum*, no. 532, p. 23. Courtesy of Northwestern University Library, Evanston, Ill.

the wide, heathy, or rushy and boggy moors. Ye may discover the whaup's lang nose half a mile aff, as the gleg-ee'd creatur keeps a watch ower the wilderness, wi' baith sicht and smell.

NORTH.

Did you shoot the whaups alluded to above, James—or the Tailor himself?

SHEPHERD.

Him—no me. But mony and aft's the time that I hae lain for hours ahint some auld turf-dyke, that aiblins had ance enclosed a bit bonny kailyard belanging to a housie noo soopt frae the face of the yerth,—every noo and than keekin' ower the grassy rampart to see gif the whaups, thinkin themselves alane, were takin' their walk in the solitude; and gif nane were there, layin' mysel doon a' my length on my grufe and elbow, and reading an auncient ballant, or maybe tryin' to croon a bit sang o' my ain, inspired by the loun and lanesome spat,—for O, sir! hae na ye aften felt that the farther we are in body frae human dwellings, the nearer are ye to their ingles in sowl?

NORTH.

Often, James—often. In a crowd I am apt to be sullen or ferocious. In solitude I am the most benevolent of men. To understand my character, you must see me alone—converse with me—meditate on what I then say—and behold my character in all its original brightness.

SHEPHERD.

The dearest thocht and feelings o' auld lang syne come crowd—crowding back again into the heart whenever there's an hour o' perfect silence, just like so many swallows comin' a-wing frae God knows whare, when winter is ower and gane, to the self-same range o' auld clay biggins, aneath the thatch o' house, or the slate o' ha'—unforgetfu' they o' the place whare they were born, and first hunted the insect-people through shadow or sunshine!

NORTH.

What a pity, James, that you were not in Edinburgh in time to see my friend Audubon's Exhibition!

SHEPHERD.

An Exhibition o' what?

NORTH.

Of birds painted to the life. Almost the whole American Ornithology, true to nature, as if the creatures were in their native haunts in the forests, or on the sea-shores. Not stiff and staring like stuffed specimens—but in every imaginable characteristic attitude, perched, wading, or a-wing,—not a feather, smooth or ruffled, out of its place,—every song, chirp, chatter, or cry, made audible by the power of genius.

SHEPHERD.

Whare got he sae weel acquant wi' a' the tribes—for do they not herd in swamps and woods whare man's foot intrudes not—and the wilderness is guarded by the Rattlesnake, fearsome Watchman, wi' nae ither bouets than his ain fiery eyne?

NORTH.

For upwards of twenty years the enthusiastic Audubon lived in the remotest woods, journeying to and fro on foot thousands of miles—or sailing on great rivers, " great as any seas," with his unerring rifle, slaughtering only to embalm his prey by an art of his own, in form and hue unchanged, unchangeable—and now, for the sum of one shilling, may anybody that chooses it, behold the images of almost all the splendid and gorgeous birds of that Continent.

SHEPHERD.

Whare's the Exhibition now?

NORTH.

At Glasgow, I believe—where I have no doubt it will attract thousands of delighted spectators. I must get the friend who gave " A Glance over Selby's Ornithology," to tell the world at large more of Audubon. He is the greatest artist in his own walk that ever lived, and cannot fail to reap the reward of his genius and perseverance and adventurous zeal in his own beautiful branch of natural history, both in fame and fortune. The Man himself—whom I have had the pleasure of frequently meeting—is just what you would expect from his works,—full of fine enthusiasm and intelligence—most interesting in looks and manners—a perfect gentleman—and esteemed by all who know him for the simplicity and frankness of his nature. I wish you had seen him, James; you would have taken to each other very kindly, for you, James, are yourself a Naturalist, although sometimes, it must be confessed, you deal a little in the miraculous, when biographically inclined about sheep, dogs, eagles, and salmon.

SHEPHERD.

The ways o' the creatures o' the inferior creation, as we chuse to ca' birds and beasts, are a' miraculous thegither—nor would they be less so if we understood better than we do their several instincts. Natural History is just anither name for Natural Theology—and the sang o' the laverock, and the plumage o' the goldfinch—do they not alike remind us o' God?

NORTH.

I never knew a Naturalist who was not a good man. Buffon was a strange devil, but not a bad fellow on the whole—with all his vanity, and sensualism. Cuvier is a most amiable character, and we need not go far from Edinburgh to find the best of men, and of Naturalists, united in one whom it is needless to name.

SHEPHERD.

That's a truth.—What thin Folio's yon sprawling on the side-table?

NORTH.

Scenery, costume, and architecture, chiefly on the western side of India, by Captain Robert Melville Grindlay—a beautiful and a splendid work.—Just look at the frontispiece, James.

SHEPHERD.

Eh, man! but she's a bonny Frontispiece, indeed! An Indian Maiden, orientally arrayed in a flowing garment, veil, shawl, plaid, gown, and trowser-lookin' petticoats, all gracefully confused into one indistinguishable drapery, from dark-haired forehead down to ringed ankles and sma' naked feet! These pure, smooth, glossy arms o' hers—hoo saftly and hoo sweetly wud they enfauld a lover stealing into them at gloamin', below the shadow o' these lofty Palm-Trees!

NORTH.

Turn over, James, and admire the shaking Minarets at Ahmedabad. It is the great Mosque erected by Sultan Ahmed early in the 15th century. His remains, with those of his family, are deposited within, in a splendid Mausoleum. The tombs are still covered, Captain Grindlay tells us, with rich tissues of silk and gold, surrounded with lamps continually burning, and guarded by Mahommedans of the religious orders, aided by innumerable devotees of the fair sex. It is, like all the other mosques and religious buildings of stone in the city and environs of Ahmedabad, ornamented with the most elaborate sculpture, and evidently copied from the remains of Hindoo architecture of very remote antiquity.

SHEPHERD.

It is a splendid structure; and can naebody tell why the Minarets shake? But I canna get the image o' that Indian maiden out o' the ee o' my mind—let me look at her again. Oh! the bonny brown Cretur, but she wad mak a pleasant companion in the way o' Wife!

NORTH.

There, James, is an Ancient Temple at Malmud, on the Peninsula of Guzerat, which was the scene of the chief exploits, and finally of the death of Krishna, the Indian Apollo, and still contains architectural remains of the highest antiquity, and of extraordinary richness and beauty.

That Audubon's drawings received immediate, favorable attention in Britain is evidenced by this 1827 appreciation in *Blackwood's Magazine*, a leading British literary periodical. The two pages of dialogue reproduced on these two pages are from *Noctes Ambrosiannae*, no.30, by John Wilson and Christopher North. Reproduced from *Blackwood's Magazine*, p.105 and 112 (Jan. 1827). Courtesy of Northwestern University Library.

Columbia Jays from Plate 96 mounted on Chinese wallpaper in Temple Newsam House, Leeds, England.

The Flicker from Plate 37 and the Florida Jay from Plate 67 mounted on Chinese wallpaper. Both photographs courtesy of Temple Newsam House.

Audubon's handwritten invitation to Frederic Tudor to an exhibition of his original drawings, held at the Boston Athenaeum. The date was late 1832 or early 1833. Courtesy of the Boston Athenaeum.

Third Return to America, 1836-1837

The Audubon party—the Naturalist, his son John, and friend Edward Harris—sailed down the Mississippi from New Orleans to the Gulf of Mexico in the last week of March on the Revenue Service cutter *Campbell*, commanded by Captain Napoleon Coste[33] (with whom Audubon had sailed off the coast of southern Florida in April and May of 1832). Provisioned for a two-month expedition, they cruised westward along the Louisiana coast toward Galveston Bay, their destination, exploring the bayous, lagoons, islands, and keys to observe and collect the birds and other species of the region. On 3 April the expedition was joined by another Revenue Service vessel, the schooner *Crusader*, under command of Captain W. B. G. Taylor, sent to serve as a tender for the larger *Campbell*.

That same day they dropped anchor off Barataria Island and landed. Here they stayed for a few days, collecting several species of birds—sandpipers, gulls, cormorants, curlews, rails, and pelicans, both brown and white—but not a new bird among them. Some snakes and small mammals also were collected before the expedition went on its way.

Proceeding westward, for the next three weeks, Audubon and his party, having transferred to the smaller *Crusader*, scoured the islands, bayous, and marshes along the coast for specimens. Thus, at journey's end, there were three casks filled with specimens to be sent to Europe, but without a new bird among them.[34] By 18 April they were at "Côte Blanche, in Sallé Bay" (Lake Sabine, near Port Arthur), where they spent several days. The Naturalist described in some detail his visit to the plantation of a Major Gordy there located.[35] However, he found the flat and marshy countryside to be "not so abundantly supplied with Birds"[36] as he had hoped.

Audubon provided a graphic account in his journal of what he and his party encountered at the capital of the short-lived republic of Texas, describing its president, Samuel Houston, his quarters, the Mexican prisoners then gathered there, and its drunken Indians "halooing and stumbling about in the mud in every direction."[37]

The Audubon party departed Texas on 18 May and arrived in New Orleans nine days later. The hardships endured by the Naturalist during the expedition had fatigued him greatly and caused him a loss in weight of twelve pounds.[38] In his account of this expedition Audubon stated that although he and his companions had not encountered a single new species, he believed that the migrations he had observed would enable him to write with more authority and competence of a good number of species which visit the United States during the breeding season. In addition, his observations would enable him to define more accurately the geographical distribution of those species which at various times make their appearance in the different sections of North America.[39]

Once back in New Orleans, Audubon and his party did not tarry long. Early in March, soon after his arrival in that city, Audubon had found economic conditions to be depressed and had written to Bachman that "the failures at New Orleans have dampened the spirits of every one who speculates on Cotton, Land, or Dollars." On his return visit, Audubon found that conditions had worsened so much that the "commercial revolution which had taken place during an absence" prompted him to leave at once. Hence Audubon, with his son, set out for Charleston via Mobile, Montgomery, Columbia, and Augusta, arriving at the Bachman home on 5 June.[40] Harris, who had traveled a different route, arrived a few days later. Although the stay in Charleston was brief, it was at this time that John, Audubon's younger son, and Bachman's oldest daughter, Maria Rebecca, were married.[41]

In the year 1837 the United States was beset by a serious economic depression. Audubon had commented on the depressed financial conditions in New Orleans, and as he traveled north from Charleston, the effects of the unsettled economic state of the country became more evident. In a letter to Bachman from Moorestown, where he was visiting Harris, Audubon commented:

> There is scarcely a Dollar of silver in Circulation, and the present thrashy Paper medium is beyond indurance, at every change of State or Towns you are obliged to see what you have and spend or give it away, for in fact it soon becomes useless–Business of all description is at a stand, and it is not every one who cries in sorrow of Van Buren I assure you.[42]

Many causes had led to the panic of 1837, one of the most severe on record in the United States. Among these were:

> First:—The great absorption of Capital in the United States during the ten or fifteen years preceeding 1837 in works of permanent improvement, railroads, canals, inventions of various kinds, and the great extension of agriculture.
>
> Second:—The action of President Jackson in 1832 in vetoing the bill for the renewal of the charter of the Bank of the United States, and in the following year withdrawing eight million dollars of public deposits which compelled the bank to curtail its discounts to such an extent as to make money for the time very tight. This was followed by the formation of a large number of state Banks, resulting in a great expansion of currency, reckless extension of credit, and wild speculation of all kinds.
>
> Third:—A year of apparently great prosperity in 1835, inducing great extravagances, both in personal and business expenditure.
>
> Fourth:—The great fire in New York, destroying a great amount of property.
>
> Fifth:—The order issued by the Treasury Department in 1836 requiring payment for public lands in gold, thus suddenly checking the wild speculation in land at fictitious prices.
>
> Sixth:—The short crops of 1835 and 1836, and the fact that in the spring of 1836 money became dearer, and could be had only at increasing rates until in the early months of 1837 it was difficult to obtain it at any price.[43]

Under conditions as then obtained, it was not surprising that Audubon endeavored to collect from his subscribers as much of the monies owed him as possible before returning to England. Prior to his departure from Charleston he had written Dr. Samuel G. Morton, the corresponding secretary of the Academy of Sciences in Philadelphia, reminding him:

> When last I saw you in Philadelphia you were so good as to promise to me you would attend to the collecting of the account due me on my work by the Academy of Natural Sciences of Philadelphia. I feel at present greatly in need of funds and should like much to receive the balance during my short stay in your city, where I expect to be early in the month, previous to my embarking for England—the balance amounted last winter to 195 Dollars, up to No. 66 and now 50 dollars will have to be added for No's 67, 68, 69, 70, 71, (prints 331–355) which the Academy received lately.[44]

Then the group, consisting of Audubon, his son and daughter-in-law, with friend Harris, proceeded north by schooner to Norfolk and then to Washington, where Audubon presented to President Martin Van Buren the letter of introduction he had received from Washington Irving.[45] The visit to Washington was but a short one, and the Audubons, with brief stopovers at Baltimore, Philadelphia, and at the Harris home in Moorestown, arrived in New York early in July. Here the Naturalist remained a week while John and his bride visited Niagara Falls. All three embarked for Liverpool on 16 July on the packet ship, the *England*, under the command of Captain Robert Waite, the voyage costing three hundred and fifty dollars for the three of them.[46]

On the journey from Washington to New York Audubon had collected $499 from his Baltimore subscribers and in Philadelphia $165, no doubt from the Academy of Natural Sciences in response to the earlier letter written Dr. Morton.[47] Soon after arriving in New York another payment of $105 came from Philadelphia. While in New York there reached the Naturalist a payment of $660 for the three volumes of *Birds of America* which had been delivered to Loammi Baldwin of Boston. Audubon also had brought with him an order for $500 from John Hunt, his subscriber in Mobile, to the New York bankers, Parrish and Company.[48] Additional monies which he had hoped to receive while in New York was a payment of $360 from the Library of Congress and an unspecified amount from the State of Maryland under arrangements made previously. Finally William Gaston of Savannah had promised the Naturalist to pay him two hundred pounds in London before the first of January next.[49]

Just before sailing to Liverpool Audubon wrote Dr. Shattuck in Boston, again commenting on the depressed state of the economy:

> But alas! the present commercial and monetary revolution has caused me to loose a good number of subscriptions through whose support I did hope to realize a few thousand dollars to comfort and supply with the wants of our later days my Beloved wife and my poor self, Trusting however and for ever in that Providence, and in the care of *Him* who supports us all, until called to his Bosum, I hope to see a less clouded Sky than the one hovering over our beloved country at present, and be permitted to end our lives in peaceful enjoyment of health and purity of Mind.[50]

THE DOUBLE ELEPHANT FOLIO

That fortune had been kind to him, especially under the conditions then prevailing, Audubon realized full well. The day before he sailed for England he wrote Bachman:

> In the way of business I have considering the Times, been I think very fortunate.—I carry with me *Nine hundred and Eighty one half Eagles*, and *One hundred and Twenty five soverigns* equal to 1106 pounds sterling [$5530]. This of course *I have insured*. Now barring accidents this sum will suffice us to finish our Work with the usual annual collections we make in England. I leave behind us about 8000 dollars—I procured a new subscriber yesterday. I have settled my accounts with my Brother-in-Law Berthoud in full to the present day [The depression had forced Berthoud to suspend payments]; and we will go on as usual as he is willing to be yet my agent here. All this is very gratifying to me, and will I daresay be equally so by yourselves. I leave a few Volumes of my Work with N. Berthoud, and some biographies, and one volume in the hands of John B. Morris of Baltimore, I have delivered all the rest, and will collect the money when we return, to purchase a Place somewhere in our Country! N. Berthoud calls me one of the Happiest of Men—Free of debts and having *available funds* and *Talent!*[51]

14

COMPLETION OF THE "GREAT WORK"
1837-1839

In seventeen days the *England* brought her passengers to Liverpool. After a short visit with friends in that city, the Audubon party joined the other members of the family, Lucy Audubon and Victor, in London on 7 August. There the Naturalist found that the publication of the *Birds of America* was proceeding in a satisfactory manner. On 14 August he wrote Bachman that "Nos 72, 73, 74, 75, & 76 gets off to New York next Week and I hope will soon be with you."[1] When Audubon wrote this letter he felt that the work would be completed by "the last day of the present year" and that 400 plates would be the total needed.

Audubon had not been long in London before he was faced with serious problems relating to the engravings for the *Birds of America*. He wrote of his dilemma in the introduction to the fourth volume of the *Ornithological Biography* as follows:

> I found the publication of the "Birds of America" in a satisfactory state of progression, but received the disagreeable intelligence that a great number of my British patrons had discontinued their subscriptions, and that most of those who still received the numbers as they came out, were desirous of seeing the work finished in Eighty Numbers, as I had first anticipated [and as he had stated in his prospectus]. On this account, I found myself obliged to introduce, and in some instances to crowd, a number of species into one and the same plate, in order to try to meet the wishes of those who had by their subscriptions in some measure assisted me in the publication of that work. This, however I did in such a manner as seemed best to accord with the affinities of the species. But, Reader, Dr. Townsend meantime returned to Philadelphia, after an absence of four years and with a second collection, containing several rare and new birds, which after meeting with some difficulties as on the former occasion, in consequence of the opposition of various enlightened persons at Philadelphia, although Dr. Townsend was extremely desirous that every thing new or rare belonging to our Fauna, should be given to me, I received only a few weeks before closing the engraving of my plates. A few others did not reach me until several days after, What was I to do? Why, Reader, to publish them

to be sure; for this I should have done, to the best of my power, even if every subscriber in Europe had refused to take them. What! said I, shall the last volume of the "Birds of America" be now closed, at a time when new species are in my hands? No! And in spite of threats from this quarter and that, that such and such persons would discontinue their subscriptions (which indeed they have done, and refused to take the few numbers that would have rendered their copies complete), my wish to do all that was in my power has been accomplished: All Dr. Townsend's species, as well as some received through different channels, have been published.[2]

The first plate on which "affinities of species" is introduced is number 353.

The Naturalist faced further problems during the last two years of his stay in England. He had yet to write two additional volumes of the *Ornithological Biography* as well as his *Synopsis of the Birds of North America*. Furthermore he had determined to include anatomical descriptions of at least one bird of each Genus.[3] To carry this out, the fourth and fifth volumes of the *Ornithological Biography* contain anatomical descriptions of many species as well as wood engravings of elements of bird anatomy. These anatomical descriptions with which MacGillivray was helping made it necessary for Audubon continually to press his many friends in the United States to send him the desired specimens.[4]

Once again Audubon worked like "a Trojan." By early October Number 78 (plates 386–90) was out. At that time the Naturalist wrote Bachman: "My last volume will be made up of 83 [23 was probably intended here, since each "number" or fascicle always included five separate plates] numbers of 115 plates without Eggs and will contain 159 species, as good as ever flew or swam . . . and the whole will be finished in March Next."[5] Shortly after writing this letter he learned from Edward Harris that Townsend had returned to Philadelphia with additional specimens from which Harris was selecting some for Audubon.[6]

With the receipt of this news Audubon immediately wrote Harris to impress him with the urgency of his receiving

> . . . the Bird skins very soon, for depend on it, now or never is for me the period to push my publication. . . . My work *must* soon be finished, and unless *all is received* here by the month of May next why I shall have to abandon to others what I might myself have accomplished. . . . I have taken upon myself the risk of publishing *his* (Townsend's) names to the Birds on my plate, but which of course I am obliged to correct in my letter press. *The little beautiful owl* [plate 432], I would venture to say has been described by Vigors at least ten years ago, &c., &c.[7]

When the skins were not forthcoming Audubon wrote Harris again on 19 January:

> My present situation is probably the most precarious of my whole life. I have about 40 men employed on my publication and in six weeks from this date the whole of them must be idle and yet under wages until I receive these birds and have prepared them for the engraver. My subscribers are all grumbling and

Completion of the "Great Work," 1837–1839

some say it is my intention to go on with the Birds of America for twelve years longer.[8]

Again on 6 February he wrote Harris:

> You cannot well conceive the amount of my disappointment.—I was in full expectation that immediately after having selected the Birds from Townsend's Collection for me, that you would *at once* have taken possession of them, and started the Box to New York; after which they might have been shipped and might have been in my hands about six weeks ago. This being deffered, and the curious difficulties which you describe having occurred, I greatly fear these Birds will never be suffered to be shipped to me? Indeed, I am much surprised that Townsend should not have at once told you of his painful situation, and again that he should not have shipped *the whole* of his collection for this country, and if not to me, at least to some one with whom I might have joined in the trying to dispose of the whole collection for cash and at the best prices in my power?—The M/S might have followed, I would have had many of the Drawings now finished and indeed on Copper &c—
>
> I Know you so well and depend so much upon your good Judgment and prudence that I have still some hopes that I may receive these specimens; but when you will understand that for the immediate want of them, my Publication is almost at a stand, for as I am forced to finish my Work in as few numbers of Plates as possible (not to Lose any more subscribers in this country) I am forced to introduce as many new species of the same Genera in the same plate, as circumstances will afford.—And Now I am at a standstill for the Birds which you have mentioned in your interesting lists.[9]

[At the College of Physicians of Philadelphia is a very long letter, dated 31 May 1838, written by Audubon from London to Townsend requesting detailed information regarding many (30) species.]

In the latter part of the previous September Charles Lucien Bonaparte had arrived in London, there to spend much of his time with Audubon. He promised the Naturalist some new species he had on hand

> and which he contemplated publishing, and I am to figure them and present them to the World very soon. The Number of these species does not exceed six or seven, but all tend to render my Work the more Compleat.[10]

It is doubtful if these species were ever figured by Audubon, for in April 1838, the Naturalist wrote to Bachman:

> Charles Bonaparte has treated me shockingly—he has published the whole of *our* Secrets, which I foolishly communicated to him after his giving me his word of honour that he would not do so, and now I have *cut him,* and he never will have from me The remaining unpublished Numbers of my Work.—(which by the bye he calls a poor thing) and the latter simply because I at last refused to give him my Knowledge of the Migratory or Geographical distribution of our Birds—So much for *a Prince!*[11]

Some indication of the pace at which Audubon was working to complete the *Birds of America* is given in the same letter:

> Will you believe that since Bona[parte] has left London I have drawn One Hundred Birds; Indeed I feel quite fagged, and now think that I never laboured harder than I have done within the last Two Months.[12]

These labors included the writing of Volume IV of the *Ornithological Biography*. Although the completion of the drawings for the *Birds of America* was his first consideration, the work on the *Biography* had begun with his arrival in London, and by the end of October of the previous year, he had completed thirteen articles and "would have done more in that way had I not been a good deal taken up by Bonaparte."[13]

With the complications that ensued from the delayed arrival of the specimens from the Townsend collection, the completion of the engraving of the plates for the *Birds of America* was not accomplished by "the last of the present year" as Audubon had expected when he had written Bachman the previous September, soon after the Naturalist's return to England. In fact, twelve species arrived too late to be included in the "Large Work," for a delay of practically six months had occurred.[14] On 25 June Audubon wrote his friend Dr. Samuel Morton, the corresponding secretary of the Academy of Natural Sciences of Philadelphia:

> The Birds of America were finished on the 16 inst. [June] consisting of 435 plates including 497 species! An immense weight from my shoulders and a great relief to my ever fidgety anxious mind respecting the Immense undertaking.[15]

The letter to Morton had been written at Edinburgh, where Audubon had gone to be with his collaborator MacGillivray to complete the two remaining volumes of the *Ornithological Biography* and prepare his *Synopsis*.

On 1 July the Naturalist wrote his family from Edinburgh:

> We begin printing *tomorrow 2 of July 1838!!* [referring to the fourth volume of the *Ornithological Biography*]. remember that Mesdames and Messieurs! and I intend to proceed with all possible despatch and care. *All* the birds in rum will be inspected as far as internals or digestive organs, trachea &c are concerned, and I am constantly present in the dissecting room, I think I shall know something about the matter anon. . . . I have seen no one hardly since my last, I am indeed as busily engaged as ever, and rarely go to bed before eleven—being with Mr. MacGillivray until generally past ten describing etc. I rise at four or earlier, he at ten; but I go to bed at eleven, he at two—[16]

By the end of September Audubon was able to write Bachman who was visiting Europe and was in Paris:

> The *Book* has now increased to 512 pages, Seven Sheets more will finish the *first part* of the 4th Vol. for I now find that one Vol. of 1200 pages would not do. I expect this first part to be before the World on the 1st of Decr it will contain Just one hundred species, and the second part 110 or 115 besides the appendix,

the Geographical lists, and the *Synopsis!* of the latter I intend to throw off 500 copies.[17]

On 20 October the Naturalist again wrote to Bachman who was still in Europe: "My fourth Vol. is finished and in 10 days I will have 200 copies of it at London where I hope you will be and receive several Copies to take over with you, for yourselves and others as then directed."[18] He even advised Bachman that: "I hope that about the first of March next my fifth and last Vol. of Biographs *including* SYNOPSIS Geographical list &c&c will be finished when I hope we will soon sail for our own Dear Woodlands of Old, and there Stay!" The last pages of Volume IV were actually received by Audubon on 26 October.[19] The introduction to the volume is dated "Edinburgh 1st November 1838."

Two weeks later, in another letter to Bachman, Audubon stated that: "My 5*th* Vol. is begun and I hope will be finished printing by the 1*st* of April, and that on the first of May next, we will all go back to America, there to stay to the last days of our Lifes!"[20]

While the Naturalist was busily engaged with his writing, his son Victor attended to the business affairs connected with the engraving and publication of the *Birds of America*. The evidence available indicates that Victor made little or no attempt to obtain new subscriptions, but that his efforts were concerned mainly with the collection of money due on subscriptions.

Following Audubon's return to England in August 1837, there is in his correspondence only one reference to a new subscription. In the letter of 30 January 1839 to Havell the Naturalist wrote: "Let me know when the copy half bound for the *State of Michigan* [is ready?] and do not forget that that set is to have Locks &c as per memorandum left with you."[21] This subscription is the last to appear on the original subscription list and is entered as "State of Michigan, by Govr Mason." Immediately preceding this entry is that of "Tho*s*. Metcalf, Esq., Augusta, Georgia." It is possible that Audubon obtained the latter subscription during his visit to Augusta in February 1837 while en route to the Gulf of Mexico. When his son Victor sailed for America in January 1839, Audubon once again had to assume oversight of his business affairs with the engraver.[22]

Even as the publication of the *Birds of America* drew to a close, Audubon found reasons to remonstrate with his engraver. On 13 March he wrote Havell:

> When next we meet I will tell you how grossly, have been the mistakes that have occurred in the Packing of Prints of my Work and in the forwarding numbers where they were not wanted, such as will make you stare; and all this through the carelessness of the Individuals where you have had an attendant in your shop, and towards the salary of whom I foolishly [have] contributed, though in an indirect manner.—only think that I have of late received *here* no less than twelve N*os* in return, some of them containing, not the plates in regular order, but 3 and 5 copies of the same plate instead of *a number*. How much I have lost in this manner, it is impossible to tell, but the id[d]le rascals who did the like of this deserve the severest punishment. In some parcels I find

Land and Water Birds mixed in Numbers published when no Land and Water Birds had yet been issued. The Canada Goose of the Third Volume, was found rolled up with the *Carrion Crow* of the *Second Volume* &c &c &c—Alas! Alas! depend on it, that a clever young man as a clerk is worth a hundred of thick heads. How can you tell for Instance that *Mr* Baker has not paid his balance to you because he has not received the numbers intended for *him* but some parcels as [curiously] erroniously and foolishly arranged as those which I have lately received and now have in my possession? Do you not remember the piece of Beef found by Lord Kinnoul among some of the plates that were sent to him, and on account of which we no doubt lost his subscription—I write all this not to vex you, but to put you on your guard, to have your eyes broad open, and to Watch what is going on round you even at this late period, I speak from the heart, as your friend.[23]

At this time, Havell was making preparations to leave for America. The decision to leave England had been made some time ago, for on 8 October 1837 Audubon had written Bachman: "Havell seems to have made up his mind to go to America to live and I think that he will go pretty soon after our work is finished, if he does not undertake the Engraving of Bonapt' continuation of Wilson."[24] In March Havell wrote to Audubon that he was disposing of his premises and selling off his stock and was "as busy as a Bee in a tar barrel."[25]

From his correspondence with his engraver it is known that Audubon was finding it difficult to defray the heavy expenses incurred in the completion of the engravings of the *Birds of America*. In a letter to Havell dated 21 March he wrote:

As you say that Mr. Baker has called upon you, and has paid you in full Eighty six pounds two shillings, and I find that we are not credited for that sum, I have debited your account with the same, with the wish that when my son Victor's first note to you becomes due at Wright & Co this sum will go as part payment of the one hundred and fifty pounds due to you the 21-24 April, and I will be glad to hear from you on the subject.[26]

Again, shortly before Havell sailed for America Audubon wrote him: "Will you have the goodness to tell me if it Would suit you as well to be paid in America for the setts extra or not. To me it would prove quite an accomodation!"[27]

Of all the matters to which Audubon desired his engraver to attend in London, nothing seemed to be of greater importance than the care of the copper plates. His first request made in March was that these be removed "from your present Dwelling to the London Docks, so that no squable may take place hereafter, between these two assurance companies and myself, in the case of a loss by fire."[28] Next was the matter of the proper insurance for the plates. The amount was first to have been three thousand pounds, but Audubon instructed his engraver to increase this to five thousand.[29]

Audubon continued to make complaints to Havell regarding errors in the shipment of prints. On 4 May he wrote that his New Bedford subscriber, James Arnold, had neither received Numbers 50, 51, and 52 nor Numbers 82 to 87, both inclusive. Also, from this letter we learn that the fifth volume of the *Biography* was completed and that the Naturalist hoped to have the *Synopsis* finished in another month.[30]

There are in the Houghton Library at Harvard University a number of letters written by Victor Audubon to Havell during the period from August to December 1838, while the son was actively supervising the engraving of the prints and the father was absorbed with the writing of the *Biography*. In these letters is the clue to the origin of certain extra prints which have been found in some of the extant sets of the folio.

Originally Audubon had hoped to show on each plate the male and the female of every species as well as the young. However it was not always possible for him to carry this out, as occasionally he had not been able to locate both sexes and the young at the same time. Therefore on some of the drawings only the male or the female were figured. Eventually both the female and male as well as the young of a species were obtained and drawn. Audubon had written to his engraver at some time prior to August 1838 and instructed him to make "6 copies of the plate that have the old birds on one plate and the young or the female on some other."[31] Extant sets which contain some of these extra plates are the following:

> Library of Parliament in Ottawa, Canada
> The New York Society Library
> H. J. Lutcher Stark Foundation in Orange, Texas
> Field Museum of Natural History in Chicago.

Only the Field and the Stark folios contain all the extra plates.

From Victor's correspondence with the engraver it is also known that some subscribers were discontinuing the work. As late as December 1838 Victor wrote that Thomas Sowler, the agent at Manchester, was returning the following prints:

> viz. 2 Setts Nos. 61 to 87 complete say 54 Nos.
>   1 Sett   " 58 to 72   "   " 30 Nos.
>   1 Sett   " 81 to 87   "   " 7 Nos.
>   Total 91 Nos.[32]

It was Victor's hope that the engraver might use these to complete some incomplete fourth volume.[33]

By 30 June the *Synopsis* was completed and the Naturalist was making ready to depart England.[34] His younger son, John Woodhouse, who was accompanied by his wife and child, had sailed on 10 June.[35] Havell and his wife also had expected to leave at the same time as the younger Audubons, but their sailing was postponed and they did not arrive in New York until September.[36]

Audubon and his wife left Edinburgh on 11 July, going to Carlisle, Manchester, and Liverpool, with a visit to John Heppenstall at Sheffield. They planned to sail for America on 1 August.[37] Their departure evidently took place near that date, for the passenger list of the ship *George Washington*, of Liverpool, which arrived in New York on 2 September 1839, includes the names of John J. and Lucy Audubon.[38]

There is among the Auduboniana in the museum at the Audubon State Park, Henderson, Kentucky, a memorandum written in ink by Audubon wherein he set down the cost of publishing the *Birds of America*, as follows:

<pre>
Actual cost of the Birds of America.
1827—Publication to 1832   £ 8,533-16- 6
1837—To January of that year   9,233-10-10½
1838—up to Dec of that year   6,431- 3- 9
1839— "   " May " . "   "   3,601- 9- 6
1839—Residue to end of year   1,110-15- 2
                                   £28,910-13- 7

[The following is in pencil]
                                    28,910
                                         4
Cost in dollars.   115,640
</pre>

Not calculating any of my expense, or that of my family for upwards 14 years.

The whole of the memorandum appears to be in Audubon's handwriting. The outside fold of the paper bears the following penciled notation: "Found in Mother's papers. T. 3/1/27." T. is probably a member of the Tyler family; the mother, Delia Tallman Tyler (Mrs. Morris Frank Tyler) was the daughter of Victor Gifford Audubon and Georgiana Richards Mallory, Victor's second wife.

15

SALE OF
THE REMAINING FOLIOS

After his arrival in New York in September 1839, Audubon at once turned his attention to whatever unfinished business still remained with the "Large Work." In the prospectus it had been stated that "The Price of Each Number will be Two Guineas [$10] payable on delivery." It had not been possible, except in rare instances, to obtain payment for the numbers immediately upon delivery. Whenever he could, the Naturalist would call on the subscriber and endeavor to collect the payment for the numbers which had been delivered but not paid for. Occasionally he had been fortunate to be paid in advance for a single volume of one hundred plates and even for the entire four-volume set, as had been the case with certain Savannah and Boston subscribers. Thus when he returned from England there were payments due him from twenty-nine American subscribers amounting to $10,610.06.[1]

Not only was there the collection of the payments due Audubon, but there was also the disposal of those sets of the folio which had been in the possession of Havell when the engraving was completed. On page 165 of Audubon's Ledger "B," which is presently at the Audubon Museum in Henderson, Kentucky, there is the following penciled notation, under the heading "Robert Havell":

> When you settle with Havell for the fifteen sets the
> process will be as follows. Each
>
> | | | |
> |---|---|---|
> | 1,2,3rd Volume | | 12-2-0 |
> | Each 4th " | | 16-7-2 |
> | Binding each 1,2,3rd Vol. | | 4-4-0 |
> | Binding each 4th | " | 4-11-0 |
> | [Approximate U.S. Payment—Vols. 1,2,3 | | $60. |
> | | 4th | 80. |
> | Binding—1,2,3 Vols. $20. 4th Vol. $21.] | | |

115

Two references to these fifteen sets of the *Birds of America* while they were still in the possession of the engraver have been found. On 8 December 1838 Victor Audubon wrote Havell to ask "When will the 15 setts be ready."[2] Then on 23 February of the following year Audubon wrote to Havell, "I now perfectly understand about the loose setts, and think as well as you do that it will be best to pack the whole as you advise in your letter."[3]

In addition to the loose prints (sheets) brought to America as late as August 1912, a considerable number were found in a bookshop in New Oxford Street, London; twelve were uncolored and several had the appearance of rejects. Moreover, in a collection of these plates received in the United States from England in 1910, there were nine copies of the Painted Bunting (Number 11, plate 53).[4] Furthermore, a large collection of uncolored prints was presented to the American Museum of Natural History of New York by the Misses Florence and Maria R. Audubon.[5]

Audubon had not been long in New York before he disposed of the first of these remaining sets. During the month of November, after two calls he succeeded in selling John Jacob Astor (1763–1848) "the full bound copy and also 5 volumes of Letter Press for $1050. payable early in January."[6] Shortly after the Astor transaction, a folio was sold to Colonel James Watson Webb (1802–1884), a prominent New York newspaper publisher. This transaction is recorded in one of Audubon's journals, also used in part as a ledger and daybook, as follows:

December 13, 1839
79— J. W. Webb   Vol. 1-4.   Full bound.   1070.

These volumes were in all probability delivered to Webb, but no trace of the set has been found.

In September 1836, while in New York, Audubon had written his wife, "I have *almost* obtained 2 subscriptions yesterday. One Coll Webb! The other Mr. Swartout of the Custom House."[7] In the fifth volume of the *Ornithological Biography*, published in Edinburgh in May 1839, and which contained the list of final subscribers, both the Webb and Swartout names are included.[8]

Samuel Swartout (1783–1865) was Collector of the Port of New York, having been appointed by President Jackson, at the time Audubon had hoped to obtain his subscription. In 1838 Swartout resigned his post and sailed for England. After his departure it was discovered that during his term in office he had appropriated more than a million dollars in public funds.[9] No bookkeeping entries covering the Swartout subscriptions have been found and under the circumstances it is doubtful that any prints of the *Birds of America* were delivered to him.

Another journal entry, made by Audubon, which probably referred to the sale of one of the folios brought over from England is the following: "Dec. 13, 1839—J. R. Peters-Balance for Large Work $430."[10] This in all likelihood was Samuel J. Peters of New Orleans, at the time president of the City Bank. In November 1839, soon after the return of the Naturalist to America, James Grimshaw of New Orleans had visited the Berthouds in New York. Lucy Audubon's sister, Eliza, was the wife of Nicholas Berthoud, Audubon's agent in New York, and their daughter had married Grimshaw. Grimshaw had aided the Naturalist in his search for subscribers in New Orleans and may have brought a subscription from Peters with him at that time.[11]

Only one additional reference to a Peters folio has been found, this in an old notebook belonging to Franklin Peters, the son of Samuel James Peters, and now included in the "La Monnier" papers at Tulane University in New Orleans. This notebook contains a catalog of books, paintings, and the like, bequeathed to B. F. Peters by his father Samuel Jarvis Peters in 1855. Among the books listed are "Audubon's Birds 4 vol."[12] No further trace of this folio has been found.

Early in February 1840 another set was sold. An entry in the Audubon journal-daybook shows a payment of $1,100. by J. Lennox (Lenox), "for a full bound copy of the Large Work and the 5 vols. of Biography with Synopsis."[13]

In his attempt to sell the remaining sets of the "Large Work," Audubon sent copies to various cities. A record of such consignment was kept in one of the Audubon journals; among these were the following:

> 1839—One complete set of the large work is at the Library in Baltimore, belonging to us in care of the Librarian, Mr. Owen.[14]
>
> 4 Jan. 1840—Sent box to N. Berthoud, Louisville with 4 sets unbound of large work complete. (written over in ink—Returned to our house Aug. 6, 1840. VGA).[15]
>
> 8 Jan. 1840—One complete set of the large work full bound sent to Parkman. (Boston)[16]
>
> 13 February 1840—Shipped Schr. Manchester to Richmond, Va. to Jos. Fisher & Son 1 Box containing 1 set of the Work half bound—4 sets Vols. 1–5 Biography—7 Synopsis (Feb. 15 insured same and paid $10.25 to the Jackson Fire office).
>
> This copy of the large Work and 1 set of the Biography & 6 Nos of the Little Work forwarded by J. J. Audubon to the University of Virginia from Richmond April 17, 1840—Sent to W. Wirtimbaker [William Wertenbaker] (Returned September 1840).[17]

Audubon had several times attempted to effect a sale of the *Birds of America* in Virginia. He even made an appeal to the governor of that state whom he had met through his agent, William Richardson, the State Librarian, only to be told that the "State of Virginia has no dispensible fund at present for the purchase of our Great Work."[18] His efforts with the University of Virginia, even after sending a folio to the university, proved unsuccessful.

It was not until July 1840 that there is a record of another folio being sold. In the museum at Audubon State Park at Henderson, Kentucky, are fourteen loose pages torn from one of the Naturalist's journals, also used as an account book. On page 88 there is the following detailed memorandum covering the shipment of a folio to Russia:

> July 7, 1840—sent per Harndry car for Boston
> 1 Copy of the Large Work
> 1 Set of the Biography
> 1 Synopsis
> 12 Nos little work
>
> in a box marked "Sa Majesté Imperiale au department des relations Interieure du Ministere des Affaires Etrangeres St. Petersburg
> pr. Barque Razan—care of C. E. Hatitch [Hartrich], Esq. Swedish Consul 70 State Street—Boston."

There are at the present time three sets of the Audubon folio of the *Birds of America* in Russia, one of which is at the State Library in Leningrad. Each one of the four volumes in Leningrad bears a stamp, written in Russian, as follows:

> No.   11.
> The Emperor's Hermitage
> Foreign Library
>
> Case Number 5 Shelf 1.

In addition, on the spine of each volume is a small blue dot on which there is a call number indicating that the set belonged to the Czar's library. The folio was transferred to the State Library sometime after the Bolshevik revolution. It has not been possible to determine through what means Audubon was able to sell this folio to "Sa Majesté Imperiale au department des relations Interieure du Ministere des Affairs Etrangeres."

A month later, in August, Audubon succeeded in selling two sets of the folio in loose prints. He had gone to New England for the purpose of obtaining subscriptions to the Octavo edition[19] of the *Birds of America*. As he wrote his family from Providence on 9 August:

> I had the fortune to sell 2 copies of the Large Work in sheets to a Mr. [Joseph] Seabury, each copy 874$. He paid me all except a balance of 397$ which I will receive next week. He purchased these copies for the purpose of selling the plates singly on spec and I hope he will do well with them.[20]

A New Bedford (Massachusetts) bookdealer, F. L. Alden, seems to have participated in this transaction, for in Audubon's journal entry of 14 August the Naturalist wrote: "Alden Purchases from Seabury one third of the 2d copy of the large work, on which I gave him 90 days credit, but for which he having given me his note for $291.67 it was discounted."[21]

Not much information about Joseph Seabury has been found. He was born in New Bedford in 1811. At the time Audubon met him, he was engaged in the banking business. The New Bedford directory of 1839 and again in 1846 lists him as "a book-keeper in the Bedford Commercial Bank." His death occurred on 30 September 1846.²²

In addition to the two copies of the "Large Work" in sheets sold to Joseph Seabury of New Bedford, Audubon sold other residents of that city the following oil paintings of the *Birds of America* which undoubtedly were the Kidd reproductions:²³

Bird of Washington Pl. XI to George Howland, Jr.	$100.
Turtle Doves [Mourning Doves] Pl. 17 to George Howland, Jr.	75.
Red-Shouldered Hawk Pl. 56 to George Howland, Jr.	50.
White Headed Eagle Pl. 31. to Charles Morgan	100.
Tetrao umbellus (Ruffed Grous) Pl. 41 Charles Morgan	75.
Peregrin Falcon (Great-footed Hawk) Pl. 16 Samuel Rodman	75.
Purple Grakles Pl. 7 Samuel Rodman	40.²⁴

Audubon's New England tour included a trip to Portsmouth, New Hampshire, where he exhibited the folio of the "Large Work" at the Athenaeum and presented several letters of introduction obtained in Boston. No purchaser was found in Portsmouth, as his journal entry of 15 September wryly noted, where the folio was "perhaps greatly admired but $1000 is *here* quite a sum!"²⁵ Upon the Naturalist's return to Boston, he obtained the subscription of a Colonel Thayer of the U.S. Engineers to the Octavo edition. Thayer "promised to write to West Point about the Large Work,"²⁶ but no set of the folio was ever sold to that institution.

On 12 December, while returning to New York, Audubon stopped off at Worcester, where he had hoped to dispose of a set of the folio to either "the famous Black Smith *Burrit*" or "Isaac Davis a Lawyer who has made a rapid fortune." But in neither instance was the Naturalist successful and he arrived back in New York shortly before Christmas.²⁷

That Audubon had hoped to sell a copy of the folio to the Mercantile Library Association of New York is known from a letter to his family, written in Baltimore on 21 February 1840, wherein he instructed his son Victor, "Call from time to time at the Mercantile Library."²⁸ The funds to be appropriated for the purchase of the folio were to have been raised by "a subscription in which the amount to be given by each subscriber was limited to Fifty-Cents" and it now can be ascertained that these subscriptions did begin in 1840. Two months later, writing from Charleston, again to Victor, Audubon asked him, "How comes the subscription at the Mercantile Library? It seems that these Gents ought to take a copy now."²⁹ Finally, in January of the following year, he wrote once more to Victor, "There is a running rumour in town (New York) that the Mercantile Library will at last buy a copy of the Large Work, *Nous Verrons?*"³⁰ Buy they did, for in 1939 a set of the folio belonging to the Mercantile Library Association of New York was purchased by a print dealer and broken up. In each volume of this folio had been pasted a broadside, printed on silk, which not only indicates that "the work was placed in the Library on the fourth day of March 1841," but also makes it clear that the plan for raising the funds by contributions of fifty-cent donations had to be supplemented with other methods for collecting the money.[31]

Eighteen months elapsed before another set of the folio was sold. Early in July 1842 Audubon again left New York, this time on a journey which took him to Philadelphia, Baltimore, Washington, and Richmond. On 25 July, while in Washington, he called on the British Ambassador, Lord Ashburton (Alexander Baring [1774–1848]), whom he had met through Daniel Webster who, shortly before, had been appointed Secretary of State by President Tyler. At the time Webster and Lord Ashburton were members of a special commission charged with settling the boundary dispute between Maine and the British provinces. Not only did Lord Ashburton purchase a copy of the folio but Audubon was paid $1,000 in gold, which, perhaps, was not too surprising since the ambassador was a member of the distinguished English banking firm, Baring Bros.[32]

In September of the same year Audubon went to Canada, reaching Montreal on the 15th. He had taken with him two boxes containing numbers of the Octavo edition, plates of the *Quadrupeds*[33] and one copy of the folio. When arranging to ship the boxes to Quebec, the Naturalist was required to pay a duty of £32 8s. 10d. on their contents, a matter of some consternation to him for he wrote of it thus to his family: "Think of this very dearest friends. Well it could not be helped and of course I had them put on board the Steamer Queen promising to pay at Quebec on my arrival there."[34]

Audubon reached Quebec the following day and immediately endeavored to see Lord Caledon, the 3d Earl of Caledon, who at the time was a Captain of the Coldstream Guards stationed in Canada, only to learn that Caledon had gone fishing and was not expected to return for some days.[35] By the 21st the earl had returned and the plates were shown him, but to no avail.[36]

At a dinner party which was given by G. H. Ryland in Audubon's honor a few days after his arrival in Quebec and at which the Naturalist had displayed the folio, the host proposed " . . . that a Raffle of the Large Work should be attempted at a share of £5 each, he taking two." Nothing seems to have come of this.[37] Finally, on 26 September (the folio having been examined several times previously by the Earl of Caledon after his return to Quebec and a subscription as well to the *Quadrupeds* obtained),

> . . . After much anxiety at 3 o'clock Lord Caledon, Lord Stopford, and another officer at last came and I showed them the 2nd volume. They were highly pleased. I was asked to pack it up by Lord Caledon and to send it to his rooms. He came afterwards to my bedroom and there wrote an order to the Pay-Master J. Payne Esq. for £250.—I now felt as if a weight had been taken off my breast.[38]

The following morning Audubon sent his son Victor a draft for $1,000.[39] An entry for this amount is to be found in the books of account under the date of 15 October 1842.

Audubon left Quebec immediately after selling the folio to Caledon, going

Sale of the Remaining Folios

first to Montreal and then to Kingston, at the time the capital of Canada, where he arrived on 2 October. Both Houses of Parliament were in session. The following morning the Naturalist repaired to the

> ... house of Assembly, and ere 10 o'clock had delivered several of my letters and had been introduced to Mons. Vivia, the uncle of Young Des Soules, also to Monsieur Papineau, brother to the renowned man of that name, to Mons. Lafontaine, whose head resembles that of Napoleon! I shook hands with almost every member of both houses, and was received with a marked attention which I must acknowledge was gratifying to my poor heart & feelings.—Every one was in favor of purchasing one, 2 or even three Copies of the Large Work. The plates of the Quadrupeds were shown to every body, and in fact I was taken quite by surprise at all that I saw, heard, and that was done for me.—I attended to the meetings of both houses and heard several arguments; and I say it with pleasure, that I was delighted to see the good order, the calmness and indeed the polite attentiveness exhibited from every member towards their Colleagues of the opposition party. I found the Librarians truly well informed men, and derived great benefit from their conversations & advice.— Being anxious to pay my respects to the Governour General, Sir Charles Bagot, I was induced to enclose the letter of our President Tyler and that of Lord Ashburton to Cap*n* Jones one of his Secretaries with a request that they should be laid before his Excellency &c—and whilst I was at dinner a Lancer came [and] delivered a Packet, and waited for my answer which I wrote in great hurry accepting however the invitation to dine with Sir Charles tomorrow evening at 7.[40]

The following morning Audubon returned to the House of Assembly:

> My plates were looked over & over by Ladies and Gents. I was admitted within the Bar of the Council of the Upper House which [was] in Session. Mr. Armour who had been very attentive to me, had a preamble presented to this Council along with my Credential-letters and it was immediately taken in consideration, where it was unanimously agreed & carried that a copy of the Large Work should be purchased and also a Subscription to the Quadrupeds. I was glad to find that both Houses have good incomes from the Government which enables them to procure such costly works as our own.—Mr. Armour told me that to-morrow, the same would be done in the Lower House, and that he hoped that Warrents would be opened and given me to receive the amounts and go homeward! May it all prove so.[41]

It did indeed "prove so." Two copies of the "Large Work" were purchased by the House of Assembly and Audubon received $2,000, a sum properly entered in the book of accounts under the date of 27 October 1842.[42]

Both sets were later taken to the Old Parliamentary Library when the capital was moved to Montreal. The two sets were destroyed on 25 April 1849 when the building was set afire by a mob led by opponents of the Rebellion Losses Bill which had been approved by the Earl of Elgin, the Governor General, earlier in the day.[43] Audubon had hoped that he might dispose of another copy of the "Great Work" in Canada. However, on his return to Montreal en route home he learned that "The St. Sulspice College declined purchasing the Large Work to my great mortification & surprise, and only bought a set of the Little Work, and subscribed to the Quadrupeds."[44]

Audubon on many occasions had expressed a desire to travel in the western regions of the United States, a wish he had not been able to gratify during his visits to America while his drawings were being engraved. However, early in 1843 preparations were undertaken for such a journey on which the Naturalist was to be accompanied, among others, by his friend Edward Harris.

In March 1843, the day Audubon was to leave, he was visited by Andrew Coates (1814–1900). Coates had come to America in 1839 from Paisley, Scotland, to act as agent for the thread business which his brothers, James, Peter, and Thomas Coats were building up in Paisley. While in America Andrew had changed the spelling of his name to Coates.

An account of this visit was given by Andrew Coates in a paper which was read to the Perthshire Society of Natural Sciences on 5 March 1894. In his recollection of the visit Coates stated that it took place the day before "Mr. Audubon was to take his departure for the Rocky Mountains." After describing the home and the family at "Minnies Land" he stated that in discussing the publication of the *Birds of America* he

> ... was told that there now only remained three copies unsold. One copy they kept for themselves, but that, they told me, was an expensive luxury which they meant to part with. I afterwards purchased the whole three copies, one for myself and the others for my two brothers in Paisley. One of these was afterwards presented to the Paisley Free Library, where it now is.[45]

That folio remains at the library; one set, presented to a brother, was sold later to an American bookdealer; and of the third, no trace has been found.

Before the death of the Naturalist in January 1851, two additional sets of the folio were sold. In the summer of 1844, while traveling in central New York State soliciting subscriptions to the Octavo edition and the *Quadrupeds*, Audubon visited Union College at Schenectady, New York, and sold a set of the folio to the Reverend Eliphalet Nott.[46] And in February 1850, Oscar Sturtevant, President of the Board of Aldermen of the City of New York introduced "To the Honourable—The Board of Assistant Aldermen of the City of New York—a communication and Resolution to purchase Audubon's Birds of America for the City Library." This resolution was passed on 25 February 1850, and $1,000 appropriated to purchase the copy of the *Birds of America*.[47] The Naturalist at this time was already in failing health, and the negotiations leading to this purchase were made by his son Victor. This folio is now at The City College of The City University of New York.

From September 1839, when Audubon had returned from England, until his death on 27 January 1851, bound sets of the folio had been sold to the following:

Sale of the Remaining Folios

in 1839 to	John Jacob Astor
	Col. J. W. Webb
	Samuel J. Peters
1840	J. Lenox
	Czar Nicholas of Russia
1841	Mercantile Library Association of New York
1842	Lord Ashburton
	Lord Caledon
	Parliament of Canada (2 sets)
1843	Andrew Coates (3 sets)
1844	Union College
1850	Board of Aldermen, City of New York

a total of fifteen sets. In addition, Joseph Seabury and F. L. Alden of New Bedford, Massachusetts, purchased two sets in sheets.

Upon the completion of the *Birds of America*, based on the notation found in Ledger "B," there remained in the hands of the engraver fifteen bound sets of the folio which later were taken to America. In addition there was a collection of loose sheets of an undetermined number.

The foregoing recapitulation shows that when Andrew Coates visited the Audubon home there actually remained five sets of the folio, three of which he purchased. The two remaining sets were sold prior to the death of the Naturalist.

Furthermore, there is a record of the sale after Audubon's death of two additional bound sets of the folio. On 29 December 1852, Victor Audubon wrote to John Bachman: "I have sold a Copy of the Large 'Birds' to the Government & also copy of the Large 'Quadrupeds' to go to Japan with the expedition [Perry], what do you think his Majesty (Brother of the Moon, etc.) will say when he sees these works?"[48] In Commodore Perry's *Narrative of the Expedition*, both folio and *Quadrupeds* are mentioned as having been included among the gifts to the Japanese.[49]

In May 1853 Victor, while in the South on a canvassing trip for subscribers to the *Quadrupeds*, wrote from Vicksburg to John Bachman, "I have obtained in all at Mobile, New Orleans, Natchez & this place 300 subscribers, and have sold one Copy of the Large Birds and 7 copies of the small birds which will have to be printed and coloured so I have done pretty well on the whole."[50] The purchaser of this set remains unknown.

In the *New York Sun* for 17 February 1896 there appeared an article about a bookdealer, name not given, of 115 Nassau Street, who had for sale an Audubon folio with five volumes of the *Ornithological Biography*. On the flyleaf of one of the volumes appeared the name of Haller Nutt of Natchez. It is known that Dr. Haller Nutt, a very wealthy planter of Natchez, possessed an outstanding library. After his death the library came into the possession of his son, Prentiss Nutt, who became a resident of Washington, D.C. It may have been Dr. Haller Nutt of Natchez who in May 1853 purchased the folio from Victor.

Although there were two sets of the folio in loose sheets, those sold to Joseph Seabury of New Bedford, it has not been possible to determine how many loose sheets were available for additional complete sets. However two bound sets have been found in which loose sheets were used. As has been previously recorded, two sets of the folio sold to the Canadian Parliament were destroyed by fire in 1849. Some years later, after the capital had been moved to Ottawa, another set of the folio was purchased by the Parliamentary Library in Ottawa. An examination of the prints of this set clearly shows that loose sheets were used in the preparation of the four volumes of the folio.[51]

There remains one other set where again there is internal evidence which clearly indicates that the folio was made up of leftover prints. In 1963, in the will of Mrs. Charles T. Church there was bequeathed to the Audubon Shrine and Wildlife Sanctuary, Mill Grove, near Audubon, Pennsylvania, the four volumes of the *Birds of America* which had originally been purchased by her husband, Charles T. Church.

Prior to the purchase by Mr. Church, the folio had been in the possession of a Barret family for many years. The set was sold by Cecil Barret whose grandfather had moved to Henderson, Kentucky, in 1833. He and his brother John H. Barret were successful tobacco merchants.[52] In letters and papers from the Barret family deposited with the folio at the Audubon Shrine in Mill Grove, it is stated that the Barret subscription, though not listed, was the last one to be received by the Naturalist. When this set was examined, it was discovered that the prints had been bound by a Philadelphia binder named Pawson, who is listed in the directory of that city for the years 1849–1868. In addition, a flyleaf in the set is not Whatman paper and has a watermark dated 1858. It is therefore possible that the Barret set of the folio was assembled from loose sheets which were on hand when the engraving was completed.

When Andrew Coates wrote about his visit with Audubon in 1843, he stated that the family had considered their copy of the folio an "expensive luxury" with which they meant to part. However, it was to be nearly twenty years before the folio would leave the possession of the Audubon family, and then under sad circumstances.

Lucy Audubon remained hale and alert for many years after the death of her husband in 1851. She even resumed her old vocation, that of schoolmistress. In 1857, when this doughty lady was in her seventieth year, she started a small school to teach some of her grandchildren and a few other pupils, the children of neighboring families, in the house of her son Victor.[53] But a succession of reversals was soon to affect the remainder of her years.

In 1859 her younger son John Woodhouse entered into an ambitious project of reproducing the *Birds of America* by a lithographic process.[54] With the outbreak of the Civil War and the unscrupulous dealings of his business partners, this venture ended in disaster.[55] Furthermore, the son had borrowed funds to promote

Sale of the Remaining Folios

the enterprise, and, with its failure, the mother had to use the money received from the sale of her late husband's original paintings to pay off bank loans which she had endorsed. This left her practically penniless.[56]

As a result, in November 1861, the family folio was sold for $600 to John Taylor Johnston (1820–1893), one of the founders of the Metropolitan Museum of Art, New York. This folio is now at the H. J. Lutcher Stark Foundation in Orange, Texas.

And finally the engraver's own copy, which Robert Havell brought with him to America in 1839, was sold in the 1880s. Through a donation, this copy is now in the collections of the Trinity College Library of Hartford, Connecticut. Thus neither the Naturalist nor his engraver was able to bequeath his personal copy of the "Large Work" to his descendants.

16

AUDUBON, ARTIST AND SCIENTIST

During the summer of 1845, Audubon's old friend, the Reverend John Bachman, accompanied by two of his daughters, went north to attend a meeting of the General Synod of the Lutheran Church, and being nearby, also spent a few weeks at the Naturalist's home on the Hudson River. At this time Audubon was busily engaged with the drawings for the *Quadrupeds* as well as with obtaining subscribers and the large sums of money necessary to keep his great enterprises in orderly movement. Bachman, for his part, was working on the letterpress for the *Quadrupeds* and was importuning the Naturalist for specimens and books to facilitate his writing.[1]

The meeting between the two men has been described by Bachman's grandson as follows:

> Audubon and Bachman clasped hands as of yore. The beautiful Hudson flows at their feet; their grandchildren play at their knees—and they are happy—very happy! Soon, however, Bachman's observant eye and loving heart detected in Audubon the unusual absence of mind, that for some time had been noticed by his family and friends. Yet, during this visit Audubon painted with his unrivaled skill, "*Leconte's Pine Mouse;*" his friend is delighted, and thinks that rest is all that is needed to restore Audubon to health of mind and body.[2]

But such was not to be, as is known from the account of a visit made to Minnies Land on the Fourth of July, 1846, by another friend of Audubon's, Dr. Thomas Mayo Brewer (1814–1880):

> The patriarch, then about sixty-six years old,[3] had greatly changed since I had last seen him. He wore his hair longer, and it now hung down in locks of snowy whiteness over his shoulders. His once piercing gray eyes, though still bright, had already begun to fail him. He could no longer paint with his wonted accuracy and had at last, most reluctantly, been forced to surrender to his sons the task of completing the illustrations of his Quadrupeds of North America.[4]

The deterioration of mind and body continued. In December 1849 Mrs. Audubon wrote to Mrs. Benjamin Phillips, the wife of her London physician:

> ... and I alas! have only the material part of my old friend all mind being gone, it is melancholy to me to see him, and I am obliged to reflect from Whom these trials come, and believe he at least feels no pain, to be at all reconciled to such a sad change.[5]

A little more than two years later, on 27 January 1851,

> the spirit of its great master had taken its final flight. The "American Woodsman," the unequaled painter, the gifted historian of nature had died as he had lived, surrounded by all that
>> "Should accompany old age,
>> As honor, love, obedience, troops of friends."[6]

With the death of the Naturalist, laudatory obituaries appeared in the daily and weekly papers of the larger cities of the United States; these were copied later by the press of the towns. Within a little more than two weeks similar recognition was paid in foreign cities. The monthly periodicals likewise printed long eulogies.

A writer for the *National Intelligencer* of Washington labeled Audubon "this venerable and highly distinguished naturalist to whom the country, and indeed the world, owe so much for the extent and character of his researches and publications."[7] A writer for the *Boston Daily Advertiser*, describing the Double Elephant Folio of the *Birds of America*, stated that:

> These herculean labors were the work of many years, and have been accompanied by personal privations, pecuniary sacrifices, severe researches and physical endurance that can hardly be credited by the superficial observer. His productions most strongly recommend themselves to public approbation by their beautiful pictorial illustrations, and felicitous language of the descriptions. They are an honor to the country and a permanent monument to the memory of the author.[8]

In the *Boston Daily Atlas*, the obituary, written by the editor, Dr. Thomas Mayo Brewer who had known Audubon for many years and who had visited him not long before his death, was particularly long. Brewer's eulogy began thus:

> The Telegraph has already communicated to you the intelligence that we have lost from among us one of our most distinguished citizens—John James Audubon is no longer among the living. He who has done so much alike for his own fame, and that of his country—so much to illustrate the natural history of his country, and by his great example to arouse among his countrymen an interest in the study of the natural sciences, has departed. Another great name must be stricken from our roll of living fame, to be placed in that of the imperishable dead. This event, although not unexpected to the friends of the departed, involves a public loss which should not be permitted to be passed over in silence. His life has been too remarkable, his fame too extended, his example too important, his claims upon our admiration are too prominent, for the cold

grave to be suffered to close over the mortal remains that enclosed his gifted spirit, without our publicly expressing our deep sense of the great loss we sustain when so great a light goes out from amongst us.[9]

The death of the Naturalist was also recorded by Philip Hone, the prominent New York Merchant in his famous historical diary:

> Wednesday, Jan 29.—*Death of Audubon.* The celebrated ornithologist John James Audubon died on Monday, aged seventy-six years. He was a most ardent and enthusiastic follower of his science, in the pursuit of which he did not hesitate to explore the hyperborean regions in search of a nondescript bird, or to plunge into the dismal swamps of the South to examine the formation of a bird's nest of some new construction; all of which indefatigable exertions resulted in the greatest work in ornithology which has ever been produced. The subscription price of the first one hundred and fifty copies was one thousand dollars, and they are to be found in most of the public libraries and in several private collections. Mr. Audubon has lived for the last few years in retirement in Harlaem; I have reason to believe in a state of mental derangement.[10]

Shortly before Audubon's death there had been published in New York *The Gallery of Illustrious Americans* containing portraits and biographical studies of twelve of the most eminent citizens of the American Republic since the death of Washington. Numbered among these notables was John James Audubon. The writer of one of the obituaries included the words used by the editor of *The Gallery* in Audubon's biography:

> ... an imperishable name—a name that is not in the keeping of history alone. From every deep grove the birds of America will sing his name. The wren will pipe it in our windows—the oriole carol it from the meadow grass—the turtledove roll it through the secret forests—the many voiced mocking bird pour it along the evening air—and the bird of Washington, from his craggy home far up the rocky mountains, will scream it to the tempests and the stars.[11]

As might be expected, some of the obituary notices included such poetical expressions of praise as the following "Impromptu":

> Bright, as the varying tints his pencil drew,
> Swift, as the wings which once entranced his view,
> Upward, as oft before his eager eye
> The feathered songster cleft the azure sky,
> Would we believe that spirit-bird has sped
> From the loved form we number with the dead?
>
> How faithfully the hand, now silent laid,
> Has on the glowing canvas oft portrayed
> Those gentle denizens of field and bower,
> Whose carol charms us with its native power:
> And woke, responsive to his glorious art,
> A rapturous sympathy of eye and heart.

> The stooping form which marked his late career,
> The trembling steps which shook his closing year,
> Have not in vain borne onward to its goal
> The undimmed jewel of his glowing soul:
> For he has shown us with unerring skill,
> The hidden wonders of our Father's will.
>
> Henceforth above that form be hallowed ground,
> And bird-like voices chaunt familiar sound,
> For with those fluttering ministers of the air
> Has he his fellows led to realms more fair.
> And with that vigorous hand bade us define
> The wondrous wisdom of the Hand Divine.[12]

The obituary in the *Illustrated London News* included a detailed critique of the Naturalist as an artist:

> As a delineator of birds, Audubon never had an equal; his subjects breath of all the freshness, character, and vigor of living nature. His attitudes are of the most spirited description, infinitely varied and all appearing as in their native haunts. They are entirely divested of that formality which too frequently characterises natural history plates, while at the same time, they are remarkable for the accuracy and imitation of the feathering; and in those parts most essential to the naturalist, namely, the beaks and feet, they are drawn with matchless skill and beauty.[13]

Considering the large number of honorary and scientific societies to which Audubon had been elected, it has been difficult to find the record of the resolutions the members undoubtedly adopted when they were apprised of his death.[14] One which has been discovered is that of the Academy of Natural Sciences of Philadelphia, to which the Naturalist had been elected a member on 25 October 1831. In the proceedings of the meeting of 4 February 1851 are recorded the following:

> Dr. Morton [Samuel G. Morton, 1799–1851] announced the decease of Mr. John J. Audubon, a member of this Society; and after some appropriate observations upon the life and character of this distinguished zoologist, moved the following Resolutions, which were unanimously adopted:
>
> *Resolved*, That the Society has heard with profound regret of the death of their esteemed and venerable colleague John James Audubon at his residence near the city of New York, on the 27th ultimo.
>
> *Resolved*, That by the demise of this truly great man, Science has lost one of her most zealous and gifted disciples of the Arts, a master in the branch he cultivated.
>
> *Resolved*, That we recognise in Mr. Audubon a man who has happily lived to fulfill his destiny as an explorer of the great field of American Zoology, while the splendid volumes which are the fruit of his labors, will diffuse the knowledge and love of science to the latest generations.

Resolved, That a copy of these Resolutions, signed by the officers, together with the sympathy of the members of the Society, be respectfully tendered to the family of Mr. Audubon.[15]

Among the many obituaries read by this researcher, it has been interesting to note that nearly all contain two misstatements of fact, namely: one, that Audubon's age at the time of his death was 76 years, although he was actually 66, as it is known that he was born on 26 April 1785; and two, that he was born in Louisiana, whereas the place of his birth was Les Cayes, Santo Domingo!

How do such encomiums as "a delineator of birds, Audubon never had an equal," or "Science has lost one of her most zealous and gifted disciples," and finally, "the Arts, a master in the branch which he cultivated" stand the test of time? When writing about "American Watercolor and Winslow Homer," Lloyd Goodrich (1897–), the former director of the Whitney Museum in New York, devoted a major portion of his monograph to the work of Audubon. What he wrote follows in part:

> His originals in watercolor, with some colored crayon, are among the greatest triumphs of the medium. . . . His figures are full of life and movement. . . . In displaying their anatomy and markings he placed them in positions to show these characteristics in the most striking way, as when a wing is extended to show its structure. . . . Audubon had a superb decorative sense. The patterns of plumage and markings, the rich profusion of foliage, flowers, blossoms and fruit in which he placed his creatures, were composed into stunning decorative designs.[16]

A cogent analysis of the Audubon drawings of the *Birds of America* made by Dr. Robert Cushman Murphy, (1887–1973), late Curator Emeritus of Birds and Research Associate in Oceanic Birds at the American Museum of Natural History follows:

> Baron Cuvier [Etienne Geoffray de St. Hilaire, 1772–1844], foremost savant of the time, called Audubon's work "le plus magnifique monument que l'art ait encore élevé à la nature." There were numerous lengthy reviews in both Europe and America. As a good example we may select that written in the spring of 1828 by the distinguished ornithologist William Swainson, Fellow of the Royal Society.
>
> Swainson hailed Audubon as a new genius who had appeared as a gift to mankind. . . . His first apprisal had come through a short note published in the *Zoological Journal*, which recalled to him the freshness and originality of several of Audubon's short essays and led him to hunt up and examine the early issues of the plates. Swainson was quick to recognize the contrast between Audubon's conception and execution and the figures of birds that had preceded them. Here, for the first time, the subjects were displayed as living beings and as exquisite designs, instead of as stiffly conventional profiles. Of the busy brood of chicks in the female wild turkey plate, Swainson noted that the

particular merit of the picture lay in the various employment of the young: "Some," he notes, "are picking the leaves of plants, others looking about for insects, one is trimming its tail and all are busy. The grouping of these little creatures cannot be surpassed; it would do honor to the pencil of Rubens. The pencilling is such a perfect copy of nature, that, although the attitudes are difficult, and perhaps uncommon, we fancy we have seen them over and over again."

Swainson then proceeded to comment on ten additional plates, pointing out and admiring the foreshortening in the details, stating that "every object speaks, either to the senses or to the imagination," (which, after all, is the essence of art,) and adding that "to represent the passions and the feelings of birds, might, until now, have been well deemed chimerical." This keen and appreciative critic closes at the end of nearly ten pages of text, in the first volume of the *Magazine of Natural History*, a technical journal which is still being published in London, with these words: "I have no previous acquaintance with M. Audubon. I never even saw him; the copy of his work which furnishes these remarks has been lent to me . . . but I can appreciate genius; and I shall ever employ my poor abilities to make it known."

Swainson's appreciation, today no less than in 1828, is a fair estimate of Audubon's natural history and of his creative artistry. If you doubt it, seek the Audubon plates and contemplate the richness of the snowy heron and the black-billed cuckoo; the charming composition and rhythm of logger-head shrikes in the smilax vine; the sweep and color of Collie's magpie-jay; the texture of plumage in the whip-poor-will; the vitality of the wood duck family; the poise and dignity of the brown pelican; the singularly dramatic challenge of the great black-backed gull with the broken wing.

The trouble with most ornithologists is that they seek in a bird portrait not what can be seen in the light and shade of the open air, but, rather, what they *know* to be there, which is quite another matter. Audubon knew the meaning of *ambiance*. He knew that a work of art must capture a mood as well as represent an object. He could not, of course, be at his best in each of 435 plates, but neither was he, as is sometimes alleged by ornithologists, merely "a good bird painter for his day." On the contrary, America has not yet seen his equal.[17]

Another critic, A. Hyatt Mayor (1901–), resorted to poetic imagery when he wrote:

Audubon's contact with the high style of Paris (referring to his study under the French painter David), even though it was only for a matter of months, nevertheless gave him a sense of the theatrical action and of the elegant disproportion of the fashion plate, which sets his pictures of birds and beasts apart from any others. His Night Hawk instructing its young to kill is the *Oath of the Horatii* in a tree top. His *Wild Turkey* and his *White Egret* are the *Incroyable* and *Merveilleuse* of the American forest, strutting forth in the assurance of their singularity. Audubon's birds live through the force of his romantic dream of a virgin world, which he imbibed from Buffon and Rousseau, and perhaps from the first years of his life in Santo Domingo.[18]

An English critic, Sacheverell Sitwell, who has dealt with Audubon's work in great detail, comments:

> "The Birds of America" is a heroic undertaking, and that one man should have endured the hardships and ardours of so many long and lonely years, painted the pictures, written the text, and continued the publication upon so gigantic a scale, puts him among the immortals. Audubon's Birds of America is one of the most valuable books in the world. . . . Audubon is the greatest of bird painters.[19]

Admiration of and inspiration from Audubon's work have been expressed by many artists who today are recognized as outstanding in the field of avian art, none of these more than Louis Agassiz Fuertes (1874-1927) considered by many a noteworthy successor to Audubon. In a letter to Frank M. Chapman (1864-1945), Fuertes wrote:

> As usual, you send me some touchingly appreciated remembrance [Herrick's 2 v. *Audubon*]. I had read of this new Audubon, but hadn't seen it. It is a splendid thing to have, and I have already started to read it. I shall make it a part of my "historical background"—but in spite of your more than flattering dedication I could never arrange myself against it in a really convincing manner—me with my 1917 clothes, notions, shotgun, means of getting to my inspiration and field—as against his romantic and picturesque day and experience. I don't know whether you knew that here, in the town library, we have one of the first 175 copies (the orig. output) purchased by E. Cornell from the orig. subscriber, and used as the nucleus of the "Cornell Library" which antedates the University by 18 or 20 years. This set was for ten years or more my daily bread; by it I was thrilled so that it melts me now to remember it, and many—so very many—of the plates are still as familiar to me as the wallpaper in the hall of the first house I remember living in! By those lovingly done things I was moved—and still am—in a way I would find it hard to express. For most of these bore the authentic stamp of the fresh bird. Frequently their strained positions are at a variance of my point of view, or what characterises the species to me, but I drew myself, for years, by his method of laying the bird on the paper and tracing around it, in true profile—and his ardor was so transparent to me, and mine so responded to it, that I could never do other than admit the enormous influence on my almost aching ardency to 'go and do likewise'. If he hadn't been so patently and helplessly stormed by his love of form and beauty of birds, I should have followed him, blindly, instead of his inspiration, for I was too young to differentiate, except for the very positiveness of his real source of inspiration. But I doubt if I should ever have had the stamina to work as he had to; I should have failed to stem the tide of adversity—and I know I could never, in his time or mine, have negotiated the great folio reproduction and its attendant enormous financing. What a monumental thing for a reed bent by the faintest breath of emotion, as he was, to have accomplished. That, to me, is quite as wonderful as his actual response to his creative lust— for nothing else expresses the desire to perpetuate the evanescent

beauty of bird or flower for future enthusiasts to respond to.[20] On 7, February 1918, Fuertes again wrote Chapman, "I have finished the Audubon, and have enjoyed it more than any book I ever read."[21]

Fuertes, as have others, criticized some of the Audubon birds, when he noted that: "Frequently their strained positions are at variance with my point of view or what characterises the species to me." However, over the many years as this researcher has examined the prints, he has come to the belief that the Naturalist may have, in many instances depicted strained positions for a particular purpose, namely to show thereby characteristics which the casual observer in the field might never see. On plate 27, the "Golden-winged Woodpecker," now called the flicker, there is one of the birds perched on a twig with wings outstretched to show the golden color of the underparts. On plate 128, the "Cat Bird," the artist drew one of the birds with tail raised to point up the brown upper tail coverts. Neither the gold under-wing coloration of the flicker, nor the brown tail coverts of the catbird are readily evident to the observer in the field.

"I am not a learned naturalist. I am only and that to a very great extent a practical one."[22] Thus did Audubon write to Charles Lucien Bonaparte in July 1830. He then added, in what was in effect for Audubon an unusually self-deprecatory tone, that he had scarcely read a book on the subject of ornithology. This, however, is known to be far from true, as has been pointed out frequently in these chapters. Audubon learned what he needed to know, and he did so by reading widely in the standard ornithological works of his day. His technical knowledge of the science of ornithology increased rapidly under the tutelage of his friend and collaborator, William Macgillivray. So effective was this Scottish savant in imparting technical knowledge to Audubon that he served essentially as a substitute for formal higher scientific education. Supplementing the instruction that derived from his long association with Macgillivray were Audubon's superb natural talent and acuity of observation.[23] As Robert Cushman Murphy[24] pointed out, the *Ornithological Biography* constitutes a "half-forgotten treasure." He further commented on the ironic discomfiture of many modern ornithologists who, thinking they have made some startlingly new discovery in bird behavior, find, upon reading this "half-forgotten treasure," that Audubon had described the same phenomenon more than a century earlier.

Ultimately, one may conclude that Audubon's supremacy as a delineator of birds derived from the unique fusion of the artist and the naturalist in the mind of a single person. Such a fusion of skills alone could never have produced the *Birds of America*, but combined with industry, vitality, ambition, and audacity, traits which Audubon had in abundance, that fusion could and did produce the world's most eminent ornithological artist. Although, prior to its appearance, no philosopher or seer could have predicted the production of the *Birds of America*, retrospectively it is possible in these terms, at least partially, to account for the extraordinary phenomenon that was John James Audubon.

II

SUBSCRIBERS
SETS
AND COSTS

17

SUBSCRIBERS

On 22 September 1826, two months after he had arrived in England and two months before he had found an engraver, Audubon, while in Manchester where the original drawings were being exhibited, was visited by the American Consul, Joshua S. Brooks, who advised him to have a subscription book for his work.[1] The following day the Naturalist wrote in his journal: "I have concluded to have a 'Book of Subscriptions' open to receive the names of all persons inclined to have the best illustrations of American Birds yet painted; but alas! I am but a beginner in depicting the beautiful works of God."[2] A few days later, upon his return to Liverpool, while dining with Dr. Traill and William S. Roscoe, Audubon brought up the subject of a subscription book and found that Roscoe thought well of the idea.[3]

When "A National Exhibition of the Works of John J. Audubon, Commemorating the Hundredth Anniversary of the Publication of the Double Elephant Folio—The *Birds of America*" was held from 26 April to 1 June 1938 at the Academy of Natural Sciences of Philadelphia, there was exhibited "The Original Subscription List of the Birds of America," lent by Victor H. Tyler, a great-grandson of the Naturalist.[4] This list is presently in the possession of Joseph Verner Reed, Greenwich, Connecticut, a private collector.

The names on the list are written on individual sheets which measure approximately 4½ inches by 8¼ inches. The individual sheets have been pasted on both sides of a linen cloth and framed in glass panels 45 inches in length. There are five of these panels. The names of the subscribers to the Double Elephant folio of the *Birds of America*, which number 308, fill one panel and the front and part of the back of a second. The balance of the second panel and three others contain the names of subscribers to the Octavo edition. The individual sheets enclosed in the glass panels seem originally to have been kept in a book or portfolio. Among the Auduboniana at the Audubon Museum at Henderson, Kentucky, there is a folder in which a book of sheets of the size of those enclosed in the panels evidently fitted. The case with the prospectus for the Octavo edition indeed shows that sheets have been torn from it.

When the 308 names of the subscribers to the Double Elephant folio of the *Birds of America* were examined by the present author it was evident that many were written by the subscribers themselves. In one instance Audubon pointed this out, for following the signature of "S.A.R.—le Duc d'Orleans" he had noted, "his handwriting." On 28 December 1826, when the Naturalist had received a subscription from the Countess of Morton he wrote in his journal: "The Countess asked for my subscription book and wrote with a steel pen, 'The Countess of Morton'. She wishes to pay for the first number now, but I declined."[5] For the subscription of the Hon. W. C. Wentworth Fitzwilliam, at the time a student at Cambridge University, Audubon observed, "I asked him to write immediately above the Countess of Morton, and he wrote in a beautiful hand, which I wish I could equal, 'Hon. W. C. Wentworth Fitzwilliam.' "[6] The names have become separated in the framing of the sheets.

Among the American subscribers, president Josiah Quincy signed for Harvard; for Columbia College, the signature is that of president W. D. Duer; and for the Library of the General Court of Massachusetts, State Senator A. H. Everett did the signing.

A puzzling signature is the following, "Gentleman of Boston—one copy by S. E. G." The name is not found on any of the printed lists of subscribers. It has been possible to determine that the "Gentleman of Boston" was Thomas Lindell Winthrop who gave his set to the Massachusetts Historical Society. The society later sold the folio.

Although many of the names were actually written by the subscribers themselves, in several instances names were entered on the list by a hand other than that of the subscriber. Examples are the names of the Savannah and South Carolina subscribers. Beginning with the name of William Gaston of Savannah, the twelve names that follow all had been written in the same legible spencerian script which resembles the handwriting of Audubon's wife, Lucy.

That Audubon carried the subscription list on his travels, even to America, is known from a letter the Naturalist wrote at New York on 9 September 1833 to his son Victor, who was then in London supervising the engraving and publication of the prints: "I do not like to send you the original list of subscribers to you now—it has considerable effect in the eyes of those who think of subscribing here, but I can send you the names of *all who have signed it* and shall do so."[7]

The first printed list of subscribers was included in a prospectus issued in the spring of 1828 when six numbers (thirty plates) had been engraved. Here 124 names were listed. Later in the same year when the completed numbers reached ten (fifty plates), another prospectus was printed with a list of 131 names, the French subscribers having been added. Finally, with the completion of twenty numbers (100 plates) late in 1830, yet another prospectus with 180 names was issued.

When the first volume of the *Ornithological Biography* was published in March 1831, there were included the names of 180 subscribers.[8] The second volume of the

Subscribers

Ornithological Biography, published in December 1834, has on pages 581 and 582 a list of subscribers "obtained since the publication of the first volume." These number sixty-three and all but seven were American subscribers.[9] In the third volume dated December 1835, six names were listed, all but one American subscribers.[10] With Volume 4 there were added twenty-seven names, only eight of which were European, all the others being American.[11]

In the final volume, on pages 647–651, there are separate lists of American and European subscribers.[12] There appear 161 names on the two lists; of these eighty-two were American and seventy-nine were European. However, the total number of copies subscribed for is 166, since the subscription of "Vicounte Simeon, for the Ministry of the Interior" called for six copies. A listing of all subscribers whose names Audubon published, with reference to sources from which the names were obtained, appears in Appendix L.

The original subscription list contained 308 names, the subscribers listed in the four volumes of the *Ornithological Biography* total 279, but in the fifth volume the number has been reduced to 161. On page xxiv of the introduction to the fifth volume of the *Ornithological Biography* Audubon wrote:

> At the end of the volume you will find the names of all my subscribers who have continued to receive fasiculi of my plates until the work has been completed. Those who have stopped short, and discontinued their subscription it is unnecessary to mention; but of them there are now upwards of one hundred and twenty."[13]

On page 140 in Audubon's Ledger "B," now at Henderson, Kentucky, is found the following heading: "Subscribers discontinued with amounts paid by them." There are fifty-four names on this list. Since the list was not dated, the period it covers is not clear, but it would appear to include early subscribers. The detailed list of discontinued subscribers is given in Appendix M.

From the amount of money paid by those who discontinued their subscriptions it is possible to determine how many numbers of the *Birds of America* each had received. With the cost of the number in England and Scotland at two guineas (£2 2s.), it appears that none who had discontinued had received more than twenty-one numbers (105 prints) and many only one number (5 prints). Death intervened in many instances with the completion of the subscriptions, as was the case with George IV of England.

The question is often asked, how many *complete* sets of the Double Elephant folio of the *Birds of America* were issued? The answer to this will probably never be known. It is difficult even to make an estimate. While Audubon had included 161 names on the final list, examination reveals that there were listed some who did not receive the complete set. Of the six Savannah subscribers, four died shortly after Audubon had obtained their subscriptions; thus it is doubtful that they received more than the first volume for which they had paid in advance. As to the subscription of Daniel Webster, it had been difficult for Audubon to collect the monies due him for that part of the work sent Webster prior to the completion of the work. At the sale of Webster's library in 1875, only three volumes were offered for sale.

On the other hand, the final list of American subscribers does not include the name of "Nat. Potter, M.D. Professor of Medicine, Baltimore." This subscription was obtained in the spring of 1830, and was included in the list of subscribers shown in the first volume of the *Ornithological Biography*. This set of the folio is presently at the New York Public Library.

Also, when the work of engraving the plates was completed in June 1838, there were fifteen complete sets left over, some bound, others in loose prints. These were shipped to America. Purchasers of these have been established.

There is a statement from Audubon himself as to the number of complete sets of the folio. In the 6 January 1838 issue of *The Athenaeum* of London he had inserted an announcement dated 1 November 1837. This began with a statement reading:

> When only a few numbers of this Work [the *Birds of America*] had been published, Mr. Audubon was informed that many Noblemen and Gentlemen, as well as a considerable number of Natural History Societies, Libraries, &c. were desirous of possessing it, but that the time to be occupied in the publication (16 years) was so great, the casualities of life so many, and the probability of its ever being finished, therefore, so remote, they determined to await its completion before they subscribed. With respect to many Societies, moreover, the rules preclude them, for the above reasons, from subscribing to any work of this kind published periodically.
>
> Mr. Audubon, therefore, feels desirous for the information of such persons or Societies, to announce that seventy-eight numbers have now appeared, and that with seven more it will be completed. He confidently expects to present the last Number to his Subscribers on the 1st of April or May next.

In the final paragraphs the Naturalist stated that: "The number of perfect copies at present subscribed for does not exceed 190, of which upwards of 80 are subscribed for in America; and the expense of getting them up is so great, that not more than ten or fifteen copies, above the number subscribed, will be prepared."

Some years later, the son, Victor Gifford Audubon, when asked how many copies of the *Birds* were in existence, wrote: "About 175 copies, of which I should say 80 were in our country. The length of time over which the work extended brought many changes to original subscribers, and this accounts for the odd volumes which are sometimes offered for sale."[14]

As was stated earlier, the exact number of complete sets of the Double Elephant folio of the *Birds of America* probably will never be known. The evidence suggests that the figure would certainly be less than 200, with the actual number somewhere between 175 and 200 copies.

At this time it would be well to record that while the complete sets of the *Birds of America* were limited to fewer than two hundred, many additional prints of the early numbers were issued for those subscribers who either had cancelled or allowed their subscriptions to lapse as the work progressed.

18

ORIGINAL SUBSCRIPTION LIST

Audubon's records containing the names of the subscribers to the Double Elephant folio of the *Birds of America* and to the Octavo edition have been framed in five glass panels which measure 44½ inches in height and 9 inches in width. The individual sheets on which the subscribers' names were written measure approximately 4¼ by 8¼ inches. These have been pasted on linen cloth, covered by glass, then framed in the panels; now in the possession of Joseph Verner Reed.

GLASS-FRAMED LIST

Panel 1

Front

1. His Most Gracious Majesty George IV
1. Her Royal Highness the Duchess of Clarence
1. The Marquis of Londonderry
1. His Grace the Duke of Rutland
1. S.A.R.—le Duc d'Orleans   his handwriting*
1. His Christian Majesty Charles X
1. Le Prince Massena
1. S. A. R. Mademoiselle d'Orleans
1. B. G. Cuvier

[*fold*]

1. The Library of the Congress of the United States of America, by E. Everett Meehan. Librarian.
1. Baron Krudener   Env. Extr. from Russia
1. Robert Gilmor, Baltimore, Md.

---

* There appears on the original sheet (now part of Panel 1) beside the signature of le Duc d'Orleans this annotation written by Audubon.

THE DOUBLE ELEPHANT FOLIO

1. Nat Potter, Baltimore Proffr of Med
1. John B. Morris Baltimore Md.

1. Isabella Anne Ingram Hertford

Honble W. C. Wentworth Fitzwilliam—No. 5 Halkin Street—Grosvenor Place London

[Sheets joined]

Hon*ble* Th——dele [Thaddele?]   Ravensworth Castle
Lady Ravensworth   Percy's Cross   Gates head
                                Fulham   Durham

1. 2. H.R.H. Princess Elizabeth Landgravine of Hesse Homburgh—Kings Palace St. James London
1. Richard Harlan, M.D. Philadelphia
1. Edward Harris, Esq. Philadelphia
1. John P. Wetherill Philadelphia
1. M. Vaughan Librarian of American Philos. Society
1. R. Harlan, M.D. For Philadelphia Academy of Natural Sciences
1. Carrick N. Buchanan Esq. London

[Fold]

1. G. Holford Esq. London
1. Tho*s* Butler King Esq. St. Simons Island Georgia
1. T. H. Perkins   Boston   One Copy
1. Sam*l* Appleton   Boston   One Copy
1. J. P. Cushing   One Copy
1. Gustavus Schmidt   New Orleans
1. Geo. C. Shattuck   Boston   One Copy
1. P. J. Jackson   Boston   One Copy
   James Brown West   Cambridge   One Copy
   Frederic Tudor   Boston   One Copy
   Gentleman of Boston   One Copy   by S.E.G.

[Sheets joined]

[*That which follows seems to be a continuation of the original sheet which ended with Audubon's annotation of the Fitzwilliam transaction.*]

1. The Countess of Morton, Dalmahoy, Scotland P. Folio [*pencil mark through P. Folio*]
1. The University of Edinburgh
1. The Wernerian Society of Edinburgh
1. The Advocates Library of Edinburgh
1. The Society of Writers to His Majesty's Signet, Edinburgh
1. P. J. Selby Esq. of Twizel, Northumberland
1. Sir W*am* Jardine, Baronet of Jardine Hall
1. James Wilson, Esq. Edinburgh
1. John Lizars, Esq. Surgeon Edinburgh
1. H. W. Williams Esq. Edinburgh

142

Original Subscription List

1. Reverend John Thomson, Duddingston
5. Daniel Lizars Bookseller Edinburgh
1. W*am* Mc Cleham Esq—Mount Stuart, Trinidad
1. W*am* Stuart Esq. of Alderston
1. Henry Witham Esq. Edinburgh
1. Lieutenant-General Graham, Stirling Castle
1. Miss Harriet Douglas of New York   Port Folio
1. Sir W*am* Allsworth Bar*t* Edinburgh
1. M*rs* Hamilton Nisbet Ferguson Edinburgh
1. M*rs* John Foster, Liverpool
1. John Rutter M.D., Liverpool
1. Doctor Bickersteth Liverpool—Dr. Bickersteth
1. x Matthew Burrell Esq. Broompark Alnwick
1. Thomas Forster Esq. Adderstone House Belford ⎫
1. Reverend A. Sharp, Bamburgh, Belford   ⎬ Northumberland
1. Thomas Bewick, for the Literary and Philosophical [Society] of Newcastle Tyne
1. John Bulman, Percy Street Newcastle
1. John Walker Benwell House Newcastle
1. James Graham Clarke Fenham Hall Newcastle on Tyne
1. Mansfeldt de C. Lawson Esq. Cromlington, Newcastle Tyne
1. John Broadley Esq. South Ella near Hull Tyne Yorkshire
1. Thomas Crawhall Newcastle upon Tyne
1. Armorer Dunkin Newcastle on Tyne
1. Major Norcliffe York [*additional words struck out*]
1. Colonel Chomley, Hawshaw York
1. M. Foulis Heslerton-Malton Yorkshire
1. The Yorkshire Philosophical Society—York
1. Mrs. Wilson, Ledston Hall near Ferrybridge, Yorkshire
1. John Clough, Oxton Hall Tadcaster Yorkshire (Portfolio)
1. N. E. Yarburgh, Heslington Hall near York (Portfolio)
1. Captain Windowe York (deceased)
1. Mrs. Foulis York
1. Jos*a* S. Crompton J*r* ⎰ or York
                            ⎱ Esholt Hall Bradford Yorks (Portfolio)
1. Thomas Walker Esq. Killinbeck near Leeds
1. Leeds Philosophical Society & Literary Society Philosophical Hall Leeds (*Portfolio*)
1. John Marshall Jun*r* Headingley Leeds
1. John Gott Leeds (Portfolio)
1. Geo. Banks, Leeds (Portfolio)*
   Portfolio Robert Hindley Manchester
1. Daniel & Peter Jackson 83 Market Street Manchester [?]
1. E. W. Sergeant Manchester (Portfolio)
1. W. Birch St. Johns Street Manchester
1. Thomas Hardman Manchester

* Many names on this list evidently had been written by the subscribers themselves; among these were Geo. Banks, Robert Hindley, Thomas Ridgway, and John Marshall.

THE DOUBLE ELEPHANT FOLIO

1. Thos Ridgway Esq. Wallsuchess.   Bolton
1. Robert Gee   Hollywood near Stockport   (Portfolio)
1. Sam. Greg   Quarry Bank near Manchester
1. S. H. Haslam   Green Bank near Bury Lancashire
1. John Barton Swixton Manchester
1. R. W. Barton   Springwood [?] Manchester

[*End of Panel 1, front, of glass-framed list*]

PANEL 1

Back

1. Edward Loyd   Greenhill near Manchester
   Manchester Society for the Promotion of Natural History (Portfolio)
1. The Rev. Peter Hordern M.A. for the Cheetham Library
1. S. R. Brooks Manchester   Dy Consul of U. S. America & Agent
       Commercial Relation of the Republic of Columbia
1. George W. Wood   Manchester
1. Tho. Hoyle   Manchester   X————
1. Joseph Winter   Stand near Manchester
1. B. A. Heywood—Claremont near Manchester

[*Beginning with the Loyd entry, the names of subscribers appear to be on separate slips of paper. Also the entries from Brooks to Heywood appear to be on a separate sheet of paper.*]

1. John Clayton, Esq. New Castle Tyne
1. Daniel Lizars Bookseller   Edinburgh
1. Patterson Ellames Esq. Allerton Hall near Liverpool
1. Mrs. Rathbone   Green Bank Liverpool
1. Mrs. P. Ainsworth, Hall, near Bolton
1. J. G. Children   British Museum
   copy one Th. Hardwicke   16 Pall Mall
1. Earl of Carnarvon   Grosvenor Square
x. Robert Mitford, Esq. Tax Office
x. ——— Mash [?]   Solicitor of the Treasury.
x. Sir Peter Laurie [?]   Regents Park
1. Earl of Darnley   Berkley Square
1. Rev. Mr. Dunbar, Applegarth   ⎫
1. Reverend Mr. Gibson   Lockmabar [?] ⎬ Scotland
1. S. P. Atkins, Esq.   Walbrook, London
1. Lord Stanley, Knowseley Liverpool
1. William Brodrick   21 Gower Street, London
1. Sir John Swinburne   Cupheaton near Newcastle
1. Cha*s* Elley   Hampstead near London
1. Mrs. Case   Liverpool
1. Reverend J. Clowes Manchester
1. George Hibbert No. 38 Portland Place, London
1. Hon*ble* W*m*. S. Ponsonby   19 St. James Square London
1. Earl Spencer   St. James Place, London.

Original Subscription List

1. John Heathcoate Esq.   41 Charles Street Berkley Square (November–March)
1. Charles Peers, Esq.   Chislihampton Lodge near Wallingford, Oxfordshire
1. Lieut-Colonel Charlewood   40 York Terrace Regents Park
1. Tho. Ponton Esq.   4 Hill Street Berkley Square
1. Charles L. Bonaparte   Prince of Musignano
1. Robt. Barclay, Esq.   Bury Hill Dorking Surrey
1. Lady Helen Hall   near Edinburgh

[End of sheet]

1. Philip John Miles   Little Court [?] near Bristol
1. W. Ogilvie Esq.   [in pencil] Glasgow
1. James Burton   Regents Park
1. Miss Maria Woodroof Smith, Aire [?]   Lane, Clapham
1. Fras. Chas. Parry   4 Onslow Terrace, Brompton (To be left at Somerset Coffee House, Strand)
1. William Cririe   Manchester
1. Sir Wathen Waller, Bart.   K.C.H., Popes Villa near Pickenham
1. Joseph John Gurney, Esq.   Earlham Hall   Norfolk
1. Samuel Gurney, Esq. 23 Lombard St. London
1. Joseph Gurney, Esq. Lackenham Grove, Norwich
1. Thomas Heywood   Manchester

[End of sheet]

1. Edward Holme M.D.   F.L.S.   Manchester
1. D. Grant, 4 Mosley Street   Manchester
1. James Darbishire, Green Heys   Manchester
1. John Blackwall, F.L.S.   Crumptsell [?] Manchester
1. Robt. Garnett Oak Hill, Cheetham [?] near Manchester
1. Lawrence Fort, Birch Hill near Manchester
1. Tho. Joseph Trafford, Trafford Park   Manchester
    (to be sent to Jackson)
1. Thos. Haigh   Cheetham Hill near Manchester [*Includes the note*, "from Thomas Heywood through Thoas Haigh" *and on the left edge of the sheet is another note reading* "Manchester Sept–1827"]
1. Matt*w* Culley, Coupland Castle,—Woler Northum (saw castle [in ink])
1. A. J. Cresswell Baker, Cresswell [*With the note*, "to be sent New Castle Tyne" *and above the initials* "A. J." *is the pencilled notation* "100"]
1. William Burrell, Esq. of Broomepark [*Includes the note*, "from N. C. to Graham Bookseller—Alnick"]

[End of page or sheet]

1. The Rev*d*. Edward Craig, 59 Great King Street, Edinburgh
1. Joseph Ridgway, Esq. Ridgemont near Manchester
1. Earl of Kinswull [Kinnoul]   51 Grosvenor St. London
1. Colle*ge* of Glasgow as Trustees of the Hunterian Museum
1. J*no* Buddle, Esq. Walls end, New Castle Tyne

THE DOUBLE ELEPHANT FOLIO

1. J. Backhouse, Darlington   New Castle at the Bank
1. The York Subscription Library—York
1. X   Joseph Harris 8 Queen Anne Street, Liverpool
1. George Smith, Esq.   Tythe Back Street Liverpool
1. W. Roscoe, Foxteth Park near Liverpool
1. Cuthbert Rippon, Esq.   Stanhope Castle, Durham
1. Kirk Patrick, Esq.   [*Includes the pencilled note,* "115"]
1. Doct*r* Stephenson, New Castle Tyne

[*End of sheet*]

1. T.B.L.L. Baker   Ch. Ch.   Oxford
1. R. H. Hay   Colonial Office, Downing Street
1. The University Library, Cambridge–Dr. Lodge.—86 Whimpole St.
1. George Thackeray, D.D.   Provost of Kings Coll. Cambridge
1. The Cambridge Philosophical Society
1. The Fitzwilliam Museum by M. Davy vice-chancellor
1. W*am* Gambier, Esq.   Sacombe Park near Warre
1. The Anatomical School, Christ Church, Oxford, by Dr. Kidd
1. The Radcliffe Library—Oxford by Dr. Williams
1. David Lyon, 29 New Norfolk Street,

[*End of sheet*]

1. James Pickering Ord, Esq.   Edge-hill, near Derby
1. N. A. Vigors, Esq.   33 Bruton Street, London
1. The Honorable & Reverend J. G. Greenville—Master. Mag*e* C. Cambridge
1. Viscount Milton, Grosvenor Place, London
1. The Rev*d* Henry Pearson, Norton Vicarage near Derby
1. La Bibliotheque de l'Institut Royal de France par M*r* Feuillet
1. La Bibliotheque particuliere du Roi. Galerie du Louvre Paris
6. Ministere de L'Interieur par le Vicounte Simeon
1. Pitois—Paris
1. J. P. Redouté—Paris [*The French subscriptions do not appear to be in Audubon's handwriting.*]
1. Mrs. Warden—London
2. Hearne—Bookseller—Strand London

[*End of sheet*]

2. x[*in pencil*] Rees Davies—Bookseller—Hull
1. James Knight, Esq.   Rhual, near Mold Flintshire [Pool & Harding Chatter(?)]
1. Henry Ellison, Esq.   Beverley, Yorkshire—R. Davies [?]
1. Joseph Eglin, Esq.   Coltingham Yorkshire—R. Davies [?]
1. John Sharpe, 9 Northwick Terrace, Edgeware Road
1. Benj*n*. Smith, Esq.   at Sam*l* Smith 16 Duke Street Westminster, London
1. Miss Rhodes, Park Place   Leeds—Yorkshire
2. Alex*r* Hill, Bookseller   Edinburgh

Original Subscription List

2. Right Hon*ble* Viscount Kingsborough. [*Includes the note,* "having subs(cribed) for the second 'c' July 24 18——"]
1. Treuttel & Wurtz. Booksellers—Soho, London
1. Earl of Bradford—Pall Mall, London
1. George Humphreys, Esq. 42 Oxford Road, Manchester

[*End of Panel 1, back, glass-framed list*]

Panel 2

Front

1. Tho*s* Frost   Gorton Hall near Manchester
1. John Potts, Esq.   New Mills near Manchester
1. John G. Reeves   Birmingham
1. P. Hussey   Wyeslely Grove   near Walsall Staffordshire
1. Birmingham Old Library   by Beilby, Knott and Beilby
1. Tho*s* Barker, Esq.   Oldham near Manchester
1. Joseph C. Dyer   Manchester
1. John Kennedy   Manchester
1. Benjamin Gott   Armley House Leeds
1. Mess*r* Longman & Co.   Booksellers   London

[*End of sheet*]

1. Alex. Barclay   Bookseller   York
1. Mr. Walker   Ravenfield near Doncaster
1. George Lane Fox, Esq.   Yorkshire
1. George H. Head   Banker Carlisle*
1. Boston Atheneum, *ca*   by Hon*ble* T. H. Perkins
1. Mrs. Euphemia Gifford   Duffield Bank Derby
1. Colnaghy   Bookseller Pall Mall London
1. Eedes, Esq.   London Lampeth Place
1. Garnett Duncan   Louisville, Kentucky
1. William Gaston, Savannah Georgia
1. James Potter, Savannah Georgia

[*End of sheet*]

1. Alexander Telfair   Savannah Georgia
1. Dan*l* Blake   Savannah Georgia
1. Tho*s* Young   Savannah, Georgia
1. John David Mongin   Savannah, Georgia
1. Legislature of So. Carolina   Columbia, S. C.
2. Legislature of Louisiana   New Orleans, La. [*It appears that Audubon had originally placed the number "2" before subscription and written "1" over the "2".*]

---

* See p. 12–15, back matter of Volume 1 of the *Ornithological Biography;* the last name on this list is that of George H. Head, Esq., Banker, Carlisle.

147

THE DOUBLE ELEPHANT FOLIO

1. Charleston Library   Charleston, S.C.
    [*Over the word* "Charleston" *there has been written in pencil* "168"]
1. Charleston Soc*y* Nat. History   Charleston, S.C.
1. Charleston Citizens private Library   Charleston, S.C.
1. Doct*r* John Croghan   Louisville, Ky.

[*Beginning with William Gaston and ending with Dr. John Croghan, the subscribers' names are transcribed in the same handwriting.*]

1. John Neal   Portland, Maine   [*Neals own handwriting(?)*]
1. Miss Burley   Salem, Mass   [*probably her own handwriting*]
1. Providence Atheneum—Rhode Island
1. The Earl of Dartmouth
1. James Arnold   New Bedford by Thomas A. Greene
1. William Oakes   Ipswich, Massachusetts
1. W*am* Sturges   Boston   Massa*ts*
1. A. H. Everett for the Library of the General Court of Massachusetts
1. Josiah Quincy for the Library of Harvard University
1. Boston Society of Natural History
1. Ed*d* Prime, Esq. New York

[*End of sheet*]

1. James G. King   New York
1. W. A. Duer for the Library of Columbia College
1. C. Low (Cornelius) New York
1. Rob*t* Ray Esq.   New York
1. J. L. Joseph   esq.   New York
1. State of Maryland [*in another handwriting,* "Little, D. Teakle, Librarian, Annapolis, M.D."]
1. P. G. Stuyvesant   621 Broadway, New York
1. Stephen VanRenselaer   by CK
1. Mrs. B. Bailey by W. G. Brunner [?]   #10 LeRoy Place   New York

[*End of sheet*]

1. Richard F. Carman   No. 42 Broadway   New York
1. Copy L. Reed   13 Greenwich Street   N. York
1. Copy State of New York   John A. Dix, Secretary
1. Copy—Greenwood, Esq.   Boston Museum   Mass*ts*
1. Copy E. Harris, Esq.   London
1. Copy Joseph E. Walker   Baltimore Museum   Baltimore St. Maryland [*In front of this and the next two are pencilled* "Xs"]
1. John S. Donnell   Baltimore M*d*   failed
1. Evan Poultney   Baltimore   failed
1. E. Geddings   Baltimore
1. Haarlem Library   Holland

[*End of sheet*]

148

Original Subscription List

1. William J. Rees of Sumter—Dist Stateburg *So Ca*
    or John Frason [?] Charleston [?]
1. T. Edmondson Jr.   Franklin St. Baltimore

[*The next two lines, having been ruled through, are practically illegible. The two lines may have been references to:*

   Mrs. Nanny Belmont }
   A(r) Llanrust Derbyshire }   Pool & Boult Chesham May 20 1834 [?]

1. Chas. Fox   Perran near Truro
1. N. M. Rothschild   Esq.   London
1. His Grace the Duke of Buccleugh.   Dalkeith Palace
1. John Tobin   Liverpool
1. London Institution per Mr. Brayley
    James Hickson, Esq.   [Dickson, *the* "H" *written over.*]

[*End of sheet*]

[*The following notation and the two names appear to have been written on a separate sheet of paper 2⅞″ × 8″ and sewn to the background cloth.*]

His Imperial and Royal Highness the
Grand Duke of Tuscany etc etc Florence
Vol III and 4 to be sent to C. F. Moline [?]
14 Paternoster Road   London

Ogden Haggerty, Esq.   New York
W. A. Coleman   New York

[*End of sheet*]

R. O. Anderson Esq.   Georgetown, S.C.
Mrs. Ford   Philadelphia
Edw*d*   Hecksher   Esq. New York
Benj*n*   Phillips Esq.   F.R.S.   17 Wimpole Street London
Henry Clay Jun.   Ashland Kentucky
His Grace the Duke of Northumberland, by T. Liddell—May 27, 1836
[*The next two names are crossed out in pencil*]
1. Col*l* Lloyd Phillips, Aberryscivish, North Wales by Havell May 28th ——36
    W*am*   Warren, Esq.   24 Queen Street Brompton
    James Grimshaw   New Orleans

[*End of sheet*]

Earl Hardwicke   Wimpole Arrington, Cambridgeshire by T. H. Liddell
John Moggridge Esq.   Gabalva near Cardiff [*this name has been pencilled out*]
Miss Elizabeth L. Pickman   Salem, Mass.
Salem Athenaeum   Salem, Mass.

THE DOUBLE ELEPHANT FOLIO

Augustus Thorndyke Esq.   Boston, Mass.
Dan*l* Webster Esq.   Boston, Mass.
J*no* Hunt, Esq.   Mobile, (Alabama)
Sam*l* Swartwout Esq.   New York
James Watson Webb Esq.   New York

[*End of sheet and end of Panel 2, front*]

PANEL 2

Back

Tho*s* H. Faile Esq.   New York
J. J. Hughes Esq.   Manchester, Miss*ii*
L. Baldwin, Esq.   Civil Engineer, Boston
Lewis Rogers, Esq.   Paris
Col*o* Thorne   Paris
Henry Hitchcock, Esq. of Mobile
J. VanRensellaer, Esq.   M.D.   New York
Hon. Levi Woodbury for the Dep*t* of State Washington
H. C. DeRham Esq.   New York
John Hewson, Esq.   Lincoln

[*End of sheet*]

Sir Jacob Astley   Bart.   7 Cavendish Square   London
British Museum, London
Tho*s* Metcalf Esq., Augusta, Georgia
State of Michigan, by Gov*r* Mason

[*Also on this panel are ninety names of subscribers to the Octavo edition*]

19

FINAL LISTS OF SUBSCRIBERS

On pages 647 to 651 of the fifth and final volume of the *Ornithological Biography*, the letterpress to the "Great Work" which was published in 1839, Audubon had included in two lists the names of American and European subscribers to the *Birds of America*. Following the names of Audubon's subscribers the author has included information his own research has brought to light—information he has found in the Naturalist's Ledger "B," journals, and ledgers; in book auction records; in the archives, libraries, and museums he has visited; and in his personal correspondence with librarians, archivists, descendants of original subscribers, print dealers, rare bookdealers, and current owners of the sets of extant folios.

In the case of the European subscribers, while the notation "X" was used in Ledger "B" to indicate uncompleted subscriptions, it is possible, from the fact that some so marked have been located as completed sets, that payments had been made to and prints received either from an agent or the engraver Havell, with no corresponding entries to the accounts of these individuals in Audubon's records. (The notation "C" in Ledger "B" entries indicated that a subscription had been completed.) There may also have been an additional ledger containing that information (as, for example, number 14 in the list of European subscribers, the subscription of Armorer Donkin).

This compilation thus provides the essential clues to the ultimate disposition of the sets and summarizes that information which is developed and elaborated upon later in chapters 20 to 23 and in chapters 26 to 28 (the provenances of the extant sets).

AMERICAN SUBSCRIBERS

1. LIBRARY OF THE CONGRESS OF THE UNITED STATES, Washington City
   In situ.

2. STATE DEPARTMENTS, Washington City
   In the Library of Congress.

3. LIBRARY OF THE GENERAL COURT OF MASSACHUSETTS
   In situ.

4. LEGISLATURE OF SOUTH CAROLINA, for the Columbia College

This folio is now in McKissick Memorial Library, University of South Carolina, Columbia, S.C.

5. LEGISLATURE OF LOUISIANA
The folio is in the Louisiana State Museum, The Cabildo, New Orleans, La.

6. LEGISLATURE OF MARYLAND
State Library, Annapolis, Maryland

7. LEGISLATURE OF NEW YORK
On 29 March 1911, the New York State Library was almost totally destroyed by fire. In the 14th Annual Report of the N.Y. State Library (no.60, 1911) there is a photograph with this caption: "The folio edition of Audubon's Birds of America as saved from the ruins." However, inquiry in person at the library has failed to find any trace of the folio at the present time.

8. LEGISLATURE OF MICHIGAN
The folio is now at the University of Michigan Library, Ann Arbor, Mich.

9. BOSTON ATHENAEUM
In situ.

10. HARVARD UNIVERSITY, Cambridge, Massachusetts
In situ.

11. PROVIDENCE ATHENEUM, Rhode Island
In situ.

12. SALEM ATHENEUM, Salem, Massachusetts
This folio was sold to a Boston bookdealer on 10 May 1923 and broken up.

13. AMERICAN PHILOSOPHICAL SOCIETY, Philadelphia
In situ.

14. ACADEMY OF NATURAL SCIENCES, Philadelphia
In situ.

15. COLUMBIA COLLEGE OF NEW YORK
In situ at Columbia University.

16. BOSTON NATURAL HISTORY SOCIETY
The subscription copy was sold in 1840. A second copy had been given to the society by Colonel Thomas H. Perkins on 19 February 1840. This copy was also sold and is presently at the Allan Hancock Foundation, Hancock Library of Biology and Oceanography, University of Southern California, Los Angeles, California. (See also set 43.)

17. CHARLESTON LIBRARY, South Carolina
In situ.

18. CHARLESTON NATURAL HISTORY SOCIETY, South Carolina
The folio is now at the Charleston Museum.

19. CHARLESTON CITIZENS' LIBRARY, South Carolina
This subscription has remained a mystery. In November 1831, shortly after Audubon had arrived in Charleston, S.C., on his second trip to America to seek subscribers and to make additional drawings of bird species, a plan was evolved whereby it was hoped subscribers might be procured in that city. To this end subscription papers were distributed, "each to be filled with twelve names at 5 Dollars per annum and 19 Dollars cash to pay for the first volume, he expects by that means to procure half a dozen, Subscribers, Companies, to the Work."[1]

It is known that in this manner the subscription of the Charleston Library and that of the Charleston Natural History Society were obtained, and the probability is that the subscription of the Charleston Citizens' Library fell into this category. On the original subscription list the name is recorded immediately beneath that of the Charleston Society of Natural History as "Charleston Citizens' Private Library." No further information concerning this subscription has been found until the completion of the work and Audubon's return to America, when the name appears on the list of delinquent accounts recorded in a journal entry on 13 December 1839 thus: "Citizens Private Library $750 for the Large Work."[2] In Ledger "B" the notations indicate that the subscription was designated "Completed." In addition, it appears that the prints were supplied loose, not bound.

Only one other reference to the prints has been found, this in a letter Audubon wrote on 7 May 1840 from Charleston to his son Victor:

Nothing can be done with the "Citizens private Library" except to take the parts of the work mutilated as it may be, as the Subscribers have either died or abandoned their wishes to fulfill their former promises to pay.[3]

20. RICHARD HARLAW [Harlan], Esq., M.D. Philadelphia

Not located. This set may have been composed of loose prints. Ledger "B" shows completion of subscription.

21. JOHN P. WETHERELL, Esq., Philadelphia

The folio remained in family for many years but was eventually sold. No further trace has been found.

22. MRS. FORD, Philadelphia

See chapter 26, Mrs. Frederick W. Beinecke copy.

23. MRS. DOUGLAS CRUGER, New York [Harriet Douglas]

She was the first American subscriber. This subscription was completed but the folio cannot be traced.

24. EDWARD PRIME, Esq., banker, New York

Ledger "B" states the set had been completed and four volumes provided, but there is no trace of set.

25. JAMES G. KING, Esq., banker, New York

Ledger "B" shows completion of subscription. The author was advised 19 April 1963 by Harry Shaw Newman, proprietor, Old Print Shop, New York, that he had broken up this set.

26. CORNELIUS C. LOW, Esq., New York

Details in Ledger "B" show that the subscription was completed but no trace of the folio has been found.

27. P. J. STUYVESANT, Esq., M.D., New York

Ledger "B" indicates that set was completed but no trace of folio has been found.

28. ROBERT RAY, Esq., New York

Ledger "B" indicates set was completed but in loose prints.

Robert Ray (1794–1879), a member of the banking firm of Prime, Ward, Daniels, King & Co., was the son of Cornelius Ray (1755–1827), a prominent New York merchant.[4]

It is possible that these prints were burned in the destruction of the Ray mansion in the disastrous fire which occurred in New York City on 19 July 1845. An account of this fire is to be found in the *Diary of Philip Hone* who wrote, "The flames ran up Exchange Place to the Waverly House, which is a magnificent ruin; thence all the fine buildings down Broadway to Marketfield Street, including Abraham Schemerhorn's hotel, at the corner of Beaver Street, are gone. Here it crossed the widest part of Broadway and burned all the houses from Morris Street, including Robert Ray's great granite edifice."[5] It was in this fire that the warehouse containing the Audubon copper plates was burned, damaging many of the coppers.

However, evidence has been uncovered which would indicate that the folio was not destroyed. A letter to the author written 24 May 1971 from David Randall, the librarian of the Lilly Library at the University of Indiana, states that each of the four volumes of the Audubon folio at that institution contains the bookplate of one Robert Ray, on which there is the motto, "J'Espere en Dieu."

29. J. L. JOSEPH, Esq., New York

Ledger "B" indicates that subscription was completed but no trace of folio has been found.

30. RICHARD N. CARMAN, Esq., New York

The folio was given to the Sage Library of the Theological Seminary at New Brunswick by Carman, the father-in-law of Colonel Garner A. Sage of New York, who gave the funds to build the seminary library. The seminary sold the folio in 1946. It was later broken up by a New York print dealer.

31. MRS. BAILEY, New York

Ledger "B": "Bailey, Mrs. B. (now Paine) New York—Completed—Last delivered 1838; May 1833 Cash to Audubon—49-10-0."

No trace of this folio has been found.

32. STEPHEN VAN RENSSELAER, Esq., Albany, New York

Ledger "B": "Van Rennselaer, Gen

Albany. May 1833—Vol. 1—Bound pd. Audubon 49-10-0. Nov. 10, 1838. Vol. 4." Folio is now at Princeton University.

33. HOGDEN HAGGERTY, Esq. New York
Ledger "B": "Ogden Haggerty, New York. Completed Bound—began in 1836." No trace of the folio has been found.

34. W. L. COLMAN, Esq. New York
Ledger "B": "Coleman, W. A. New York

  February 12, 1836—No. 50
  July 1836 " 87

50-87 inclusive." An "X" indicates the subscription was not completed.
Additional entries in Ledger "B": "W. A. Coleman

 1836—Feb. 1—No. 51 18-18-0
 1837—J. E. Walker 21-18-0
 July 1838—82-87 12-12-0."

On 10 April 1850 and continuing for seven days there was a sale of "Books, Drawings, Paintings, and Statuary of William A. Coleman [sic] Long known as a Collector and Dealer of Rare Books and Works of Art. By Cooley and Keese, John Keese, Auctioneer, No. 304 Broadway, N.Y. By the order of the Assignee and administrator of the late William A. Colman."

Item 2115, p.106: "Audubon's Great Work, The Birds of America, 4 vols., imperial folio, contains 435 plates with five volumes of letter press, half bound. A Subscriber's Copy."

Item 2554, p.128: "A set of the Ornithological Biography."[6] No further trace.

35. SAMUEL SWARTOUT, Esq. New York
There is no record of this subscription in Ledger "B." Hence it would appear that no prints were ever delivered to Swartout.

Audubon wrote his wife in London on 7 September 1836: "I have *almost* obtained 2 Subscribers yesterday. One *Coll* Webb! The other Mr. Swartout of the Custom house."[7] At the time Swartout was Collector of the Port of New York, having been appointed to the position by President Jackson in 1829. He retained that office until 29 March 1838. Upon his retirement it was discovered that, beginning within a few months of his appointment, he had appropriated more than a million dollars of public funds. In August 1838 Swartout sailed for England, hoping to meet his shortage by disposing of certain valuable coal and iron lands. Failing this, he remained abroad until 1841. Then, assured that he would not be prosecuted, inasmuch as his properties had been surrendered to meet claims, he returned to the United States and lived in retirement until his death in New York on 21 November 1865.[8]

36. JAMES WATSON WEBB, Esq., New York
Audubon did not obtain the subscription in 1836 as he had hoped.[9] However, a folio was sold to Webb in 1839.[10]

Webb, a newspaper publisher, suffered financial reverses shortly after the purchase of the folio. In 1842 he took advantage of the Federal Bankruptcy Law and surrendered his personal property to the sheriff, his real estate already having been mortgaged beyond its value. It is possible that the folio was disposed of at this time.[11]

37. THOMAS H. FAILE, Esq. New York
Ledger "B": "T. H. Faile, New York. May 23, 1838 Vols. 1, 2, 3. 168-15-0 by cash 1000 to N. Berthoud—225-0-0." [This set was bound, and the subscription probably was completed.] No trace of this folio has been found.

38. LEWIS ROGERS, Esq. New York
Ledger "B": "Rogers, Lewis by Mr. Bremmer [?] Vols. 1, 2, 3 (bound). May 23, 1838." The subscription was not completed and no trace of the three volumes found.

39. JER. VAN RENSSELAER, Esq., M.D., New York
Ledger "B": "Rensselaer, J. M.D., New York First 3 in 1837, 4th volume Nov. 10, 1838 ½ Bound—all payments to N. Berthoud." No trace of this set has been found.

40. H. C. DE RHAM, junior, Esq., New York
Ledger "B": "De Rham, New York—completed Nov. 10, 1838 Vols. 1, 2, 3, shipped to New York March 18, 1837 half-bound."

On 30 December 1957, Mr. Casimir de Rham wrote: "In regard to your question about the Elephant Folio of Birds of America which was recorded in the name of H. C. deRham Jr., who was my great uncle and quite an Ornithologist in his own right, these folios were eventually inherited by his nephew and my father who had the same name. These books passed to my mother in 1916 on my father's death, and unfortunately were sold in the early 1920's. There is no record available as to the purchaser, but I think it was a dealer."

41. STEPHEN A. HALSEY, Esq., Long Island, New York

No record of this subscription was recorded in Ledger "B." No trace of the set has been found.

42. EDWARD HARRIS, Esq., Moorestown, New Jersey

Ledger "B" record is not clear—would appear to have received loose prints.

On 7 January 1959, William U. Harris [a grandson of Edward Harris] of Jackson, Ala., wrote: "In his papers I have some recollection of some memorandum relative to it, but it was actually a receipt of some nature. I have no recollection of seeing it in my childhood, and at a time when the rest of our Audubon material was in our possession. We had a number of individual sheets from this folio which I still have in Montgomery, there are several more scattered among the family. Other relatives have also written that they have loose prints."

In a scrapbook containing many items concerning the Audubon folios, which had been compiled by the late Ruthven Deane of Chicago, now in the possession of Albert E. Lownes of Providence, R.I., is included the following:

1905—Franklin Bookshop, Samuel N. Rhoades, 1105 Walnut Street, Phila., Pa. Folio with 5 vols. O.B. "A subscriber's autograph copy." $3,000. (at the same time was offering four original letters from Audubon to Harris).

It is possible that the folio referred to in the above summary was the one subscribed for by Harris.

43. THOMAS H. PERKINS, Esq., Boston

Ledger "B": "Perkins, Thomas H. Boston. June 7, 1833, First Vo. Full Bound. Vols. 2 & 3. Full bound. 56-5-0—Set completed."

This set is presently at the Hancock Library of Biology and Oceanography, University of Southern California, Los Angeles. (*See* also set 16.)

44. J. G. CUSHING, Esq., Boston

Ledger "B": "3 vols. Last in June 1836—bound Payments to Dr. Parkman Jan. 1837 for vol. 3—£56-5-0." Not completed [?].

No trace of this set has been found.

45. SAMUEL APPLETON, Esq., Boston

Ledger "B": "Appleton, Samuel of Boston 3 vols. Paid. Dr. Parkman."

The folio presently at the Boston Public Library seems to have been the Appleton set.

46. GEORGE C. SHATTUCK, Esq., M.D., Boston

Ledger "B": "Shattuck, G. C. Nov. 10, 1838 (1st Vol.) £52-2-0. Dec. 10, 1832 £52-10-0, May 1833, £49-1-0 Subscription completed."

Around 1905 this folio came into the possession of John Lewis Childs, a prominent floriculturist of Floral Park, N.Y. Childs was much interested in ornithology and published a magazine, *The Warbler* (of which see 1:3 [Jan. 1905] for the story of the acquisition of the folio). After his death, the folio was sold at the Anderson Galleries on 26 March 1923. The purchaser, Brick Row Book Shop, then sold it to James Cox Brady. In the early 1940s Brady's widow sold the set and it was broken up by a New York book firm.

47. P. J. JACKSON, Esq., Boston [Patrick T(racy) Jackson]

Ledger "B": "Vol. 1. pd. 52-10-0. Balance in parts—Set completed."

On 26 May 1967 this folio was located at the University Library, Scientific and Medical Department, in Copenhagen, Denmark.

48. JAMES BROWN, Esq., Boston

Ledger "B": "Brown, James Bookdealer, Boston. 1st volume bound—Balance loose. Completed July 1838."

Brown, in 1818, was hired by William Hilliard to work in his Cambridge bookstore, and in 1826 was taken into the firm as a partner. He also acquired an interest in

Hilliard, Gray and Co., his partner's Boston business. During the depression of 1837, Brown entered into a partnership with Charles C. Little. They bought both businesses and merged them under the name of Charles C. Little and Co., which eventually became Little, Brown and Co.

On 8 Dec. 1960, the widow of one of the grandsons of James Brown wrote that she had no knowledge of what had become of the James Brown set of the Audubon prints.

49. FREDERICK [Frederic] TUDOR, Esq., Boston

Ledger "B": "Tudor, F. Boston"—entry shows two volumes of Number 1. However, Audubon's letter of 1 April 1833 to Victor in London clarifies this: "Frek. Tudor wishes full Bound copy. The ½ bound he had was returned, although paid for, & given to Miss Burley who has paid for it."[12]

Tudor was one of the founders of the Boston natural ice trade for export. He may have received only three volumes, for the ledger notation "X" is an indication that the set was not completed. No trace has been found of the volumes.

50. THE HONOURABLE DANIEL WEBSTER, Boston

Ledger "B": "Webster, Daniel, Boston, Mass. 1837 Vols. 1, 2, 3. for £148-10-0."

The ledger notation "X" indicates the subscription was not completed. The three volumes are presently at Dartmouth College Library, Hanover, N.H.

51. AUGUSTUS THORNDIKE, Esq., Boston

Not recorded in Ledger "B." In a letter to Edward Harris (then in Paris) on 19 December 1838 from Edinburgh, Audubon wrote: "I should also like you to try to find Mr. Augustus Thorndike to whom Victor wrote a few days ago with a view to enquire from that Gentleman when he wished *his* copy of the Birds of America to be delivered. Victor addresses his letter to 'his Hotel' or to the care of the 'American Embassy,' We are not sure, however whether he is in Paris at Present, and let me know what discoveries you have made as regards this—"[13] No trace of the folio has been found.

52. L. BALDWIN, Esq., Civil Engineer, Boston

Ledger "B": "3 vols. ½ Bound. July 1838." This set was completed and is presently in the Library of the Buffalo Museum of Natural History, Buffalo, N.Y.

53. E. GREENWOOD, Esq., Museum, Boston

Ledger "B": "Greenwood, Boston. Nos. 1-87 inc. Portfolio—loose. Pd. by note in Dr. Parkman's hand—112-10-0." That Audubon had difficulty collecting payment is known from his letter written from Worcester on 12 August 1842 to Victor, who was then at 77 William Street, New York.[14]

Nathan A. Greenwood bought out the management in a museum 1 Jan. 1825 and located on Court Street in Boston. This was known as the New England Museum and because of its popularity at that time was considered valuable. In 1839 the assignees of Greenwood sold the New England Museum collection to Moses Kimball for his Boston Museum, which was opened in 1841 at a corner of Tremont and Bromfield Streets, and in 1846 was moved to the new Museum building near Court Street.[15] The Greenwood account is listed in detail in Ledger "B." No trace of the prints has been found.

54. GEORGE PRATT, Esq., Boston

Ledger "B": "George W. Pratt—Boston—First vol.—December 11, 1832—4 vols in Hf. russia."

No trace of the volumes has been found.

55. WILLIAM STURGES [Sturgis], Esq., Boston

Ledger "B": "Bound set completed 1838." This folio is now at the Museum of Art, Boston, Mass.

56. ROBERT GILMOR, Esq., Baltimore

Ledger "B": "Gilmor, Robert, Baltimore Vol. 1; 22-87 (Loose)
Jan. 7, 1831 by cash to Wm. G. Bakewell Louisville."

This set is presently at the Peabody Institute of the City of Baltimore (now a branch of the Enoch Pratt Free Library).

57. JOHN B. MORRIS, Esq., Baltimore

Ledger "B": "Morris, John B. Baltimore 1-71 inc. March 18, 1837. X."

Morris, a banker, appears to have helped Audubon with the Maryland subscribers. When the Bank of Maryland closed its doors in 1834, he was appointed one of the trustees for the bank. He was most reluctant to turn the business of the bank over to the creditors. When, during the summer of 1835, the status of the bank remained in doubt, the creditors became restless. As a consequence, on 9 August, a mob invaded Morris's home, burning the furniture and other things (including individual numbers of the *Birds of America*).[16]

Audubon, on 22 January 1836, alluded to this in a letter to Bachman, "The Riots at Baltimore were also much against us and there we have lost many a number unpaid and undelivered of the Birds of America."[17]

However, the Naturalist was reimbursed for his loss, as is known from the following letter written to his wife at New York on 7 Sept. 1836: "The State of Maryland have passed an act to compensate all the sufferers by the Riots to the full amount of their Losses and N. B. [Nicholas Berthoud] in consort with J. B. Morris have claimed 120$ for the Nos. lost at the time, and we have a bound for the amount."[18]

In Ledger "B," on p.72, the account of N. Berthoud under Baltimore shows a credit of £27-0-0 for 7 January 1837, the amount collected as compensation for loss by riot at Baltimore.

Morris died on 24 December 1874 in his 90th year. No trace has been found of the prints he had acquired.

58. ——— SMITH, Esq., Baltimore

There is no record in Ledger "B" of any subscriber with the name of Smith in Baltimore. It is possible that this may have been Gideon B. Smith, who was Audubon's agent in Baltimore for the Octavo edition.[19] No trace of any folio belonging to Smith has been found.

59. THOMAS EDMONSTON [Edmondson], jun. Esq., Baltimore

Ledger "B": "First Volume—June 1834—Completed subscription—Paid—J. B. Morris Nov. 10, 1838."

The four volumes are presently at the Public Library of Cincinnati and Hamilton County in Cincinnati.

60. WILLIAM GASTON, Esq., Savannah, Georgia

Gaston, a prominent and wealthy merchant, not only subscribed himself, but was instrumental in obtaining for Audubon the subscriptions of James Potter, Alexander Telfair, Thomas Young, John David Mongin, and David Blake, all of Savannah. No account has been found in Ledger "B" for any of these five subscribers. However, there are many transactions in that of Gaston, who acted as Audubon's agent in Savannah, so that payments from the five subscribers evidently were included.

It has not been possible to determine if the Gaston subscription was completed, nor has any trace been found of the prints. Gaston died on 12 Sept. 1837. It is possible that he had obtained only two volumes before he died, since there is the following entry in Ledger "B": "1838—Third Volume trans. to T. B. King a/c." King was a subscriber from St. Simon's Island, Ga.

On 9 Mar. 1834, Audubon, then in Baltimore, wrote his son Victor in England, "I forwarded you 252£ from W*am* Gaston for all the Subscribers 2d Vols at Savannah except Mr. King of St. Simon Island whose amount will be forwarded to the Rathbones for you shortly if not already done by W*am* Gaston, who proves to be a man in a million."[20] Since Telfair, Young, and Mongin, all Savannah subscribers, were dead at the time, the reference to "all the Subscribers 2d Vols at Savannah" is not quite clear. Telfair and Young had died in 1832. Audubon referred to this in a letter written to Gaston on 19 Feb. 1833: "I regret the loss of two subscribers in your hospitable land."[21]

61. JAMES POTTER, Esq., Savannah, Georgia

Potter's seems to have been the only Savannah subscription completed. The four volumes subscribed for by Potter are presently at the Houghton Library, Harvard University.

62. ALEXANDER TELFAIR, Esq., Savannah, Georgia

Telfair died 9 Oct. 1832. He received the first volume, for which he paid in advance, but it is doubtful if he received any other prints. No trace of any prints which Telfair may have received has been found.

63. THOMAS YOUNG, Esq., Savannah, Georgia

Young died on 6 Aug. 1832. He had paid for and received Volume I of the *Birds of America*, as indicated in a letter written by Audubon on 13 March 1832 from Charleston to his wife: "I have another Subscriber at Savannah through that most extraordinary man W*am* Gaston—the name of Whom is Thomas Young, Esqr. I have Rec*d* the money for the first Volume."[22] That Young received any other prints is doubtful. No trace of the first volume has been found.

64. JOHN DAVID MONGIN, Esq., Savannah, Georgia

Mongin died between 12 September 1833, the date of his will, and 18 November 1833, the date the will was probated [from the letter of 23 April 1957 to the author sent by Mrs. Lilla M. Hawes, Director of the Georgia Historical Society]. On 30 March 1832, while in Charleston, Audubon wrote his wife: "I have received 232 Dollars from W*am* Gaston for John David Mongin Esq. pay*t* of the 1st Volume Birds of America, and the 32 Copies of biography [*Ornithological Biography*] which he has sold." No trace of the Mongin prints has been found.

65. DANIEL BLAKE, Esq., Savannah, Georgia

"Daniel Blake died late in 1834 or prior to Jan. 19, 1835, the date of his administrator's notice" [Quoted from the letter of Mrs. Lilla M. Hawes, Director, Georgia Historical Society, 23 April 1957]. There is no further information nor any trace of the prints.

66. THOMAS BUTLER KING, Esq., St. Simon Island, Georgia

Ledger "B" provides few details concerning this subscription which probably was included in the Gaston account. Audubon had obtained King's subscription in November 1831, while en route to St. Augustine, Fla.[23] However, he was collecting payments as late as 1 May 1840 from King, who was at that time a representative from Georgia in the United States Congress.[24] King died on 10 May 1864. His folio of the *Birds of America*, it is believed, was acquired by James Hamilton Couper, in payment of a debt.

Couper owned a plantation, Altama, near Darien, Ga. He also built a summer home in Atlanta during the 1880s. There is reference to a set of Audubon prints in the library at Altama in *Plantation South* by Katherine Jones (Indianapolis: Bobbs-Merrill, 1957). The library of some 5,000 volumes was eventually removed from Altama Plantation to the Couper home in Atlanta. Upon Couper's death this library, including the Audubon folio, was inherited by the son, James Maxwell Couper. A daughter, Mary Harper Couper, married George McDonald Traylor, who purchased the Couper home in Atlanta. The letter of 24 March 1957 to the author from Mrs. R. J. Thiesen of Atlanta, a great-granddaughter of James Hamilton Couper, indicates that the Audubon folio was sold prior to the beginning of the present century. It has not been possible to trace this folio further.

67. THOMAS METCALF, Esq., Augusta, Georgia

Ledger "B": "Metcalf, Thomas S. 1838 by cash to N. Berthoud [Audubon's brother-in-law and his New York agent] $660–148–10–0." No trace of the prints has been found.

68. E. GEDDINGS, Esq., M.D., Charleston, South Carolina

The entry in Ledger "B" shows his address as Baltimore and the subscription completed.

On 28 May 1958, Miss Elizabeth Williams, Associate Librarian of the Medical College of South Carolina, Charleston, S.C., wrote the author, "Dr. Eli Geddings left no will. His library was appraised at $125, and the books sold for $300. There is no mention of the Audubons."

G. Edmund Gifford, Jr., M.D., Watertown, Mass., advised the author on 8 June 1962, "Gedding's library burned in the Civil War."[25]

69. WILLIAM J. REES, Esq., Stateburgh, South Carolina

From Ledger "B" it is known that in 1836 Rees received the first three volumes of the prints and that the fourth was paid for directly to Audubon in January 1837. Audubon's letter of 13 February 1837, written at Charleston, mentions the Rees payment.[26] No trace of the volumes has been found.

70. R. O. ANDERSON, Esq., Georgetown, South Carolina

Ledger "B" lists only three volumes and is marked "X" which indicates the subscription was not completed. It had originally been obtained by Audubon's friend and benefactor, the Rev. John Bachman, of Charleston, S.C., in 1835.

In 1758 there was received by the Winyah Indigo Society of Georgetown, S.C., a royal charter from King George II. The society founded a school which became "the School for all the country lying between Charleston and the North Carolina line for more than one hundred years." In 1834 the society erected a new building called the Academy. In addition to the school and a meeting place for the members of the society, the building also included a library. During the Civil War the Academy building was occupied by Union forces, at which time the building and the surrounding premises were much abused by the soldiers. The best and most valuable works in the library were appropriated and carried off, including Audubon's great work on ornithology.[27] On the other hand, there is a record of the sale in 1853 of Keithfield, the plantation of R. O. Anderson, to James H. Trapeir. The Audubon folios may have been included in the sale.[28]

There is a letter in the Princeton University Library which Audubon wrote to Anderson at the time the third volume of the *Birds of America* was being sent to this subscriber. The Naturalist hoped that Anderson might be able to send him specimens from his "country" (which Audubon had not visited) of birds Anderson did not find represented in the three volumes. These specimens were to be "put in Common Whiskey or Rum in Stone Jars or whatever else may prove convenient."

71. MISS BURLEY, Salem, Massachusetts

From Ledger "B" it appears that the first volume of 100 prints was bound and the balance of the set supplied in loose prints. Final payment was made to Dr. Parkman in July 1838.

Some, at least, of the Audubon prints received by Susan Burley came into the possession of Mr. John Saltonstall from his "aunt," Susan Burley Cabot, who was actually no relative, but who left his family money and property. Susan Burley Cabot lived at the corner of Beacon and Joy Streets (now the Little, Brown Building) and at Pride's Crossing in the summer. Mrs. Henry A. Murray who furnished the information about Mrs. Susan Burley Cabot on 27 October 1960 also stated that she recalled seeing Audubon prints when she called on the lady.

Finally, there are some Audubon prints at the Groton School, Groton, Mass., the gift of a member of the Saltonstall family. It is possible that these are Susan Burley's prints.

72. MISS ELIZABETH L. PICKMAN, Salem, Massachusetts

Ledger "B" states that the fourth volume was delivered 10 Nov. 1838. This set is presently at the Peabody Museum, Salem, Massachusetts, on deposit from the Essex Institute, Salem, Mass.

73. WILLIAM OAKES, Esq., Ipswich, Massachusetts

Ledger "B" indicates that this set was in loose prints and completed 18 July 1838, payment having been received through Dr. Parkman.

Oakes was a lawyer, botanist, and naturalist whose fame as a botanist eclipsed his fame as a lawyer. He was drowned on 31 July 1848, "while passing from Boston to East Boston, under circumstances which left it doubtful, whether by accident, or in a temporary fit of insanity, to which he was subject."[29] No trace of these Audubon prints has been found.

74. JAMES ARNOLD, Esq., New Bedford, Rhode Island [sic]

Ledger "B" indicates this set was completed July 1838, payment having been made through Dr. Parkman in the amount £22-10-0. This folio is presently at the New

Bedford Free Public Library, New Bedford, Mass.

75. GARNET DUNCAN, Esq., Louisville, Kentucky

The first entry in Ledger "B" was dated 10 December 1832, the last, July 1838. This set appears to have been loose prints, as is evident from a letter Duncan wrote to Doctor John Croghan, another of Audubon's subscribers, on 22 June 1838: "I have got a man at work binding my Audubon—Upon examining them to make the volumes I find I have not got plates 236 to 260 inclusive—I think it highly probable that you may have those plates of mine as I did not run over critically those which were sent to me for you. Please examine this Evening Carefully whether you have from 236 to 260 and whether you have not got duplicates of those numbers and let me know in the morning." [Copy of a letter sent to the author 4 June 1966 by Dr. S. W. Thomas of Louisville, Ky. The original was found among the Croghan papers in the Henry Huntington Library, San Marino, Cal.]

Duncan died in Louisville on 25 May 1875. A surviving son, Col. Blanton Duncan, moved to Los Angeles around 1892. [Information obtained by the author 25 Nov. 1958 from Miss Mable Weeks, Archivist, Filson Club, Louisville, Ky.] The name of Blanton Duncan appears in the Los Angeles city directory for 1894-1900 as residing at 3016 South Figueroa Street. No trace of the folio has been found.

76. JOHN CROGHAN, Esq., M.D. Louisville, Kentucky

Ledger "B" states that this set was completed July 1838, that Croghan had been sent loose prints, and finally, that he had paid cash to Audubon on 8 May 1833 in the amount of £73-8-0. (*See* item 75, the account of Duncan subscription for additional information about the folio.)

Dr. Croghan, born 14 April 1790 near Louisville, Ky., was the son of Maj. William Croghan and Lucy Clark Croghan, as well as a nephew of Gen. George Rogers Clark. Croghan, who resided at Locust Grove, Ky., which is near Louisville, owned Mammoth Cave. He died at Locust Grove on 11 January 1849 [from information supplied the author 24 March 1958 by Miss Mable Weeks, Archivist, Filson Club, Louisville]. No trace of the folio has been found.

77. HENRY CLAY, jun. Esq., Ashland, Kentucky

Ledger "B": 3 Vols. Biog., 3 Vols. Birds of America March 1836." In July 1836 Clay was billed by Audubon for guns amounting to £58-0-0. There is another entry in Ledger "B," dated June 1838, under Berthoud, showing a receipt from Clay for $1000 (£225-0-0).

Henry Clay, Jr., was born in 1811 and died 13 February 1840 in the battle of Buena Vista in the Mexican War. In 1958 Eugene Simpson of Lexington, Ky., a descendant of Henry Clay, made an exhaustive inquiry of many of the living descendants of Ann Clay (Mrs. Henry McDonald), a daughter of Henry Clay, Jr., and the only member of his family of six children who left issue. He was unable to find any trace of the prints.

78. JAMES GRIMSHAW, Esq., New Orleans

Ledger "B": "3 Vols. Bound—Jan. 7, 1837 £168-15-0. X [not completed]."

With the help of Miss Louise Hubert Guyol, the following information regarding the Grimshaw prints was obtained. On 24 April 1959, Frederick D. Barham of New Orleans wrote Miss Guyol, "I remember when I was a boy seeing some of the large prints in the house of my uncle, James Grimshaw Duncan, on Henry Clay Avenue and I believe that there was a whole folio of these prints in his possession and that it was possibly the elephant folio. Some years later the house was completely destroyed by fire. Many years afterward, when I inquired about the Audubon prints, I was told that they had burned up with the house. It is quite possible however that I was mistaken in believing that my uncle owned the elephant folio. I have spoken to Mildred and Sylvia Norman Duncan but neither one can tell me anything definite.

It may be of help to you in running down these prints for me to outline some of the family connections. Audubon married Lucy Bakewell, daughter of William Bakewell of Derbyshire, England. Another Bakewell daughter married Nicholas Berthoud. My great-grandmother was a Berthoud and married Mr. James Grimshaw, an Englishman in the cotton business in New Orleans. After the Civil War Mr. Grimshaw sold all of his art collections and similar possessions in New York.... Some Audubon folios may have been included in his collection.... I do not believe that any of the sons and grandchildren of Mr. Grimshaw had any prints during the period in which I would have heard about it."

79. GUSTAVUS SCHMIDT, Esq., New Orleans

"Ledger B" shows the subscription was completed. In 1965 the following information was sent to the author by Mrs. Frederick Swigart of New Orleans, La.: "There were recently given to the Department of Archives of the Howard-Tilton Library of Tulane University in New Orleans the papers of the de la Vergne family. Mrs. de la Vergne who died some 5–6 years ago was a granddaughter of Gustavus Schmidt. She was first married to Jules de la Vergne and later to Henry Landry de Freneuse. Included among the papers is a draft of a letter written in French in 1910 on the stationary of the Hotel Rydbergs, Stockholm. In the letter, the purpose of which seems to have been that of asking an audience with the King, she relates that her grandfather, Gustavus Schmidt, had been born in Manestad of a family closely attached to the Swedish King Oscar, and were protégés of his. Further, that her grandfather had left Sweden at the age of 21 and set out to make his fortune in America, had studied and practiced law in New Orleans and built up a large clientele. Finally she states, "When the works of Audubon's Birds were published he (Gustavus Schmidt) sent a copy to King Oscar."

With the help of Mr. J. Graham Parsons, the American Ambassador at Stockholm, contact was made with Nils F. Holm, Keeper of the Royal Family Archives. On 13 August 1965, Mr. Holm wrote that he had found in the Archives of King Oscar a letter from Gustavus Schmidt to the King, dated 4 July 1844, and a copy of the King's answer, dated 2 October 1844. Holm went on, "In the letter written in French Gust. Schmidt affirms to the King his affection for him and his native country etc., but the book he sends is 'History of the Indian Tribes of North America etc.' by Th. L. M. Kenney and James Hall, 3 vols., publ. 1838–1844. In his very kind answer the King thanks for that bookwork...." Holm further stated: "As regards the works of Audubon's Birds no letter from G. Schmidt to King Oscar is to be found in the Family archives...."

Schmidt died in 1877. It appears that he had reverses in business just before his death and his entire collection of books was sent to St. Louis to be sold. The firm of Soule, Thomas and Wentworth had them for sale. They had a catalog printed listing all the books. No Audubon folio was included.

80. J. J. HUGHES, Esq., Manchester, Mississippi [now Yazoo City]

Ledger "B": "Jan. 23, 1837 Vol. 1, 2, 3, Bound." While "X" is included in margin, there is additional information about the subscription. In a letter dated, New York, 7 September 1836, written to Mrs. Audubon in London, Audubon stated: "Our Dear Victor will mark—what follows—J. J. Hughes Esq. of Manchester, Mississippi a New Subscriber has received and paid for 1, 2, & 3rd Volumes, and desires the 4th half bound when finished to be forwarded to N. Berthoud."[30]

Hughes was a prominent Whig, a banker [Commercial Bank of Manchester], and a planter. He was appointed a captain of the 20th Regiment of the Mississippi Militia in July 1845. Hughes seems to have been a bachelor and in 1850 was living in the household of Dr. and Mrs. S. Mansfield. He was not, however, listed in the 1860 census. [Information provided the author by Mrs. Carl Black, Jr., of the Department of Archives and History, State of Mississippi, Jackson, Miss., 12 June 1958.] No trace of this set has been found.

81. JOHN HUNT, Esq., Mobile, Alabama

In connection with this subscriber Audubon, while in Moorestown, N.J., wrote his wife on 2 July 1837: "*John Hunt* a new subscriber from Mobile gave me an order for $500 on Messrs Parish of New York on a/c of his Copy although not yet received."[31] No trace of the prints has been found.

82. HENRY HITCHCOCK, Esq., Mobile, Alabama

At the Audubon Museum, Henderson, Ky., there are some loose pages torn from one of Audubon's journals. From certain entries (loose journal pages 95 and 96) it is known that Judge Hitchcock died before the folios were sent to him. The subscription had not been obtained until 1838. The entry in Ledger "B" reads: "Henry Hitchcock—1838—to Vols. 1, 2, 3 Full Bound. Shipped to N. Berthoud, N.Y. 168-15-0." After the death of Judge Hitchcock, his widow first moved to Nashville and then to Lexington, Ky. On 20 February 1841 Audubon wrote her that the four volumes of the folio and the *Ornithological Biography* were being sent to her brother, James W. Erwin, in New Orleans, but who later moved to Lexington, Ky. No trace has been found of this set of the folio.

EUROPEAN SUBSCRIBERS

1. HER MOST EXCELLENT MAJESTY, QUEEN ADELAIDE, England

Born Adelaide of Saxe-Meiningen 13 August 1792, she married the Duke of Clarence, third son of George III on 4 July 1818. The Duke of Clarence became William IV on 28 June 1830. William died in 1837. In November 1831 Parliament passed a bill making Adelaide regent in case a child of hers should survive the king, and provision was made for her widowhood by a settlement of £100,000 a year. She died in 1849.

The record for this account in Ledger "B" follows:

"I. Adelaide Queen of England

1830—First vo.		42- 0-0
1831 No. 21 & Biog. delivered by Havell		3- 0-0
1835 22 to 31 Inc.		21- 0-0
Contra		
By cash at Sundry times		42- 0-0
1832 Dec. 11 By cash R. Havell		18-18-0
" 17 J.J.A.		5- 5-0
		24- 3-0"

From the foregoing it would appear that the queen received the first volume and additional plates to Number 155, and the first volume of the *Ornithological Biography*. There may have been other transactions direct with Havell.

2. (HIS MOST CHRISTIAN MAJESTY, CHARLES X)

Audubon had obtained a subscription from Charles X on 26 October 1826.[32] The king was deposed by the July Revolution of 1830. He was exiled from France and came to Edinburgh in 1830.

Ledger "B" shows the following:

"King of France—Private Library 1831—
May to No. 1-21
Inclusive and Biography   45-3-0
            Contra
1831—May By cash from Pitois   45-3-0"

The king had received twenty-one numbers of 105 prints and Volume 1 of the *Ornithological Biography* which were paid for through Audubon's agent.

3. HIS MAJESTY PHILIPPE I, KING OF THE FRENCH

Audubon had obtained the subscription of the Duc d'Orléans (the future King Philippe) on 30 September 1828, with the aid of the artist Redouté. When Audubon opened his portfolio containing the plates and displayed that of the Baltimore Oriole, the duke exclaimed: "This surpasses all I have seen, and I am not astonished now at the eulogiums of M. Redouté."[33] King Philippe reigned until 1848.

The account of King Philippe as shown in Ledger "B" follows:

"1831 May—to Nos., 1-21 and
    Biography   45- 3-0
1833 June Nos., 22-25 Inc.   8- 8-0
     July   26-33 "   16-16-0
1834 June   34-37 "   8- 8-0
     July   38-41 "   8- 8-0
                                 42- 0-0

Final Lists of Subscribers

1835 Jan 19	42–47 [Inc.]	12–12–0
1836 Feb 12	48–57 "	21– 0–0
" 12	58–62 "	10–10–0
October	63–67 "	10–10–0
		54–12–0

Contra

1831 May—By cash-sundry times		45– 5–0
1834 July Cash		42– 0–0
1837 Pitois		54–12–0"

According to the foregoing, the king received 335 plates of the *Birds of America* as well as the first volume of the *Ornithological Biography*. The evidence indicates that the prints were obtained unbound.

4. HER ROYAL HIGHNESS MADEMOISELLE D'ORLEANS

The sister of le Duc d'Orléans, her subscription was received by Audubon on 21 October 1828 in Paris [through Redouté].[34] Ledger "B" shows that the duchess also received 335 plates and the first volume of the *Ornithological Biography*. Deliveries of the plates were made on the same dates as those sent to her brother.

5. PRINCE MASSENA, Paris

Audubon obtained this subscription on 10 September 1828, while in Paris.[35] The entry in Ledger "B" shows that the subscriber received and paid for the first twenty-one numbers (105 plates) and the first volume of the *Ornithological Biography*. In 1958 Prince Massena d'Essling stated that the library of his grandfather was dispersed in 1850 and that he could give no further information.[36]

6. HIS GRACE THE DUKE OF RUTLAND, London

On 23 September 1958, John P. Mudd of Belvoir Estates Limited, advised the author: "I have asked the Duke about this (whereabouts of the Audubon set) but unfortunately he has no idea what happened to it; he thinks it probably went to the U.S.A." According to the records in Ledger "B" the set was not completed. The account as recorded in Ledger "B" follows: "Rutland, Duke of, London—Vol. 1, Biog., 21–31 April 1831."

It would appear from this that the duke had obtained the first volume—probably bound—and prints from 101 to 155 inclusive.

7. THE HONOURABLE W. C. WENTWORTH FITZWILLIAM, London

Ledger "B" indicates this set was not completed: "Wentworth Fitzwilliam, London Vol. I, No. 21, Biog. 22, 23–31 Inc. 3/21/1833."

Audubon obtained this subscription at Cambridge, where Fitzwilliam was a student. On 7 March 1828, he wrote in his journal: "I was called from here to show my work to Lord Fitzwilliam, who came with his tutor. The latter informed me the nobleman wished to own the book. I showed my drawings, and he being full of the ardor of youth, asked where he should write his name. I gave him my list; his youth, his good looks, his courtesy, his refinement attracted me much, and made me wish his name should stand by that of some good friend. There was no room by Mrs. Rathbone's, so I asked that he write immediately above the Countess of Morton, and he wrote in a beautiful hand, which I wish I could equal, 'Hon. W. C. Wentworth Fitzwilliam.'"[37]

On 23 November 1966, the present Earl of Fitzwilliam wrote to the author, "The Fitzwilliam family formerly possessed two copies of Audubon's Birds of North America. One belonged to the senior branch of the family at Wentworth Woodhouse, the other belonged to my junior branch of the family at Milton.

"I sold my copy about thirty years ago and believe it was eventually acquired by the University of California, but I am not certain of this."

8. THE RIGHT HONOURABLE THE COUNTESS OF RAVENSWORTH, Ravensworth Castle

The account is carried in Ledger "B" as follows: "*Lidell, Thomas*—Ravensworth Castle (or Lady Ravensworth) near New Castle. 1–31 Inc. Biog. March 21, 1833 (Box.)"

"Plates 1 to 155 inc. and the 1st Vol. of the Biog."

There is no current information about this subscription. The set was not completed.

9. THE UNIVERSITY OF EDINBURGH
   In situ.

10. THE SOCIETY OF WRITERS TO HER MAJESTY'S SIGNET, Edinburgh
    This folio was sold by the Society at Sotheby's 19 October 1959 for £13,000 ($36,400) to Messrs Sotheran and resold to Mr. Stanley Smith, London, for his daughter, Barbara Stanley Smith.

11. HENRY WITHAM, Esq. of Lartington, Durham
    Ledger "B": "to July 1838 Bound with locks June 1831 53-18-0."
    See the provenance of the Lord Hesketh folio in chapter 27.

12. JOHN RUTTER, Esq., M.D., Liverpool
    Ledger "B": "Rutter, John M.D. Liverpool—Vol. 1., Biog. 21-22."
    This subscription was not completed.

13. DOCTOR BICKERSTETH, Liverpool
    Ledger "B": "Bickersteth, Dt. Liverpool up to 22 & Biog. 6/24/1831."
    The set was not completed.

14. ARMORER DONKIN, Esq., Newcastle-upon-Tyne
    Ledger "B": "Donkin, Armorer, Esq. Vol. 1, Biog, 21-22."
    According to *Auction Book Prices Current 1925*, on 25 November 1924 there was sold at the Anderson Galleries in New York "The Valuable Ornithological Library of the late W. J. M. de Bas, The Hague, Holland." Included in the sale was item #12, "Audubon, John J., *Birds of America* from Original Drawings—435 of the finest and largest ornithological plates ever made. . . . London, Published by the Author, 1827-38. An unusually large copy with the plates measuring 38½ × 25¾ inches, with the *Armorer Donkin bookplate in each volume* [italics the present author's]. Sales Price, $3,100."

15. YORKSHIRE PHILOSOPHICAL SOCIETY, York
    This set is now in the possession of Joseph Verner Reed, Greenwich, Conn.

16. JOHN CLOUGH, Esq., Oxton Hall, Yorkshire
    Ledger "B": "Clough, John. Todcaster, Oxton Hall, Yorkshire. up to 31 inc. Biog."
    Although the ledger indicates noncompletion of this subscription, there is presently a set at Vassar College which seems to have been subscribed for by Clough.

17. JOS. S. CROMPTON, jun., Esq., Eshott [Esholt] Hall, Bradford, Yorkshire
    Ledger "B": "Crompton, Josiah, Esholt Hall near York Vol. 1, Biog. and up to Nos. 31 inc." The set was not completed.

18. THOMAS WALKER, Esq., Killinbeck, near Leeds
    Ledger "B": "Vol. 1., 21-22 to April 1831. Chg. to M. Robinson."
    This folio was presented by Mrs. Carll Tucker to the Audubon Museum, Audubon State Park, Henderson, Ky., in 1966.

19. LEEDS PHILOSOPHICAL AND LITERARY SOCIETY
    Ledger "B": "Vol. 1, Biog., 21 & 22. April, 1831–not completed."
    However, D. Cox, Deputy Librarian, Brotherton Library, University of Leeds, advised the author that the Sixty-ninth Report of the Council of the Leeds Philosophical & Literary Society, at the close of the session, 1888-89 (Leeds, 1889), contains the following information: "The debt of the Society has been reduced from £468 18s 11d. to £225 15s 11d. This was effected chiefly by the sale of Audubon's 'Birds of America.'" Audubon had obtained the subscription 2 May 1827.[38]

20. JOHN MARSHALL, jun., Esq., Headlinglay, Leeds
    Ledger "B": "Vol. 1. Biog. 21 & 22. (Charged to Mary Robinson Bookseller at Leeds—)."
    The folio is now at Duke University, Durham, N.C.

21. SAMUEL GREG, Esq., Quarry Bank, near Manchester
    Ledger "B": "Samuel Greg—Manchester. Vol. 1, Nos. 21-22 Biog.—Apr. '31 X [not completed]."
    In a Sotheby (London) auction catalog, dated 16-20 December 1929, is the following: "Item 373. Audubon (J.J.) The Birds of America. 4 vols. consisting of 435 beautiful

colored plates by R. Havell, each bird being represented the full size with its prey, half morocco (red) g.e. slightly rubbed and the top of the spine of vol. IV a little broken. A magnificent copy. elephant folio (3 feet, 2¼" by 2 feet, 1½") for the author 1837–38. The Property of Major H. S. Greg, Woodcroft, Haverthwait, Ulveston." The folio was purchased by the American rare bookdealer Gabriel Wells for £1,300.

With the assistance of Major Osbert M. Greg, London, a great-grandson of Samuel Greg of Quarry Bank, and Miss Sylvia England, it has been possible to determine that the folio sold by Sotheby on 17 December 1929 was the one originally subscribed for by Samuel Greg of Quarry Bank.[39] The present whereabouts of this folio has not been ascertained.

22. EDWARD LLOYD, Esq., Greenhill, near Manchester

Ledger "B": "Lloyd, Edward—Banker—Vol. I., 21 & 22. Biog. (Refer to Sowler.)" An "X" indicates the set was not completed.

23. THE MANCHESTER SOCIETY FOR THE PROMOTION OF NATURAL HISTORY

Ledger "B": "Society of Natural History—Manchester—Vol. 1, 21 & 22. Biog. Charge to Sowler. X." The "X" in this ledger entry indicates that this set was not completed.

Miss Hilda M. McGill, Reference Librarian of the Central Library, St. Peter's Square, Manchester 2, England, wrote the author on 23 March 1959: "The Manchester Society for the Promotion of Natural History was discontinued in 1868. In 1862 a catalog of the library was published and this included the Audubon (call number 016.5 M7). When the Society was wound up, part of the library was sold, and part was handed to the Manchester Museum which ultimately became part of Owens College, now the University. The 1895 printed catalogue of the Museum indicated that this or another copy of the large Audubon was contained in the library. The call number was 598.297 f Au2."

Dr. D. E. Owen, Manchester Museum, University of Manchester, wrote the author on 22 June 1959, "I am very sorry to say that although we had a copy of Audubon's *The Birds of America*, it was sold many years ago when the museum was short of funds."

24. THE REVEREND PETER HORDEN, M.A., FOR THE CHEETHAM LIBRARY, Manchester

Ledger "B": "Library, Cheetham, Manchester—Vol. 1 Portfolio—21 & 22. Biog. April 1831 [last entry]." Although "X" indicates the subscription was not completed, it actually was.

This folio, with erasures on plate 2, remained in Chetham's Library until early in 1972, when it was put up for sale with Sotheby & Co. of London. The sale was held 26–27 September 1972. The four volumes of the folio and the five of the letterpress (item 72 in the sale catalog) were purchased for £62,000 by J. N. Bartfield, the New York bookdealer. In July 1973 the folio was sold to Rawlston D. Phillips, Jr., of Baton Rouge, La.

25. G. W. WOOD, Esq., Manchester

Ledger "B": "Vol. 1, 21 & 22. Biog. to April 1831. Chg. to Thos. Sowler."

On 12 August 1958, Robert W. Oates, of the Oates Memorial Library and Museum, Selborne, Hants, advised the author, "Two of my relatives gave Audubon orders, viz. George W. Wood, M.P. who sold his copy through Sotheby when it fetched about £100."

26. MRS. RATTSBONE, Greenbank, Liverpool

Ledger "B": "Rathbone, Mrs., Green Banks Liverpool Vol. 1., Nos. 21 & 22. April '31." This set remained in the family until sold by F. W. Rathbone at Sotheby's 16 March 1937 (item 345). It was purchased by Colnaghi for £1,475 and resold to the Kennedy Galleries, New York.

27. J. G. CHILDREN, Esq., British Museum, London

Ledger "B": "Children, J. Head of British Museum, Vol. 1, 21 & 22; 23–31 inc. [plates 1–155]."

Children was associated with the British Museum from 1823 to 1840. *See* also in this list entry 76, The British Museum.

28. **The Right Honourable the Earl of Caernarvon,** London

Ledger "B": "Earl of Caernarvon—Vo. 1, Biog. up to 32 inc." [plates 1–160].

29. **S. P. Atkins, Esq.,** Walbrook, London

Ledger "B": "Atkins, S. P. London up to 31 inc. X [plates 1–155]." The name of this subscriber does not appear in the *Dictionary of National Biography*. No trace was found of the folio.

30. **The Right Honourable the Earl of Derby,** P.Z.S. [President of the Zoological Society], &c. &c. &c.

Ledger "B": "Lord Stanley 112 Upper Grosvenor St. London Vol. 1., 21–31 inc. Biog. Mar. 21 1833 Charged to Havell."

Lord Stanley, Edward, fourteenth Earl of Derby (1799–1869), had not only been a Member of Parliament, but also had been Chief Secretary for Ireland, Secretary of the Colonies, First Lord of the Treasury, and Prime Minister during his public career.

This set of four volumes, containing four hundred prints only, was purchased by Edward Speelman Ltd. in 1966. It was resold to an American print dealer and broken up.

31. **The Right Honourable Earl Spencer,** London

Ledger "B": "Earl Spencer London. Vol. 1., 21–31 inc. Biog. March 21, 1833 Cg to Havell. X."

On 24 June 1959, Ronald Hall, Keeper of Printed Books at the John Rylands Library, Deansgate, Manchester 3, England, advised the author, "The Librarian has now had a reply from Lord Spencer who says that their copy of Birds of America is no longer at Althorp and he is unable to say what happened to it."

32. **John Heathcote, Esq.,** London

Ledger "B": "Eatcoat (41) (Heathcoat) Berkeley Square 41 Charles St. V. 1. No. 2-21, 22, 23 to 31. inc."

This folio was sold 21 March 1955 by Sotheby's for £9,200 ($25,760) to a dealer by the name of Lionel Robinson who resold it to H. Bradley Martin of New York.

33. **Joseph John Gurney, Esq.,** Earlham Hall, Norfolk

Ledger "B": "John J. Gurney—Norwich. 1830—Jan. 31, 1st. Vol. 42- 0- 0—April 31—No. 21 & Biog. June No. 22—5- 0- 0 May 21, 1833—Nos. 23-31 inc."

See entry for the Earl of Crawford and Balcarres in chapter 27.

34. **James Darbyshire, Esq.,** Manchester

There is no record in Ledger "B" of this folio.

35. **John Blackwall, Esq.,** Manchester

Ledger "B": "Blackwall, John. Manchester. Vol. 1. Biog. & No. 21 X."

The "X" indicates the subscription was not completed.

36. **A. J. Cresswell Baker, Esq.,** Prowin Park

The original subscription list reads: "A. J. Cresswell Baker, Cresswell—to be sent New Castle Tyne." There is no record of this subscription in Ledger "B."

37. **Reverend Edward Craig,** Edinburgh

Ledger "B": "Craig, Rev. Edward Edinburgh (unbound) Through Burton Latimer, near Kettering—Northamptonshire, Alex Hill agent."

Hill was Audubon's agent in Edinburgh. Ledger also shows "C," indicating that the subscription was completed.

38. **The College of Glasgow,** as Trustees of the Hunterian Museum

Ledger "B": "Glasgow, College of—Jan. 1830 42- 0- 0. for 1st vol. B. of A. 1831—April No. 21 & Biog. 1833 June No. 22."

This set is presently at the Library of the University of Glasgow.

39. **John Buddle, Esq.,** Newcastle-upon-Tyne

Ledger "B": "Buddle, John New Castle-on-Tyne, Vol. 1., Biog. & No. 21. X."

40. **The York Subscription Library,** York

The society decided to sell the folio in 1889 and its sale was finally consummated in 1896. It is presently in the possession of The William Henry Smith Memorial Library of the Indiana Historical Society in Indianapolis,

Final Lists of Subscribers

Ind. There is no record of this subscription in Ledger "B."

41. KIRK PATRICK, Esq., London

    Ledger "B": "Patrick, Kirk London Vol. 1. Biog. 21-31 inc. March 21, 1833. X."

42. T. B. L. L. BAKER, Esq., Christ Church, Oxford

    Ledger "B": "Baker, T. B. L. L. Harwick Court Gloucester Vol. 1. up to 31 March 21, 1833 X."

    T. B. L. L. Baker was Thomas Barwick Lloyd Baker (1807-1886), only son of Thomas John Lloyd Baker of Uley, Gloucestershire. He matriculated at Christ Church 14 March 1826, at age 18, and in 1828 was a student at Lincoln's Inn. Baker later owned Harwicke Court, Gloucestershire, and served not only as a J.P.[?] and as a D.L.[?] but also as High Sheriff of Gloucestershire in 1847. He was much involved with the suppression of vagrancy and school reform.

43. DOCTOR LODGE, FOR THE UNIVERSITY LIBRARY OF CAMBRIDGE

    Ledger "B": "Library, University of Cambridge—Prof. Henslow July 1838 Final. (Loose) C."

    The folio is presently at the Library of Cambridge University, Cambridge, England.

44. GEORGE THACKERAY, D.D., PROVOST OF KINGS COLLEGE, Cambridge

    Ledger "B": "Thackeray, George D.D., Kings College Cambridge, Vol. 1, 21 & 22 Inc. 23-31. Biog. March 21, 1833 chg. Havell X."

    A. N. L. Mumby, in a letter to the author, dated 18 July 1957, wrote: "... sold at Sotheby's during the year ending October 1923 for £455." Also, "Shortly after the first world war the library was extremely short of funds and one of my predecessors sold it at Sotheby's and devoted the proceeds to less splendid but more immediately useful purchases."

45. THE CAMBRIDGE PHILOSOPHICAL SOCIETY

    Ledger "B": "Philosophical Society—Cambridge—(July 1838 with Briggs through Henslow) Loose C."

    Miss L. E. Larter, Librarian at the Cambridge Philosophical Library, Free School Lane, Cambridge, on 14 July 1959, wrote the author: "The copy belonging to the Cambridge Philosophical Society was sold in 1924 to Gabriel Wells, Rare Book Dealer, 489, 5th Avenue, New York for £400." Again, on 24 July 1959: "The copy of Audubon's *Birds of America* of which you enquired was sent to Gabriel Wells' London agent, Robert Riviere & Son, Bookbinders and Booksellers, 29-33 Heddon Street, Regent Street, London W.1, who undertook the binding." The present whereabouts of this folio has not been ascertained.

46. THE FITZWILLIAM MUSEUM, by M. Davy, Vice Chancellor

    Ledger "B": "Fitzwilliam Museum Cambridge & Biographies loose—5th Vol. Bio. missing. C"

    On 13 June 1959, Phyllis N. Giles, Librarian, Fitzwilliam Museum, Cambridge, wrote: "We still have in the Fitzwilliam Museum Library a set of Audubon's Birds of America."

47. DR. KIDD, FOR THE ANATOMICAL SCHOOL, CHRIST CHURCH, Oxford

    Ledger "B": "Anatomical School Oxford—up to 31 X."

    W. G. Hiscock, Deputy Librarian, wrote the author on 22 July 1958, "... there is no doubt that our set is no. 47 subscribed for Christ Church in Kidd's name."

48. DOCTOR WILLIAMS, FOR RADCLIFFE LIBRARY, Oxford

    Ledger "B": "Library Radcliffe—Oxford Vol. 1—Nos. 21-23 inc. Biog. March 21, 1833 [last entry]."

    On 19 May 1959 Mr. H. F. Alexander, Superintendent of Radcliffe Science Library, wrote the author: "However I can substantiate the fact that the set bought by Dr. G. Williams for the Radcliffe Library is still in this Library."

49. JAMES PICKERING ORD, Esq., Hedge Hill, near Derby

    Ledger "B": "Ord, James Pickering, Edge Hill near Derby Vol. 1. Biog. 21 & 22 Settled March 21, 1833 X."

THE DOUBLE ELEPHANT FOLIO

50. THE RIGHT HONOURABLE VISCOUNT MILTON, London

    Ledger "B": "Milton, Viscount (now Earl Fitzwilliam London) Vol. 1. Biog. 21-23 inc. March 21, 1833 X."

    See entry 7, The Honourable W. C. Wentworth Fitzwilliam, London, in this list.

51. M. FEUILLET, FOR THE LIBRARY OF THE ROYAL INSTITUT OF FRANCE

    It has not been possible to locate this folio.

52. VICOUNTE SIMEON, FOR THE MINISTRY OF THE INTERIOR, 6 Copies

    Ledger "B": "Ministry of the Interior—Rue Grenelle Paris
    6 vols. #One ⎫
    6 No. 21 (Pl. 101-105) ⎬ Paid May 18 1831"
    6 Biog. ⎭

    No trace has been found of the six copies of Volume 1 which, it appears, were sent to the Ministry of the Interior.

53. M. PITOIS, Paris

    Ledger "B": "Pitois of the House of Leverault Pitois & Co." and in yet another entry, "House of Levrault—Pitois.
    May 23—to nos, ea.
    Prince Messina
    Institute of France
    King of France Private Library
    Ministry of the Interior."
    Pitois was then Audubon's Paris agent.

54. MRS. WARDEN, London

    Ledger "B": "Mrs. Warden, London. Vol. 1, 21, 22, 23-31 inc. Biog. Mar. 21, 1833 X."

55. MR. HEARNE, bookseller, London

    Ledger "B": "Hearne, Bookseller, Strand, London, March 31, 1833—No. 1-31 inc. (Pl. 1-155) X."

56. HENRY ELLISAN, Beverly, Yorkshire

    Ledger "B": "Henry Ellison, Cottingham near Hull. vol. 1—Biog. 21, 22-31 inc. 1833 Mar 21 X."

57. BENJAMIN SMITH, Esq., M.P. London

    Ledger "B": "Smith, Benjamin. Westminster, London Vol. 1. Biog., 21-31 March 21, 1833 X."

58. RIGHT HONOURABLE EARL OF BRADFORD, London

    Ledger "B": "Bradford, Earl of Vol. 1; Biog. up to 31 X."

59. THOMAS FROST, Esq., Gorton Hall, near Manchester

    Ledger "B": "Vol. 1. 21, 22 Biog. Jan. 7, 1830 X."

60. JOHN G. REEVES, Esq., Birmingham

    Ledger "B": "Reeves, John G.
    Aug. 8, 1830   1-17 Portfolio
    Jan. 7, 1831   18, 19, 20
    Apr.   "   21 & Biog.
    June   "   22 [The last two entries bear the notation, 'Charged to Beilby, Knott & Beilby.']."

    F. J. Patrick, Birmingham Public Libraries, wrote the author on 8 March 1954, "The only facts discovered are that John G. Reeves appears in the directories of Birmingham between 1829 and 1852. He is described as a merchant and factor and his firm had premises on Moor Street. Not possible to trace his copy of Audubon."

61. BIRMINGHAM OLD LIBRARY, by Beilby, Knott, and Beilby

    Ledger "B": "Old Library, Birmingham 1-17 Portfolio 18-22 & Biog. Charge to Beilby, Knott & Beilby 1831 X."

    In a letter dated 26 March 1958, V.H. Woods, City Librarian, Birmingham Public Library, wrote, "The Birmingham Library itself was an original subscriber through the Birmingham book sellers, Beilby, Knott and Beilby. It was no. 61 on the list of European subscribers. . . . it is there described as the Birmingham Old Library to distinguish it from a secondary institution which for a time existed independently as the Birmingham New Library."

62. JOSEPH C. DYER, Esq., Manchester

    Ledger "B": "Manchester, Dyer, Joseph C. Vol. I, Biog. No. 21 & 22 X."

    Miss Hilda M. McGill, Reference Librarian, Central Library, Manchester, England, wrote the author on 23 March 1959, "The library of Joseph Chessborough Dyer was sold in 1868, although he did not die

Final Lists of Subscribers

until 1871 (for his life see *Dictionary of National Biography*, v.6, p.287-88). The sale catalogue does not contain any notice of his copy of Audubon."

63. THOMAS WALKER, Esq., Ravenfield, near Doncaster

    Ledger "B": "Walker Thomas, Ravensfield near Doncaster. (Loose Prints) to July '38— Biog. & Portfolio. C."

    No trace of this set has been found.

64. GEORGE LAMB FOX, Esq., Yorkshire

    Ledger "B": "Fox, George Lane, Branham near Wetherby Yorkshire, loose, July 1838 to Robinson. C."

    This subscriber's name should have been listed as "George Lane Fox" (*see* entry 68 in this list), according to a letter Audubon wrote Havell, his engraver, from Edinburgh, Sunday 31 October 1831: "I am glad that *Mr.* Calvert procured the subscription of George Lane Fox (Yorkshire)— do you know where that Gent*n* resides in Yorkshire?"⁴⁰

    On 27 July 1909 there was sold a set of the folio, the property of G. R. Fox, M.P., by Sotheby, Wilkinson & Hodges to Quaritch for £380. It has not been possible to trace this set any further.

65. HAARLEM LIBRARY, Holland

    Ledger "B": "Tylerian Library— Haarlem—July 1838
    August 24*th* 1833 Cash pd. VGA
       Van Marum   40-0-0 Loose prints
    1834 Draft   "   45-0-0
       Van Marum—Librarian C."

    This set of the folio is presently at Teyler's Stichting Bibliotheek, Haarlem, Netherlands.

66. MRS. EUPHEMIA GIFFORD, Duffield Bank, Derby

    Ledger "B": "Gifford, Mrs. Euphemia— Duffield Bank near Derby. Complete Set Plus Binding—Plus Ottaman (£20.) C."

    See the Field Museum of Natural History entry in chapter 26.

67. CHARLES FOX, ESQ. Perrair, near Truro, England

    Ledger "B": "26-9-6 X"

68. GEORGE LANE FOX, Esq. Yorkshire

    See entry 64 in this list. Audubon must have duplicated names in making up the list, for there is no George Lamb Fox, Yorkshire listed in Ledger "B."

69. SIR JOHN TOBIN, Liverpool

    Ledger "B": "Tobin, Sir John. (unbound) Jan. 19, 1835 to July 1838—Loose— C."

    No trace of this set of the folio has been found.

70. HIS GRACE THE DUKE OF BUCCLEUCH, Dalkeith Palace, Scotland

    Ledger "B": "Four volumes full bound. July 1838."

    In 1942 this set was broken up by a New York print dealer.

71. HIS IMPERIAL AND ROYAL HIGHNESS THE GRAND DUKE OF TUSCANY, &c. &c. &c.

    Ledger "B": "1834 July—1 & 2nd. Volumes 93-5-0 Cash July 1834 from Molini of Paternoster Row."

    On 29 April 1960, Frederick H. Jackson, a graduate student at Syracuse University (under Professor Antonio Pace), went to the Biblioteca Nazionale Centrale in Florence, Italy, and "after one hour's searching and with the aid of Baglioni I found in the lower recesses of the Inner Sanctum a large (about 4 1/2 by 3 ft) volume of Audubon's 'The Birds of America.' It had no 'dedic' [dedication] I could find no mention of No-Fl. It was printed in London and the catalogue number for your information is 22-I-2-II. There are four volumes, I believe, to the set and they are here."

72. LONDON INSTITUTION. by Mr. Bradley, Librarian

    There is no record of this subscription in Ledger "B." On 5 September 1835 Audubon wrote his engraver from Edinburgh, "I have received this day a letter from the (———) of the *London Institution* Mr. E. W. Brayley, Junior, who informs me that this Institution has subscribed for a Copy of the 'Birds of America'.—and requests all the numbers published to be sent them, along with an account or bill which will be payable at the Monthly Meeting of the Managers.—I therefore wish you to see that this Institution does receive at your hands an excellent copy collected and examined by yourself, and see Mr. Brayley to whom please deliver the enclosed."[41]

On 31 August 1967, Miss P. M. Baker, Assistant Librarian, University of London, wrote the author: "The Institution must have received this copy some time after the main catalogue was published as it only appears in a supplementary volume published in 1843.... Edward William Brayley (1802–70) was joint librarian of the Institution with Richard Thomson for some years from August 1834 ... by 1905 the Institution was almost moribund and it closed in 1910. The University of London acquired the building in 1917 for its newly founded school of Oriental Studies. The library was also acquired and the books of oriental interest retained for the use of the school. The rest of the library was divided between the three principal libraries of the University, the University Library itself, University College, and King's College. A few books went to the British Museum and a small collection to the Guidhall Library. What has happened to the Audubon volumes remains a mystery, however: they do not appear now to be in any of the libraries which received books from the Institution Library. One cannot of course be sure that they were still in that library when the books were dispersed by the Institution, or gone amissing at an earlier date."

73. BENJAMIN PHILLIPS, Esq., F.R.S.L., &c. &c. &c. 17 Wimpole Street, London [Physician to the Audubon family]

Ledger "B": "Phillips, B. 17 Wimpole St. London Vols.1,2,3. (unbound) £126-0-0."

John C. Page-Phillips, a great-grandson of Dr. Phillips, advised the author 7 June 1965 that the set had been sold at auction, probably at Sotheby's.

74. HENRY G. BOHN, Esq., London

This subscription was not recorded in Ledger "B." Bohn was an antiquarian bookseller and publisher whose business was taken over in 1864 by George Bell, Portugal Street, London.

A large number of the Audubon prints which appear to have been those originally belonging to Bohn are presently in the possession of B. Juriev, Junior Research Assistant, Zoology Institute, Academy of Sciences, Leningrad, USSR. These prints and supporting evidence of their provenance were seen by the author during a visit to Leningrad in 1967.

75. CHARLES J. WARDE, Esq., Welcomb, near Stratford-on-Avon

Ledger "B" contains no record of this subscription.

76. THE BRITISH MUSEUM, London [in part]

Ledger "B": "British Museum [in part]
May 1838   49–82

July 1838   83–87
Paid Victor   Jan. 19, 1839."

The foregoing means that Numbers 49 to 82, plates 242 to 410, were delivered in May 1838 and Numbers 83 to 87, plates 411 to 435, were delivered in July 1838.

On 11 December 1959, C. N. Dodd for the Superintendent of the British Museum, the Reading Room, wrote: "I am afraid that the only further information I have discovered concerning their receipt [Museum set of Audubon's folio] in the British Museum is contained in an entry dated 11 January 1839 in an acquisitions register which states that plates 411–435 and the title page of Volume 4 were purchased of Audubon for ten guineas."

The date Jan. 19, 1839, entered in Ledger "B" as the date of payment, could have been an error made during transcription of that information. Also Ledger "B" shows that plates 411 to 435 were delivered in July 1838. *See* the British Museum, Reading Room entry in chapter 27.

77. HIS GRACE THE DUKE OF NORTHUMBERLAND, &c. &c. &c.

Ledger "B": "Duke of Northumberland—full bound, completed Jan. 28, 1839."

Final Lists of Subscribers

The set is presently in the possession of Louisiana State University, Baton Rouge, La.

78. EARL HARDWICKE, &c. &c. &c.
Wimpole, Arrington, Cambridge

In Ledger "B" the only Hardwicke is "Hardwicke, Major General Thomas, Pall Mall, London—Vol. 1.—21-31 inc. Mar. 21, 1833 and Biog. X."

A set of the folio with the bookplate of the Earl of Hardwicke presently is in the collection of the Library of Northwestern University, Evanston, Ill.

79. SIR JACOB HASTLEY, Bart. &c. &c. &c.
Cavendish Square, London

No record of this set was made in Ledger "B." The folio at the Carnegie Museum, Pittsburgh, Pa., is believed to be this one.

20

COMPLETE AND INCOMPLETE SETS

COMPLETE SETS:
UNITED STATES AND CANADA

THE ACADEMY OF NATURAL SCIENCES
Philadelphia, Pa.

THE AMERICAN MUSEUM OF NATURAL
HISTORY
New York, N.Y.

THE AMERICAN PHILOSOPHICAL SOCIETY
Philadelphia, Pa.

AMHERST COLLEGE
Amherst, Mass.

AUDUBON SHRINE AND WILDLIFE
SANCTUARY
Audubon, Pa.

AUDUBON STATE PARK MUSEUM
Henderson, Ky.

BARTFIELD, J. N.
New York, N.Y.

BEINECKE, MRS. FREDERICK W.
New York, N.Y.

BOSTON ATHENAEUM
Boston, Mass.

BOSTON PUBLIC LIBRARY
Boston, Mass.

BOWDOIN COLLEGE
Brunswick, Me.

BROWN UNIVERSITY
Providence, R.I.

BUFFALO AND ERIE COUNTY PUBLIC
LIBRARY
Buffalo, N.Y.

BUFFALO SOCIETY OF NATURAL SCIENCES
Buffalo Museum of Science
Buffalo, N.Y.

CALIFORNIA ACADEMY OF SCIENCES
San Francisco, Calif.

THE CALIFORNIA STATE LIBRARY
Sacramento, Calif.

CARNEGIE INSTITUTE
Carnegie Museum
Pittsburgh, Pa.

CHARLESTON LIBRARY SOCIETY
Charleston, S.C.

THE CHARLESTON MUSEUM
Charleston, S.C.

THE CITY COLLEGE OF THE CITY
UNIVERSITY OF NEW YORK
New York, N.Y.

THE CLEVELAND MUSEUM OF NATURAL
HISTORY
Natural Science Museum
Cleveland, Ohio

COLUMBIA UNIVERSITY
New York, N.Y.

The ownership and location of the sets of the folio listed in chap. 20 are current as of 1 Oct. 1973.

Complete and Incomplete Sets

COMMONWEALTH OF MASSACHUSETTS
STATE HOUSE LIBRARY
Boston, Mass.
CORNELL UNIVERSITY
Ithaca, N.Y.
DELAWARE ART MUSEUM
Wilmington, Del.
DICK, JOHN HENRY
Meggett, S.C.
DUKE UNIVERSITY
Durham, N.C.
ENOCH PRATT FREE LIBRARY
George Peabody Branch
Baltimore, Md.
EVANS, MRS. DANIEL W.
Merrie Hill Farm
Cobham, Va.
FIELD MUSEUM OF NATURAL HISTORY
Chicago, Ill.
FREE LIBRARY OF NEW BEDFORD
New Bedford, Mass.
THE GROTON SCHOOL
Groton, Mass.
HARVARD UNIVERSITY
Houghton Library
Cambridge, Mass.
HARVARD UNIVERSITY
Widener Library
Cambridge, Mass.
HENRY E. HUNTINGTON LIBRARY AND ART
GALLERY
San Marino, Calif.
INDIANA HISTORICAL SOCIETY
The William Henry Smith Memorial
Library
Indianapolis, Ind.
INDIANA UNIVERSITY
Lilly Library
Bloomington, Ind.
JAMES J. HILL REFERENCE LIBRARY
St. Paul, Minn.
JOHN CRERAR LIBRARY
Chicago, Ill.
JOHNS HOPKINS UNIVERSITY
The Evergreen House Foundation
Baltimore, Md.
JOHNSON, MRS. GRACE PHILLIPS, ESTATE OF
New Castle, Pa.

LAVAL UNIVERSITÉ
Quebec, Que., Canada
LEGISLATIVE LIBRARY
Fredericton, N.B., Canada
LEHIGH UNIVERSITY
Bethlehem, Pa.
LIBRARY ASSOCIATION OF PORTLAND
Portland, Ore.
LIBRARY OF CONGRESS
Washington, D.C.
LIBRARY OF CONGRESS
Washington, D.C.
War Department copy
LIBRARY OF PARLIAMENT
Ottawa, Ont., Canada
LOUISIANA STATE MUSEUM
New Orleans, La.
LOUISIANA STATE UNIVERSITY
Baton Rouge, La.
MARTIN, H. BRADLEY
New York, N.Y.
McGILL UNIVERSITY
Montreal, Que., Canada
MELLON, PAUL
Upperville, Va.
MILWAUKEE PUBLIC LIBRARY
The Charles Allis Art Library
Division of Art and Music
Milwaukee, Wis.
MINNEAPOLIS ATHENAEUM
Minneapolis, Minn.
MITCHELL WOLFSON FOUNDATION, INC.
The Audubon House
Key West, Fla.
MUSEUM OF FINE ARTS
Boston, Mass.
NATIONAL AUDUBON SOCIETY
New York, N.Y.
NATIONAL GALLERY OF ART
Washington, D.C.
NEW-YORK HISTORICAL SOCIETY
New York, N.Y.
NEW YORK PUBLIC LIBRARY
New York, N.Y.
Tilden set.
NEW YORK PUBLIC LIBRARY
New York, N.Y.
Lenox set.

NEW YORK PUBLIC LIBRARY
New York, N.Y.
Stuart set.

NEW YORK PUBLIC LIBRARY
New York, N.Y.
Provenance unknown.

NEW YORK SOCIETY LIBRARY
New York, N.Y.

NORTH CAROLINA STATE LIBRARY
Raleigh, N.C.

NORTHWESTERN UNIVERSITY
Evanston, Ill.

NORTON, RICHARD W., ART GALLERY
Shreveport, La.

PEABODY INSTITUTE
Eben Dale Sutton Reference Library
Peabody, Mass.

PEABODY MUSEUM
Salem, Mass.

PECK, MISS CLARA
New York, N.Y.

PFLAUMER, ARTHUR E.
Haverford, Pa.

PHILLIPS, RAWLSTON D., JR.
Baton Rouge, La.

PHILLIPS ACADEMY
Oliver Wendell Holmes Library
Andover, Mass.

PIERPONT MORGAN LIBRARY
New York, N.Y.

PRINCETON UNIVERSITY
Princeton, N.J.

PROVIDENCE ATHENAEUM
Providence, R.I.

THE PUBLIC LIBRARY OF CINCINNATI AND HAMILTON COUNTY
Cincinnati, Ohio

REED, JOSEPH VERNER
Greenwich, Conn.

ST. LOUIS MERCANTILE LIBRARY ASSOCIATION
St. Louis, Mo.

SMITHSONIAN INSTITUTION
Washington, D.C.
The Smithsonian has a set on loan from the National Academy of Sciences of the United States of America.

STARK (H. J. LUTCHER) FOUNDATION
Orange, Texas

STATE LIBRARY
Annapolis, Md.

SYRACUSE UNIVERSITY
Syracuse, N.Y.

TORONTO PUBLIC LIBRARY
Toronto, Ont., Canada

TRINITY COLLEGE
Hartford, Conn.

UNION COLLEGE
Schaffer Library
Schenectady, N.Y.

UNIVERSITY OF ILLINOIS
Urbana, Ill.

UNIVERSITY OF MICHIGAN
Ann Arbor, Mich.

UNIVERSITY OF MINNESOTA
Minneapolis, Minn.

UNIVERSITY OF PENNSYLVANIA
Philadelphia, Pa.

UNIVERSITY OF PITTSBURGH
The Darlington Memorial Library
Pittsburgh, Pa.

UNIVERSITY OF SOUTH CAROLINA
McKissick Memorial Library
Columbia, S.C.

UNIVERSITY OF SOUTHERN CALIFORNIA
Hancock Library of Biology and Oceanography
Los Angeles, Calif.

UNIVERSITY OF WISCONSIN
The Memorial Library
Madison, Wis.

VASSAR COLLEGE
Poughkeepsie, N.Y.

WILLIAMS COLLEGE
Chapin Library
Williamstown, Mass.

YALE UNIVERSITY
New Haven, Conn.
Art Gallery copy

YALE UNIVERSITY
New Haven, Conn.
Henry Farnum copy

Complete and Incomplete Sets

AUSTRALIA

THE STATE LIBRARY OF VICTORIA
  Melbourne

ENGLAND AND SCOTLAND

BIRMINGHAM PUBLIC LIBRARIES
  Reference Library
  Birmingham, England
BRITISH MUSEUM
  Natural History
  London, England
    Set #1 (from the British Museum in Bloomsbury)
BRITISH MUSEUM
  Natural History
  London, England
    Set #2 (Bequest of Baron Rothschild)
BRITISH MUSEUM
  Reading Room
  London, England
    Bequest of General Hardwicke
CAMBRIDGE UNIVERSITY
  Fitzwilliam Museum
  Cambridge, England
CAMBRIDGE UNIVERSITY
  University Library
  Cambridge, England
CRAWFORD, EARL OF
  Colinsburgh, Fife, Scotland
DEVONSHIRE, DUKE OF
  Chatsworth, Bakewell, England
FANE, MRS. BARBARA
  London, England
FITZWILLIAM, THE HONOURABLE LORD
  Milton, Peterborough, England
GLASGOW, THE COLLEGE OF
  Glasgow University Library
  Glasgow, Scotland

HESKETH, THE HONOURABLE LORD
  Easton Neston
  Towcester, England
THE JOHN RYLANDS LIBRARY
  Manchester, England
LIVERPOOL PUBLIC LIBRARIES
  Picton Reference Library
  Liverpool, England
THE MITCHELL LIBRARY
  Glasgow Corporation Public Libraries
  Glasgow, Scotland
OXFORD UNIVERSITY
  Christ Church Library
  Oxford, England
OXFORD UNIVERSITY
  Radcliffe Science Library
  Oxford, England
PAISLEY PUBLIC LIBRARY
  Corporation, of Paisley, Scotland
PORTLAND, DUKE OF
  Welbeck Abbey, Workshop
  Nottingham, England
ROYAL LIBRARY
  Windsor Castle
  Windsor, England
UNIVERSITY OF EDINBURGH
  Old College
  Edinburgh, Scotland
VICTORIA AND ALBERT MUSEUM
  South Kensington, England

DENMARK

UNIVERSITY OF COPENHAGEN
  Scientific Library
  Copenhagen

DEUTSCHE DEMOKRATISCHE REPUBLIK

STAATLICHE MUSEEN
  Natural Science Department
  Meiningen (Thuringia)
    In this set the following plates are missing:
    106, 131–35, and 166–70.

FRANCE

BIBLIOTHÈQUE DE L'INSTITUT DE FRANCE
  Paris

MUSÉUM NATIONAL
  D'HISTOIRE NATURELLE
  Bibliothèque Centrale
  Paris

IRELAND

GALVIN, JOHN
  Loughlinstown House
  Co. Dublin

ITALY

BIBLIOTECA NAZIONALE CENTRALE
  Florence

THE NETHERLANDS

BIBLIOTHEEK VAN TEYLER'S STICHTING
  Haarlem

NORTHERN IRELAND

CALEDON, 6th EARL
  Caledon Castle
  Caledon, Tyrone

PORTUGAL

BIBLIOTECA NAÇIONAL DE LISBÕA
  Lisbon

UNION OF SOVIET SOCIALIST REPUBLICS

DARWIN MUSEUM
  Moscow
STATE LIBRARY
  Leningrad

ZOOLOGICAL INSTITUTE
  Academy of Sciences
  Leningrad

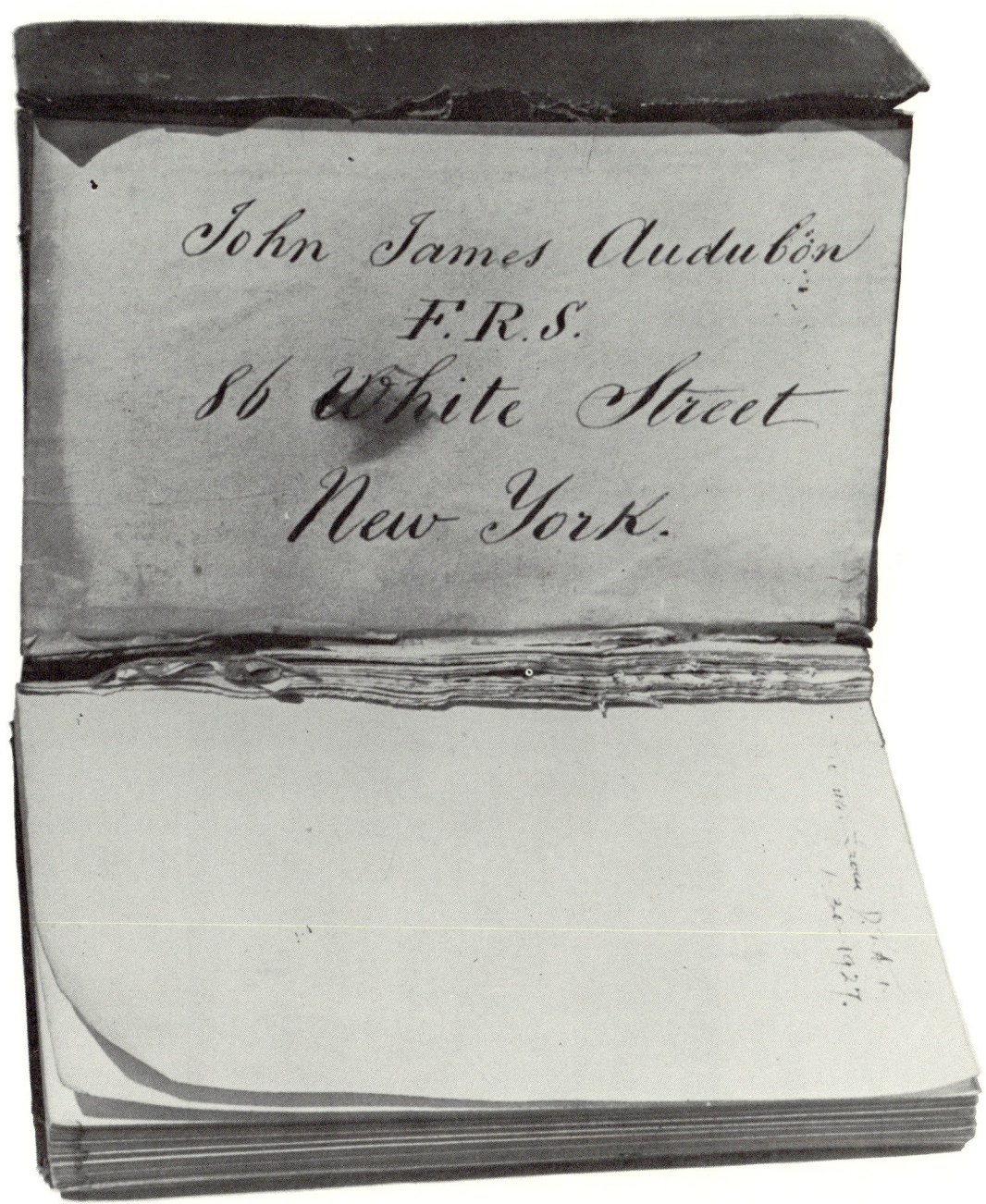

Audubon's folder of subscribers' names for which pages have been torn. Courtesy of the Audubon State Park Museum, Henderson, Ky.

1 His Most Gracious Majesty George IV
1 Her Royal Highness the Lady Clarence
1 The Marquis of Londonderry
1 His Grace the Duke of Rutland
1 S. A. R. le Duc d'Orleans
1 His Christian Majesty Charles X
1 S. A. R. Mademoiselle d'Orleans

1 The Library of the Congress of
the United States of America, by Edward

1 [illegible]
1 [illegible]
1 [illegible] Potter, Baltimore [illegible]
1 John B. Morris Baltimore
1 Isabella [illegible] Hartford

1 H. R. H. Princess Elizabeth [illegible]
1 Richard Harlan M.D. Philadelphia
1 Edward Harris Esqre Philadelphia
1 [illegible]
1 J. Vaughan Librarian of American Philos. Society
1 R. Harlan M.D. for the Philadelphia Academy of Natural Sciences
1 [illegible] Buchanan Esq. London
1 [illegible]
1 Thos Butler King Esq. [illegible] Georgia
  M. Pickens Boston One Copy
1 Saml Appleton Boston One Copy
1 J. P. Cushing Boston One Copy
1 Gulian [illegible] New Orleans
  Geo. C. Shattuck Boston One Copy
1 [illegible] Boston One Copy
  James Brown West Cambridge One Copy
  [illegible] Boston One Copy
  Gentleman of Boston one Copy [illegible]

1 The Countess of Morton [illegible] Portland [illegible]
1 The University of Edinburgh
1 The Wernerian Society of Edinburgh
1 The Advocates Library [illegible]
1 The Society of Writers to his Majesty's Signet Edinburgh
1 P. I. Selby Esqre of Twizel Northumberland
1 Sir Wm Jardine Baronet of Jardine Hall
1 James Wilson Esqre Edinburgh
1 John Syme Esqre [illegible]
1 D. W. Witham Esqre to be [illegible]
1 Revd John Brown [illegible]
5 Daniel Lizars Bookseller Edinburgh
1 Wm M. M'Lelan Esqre Mount [illegible] Dunkeld
  Stacy Esqre of Aldenton
1 Henry Witham Esqre [illegible]
1 Lieutenant General Graham Stirling Castle
1 Jeff Harris Dunlop of New York [illegible]
1 [illegible]
1 Mr. [illegible]
1 Mrs John Potter Liverpool
1 John [illegible] M.D. [illegible]
1 Doctor Bickersteth Liverpool [illegible]
1 Mathew Burrell Esqre of Broompark Alnwick
1 Thomas Forster Esqre Addenton [illegible] Belford
1 Reverend A. Sharpe Bamburgh Belford [illegible]

Opposite, the upper portion of a glass-framed list of subscribers, Panel I (front). Above is the lower part of the same list. The list appears in full in chapter 18. Courtesy of the Academy of National Sciences of Philadelphia and of John Verner Reed, Greenwich, Conn.

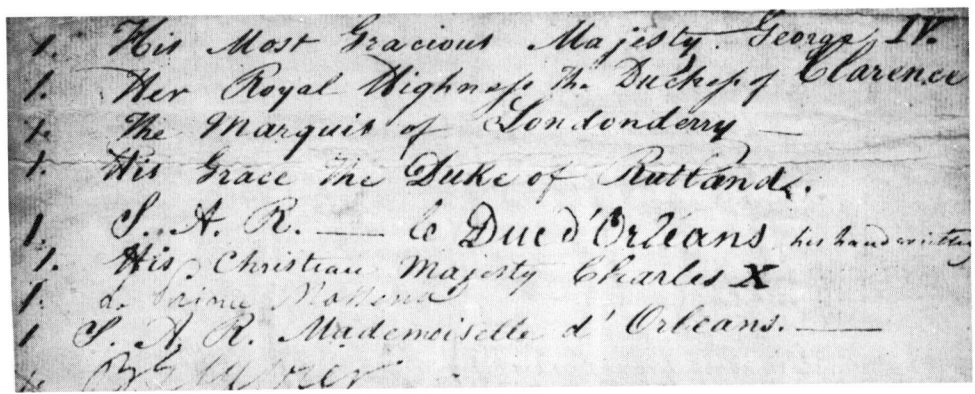

Detail of Panel I, showing inter alia the signature "S. A. R.—le Duc d'Orleans." Audubon's note "his handwriting" is clearly visible. Courtesy of Academy of National Sciences of Philadelphia and of John Verner Reed, Greenwich, Conn.

Detail of Panel I, showing the subscription of the Library of Congress, signed for by Edward Everett. Courtesy of the Academy of National Sciences of Philadelphia and of John Verner Reed, Greenwich, Conn.

THE BIRDS OF AMERICA,

FROM

DRAWINGS MADE IN THE UNITED STATES

AND THEIR TERRITORIES.

BY JOHN JAMES AUDUBON, F. R. SS. L. & E.

FELLOW OF THE LINNEAN AND ZOOLOGICAL SOCIETIES OF LONDON, MEMBER OF THE LYCEUM OF NEW YORK, OF THE NATURAL HISTORY SOCIETY OF PARIS, THE WERNERIAN NATURAL HISTORY SOCIETY OF EDINBURGH, HONORARY MEMBER OF THE SOCIETY OF NATURAL HISTORY OF MANCHESTER, AND OF THE ROYAL SCOTTISH ACADEMY OF PAINTING, SCULPTURE, AND ARCHITECTURE; MEMBER OF THE AMERICAN PHILOSOPHICAL SOCIETY, OF THE ACADEMY OF NATURAL SCIENCES AT PHILADELPHIA, OF THE NATURAL HISTORY SOCIETIES OF BOSTON, OF CHARLESTON IN SOUTH CAROLINA, THE QUEBEC LITERARY AND HISTORICAL SOCIETY, THE ORNITHOLOGICAL SOCIETY OF LONDON, THE SOCIÉTÉ FRANÇAISE DE STATISTIQUE UNIVERSELLE DE PARIS, &c. &c.

PROSPECTUS.

To those who have not seen any portion of Mr. Audubon's collection of Original Drawings, it may be proper to state, that their superiority consists in the accuracy as to proportion and outline, and the variety and truth of the attitudes and positions of the figures, resulting from peculiar means discovered and employed by him, and his attentive examination of the objects portrayed, during a long series of years. Mr. AUDUBON has not contented himself with single profile views, but in many instances has grouped his figures, so as to represent the originals at their natural avocations, and has placed them on branches of trees decorated with foliage, blossoms and fruits, or amidst plants of numerous species—some are seen pursuing their prey through the air, searching for food amongst the leaves and herbage, sitting on their nests, or feeding their young; whilst others, of a different nature, swim, wade, or glide in or over their allotted element. The insects, reptiles and fishes that form the food of some of the birds, have now and then been introduced in the drawings. In nearly every instance where a difference of plumage exists between the sexes, both male and female have been represented, and the extraordinary changes which some species undergo in their progress from youth to maturity, have been depicted.

The Plants are all copied from nature, and as many are remarkable for their beauty, their usefulness, or their rarity, the Botanist cannot fail to look upon them with delight.

The particulars of the plan of the work may be reduced to the following heads:

1. The size of the work is royal octavo, the paper being of the finest quality.
2. The Plates representing the Birds are correctly reduced from the original drawings, and are coloured in the most careful manner.
3. The work will appear in numbers, on the first and fifteenth of every month.
4. Each number will consist of Five Plates, accompanied with full descriptions of the habits and localities of the birds, their anatomy and digestive organs, (with occasionally wood cuts representing the latter,) and will be furnished to subscribers for one dollar, payable on delivery.
5. The work will be published in accordance with a scientific arrangement of the genera and species, and will complete the Ornithology of our country, it is believed, in the most perfect manner.

Persons desirous of subscribing to the above work are respectfully requested to apply to J. J. AUDUBON, 86 White street, or W. A. COLMAN, Broadway, New York, or to J. B. CHEVALIER, 72 Dock street, Philadelphia.

Prospectus for the Octavo edition showing sheets that have been torn from it. Courtesy of the Audubon State Park Museum, Henderson, Ky.

Display of individual prints from *Birds of America* at the Shelburne Museum. Courtesy of Shelburne Museum, Inc., Shelburne, Vermont 05482.

Display of individual prints from *Birds of America* at Manoir Richelieu. The collection of prints is now in the Public Archives of Canada, Ottawa. Courtesy of Manoir Richelieu, Murray Bay, Quebec.

PRICES *of* AUDUBON PRINTS
1827-38 EDITION
Elephant Folio

1	The Wild Turkey	224.00
2	Yellow-billed Cuckoo	10.89
3	Prothonotary Warbler	8.94
4	Purple Finch	14.89
5	Bonaparte's Fly Catcher	4.96
6	Great American Hen and Young	104.00
7	Purple Grackle	14.89
8	White throated Sparrow	10.89
9	Selby's Flycatcher	4.96
10	Brown Lark	4.96
11	Bird of Washington	34.50
12	Baltimore Oriole	24.89
13	Snow Bird	6.94
14	Prairie Warbler	6.94
15	Blue Yellow backed Warbler	6.94
16	Great-footed Hawk	24.89
17	Carolina Turtle Dove	29.75
18	Bewick's Wren	8.94
19	Louisiana Water Thrush	4.96
20	Blue-Winged Yellow Warbler	10.89
21	Mocking Bird (with Rattlesnake)	29.75
22	Purple Martin. Nest, Gourd	10.89
23	Yellow-breasted Warbler	8.94
24	Roscoe's Yellow Throat	4.96
25	Song Sparrow	14.89
26	Carolina Parrot	34.50
27	Red headed Woodpecker	17.89
28	Solitary Vireo	4.96
29	Towhe Bunting	17.89
30	Vigors' Warbler	4.96
31	White-Headed Eagle (with Yellow Cat-fish)	34.50
32	Black-billed Cuckoo	17.89
33	Yellow Bird or American Goldfinch	14.89
34	Worm-eating Warbler	8.94
35	Children's Warbler	6.94
36	Stanley Hawk	19.89
37	Golden-winged Woodpecker	34.50
38	Kentucky Warbler	10.89

Prices of Audubon prints offered by Macy Galleries in May 1931. Courtesy of Macy Galleries, New York.

The Double Elephant folio saved from the ruins of a fire that destroyed the New York State Library on 29 March 1911. The photograph is taken from the 14th Annual Report of the Library. Courtesy of the New York State Library, Albany.

Complete and Incomplete Sets

INCOMPLETE SETS: UNITED STATES

BAKEWELL, MRS. DONALD
Sewickley, Pa.

Volume 1. This probably belonged to Thomas Woodhouse Bakewell, brother of Lucy Audubon. It has been handed down in the Bakewell family.

BOSTON PUBLIC LIBRARY
Boston, Mass.

Volume 1, loose prints.

BUFFALO AND ERIE COUNTY PUBLIC LIBRARY
Buffalo, N.Y.

Volumes 1, 2, and 3; these were originally purchased by The Young Men's Association which merged with the Buffalo Public Library.

DARTMOUTH COLLEGE LIBRARY
Hanover, N.H.

Volumes 1, 2, and 3, the original Daniel Webster subscription (*See* Dartmouth College entry in chap. 26).[1]

HARVARD UNIVERSITY
Houghton Library
Cambridge, Mass.

Volumes 1 and 2. These volumes of the Audubon folio were presented to the University 14 March 1904 by the following:

An Anonymous Friend
William Brewster
Arthur F. Estabrook
Francis H. Peabody
Louis Cabot
Augustus Hemenway
Dudley L. Pickman
John Eliot Thayer.

The folio had been sold at auction on 18 June 1903 by Sotheby, Wilkinson & Hodge, London, for £51 ($255); the purchaser was listed as "Stevens."[2]

LOUISIANA STATE UNIVERSITY
Baton Rouge, La.

Volume 1. This volume of the *Birds of America* appeared in the catalog of Charles W. Traylen, 49–50 Quarry St., Guilford, England, no.62, item #41, where it is described as follows:

Volume 1 of the ORIGINAL EDITION, containing 100 most beautiful colored aquatint-plates of the birds in their natural size, elephant folio, full brown calf, old rebacking, loose in case and binding, rubbed *London*, 1827–1830. £6,000 ($16,800).

This volume had been purchased by Traylen from Messrs Sotheby's in London and it is believed to be Lord Onslow's copy from Clandon Park, Surrey.[3]

STARK (H. J. LUTCHER) FOUNDATION
Orange, Texas

Volume 1, The Bachman Copy (gift of Audubon to John Bachman).

In a letter written to Audubon, who was then at St. Augustine, Fla., by the Rev. John Bachman on 31 December 1831 from Charleston is the following: "My sister Maria, paints birds better every day; she fails only in setting them up. Your book, however, will soon be here, and she will study the attitudes of your birds."

A footnote applying to "book" states, "The book alluded to is the First Volume of 'Audubon's Birds of America.' This valuable gift, bound in fine Russian leather, is still in the possession of the Bachman family. It was the first impression struck from the copper plates, and is peculiarly clear-cut. It was Audubon's traveling companion through England and France, when George IV, and Charles X, placed their names at the head of his subscription list, on which occasion Cuvier pronounced Audubon's drawings, 'the most splendid monument which art had yet erected in honor of ornithology.' It was no wonder that the admiration of appreciative friends kindled into enthusiasm."[4]

The above statement is not based on the facts. It so happens that the completion of the engraving of the first one hundred plates contained in Volume 1 of the *Birds of America* did not occur until the fall of 1830.[5] Audubon's visit to Paris took place in 1828 and the subscription of Charles X was obtained on 26 October of that year, while that of George IV came to him on 27 September of the previous year.[6]

Before Audubon sailed for America in August 1831 he had arranged with his engraver to have shipped to him a number of copies of the first one hundred prints bound.[7] Thus when the American subscriptions were obtained it was in many instances possible to provide the subscribers with a bound copy of the first 100 prints.[8]

The word "book" as used by Bachman refers to one of these volumes being sent at the time to those Charleston residents whose subscription had been obtained after Audubon had visited the city in October and when the two had first met. It could very easily have been the bound copy of Volume 1 which Audubon had sent shortly before 13 November to Professor Gibbs at Columbia College (Univ. of South Carolina) where he hoped to obtain a subscription.[9]

The volume for the Bachman family regarding which Audubon was to write "I beg you to accept it from your old friend in part atonement for the troubles I have given you and the leatherings which you may receive at my hands at Chess!!!" reached Charleston in March 1834.[10]

The "superb book" (full calf binding over paper board, gilt edged, gold tooled on edges of cover, about ¾" in width) remained with the Bachman family until 1884 when it was purchased by Robert J. Hubbard of Cazenovia, N.Y.[11] The volume remained in the Hubbard family for three generations and was given to the Cazenovia Public Library by Mr. Hubbard's grandchildren with the right to sell should the library so desire.[12] In 1963 it was purchased by Mr. Stark.

TULANE UNIVERSITY
Howard-Tilton Memorial Library
New Orleans, La.
Volumes 1, 2, and 3.

AUSTRALIA

NATIONAL MUSEUM OF VICTORIA
Melbourne
Volumes 1 and 2.

ENGLAND AND SCOTLAND

HIS GRACE, THE DUKE OF BEDFORD
(13th Duke of Bedford,
John Robert Russell, 1917–   )
Woburn Abbey, Bletchley, England
Volume 1.

ROYAL FACULTY OF PHYSICIANS AND
SURGEONS
Glasgow, Scotland
Volumes 1 and 2.

UNIVERSITY OF ABERDEEN
Marischal College
Aberdeen, Scotland
Volume 2.

Complete and Incomplete Sets

FRANCE

Bibliothèque Nationale
Départment des Estampes
Paris
  Volumes 1 and 2.

POLAND

Institute of Zoology
Academy of Science
Warsaw

Volume 4. It is of interest to note that Volume 4 of the *Birds of America* at the Institute of Zoology, Academy of Science, in Warsaw, is accompanied by the first four volumes of the *Ornithological Biography*, while the fifth volume is missing.

Also, the one volume of the *Birds of America* and the four volumes of the *Ornithological Biography* are similarly bound in half morocco or stamped calf, gold only on the spine and with a crown above two interwoven letters on top. At the bottom of the spine on both the volume of the *Birds of America* and the four volumes of the *Ornithological Biography* is found "SIMIER. R. DU ROI" in gold capitals. These have the same type of mottled paper observed in the two volumes of the folio at the Bibliothèque Nationale, Départment des Estampes in Paris.

Finally the circular stamp of "Bibliothèque du Roi—Palais Royal" appears in both Volume 4 of the *Birds of America* and in the four volumes of the *Ornithological Biography*.

COLLECTIONS OF INDIVIDUAL AND LOOSE PRINTS

Amon Carter Museum of Western Art
Fort Worth, Tex.

21 prints. Among these are fifteen prints, probably the first to have been sent to America. These fifteen prints Audubon had originally sent to his friend Charles Lucien Bonaparte in America on 1 December 1827. The prints had been mislaid in the New York Customs House and came into possession of William Cooper, Bonaparte's friend, one of the founders of the Lyceum of Natural History of New York and editor of the last two volumes of Bonaparte's *American Ornithology*. They remained in the possession of the Cooper family until sold to a New York print dealer who then sold them to the museum.

Audubon State Park
Henderson, Ky.
  122 prints.

Bonbright, James C. H.
Washington, D.C.
  130 prints.

Brown University
Providence, R.I.
  16 prints—Koopman Collection.

Case-Western Reserve University
Cleveland, Ohio
  229 prints.

Colorado Springs Fine Arts Center
Taylor Museum
Colorado Springs, Colo.
  160 prints.

Currier Gallery of Art
192 Orange St.
Manchester, N.H.
  28 prints.

GEORGIA MUSEUM OF ART
   University of Georgia
   Athens, Ga.
   12 prints.

GIBSON, MR. & MRS. FRANK R.
   Lake Charles, La.
   42 prints.

THE HENRY FRANCIS DU PONT
WINTERTHUR MUSEUM
   Winterthur, Del.
   258 prints (10 duplicates).

JURIEV, DR. K. B.
   Leningrad, USSR
   175 prints. The original subscriber to this collection of prints was Henry G. Bohn of London.

LENOX LIBRARY ASSOCIATES
   Lenox, Mass.
   55 prints.

MCCOY, DR. WALTER C.
   Birmingham, Ala.
   30 prints.

MARCH, DAVID H.
   Salisbury, Conn.
   223 prints.

THE MORTON ARBORETUM
   Lisle, Ill.
   13 prints.

NEW YORK PUBLIC LIBRARY
   New York, N.Y.
   75 prints (in a volume).

OBERLIN COLLEGE
   Oberlin, Ohio
   80 prints.

PUBLIC ARCHIVES OF CANADA
   Ottawa, Canada
   181 prints. In 1970, 191 prints were purchased from Manoir Richelieu (Murray Bay, Que.). Ten of them were sold at auction 29 April 1971.

ROYAL SCOTTISH MUSEUM
   Edinburgh, Scotland
   At present the museum has a bound volume containing 29 plates, Numbers 2–30, of Audubon's *Birds of America*. There is no evidence that Plate 1 was ever included. The provenance of this volume has not been ascertained.
   In addition, in 1966 when the museum officials were asked to clear out the old museum of the Free Church College of the Church of Scotland, the museum acquired a tightly rolled bundle of what turned out to be 16 Audubon prints. Again, it has not been possible to determine how and when these prints came to the Free College.[13]

SHELBURNE MUSEUM
   Shelburne, Vt.
   60 prints.

WEEKS, MANGUM
   Alexandria, Va.
   112 prints.

YOUNG, JOSEPH RUTLEDGE
   Charleston, S.C.
   In July 1970, when the premises at 28 Broad Street, Charleston, S.C., were being renovated and restored, a well-hidden closet was uncovered. Among other old books and papers covered with years of dust was found the first volume of the Double Elephant Folio of Audubon's *Birds of America*. The title page was missing and print no. 1, that of the Wild Turkey, as well as others had been "yanked" out of the book. The remaining 65 prints, although stained at the bottom, are in good condition.
   The building has been in the possession of the family of the present owner, Joseph Rutledge Young, for many years and it is believed that the volume may have been placed in the closet for safekeeping during the Civil War. The original owner of the volume of 100 prints has not been determined.[14]

21

SETS BROKEN UP OR DESTROYED

SETS BROKEN UP

ABERCROMBIE & FITCH CO.
New York, N.Y.

A set of the folio was purchased for $11,700 at the George D. Smith sale in April 1939 and was subsequently broken up. *Antiques* (36(3): 138 [Sept. 1939]) carried the following account of the Abercrombie & Fitch sale of the prints: "Prices cover a wide range up to $900 for the famous Wild Turkey. In 1935 a set brought $5,750 and in 1939 it brought $11,700 (the price paid by Abercrombie & Fitch on 11 April 1939 at Parke-Bernet). Abercrombie & Fitch confidently expect to realize nearly ten times that amount."

AMERICAN ACADEMY OF ARTS AND LETTERS
New York, N.Y.

It is believed that this set was originally owned by Collis P. Huntington, then, in turn by his son Archer Milton, who gave it to the academy. It was sold at the Parke-Bernet Auction Galleries in May 1966 and purchased by the New York rare bookdealer, J. N. Bartfield. Later it was sold to a Baton Rouge, La., interior decorator who broke up the folio, selling the individual prints.

BARRETT, MRS. THOMAS
Augusta, Ga.

In August 1958 Mrs. Thomas Barrett of Augusta, Ga., advised the author as follows: "I once had two complete Elephant Folios, Havell & Lizars sets of Audubon. I bought them in Atlanta from a 2nd hand bookdealer. I gave my sister-in-law 10 plates in one book. All the others sold as pictures & cut out. I only have one Elephant Folio Binder, no plates."[1] It was further learned that Mrs. Barrett had paid $5,000 for each set of the folio.[2]

BUCCLEUCH, DUKE OF
Dalkeith Castle, Edinburgh, Scotland

This is #70 on Audubon's list of European Subscribers (vol. 5 of the *Ornithological Biographies*, p.647-51). The folio was purchased in 1941 by the Old Print Shop of New York and broken up. With the purchase of each print there was given a certificate certifying that the print was from the set originally subscribed for by the Duke of Buccleuch.

The Old Print Shop advertised this sale in *The Art Digest* 16(3):15 (1 Nov. 1941), as follows: "offering separately the prints from the original Elephant folio . . . the magnificent set of the Duke of Buccleuch from Dalkeith Castle, Edinburgh."

COLEMAN, GEORGE DAWSON
Lebanon, Pa.

Folio broken up by Old Print Shop which had obtained it through the Philadelphia dealer, Charles Sessler, Inc.[3]

EARL OF DERBY
London, England

The folio of "The Right Honourable the Earl of Derby, P.Z.S. (President of the Zoological Society), &c.&c.&c.," European subscriber, no.30 (*see* List of Subscribers, v.5, *Ornithological Biography*, p.647–51), was sold by a London dealer to an interior decorator in Baton Rouge, La. This set was said to have contained only four hundred prints.

DONNELL, JOHN J.
Baltimore, Md.

Only one volume of the folio was involved in this instance. The subscription was recorded by Audubon among others in "Subscribers to 'Birds of America' Obtained Since the Publication of the First Volume," included in Volume 2 of the *Ornithological Biography*.[4] However, Donnell did not complete his subscription. Although the first volume was delivered and paid for in June 1834,[5] the second was returned in 1837.[6] Volume 1 of the *Birds of America* was inherited by the mother of J. Donnell Tilghman. She sold it to a New York dealer who broke it up for the individual prints.[7]

FIELD MUSEUM OF NATURAL HISTORY
Chicago, Ill.

When, in 1970, the Field Museum of Natural History acquired the Euphemia Gifford set of the folio, its earlier set, which had been presented to the museum by Mr. Edward E. Ayre and later mutilated by the theft of prints, was acquired by a Chicago rare book dealer who sold the remaining prints to the public.

According to the historical preface to the *Catalogue of the Edward E. Ayre Ornithological Library*, written by Wilfred H. Osgood, then Curator of Zoology of the Field Museum of Natural History: "In the early eighties, one of Mr. Ayre's (1841–1927) recreations was duck shooting in the Mississippi Valley and no season passed without seeing him in the field, not only near home but elsewhere, from Minnesota to southern Illinois. This brought his attention to birds more especially than formerly and he began buying a few of the more important books about them. These included Audubon's 'Birds of America' and other large illustrated works which were added from time to time until he had in his home a considerable collection of choice ornithological books."

Dr. Osgood's preface states further that, "After the World's Columbian Exposition in 1893, Mr. Ayre was the leader of the small group of far-seeing men who took an active part in founding the Field Museum. In fact, he became the first president of its board of trustees, and, although he retired from this heavily responsible office in 1899, he continued to serve with unceasing interest in the welfare of the Museum, as a member of the board until the present time (1926). Among the first acts, after the organization of the Museum, was the presentation to it of his library of ornithological books. Thereafter he provided funds for additions to it, especially in the purchase of books sumptuously bound and profusely illustrated with colored plates."[8]

The *Birds of America* was accessioned by the museum on 1 December 1900.[9] It has not been possible to ascertain where Mr. Ayre obtained the set of the folio. The four volumes were listed in the *Catalogue of the Edward E. Ayre Ornithological Library*.[10]

In the early 1930s one hundred and ninety-two plates were extracted from the four volumes and are missing. In addition many of the remaining 243 plates have been cut along the inner edges and are loose in the bindings. The stolen plates bore the Museum's perforated stamp of ownership.[11]

GATES, THOMAS
Philadelphia, Pa.

The folio was originally sold to Gates by Kennedy Galleries of New York. It was then purchased by Richard Van Hoosear who sold it to Sessler's of Philadelphia, who sold it to the Old Print Shop in New York, where it was broken up.[12]

HARVARD UNIVERSITY
Cambridge, Mass.

An entry in the accession list of the Library at the Museum of Comparative Zoology, Harvard University, shows that Audubon's four volumes of the elephant folio, and five volumes of his *Ornithological Biography* were presented to the Library by J. C. Phillips. A note added later in the margin of the entry reads: "Elephant folio vols. sold." The sale was actually made in 1939 to the firm of Hamill & Barker of Chicago, who broke up the set.

HORNBLOWER, RALPH

On 2 July 1958, the author was advised by Mr. Hornblower as follows: "I bought my Audubon set from Charles E. Lauriat Co., kept it several years and sold it." "Sale apparently consummated in August 1936."

In May 1968, the author was advised by the Rare Book department of Scribners that the folio had been sold in September 1938 to R. H. Macy & Co., who broke it up.

ITHACA PUBLIC LIBRARY
Ithaca, N.Y.

The folio was purchased by Ezra Cornell (for the Library) in 1865 at the sale of books of John Taylor of Albany, N.Y. The purchase price was $1075. In the archives of Cornell University is a long letter written to Mary Ann Cornell, his wife, immediately after the auction in which Cornell relates the details of the sale. At a meeting of the Trustees of the Ithaca Library held on 6 June 1944, the sale of the folios was authorized, the purchaser being the Old Print Shop of New York, for $14,000. The folio was broken up.

KING, JAMES G.
New York, N.Y.

A letter dated 19 April 1963, from the Old Print Shop, New York, states "We broke up the King set in 1941, 22 years ago. King was an original subscriber." *See* v.5, *Ornithological Biography*, p.647-51.

LEIBOLD, MRS. CARL PETER
Birmingham, Ala.

In 1941 Mrs. Leibold purchased from a Philadelphia dealer, Campion & Co., a set of the folio which she broke up, selling the individual prints in many southern cities of the United States.

MACCOY, W. LOGAN
Philadelphia, Pa.

Mrs. W. Logan MacCoy of Haverford, Pa., believed the folio to have belonged to her grandfather Wistar Morris. It was purchased by Charles Sessler, Inc., of Philadelphia and broken up.

MACY, R. H.
New York, N.Y.

In a period from 1931 to 1935 this firm purchased either four or five complete sets of the Audubon double elephant folio of the *Birds of America* which were broken up and the prints sold to the public.[13]

MERCANTILE LIBRARY
New York, N.Y.

One of the sets purchased from Audubon in New York after the completion of the engraving of the prints, it was broken up in 1939 by Harold Potter who operated the Old Print Exchange at 13 East 48th Street in New York.

When the folio of the Association was sold, the purchaser found in the volumes a "Bookplate, printed on silk" which reads in part as follows: "Presented to The Mercantile Literary Association by a number of its Members and Friends. The funds appropriated to the purchase of this work have been raised as follows: A *Subscription* in which the amount to be given by each subscriber was limited to fifty cents, was commenced in 1840. At the annual meeting in 1841, it was reported that the sum raised by this subscription amounted to One Hundred and Twenty Five Dollars.

"Another *Subscription* was subsequently started at a meeting of Members of the Association which resulted in the collection of the sum required for the purchase. The work is accordingly placed in the library this Fourth Day of March, Eighteen Hundred and Forty One."[14]

PERRY, WILLIAM
Boston, Mass.

A set purchased by Perry from Rosenbach, the rare book dealer, was sold by him to Weyhe Galleries of New York and broken up. It has not been possible to determine exact date of the latter transaction but it probably took place in the late 1930s or early 1940s. Rosenbach had purchased the folio in the 1930s from the Coates family of Paisley, Scotland. The story of the original purchase of the folio is to be found in the "Personal Reminiscences of Audubon" by Andrew Coates, published in the *Proceedings of the Perthshire Society of Natural Sciences*, v.2, p.xxiv-xxvi, 8 March 1894.

SALEM ATHENAEUM
Salem, Mass.

In 1838 ten proprietors united in subscribing to the *Birds of America* for the Salem Athenaeum. On 10 May 1923, the folio was sold to Charles Goodspeed of Boston and broken up. This was no.12 on the list of original American subscribers.[15]

SHATTUCK, GEORGE C.
Boston, Mass.

This was set No.46 on the original list of American subscribers.[16] It was sold by the Shattuck family to the Long Island seedman, George L. Child. After Child's death it was purchased at an auction held 26–27 March 1923 by the Brick Row Book Shop for $4,000 and resold to James Cox Brady of New York. In the 1940s Brady's widow sold the folio through A. G. Baker & Co. to Charles Scribner's Sons. The set was broken up and sold.

SHEPARD, MRS. HELEN GOULD

The set, originally the property of her father, Jay Gould, was purchased by Brentano's of New York, resold to Weyhe Galleries, and broken up.

THAYER, COL. JOHN ELIOT (1862–1933)

The following information was received from Frank Walters, one-time prominent rare book dealer in New York City: "The Colonel Thayer bird library was bought by Kennedy & Co., print-sellers, and myself. Kennedy kept for themselves only the Audubon's Birds, both folio and octavo, and immediately broke them up."

THEOLOGICAL SEMINARY
New Brunswick, N.J.

The folio had been given to the Library by Gardner A. Sage of New York. The second wife of Sage was Frances Carman, a daughter of Richard Carman, an original subscriber to Audubon's *Birds of America*. Around 1947 the folio was sold and eventually came into the possession of a New York print dealer who broke it up.

WINTHROP, THOMAS LINDELL
Boston, Mass.

On the original subscription list there is included the following: "Gentleman of Boston One Copy by S.E.G." (but not included in Audubon's list of final American subscribers).

The records of the Massachusetts Historical Society show that this was Thomas Lindell Winthrop (1760–1841), who gave his volumes to the society in 1837. The set was completed. The five volumes of the *Ornithological Biography* were also presented by Winthrop to the Society. On 9 April 1905, the Council authorized the sale of the set to a local Boston bookdealer for $2,000. The folio was broken up by the bookdealer. The folio and the volumes of the *Ornithological Biography* are listed in the catalog of the society, dated Boston, 1859, p.86. The gift to the Society is recorded in the "Proceedings of the Massachusetts Historical Society," published in 1880, v.1 (1835–1855), monthly meeting of 30 March 1837, p.77; annual meeting of 27 April 1837, p.80.

SETS DESTROYED BY FIRE

BENHAM, COMMANDER TIMOTHY GREEN

The following appears in the book, *The Captains and the Kings*, written by Edith Benham Helm (Mrs. James M.), who for many years was a White House social secretary:

> One of the treasures of my grandfather's house was John J. Audubon's great life work, *The Birds of America*. This beautifully illustrated tome was considered so important that it was kept upstairs and brought out only on rare occasions. As a child, I was told that Audubon was a friend of my grandfather's, and that he had tramped all over Staten Island in his study of birds. And when I was shown the picture of the marsh wren, it was with the information that it had been painted right there on Staten Island near the old home.[17]

In response to a request for additional information, Mrs. Benham advised that from a cousin, Mrs. A. I. Dorr, the following had been received:

> Audubon
> 1st Folio
> (Elephant Folio)

Audubon stayed at the home of Timothy G. Benham, Green Ridge, Staten Island. While there painted the Marsh wren on the Benham property. Timothy subscribed to the first edition. Timothy's house burned in 1898 (?) and the Audubon was burned.[18]

No other record of this subscription has been found nor is the Benham name included on the original list of subscribers to the Double Elephant edition of the *Birds of America*. The book described may have been one of the Bien Chromolithograph one-volume edition of 1859–1860.

LIBRARY OF PARLIAMENT
Montreal, Canada
2 sets

On 5 October 1842, while at Kingston, Ontario, Canada, at that time the capital of the country, Audubon obtained from the Assembly a subscription to the *Birds of America*, Elephant folio. The following day he received a second subscription from the Upper Chamber. These two sets were removed to the Library of Parliament in Montreal when the capital was moved to that city.

On 25 April 1849, the Parliamentary Library was destroyed in the burning of the Parliament building. The building had been set afire by a mob led by the opponents of the Rebellion Losses Bill which had been approved by the Earl of Elgin, the Governor General of Canada, earlier in the day. Included in the collections lost were the two sets of the *Birds of America*.[19]

MECHANICS MERCANTILE INSTITUTE OF SAN FRANCISCO
San Francisco, Calif.

The purchase of the folio had been made through subscription. In the Fifth Annual Report of the Mercantile Library Association, dated 1858, it is stated: ". . . permit me to call the attention of the members of the Association to one extremely valuable work of art, now attainable by a very small sacrifice on the part of a few of our members. I refer to Audubon's great national work, the 'Birds of America.' This work from its beauty and importance as well as its rarity, deserves a place in every great public Library, and if we can secure the copy now within our reach, we may regard ourselves as having gained a rich prize. The Directors have not felt justified in appropriating the general funds of the Association to the purchase of a single work of so high cost, but a private subscription has been started with the hope that in that way the object might be secured. The subscription now amounts to $400. about one-half the sum necessary."

In the *Sixth Annual Report of the President of the Mercantile Library Association of San Francisco, 1859*, on page 7, the librarian's report includes the following: "Many of the works secured to the Library are of a permanently interesting and highly valuable character, among which may be found the following: Audubon's Birds of America, in 5 volumes imperial octavo [the *Ornithological Biography*] and 4 volumes elephant folio of colored plates."

In 1906 the Mechanic's Institute of San Francisco absorbed the Mercantile Library and in the same year the library was completely destroyed by the earthquake and resulting fire.

NEW YORK STATE LIBRARY
Albany, N.Y.

On 29 March 1911, the New York State Library was almost totally destroyed by fire. The losses sustained by the library were detailed in *New York State Library*, 94th Annual Report, 1911 (Albany, N.Y.: Univ. of the State of New York, 1913). Among the illustrations following p.34 is a picture of the charred remains of the Audubon folio. The writer has visited the library but the staff have not been able to locate any trace of the set.

UNIVERSITY OF TORONTO
Toronto, Canada

A set of the folio listed in the *Alphabetical Catalogue of the Library of the University of Toronto* (Toronto, Henry Boswell, 1957) was lost when fire destroyed the library on 14 February 1890. The writer has been unable to trace the donor of the set.

VANDERBILT, CORNELIUS
New York, N.Y.

Vanderbilt's name appeared on the list prepared by Anthony Woodward, Ph.D., on 21 March 1901, under the heading: "A Brief Record of the Elephant Folio Edition of Audubon's 'Birds of America,' to whom they have belonged and where they can be found. This copy destroyed by fire." (It has not been possible to verify the destruction of the set by fire.)

SETS DESTROYED OR LOST IN WARS

CALLET
Charleston, S.C.

The folio was destroyed by Sherman during the Civil War in 1863. This information obtained from "A Brief Record of the Elephant Folio Edition of Audubon's 'Birds of America,' to Whom They Have Belonged and Where They Can Be Found," by Anthony Woodward, Ph.D., dated 23 March 1901.

A copy of this list was found by the writer in the files of the Buffalo and Erie County Public Library. Anthony Woodward was the first librarian at the Museum of Natural History in New York, N.Y.

DELACOUR, JEAN
Research Assistant, The American
Museum of Natural History
New York, N.Y.

On 25 July 1960, Dr. Delacour wrote to the author as follows: "There was a copy of the Folio Audubon in my library which was destroyed at my home in France by fire in 1939. As far as I remember I bought that copy in 1918 from a bookseller in Paris called Hermann who had himself bought it from a private collection which I do not quite remember. I have no idea if this was one of the copies subscribed in France or whether it was brought from another country." In another letter dated 4 August 1960, Dr. Delacour states that the fire was not caused by bombing, but probably deliberately put on.

LIMERICK HOUSE
(near) Charleston, S.C.

Limerick House, on the east branch of the Cooper River, near Charleston, was the home of the Hugger family. It was occupied in 1865 by William J. Ball and family when raided by Union troops under the command of Gen. E. E. Potter. An account of the raid and its consequences is to be found in *A Day on the Cooper River* by John D. Irving, M.D.:

> The soldiers left behind a single vehicle, the carriage, "for the old lady." Of the poultry, a goose setting on an island in the big duck-pond and a hen similarly occupied under the barn were all that remained.

> The lawn was littered with papers in which the men had brought their dinner. They were engravings torn from elephant editions of Audubon's works on the "Birds" and "Quadrupeds of America"![20]

WILKS
Langdon Hall,
Blair, Ont.

On 16 Dec. 1958, Paul Hahn of the Royal Ontario Museum, Toronto, Canada wrote the author relative to the Wilks folio as follows: "Regarding the Audubon you mention which was destroyed during the last war (World War II) in her chalet in France. This copy belonged to the Langdon Wilks family now living at Langdon Hall, 1300 Acres, Blair, Ontario. I have sent Mrs. Langdon Wilks your letter. Her husband was a grandson (sic) of John Jacob Astor of New York." In 1840 Matthew Wilks married Eliza Langdon, the granddaughter of John Jacob Astor.

In a postscript he writes further: "Regarding the Langdon Wilks 'Audubon' this is my story. Just before the last war I had luncheon with Mrs. Langdon Wilks (a relative of my wife). I said, 'Would you not like to give the Audubon you have to the Royal Ontario Museum? She hesitated then said I will think it over.' The next time at a dinner party at *our* house, she said 'I am sorry I did not give the 'Audubon' to the Royal Ontario Museum as in the war my Chalet in France was destroyed and the 'Audubon' too.'"

Another letter relating to this folio is that written by Mr. Wilks Keefer, Cruickston Park, Blair, Ont., 15 January 1959, who wrote to Mr. Hahn, as follows: "Mrs. Wilks tells me that she does not know from whom her husband, Langdon Wilks, obtained the Audubon folio but I think it came from his mother who was the granddaughter of John Jacob Astor. The volume was in my uncle's Chateau in France during the war and after the occupation it was found that a number of articles of value had been removed including this volume."

From the foregoing there remains the question as to whether the folio was destroyed or stolen during World War II.

22

SETS RECORDED BUT PRESENT LOCATIONS NOT KNOWN

Boston Natural History Society
Boston, Mass.

On 25 October 1836 there was donated to the society a subscription to Audubon's *Birds of America* by the following eleven persons: Messrs. Amos Lawrence, Benjamin D. Greene, Samuel A. Eliot, David Eckley, George B. Emerson, William Ingalls, George Parkman, Charles Amory, George C. Shattuck, George Shattuck, Jr., and Mrs. A. A. Shattuck. This subscription had been voted upon at a meeting held on 21 September 1836.[1] The Shattuck family contributed funds covering one-fourth of the cost which amounted to $880.[2]

When, sometime later, Colonel Thomas H. Perkins generously donated his set of the folio to the society, consent was asked and readily obtained of the donors of the original set to its disposal by the society for other works. A committee was therefore appointed to effect such an exchange. Messrs. Little and Brown, who had always maintained a very friendly feeling in behalf of the society, purchased the work, agreeing to allow $625 and to deliver in return for it such books as might be ordered from time to time through the committee.[3]

Centenary College of Louisiana
Shreveport, La.

The following information concerning the possibility that there was a set of the folio in possession of Centenary College is taken from the letter of 8 November 1958, written to the author by Mrs. Kathleen M. Owens, Acting Head Librarian, Centenary College of Louisiana:

Thank you for your letter of November 5th concerning the Audubon print, namely Plate V, Bonaparte Fly Catcher, which we have in the Centenary Library. We had the watermark checked yesterday and find it to be J. Whatman 1826.

I believe this confirms the fact that we have one of the first ten plates engraved in Edinburgh by W. H. Lizars in the Library and that it is very likely that the college did, at one time, own the Birds of America (Double Elephant Folio).

As I wrote in my previous letter, it has been traditionally understood that the college owned both the Birds and the Quadrupeds in 1860's when the college was located at Jackson, La., and that the Birds were sold at a time when the college was in financial difficulty.

[*Signed*] (Mrs.) Kathleen M. Owens
Acting Head Librarian

Graves, J. K.
Dubuque, Iowa

On 11 March 1971 the author received from George G. Kalbach of Des Moines, Iowa, the following information concerning an Audubon folio which it is believed was at one time in the possession of J. K. Graves:

My grandfather was J. K. Graves, born September 29, 1837, at Keene, New Hampshire, he died December 9, 1898, at Dubuque, Iowa where he had been a banker and industrialist for about 40 years.

My mother Sara, born in 1873 at Dubuque, was one of several children of J. K. Graves and spent her early life in the Graves home. She married George Kalbach of Oskaloosa, Iowa, in 1909. During my own childhood in Oskaloosa, she often spoke of 'a set of the original Audubon bird books' that J. K. Graves owned, and of his having commissioned a Chicago cabinet-maker to build the carved case in which she remembered their being kept. Old photos of the J. K. Graves home show the case, standing closed, in the library or music room.

There are two views within the family as to what happened to the books. One is that the books, but not the case, were sold either before or shortly after J. K. Graves' death, and that the case alone was inherited by one of Graves' sons, Luin Graves, of Dubuque. The other view is that both case and books were inherited by Luin Graves and that either he sold them within a few years, or his wife sold them as late as 1920 or so to a firm in Chicago.

In either event, the empty case later passed along to Luin's son Alan, also of Dubuque, who passed the case to me 15 or more years ago.

Since complete sets of the folio, 435 prints, are usually bound in four volumes and the case held only one volume, it is possible that this may have been the one-volume Chromolithograph edition of the *Birds of America* published in 1859–60 by the son John Woodhouse Audubon.

HEPPENSTALL, JOHN
Sheffield, England

The name of John Heppenstall neither appears on Audubon's final list of subscribers nor on the original subscription list.[4] However, Ledger "B" includes an entry showing that Heppenstall received all 435 prints.[5]

Audubon had completed a large oil painting, "English Pheasants Surprised by a Spanish Dog," in the summer of 1828. This the Naturalist had thought to present to King George but was persuaded from doing so by Sir Thomas Lawrence, then head of the Royal Academy, since in all probability the painting merely would be accepted and placed in the king's collection without accruing any benefit or recognition to the donor. Sir Thomas also advised Audubon that the painting was worth 300 guineas. The painting was eventually sold to John Heppenstall and is now at the American Museum of Natural History in New York.[6]

It is also recorded that the Naturalist, when returning to England from a visit to America, was bringing with him a number of wild passenger pigeons as a gift to Heppenstall. Unfortunately most of them died en route.[7] And in 1839, just before returning to America upon completion of his endeavors in England, the Audubon family spent "two most pleasant days with our worthy Friends the Heppenstalls."[8]

In June 1890 the Heppenstall folio together with the five volumes of the *Ornithological Biography*, the fifth volume of which had been autographed by Audubon and his wife, were sold at auction by Sotheby, Wilkins & Hodges. The purchaser was the dealer Quaritch, but additional information regarding this folio is not available since many of the Quaritch records were destroyed during World War II.[9]

HOPKINS, MAJOR ROBERT E. (1833–1901)
Tarrytown, N.Y.

While serving in the Army of the Potomac Hopkins was captured in the battle of Chancellorsville (3 May 1863) and imprisoned in Libby Prison, Richmond, Va. He became trustee and one of the five managers of the Tidewater Pipe Co. Ltd., also secretary and director of Tidewater Oil Company, and was a long-time resident of Tarrytown, N.Y.

Some years ago when Thomas C. Roberts presented to Princeton University a long letter that Audubon had written to his engraver Havell on 8 March 1831, the donor stated that this letter had originally been in the possession of Major Hopkins who had also been the owner of a set of the folio which had been sold by his son, Robert Ernest Hopkins, about 1940. The information about the letter and the folio had been given him by Miss Elizabeth Chambers of Newtown, Bucks County, Pa., she being the last of the Major's generation. With his long residence in Tarrytown it is conceivable that the Major had become acquainted with the Havell family who lived in that town. No further trace of folio has been found.[10]

JAPAN

On 20 December 1852 Victor Gifford Audubon wrote the Reverend John Bachman, "I have sold a Copy of the Large 'Birds' to the Government & also a Copy of the Large 'Quadrupeds' to go to Japan with the expedition. What do you think his Majesty (Brother of the Moon etc.) will say when he sees these works?"[11] Some days later, on the 29th of the month, in another letter to the Reverend Dr. Bachman, he again mentions selling the Large "Birds" and "Quadrupeds" to the State Department to be sent to Japan with the Perry expedition.[12]

That these volumes were taken to Japan by Commodore Perry is known from the official account of the expedition.[13]

In the hope of locating the present whereabouts of the Audubon volumes, enquiry was made of Dr. Nagahisa Kuroda, Yamashina Museum of Birds. He replied to the inquiry, stating that neither the Imperial Library nor the Ueno National Library record such books in their registered list. It was suggested by him that contact should be made with the Library of the Imperial Household.[14]

The librarian of that institution, Miss Kuniko Aoki, upon request for information concerning the matter, pointed out that the gifts, including the Audubon books, were presented to the Shogun of that time, not to the Emperor's household.[15] However, she did attempt to trace the volumes and reported as follows: "I have investigated many historical documents relative to the case. Even though I can not have found any record connected with which format of Audubon's works was taken to Japan, there is only a material written in *Dainihon Komonjo, Bakumatsu Kankeimonjo*, v. 4 (Documents Relating to Foreign Affairs in the Last Days of the Shogunate, 1853–68). We guess it means as follows: there are nine volumes of the pictures of the birds in various places of America, which are said described in life-size as they are, including the explanatory remarks in the list of gifts presented to the Shogun in March, 1854."[16] The mention of nine volumes would seem to indicate that with the "Large Birds" were included the five volumes of the *Ornithological Biography*.

In addition, the librarian did inquire of several libraries and museums which have some connection with the Tokugawa Shogunate, but none could furnish any information regarding the matter.[17]

Finally, Dr. Oscar M. Root and Mrs. D. D. Power, while visiting Japan, endeavored to obtain information regarding the Audubon books, but to no avail.

JENKINS, JOHN CARMICHAEL (1810–1855)
Elgin Plantation, near Natchez, Miss.

A granddaughter of John C. Jenkins wrote the author[18] that as a child she had seen the Audubon folio at Elgin but that it had been sold later by her uncle, W. D. Jenkins.

There is in the possession of the granddaughter a diary of John C. Jenkins from 1842–1855, in 12 volumes. The Department of Archives of Louisiana State University has a typescript. In the diary under the date of 15 January 1846, Jenkins had written:

> Shot a Hawk to-day of the species Falco Harrisii or Louisiana hawk of Audubon, see page 30 (actually v. 5, *Ornithological Biography*) of Birds of America. This bird is very seldom seen in this country and the only specimen now in any museum or cabinets are the two I shot—viz—the first one in October 1837 near Pinckneyville [located between Bayou Sara and Natchez] and which I presented to the Academy of Natural Sciences in Philadelphia. . . . They both were females and full or adult age. Mr. Audubon obtained my first specimen, and described and named it without my knowledge or consent. I had described and named this beautiful bird after my friend Dr. Morton of Philadelphia.[19]

Writing about the Louisiana Hawk, *Falco Harrisii*, Audubon stated, The species now before you belongs to the group of what may be called indolent or heavy-flying Hawks. The specimen from which I made my drawing was procured by a gentleman residing in Louisiana, who shot it between Bayou Sara and Natchez. A label attached to one of its legs authorizes me to say that it was a female; but I have received no further information respecting its habits; nor can I at present give you the name of the donor, however anxious I am to compliment him upon the valuable addition he has made to our Fauna, by thus enabling me to describe and portray it.[20]

KEMBLE, WILLIAM H.
Philadelphia, Pa.

On 19 & 20 April 1906 at the Book Auction Rooms of Davis & Harvey, 1112 Walnut St., Philadelphia, Pa., there was conducted by Stan V. Henkels the sale of the elegant library of the late William H. Kemble, Esq., of Philadelphia. In the catalog of the sale (No.949) item no. 27 is listed as the "Original Elephant Folio Edition of Audubon's Birds and Quadrupeds." The four volumes of the folio are described as "full Russia, gilt, gilt edges." For the *Quadrupeds* the description reads, "and Text, 3 vols. Imperial 8vo. three-quarter Russia, gilt, top edge gilt. New York, 1846."

Both works were encased in a handsomely carved black walnut cabinet with sliding apartments for the larger volumes, and a shelf for the descriptive volumes. The folio and the *Quadrupeds* sold for $4,350.

William Kemble had been prominent both in the business and political life of the city of Philadelphia and the state of Pennsylvania. In addition to being listed as a merchant in the directories, he had served as treasurer of the state (1865–67), was president of the People's Bank, as well as president of the Philadelphia Traction Co. & Union Passenger Railway.[21] No trace of the folio has been found.

KENT, EDWARD G.
Madison, N.J.

On 20 August 1962, Mrs. John C. Hubbard, of Madison, N.J., wrote that "we owned the first volume in folio (105 plates) which father (Edward G. Kent) purchased from Quaritch in London in the 20's. Subsequently, I believe through Southeby's [sic], he bought a complete set of four volumes bound in green morocco in the late 1930's, by Rivière [Robert Rivière (1808–82)]. This set he sold in the late 1930s to Scribners. Mr. David Randall was then at Scribners and I believe he made the purchase for a library."

Mr. Randall, Librarian of the Lilly Library at the University of Indiana, wrote on 19 October 1967: "I am sorry to say that the particular Audubon you mention from the Hubbard family of Madison, New Jersey, bound in green morocco by Rivière, four volumes folio, rings no bell with me whatsoever." Previously, Mr. Carroll Bradford Merrit, one time vice president of Charles Scribner Sons, had written: "Mrs. Edward G. Kent of Prospect Street, Madison, did own a set of the 'Audubon' and as one recollects it went to the famous, was it, the Old Corner Book Store in Boston? At the time of the sale I was connected with Charles Scribners' Sons in the capacity of Vice President and we made an offer for it which was exceeded by the Boston bookstore." No further trace of folio has been found.

KLUCKAUF, DR. WALTER Z.
Mexico City, Mexico

On 6 January 1958, the author was advised by Dr. Kluckauf of Paseo de la Reforma 402, Mexico 6, D.F., that prior to World War II he had purchased a set of the Double Elephant folio of Audubon's *Birds of America*. In a letter dated 24 July 1958, he wrote, "Regarding my set I cannot trace it further back than to Geneve (?) where I bought it from Mr. Kundig in 1952. Mr. Kundig died since."

The information concerning this folio had been given to the author by William Kaye Lamb, National Librarian for Canada at Ottawa. Dr. Lamb had further advised that in the four volumes, plates 101, 303, 335 and 409 were missing but that otherwise the set in original binding was in perfect condition. When writing in 1958, Dr. Kluckauf had stated that the volumes were in the safe deposit of a friend in New York. The folio has never been seen by the author nor has it been possible to obtain any further information from Dr. Kluckauf.

On 12 January 1970 Dr. Lamb wrote the author that Dr. Walter Kluckauf had died in the late autumn of 1969 but that he had not heard from Mrs. Kluckauf as to what disposition had been made of his library.

MERRILL, ADAMS HUSE
Brownville, Me.

This folio is included in the list prepared by Anthony Woodward as follows: "A. H. Merrill, of Brownville, Maine, 1886. His heirs wish to sell it."

Definite information relative to this folio was furnished by Lillian E. Fredin, a great-granddaughter of Adams H. Merrill. Papers in possession of the Merrill family show that on 5 August 1848, A. H. Merrill signed the following document:

> I, having this day bought of Joseph Lamson one set of Audubon's Birds of America with 5 volumes of Ornithological Biography, do hereby engage to pay to said Lamson one fourth part of the proceeds of said work when it shall be sold.

When this agreement was made, Lamson appears to have been in need of funds which were given to him by Merrill, with the *Birds of America* as security. It is not until 29 January 1889, that further information about the matter is available. Merrill had died the previous year and Lamson had appealed to a son, Henry Merrill, for payment even though the folio had not been sold. From a letter written by Lamson it is known that the amount Merrill had lent him was $600. However, in his letter to the son, Lamson states that "I had four-hundred dollars in that work against his six (600)." How the matter was settled with Lamson is not known other than an attorney for Merrill suggested that "had you not best let him have it." The folio was not sold until 1910 as witnessed by the fact that among the Merrill papers is a statement of sale showing the receipt from C. E. Goodspeed of $1,800, shipment of prints having been made to Dodd & Livingston in New York, N.Y. The sale of the folio was made by Mrs. (Marie) M. (Merrill) Jenks, a daughter of Adam Huse Merrill.

NASH, NATHANIEL CUSHING
Boston, Mass.

It is not known how the folio came into possession of the Nash family. It was sold by Stan Henkels of Philadelphia on 12 December 1916 for $4,200. The purchaser is believed to have been Gabriel (Weiss) Wells and to have been sent by him to Chicago.[22]

Evidence to the folio having gone to Chicago is found in a letter dated 13 November 1922, by Ruthven Deane to Frank Chapman of the American Museum of Natural History, in which it was stated, "is now [the folio] in Chicago, owner paid $5,000 with Quadrupeds beautifully bound in full morocco with ebony stand with gold decorations and accompanied by a folding table."[23] No further information regarding this folio is available.

PAUL, JOHN JAY

In March 1971 there was found on the bibliographical shelf at the Howard-Tilton Memorial Library of Tulane University by Professor Joseph Ewan[24] of the Biology Department a catalog, the title page of which reads as follows:

> A Catalogue of
> THE LIBRARY OF
> JOHN JAY PAUL
> Watertown, Florida
> Principally works on
> American Ethnology, Mammalogy
> Ornithology, Herpetology
> and Botany
> Privately Printed
> Philadelphia
> 1912

There is listed on page 21 in this catalog the following:

Item #75 Audubon, John James. The Birds of America, from original drawings by John James Audubon. London, published by the author, 1827–30. 4 vols. 435 hand-colored plates. Elephant folio, half black morocco; by Riviere.
"This is by far the most sumptuous ornithological work ever published."—Coues

Item #76 The 5 vols. of the Ornithological Biography-also bound in half black morocco; by Riviere.

It has not been possible to find any trace of these four volumes of the folio or those of the *Ornithological Biography*. Nor has it been possible to identify the owner of this outstanding library of natural history subjects.

It is thought that John Jay Paul might have been a resident of Philadelphia, since the catalog was printed in that city. However, inquiry at the Academy of Natural Sciences of Philadelphia[25] and at the Free Library of Philadelphia failed to elicit any information concerning John Jay Paul.[26]

Rosedown Plantation
St. Francisville, La.

In 1957 the author was advised by a Mrs. R. W. Siegel of Buffalo, N.Y., that, "In February, 1940, I visited Rosedown Plantation at St. Francisville, La. (about halfway between Natchez, Miss. and Baton Rouge). This plantation was completed in 1825 or thereabouts and had always been in the same family. The owners then were the Misses Bowman, two elderly spinsters. During the Civil War the entire establishment had been under Federal protection, Miss Bowman informed me, because her grandmother was a sister of General Sherman's wife. Nothing had been burned, destroyed or looted, and in 1940 the house was in a perfect state of preservation. I was astonished to find on a table in the library a complete set (so I believe) of Audubon's folio, stacked in black leather folders. I examined them." Then in 1958 the author received a letter from Mrs. Richard G. White of Charleston, S.C. She wrote "Once when we were in St. Francisville, La., we called on a Miss Bowman at Rosedown Plantation and she showed us the beautiful large Audubon Books, the small ones, and a lovely portrait Audubon painted of their mother."

Inquiry regarding the folios was made of James P. Bowman III, Shreveport, La., whose father was a brother of the Bowman sisters. In 1958 he wrote: "You were correctly informed that a set of the Folio had been at Rosedown Plantation, but I am sorry that I cannot tell you the whereabouts of this set now. For several years Rosedown was occupied by my Father's Sisters all of whom are now deceased. After the death of the last one two and a half years ago, the estate was inventoried and most of it has been sold. In the settlement I represented my Father who lives in Tulsa, Oklahoma and is very old and feeble. In making this inventory it was necessary to examine more than two thousand books in the library of the Plantation, but no sign of the Elephant Folio was found nor any record of its disposal. We examined bank deposits of my Aunts with the thought that at some time they may have needed cash and sold the set but this revealed nothing."

23

DISTRIBUTION OF THE SETS AND STATISTICAL SUMMARY

UNITED STATES AND CANADA

ACADEMIES
   The Academy of Natural Sciences Philadelphia, Pa.
   American Philosophical Society Philadelphia, Pa.
   California Academy of Sciences San Francisco, Calif.

ART GALLERIES
   Delaware Art Museum, Wilmington, Del.
   Henry E. Huntington Library and Art Gallery, San Marino, Calif.
   Museum of Fine Arts, Boston, Mass.
   National Gallery of Art, Washington, D.C.
   Norton Art Gallery, Shreveport, La.

ATHENAEUMS
   Boston Athenaeum, Boston, Mass.
   Minneapolis Athenaeum, Minneapolis, Minn.
   Providence Athenaeum, Providence, R.I.

AUDUBON SOCIETIES
   Audubon Shrine and Wildlife Sanctuary Audubon, Pa.
   Audubon State Park Museum, Henderson, Ky.
   National Audubon Society, New York, N.Y.

COLLEGES AND UNIVERSITIES
   Amherst College, Amherst, Mass.
   Bowdoin College, Brunswick, Me.
   Brown University, Providence, R.I.
   The City College of the City University of New York, New York, N.Y.
   Columbia University, New York, N.Y.
   Cornell University, Ithaca, N.Y.
   Duke University, Durham, N.C.
   Harvard University, Cambridge, Mass. 2 sets.
   Indiana University, Bloomington, Ind.
   Johns Hopkins University, Baltimore, Md.
   Laval Université, Quebec, Canada
   Lehigh University, Bethlehem, Pa.
   Louisiana State University, Baton Rouge, La.
   McGill University, Montreal, Canada
   Northwestern University, Evanston, Ill.
   Princeton University, Princeton, N.J.
   Syracuse University, Syracuse, N.Y.
   Trinity College, Hartford, Conn.
   Union College, Schenectady, N.Y.
   University of Illinois, Urbana, Ill.
   University of Michigan, Ann Arbor, Mich.

University of Minnesota, Minneapolis, Minn.
University of Pennsylvania, Philadelphia, Pa.
University of Pittsburgh, Pittsburgh, Pa.
University of South Carolina, McKissick Memorial Library, Columbia, S.C.
University of Southern California, Los Angeles, Calif.
University of Wisconsin, Madison, Wis.
Vassar College, Poughkeepsie, N.Y.
Williams College, Williamstown, Mass.
Yale University, New Haven, Conn. 2 sets.

FOUNDATIONS
H. J. Lutcher Stark Foundation Orange, Tex.
Mitchell Wolfson Foundation, Inc. Key West, Fla.

HISTORICAL SOCIETIES
Indiana Historical Society, Indianapolis, Ind.
The New-York Historical Society, New York, N.Y.

INDIVIDUALS
J. N. Bartfield, New York, N.Y.
Mrs. Frederick W. Beinecke, New York, N.Y.
John Henry Dick, Meggett, S.C.
Mrs. Daniel W. Evans, Merrie Hill Farm, Cobham, Va.
Estate of Mrs. Grace Phillips Johnson New Castle, Pa.
H. Bradley Martin, New York, N.Y.
Paul Mellon, Upperville, Va.
Miss Clara Peck, New York, N.Y.
Arthur E. Pflaumer, Haverford, Pa.
Rawlston D. Phillips, Jr., Baton Rouge, La.
Joseph Verner Reed, Greenwich, Conn.

INSTITUTIONS
Peabody Institute, Eban Dale Reference Library, Peabody, Mass.
Smithsonian Institution, Washington, D.C. (on loan from the National Academy of Science of the United States of America)

LIBRARIES
Boston Public Library, Boston, Mass.
Buffalo and Erie County Public Library, Buffalo, N.Y.
Charleston Library Society, Charleston, S.C.
Enoch Pratt Free Library, Baltimore, Md.
Free Library of New Bedford, New Bedford, Mass.
James J. Hill Reference Library, St. Paul, Minn.
John Crerar Library, Chicago, Ill.
Legislative Library, Fredericton, N.B., Canada
Library Association of Portland, Portland, Ore.
Library of Congress, Washington, D.C. 2 sets.
Library of Parliament, Ottawa, Canada
Milwaukee Public Library, Milwaukee, Wis.
New York Public Library, New York, N.Y. 4 sets.
New York Society Library, New York, N.Y. (*See* provenance, chap. 26.)
Pierpont Morgan Library, New York, N.Y.
Public Library of Cincinnati and Hamilton County, Cincinnati, Ohio
St. Louis Mercantile Library Association, St. Louis, Mo.
Toronto Public Library, Toronto, Canada

MUSEUMS
American Museum of Natural History New York, N.Y.
Buffalo Society of Natural Sciences Buffalo Museum of Science, Buffalo, N.Y.
Carnegie Institute, Carnegie Museum Pittsburgh, Pa.
Charleston Museum, Charleston, S.C.
Cleveland Museum of Natural History Cleveland, Ohio
Field Museum of Natural History Chicago, Ill.
Peabody Museum, Salem, Mass.

Distribution of the Sets and Statistical Summary

SCHOOLS
The Groton School, Groton, Mass.
Phillips Academy, Andover, Mass.

STATES
California State Library, Sacramento, Calif.
Commonwealth of Massachusetts, State House Library, Boston, Mass.
Louisiana State Museum, New Orleans, La.
State Library, Annapolis, Md.
North Carolina State Library, Raleigh, N.C.

FOREIGN COUNTRIES

ACADEMIES
Academy of Science, Zoological Institute, Leningrad, USSR.

INDIVIDUALS
Lord Caledon, 6th Earl of Caledon Castle, Caledon, Tyrone, N.I.
Earl of Crawford, Collinsburgh, Fife, Scotland
Duke of Devonshire, Chatsworth, Bakewell, England
Mrs. Barbara Fane, London, England
The Honourable Lord Fitzwilliam, Peterborough, England
John Galvin, Loughinstown, Co. Dublin, Ireland
The Honourable Lord Hesketh, Easton Neston, Towcester, England
Duke of Portland, Welbeck Abbey, Workshop, Nottingham, England

LIBRARIES
Biblioteca Naçional de Lisbõa, Lisbon, Portugal
Bibliotheca Nazionale Centrale, Florence, Italy
Bibliotheek van Teyler's Stichting, Haarlem, Netherlands
Bibliothèque de l'Institut de France, Paris, France
Bibliothèque Centrale, Muséum National d'Histoire Naturelle, Paris, France
Birmingham Public Libraries, Reference Library, Birmingham, England
John Rylands Library, Manchester, England
Liverpool Public Libraries, Picton Reference Library, Liverpool, England
Mitchell Library, Glasgow Corporation Public Libraries, Glasgow, Scotland
Paisley Public Library, Corporation of Paisley, Scotland
Royal Library, Windsor Castle, Windsor, England
State Library, Leningrad, USSR
State Library of Victoria, Melbourne, Australia

MUSEUMS
British Museum, London, England. 3 sets.
Darwin Museum, Moscow, USSR
Staatliche Museen, Meiningen (Thuringia), Deutsche Demokratische Republik
Victoria and Albert Museum, London, England

UNIVERSITIES
Cambridge University, Cambridge, England. 2 sets.
Glasgow, College of, Glasgow, Scotland
Oxford University, Oxford, England. 2 sets.
University of Copenhagen, Copenhagen, Denmark
University of Edinburgh, Edinburgh, Scotland

Complete sets
    United States — 94
    Canada — 5
    Australia — 1
    Denmark — 1
    Deutsche Demokratische Republik — 1
    England — 17
    France — 2
    Ireland (Eire) — 1
    Italy — 1
    The Netherlands — 1
    North Ireland — 1
    Portugal — 1
    Scotland — 5
    Union of Soviet Socialist Republics — 3
                  134*

Incomplete sets
    United States — 8
    Australia — 1
    England — 1
    France — 1
    Poland — 1
    Scotland — 2
                  14
Sets broken up — 28
Sets destroyed by fire (Library of Parliament, Canada, 2) — 7
Sets destroyed in wars — 4
Sets recorded but present locations not known — 14
Collections of individual and loose prints
    Scotland — 1
    United States & Canada — 20
    USSR (Russia) — 1
                  22

* All but six of these have been examined by the author.

24

ORIGINAL COST AND SUBSEQUENT PRICES

In his prospectus Audubon had advised the subscribers that the price of "Each Number [composed of five prints] will be Two Guineas [£2. 2s.], payable on delivery." As the numbers began to be delivered to the English subscribers, payment was made on this basis. A receipt given by Audubon on 13 March 1828 to John Lodge, University Library, Cambridge, England, shows a payment of 10 pounds, 10 shillings [£10. 10s.] for five numbers consisting of twenty-five plates.

When the first 100 plates, or 20 numbers, had been engraved, they were sold for £42.0.0. According to the prospectus there were to have been 400 drawings; however, before the work was completed 435 were engraved, resulting in an additional cost for the fourth volume. Also, the cost was increased when subscribers requested that their volumes be bound, depending on the type of binding provided. Among the English subscribers included in Ledger "B" and the amount of their payments were:

Adelaide, Queen of England	Vol. 1	42-0-0 (loose prints)
Armorer Donkin	Vol. 1	42-0-0 (loose prints)
Henry Witham	Vol. 1	54-8-0 (bound, with locks)
Euphemia Gifford	Vol. 1	42-0-0
Binding		4-12-0.

Nearly all of the American subscriptions were obtained after the first 100 plates had been engraved. Audubon had arranged, therefore, to have bound copies sent to America in 1831 on the occasion of his second return trip from England. As a result he was receiving cash payments from subscribers for this volume. In March 1832 when he had obtained the subscription of the Savannah merchant, William Gaston, he received $200 for the first volume.[1] The Naturalist also had received similar payments from other Savannah subscribers.[2] The following year when he acquired subscribers in Boston, many of them received the first volume, paying him $220 for it.[3] However, in Ledger "B," the payments from many subscribers, as shown below, were recorded in English currency:

THE DOUBLE ELEPHANT FOLIO

State of Louisiana 1st. Vol. Hf. bound.	49-10-0
L Reid New York	
Vols. 1, 2, 3 Hf. bound (each)	49-10-0
Fourth Volume Hf. bound	65- 5-0
Columbia College Vols. 1, 2, 3 (each)	49-10-0
Vol. 4	65- 5-0

In March 1830, just prior to his return to England after his first visit to America, Audubon had received the subscription of John B. Morris of Baltimore. Since at that time the first 100 plates had not been completed, Morris was supplied with loose prints as shown by the Ledger "B" entry, "John B. Morris—Baltimore (loose prints) 42-0-0."

As has been mentioned previously, the cost of each number of five prints was to be 2 guineas (£2. 2s.). At the rate of exchange current in the years 1828–1838, which rate varied from $4.44 to $4.80 to the pound, the cost of one number of the prints (£2. 2s.) was approximately $10, or $2 per print.

On 17 March 1838, before completion of the engraving of the *Birds of America*, while Audubon was still in England, he wrote to his New York agents, Forrestall Brothers & Berthoud, in reply to a letter from Charles Fothergill of Toronto, Canada, setting the following prices for the folio: $870, $950, and $1070. These would seem to apply first to a set of the loose prints, then to a set with half-leather binding, and finally to the folio full bound in leather.[4] After completion of the "Large Work," Audubon received $1050 for each of the bound sets taken to America.

The first set of the folio to be offered for sale by someone other than the Naturalist appears to have been the one listed in the "Catalogue of Books, Drawings, Paintings, Engravings and Statuary of William Colman." Included among the items which were auctioned by Cooley & Keese, 304 Broadway, New York, on 10 April 1850, was "A Subscriber's Copy of Audubon's Birds of America," with five volumes of the *Ornithological Biography*.[5] It has not been possible to determine the subscriber or the purchaser of this set.

On the other hand, the first auction of prints of the *Birds of America* had taken place some sixteen years earlier. In 1834 there were being sent from London Numbers 34 and 35 for the American subscribers. All the copies of these numbers, sent by the ship *President*, were, as Audubon wrote his son, "so wet & good for Nothing [that] These have been sold at auction in N.Y., and I have been vexed enough on that account."[6]

In the last half of the nineteenth century, offerings of the folio began to be listed in dealers' catalogs. In 1855 in a "Trade Circular of English Books Consigned for Private Sale," published by Bangs, Brother & Son, 13 Park Row, New York, a set of the folio and one of the *Quadrupeds* were listed. In 1862 an auction catalog of Puttick & Simpson of London for a sale to be held on 29 March included item 103, "One volume of 75 prints."

Toward the end of the century the folio began to be offered frequently in auction sales, both in England and the United States.

Original Cost and Subsequent Prices

AUCTION HOUSE	DATE OF SALE	LOT OR ITEM NO.	SUBSCRIBER'S OR COLLECTOR'S NAME	DESCRIPTION	PURCHASER	PRICE
ENGLAND						
Sotheby, Wilkinson & Hodges (SW&H)	14–17 June 1890	311	John Heppenstall	v. 1 bound, v. 2–4, loose prints, plus 5v. O.B. with autograph inscription of Audubon and wife in v. 5.	Quaritch	£300
SW & H	4–6 April 1892	2607	John Winfield Larking	4v. bound	Sotheran	£345
SW & H	21–23 Dec. 1892	305	George Dennis	4v.	Quaritch	£290
Christie, Manson & Woods	9 May 1893	Lot 184	Lord Hastings	4v. plus 5v. O.B.	Sotheran	£235
Puttick & Simpson	13–15 Dec. 1893	Lot 224	S. Simon and others	4v.	Sotheran	£137
UNITED STATES[7]						
Rice	Mar. 1870	81	Not Known	4v.	Not Known	$ 810
Leavitt	Dec. 1873	286	"	4v.	"	$1,134
Leavitt	Jan. 1889	—	"	4v.	"	$2,430
Libbie	4 Dec. 1889	53	"	4v.	"	$1,200
Bangs	6 Feb. 1896	25	"	4v.	"	$1,260

After the turn of the century the set of W. H. Kemble, together with the five volumes of the *Ornithological Biography*, was sold at the auction held 19–20 April 1906 by Stan Henkels of Philadelphia for $4,350. In England the folio of G. R. Lane-Fox, M.P., was sold by Sotheby, Wilkinson, & Hodges on 27 July 1909 for £380 ($1850).

Although a number of sets were sold both in England and in the United States between 1909 and 1930, it was not until 1933 that the price obtained for the Kemble set was exceeded. In February of that year a folio with the five volumes of the *Ornithological Biography* brought $5,200.

From then on the price of the folio gradually increased until 1939 when a sale was recorded in the United States at $15,600. From 1942 until 1963 there were no complete sets sold in the United States. Then in May 1966, at the Parke-Bernet Galleries in New York a set of the folio sold for $60,000.

In England, beginning with 1919, the number of folios offered at auction exceeded by a considerable number those offered in the United States. After the first World War sets were sold by English universities, natural history societies, and other like institutions to obtain needed funds for the restoration of war-damaged library buildings.

Following is a list of English auction sales prices of the folio to 1973:

1919 (with O.B.)	£ 545	($2,650)
1922 (with 13 extra plates)	£ 600	($2,900)
1923 (with O.B.)	£ 420	($2,000)
1923 (with O.B.)	£ 500	($2,450)
1925	£ 540	($2,600)
1929	£ 1,300	($6,300)
1932 (depression of the '30s.)	£ 530	($2,575)
1936	£ 1,475	($6,200)
1937	£ 2,400	($11,600)
1945	£ 3,700	($18,000)
1951 (pound devalued to $2.80)	£ 7,000	($34,000)
1955	£ 9,200	($25,760)
1959	£13,000	($36,400)
1969 (with 13 extra plates)	£90,000	($216,000)
1972	£62,000	($151,280)[8]

In addition to the sales of complete sets, there frequently occurred sales of partial sets—one, two or even three volumes (100, 200, 300 prints), as well as loose prints from 15 up to 137, 150, 185, and in one instance, 240. That there should have been so many broken sets offered is not surprising when it is recalled that many of the English subscribers did not complete their subscriptions.

A check of print dealers' catalogs has made it possible to trace the fantastic increase in the price of individual Double Elephant folio prints since these were first offered to the public. As early as 1893 there appeared in the *Oölogist* an advertisement of Estes, Lauriat, of Boston, offering prints, but no prices were given.[9] In May 1905 and again in 1906 the Boston bookdealer, Charles E. Goodspeed, advertised prints, the prices of which varied from $7.50 to $25, with the exception of Plate 1, the Turkey Cock, which was priced at $200.[10]

Among the prints offered were the following:

Plate			
96	Columbia Jay	Price	$20.00
104	Chipping Sparrow		7.50
145	Yellow Red-Poll Warbler		7.70
222	White Ibis		20.00
231	Long-billed Curlew (view of Charleston)		20.00
269	Greenshank (view of St. Augustine)		15.00
281	Great White Heron (view of Key West)		25.00
226	Hooping Crane		25.00
242	Snowy Heron		25.00
216	Wood Ibis		25.00
297	Harlequin Duck		20.00
246	Eider Duck		15.00

Original Cost and Subsequent Prices

Prices remained low for some years. In 1919 the Franklin Book Shop in Philadelphia, owned by Samuel N. Rhoades, issued a catalog of Auduboniana which included a large number of "Plates from the original elephant folio edition of Audubon's Birds of America, engraved by Lizars and Havell." It is possible that the collection of prints to be sold were those of the subscriber, Edward Harris of Moorestown, for Rhoades had obtained much of his stock of Auduboniana from Harris descendants.[11] The prices of individual prints varied from $7 to $60, as shown by the following sampling:

Plate		Price
89	Nashville Warbler	$ 7.00
9	Selby's Flycatcher	7.00
5	Bonaparte's Flycatcher	9.50
48	Cerulean Warbler	9.50
138	Connecticut Warbler	9.50
38	Kentucky Warbler	9.50
3	Prothonotary Warbler	12.00
2	Yellow-billed Cuckoo	15.00
27	Red-headed Woodpecker	22.00
211	Great Blue Heron	35.00
326	Gannet	22.50
321	Roseate Spoonbill	30.00
397	Scarlet Ibis	35.00
62	Passenger Pigeon	60.00

The warblers and flycatchers, being among the smaller birds, have always commanded lower prices. The high cost of the passenger pigeon print is no doubt attributable to the extinction of the species.

On 1 October 1929, Goodspeed's of Boston issued a catalog of all 435 prints of the *Birds of America*. This probably indicates that a complete set had been acquired and broken up.[12] It is of interest to compare the 1929 prices of the prints with those from the catalogs of 1905–1906.

Plate		1905–6	1929
96	Columbia Jay	$20.00	$ 75.00
104	Chipping Sparrow	7.50	17.50
145	Yellow Red-poll Warbler	7.50	15.00
269	Greenshank (view of St. Augustine)	15.00	50.00
246	Eider Duck	15.00	150.00
222	White Ibis	20.00	50.00
231	Long-billed Curlew (view of Charleston)	20.00	150.00
297	Harlequin Duck	20.00	60.00
281	Great White Heron (view of Key West)	25.00	100.00
226	Hooping Crane	25.00	75.00
242	Snowy Heron (view of Plantation)	25.00	60.00
216	Wood Ibis	25.00	50.00

Prints of ducks (such as Pl. 246, Eider Duck) had become popular among sportsmen; also those with background views (Pl. 231, Charleston) were in demand.

Beginning with the early 1920s the Audubon prints, either loose or occasionally in complete sets, began to be an important item of trade among print dealers. In New York these were to be found included in the catalogs of the following: The Old Print Shop (Harry Shaw Newman), E. Weyhe, Inc., Kennedy Galleries, Inc. (H. Wunderlich), Charles Scribner's Sons, J. N. Bartfield, Edward Eberstadt & Sons, as well as in those of lesser known shops. Certain of the print dealers listed, as well as Dr. A. S. W. Rosenbach and Gabriel Wells (Weiss), rare bookdealers who made many of their purchases abroad, confined their sales to complete sets of the folio.

In the period from 1935 until 1941, when the market in Audubon folios and prints was particularly active, David A. Randall, for many years associated with the rare book department of Scribners and presently the librarian of the Lilly Library, Indiana University, bought and sold seven copies of the folio, some of which were broken up and others sold to new owners.[13]

For many years the Old Print Shop in New York carried a large inventory of the Audubon prints. From the early 1940s until the death of the founder a few years ago there would be in stock prints, at times in large numbers. These often were listed in the house organ, "Portfolio," issued frequently during the year. While it has been impossible to determine how many complete sets of the folio Newman broke up, at least five have been identified. One of the last of these was the folio which had been subscribed for by the Duke of Buccleuch of Dalkeith Castle (Edinburgh).[14] Each purchaser of a print from this set was furnished with a certificate stating that the print had come from the Buccleuch folio. Some of the prices commanded by the Buccleuch prints are shown below:

Plate			Price
6	Wild Turkey, female and young		$550.00
11	Bird of Washington		125.00
12	Baltimore Oriole		375.00
25	Carolina Parrot		250.00
47	Ruby Throated Humming Bird		275.00
64	Swamp Sparrow		55.00
96	Columbia Jay		475.00
113	Blue Bird		300.00
131	American Robin		350.00
217	Louisiana Heron		375.00
246	Eider Duck		275.00
251	Brown Pelican		375.00
297	Harlequin Duck		85.00
307	Blue Crane or Heron		325.00
321	Roseate Spoonbill		675.00
386	White Heron		475.00
397	Scarlet Ibis		185.00

Original Cost and Subsequent Prices

Undoubtedly the most extensive disposal of Audubon prints resulted from the numerous sales by R. H. Macy of New York in the period from 1931–1935. It was in 1930 that the "World's Largest Department Store" had opened, on the 8th floor, its Art Gallery. At the time the buyer for the Gallery was Margaret A. McKinlay. A printdealer acquaintance sent her the one volume of the Bien Chromolithograph prints of the folio on consignment.[15] She relates, "I broke it up, advertised the prints, sold out in an hour, and that started Macy's off on the Audubon project."[16]

From 1931 until 1935 either four or five sets of the Double Elephant edition of the *Birds of America* were purchased, broken up, and sold to the public. A priced catalog was published for the opening sale, but, when additional catalogs were issued, prices were not included, "for the prices went up so fast, as the buying of the plates became more and more furious!"[17] It has not been possible to determine the owners of the folios which were broken up. The Macy affiliate in Newark, Bambergers, participated in the sale of the last one.

The author is fortunate to have a copy of the original priced catalog issued May 1931, of which only 300 copies were printed. While it should be recalled that the United States had entered into a depression, nevertheless the prices at which Macy's was offering the Audubon prints at that time is well nigh unbelievable. Here is a sampling from that catalog:

Plate			Price
1	Wild Turkey (none priced higher)		$224.00
2	Yellow-billed Cuckoo		10.89
3	Prothonotary Warbler		8.94
6	Great American Hen & Young (early state of the print)		104.00
12	Baltimore Oriole		24.89
17	Carolina Turtle Dove		29.75
21	Mocking Bird (with rattlesnake)		29.75
37	Golden-winged Woodpecker (Flicker)		34.50
47	Ruby-throated Humming Bird		34.50
62	Passenger Pigeon		49.75
64	Swamp Sparrow (plate with Lucy's name on it)		8.94
95	Yellow Warbler		8.94
110	Hooded Warbler		4.96
116	Ferruginous Thrush (with black snake)		19.80
226	Hooping Crane		49.75
231	Long-billed Curlew (view of Charleston)		104.00
242	Snowy Heron (rice plantation, S.C.)		39.75
246	Eider Duck		104.00
301	Canvas-backed Duck (view of Baltimore)		174.00
321	Roseate Spoonbill		74.50

At the prices listed in this catalog R. H. Macy realized slightly over $12,200 from the sale of the 435 prints. In the period from the first sale in May 1931 until the completion of the final sale in 1935, Audubon prints in the amount of $120,000 were sold.[18]

As was earlier stated, when additional sets were purchased the pricing of catalogs was discontinued. The extent of the price increases is shown by a comparison of the prices in an advertisement prepared for one of the later sales with those listed in the original catalog. In some instances the prices were practically doubled. However, for some unknown reason the price of one plate was actually lowered. No mention is made of prints being available at $4.89, a price at which many prints were offered at the first sale.

			Adv.	1st Sale
Plate	211	Great Blue Heron	$ 59.75	$ 39.75
	231	Long-billed Curlew (view of Baltimore)	204.00	104.00
	201	Canada Goose	224.00	104.00
	209	Wilson's Plover	10.89	17.89
	236	Night Heron	49.75	39.75
	256	Reddish Egret (Purple Heron)	69.75	49.75

In writing about her purchase and sales of the Audubon prints Miss McKinlay has recounted a particular sale amounting to $10,000 to one customer. The purchaser was Mrs. Brooks Thayer of Oyster Harbor, Mass., described by Miss McKinlay as "one of the few perfect ladies I ever met in my long sojourn at Macy's. I shall never forget her kindness," she writes, "nor her beauty of character, nor cleverness in securing what she wanted to buy."[19]

This lady, when she learned that there was to be a sale of the Audubon prints, had gone to the Gallery to purchase some but was informed that none would be sold until the day of the sale. She arrived in the store promptly after the public was admitted only to find many other customers waiting for the elevator which was to take them to the 8th floor. However she spotted an employees' elevator already running which she immediately entered and arrived at the 8th floor before the other customers. No sooner had she entered the Art Gallery than she told a clerk that she wanted *all* the prints in view except the gory ones! The prints purchased by Mrs. Thayer she later presented to the Winterthur Museum (Winterthur, Del.).

When the dealers were offering the Audubon prints in New York these could also be found in other cities on occasion. In Boston there were those early sources, Goodspeed's and Lauriat. In Philadelphia, Mabel Zahn of Charles Sessler Inc., generally had a few on hand, and on occasion she would sell a complete set of the folio.

However, in the late 1950s the prints became a scarce item in print dealers' inventories. Also, the prices had risen appreciably, as will be shown by a comparison of those selected from a catalog issued in 1968 with those appearing in a copy of "Portfolio" (Old Print Shop, New York), dated January 1947.

Original Cost and Subsequent Prices

		A[20]	B[21]
Plate 13	Snow Bird (Junco)	$ 35.00	$ 325.00
28	Solitary Flycatcher	40.00	350.00
45	Traill's Flycatcher	37.50	300.00
57	Loggerhead Shrike	65.00	575.00
67	Red-winged Starling	75.00	575.00
107	Canada Jay	175.00	550.00
116	Ferruginous Thrush	90.00	750.00
126	White-headed Eagle	45.00	725.00
172	Blue-headed Pigeon	100.00	550.00
246	Eider Duck	225.00	900.00
256	Purple Heron	300.00	1,500.00
269	Greenshank (view of St. Augustine)	75.00	350.00
322	Red-headed Duck	135.00	850.00
391	Brant Goose	65.00	950.00
403	Golden-eye Duck	65.00	500.00

In 1969 a large number of prints were purchased in Paris by two American print dealers. The following examples from the catalog issued for the sale of these prints is further evidence of how their value has continued to rise:

Plate 13	Snow Bird (Junco)	Price $475
57	Logger-headed Shrike	675
67	Red-winged Blackbird	750
172	Blue-headed Pigeon	850

The Old Print Shop of New York in the autumn of 1971 acquired 135 prints of the Double Elephant folio, namely plates 301 to 435.[22] A comparison of a few of this dealer's prices for the Audubon prints in 1971 with those in 1968 is indicative of the continuing upward trend.

		1968	1971
Plate 322	Red-headed Duck	$850	$1,500
391	Brant Goose	950	1,760
403	Golden-eye Duck	500	800

Although individual Audubon prints were rarely found in the catalogs of foreign dealers, English dealers—Bernard Quaritch Ltd., Southeran's, Lionel & Philip Robinson Ltd., Christie, Manson & Woods Ltd., B. F. Stevens, and Traylen—have been active over the years in the purchase of complete sets at auction sales or from institutions and libraries, mostly for resale to purchasers in the United States.

III

CENSUS AND SURVEY OF EXTANT COMPLETE SETS

25

QUESTIONS OF INTERNAL EVIDENCE: LEGENDS AND WATERMARKS OF PRINTS OF THE FIRST TEN PLATES

When the decision was made actively to pursue the search for complete extant sets of the Double Elephant folio of the *Birds of America*, it was determined, if at all possible, to examine each set. As a result, all but one of the sets located in the United States and Canada and five of those found elsewhere have been carefully scanned.

Although each one of the 435 prints of the sets came under scrutiny, it was decided that only information regarding the first ten plates should be recorded and for this reason transcripts of the legends of these plates were made. In addition, some information was also obtained through correspondence from the owners of those sets located overseas but not seen.

It will be recalled that the first ten plates were originally engraved by W. H. Lizars of Edinburgh, while the remaining 425 were the work of Robert Havell, Jr., of London. While Havell also retouched certain of the first ten plates, which meant for the most part the use of aquatint in the larger plates, no evidence has been found to indicate that he had reengraved any of these plates in entirety.

The examined sets of the folio varied considerably in preservation. There were instances where the volumes had received most careful treatment, as is evident with the set at Trinity College, Hartford, Connecticut. This set had been brought to America by the engraver, Havell. Another set in excellent condition is the one at the Legislative Library, Fredericton, New Brunswick, Canada. The set of Providence collector Albert E. Lownes, later given to Brown University, had been interleaved with sheets of Whatman paper and bound in six volumes which resulted in all 435 prints being in excellent condition. In contrast, both the set at the State House Library of Massachusetts and that at the Free Public Library of New Bedford had suffered from improper handling, especially the first volume. In many sets there were individual prints showing small tears, creasing, foxing and offsetting. In some instances the complete outline of the bird had been transferred to the back of the preceding print. It is believed that the pressure resulting from the placing of one heavy volume on top of another caused the coloring to be absorbed by the paper of the preceding print. The prints of the larger birds on which the surfaces covered were greater were especially subject to such offset.

The size of the prints varied considerably, depending how severely they had been trimmed when bound. At times trimming had been so severe that parts of the legends, such as "No." (fascicule) and "Plate No." or the artist's and engraver's credits at the bottom of the print, were entirely cut off. Happily, there were but few examples of careless work by the colorists.

Examination of the many sets revealed that rarely had the owner of a set made a collation of the prints. There was one outstanding exception. In 1932 J. Christian Bay, then librarian of the John Crerar Library of Chicago, had prepared "The John Crerar Library Reference List No. 17" and the "Alphabetical Index to the Birds of America by John James Audubon, London 1827-1838, 4 vols." This list was made available to other librarians in a mimeographed edition at a very slight cost.

As more and more sets were examined and transcripts made of the first ten plates, differing legends for the same plate came to light. It is generally believed that the legend for plate 1 is "Wild Turkey," but before long, prints with an early watermark, such as 1826, and the legend "Great American Cock" were found. Other discrepancies also emerged; on prints with the "Wild Turkey" legend, the artist's credit was found to be, "Drawn from nature by J. J. Audubon F.R.S. F.L.S.," but on those bearing the "Great American Cock" legend the artist's credit read, "Drawn by J. J. Audubon M.W.S." The initials following the artist's name in the latter instance refer to Audubon's election to the Wernerian Society very soon after his arrival in England in 1826. Thus the initials "M.W.S." were used on the early state of the print. Later, after the Naturalist had been elected to other scientific societies—such as the Royal Society of Edinburgh (F.R.S.E.), the Linnaean Society (F.L.S.), and then the crowning honor, the Royal Society of London (F.R.S.)—the initials denoting membership in these societies were used instead.

There were variances, too, in the numbering of the plates; sometimes Arabic numerals and at other times Roman were used. Even the location of the legends for the same plate differed. In some instances, these were placed in a corner of the sheet instead of being centered at the bottom. The variations in the legends for the same plate are given in detail later in this chapter. However, the story in connection with the discovery of a print on which the name of the bird was incorrectly labeled warrants relating.

In 1906 Dr. Witmer Stone of The Academy of Natural Sciences of Philadelphia published in *The Auk* an article entitled "A Bibliography and Nomenclature of the Ornithological Works of John James Audubon."[1] Stone stated that

> Parts 1 and 2, pls. I–X, then are the work of Lizars, and Parts 3–87, pls. XI–CCCCXXXV, the work of Havell.... This is not the whole story however, for it seems that in 1829, Havell retouched some of Lizars and entirely reengraved some others.* Thus, in the copy of the folio in the library of The

---

* This writer has found no evidence that Havell had reengraved any of the first ten plates of the *Birds of America*. Prof. Francis H. Herrick in his definitive two-volume work, *Audubon the Naturalist*

Questions of Internal Evidence

Academy of Natural Sciences of Philadelphia plates VIII and IX are marked "Engraved by W. H. Lizars, Edin*r*.; Plates I, II, VI, VII," "Engraved by W. H. Lizars Edin*r*. Retouched by R. Havell Jun*r*." (some have London added after Havell's name, and plate II and VII bear date 1829); plates III, IV, V, X, "Engraved, Printed & Coloured by R. Havell Jun*r*." Being curious to know whether other American copies agreed with this one or whether some of them contained all of the original Lizars plates, and whether the name "Dacnis protonotarius" quoted for the Prothonotary Warbler might not occur in them I corresponded with several gentlemen who owned or had access to copies, and obtained data upon six sets. Five of these were exactly like the Academy set while the one at the Museum of Comparative Zoology at Harvard University contained the original Lizars plates for which I had been searching. Correspondence with Dr. Walter Faxon brought out the fact that he had long since been aware of those two editions and through his kindness I am able to present transcriptions of the Lizars plates.[2]

There is yet another record of a comparison of the legends of the *Birds of America*, that made by Professor Francis H. Herrick to illustrate what he called successive editions of Audubon's plates. Herrick compared the legends of "two or three of the most famous, taken from copies in the British Museum and Boston Society of Natural History or from detached plates obtained in London in 1903." These were plates 1, 6, and 31.[3]

Also, in 1941 E. F. Hanaburgh published *Audubon's 'Birds of America': A Check List of First Issues of the Plates in the First Folio Edition 1828–1838*. This was based on the study of twelve completed sets of the double elephant folio of *Birds of America*, six in public institutions and six that were either in private possession or that had been sold at public auction, together with many individual prints.[4] Hanaburgh made no comparison of the plates found in the sets examined but merely recorded what he believed to be the date of the earliest issue of each of the plates in these folios.

Stone listed transcripts of six plates; one of particular interest is the following:

> Plate II. "Black-billed Cuckoo, Coccyzus erythropthalmus." Corrected in the retouched plate to "Yellow-billed Cuckoo, Coccyzus americanus."

This indicates that in the set at the Museum of Comparative Zoology there was included a print of a plate on which originally the incorrect name of the species had been engraved. Herrick in his definitive work on Audubon, stated that in 1914 he had been shown the print by Dr. Samuel Henshaw, then director of the museum.[5] There are presently at Harvard two complete sets of the folio and two additional volumes containing the first two hundred prints. In each set the legend for plate 2 reads "Yellow-billed Cuckoo." However, some years ago a third set which had belonged to the Museum of Comparative Zoology was sold. It is probable that the print of plate 2 with the incorrect title was in that set.

(New York & London: D. Appleton and Co., 1917), v. 1, p. 383–84, stated that he was unable to verify the story that Havell had reengraved plate 11 [sic], the Prothonotary Warbler. Herrick, however, did err in his numerical identification of this engraving, for it is actually plate 3.

As the search for the extant copies of the folio progressed, prints of plate 2 were found on which the legend had been placed in the upper lefthand corner instead of at the bottom. Finally there was found a print with the legend so placed upon which there evidently had been made an erasure in part of the common and specific names of the bird and the words "Yellow" and "Carolinensis" added in fine Spencerian script. Always likely was the possibility that there would be found a set in which the legend on plate 2 would be "Black-billed Cuckoo, Coccyzus Erythropthalmus." Eventually, when the Art Museum (Garvan) copy of the folio at Yale University was examined, the uncorrected legend for plate 2 appeared. Before the search for the extant sets was completed, there were discovered three other sets which contained the print with the incorrect title: at Evergreen House, Johns Hopkins University in Baltimore, at the Indiana Historical Society Library in Indianapolis, and at the Darwin Museum in Moscow.

In addition to the variants in the legends of the first ten plates, others have been found among the later prints. Examples of these comprise Appendix K. In some instances alterations in the legends were due to mistakes made by the engraver while the Naturalist was in America.

It was on 21 July 1832 that Victor Audubon, writing from Philadelphia, advised Havell, "My father is delighted with the Engravings of the last nos received here. . . . Plate 122 Blue Grosbeak, you called Fringilla *corulea*, instead of coerulea. . . ."[6] On 1 April 1833 in a letter written in New York to Victor, then in London supervising the work of publishing the *Birds of America*, Audubon advised that, "he [Havell] has written under the Turkey Buzzard—Cathartes Atratus—it ought to be C. *Aura*."[7] In the next year, on 14 January 1834, while in Charleston, again in a letter to Victor:

> This morning I brought Nos. 35 & 36 for the subscribers here, & the Columbia College [Univ. of South Carolina] I have opened them and I tell you with pleasure that I think them *very fine*. all I regret is the *errors* in nomenclature, which however may be corrected so that you may have them correct for those persons who have not yet been supplied,—as follows plate [—] instead of Gray Tyrant have Pipiry Fly Catcher—Muscicapa *Matinatus* Plate [—] [pl. 170, No.34] *Muscicapa Cooperii*—also have the *black headed Titmouse* (*for it is a new Species*) The Lesser black headed Titmouse—*Parus Caroliniensis* [pl. 160, No.32]. My letter press will do the rest.—I write to Havell.—[8]

Finally, on 26 September 1835, this time from Edinburgh where he was working on his letterpress, the *Ornithological Biography*, Audubon wrote Havell, "I forgot in my last to you by all means, the letter D is to be placed in the English name as well as in the Latin of 'Richardson's Yeager' 'Lestris Richardsonii.' "[9]

That Audubon himself became aware of and was disturbed by the variations in the legends of the plates is known from a letter written to his engraver on 29 June 1830. Early in the month the Naturalist had arranged an exhibition of his prints in Birmingham, one of the cities he was visiting on a trip through England and Scotland during which he was collecting moneys due him, searching for new subscribers, as well as trying to reactivate some subscriptions which had lapsed. He wrote,

> I have examined you may depend at great leisure all the Plates as they hang on the wall around me and I am surprised myself to see how carelessly *I have past over faults* which no difference of time in the engraving or colouring could not have greatly improved—Your letter Engraver must be dismissed or become considerably more careful and in fact must now correct his past errors.—When I return to London *you & I* must have a regular and compleat overhauling of the Coppers, and see what can be done to redeem the caracter of a work of this Magnitude and one which you cannot but conceive of Importance to your own standing, as a good Engraver and a Good man.[10]

Audubon's trip through England and Scotland continued until the middle of October when he arrived in Edinburgh where he at once resumed his writing of the *Ornithological Biography*. This activity kept him so occupied that he did not get to London for the meeting with his engraver. However, on 2 March 1831 Audubon sent Havell a very long letter, some four pages written on foolscap measuring 16 ½ inches by 10 ⅛ inches. The purpose of the letter was set forth in the first paragraph:

> I wish you to set about having the Plates re-engraved I mean the lettering as soon as possible and to employ such engravers as will do justice to the whole of it.—I think that if you can have it done under your roof it will be of great advantage, You must push this because I want ten copies bound up by the 1st of August next [when JJA was planning a second trip to America.]—Next week I will send you the remainder of the list—[11]

One entire page of the letter sets forth in great detail the arrangement, lettering, and style of the legends.

The following arrangement to be adopted generally.

No. 2   PLATE IX
                                                    (always in Roman Letters)

(*Always at the bottom of the Plate*)
Selby's Flycatcher.
Muscicapa Selbii. Aud.
Male.
Flos Adonis. Adonis autumnalis.

Drawn from nature by J. J. Audubon. F.R.S. F.L.S.   Engraved, printed and coloured by
                                                                                    R. Havell, Jun.

When the space left at the bottom of the plate is small, let the names run on in a continuous line thus.

Wild Turkey. Meleagris Gallopavo. Linn. Male. American Cane. Miegia macrosperma

Let the naming be uniform in all the plates, that is, let the English names of the birds be all in one character, the Latin names also in one character, &c.

Carolina Turtle Dove
COLUMBA CARLINENSIS. Linn.

Males, 1. Females, 2.
White-flowered Stuartia. Stuartia Malacodendron.

The above announcement and
lettering to be adopted throughout.

For the largest plates, let the letters not be larger than those of
Plate 46. N. 10.
For the middle-sized plates, let them be the size of Plate 47. N. 10
For the small plates, as in   *Plate 64. N. 13.*

Be sure not to have any at the top of the plates,
not to make capital letters where they should be small,
and to have the whole uniform.
no flourishes,
The dots (.,) to be as in the manuscript.

On two other pages there are listed 44 plates with the common and specific names of the bird, sex, common and specific name of the shrub, plant, flower, or tree used in the drawing. As he had written in his letter, the following week he planned to send the remainder of the list, referring to the other 56 plates of Volume I.

Hereafter, the legends of all the plates in the first volume would follow the instructions set forth in this letter of 2 March 1831, which would cover most of the sets of the American subscribers.

While Havell undoubtedly immediately followed these instructions and had the plates reengraved where necessary, so that the ten volumes which Audubon was to take to America later in the year contained prints from the reengraved plates, there have been found sets subscribed for or purchased several years after this time which contain prints made and colored before the instructions of 2 March 1831 had been issued.

Such a set is the one at Union College, Schenectady, New York, which was purchased by the president of the college directly from Audubon, but not until 1844. In this set the legend on plate 6 is: "Engraved by W. H. Lizars, Re-touched by R. Havell, Junr.," rather than "Engraved printed and coloured by R. Havell, Jun," as prescribed in the letter. This set also is printed on paper with an 1830 watermark.

The explanation for these earlier prints appearing in some sets arises from the fact that on numerous occasions prints had been returned by agents appointed by Audubon in England and Scotland when subscriptions had been cancelled. There was even one occasion when Audubon himself, while in America, returned prints and advised that Havell "work them into the Volumes which I have requested Victor to have coloured & bound as soon as possible."[12]

Questions of Internal Evidence

VARIATIONS IN THE LEGENDS OF THE FIRST TEN PLATES

NUMBER 1

Plate 1 (3 variants found)

PLATE I.

Great American Cock Male—Vulgo (Wild Turkey—)
Maleagris Gallopavo

Drawn by J. J. Audubon M.W.S.   Engraved by W. H. Lizars Edinr.

Rawlston D. Phillips, Jr., Baton Rouge, La.	J. Whatman	1826
Duke University, Women's College Library	J. Whatman	1826
New-York Historical Society	J. Whatman	1826
Vassar College	J.W.T.M.	1826
Bibliothèque Nationale, Bureau l'Estampes, Paris, France	J.W.T.M.	1827
Brown University	J.W.T.M.	1827
Indiana Historical Society	J.W.T.M.	1827
Public Library, Corporation of Paisley, Scotland	J.W.T.M.	1827
Yale University, Garvan set	J.W.T.M.	1827
Zoological Institute, Academy of Science, Leningrad, USSR (Loose prints)	J.W.T.M.	1827

No. 1   PLATE I

Great American Cock Male—Vulgo (Wild Turkey—)
Maleagris Gallopavo

Drawn by J. J. Audubon F.R.S.E. F.L.S. M.W.S.   Engraved by W. H. Lizars Edinr.
                                        Retouched by R. Havell Junr. London 1829.

Amherst College	J. Whatman	1830
Pierpont Morgan Library	J. Whatman	1830
H. J. Lutcher Stark Foundation (Bachman copy)	J. Whatman	1830
Reference Library, Birmingham Public Libraries, England	J. Whatman	1830

215

No. 1 PLATE I

Wild Turkey. Meleagris Gallopavo. Linn, Male
American Cane. Miegia macrosperma.

Drawn from nature by J. J. Audubon F,R,S. F,L,S. Engraved by W. H. Lizars Edinr.
Retouched by R. Havell Junr.

University Library, Scientific and Medical Dept., Copenhagen, Denmark	J. Whatman 1832
Yale University, Farnam set	J.W.T.M. 1833
Library of Congress (War Dept. copy)	J.W.T.M. 1834
Cornell University	J. Whatman 1836
Library of Parliament, Ottawa, Canada	J. Whatman 1836
Windsor Castle, Berkshire, England	J. Whatman 1836
National Academy of Sciences (On loan to the Smithsonian Institution)	J. Whatman 1838
Liverpool Public Library, England	J.W.T.M. (date shaved)

Plate 2 (4 variants found)

PLATE II.

Black-billed Cuckoo, Coccyzus Erythophthalmus.
Plant Popaw Porceliatriloba.

Drawn by J. J. Audubon M.W.S. Engraved by W. H. Lizars Edinr.
[Legend is in upper left corner of plate]

Johns Hopkins University, Evergreen House	J.W.T.M. 1826
Indiana Historical Society Library	J.W.T.M. 1827
Yale University, Garvan set	J.W.T.M. 1827
Darwin Museum, Moscow, USSR	J.W.T.M. 1827

PLATE II.

Yellow-billed Cuckoo. Coccyzus Carolinensis.
Plant Popaw Porceliatriloba.

Drawn by J. J. Audubon, M.W.S. Engraved by W. H. Lizars Edinr.
[Legend in upper left corner of plate]

John Rylands Library, Manchester, England (Erasure evident)	J. Whatman 1826
Paul Mellon (Erasure evident)	J.W.T.M. 1826
Rawlston D. Phillips, Jr., Baton Rouge, La. (Erasure evident)	J.W.T.M. 1826
Brown University (Erasure evident)	J.W.T.M. 1827
University of Illinois	J.W.T.M. (date not seen)

Questions of Internal Evidence

No. 1   PLATE II

Yellow-billed Cuckoo
Coccyzus Carolinensis
Plant Popaw Porceliatriloba

Drawn by J. J. Audubon F,R,S,E. F,L,S. M,W,S.   Engraved by W. H. Lizars Edinr.
Retouched by R. Havell Junr. London 1829
[Legend in upper left corner of plate]

Boston Athenaeum	J. Whatman 1830
Williams College	J. Whatman 1830

No. 1.   PLATE II.

Yellow-billed Cuckoo, Coccyzus americanus. Bonap,
Male .1. Female .2.
Pawpaw Tree. Porcelia triloba.

Drawn by J. J. Audubon. F.R.S.E.   Engraved by W. H. Lizars Edinr.
Retouched by R. Havell Junr. London 1829.

Academy of Natural Sciences of Philadelphia	J. Whatman 1830
California State Library	J. Whatman 1833
Yale University, Farnam set	J.W.T.M. 1833
City College of New York	J. Whatman 1836
Toronto Public Library	J. Whatman 1836

Plate 3 (2 variants found)

PLATE III.

Prothonotary Warbler.
Dacnis Protonotarius.
Plant Vulgo Cane Vine.

Drawn by J. J. Audubon M.W.S.   Engraved by W. H. Lizars Edinr.

Brown University	J. Whatman 1825
Tulane University	J. Whatman 1825
Estate of Mrs. Grace Phillips Johnson	J. Whatman 1826
Christ Church, Oxford University	J. Whatman 1827
Yale University, Garvan set	J.W.T.M. 1827
American Museum of Natural History	J. Whatman 1830

No. 1   PLATE. III.

Prothonotary Warbler.
Sylvia Protonotarius. Lath.
Male .1. Female .2.
Cane Vine.

Drawn from nature by J. J. Audubon F,R,S. F,L,S.   Engraved, Printed & Coloured, by
                                                                                               R. Havell Junr.

Charleston Library Society	J. Whatman 1831
Audubon Shrine and Wildlife Sanctuary, Audubon, Pa.	J.W.T.M. 1834
University of Minnesota	J. Whatman 1837
Trinity College	J. Whatman 1838
Yale University, Farnam set	J.W.T.M. (*date trimmed*)

Plate 4 (3 variants found)

PLATE IV.

Purple Finch.
Fringilla Purpurea.
Plant Pinus pendula.

Drawn by J. J. Audubon M.W.S.   Engraved by W. H. Lizars Edinr.

Audubon Sanctuary, Key West	J.W.T.M. 1826
Paul Mellon	J. Whatman 1826
Estate of Mrs. Grace Phillips Johnson	J.W.T.M. (*date bound in*)
University of Edinburgh, Scotland	J.W.T.M. (*date bound in*)

PLATE IV.

Purple Finch.
Fringilla Purpurea.
Plant Pinus pendula.
Vulgo Black Larch.

Drawn by J. J. Audubon M.W.S.   Engraved by W. H. Lizars Edinr.

H. Bradley Martin	J. Whatman 1826
Yale University, Garvan set	J. Whatman 1827
Brown University	J.W.T.M. 1827
Daniel W. Evans	J.W.T.M. 1827
New York Public Library, Tilden set	J.W.T.M. 1828

Questions of Internal Evidence

No. 1.   PLATE .IV.

Purple Finch Fringilla Purpurea. Gmel,
Male .1. 2. Female .3.. Red Larch—Larix americana.

Drawn from nature by J. J. Audubon F,R,S. F,L,S.	Engraved, Printed & Coloured, by R. Havell, Jun*r*.
J. N. Bartfield, New York, N.Y.	J. Whatman 1830
Laval Université	J. Whatman 1832
Yale University, Farnam set	J.W.T.M. 1833
City College of New York	J. Whatman 1837

Plate 5 (2 variants found)

PLATE V.

Bonaparte Fly Catcher.
Muscicapa Bonapartii.
Plant seed pud Magnolia grandiflora.

Drawn by J. J. Audubon M.W.S.	Engraved by W. H. Lizars Edin*r*.
The College of Glasgow, Scotland	J. Whatman 1825
American Museum of Natural History	J. Whatman 1826
Brown University	J. Whatman 1826
Yale University, Garvan set	J. Whatman 1827
University Library, Cambridge, England	J.W.T.M. 1827
Boston Athenaeum	J. Whatman 1830
Pierpont Morgan Library	J. Whatman 1830

No. 1.   PLATE .V.

Bonaparte's Flycatcher, Muscicapa Bonapartii. Aud,
Male. Great Magnolia—Magnolia grandiflora.

Drawn from nature by J. J. Audubon F,R,S, F,L,S.	Engraved, Printed & Coloured, by R. Havell Jun*r*.
Providence Athenaeum	J. Whatman 1830
State Library of Victoria, Melbourne, Australia	J. Whatman 1832
University of Southern California	J.W.T.M. 1832
City College of New York	J. Whatman 1838
Yale University, Farnam set	J.W.T.M. (*date bound in*)

NUMBER 2

Plate 6 (3 variants found)

PLATE VI. No. II.

Great American Hen & Young.
Vulgo, Female Wild Turkey.—Meleagris Gallopavo.

Drawn from Nature by John J. Audubon F.R.S.E.M.W.S.   Engraved by W. H. Lizars Edinr.
[*No snail in lower right corner.*]

Brown University	J. Whatman 1827
Rawlston D. Phillips, Jr., Baton Rouge, La.	J. Whatman 1827
Christ Church, Oxford University	J.W.T.M. 1827
Daniel W. Evans	J.W.T.M. 1827
Yale University, Garvan set	J.W.T.M. 1827

PLATE VI.   No. II

Great American Hen & Young   Vulgo Female Wild Turkey
Meleagris Gallopavo

Drawn from Nature by John J. Audubon F.R.S.E.F.L.S.M.W.S.   Engraved by W. H. Lizars Edinr.
Retouched by R. Havell Junr. London 1829
Coloured by R. Havell Senr.
[*Snail is in the lower right corner but colored same green as foliage, making it difficult to see.*]

Audubon Shrine and Wildlife Sanctuary, Audubon, Pa.	J. Whatman 1828
Boston Athenaeum	(*Watermark not discernible*)

No. II   PLATE VI

Wild Turkey, Meleagris Gallopavo. Linn Female and Young.

Drawn from Nature by J. J. Audubon F,R,S F,L,S   Engraved by W. H. Lizars
Retouched by R. Havell, Junr.
[*Snail, usually colored tan or brown, is visible in lower right corner.*]

Princeton University	J. Whatman 1832
University Library, Scientific and Medical Dept., Copenhagen, Denmark	J. Whatman 1832
Buffalo Museum of Science	J.W.T.M. 1834
Louisiana State University	J.W.T.M. 1834
Windsor Castle, Berkshire, England	J. Whatman 1836
City College of New York	J. Whatman 1837
Yale University, Farnam set	J.W.T.M. 183(?)

Questions of Internal Evidence

Plate 7 (3 variants found)

PLATE VII. No. II.

Purple Grackle Quiscalus Versicolor.
1. Male 2. Female.
Plant Vulgo, Indian Corn.

Drawn from Nature by John J. Audubon F.R.S.E. M.W.S.   Engraved by W. H. Lizars Edinr.
Printed & Coloured by R. Havell Senr.

Audubon Sanctuary, Key West	J. Whatman 1826
H. Bradley Martin	J. Whatman 1826
Paul Mellon	J. Whatman 1826
Brown University	J. Whatman 1827
Rawlston D. Phillips, Jr., Baton Rouge, La.	J. Whatman 1827
Christ Church, Oxford University	J.W.T.M. 1827
Daniel W. Evans	J.W.T.M. 1827
Yale University, Garvan set	J.W.T.M. 1827

No. II   PLATE VII

Purple Grackle, Quiscalus Versicolor
1. Male 2. Female
Plant Vulgo, Indian Corn

Drawn from Nature by John J. Audubon F,R,S,E. F,L,S. M,W,S.   Engraved by W. H. Lizars Edinr.
Retouched by R. Havell Junr. London 1829
Printed, & Coloured by R. Havell Senr.

Legislative Library, Fredericton, New Brunswick, Canada	J.W.T.M. 1828
Williams College	J. Whatman 1830

No. II.   PLATE VII.

Purple Grakle or Common Crow Blackbird, Quiscalus
versicolor. Vieill.
Male .1. Female .2. Maize or Indian Corn. Zea Mays.

Drawn from Nature by J. J. Audubon, F,R,S. F,L,S.   Engraved by W. H. Lizars Edinr.
Retouched by R. Havell Junr. London 1829.

American Philosophical Society	J. Whatman 1830
University Library, Scientific and Medical Dept., Copenhagen, Denmark	J. Whatman 1832
California State Library	J. Whatman 1833

221

Cleveland Museum of Natural History J. Whatman 1833
Public Library of Cincinnati and
 Hamilton County J. Whatman 1833
Yale University, Farnam set J. Whatman 1833
Audubon Shrine and Wildlife Sanctuary,
 Audubon, Pa. J. Whatman 1836
Royal Library, Windsor Castle, England J. Whatman 1836

Plate 8 (2 variants found)

PLATE VIII. No. II

White Throated Sparrow
Fringilla Pensylvanica.
1. Male 2. Female
Plant Cornus Florida—Vulgo Dog Wood.

Drawn from Nature by John J. Audubon F.R.S.E. M.W.S. Engraved by W. H. Lizars Edinr.
Printed & Coloured by R. Havell, Senr.
[*Legend in lower left corner of plate.*]

Joseph Verner Reed J. Whatman 1826
Brown University J. Whatman 1827
John Rylands Library, Manchester, England J. Whatman 1827
Yale University, Garvan set J.W.T.M. 1827
Christ Church, Oxford University J.W.T.M. 1828
Boston Athenaeum J. Whatman 1830
New York Public Library, Tilden set J.W.T.M. (*date bound in*)

No. 2. PLATE .VIII.

White throated Sparrow
Fringilla pennsylvanica. Lath,
Male .1. Female .2.
Dog-wood, Cornus florida.

Drawn from Nature by John J. Audubon F,R,S. F,L,S Engraved by W. H. Lizars Edinr.

Academy of Natural Sciences of Philadelphia J. Whatman 1831
California State Library J.W.T.M. 1833
Yale University, Farnam set J.W.T.M. 1833
City College of New York J. Whatman 1837
Picton Reference Library, Liverpool
 England J.W.T.M. (*date bound in*)

Prothonotary Warbler.

DACNIS PROTONOTARIUS.

Plant Vulgo Cane Vine.

Drawn by J. J. Audubon M.W.S.   Engraved by W. H. Lizars Edin^r.

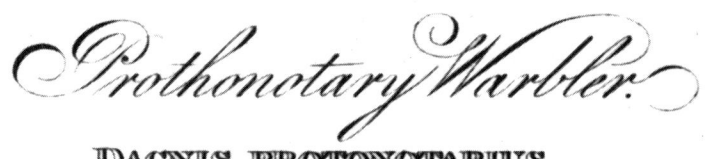

Prothonotary Warbler.

SYLVIA PROTONOTARIUS. Lath,
Male. 1. Female. 2.
Cane Vine.

Drawn from nature by J.J. Audubon F, R, S. F, L, S.

Engraved, Printed & Coloured, by R. Havell Junr.

Two representations of two legends of Plate 3 showing differences in the artist and engraver credit lines and in scientific nomenclature. The first state is shown in the two upper photographs and the second state in the two lower. The lower photograph in each set has been reduced to exhibit all of the elements of the legend in their actual spatial relationships. The upper photographs distort the original placement of elements but show them in a legible size. For names of individuals and institutions owning sets with these variants, see pages 217–18.

Selby's Fly Catcher

MUSCICAPA SELBII.

Plant Vulgo. Pheasants Eye.

Drawn from Nature by John J. Audubon F.R.S.E.M.W.S.

Engraved by W. H. Lizars Edin.

Printed & Coloured by R. Havell, Sen.

Selby's Fly Catcher
MUSCICAPA SELBII.
Plant Vulgo. Pheasants Eye.
Drawn from Nature by John J. Audubon F.R.S.E.M.W.S.   Printed & Coloured by R. Havell, Sen.   Engraved by W. H. Lizars Edin.

Selby's Flycatcher.

MUSCICAPA SELBII. Aud.
Male.

Flos Adonis.   Adonis autumnalis.

Drawn from Nature by J. J. Audubon, F.R.S. F.L.S

Engraved by W. H. Lizars Edin.

Drawn from Nature by J.J. Audubon, F.R.S. F.L.S.   *Selby's Flycatcher.* MUSCICAPA SELBII. Aud, Male. Flos Adonis Adonis autumnalis.   Engraved by W. H. Lizars Edin.

Two representations of two legends of Plate 4 showing differences in the artist and engraver credit lines and in scientific nomenclature. The first state is shown in the two upper photographs and the second state in the two lower. The lower photograph in each set has been reduced to exhibit all of the elements of the legend in their actual spatial relationships. The upper photographs distort the original placement of elements but show them in a legible size. For names of individuals and institutions owning sets with these variants, see pages 218-19.

Bonaparte Fly Catcher.

MUSCICAPA BONAPARTII.

Plant seed pud Magnolia grandiflora.

Drawn by J.J.Audubon M.W.S.   Engraved by W.H.Lizars Edin.

Bonapartes Flycatcher,

MUSCICAPA BONAPARTII. Aud,

Male.

Great Magnolia — Magnolia grandiflora.

Drawn from nature by J.J.Audubon F.R.S.F.L.S.

Engraved, Printed & Coloured by R.Havell Jun.

Two representations of two legends of Plate 5 showing differences in the artist and engraver credit lines and in scientific nomenclature. The first state is shown in the two upper photographs and the second state in the two lower. The lower photograph in each set has been reduced to exhibit all of the elements of the legend in their actual spatial relationships. The upper photographs distort the original placement of elements but show them in a legible size. For names of institutions owning sets with these variants, see page 219.

Purple Finch

FRINGILLA PURPUREA.

Plant Pinus pendula

Vulgo Black Larch.

Drawn by J.J. Audubon M.W.S.  Engraved by W.H. Lizars Edin.

Purple Finch

FRINGILLA PURPUREA, Gmel,
Male. 1. 2. Female. 3.
Red Larch — Larix americana.

Drawn from nature by J.J. Audubon F, R, S. E, L, S.

Engraved, Printed & Coloured, by R. Havell. Jun.

Two representations of two legends of Plate 9 showing differences in the artist and engraver lines and in scientific nomenclature. The first state is shown in the two upper photographs and the second state in the two lower. The lower photograph in each set has been reduced to exhibit all of the elements of the legend in their actual spatial relationships. The upper photographs distort the original placement of elements but show them in a legible size. For names of individuals and institutions owning sets with these variants, see page 223.

Questions of Internal Evidence

Plate 9 (2 variants found)

PLATE IX.   No. II.

Selby's Fly Catcher
Muscicapa Selbii.
Plant Vulgo, Pheasants Eye.

Drawn from Nature by John J. Audubon F.R.S.E. M.W.S.   Engraved by W. H. Lizars Edin*r*.
Printed & Coloured by R. Havell. Sen*r*.

Brown University	J. Whatman 1827
John Rylands Library, Manchester, England	J. Whatman 1827
Indiana Historical Society Library	J.W.T.M. 1827
Yale University, Garvan set	J.W.T.M. 1827
Williams College	J. Whatman 1830

No. 2.   PLATE. IX.

Selby's Flycatcher,
Muscicapa Selbii. Aud,
Male.
Flos-Adonis. Adonis autumnalis.

Drawn from Nature by J. J. Audubon, F,R,S,E. F,L,S.   Engraved by W. H. Lizars Edin*r*.

Providence Athenaeum	J. Whatman 1831
Harvard University	J. Whatman 1832
Mrs. Frederick W. Beinecke	J.W.T.M. 1833
Yale University, Farnam set	J.W.T.M. 1833
New York Society Library	J.W.T.M. 1834
Picton Reference Library, Liverpool, England	J.W.T.M. (*date bound in*)

Plate 10 (2 variants found)

PLATE X.   No. 2.

Brown Lark
Anthus Aquaticus.
1. Male 2. Female.

Drawn from Nature by John J. Audubon F.R.S.E. M.W.S.   Engraved by W. H. Lizars Edin*r*.
Printed and Coloured by R. Havell. Sen*r*.

Brown University	J. Whatman 1827
Victoria and Albert Museum, London, England	J. Whatman 1827

223

THE DOUBLE ELEPHANT FOLIO

National Gallery, Washington, D.C.	J.W.T.M.	1827
Yale University, Garvan set	J.W.T.M.	1827
Northwestern University	J. Whatman	1830
H. J. Lutcher Stark Foundation (Bachman copy)	J. Whatman	1830

No. 2. PLATE .X.

Brown Titlark,
Anthus Spinoletta. Bonap,
1. Male 2. Female.

Drawn from Nature by J. J. Audubon, F,R,S. F,L,S. Engraved, Printed, & Coloured, by R. Havell.

Providence Athenaeum	J. Whatman 1831
Indiana University	J. Whatman 1831
Bowdoin College	J.W.T.M. 1833
New York Society Library	J. Whatman 1836
Windsor Castle, Berkshire, England	J. Whatman 1836
University of Minnesota	J. Whatman 1837
Yale University, Farnam set	J.W.T.M. (date trimmed)

26

PROVENANCES OF SETS IN THE UNITED STATES AND CANADA

THE ACADEMY OF NATURAL SCIENCES
Philadelphia, Pa.

On his first trip from England Audubon had remained in America from early May 1829 until the following April. He made a short visit to Philadelphia but, as he wrote his son, his reason for coming to America was "to take your Mama over to England" and, "to redraw some of my earliest productions."[1] His visit to Philadelphia was recorded by Dr. Harlan, a member of the Academy of Natural Sciences, in a letter written 29 October 1829 to William Swainson:

> Nothing can surpass the indefatigable industry of our friend Audubon, since his residence with us. He has collected 30 or 40 of the most splendid drawings of the most interesting birds, . . . I fear he will fail in adding to his list of subscribers—we have had so much of American birds of late years, but above all, I think there is not an individual among us who ever dreamed of expending 7 or 800 dols. on a book of any dimensions, the price alone seems to frighten them. His drawings and his plates have been very much admired in the public institutions where I took pains to display them but the managers appeared not prepared at present to meet the necessary expenses of obtaining the work. Mr. A. is naturally enough mortified at this species of illiberality. I had commenced raising a subscription for the price of the work among my friends of the Acad. of Nat. Sciences of Phila. and could have succeeded, but Mr. A. declined it on such terms. He has a great deal of pride on this subject.[2]

In September 1831, immediately after his arrival in New York on his second trip to America, Audubon spent several weeks in Philadelphia. However not until 13 March 1832 is there a reference to the subscription of the academy. At that time the Naturalist wrote to his wife from Charleston and sent her a list of 22 subscribers he had obtained in America. Included among them was the "Society of Nat'l Sciences Phila."[3] It is of interest to note that although the actual subscription was not obtained until 1831, the first number of five plates of the *Birds of America* had been exhibited to members of the academy some years previously by Charles Lucien Bonaparte who had brought them to America in 1827 upon his return from England.[4]

It must have been after 20 September 1831 that the subscription was obtained, for on that day Audubon had written his engraver, "Since here [Philadelphia] I have obtained *Three* Subscribers." The academy was not one of the three.[5] On 25 October 1831, after Audubon had left Philadelphia, he was elected a corresponding member of the academy.[6] When he learned of his election he wrote Havell, "The Society of Natural Sciences has *at last* elected me one of their members, the Papers say Unanimously I dare say friend Lea was not in the way."[7]

An entry in the academy's Minute Book, dated 10 September 1833, reads, "Donation to the library 10 plates of Vol. II—Audubon's Birds of America, presented by a number of members."[8] Identification of the contributing members is made on page 41 in the bound catalog of the academy, dated 1837: "Audubon, The Birds of America . . . Messers Wm. Hembell, J. P. Wetherill, Col. S. H. Long, Wm. Norris, Jun., Thomas Fisher, Wm. Blanding, Reuben Haines, Jos. P. Smith, and Dr. Thomas F. Belton."

In one of Audubon's journals is a memorandum with the names of the academy members who subscribed and the amount of the individual payments:

```
Jos. P. Smith           pd.         $15.        pr. an. to 1837 inc.
J. P. Wetherill          "          $10.         "   "   "   "   "
W. Hembell               "          $10.         "   "   "   "   "
R. Haines Estate (by Mr. Wistar the Exc. paid to 1837 inc.)
W. Blanding    (has paid in full to V.G.A.)
Wm. Norris              pd.         $10.        pr. an. to 1837 inc.
Col. S. H. Long (has not paid since 1834)[9]
```

The memorandum appears to have been written in 1839. Audubon's receipt of 1 July 1837 to Dr. S. G. Morton on behalf of Joseph P. Smith has been found. This records Smith's payments totaling $60 (or $15 per annum) for the years 1834–1837.[10]

The minutes of the academy indicate that additional numbers were received at frequent intervals until 4 September 1839, when 30 plates arrived and the folio was completed.[11] Payments, however, were not made promptly. On 12 June 1837, Audubon wrote Dr. Samuel G. Morton from Charleston, "When I last saw you in Philadelphia you were so kind as to promise me that you would attend the collection of the amount due me on my work by the Academy of Natural Sciences. I feel at present greatly in the need of funds and should like much to receive the balance during my short stay in your city next month previous to my embarking for England, the balance amounted to 195 Dollars up to No. 66, and now 50 dollars will have to be added for Nos. 67, 68, 69, 70, 71, which the Academy has received lately."[12]

The difficulty in collecting payments from the academy continued. Audubon again wrote Morton in August 1837 and once more on 6 July 1840 when the amount owing him was, "three hundred and two dollars and 57/100."[13] However, as late as 12 August 1847 final settlement had not been made, for on that date Victor Audubon wrote to Edward Harris of Moorestown, and sent him a transcript of the academy's account showing a balance of $202.57. This letter indicates that Harris had previously endeavored to obtain payment, for Victor concludes, "Should you not be able to collect the whole we will relinquish as much as may be necessary in order to close the account after you have had so much trouble with it."[14]

THE AMERICAN MUSEUM OF NATURAL HISTORY
New York, N.Y.

This set of the folio was presented to the museum in 1904 by Archibald Rogers (1852-1928), a member of the Board of Trustees.[15] When the volumes were rebound in 1932 by the New York Public Library, earlier states of the following prints were added in Volume 1, namely, Plates 2, 3, 4, 5, 6, 7, 9, and 10. It is believed that these extra prints were obtained by Ralph W. Tower (1870-1926), who for twenty-three years occupied the dual post of curator of physiology and curator of books and publications.[16] How the set of the folio came into the possession of Mr. Rogers has not been possible to ascertain.

AMERICAN PHILOSOPHICAL SOCIETY
Philadelphia, Pa.

There are, in the library of the American Philosophical Society, two copies of a prospectus published by Audubon for his *Birds of America*. One copy was issued when the first number of five plates had been engraved, probably in May 1827. The other states that ten numbers had been completed and is, again, not dated but on the first page there has been written, "From J. J. Audibon [sic] 17 April 1829." While it was not until some years later that the subscription to the *Birds of America* was obtained, the first number of five plates had been exhibited to members of the society late in 1827 or early in 1828 by Charles Lucien Bonaparte. Bonaparte had brought the prints with him in the autumn of 1827 upon his return to America after a short visit to England.[17]

Audubon spent some time in Philadelphia in May and July of 1829, but whether he visited the society or tried to obtain a subscription to the *Birds of America* is not known. Two years later Audubon was again visiting the city and at that time, on 15 July, he was elected a member of the American Philosophical Society.

Three months later, on 7 October 1831, there appears the following entry in the Minute Book of the society and repeated in the Donations Book:

Audubon, James. The Birds of America from his drawings Vol. 1. & 3 No. of Vol. 2 grand folio 4 Vols expected subscribed for by Diverse members & presented to the Society. [The names of those subscribing members had been written in.]

Biddle, Col. Clement Cornell	Kane, John Kintzing
Biddle, Thomas	Keating, William Hypolitus
Brown, James	La Roche, Dr. Rene
Carey, Mathew	Lorich, Sverin
Chapman, Dr. Nathaniel	Meridith, William Tucker
Du Ponceau, Peter Stephen	Meigs, Charles Deluceno
DuPont, E. I.	Pollock, George
Hare, Dr. Robert	Seybert, Henry
Harlan, Dr. Richard	Short, William
Harris, Dr. T.	Strickland, William
Hembell, William	Vaughan, John
Hopkinson, Joseph	Ware, Nathaniel
Horner, William Edmonds	Wetherill, John Price

Mr. Audubon subscribed the binding. Expected cost 800$.

When Audubon left England in 1831 he took with him a number of bound volumes of the first one hundred plates of the *Birds of America* and one of these evidently was deposited with the American Philosophical Society. After the Naturalist's arrival in America he had received additional plates, those for three numbers of the second volume.

It has not been possible to find any details of the amount of the donations made by the individual members at the time of the meeting on 7 October. The only record which has come to light was that of a payment made by E. I. DuPont. This was obtained from a receipt issued to him by John Vaughan, the treasurer and librarian of the society, on which there is noted: "payment made for you on acc. of Audubon's work $20.," with the additional statement, "the Sub. to Audubon and for the completion of the work to pay pr. annum 5-."[18]

Since Dupont died of cholera on 31 October 1834, the payment referred to must have been for the four years 1831, 1832, 1833, and 1834.

As to the receipt of additional plates of the *Birds of America*, no reference could be found in the minutes of the society. However, as late as 30 June 1841, three years after the completion of the work, Victor Audubon, on behalf of his father, wrote to John Vaughan, asking his help in closing the account of the society on which there was still owing $90.00.[19]

The four hundred and thirty-five plates in possession of the American Philosophical Society are bound in five volumes, and many of the plates are backed with linen. The bookplates in the five volumes carry the notation "presented by George Ord." On the case in which the volumes are kept is this additional information "Subscribed for by diverse members and given to the Society, Oct. 7, 1831."

Provenances of Sets in the United States and Canada

AMHERST COLLEGE
Amherst, Mass.

The Audubon folio of the *Birds of America* was presented to Amherst College in 1915 by Herbert Pratt, a graduate of the class of 1895. It had been purchased by him from Bernhard Quaritch of London who wrote, on 30 November 1915, that the set came from the library of Edward Brown Lees of Thurland Castle and had been acquired by him at the sale of that library in November of 1912.[20] The record of the Sotheby auction sale of the Lees Library on 26 November 1912 shows that Quaritch purchased the Audubon folio for £540 (approx. $2700).

In the same letter, Quaritch wrote, "Nearly, I might almost say, every copy that has occurred for sale in this country has either been purchased or handled by me. I have no hesitation in describing your copy as the best of all, principally by reasons of its uncut state." In addition to commenting upon the condition of the set of the folio, Quaritch could have pointed out that it was a *unique* set from the fact that besides the title page and the hundred plates in volume one there is an engraved list of 132 subscriber's names, headed by "His Most Gracious Majesty, George IV" dated 31 December 1828. No other folio containing such an engraved list of subscribers has been located.

However, on one occasion Audubon did instruct his engraver to include a list of subscribers in a copy of the *Birds of America*. In a letter from Edinburgh to Havell on 11 November 1830, he wrote: "As I was stopping my letter George H. Head, Esq. Banker of Carlisle came in and *has* subscribed. Now do your best & find a *handsome, clean copy well coloured* & directed as above as soon as you can–of the 20 numbers with a sheet of Title, page of Contents & Subscribers names, in a good portfolio with Silver paper for the whole and write to me when this is done."[21]

It is strange that Audubon should have asked his engraver to include a "page of Contents & Subscribers names" in this instance, for he had purposely refrained from including letterpress of any kind with the engravings, as he feared that by so doing he would be subject to the copyright law requiring him to deposit a copy of his work in each of certain institutions in England, Wales, Scotland, and Ireland. At that, soon after his letter to Havell in reference to the Head subscription, he wrote him on 23 March 1831: "Your last is now before me and in reply to it I have merely to say *do not print any sheet of Contents at all*, the Birds of America will do very well without such a thing—My book of Ornithological Biography will answer all the purpose to the subscribers of the Great Work."[22] The first volume of this had been completed and was shortly to be issued.

The Head subscription is not included on the final list of European subscribers published by Audubon. However, an entry in Ledger "B" shows that Head obtained the first volume of 100 plates as well as numbers 21–31. The subscription may have been completed with the payment included in the account of one of Audubon's agents.

AUDUBON SHRINE AND WILDLIFE SANCTUARY
Audubon, Pa.

For many years this folio was on loan to the University Club of the City of New York, displayed there in the library. In April 1937 it was seen by an astute and enterprising young New York bookdealer who promptly arranged to purchase the volumes from the owner, Cecil Barret. Barret, although long a member of the club, had actually resigned a few years before.[23] The folio was soon sold to Charles T. Church, and in 1961 bequeathed to the Audubon Shrine and Wildlife Sanctuary by his widow.

There were deposited in the Audubon Shrine by the Church Estate a number of letters written to Cecil Barret concerning the folio. Much relating to the early history of the set is to be found in a letter written to Mr. Barret on 20 March 1906, by a cousin: "The edition you have is one of the original subscriptions, subscribed for by your grandfather, who, if I remember aright was the last subscriber and his name was not printed with the original subscribers but I think in one of the copies was written in by hand and I know he was one of the original number and received his copy direct from the publisher. If I am not mistaken, I think also, that he was a subscriber to the seven volume edition of 1840 and I know that he left in his will a copy of the seven volumes to Alexander Buchanan Barret Harris, who is named for him. He was a son of my uncle B. Harris. Alec sent his edition to (I think) Dodd and Mead for sale, perhaps two years ago, and they pronounced it to be a very fine copy of that edition but I do not know if the sale was affected. The copy that you have was never, so far as I know, in the possession of anybody but your grandfather and through him descended to your father, and to you."

The grandfather referred to was Alexander Buchanan Barret, born in Virginia on 18 March 1811. He went to Henderson, Ky., in 1833 and there established himself in the tobacco business. Some years later he was joined by his brother John. They became very successful merchants and Alexander was reputed to have been one of America's first millionaires. He died in New York City on 15 June 1861.

An examination of the folio lends credence to the statement that Alexander Buchanan Barret was "the last subscriber but his name was not printed on the list of subscribers." The Whatman watermarks of the first ten prints show a variation in date from 1826 to 1836, suggesting that the collection of prints had been assembled from those left over at the completion of the engraving in 1838 and later sent to America.

In volume 5 there is found the name of the binder, namely Pawson and Nicholson of 519–521 Minor Street, Philadelphia. From the city directory it was found that this firm was located at the above address from 1849–1868.[24] A flyleaf has a watermark (not Whatman, but T & F H, dated 1858).

Although Alexander Buchanan Barret may not have been exactly the last subscriber, it is evident that the folio of the 435 prints was assembled nearly twenty years after the work was completed and actually seven years after the death of Audubon.

AUDUBON STATE PARK MUSEUM
Henderson, Ky.

The original subscriber of this set was Thomas Walker of Killingbeck Hall, near Leeds, England, the son of William Walker, a wealthy cloth merchant.[25] Thomas was a connoisseur and patron of several local artists and it is believed that he also was the owner of several paintings by Gainsborough and two by Watteau.

Walker was among the early subscribers to the *Birds of America*. Although it has not been possible to determine the exact date the subscription was obtained, it probably was during the period Audubon was visiting Leeds, late in April and early May of 1827.

While Lizars was busily at work engraving the first ten plates, Audubon left Edinburgh and embarked on a trip to northern England to solicit subscribers. He left on the first of April and, after visiting Newcastle and York, he arrived in Leeds on the 28th of the month.

Writing in his journal on 2 May, while in Leeds, the Naturalist noted: "Mr. George called very early, and said that his colleague, the Secretary of the Literary and Philosophical Society, would call and subscribe, and he has done so."[26]

On the following day, 3 May, Audubon made this entry: "Until two o'clock this day I had only one visitor, Mr. John Marshall, a member of Parliament to whom I had a letter; he told me he knew nothing at all about birds, but most generously subscribed, because he told me, it was such a work as every one ought to possess, and to encourage enterprise."[27] Also on 3 May he wrote: "I have at Leeds only five subscribers— poor indeed compared with the little town of York." He had obtained 10 subscribers there.[28]

Audubon had been persuaded to carry with him a subscription book in which he endeavored to have each subscriber sign his name. Fortunately, pages from this have been preserved and are presently in the possession of Joseph Verner Reed. Upon reference to these, the subscribers in Leeds were found to be the following:

> Thomas Walker. Killinbeck [sic] near Leeds
> Leeds Philosophical Society and Literary
>   Society, Philosophical Hall
> John Marshall, Junr. Headingly
> John Gott
> George Banks.

Since the secretary of the Literary and Philosophical Society subscribed on 2 May and as Thomas Walker's name appears just ahead of that of the society, Audubon undoubtedly obtained the Walker subscription at practically the same time.

There is a reference to Walker in the introduction to Volume 2 of the *Ornithological Biography*. Here Audubon, writing about this trip to Leeds, stated: "At Leeds, the Gotts, the Bankses, the Walkers, the Marshalls, and the Davys were all extremely kind to me."[29]

The folio remained in the possession of descendants of Thomas Walker until the 1920s when it was purchased by the well-known ornithologist, Dr. Robert Cushman Murphy, who sold it to Mrs. Carll Tucker in 1935.[30] In June 1965 the folio was sent by Mrs. Tucker to the museum at the Audubon State Park, Henderson, Ky.

J. N. BARTFIELD
New York, N.Y.

When this folio of the *Birds of America* was examined in 1958 at the Cooper Union for the Advancement of Science and Art, it was possible to obtain but little information as to the provenance of the set. The librarian stated that it had been presented to the Cooper Union in 1921 by Erskine Hewitt: "It was reported that in the archives there were original papers of Hewitt but these had never been examined for clues as to how and when the folio had been obtained." In *Who Was Who, 1897–1942*, it is stated that Erskine Hewitt was born in New York on 12 January 1871, the son of Abraham Stevens Hewitt and Sarah Amelia Cooper. A grandson of Peter Cooper, Hewitt was educated at Princeton University, graduating in 1891. He received his master's degree from the same university in 1893 and an L.L.B. degree from New York Law School in the same year. He never married.

In July 1973 J. N. Bartfield purchased the folio for his personal library.

The early watermarks of the first ten plates indicate that the subscriber to the set was among Audubon's early English patrons.

MRS. FREDERICK W. BEINECKE
New York, N.Y.

Prior to the purchase of this folio by Frederick W. Beinecke in 1959 from H. P. Krause,[31] the New York dealer in rare books, the set had been for many years in the possession of the Long Island Historical Society of Brooklyn, N.Y. In the Minutes of the Society for 18 January 1866 there appears the following report: "The great work of Audubon . . . [here follows a long description of it] has been procured for our library from the estate of one of our subscribers in Philadelphia, lately deceased and it is now added to our collections."[32]

Again, in the *Third Annual Report* of May 1866, it is noted that the Society received: ". . . from Mr. George S. Stephenson the sum of $1100, for the purchase of the magnificent work of Audubon on 'The Birds of America.' "[33]

It will be noted that in the Minutes of the Society for 18 January 1866 there is the phrase, "from the estate of one of *our* [italics this author's] subscribers in Philadelphia." When the additional information in the society's *Third Annual Report*, 1866, was supplied this author, it was discerned that the correct phrase was, "from the estate of one of *the* [italics this author's] subscribers in Philadelphia, lately deceased."[34]

In the files of the society also were found three letters relating to the folio. These were dated 28, 29, and 30 December 1865 and in them was the information that the folio had been purchased from Guy Bryan Schott, administrator for the estate of William Schott, of 1522 Pine Street, Philadelphia, for $1,100 and $10 packing and shipping charges.[35] The Philadelphia Directory of 1863 lists William Schott as a wholesale druggist and Guy Bryan Schott as an attorney.

Number 22 on Audubon's final list of subscribers, is "Mrs. Ford, Philadelphia."[36] The entry for this subscription in Ledger "B" (where again neither given name nor initial is recorded) indicates that the subscription was completed.

The only other reference by Audubon to Mrs. Ford which has been found is contained in a letter to his son Victor which the Naturalist wrote from Richmond on 15 April 1840 while he was soliciting subscriptions for the Octavo edition: "This morning 6 Names.—Mrs. M. M. Elfreth is the Sister of M*rs* [Ford] of Phil*a* who Subscribed for and has the large Work."[37]

In a list of portraits painted by Thomas Sully contained in *The Life and Works of Thomas Sully (1783–1872)* are three listings which seem to offer a clue or at least a connection with the Ford folio.[38] These are found therein on the following pages:

145. "517 [among the "E" names] Olfrith, Mrs. [Alexander] and her daughter. Portrait begun April 16, 1836, finished June 3, 1836. Size 24" x 20". Price, $200.00"

153. "596 Ford, Mrs. C. Portrait painted for Thos. Bryan, begun Oct. 30th 1829, finished Nov. 20th, 1829. Head. Price, $50.00"

154. "596 Ford, Mrs. C. Head, nearly full face, lace cap and blue ribbon. Signed 'TS 1830.' Size 14" x 20". Second portrait, begun Jan. 30th, 1830, finished Feb. 1st, 1830. Price, $50.00
    "Owned [in 1921] by Miss Mary W. Schott, Phila."

Miss Mary Wagner Schott died in 1928 at the age of 82.[39] It will be recalled that the folio of the Long Island Historical Society was purchased from Guy Bryan Schott, administrator for the estate of William Schott.

Audubon and the artist Thomas Sully (1781–1871) met in Philadelphia in 1824. It is believed that at the time he applied for instruction in painting from the artist. It was Sully who gave Audubon a letter of introduction to Sir Thomas Lawrence, the English portrait painter. Sully also was active in defending Audubon against his Philadelphia critics.[40] Over the years a close friendship developed between the two men.

There are links missing in the chain, but from the records of the Long Island

Historical Society, the correspondence from Guy Bryan Schott, the administrator of the estate of William Schott, to the Society, and that of Audubon himself, the "great work of Audubon . . . procured from the estate of one of the subscribers in Philadelphia," is most probably the Ford copy of the folio. In addition, in the record of the Sully paintings there is evidence of some relationship between the Ford and Schott families.

Frederick William Beinecke died on 30 July 1971 and the folio, at this writing, is in the possession of Mrs. Beinecke.

BOSTON ATHENAEUM
Boston, Mass.

On 9 November 1830, at a meeting of the Trustees of the Boston Athenaeum, it was voted to subscribe to "Audubon's ornithology, the treasurer to appropriate $800."[41] On the original subscription list it is listed as "Boston Athenaeum aca by T. H. Perkins." Thomas Handasyd Perkins (1764–1854) was at the time president of the Athenaeum. Audubon obtained his subscription in the summer of 1832 when visiting Boston.

Notice of the Athenaeum's subscription must have been sent to England immediately for, on 20 January 1831, the engraver, Havell, wrote to Audubon in Edinburgh that he had received a subscription from the Boston Athenaeum.[42] Although Audubon had been in America from May 1829 until April 1830, he had not been in Boston.

There is the possibility that the subscription had been obtained through the efforts of Edward Everett (1794–1865), a member of the Athenaeum since 1822. The Naturalist had met Everett in March 1830 when the latter was a representative from Massachusetts and chairman of the Joint Committee of the Library of Congress from which the subscription to the *Birds of America* had been obtained. During that same time Audubon had asked Everett's help to have Congress remove the import duty on the *Birds of America*. In addition the Naturalist left with Everett some copies of his prospectus.

A year later, in May 1831, Everett had written to Audubon that "The portions of your works which arrived in Washington before I left, were publicly exhibited in the library, and attracted great satisfaction and unqualified admiration. The same is true of the copy received by the Boston Athenaeum. The plates were specially exhibited in the great hall, to the entire satisfaction and delight of those who saw them."[43]

Another reference to the Athenaeum subscription is found in the diary of John Perkins Cushing who noted that the fourth volume of the *Birds of America* had been received in Boston early in 1839 and that on 12 March a payment of $320 was made to Dr. Parkman, Audubon's agent.[44]

The first and second numbers (plates 1–10) of the Athenaeum set include examples of the early states of the prints. Plate 1 bears the legend, "Great American

Cock," Plate 6, "Great American Hen & Young," while the legend on Plate 2 is in the upper left hand corner and on Plate 8 the word "Pennsylvanica" is spelled "Pe*n*sylvanica."

Nine members of the Boston Athenaeum became original subscribers to the *Birds of America*.

BOSTON PUBLIC LIBRARY
Boston, Mass.

On page 15 of the third Annual Report of the Trustees of the Public Library of Boston, dated 15 November 1855, will be found the following: "Among the more valuable donations the Trustees feel bound to particularize . . . a copy of Audubon's Ornithology, in four volumes of the largest size and superior binding by Thomas G. Appleton, Esq."[45]

Samuel Appleton, an original subscriber to the *Birds of America*, died in July 1853 without issue. It is most likely that his copy of the folio came into the possession of his nephew, Thomas G. Appleton, who never married and who, in turn, presented it to the Boston Public Library in 1855.

Also in the possession of the library are the first 100 prints of the folio, loose. These appear never to have been bound. No information is available as to the provenance of the 100 loose prints.

BOWDOIN COLLEGE
Brunswick, Me.

In a letter dated New York, 20 September 1833, Audubon wrote his son Victor in London, "I expect shortly to be able to send you the subscription of Bowdon [sic] College Brunswick, Maine, having received a letter from Professor Cleveland [Parker Cleaveland, 1780–1858] requesting a prospectus of the work."

This was only wishful thinking, for the subscription was never received. However, in 1953, a folio was presented to the college by Roscoe H. Hupper, in memory of his mother Mary Alden Hupper (1854–1944). Mr. Hupper, who died in May 1967, was a member of the class of 1907.

The folio was at one time in the possession of the American Museum of Natural History to which it had been a gift from a prominent New York attorney, Charles Southmayd (1824–1911), for many years a member of the firm of Evarts, Southmayd and Choate.

In connection with this folio, Ruthven Deane, long a student of Auduboniana, had written on 23 September 1923 to Ralph W. Tower, one-time librarian at the Museum, "I knew Charles Southmayd well. It may interest you to know that Mr. Southmayd purchased it in New York City about 1876. The price paid was

$1,000 and $100 commission." At the time of the Southmayd accession, the Museum already owned a copy of the folio and it was for this reason that the Southmayd copy was sold.

BROWN UNIVERSITY
Providence, R.I.

This folio is listed in "The Leiter Library: A Catalogue of the Books, Manuscripts and Maps Relating to America Collected by the Late Levi Ziegler Leiter" (1834–1904). A copy of this catalog was sent to the John Carter Brown Library on 15 February 1908. Levi Z. Leiter, a prominent Chicago merchant, was elected president of the Chicago Art Institute on 27 May 1880. He later moved from Chicago to Washington where he collected a valuable library of early American history and literature. He traveled extensively in nearly every part of the world and everywhere added to his valuable library.

On page 13 of the Leiter catalog the folio is described as follows: "Audubon, John J. (1780 [?]–1851) The Birds of America from Original Drawings, London. Published by the author 1827–38. 4 volumes in 6. El. folio size, 99 x 66cm. Half red levant-morocco with corners of the same." There could have been added: In all six volumes the prints are interleaved with J. Whatman Turkey Mill sheets; also "Bound by F. Bedford, London."

The first volume contains all four of the original title pages. Each volume has an additional title page reading, "Four Volumes Bound in Six." The plates in this set of the folio are bound as follows:

Vol.	Plates
1	1–72
2	73–144
3	145–216
4	217–289
5	290–361
6	362–435.

As to the provenance of the set, the following appears in the catalog: "It was purchased of Sotheran in 1880, and was known as the Hays set. Mr. B. F. Stevens, in a letter discussing this copy says, 'I went to Sotheran's to see the Audubon birds and found it a very fine set evidently kept by a subscriber as it was received on publication.'" It has not been possible to identify "Hays" with any original subscriber.

The set and the five volumes of the *Ornithological Biography* were purchased by Mr. Lownes at the auction sale held for the American Art Association by the Anderson Galleries on 15 and 16 February 1933 for $5,200.

In May 1970, on the occasion of the fiftieth reunion of his class, Mr. Lownes presented the folio to Brown University.

Provenances of Sets in the United States and Canada

BUFFALO AND ERIE COUNTY PUBLIC LIBRARY
Buffalo, N.Y.

On 10 December 1897 there appeared in the *Buffalo Express* an article with the heading, "Birds of America," followed by the subcaptions,

>Charles H. Williams's
>Bibliophilic Treasure
>
>Audubon's Full Work
>
>After years of search the Buffalo Book-lover secures one of the few perfect copies of the great ornithologist's book—not a plate missing.

The article reports that Williams had just returned from New York, bringing with him "a prize precious to all book-lovers and above all to ornithologists." Charles H. Williams had for years had a standing order with New York ornithologists and bibliophiles for a perfect set of the folio and had traveled thousands of miles in search of one. Upon learning of the availability of the set in New York, he arranged with Prof. W. T. Hornaday and Ernest Seton Thompson, the artist, to examine it with him. After an inspection lasting six hours, the work was found complete, perfect, and genuine, with the result that Williams immediately purchased it and took it to Buffalo.

The *Buffalo Express* story contains two references to the provenance of the set purchased by Williams: "that the owner of the set was a prominent Audubon man of famed ancestors," and that "among the 82 American subscribers were four from Albany, one of whom originally owned the set now owned by Mr. Williams." Audubon's final list of American subscribers contained in volume 5 of the *Ornithological Biography* includes the name of only one subscriber in Albany, that of Stephen Van Rensselaer, Esq.

The folio was presented in 1930 to the Grosvenor Reference Library (now part of the combined Buffalo and Erie County Public Library) by Mrs. Frederick L. Pratt, the daughter of Charles H. Williams. A special case displaying the artistry and vibrant color of the 24-by-39-inch plates became a major focus of interest in the library. After the library first received the folio, a plate was turned each Monday, with the result that it would have taken one somewhat longer than eight years to view the four volumes.

In addition to the complete folio, the library also possesses three volumes with the plates bound as follows: Volume 1, plates 1–100; Volume 2, plates 300, 101–200; and Volume 3, plates 201–99. According to Richard T. Morris of the library, in a letter written to the author on 17 September 1957, these volumes were obtained by the Young Men's Association of the City of Buffalo at some time prior to 8 February 1837. The First Annual Report of the Executive Committee of the association under that date stated that:

> ... the great work of Audubon, upon the Birds of America, was thought to be indispensible to form a complete collection on the subject of Ornithology, and though the expense is great, yet considering the intrinsic value of the work, it is cheap at $800, the subscription price, and finding an opportunity of purchasing it at the subscription price upon a year's credit, they thought it fit to purchase it. The first volume is now in the Library and is really a great addition to the attraction of our Library. Fearing that this purchase might not be santioned by the judgment of our patrons, on account of the expense your Committee has resolved to make an effort to pay for it without using any of the heretofore donated funds of the Association. Considerable progress has been made with a subscription for the special purpose of paying for this work, and $80.00 have been subscribed at the Library by persons who would give like sums for no other purpose.

It has not been possible to find any additional references to the purchase of the folio by the Young Men's Association of the City of Buffalo. On the other hand the Ninth Annual Report of the Executive Committee, dated 14 February 1845, yielded the following information: "Your Committee takes pleasure in announcing that in the month of January last, Benjamin Fitch, Esq. of this city donated to this association, Mr. Audubon's 'Quadrupeds of America', now in progress of publication, the first nos. of which have been received, and that as the strongest testimony of their appreciation of the value of this donation, in the power of your Committee to give to Mr. Fitch, they elected him a life member."

The Young Men's Association changed its name to "The Buffalo Library" through an act passed by the New York State Legislature on 15 May 1886. This followed the annual meeting during which the organization's president, Mr. Jewett M. Richmond, drew attention to the confusion on the part of the community due to the resemblance of the name to that of The Young Men's Christian Association.

It was in the files of the Buffalo and Erie County Public Library that there was found a copy of "A Brief Record of the Elephant Folio Edition of Audubon's 'Birds of America,' to Whom They Have Belonged and Where They Can Be Found," by Anthony Woodward, Ph.D., dated 23 March 1901. The library also has the letter, written by Ernest Seton Thompson on 27 December 1897 to Mr. Williams, recounting in detail his examination of the folio with comments as to size of prints, condition, and the like.

BUFFALO SOCIETY OF NATURAL SCIENCES
Buffalo Museum of Science
Buffalo, N.Y.

Loammi Baldwin (1780–1838), in a letter dated Charleston (Mass.), 1 October 1836, wrote Audubon: "My wish was to enter my name with you *personally* as a subscriber to your Ornithology which appears to me a work of such great &

peculiar genius upon birds of our country."[46] Baldwin was a prominent civil engineer with business activities in Massachusetts, Pennsylvania, and Virginia.[47]

The first three volumes were sent to Baldwin on 7 July 1837 through another subscriber, George C. Shattuck, who also acted as one of Audubon's American agents, and Baldwin sent Shattuck his check for $660 in payment for these. He did not live long after this, for he died in 1838, the year the work was completed in London.

The folio came into possession of Dame Catherine Rumford Griffith of Quebec, Canada, who was the daughter of George Rumford Baldwin (1798–1888), a half-brother of Loammi. Dame Catherine also had inherited the family home in Woburn, Massachusetts, and the *Birds* remained in the library there, the family using the place as a summer home.

Dame Catherine Rumford Griffith died on 6 December 1910. One provision of her will stated: "To my cousin Loammi F. Baldwin the Old Mansion House situated in Woburn in the State of Massachusetts, built in the year 1661, together with five acres of land surrounding it, together also with the household furniture, house furnishings and other effects therein contained except as such as may be herein specially bequeathed."

Another provision of interest is: "To my cousin Dr. Roswell Park, all my paintings and one half of my silverware in Quebec, and not herein specially bequeathed."

Listed in the inventory of the Baldwin Mansion in Woburn, dated 25 January 1911, are: "Four volumes of Audubon's Birds of America—$1500."[48]

One of the sons of the first Loammi Baldwin, Benjamin Franklin Baldwin, married Mary Carter Coolidge. Their daughter, Mary Brewster, in 1836 married Roswell Park, D.D. The Reverend Dr. Park had resigned a professorship at the University of Pennsylvania to take Holy Orders, and became a pastor in Woburn.[49]

A son, Roswell, became a physician and settled in Buffalo, New York. He had often expressed great interest in the Audubon folios. Knowing this, Loammi F Baldwin, the beneficiary under the will of Dame Catherine Rumford Baldwin, shortly after her death turned over the folio to the Reverend Dr. Park, who deposited the set with the society in 1911 After he died in 1914 his sons, Julian and Roswell, gave the set of the folio to the society in honor of their father.

CALIFORNIA ACADEMY OF SCIENCES
San Francisco, Calif.

In 1893 Edward F. Searles, Esq., of Methuen, Massachusetts, conveyed to the regents of the University of California the mansion and lands on the crest of California Street, San Francisco, which had become his property through the death of his wife, the widow of the late Mark Hopkins. It was stipulated that the building should be known as "The Mark Hopkins Institute of Art."[50]

In "The San Francisco Art Association—A Survey," by Dorothy N. Colodny (an article appearing in the March 1951 issue of *Opera and Concert*, published in San Francisco), it is stated that the property was deeded in trust for the San Francisco Art Association which had been organized in 1871.

Sometime in the year 1894 Searles presented to the association a set of the Double Elephant folio. The folio was still in that organization's possession when the earthquake and fire occurred in San Francisco on 18 April 1906. Although the Mark Hopkins Institute building was destroyed in that calamity, the Audubon *Birds* were saved and taken into protective custody by the San Francisco Police Department. The set bears the Police Department's stamp to this day.

In 1941 the folio was sold by the San Francisco Art Association to Edward E. Hills (1894–1959) of San Francisco. Upon his death (20 Nov. 1959) the set was bequeathed to the San Francisco Academy of Sciences and came into the possession of the California Academy of Sciences in July 1964.

THE CALIFORNIA STATE LIBRARY
Sacramento, Calif.

It has not been possible to determine the exact manner in which the Audubon folio of the *Birds of America* was obtained by the California State Library. The four volumes were listed in the "State Library Catalogue of 1870." Since they were not listed in the earlier catalog of 1866, it is possible that the accession occurred in the latter part of 1868 or in the first part of 1869. From information provided by Dr. William N. Davis, Jr., it is known that the folios are not listed in a State Library volume entitled "Exchanges and Donations." It is possible, therefore, that they were obtained through purchase from A. Roman & Co., Booksellers, Publishers and Stationers, San Francisco, since the State Library had made substantial purchases from that firm during the 1860s.

CARNEGIE INSTITUTE
Carnegie Museum
Pittsburgh, Pa.

In 1907 a Double Elephant folio of Audubon's *Birds of America* was brought to the attention of W. J. Holland, Director of the Carnegie Museum, by George F. Denniston of the Weldin bookstore of Pittsburgh. The matter was laid before the committee of the Museum, who made the necessary appropriation and purchased the folio.[51]

The four volumes are bound in full calf with gold tooling on three surfaces of the cover and back and have gold edges on the leaves. On the inside cover of the first volume is the coat of arms of Baron Hastings.

On Audubon's list of European subscribers, no.79 is recorded as "Sir Jacob Hastley, Bart, &c., &c., &c., Cavendish Square, London."[52] However, the name appears on the original subscription list as "Sir Jacob Astley, Bart., 7 Cavendish Square, London." Jacob Astley, 6th Baronet and 16th Baron of Hastings, was born on 13 November 1797 and died on 27 December 1859.[53] His subscription was among the last Audubon had received in England.

The five volumes of the *Ornithological Biography* belonging to Sir Jacob Astley did not accompany the folio. Strangely enough, they are presently at the Henry Huntington Library and Art Gallery in California.

CHARLESTON LIBRARY SOCIETY
Charleston, S.C.

Audubon arrived in New York early in September 1832 on his second return trip to America. After a visit in Philadelphia, he went on to Charleston, S.C., arriving on 16 October. Before journeying further south in search of new species of birds to paint, he, with the unstinted aid of Dr. John Bachman, began the solicitation of subscribers to the *Birds of America*. This resulted in several subscriptions in the city and state.

One of these was that of the Charleston Library Society. The following is taken from the records of the Society:

12 June 1832—Tuesday. At a Quarterly Meeting of the Charleston Library Society held at the Library Room in the State House.

> Elias Horry   President
> William Logan Librarian and Secretary
> M. A. Waring   Treasurer

Resolved—that the Book Committee be directed to subscribe for Mr. Audubon's Work on the Birds of America, the motion was warmly advocated by Mr. King, Bishop England, Rev. Mr. Bachman, and other members—after some opposition the question was put and the Resolution agreed to.

It is of interest to note that among those warmly advocating the resolve were the Lutheran minister, Dr. John Bachman, and the Catholic Bishop of Charleston, John England, the latter being the first priest to address the House of Representatives in Washington on 8 January 1826.[54]

Audubon advised his wife (who was visiting her sons in Louisville), of this subscription in a letter written in Charleston on 29 March 1832, "The Charleston Library has subscribed to the Birds of America."[55] It should be noted that his letter was written prior to the action taken at the meeting of the Library Society on 12 June 1832.

THE CHARLESTON MUSEUM
Charleston, S.C.

In the autumn of 1832, when Audubon began soliciting subscriptions for the *Birds of America*, he noted that "Friend Bachman has Six subscription papers distributed among his acquaintances each to be filled with twelve names at 5 Dollars per annum and 19 Dollars cash to pay for the first Volume—he expects by that means to procure half a dozen Subscribers, Companies to the Work."[56]

It was hoped that in this manner a half dozen subscriptions would be procured.[57] It does not appear that these hopes were fulfilled. However, there is a record of one subscription obtained in this manner, namely that of the Charleston Natural History Society.

In the files of the library of the Charleston Museum is the record of an exhibit, dated Charleston, 19 July 1873, and signed by Caroline Gilman. Here recorded are the names of twelve members of the Natural History Society who signed one of Bachman's "subscription papers." These were:

1. Rev. John Bachman D.D.
2. Rev. Samuel Gilman D.D.
3. James Moultrie M.D.
4. J. Bellinger M.D.
5. W. J. Ramsay M.D.
6. H. R. Frost M.D.
7. Samuel Henry Dickson M.D.
8. Edmund Ravenel M.D.
9. Alexander Mazÿck, Esq.
10. Hon. Benjamin Faneul Dunkin, Legislature
11. Wm. Clarkson, Esq.
12. James L. Petigrew, Esq.

(Note the interest of the medical profession in natural history.)

This list is confirmed by a memorandum in one of Audubon's Journals where the same names are set down and beside each name the sum of $5.83 with the exception of Bachman's where the amount is $5.87 for a total of $70.00.[58] Appended to the list of payments due is the following "Left orders on all the above except Bachman's with J. P. Beile (a Charleston bookdealer) for collection—Dec. 7, 1839."

Caroline Gilman was the wife of the Unitarian minister, Samuel Gilman, one of the subscribing members of the Natural History Society. He was the author of *Fair Harvard*, which he had written for the exercises commemorating the 200th anniversary of the founding of the college on 8 September 1836. From the exhibit record it is known that each subscriber gave $100 towards the cost of the folio, and that the volumes were rolled from house to house on a specially built stand, at the pleasure of the subscribers. After the Civil War Mrs. Gilman had inquired respecting the volumes and learned that they were in a room over Dr. Frost's in

Broad Street, mouldy, mildewed, and injured in many ways. She was granted leave to take care of them until called for by a subscriber. The actual condition of the volumes she found to be as follows:

Vol. I. Binding all broken on back, engravings in good order, mildew on margins, several leaves loose.
Vol. II. Binding slightly broken, seventeen engravings a little torn, One torn quite across.
Vol. III. Binding in good order, Three engravings torn.
Vol. IV. Much torn and dilapidated.

In the final paragraph of the exhibit record, Mrs. Gilman wrote: "As I am about leaving Charleston, S.C., what disposition do you wish to make of these books. I have placed them under charge of my daughter, Mrs. Francis J. Porcher, to whom please direct your reply, care of W.G.G. (Dessausure)."

In 1873, when Mrs. Gilman had turned over the care of the volumes to Mrs. Porcher, all of the original subscribers except Mazÿck had died. The folio was to remain in possession of the Porcher family for upwards of forty years. Over the years the shares of the deceased members of the Natural History Society came into the possession of both the Charleston Museum and the Home for Mothers and Daughters of Confederate Soldiers. By 1925 the home held seven shares. An attempt to sell the folio had failed and since the proof of ownership of the shares owned by the home had been lost or destroyed by fire, it was agreed that the Audubon folio should become the sole property of the Charleston Museum.

THE CITY COLLEGE OF THE CITY UNIVERSITY OF NEW YORK

In 1850, within a year of the death of his father, who at the time was an invalid, Victor G. Audubon succeeded in selling to the City of New York a copy of the Double Elephant Folio of the *Birds of America* for $1,000, as well as a copy of the Audubon-Bachman *Quadrupeds* for $500. The latter was to be presented, on behalf of the City of New York and through one Monsieur Alexandre Vattemare, to the City of Paris.

The details of the purchase by the City of New York of both the *Birds of America* and the *Quadrupeds* are to be found in the proceedings of the Board of Aldermen from January to May 1850, (p. 201–23), and in a "Communication & Resolution to purchase Audubon's Birds of America for the City Library, prepared by Oscar W. Sturtevant, President of the Board of Assistant Aldermen."[59] It should be explained that in 1849 the New York State Legislature, in an amendment to the New York City charter, provided that "the legislative power . . . shall be vested in a board of aldermen and a board of assistant aldermen, who together shall form the common council of the city." This arrangement of the council continued until 1853.

It is in the report of the Committee of Arts and Sciences to whom had been referred the communication from V. G. Audubon, relative to selling a copy of the "double (elephant) folio edition of the 'Birds of America,'" that provides the reason for the purchase of the *Quadrupeds*. Here this was expressed as follows: "Your committee in consideration of this communication, and the subject of international exchanges between this country and Europe to which it alludes, are unanimously of the opinion that the city of New York is largely indebted to the city of Paris, particularly for the many valuable literary and scientific contributions received through the zealous and successful efforts of Mons. Vattemare, and which has recently been deposited in the Corporation library."

The communication from Sturtevant to the Board of Assistant Aldermen follows, quoted in full without comment:

To the Honourable
 The Board of Assistant Aldermen of the city of New York.
 There can be obtained, but one copy of that remarkable ornithological work of John J. Audubon, called the "Birds of America." That copy is now in the hands of the author, and may be secured, it is understood, for a thousand Dollars. In 1835, the plates from which this great work was struck, were destroyed by fire. They can never be replaced, and, consequently, the volumes can never be republished. This is probably, the only opportunity we shall have, at least in many years, to grace the City Library with this celebrated book. That Library has just been arranged and enlarged, and placed on a conspicuous and useful basis, for the benefit of the public at large. It is the library of the first City of the union—It will soon be visited, by Citizens with pride and pleasure, and by strangers as one of our attractions—It has recently, through the indefatigable exertions of M. Vattemare,[60] received large accessions from abroad, the beginnings of a delightful system of international courtesies, and exchanges.
 The work to which I have alluded, is an American work, written in America, by an adopted American [in the original the words "an adopted" have been crossed out and above written "a native born"], upon American subjects—To gather its materials, its bold and gifted author has traversed the continent—has trodden all the forests—has expended years in the wilderness—has lived aloof from civilized man,—has surpassed the Indian hunter in his lonely feats—has crossed the broad rivers—pursued the valleys,—scaled the mountains,—waded the morasses,—tracked the prairies—and left the imprint of his diligent foot, all over the American soil,—from the Aroostock to the Sabine,—in the everglades of Florida,—in the snows of the upper Lakes,—on the moss of the Rocky mountain,—and on the western slope of distant Oregon—
 No bird spreads its airy pinions over any part of the American continent, from the grey wing of that national emblem,—the american Eagle, to the gem-like elegance of that winged flower, the bright humming bird, whose lineaments, in all their peculiar characteristic form, color, expression and attitudes, are not [now] impressed, in glowing life, upon these ample leaves.—These bright inhabitants, of earth and air, which are here so perfectly repre-

sented, are the beautiful creation of the same artistic Power, by whom we live and move and have our being—

In this higher sense, also, it is most earnestly to be desired, that they should be perpetuated. These lovely tenants of the wood, can only be *thus* perpetuated; for many of them will disappear with the forests which are falling before our advancing population.

And yet, compiled of American materials—a truly National book,—the biography of the natives of the American atmosphere—the few copies which were given to the world, have, mostly, crossed the ocean, and find their homes on the tables of foreign libraries. One copy, to our honor, reposes in the state collection at Albany—Let us have the other, in the Library of the City of New York.

The distinguished author, who has added so much to the archives of Natural History, and conferred such fame on the country, and its literature,—by his high wrought and enthusiastic devotion to the pursuit of his life, is now, in his advanced and honored age, afflicted by the loss of sight,—the sense by which his great achievements have been made.

The purchase of this work, by this city, would not only enrich our library, and be a proper testimonial of our regard for worth, genius and art, and give the production an appropriate position in the Library of the Emporium,— but would, especially, in this dark hour of the author's life, would be a cheerful token of appreciation, to him and to his family—

I would, therefore, propose, and impressively urge, the adoption of the following resolution,

Resolved, that the Clerk of the Common Council of the City of New York, be directed to purchase, with the proprietors assent, the work of Audubon called "The Birds of America" now in possession of the author, at and for the price of one Thousand Dollars and that that sum be and the same is hereby appropriated therefor

Oscar W. Sturtevant
President—Bd Asst Ald.

The resolutions submitted to the two branches of the Common Council were passed, the Board of Aldermen voting 13 ayes and 2 nays, with the vote of the assistant Aldermen being 20 ayes and (?) nays. On 26 February 1850 the Mayor, Caleb S. Woodhull, approved the resolutions.

The City Library had been founded in 1849; the municipal reference library was established in 1913, acquiring as a consequence the books of the City Library. On 21 April 1919, the Audubon folio was transferred to the City College.[61]

CLEVELAND MUSEUM OF NATURAL HISTORY
Natural Science Museum, Cleveland, Ohio

Included among the papers of Amy Lowell deposited at the Houghton Library at Harvard University is a bill from the London bookdealer Quaritch, dated

11 March 1901, for the four volumes of Audubon's *Birds of America* together with the 5 volumes of the *Ornithological Biography*, cost £350 ($1575). Also listed on the bill were the three volumes of the Audubon-Bachman *Viviparous Quadrupeds of North America*, 1845-54, price £30. All these volumes were actually sent to Miss Lowell on 13 March 1901.[62]

The first volume of the *Biography* contained the signature, with some remarks, of Dr. P. Brontë, the father of the Brontë sisters. The autograph also appears in the second, third, and fourth volumes.

After the death of Miss Lowell in 1925, the folios were sold and, under date of March 1926, are listed as follows in the catalog of a Boston bookdealer: "Aubudon folio—Full Brown crushed Levant—g.e. with Ornithological Biog. same has sig. of Dr. Brontë (father of Charlotte, Emily, and Anne) autograph in Vol. I-IV with some notes in his hand in Vol. I. Price $4,750."

The four volumes of the *Birds of America* and the five volumes of the *Ornithological Biography* were purchased by John Sherwin of Cleveland, Ohio, and presented by him to the Cleveland Museum of Natural History, now the Natural Science Museum, on 29 December 1947.

COLUMBIA UNIVERSITY
New York, N.Y.

In the introduction to the second volume of the *Ornithological Biography* which was published in December 1834, Audubon, when writing about his departure from America in late April of that year, includes among the names of those of his friends of whom he had taken "hurried leave" that of "the Reverend W. (William) A. (Alexander) Duer, President of the College." The College referred to is Columbia.

An entry in the diary of George Templeton Strong (1820-1875) indicates the college had subscribed in 1833, actually in May, a date supplied by an entry in Ledger "B." Audubon had visited the college when a number of people had been invited to the President's Room to inspect his drawings. A subscription of $800 was then raised to purchase the work for the college. At that time the buildings were situated in a residential section of New York, a fenced area shaded with sycamore trees and bounded by Murray and Barclay Sts., College Place (West Broadway), and Church Street. Park Place led eastward one block to "the Park," now City Hall Park.[63]

Another reference is found in the Strong diary under the date of 23 June 1836: "Looked over Audubon to-day with Cooper (Thomas Colin Cooper, class of 1838) in Prex's private Library."[64]

Audubon recorded this subscription with the following entry in his Ledger "B": "Columbia College State of N.Y. a/c in name of W. A. Deuer [sic] May 1833. Completed Nov. 10, 1838—(Bound)."

Provenances of Sets in the United States and Canada

COMMONWEALTH OF MASSACHUSETTS
STATE HOUSE LIBRARY
Boston, Mass.

While in New York during July 1832, Audubon wrote A. H. Everett, who was at the time a state senator in Massachusetts, thanking him for his endeavors in trying to obtain a subscription for the *Birds of America* from the Commonwealth. The Naturalist sent him at the same time a prospectus and his first volume of letterpress, the *Ornithological Biography*.[65]

The following year while in Boston he wrote, on 25 February, to his son Victor, "I have waited until this moment with the Hope that I could announce the acquisition of a subscriber—*The State of Massachusetts*. Mr. Everett [to whom the Naturalist had written in July of the previous year] has offered a petition *which has been sent by the Senate* for concurrence to the Lower House; as it is well known the Senate will accede to the demand Instento. The result will be known to us pro or con on Wednesday next.—"[66]

Neither the Senate nor the Lower House acted quite as promptly as Audubon had hoped, that is, "Instento." As stated, Everett did introduce his motion "that the committee on the Library be instructed to consider the expediency of purchasing for the Library a copy of the work entitled the Birds of America." While the motion came up regularly on succeeding days it was not passed until 6 March by the Senate. In the House it finally was passed on 21 March.[67]

The *Boston Daily Advocate & Patriot* of 26 February 1833 noted the introduction of the Everett resolution: "Resolve for the purchase of a copy of the great work was yesterday reported to senate by the Committee on the Library." Another Boston newspaper reported in great detail the meeting held by the House on 21 March, to reconsider authorizing "the Committee on the Library to purchase Audubon's Birds of America provided the cost should not exceed 800 dollars." The Senate resolution had already been passed on 6 March.[68]

Evidently the resolution had been voted down at a previous meeting. *The Columbia Centennial* (Boston, Mass.) for 23 March 1833 carried the remarks of "Mr. Brinley of Boston" (Francis J. Brinley, 1800–1889), who "said he hoped the motion to reconsider would prevail. He thought the House voted under a misunderstanding of the subject. He knew the House was adverse to large appropriations but this would not be paid at one time, but would amount to about sixty or seventy dollars a year, for some years." The remarks of Stephen White (1787–1841), another legislator, were prescient when he stated: "We do not pay it for nothing: and if the State should ever arrive at Bankruptcy so it could not afford to hold such a work in its library, we can sell it for as much as we gave. It is not a gratuity that is asked but a subscription."

The *Columbia Centennial* article quoted still another legislator, Joseph Thornton Adams (1796–1878), who referred to the utility of the work "It often happens that there are large classes of birds supposed to be pernicious which turn out to be

247

beneficial. He was much gratified with a treatise he had seen in a newspaper where it was shown that some of these classes (species) did more good in destroying vermin and insects, than in depredation upon game and fruit trees. By studying this work we should find many against whom a war of extermination is declared who ought to be preserved for the service to the farmer.... The motion to reconsider prevailed after the Resolve was amended as proposed by Mr. Keys and passed."

Again writing his son Victor, this time from New York on 1 April 1833, Audubon stated that he had delivered one of the seven bound copies of volume one, which were awaiting him upon his arrival in New York, to the Library of the General Court of Massachusetts. In his Ledger "B" the entry for the State of Massachusetts shows that the volume was delivered to A. H. Everett in May and a contra entry lists a payment of £49–10–0 (approximately $220) on 6 June.

CORNELL UNIVERSITY
Ithaca, N.Y.

In 1955, shortly after the death of William R. Coe, his widow presented to the University the four volumes of Audubon's *Birds of America* which he had purchased from a London dealer sometime between 1911 and 1913.[69] At the presentation in October of 1955, besides Mrs. Coe, there was present her niece whose husband is a member of the class of 1928 at Cornell. All four volumes are uniformly bound in full light-brown coarse-grained crushed morocco. The covers and spines are ornately gilded with titles gilt stamped on front covers and spines. In volumes 2 and 3 on the front loose endleaf there is stamped, in the upper left hand corner, in black, "Bound by Hering 9 Newman St."

In 1838, after the engraving of the plates had been completed and subscribers furnished with the final numbers, there remained on hand in the possession of the engraver fifteen complete sets of the folio, some bound, others in loose prints. Eventually these were all sent by Havell to America. In 1842 Audubon sold one of the bound sets to Alexander Baring, Lord Ashburton. On 25 July of that year, while in Washington, the Naturalist was presented by Baring with a check for $1,000 in payment.[70] Lord Ashburton was in Washington at that time, engaged in negotiations with Daniel Webster (one of Audubon's subscribers), the Secretary of State under President Tyler, concerning the dispute over the northeast boundary of Maine.

In checking the English auction records,[71] it was found that on 15 April 1912, there was sold by Sotheby, Wilkinson & Hodge (Hortenstein, buyer) for £540, an Audubon folio which had been the property of Lady Ashburton of Melchet Court, near Ramsey, a direct descendant of Lord Ashburton to whom Audubon had sold a folio in 1842.[72] In the auction catalog the folio is described as follows: "Audubon, (John James) The Birds of America, from original drawings, 4 vols.

435 Fine Large Coloured Plates. Half russia gilt elephant folio. Printed for the author, 1827–38."

When the folio at Cornell was examined it was found that the Whatman watermarks of plates 1, 2, 6, 7 and 10 are dated 1836. In addition, the watermarks of the fly leaves of volumes 2, 3, and 4, are all J. Whatman 1838. An entry in Audubon's Ledger "B" shows that Hering, of 9 Newman St., whose name is found in the bound volumes of the folio, was the binder used at the completion of the engraving of the plates.

While it may not be possible to make a positive statement, the facts relating to the Coe folio recorded above would seem to indicate that the one sold to Lord Ashburton in 1842 and the one presently at Cornell are one and the same.

DARTMOUTH COLLEGE
Hanover, N.H.

The three volumes of the *Birds of America* presently in the Dartmouth College library were originally subscribed for by Daniel Webster. There is a record of the subscription in Audubon's Ledger "B," where it is listed as follows:

    74   Webster, Daniel   Boston, Mass.
          1837 Vol. 1,2,3 for £148-10-0
          1837—delivered to him half bound.

The ledger contains no record of any payments. There is an "X" at the right margin of the account entry which denotes that the subscription was not completed.

Although it is indicated that the delivery of the three volumes was not made until sometime in 1837, the subscription had actually been obtained the previous year. In a letter written from Boston by the Naturalist to George C. Shattuck on 30 September 1836, there is a postscript which reads: "As the honourable Daniel Webster subscribed to my work last evening, and as he at the same time desires our mutual friend Isaac P. Davies, Esq. (Isaac P. Davis [1771-1855], 8 Winthrop Street) to pay to myself on order the sum of Two Hundred Dollars, on the first day of each fourth ensuing January; and the said I. P. Davis promised to do so! I beg you to call on the latter on the 1st day of January next (1837), to receive the first installment of Two Hundred Dollars from him and to receipt for the same in my name. . . ."[73] On 3 October, upon the Naturalist's arrival in New York, he wrote Isaac P. Davis that he had sent him, that day, for Webster the first volume of the *Birds of America*.[74]

Webster has been described by one of his biographers as follows: "Although regarded as an authority on government finances, Webster was, in his private transactions, absolutely without a money sense. He kept no regular accounts and was never clear how his large income from law disappeared."[75]

It has not been possible to ascertain accurately how much of the "£148-10-0" (approximately $660) Audubon was able to collect. There are available a number of letters as well as journal entries from which some information can be gleaned regarding efforts to collect and payments made.

That Webster did not carry out the arrangement to pay two hundred dollars annually on 1 January beginning in 1837 is evident from a list of payments due from subscribers dated 13 December 1839, found in a journal of Audubon's presently at the Houghton Library at Harvard University.[76] On this list the full amount owed by Webster is recorded. Also, it was found that in 1840 payment had not yet been made. At that time the Naturalist, while on a trip in New England soliciting subscribers for the Octavo edition, wrote in his journal as follows: "Plymouth—August 18, 1840, I was introduced to the wife of a Phisician whom I found both handsome and amiable. She is well acquainted with D*l* Webster, where she has seen *my* great work several times, but she not knowing Mr. W. as well as I do called the Volumes there his Copy??? When paid for!"[77]

When in Boston two months later, Audubon "called on Daniel Webster twice, and finally got $100 Dollars from him on a/c of the Large Work and a memorandum authorizing me to draw upon him at Three Different dates for the balance he now owes me. To my astonishment he subscribed to the little work; and Mr. Little of Little & Brown, guaranteed me the payment thereof!"[78]

In 1842, while in Washington, Audubon endeavored on numerous occasions to see the Secretary of State but always found him busily engaged with Lord Ashburton negotiating the boundary settlement between Maine and Canada. Finally, on 25 July, he received a check drawn on New York for $100.[79]

Although no record of additional payments has been found Audubon evidently continued to press, for on 8 March 1843, he wrote Webster as follows:

> I was this day honored by your note of the 6th Inst. and although I much regret your nonconvenience to forward me any money at the present time. I cannot but express my sincere thanks for allowing me to draw upon you at Ninety Days after date for the sum of Two Hundred Dollars, which I have done this day, and which you will greatly oblige me by paying them at maturity. As one of the good Friends, whom in you I have in this poor World, you must allow me to say that I trust, and that with great sincereity, that you never dispose of the 'Birds of America' until indeed you are reduced to the direct necessity, which of course can never be the case with one who possesses such a *head* as is now so powerfully poised on your good shoulders.
>
> Health and prosperity attend you, my good Friend, and ever believe me yours,
>
> JOHN J. AUDUBON[80]
>
> The Honourable
> Daniel Webster
> Washington City D.C.

That Webster did not dispose of the volumes of the *Birds of America* during his lifetime is known, since these were included in the sale of his library, at which time they brought $675.[81] Later the three volumes were given to the Haverhill (Mass.) Public Library by E. J. H. Hale and James H. Carleton.[82]

In 1961 when the Haverhill Public Library was raising funds for the construction of a new building, several rare book dealers made offers to purchase the volumes. Details relating to the eventual disposal of the volumes were given in a letter from the librarian who, on 14 February 1966, wrote, "... at the same time we received intimations of interest on the part of Dartmouth, because of the former Webster ownership, the trustees decided that the only offer they would entertain would be one from Dartmouth. Several months ago Dartmouth renewed its interest, found a donor who would give it as a memorial to her son, and the sale went through a few days before Christmas (1965).

The decision to sell was influenced by the need of money to build the new library (about $800,000, of which we hope to raise $500,000 by public subscription). In addition your census showed that there are nine complete sets, all in good condition, presumably, between here and Boston and Cambridge, so that anyone wishing to see one would not have to make a very great effort."[83]

DELAWARE ART MUSEUM
Wilmington, Del.

The 435 loose prints of Audubon's *Birds of America*, 39 by 26½ inches in size, were obtained by Thomas Coleman duPont (1863–1930), who is believed to have purchased them from a store in London, England, possibly in 1910. The prints were presented to the Wilmington Society of the Fine Arts (now the Delaware Art Museum) on 21 September 1950 by Francis V. duPont, a son of T. Coleman duPont (1894–1962).[84]

JOHN HENRY DICK
Meggett, S.C.

This folio was purchased in 1952 by Morris Schapiro of Baltimore from Miss Mabel Zahn (Charles Sessler, Inc. Philadelphia, Pa.) in collaboration with Lionel Robinson of London, an English rare book dealer.[85] The folio had been purchased by Robinson at the Christie, Manson & Woods auction in London on 3 July 1951 for £7,000 (approx. $19,500).[86]

When the folio was examined by the author it was found that there was a print penciled notation on the title page of Volume 1 reading, "The set of John Clayton Newcastle."

John Clayton of Newcastle is not listed as one of the original subscribers. However, Audubon did meet him in Newcastle on 18 October 1827. His journal entry for that date notes, "This morning I paid a visit to old Mr. Bewick . . . I could not spend much time with him as I wished. . . . I met Mr. Adamson who went with me to dine at the Mansion House. We were received in a large room, furnished in the ancient style, panelled with oak all around, and very sombre. The company all arrived, we marched in couples to dinner and I was seated in the centre, the mayor at one end, the high sheriff at the other: we were seventy-two in number. As my bad luck would have it, I was toasted by John Clayton, Esq.; he made a speech and I, poor fellow, was obliged to return the compliment, which I did, as usual, most awkwardly and covered with perspiration. Miserable stupidity that will never leave me!"[87]

John Clayton was born in 1792. He became an attorney in 1815, undersheriff of Northumberland in 1816, and Town Clerk of Newcastle in 1822. In addition, Clayton was affiliated with the Foundation of Railways, circa 1825. A member of the Society of Antiquaries, he was a person of wealth and literary culture identified with the growth of Newcastle-upon-Tyne, where he is commemorated by Clayton Street. He died in 1890.[88]

Although John Clayton is not included by Audubon in his final list of European subscribers, the name does appear on the original subscription list, as well as on the List of Subscribers shown in Volume 1 of the *Ornithological Biography*.[89] In addition, there is an entry in Audubon's Ledger "B" which records that the first 22 numbers were sent to him as well as the first volume of the *Ornithological Biography*. It is possible that the remaining prints were received through one of Audubon's agents or directly through Havell, and the entries included in the respective accounts. Certainly the set is among the early ones prepared for subscribers since the watermarks of the Whatman paper for the first ten prints are either 1826 or 1827. In addition plate XI has the legend "Bird of Washington" or "Great American Sea Eagle" placed on the rock on which the bird is perched and not at the bottom of the plate. The four volumes are gilt edged, the prints in good condition, except that Plate 1 is slightly creased.

The folio was purchased in 1963 by Mr. Dick.

DUKE UNIVERSITY
Durham, N.C.

In the second and third volumes of this set of the Double Elephant folio of the *Birds of America* is found, written on an extra leaf, the following inscription:

Reginald Dykes Marshall
from
His Grandmother
To whom it was given
by
His Father

The name Marshall is found, also, in other places in the folio, as on the back of Plate 435 in Volume 4.

On the list of subscribers in Volume 5 of the *Ornithological Biography* among the European subscribers appears the name No. 20 "John Marshall, jun. Esq. Headlinglay, Leeds."[90] In his journal Audubon noted that he had met Marshall on 3 May 1827, and that "he told me he knew nothing at all about birds, but most generously subscribed, because he told me, it was such a work as every one ought to possess, and to encourage enterprise."[91]

John Marshall was born in 1765 and died in 1845. The Marshalls ranked among the foremost families of Leeds during the first part of the nineteenth century, and John Marshall was the first Member of Parliament for Leeds after the Reform Bill of 1832. He built a celebrated mill, known as Marshalls Mills, in the form of an Egyptian temple. The building which still stands has attracted a good deal of notice from architectural historians. John Marshall lived at New Grange, Headingly (a suburb of Leeds). He had two sons, one of whom, John II (1797–1836), was the father of Reginald Dykes Marshall.[92]

In 1930, Dr. William K. Boyd, Director of Libraries at Duke University, purchased the Marshall folio from Mrs. Margaret Barber of Williamsburg, Missouri. It has not been possible to ascertain when the folio had come into the possession of the Barber family.

ENOCH PRATT FREE LIBRARY
George Peabody Branch
Baltimore, Md.

In May 1930, the Peabody Institute Library purchased from the Maryland Historical Society a Double Elephant folio edition of Audubon's *Birds of America* for $6,000. Each of the four volumes of this set contains an Audubon autograph to Robert Gilmor, Baltimore, dated 27 February 1840. The Maryland Historical Society acquired this set in 1855 when it took over the Library Company of Baltimore. Robert Gilmor was President of the Library Company between the years 1828 and 1843, and, when in 1831 the first numbers of Audubon's work appeared, Gilmor made a gift of his own set to the Library. The gift is recorded in the minutes of the Library Company by R. H. Owen, Librarian, as follows:

> May 25, 1831. Report of R. H. Owen, Librarian.
>
> I have the rare pleasure to state that the Library is enriched with a copy of Audubon's Work on the Birds of America, as represented with the enclosed note from the Donor Robert Gilmor Esq. The number of Plates at present received is 90; the work when complete and encased in Portfolios suitable for their preservation and exhibition, agreeably to the suggestion expressed in the President's Note of presentation, will excite an interest & present attractions which must elevate the Institution in publick estimation.
>
> As this will be the most costly & magnificent production which has hereto-

fore adorned the Archives of the Library, may we not indulge the hope, that it will prove the Harbinger of other munificent Benefactions and the dawn of a brilliant era in the memorials of the company. p. 136.

The "President's Note" referred to in Owen's report is now mounted in Volume 4 of the *Birds* and reads as follows:

24 May 1831

Sir

I send by the bearer all the numbers of Audubon's magnificent work on the Birds of America, of the size of, & coloured to the life, which I present to the Library as worth their best care and preservation. As the future numbers arrive they shall be sent to you, and in the meantime I would recommend that suitable portfolios be provided to contain them as preferable to having them bound in volumes, the large size of the plates rendering them liable to be torn or otherwise injured when bound.

I am Sir
Your mo:obd^t.
Robert Gilmor

Mr. Owen (Librarian)

Other numbers of the *Birds* were presented when ready and the last notice of this gift to appear in the Minutes of the Library Company is as follows:

Nov. 15, 1838.

I omitted last month to acknowledge the receipt at the Library of 30 numbers of Audubon's Birds of America which I learn is the last of that magnificent gift of the President of the Board; the work is now complete in 435 sheets & I am pleased to be enabled to say in good preservation.

It will be noticed that Gilmor specified that the plates were to remain in portfolio and not be bound. However, sometime after 1838, the plates were bound by Hering of 9 Newman St., London, into their present set of four volumes. It seems quite likely that they had been bound prior to the autographs being entered in each of the volumes, but this is merely conjecture.

The question arises as to why this particular set should include the autographs of Audubon, which is not typical of the other sets. Although Gilmor was by no means one of Audubon's closest friends, he was probably his closest Baltimore friend during the period prior to the autographs.

Robert Gilmor, Jr. (1774-1848), was the son of a wealthy Baltimore merchant and a member of the firm of Robert Gilmor & Sons, a leading commercial house in the city. Gilmor had a lively interest in the arts and during the years 1799-1801, while on "the grand tour" of Europe, commenced to seriously collect art objects. He soon distinguished himself as a notable connoisseur in the field of art and as a sociable, cultured gentleman in Baltimore society. Gilmor was the logical person to whom an artist like Audubon would be given a letter of introduction. Such a letter was probably written by Captain Basil Hall, a friend of Audubon's in London, who had toured North America in 1827-28 and had met the best of Baltimore society in his visit to this city. Audubon undoubtedly first met Gilmor during his subscription visit to Baltimore in 1830. At this time Gilmor assisted Audubon in the display of his drawings as is indicated by the following card in the Mercantile Library Autograph Book:

> Mr. Audubon through Mr. R. Gilmor begs to inform Mr. Cox that his original Ornithological Drawings will be exhibited at the Baltimore Library from 10 untill 12 O'clock tomorrow Morning.
> Thomas's Hotel
> March 22d 1830

In connection with this exhibition the notices which follow were placed in the Baltimore newspapers:

Baltimore American, 23 March 1830:

> Mr. AUDUBON being in town with the original drawings of his splendid work on the Ornithology of America, for which he is soliciting subscriptions, has been requested to exhibit them to the public in the hope of its patronage to so magnificent an undertaking, in which every bird is drawn (and will be engraved) as large as life; and in compliance with the request will exhibit them accordingly, from 10 o'clock till 12 THIS MORNING, at the Baltimore Library in Holliday street.

Baltimore Sun, 24 March 1830:

> A large assemblage of ladies and gentlemen having attended the exhibition of Mr. Audubon yesterday morning, he is induced at their particular request to repeat it this morning. (The same announcement which had appeared in the *American* the day before was then repeated.)

Gilmor's was one of three subscriptions to the folio obtained in Baltimore during Audubon's first return to America in 1830, the other two being those of Nathaniel Potter and John B. Morris. He also was instrumental in procuring Gideon B. Smith (1793–1867) as agent in Baltimore for Audubon in 1840 for the Octavo edition of the *Birds*. Smith's name also appears on Audubon's final list of subscribers. The Naturalist as a token of his appreciation for Smith's services and friendship, gave the name "Smith's Lark-Bunting" (Plectrophanes Smithii, Octavo ed., v. 7, p. 336–38) to one of the bird species he discovered.

The presence of the autographs in Gilmor's set of the *Birds* is undoubtedly the result of Gilmor's interest in autographs. In addition to collecting art objects, Gilmor was also an avid autograph collector, one of the first three genuine collectors in America, and possibly the first. In a letter of 10 February 1846 about autograph collections, he told Robert Bolton, "I believe I was the earliest person in the Country who attempted to form one."

Gilmor gave to the Maryland Historical Society a large part of his American collection in 1845; after his death, what remained was sold to Ferdinand Dreer of Philadelphia.

Audubon had assisted Gilmor in procuring some of these autographs. They corresponded between London and Baltimore,[93] and on one occasion the loss of a parcel of autographs gave Audubon some concern. He wrote to Mrs. Bachman from New Jersey on 2 July 1837, as follows:

> A Parcel of Valuable Autographs which I forwarded from your House to Robt Gilman [editor probably misread Gilmor's name] of Baltimore have never reached him—are they with you yet by chance? and if please send them him. It was sealed and about the size of a Pamphlet, directed R. Gilman Esqr Care of Coll Theodore Anderson, Custom House Baltimore—This was soon after we reached you last November.[94]

In view of Gilmor's and Audubon's interest in autographs, it was quite natural that Gilmor would have Audubon autograph his copy of the *Birds* on the first possible occasion after it was completed. That occasion probably occurred during Audubon's visit to Baltimore in 1840.

The provenance of this folio of the *Birds of America* was prepared by F. C. Haber, during his tenure as professor of history at the University of Maryland.

MRS. DANIEL W. EVANS
Cobham, Va.

In 1955 when the ornithological library of Dr. Evans Morton Evans (1870–1955)[95] was sold at the Parke-Bernet Galleries in New York, the Audubon folio was not included.[96] The present owner of this copy of the folio is the widow of Daniel W. Evans, a son of Dr. Evans. The original subscriber to this set, to whose identity there is not a single clue, must have been among the earliest, since the first ten prints are all from the Lizar plates, with the Whatman paper bearing no dates later than 1827. The four volumes of the folio were bound by Zaehnsdorf of London. The prints are all in excellent condition.

The folio had been sold to Dr. Evans by Frank Walters, the New York rare book dealer. Regarding the folio Mr. Walters wrote the author, "Sold many years ago by Charles Scribner's Sons, N.Y., to a Mr. Anton Hardy of New York and Englewood, N.J., for $12,000 and removed by me from Mr. Hardy's fine estate at the latter place. Knowing Scribner's methods I have no doubt it was secured in England."[97] Inquiry of the Rare Book Department at Scribner's elicited no information concerning the provenance of the folio sold to Hardy. It was explained that the records concerning Audubon folios did not antecede 1936. It is likely that the Hardy set of the folio was purchased by him prior to that date.

A detailed description of the binding follows: Four volumes, all bound in full pigskin. Triple line outer edge of cover about ¼″ apart. Double gilt lines 4″ from outer edges with dark brown line between double gilt line bisection of which forms 3″ squares, four gilt dots in corners centered by tooled brown quatrefoil stylized floral design. Four gilt dots on corners of vertical and horizontal narrow section and four gilt dots at corners of four rectangular sections.

Each volume contains three flyleaves. On the inside left-hand upper corner of the first front sheet there is found, "Bound by Zaehnsdorf for G. Scribner's Sons, New York." Set into the third flyleaf is a copy of an engraved portrait of Audubon, together with his signature and the legend, "London. Published Jany 12, 1835, for the Proprietor who may have been the engraver of the portrait, Audubon himself, or Havell, by Robert Havell, Printseller, 77, Oxford Street."

The engraving is from a miniature painted of the Naturalist by the celebrated Frederick Cruikshank about 1831. The engraving of the portrait was made by Charles Turner, A.R.A. The watermark of the third flyleaf is "T. Edmonds Wycombe 1834."

FIELD MUSEUM OF NATURAL HISTORY
Chicago, Ill.

Included on the list of the subscribers to Audubon's *Birds of America* is the name of "Mrs. (Miss) Euphemia Gifford, Duffield Bank, Derby." In Ledger "B" there is recorded the following:

> 59—Gifford, Mrs. Euphemia—Duffield Bank near Derby   C
>   Complete set
>   Plus binding Plus Ottoman—£20

(Usually the ledger furnishes additional details such as dates of delivery of the separate numbers, or volumes, and price paid. In the case of Miss Gifford, only the price of the ottoman is shown).

Some additional information concerning the Gifford subscription is to be found in letters written by Audubon. For example, there is a long letter dated 27 April 1831 written from 77 Oxford Street, London, to Miss Gifford in which Audubon expressed his gratitude on learning that she had become a patroness of his *Birds of America*. He also spoke of his wife's affection for her (they were cousins) and mentioned the fact that his first-born, Victor Gifford, was named after her. In addition he wrote,

> I do not only feel grateful to be able to add to my List of Subscribers the name of one of my wife's earliest and best of friends, and in forwarding to you a copy of my work will take satisfaction in attending of the colouring and finishing of each separate Plate of Engraving,—but, my dear Madam I wish to mention that the first volume now being finished, each of my Subscribers are having that volume bound and no longer kept in their portfolios as Prints are usually kept: therefore I wish you to have the kindness to say if I may have the volume bound for you, or if you prefer having the Prints and having them bound according to your own wish?"[98]

As Havell had completed the engraving of the plates for the first one hundred prints comprising Volume 1, shortly before October 1830, the Gifford subscription was probably obtained in the winter of 1830–31.

On 29 June 1831 Audubon was to write Miss Gifford, "I have the pleasure to send you the first volume of my work bound as near according to your own directions as either Lucy or myself can conceive."[99]

In another letter, dated 29 September 1838, Lucy Audubon wrote her, "Mr. Audubon says it will not be many months before you have your volume [The engraving had been completed in June 1838]. It is strange how few complete copies of the 'Birds of America' there will be, every one believing that afterwards, it would be cheaper, and already the mistake is beginning to be felt since the Coppers are all put by—in the application of some for a few extra plates which cannot be had even now. . . ."[100]

In 1870 the following item appeared in the *American Literary Gazette and Publishers' Circular:* "Audubon's own copy of his Birds of America in four large volumes, half bound and five volumes of the letter press is advertised as being for sale in England. The four volumes are in a nest of mahogany drawers, faced in rosewood, and upholstered as an ottoman. Each draws out, the top falls over, and forms a table upon which to exhibit the volume. The price put on this interesting and curious set of books is not mentioned."[101]

As to the set having been "Audubon's own copy," this statement was in error. The Naturalist had left England in 1839 and the family set of the folio was sold by his wife in the early 1860s and is presently in Texas.

However, reference to the folio and its singular ottoman cabinet next appeared in the *Catalogue of the Valuable Library of the Property of the late Baroness Burdett-Coutts,* which was to be sold on 15 May 1922. It was listed as follows:

> 23 Audubon, J. J. The Birds of America 4 Vols. (Vol. I, 1834-5, Vol. II, 1831-34, Vol. III, 1834-35. Vol. IV, 1838 containing 448 plates (including 13 in two states.), life-size, coloured engravings by R. Havell, from the original drawings by Audubon, half russia, (enclosed in a mahogany sectional cabinet with handles, covered with baize and forming an ottoman, on castors, double atlas folio. Sold to Quaritch £600 ($3,000). The plates in this folio were especially selected by the Artist himself for his Father, who was an intimate of Audubon [This last statement is unclear as to meaning].[102]

The folio was sold to Quaritch for £600 ($3,000), who sold it in turn to J. W. Dearden.[103]

Baroness Angela Georgina Burdett-Coutts (1814-1906) was the daughter of Sir Francis Burdett (1770-1884). Sir Francis had, in 1793, married Sophia Coutts, the daughter of Thomas Coutts (1735-1822) of the great English banking family. Angela Georgina was created Baroness Burdett-Coutts of Highgate and Brookfield in June 1871. In 1881 she married William Ashmead Bartlett (1851-1921), who assumed her name. She was then 66 and he 30 years of age.[104] The Audubon folio was sold after the death of the husband of the Baroness. The details of when she had acquired the folio and from whom have not been possible to ascertain.

It should be noted that the set sold by the Baroness Burdett-Coutts contained 448 prints, 13 more than the usual 435. On 28 August 1838 Victor Audubon wrote the engraver Havell that he wished "*6 copies printed of those plates* which *have* old or young birds to add on them or females &c." There is evidence that Miss Gifford received one of these sets.[105]

The folio remained in the possession of the Dearden family until 24 November 1969, when it was sold by Sotheby & Co., of London, for £90,000 ($216,000).[106] The purchaser was Kenneth Nebenzahl, a rare book dealer of Chicago, Illinois. Early in 1970 the folio was presented to the Field Museum of Natural History in Chicago, Illinois, by an anonymous donor.

THE FREE LIBRARY OF NEW BEDFORD
New Bedford, Mass.

Audubon undoubtedly obtained the subscription of James Arnold of New Bedford (1781–1868) while in Boston during the winter and spring of 1833. This is noted on the original subscription list as "James Arnold of New Bedford by Thomas A. Greene." An entry in Ledger "B" shows that the first volume was delivered in May of that year. Also, on 6 June 1833, a payment by Arnold of "£49-14-6" is recorded in the ledger.

Some difficulties arose in the delivery of later prints. On 4 May 1839, shortly before leaving England, Audubon wrote his engraver: "One of our subscribers in America, Mr. Arnold of New Bedford, has never received Nos. 50, 51, 52 nor also Nos. 82 to 87 both inclusive."[107]

After returning to America Audubon was advised of another mishap with the Arnold prints. It appeared that in the set some plates were inverted or sewn upside down.[108]

The Trustees' Report of the New Bedford Free Library for 1866 indicates that the folio, with the five volumes of the *Ornithological Biography*, had been donated to the library by James Arnold.

A few years ago it was decided to frame the first one hundred prints since the binding of Volume I was in great disrepair and many of the prints were loose. These framed prints now are either hung on the walls of the library or put in a special display rack.

THE GROTON SCHOOL
Groton, Mass.

The subscription of Susan Burley was one of those which Audubon obtained in the spring of 1833 during his long visit to Boston.[109] At the time it was obtained, the first volume of prints was delivered to the subscriber and she in turn paid Audubon $220.

The folio remained in the possession of Miss Burley until her death in 1850. She was survived by a brother Edward and a sister Elizabeth who had married Frederick Howes. Their daughter, Susan Burley Howes, became the second wife of Joseph Sebastian Cabot, a man much older than she. The Boston home of Mrs. Cabot was located at the corner of Beacon and Joy Sts and it was here that the prints were seen by Mrs. Henry A. Murray, who graciously supplied this writer with some of the intervening history of the set prior to its being donated to the Groton School by John L. Saltonstall. She wrote the author that "they were given to her uncle, John Saltonstall by his 'aunt' Susan Burley Cabot, who actually was no near relative but who left his family money and property."[110] The prints were found in an old trunk belonging to Mrs. Cabot after her death. They were received by the school sometime around 1916.[111]

HARVARD COLLEGE
Houghton Library, Cambridge, Mass.

The subscription of Harvard College to Audubon's Double Elephant folio of the *Birds of America* was occasioned by the generous gift of eight New England gentlemen, the actual circumstances being set down in the records of the college as follows:

> The Corporation of the University in Cambridge, Massachusetts, have received a generous subscription for "The Birds of America by J. J. Audubon" with the First Volume of the magnificent Work: a Gift to the Public Library from Hon. Nathaniel Bowditch & eight other Gentlemen for which the Corporation return a grateful acknowledgement on the part of the University.
>
>   Josiah Quincy, President.
>
> Harvard College
> Cambridge April 25, 1833.   Thaddeus William Harris, Librarian

The foregoing seems to have been the statement of official thanks to the donors, for on 28 March 1833 the following appears in the records of Harvard College: "The President laid before the Board [Overseers] a donation of Audubon's North American Birds; and it was Voted, That [the] thanks of this Board be given the Donors of this Work."

The nine donors were:

> Dr. George Parkman of the Medical School faculty (uncle of Francis Parkman, the historian and victim of murder in the famous Parkman-Webster case)
> Josiah Quincy, President of Harvard
> Nathaniel Bowditch, Astronomer, Harvard overseer
> Nathaniel Ingersoll Bowditch, son of Nathaniel, Harvard graduate
> Francis Calley Gray (left to college his famous collection of engravings and large bequest of money for the Museum of Comparative Zoology)
> Jonathan Phillips, holder of an honorary degree from Harvard
> Joseph Story, eminent jurist

George Ticknor, distinguished literary man of Boston

John Welles, class of 1772, member of the Board of Overseers of Harvard College.

It has not been possible to ascertain the amounts of the individual donations. Receipt of Volume 1 of the *Birds of America* is recorded on 25 April 1833 in "Donations to the Library," but no record of the receipt of additional volumes could be found.

One of the subscribers, Nathaniel Bowditch, died on 16 March 1838. It has not been determined whether any of the other original subscribers also died before completion of the work. The corporation's certificate acknowledging the generosity of Nathaniel Bowditch and his associates was given to the library by Robert Black in 1954.

The Houghton Library also holds incomplete volumes of prints of the *Birds of America* (pl. 1–200 inc.). These were presented to the University on 14 March 1904 by the following donors:

An Anonymous Friend   Louis Cabot
William Brewster   Augustus Hemenway
Arthur F. Estabrook   Dudley L. Pickman
Francis H. Peabody   John Eliot Thayer.

These prints were purchased at the auction sale of Sotheby, Wilkinson & Hodges on 14 March 1904. The sale price, as given in *English Auction Records*, was £51 (approx. $250).

Harvard's set of the *Ornithological Biography*, which had belonged to Edward Harris, having been presented to him by Audubon, came as part of a bequest to that institution, in the Jeanes collection. The donor, the late Joseph Yerkes Jeanes, of Philadelphia, had purchased from Edward Harris II the greater part of his (Harris's) father's large collection of Audubon's original drawings.

Joseph Y. Jeanes, Jr., a member of the Harvard class of 1924, presented the collection to the Harvard College Library in May 1930. The gift included the Audubon drawings, 110 in all, the five volumes of letterpress, and a collection of original letters from the Naturalist to Harris.

Also of interest, in the Grenville Lindall Winthrop Collection at Harvard's Fogg Museum is a drawing of the European robin, made by the Naturalist at Greenbank, the home of the Rathbone family near Liverpool.

HARVARD UNIVERSITY
Widener Library

In March 1832, through the efforts of William Gaston, a wealthy merchant in Savannah and himself a subscriber, Audubon obtained three additional subscriptions in that city.[112]

Among these was that of James Potter, the owner of two large plantations near Savannah. Not long after that, Gaston procured two more subscriptions. With all these subscriptions Audubon received full payment for the first volume of 100 prints in advance.[113]

James Potter had a summer home in Princeton, New Jersey. It is believed that the folio of the *Birds of America* was moved to Princeton at the outbreak of the Civil War, for the Potter plantations, Coleran and Tweesdale (?) were burned by Sherman.[114] James Potter's only son, John Hamilton Potter, was killed at the siege of Atlanta. The latter's son, James Potter, was born two weeks before the death of his father. Soon after he became of age James sold the Princeton home, and the family moved to Philadelphia where they became friends of the Wideners.

The second James Potter was the grandfather of Mrs. Frank L. Polk, whose husband was Acting Secretary of State under President Wilson in 1919-1920. She recalls seeing the set often as a child and has told the author that "Mr. George Widener was a friend of my father's in Philadelphia and his son Harry was a friend of mine. The latter went down on the Titanic and it was in his memory his mother founded the library at Cambridge."[115] While Mrs. Polk states that Mrs. Widener purchased the set from her father, it would appear that the folio had been in the possession of the Widener family some time previously, for on the list of extant folios prepared by Anthony Woodward and dated 1901 is found "Peter A.B. Widener, Philadelphia, Pa. Informed March 22, 1901."[116]

Some years after the death of her husband, Mrs. Widener married Dr. Alexander Hamilton Rice. Shortly before 1938, his wife having died, Dr. Rice presented the folio to the Widener Library.

HENRY E. HUNTINGTON LIBRARY AND ART GALLERY
San Marino, Calif.

The Huntington folio was purchased at the Anderson Galleries auction sale held on 26 Feb.–1 March 1917 (item 529, sale of 27 Feb.), at a cost of $3,500. It had been the property of William K. Bixby of St. Louis, Mo.

Inquiry among members of the Bixby family failed to produce any information as to the previous history of the set other than that it may have been purchased through B. F. Stevens & Brown of London from whom Mr. Bixby had obtained many items.[117]

INDIANA HISTORICAL SOCIETY
The William Henry Smith Memorial Library, Indianapolis, Ind.

The Audubon folio and the five volumes of the *Ornithological Biography* were acquired in 1933 by the Library while the building was in process of construction and before a librarian was appointed.[118] The volumes had been in the possession of the Borden Institute, New Providence (now Borden), Indiana, which was established in 1884, by William Wesley Borden (?–1906). The Institute was closed in 1903. The folio as well as other books came into the possession of Borden's heirs following his death.[119]

It is believed that Borden purchased the folio in Cleveland as a wedding gift for his second wife, whom he married in 1884. The first volume of the set is inscribed, "Emma Borden from Wm. W. Borden."

The additional facts concerning the provenance of the folio were obtained in the following manner. Upon examination of the title page of volume 1 of the accompanying *Ornithological Biography* there was found the impression of a rubber stamp reading:

York
Subscription
Library

Furthermore, on the top of the title page was found the following acquisition notation:

2666
1st Vol.
6 July 31[120]

The catalog for the York Subscription Library for 1842 lists Audubon's *Birds of America* and the *Ornithological Biography* and both bear the accession number 2666.[121]

At a meeting of the members of the library held on 17 October 1889, after considerable discussion and opposition, it was voted to sell the Audubon folio to help pay for certain improvements to the library requiring an expenditure of £285. It was pointed out that "the Leeds association had recently sold (a set) for £250."[122] However, the York folio was not sold until sometime prior to January 1896.[123]

The folio in this library is unusual since it is one of only four located in which Plate 2 bears the incorrect legend, "Black Billed Cuckoo—Coccyzus Erythrophthalmus." This is evidence that the folio was that of a very early subscriber. Audubon was in York, England, from 22 April to 29 April 1827. Writing to his wife from Liverpool on 16 May 1827, he told her that he had obtained 10 subscriptions in York. That of the York Subscription Library was undoubtedly one of these.

INDIANA UNIVERSITY
The Lilly Library, Bloomington, Ind.

This folio was purchased in 1932 by Perry Hall of Philadelphia, a member of the banking firm of Drexel & Co., from Charles Sessler of Philadelphia, who had obtained it from the New York dealer, Thomas Gannon.[124]

When Mr. Hall was asked about the history of the folio, he stated "that he bought it from Sessler's in Philadelphia about 1932 and all he knows from its early history is that it came from England from a family called Ray."[125]

In the early 1940s David A. Randall, of the Scribner Book Store, purchased the folio for Joseph Kirby Lilly through Miss Belle Greene of the Morgan Library who was acting in the sale on behalf of Mr. Hall.[126]

In a letter to the author dated 24 May 1971, Mr. Randall has advised that each of the four volumes of the folio contains the bookplate (the dimensions of which are 3½" by 2⅝") of one Robert Ray, on which there appears the motto—"J'Espere en Dieu."

JAMES J. HILL REFERENCE LIBRARY
St. Paul, Minn.

It was in 1912 that James Jerome Hill (1838-1916) decided to build and endow a free reference library as a gift to his friends and neighbors in St. Paul. In 1915 the old Market House, where the Public Library had been located, was destroyed by fire. Soon after, two structures were planned to be built under one roof with a connecting door between them.

Mr. Hill died on 29 May 1916. The Audubon folio was received by the Reference Library in December 1918 during the settlement of Mr. Hill's estate, in all probability a gift from Mrs. Hill.[127]

Just when the folio was purchased by Hill is not known. A letter from one of his daughters states, "My Mother and Father moved from a house in the older part of the city to their final residence on Summit Avenue in 1892. I was nine years old at the time, and I remember that the books were there in a case with rollers. I imagine they are in the same case now, in the Library. I don't remember them in the old house where we formerly lived, but as I was only nine years old when we left it that doesn't mean much."[128] It would appear that the date of acquisition of the folio by Mr. Hill may have been prior to 1892.

The binding of the four volumes is in red morocco with gilt edges and some gold stamping. The five volumes of the *Ornithological Biography* accompanied the folio and are similarly bound. A bookseller's notation in the volumes of the *Biography* would indicate that the folio and the volumes of letterpress were sold at the same time.

THE JOHN CRERAR LIBRARY
Chicago, Ill.

On page 15 in a printed "Catalogue of the Collection of Books, Manuscripts, and Works of Art, belonging to Mr. Henry Probasco, Cincinnati, Ohio (Oakwood, Clifton), 1873," is an entry for Audubon's *Birds of America* which reads "Subscribers copy." There is, however, no elaboration.[129]

Probasco attempted to sell his collection to the Cincinnati library[130] but he was turned down, and in 1890 the Newberry Library of Chicago acquired the collection, which also included the Double Elephant folio of Audubon's *Birds of America*.[131] In 1898 the folio and the five volumes of the *Ornithological Biography* were acquired from the Newberry by the John Crerar Library of Chicago.

In 1932 J. Christian Bay, at the time librarian of the Crerar Library, carefully collated the prints of the Audubon folio and prepared an "Alphabetical Index to the Birds of America by John James Audubon, London 1827–1838, 4 vols." No other instance has been found where the prints of the Audubon folio have been collated.[132] Mr. Bay made available copies of this list to all who were interested.

JOHNS HOPKINS UNIVERSITY
Evergreen House Foundation, Baltimore, Md.

The library of John Work Garrett (1872–1942), which was bequeathed to Johns Hopkins University in 1942,[133] contained this copy of the Audubon folio. Information included in the file of the library and also the coat of arms of F. Buddle Atkinson (Deo Regi Fidelis) in the volumes indicates that the folio was at one time in the possession of the grandfather of Frank Buddle Atkinson, J. P. Gallowell House, Morpeth, Northumberland, England. It is not known when Mr. Garrett purchased the folio.

This is another set whose original subscriber must have been among the very early ones, for not only are all of the first ten prints those of the Lizars plates, with the Whatman watermarks dated either 1826 or 1827, but also Plate no. 2 carries in the upper left corner the incorrect legend "Black-billed Cuckoo."

THE ESTATE OF MRS. GRACE PHILLIPS JOHNSON
New Castle, Pa.

The Audubon folio and other Auduboniana were obtained for Mrs. Johnson in the late 1920s or early 1930s by Charles B. Randall, a New Castle bookdealer, who at that time was an agent for the well-known New York dealer, Gabriel Wells.

The first ten plates of the folio have very early Whatman watermarks, viz. 1826–1827. Plate 2, in addition, shows an erasure. This internal evidence indicates that the folio was one subscribed for in the beginning of the publication of the *Birds of America*. The set is in four volumes: Volume 1, plates 1–100; Volume 2, plates 101–200; Volume 3, plates 201–350; Volume 4, plates 351–435. Volume 1 has been rebound and placed between the prints are double elephant folio size sheets upon which have been attached the manuscripts for many of the descriptions of the 100 species found in Vol. 1 of the *Ornithological Biography*, as well as many of the "Episodes" found in Volumes 1 and 3 of that work.

In Volume 3 of the folio, the plate of the Fork tail Petrel has the number incorrectly engraved as 240 (CCXL) and it is placed between plates 253 and 255.

An additional copy of the plate of the Fork tail Petrel, with the correct number, 260 (CCLX), has been inserted in the correct place. Also, the engraving of Wilson's Phalarope, which is plate 254 (CCLIV), is incorrectly engraved plate 256 (CCLVI).

In recapitulating the manuscript material acquired by Mrs. Johnson, it was found that the collection includes all but eight of the descriptions of the 100 species in Volume 1 of the *Ornithological Biography*. As to the Episodes which Audubon interspersed in the first three volumes of the *Ornithological Biography*, the manuscripts of the following are in the Johnson collection:

from Volume 1	The Ohio	*Page*	29
	The Great Pine Swamp		52
	The Prairie		81
	The Regulators		105
	Improvements in the Navigation of the Mississippi		130
	A Flood		155
	Meadville		182
	The Cougar		205
	The Earthquake		239
	The Hurricane		262
	Deer Hunting		335
	Niagara		362
	Hospitality in the Woods		383
	The Original Painter		410
	The Eccentric Naturalist		455
	Bear Killing (Scipio and the Bear)		479
from Volume 3	A Good Horse		270
	Breaking Up Of the Ice		408
	A Long Calm at Sea		491
	Still Becalmed		520
	Natchez in 1820		539
	The Lost Portfolio		564
	Great Egg Harbour		606.

The collection also contains a manuscript entitled "Mangrove" which it has not been possible to identify.[134]

In *Audubon and His Journals*, Maria Audubon, a granddaughter of the Naturalist, included Audubon's paper, "My Style of Drawing Birds." The manuscript of this also is included in the Johnson Auduboniana.[135]

LAVAL UNIVERSITÉ
Québec, Canada

This folio of Audubon's *Birds of America* was purchased in 1861 from New York bookdealer A. Appleton & Co. of 443 & 445 Broadway. A letter from that firm dated 4 November 1861 shows that the cost was $1020.

The amount of money required was raised by subscription with 39 contributors to the fund, including a major gift of $800 by the Séminaire de Québec. Among the individual subscribers were the following:

Leverdière, Charles-Honoré, priest and librarian of the University, editor of *Relations des Jesuites* and of *Oeuvres (Works) de Champlain*
Hamel, Thomas-Etienne, Rector of Laval University (1871), president of the Royal Society, 1886
Taschereau, Elzéar-Alexandre, Bishop of Quebec (1871), first Canadian Cardinal (1886)
Ferland, J. B. Antoine, priest, historian
Lemoine, Sir James McPherson, writer, professor at Laval University, president of the Royal Society, 1896, author of *Canadian Ornithology (Ornithologie du Canada)*, 1861, the first Canadian work on birds.

LEGISLATIVE LIBRARY
Fredericton, N.B., Canada

The four volumes of the Audubon prints of *Birds of America* in the Legislative Library at Fredericton are splendidly bound in dark crimson turkey morocco, the backs and sides elaborately gilded with broad gold borders and gilt edges. The binder was John Wright of London "whose specimens are characterized by an abundance of gold." In 1862 he was awarded a medal by the Trustees of the Great Exhibition of that year "for excellence in blind tooling and forwarding."[136]

The present librarian, Maurice P. Boone, has for many years been making an exhaustive search of the library and legislative records, hoping to find definite information about the history of the acquisition of the set, as well as knowledge of the original subscriber.[137]

One reference was found in the "Journals of the House of Assembly of New Brunswick" for 1864. The Secretary of the Legislative Library in his report stated: "The copy of Audubon's magnificent work upon the Birds of America, belonging to the Library, is believed to possess an historical interest as the subscription copy of King Louis Phillippe, or of his unfortunate son the Duke of Orleans, who accidentally perished in the full vigour of health and manhood." As Mr. Boone writes,[138] the Secretary, Mr. Gowan, erred, for the King's son was not an original subscriber and the set of his father, who was an original subscriber, was burned in the Neuilly fire of 1848, from which only one volume with burnt covers was salvaged.

However, Mr. Boone was to find a manuscript book of minutes of the Library Committee, 1848–1878, which had been missing from the Legislative Library for a great number of years.[139] In this, under the date of 2 April 1852, was found the following: "Resolved that Mr. Gowan be authorized to obtain Audubon's Ornithology from Little Brown for the specified sum of £200 currency." Then, on 29 April 1853, it is further stated: "Agreeably to the order of the Committee, the 4 volumes of Audubon's American Ornithology have been purchased at a cost of $800 and are now in the Library. They were the property of the Duke of Orleans, eldest son of King Louis Philippe of France, and they have thus acquired a kind of historical interest." Mr. Boone continues: "It must be conceded that there is still a mystery concerning the question of the original subscriber. Since it cannot have been Louis Philippe's set, perhaps it is that of King Charles X, or that of Her Royal Highness, Mademoiselle d'Orleans, whose set could have passed into the hands of her nephew, the Duke of Orleans."

As for King Charles X, who was an original subscriber, it must be pointed out that when he was deposed he had received, according to Audubon's records in Ledger "B," only the first 21 numbers, or 105 plates, of the folio.

LEHIGH UNIVERSITY
Bethlehem, Pa.

Information concerning the provenance of this set of the folio of Audubon's *Birds of America* is lacking. All that is known is that it was purchased by the University and that it was accessioned on June 30, 1885.[140]

In the binding of the four volumes of the folio, the boards (¾ binding, gold tooled spine) are marbled outside and inside. The five volumes of the *Ornithological Biography* are similarly bound.[141]

LIBRARY ASSOCIATION OF PORTLAND
Ore.

The folio was presented to the Library Association by the widow of William S. Ladd in 1906.[142] Mr. Ladd (1826–1893) had been a native of Vermont and had gone to Portland, Oregon, in 1851 at the age of 25. He became a merchant and shortly thereafter opened the first bank in Portland, the Ladd and Tilton Bank. He was the first president of the Library's Board of Directors.[143]

The four volumes of the folio and the five volumes of the *Ornithological Biography* are bound in red morocco, with tooled spines, names in gilt letters, and marbled end papers. In the first volume of the latter there is the following notation:

        No. 5190   5 vols Text
                      4 " Plates.

This may represent an auction catalog number.

The first volume of the folio contains a print of Plate 2, the Yellow-billed Cuckoo, with the legend in the upper left corner. This shows an erasure in the title, the words "Yellow" and "Carolinensis" having been written in.

Plate 110 as found in the Field Museum set of the folio, one of two sets known to contain all thirteen of the composite plates. See figure 35. Courtesy of the Library, Field Museum of Natural History.

Plate 9 as found in the Field Museum set of the folio. Originally Audubon believed this bird to be a new species, named by him "Selby's Flycatcher." He later learned that the bird is an immature form of the Hooded Flycatcher. Courtesy of the Library, Field Museum of Natural History.

Composite Plate 110 as found in the Field Museum set of the folio, one of thirteen present in this set. Note that the bird originally designated "Selby's Flycatcher" appears in the lower right with flowering branch truncated. Courtesy of the Library, Field Museum of Natural History.

Ottoman (closed) built to house the Euphemia Gifford set.

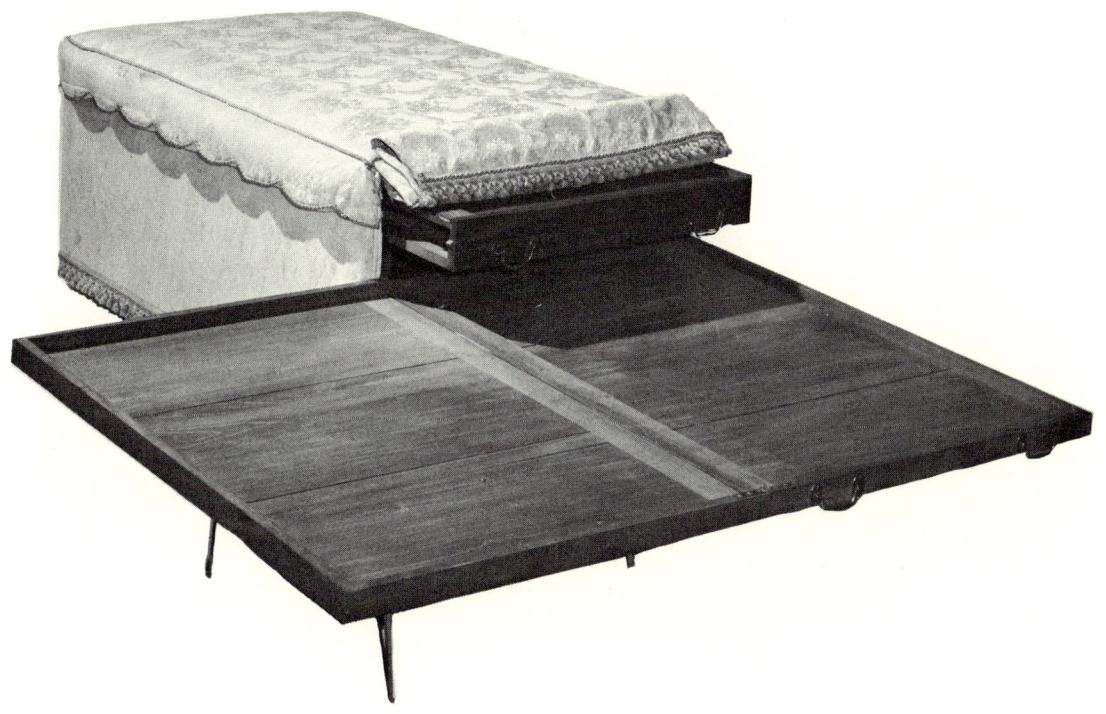

The same ottoman shown open. There are four large sliding trays which provide complete protection for the folio volumes. Both photographs courtesy of the Library, Field Museum of Natural History.

The J. Whatman watermark. Courtesy of the Library, Field Museum of Natural History.

Legend of Plate 2, showing erasures. Also visible is the J. Whatman watermark. Courtesy of the Amon Carter Museum of Western Art, Forth Worth, Tex.

Provenances of Sets in the United States and Canada

LIBRARY OF CONGRESS
Washington, D.C.

The list of American subscribers which Audubon has included in the fifth volume of the *Ornithological Biography* is headed by "Library of Congress of the United States—Washington City."[144]

That Audubon was desirous of having his adopted country be among the first to become acquainted with his *Birds of America* is made evident in an interesting manner. On 14 December 1827, when the engraving of the drawings had been in progress for a little over a year, Audubon, while in Liverpool, had written in his journal: "By the advice of our consul Mr. Maury, I have presented a copy of my work to the President of the United States and another to the House of Representatives through Henry Clay."[145] The president at the time was John Quincy Adams; Clay was the Secretary of State. It is possible that Audubon and Clay had become acquainted during the former's long residence in Louisville and Henderson, Ky. When Audubon had left for Europe in 1826, included among the many letters of introduction taken along were some given him by Clay.[146]

Even previous to this, namely on 30 May of the same year, the Naturalist had exhibited some of his drawings to Albert Gallatin, at the time Envoy Extraordinaire to the British government. Gallatin had been Secretary of the Treasury under President Jefferson.[147]

Audubon referred to the matter again in his journal entry dated London, 8 January 1828: "I have ordered one set of my birds to be colored by Havell himself, for Congress and the numbers already out will soon be enroute."[148]

It was hoped that there might be some reference to this intended gift in the Adams papers now deposited in the Archives of the Massachusetts Historical Society, but no letters addressed to President John Quincy Adams from Audubon have been found. On the other hand, there is included among the Adams papers a letter written by Audubon on 10 April 1828 at 95 Great Russell Street, London, Bedford Square, addressed to "His Excellency Gl Andrew Jackson, President of the United States."

With this letter requesting Jackson's support and patronage, Audubon had sent his prospectus which contained a list of subscribers he had thus far obtained in Europe. Also in this letter is a reference to "the letters of introduction you sent me in Louisville (Kentucky)," for which Audubon thanked him. From an entry in Audubon's journal, dated Louisville, 20 November 1824, it is known that he had received such a letter with an introduction to the Governor of Florida from General Jackson.[149] Inasmuch as Jackson was not inaugurated president until 4 March 1829, the presence of Audubon's letter addressing him as "His Excellency . . . , President of the United States" in April of 1828 among the Adams papers is baffling.[150]

There is in the diary of John Quincy Adams a reference to Audubon's *Birds of America* under date of 9 November 1830. That evening Adams had attended a meeting of the American Philosophical Society in Philadelphia. He wrote, "Audubon's Birds was there. The oriole of Baltimore is the fiery hang bird."[151]

It has not been possible to locate any letters among the Henry Clay papers in reference to the contemplated gift. And not until two years had elapsed, in 1830, was Audubon to receive the subscription of the Library of Congress.

On 1 April 1829 Audubon sailed from England for America where he planned to paint additional birds and solicit subscriptions for the *Birds of America*. He arrived in New York on 1 May 1829, but it was not until March of 1830, accompanied by his wife who was returning to England with him, that he visited Washington City. Here, after exhibiting his original watercolor drawings of his *Birds of America* before the House of Representatives, he received the subscription of the Library of Congress, authorized by the "Joint Committee on the Library of Congress."[152]

This committee included two members who were to be of considerable help to Audubon in obtaining additional subscriptions. One of these was Edward Everett, at the time a congressman from Massachusetts and chairman of the Library Committee. When Audubon listed the subscription of the Library of Congress in the first volume of the *Ornithological Biography*, he set it down as follows: "E. Everett, Esq., for the Library of Congress of the United States of America."[153]

Everett, in his effort to be of help during Audubon's Washington visit, gave him letters of introduction to individuals who themselves might subscribe or who might influence others to do so. One of these letters was addressed to Robert Gilmor of Baltimore. In this letter, dated Washington City, 18 March 1830, he wrote: "He has with him a few of his original drawings, which he is anxious you should see." He also stated: "He has not obtained a single subscription to his work in the United States of America."[154] From the date of this letter it would appear that the subscription of the Library of Congress must have been received shortly after 18 March 1830.

Another letter from Everett, written on the same date, was addressed to the Reverend Dr. Johnson Wainwright of Grace Church in New York. In this letter he bespoke the Reverend Doctor's help in obtaining subscriptions, writing: "will not your Institutions in New York or your wealthy liberal individuals take a copy?"[155]

The other member of the Joint Committee of the Library of Congress who was to be helpful to Audubon was Levi Woodbury, at the time a senator from New Hampshire. In 1836, when he had become Secretary of the Treasury under President Jackson, he aided Audubon in obtaining the subscription of "State Departments—Washington City."

During the visit to Washington Audubon met with President Jackson who "received me with great kindness as he did your mother also after-wards."[156]

Soon after receiving the subscription of the Library of Congress, Audubon and his wife left Washington. En route to New York there was a stopover in Baltimore, then on to New York from which city on 1 April 1830 the Audubons sailed for England.

Provenances of Sets in the United States and Canada

Not long after his return to England, Audubon began to send copies of the finished engravings of the *Birds of America* to the United States. One such shipment probably was made early in May, for in a letter to Robert Gilmor, whose subscription, together with two others, Audubon had obtained in Baltimore when he had visited that city the previous March, he wrote: "I take the liberty to advise you that Messrs Rathbone Brothers & Co. of the city (Liverpool) have shipped per Watchman, Nason master bound to Baltimore a box addressed first to your care and secondly the Secretary of the Congress Library at Washington City. The Case contains 4 sealed packages. (in) each is a copy of the 'Birds of America' numbered 1 to 4. No. 17 will be ready to forward to America next month."[157]

It would appear from this letter that each package contained 80 prints in all, comprising the numbers (fascicles) from 1 to 16 inclusive. While it is not possible to give the date of this letter, it was probably sent sometime prior to September 1830, for on the 13th of that month Audubon, while in York, England, wrote to his engraver Havell; "Tomorrow I exhibit Nos. 17 & 18 and my drawings at the Philosophical Society."[158] From this it seems evident that both Numbers 17 & 18 had been engraved.

On 1 November 1830 the Naturalist wrote to Edward Everett, sending him copies of the prospectus for the *Birds of America*. He wrote to Everett again on 5 March 1831. In both letters Audubon asked for Everett's help in the passage of a bill which would allow "free introduction" for the *Birds of America*, inasmuch as the prints then were being taxed for duty. Audubon also asked for information relative to United States copyright laws, since he was at the time writing the first volume of his letterpress, the *Ornithological Biography*.

Everett replied to both of these letters on 19 May 1831 from Charleston, where he had been recuperating from illness. He wrote: "The portions of your work which arrived at Washington before I left it were publicly exhibited in the Library, and attracted great attention and unqualified admiration." He furthermore told Audubon that he had distributed a part of the prospectuses and would do the same with the rest "in a manner that seems most likely to promote your interests." With this letter he also furnished Audubon the desired information regarding the copyright laws.[159]

In the summer of 1831, after completing the writing of the first volume of the *Ornithological Biography* and with the engraving of the plates for the second volume of the *Birds of America* underway, Audubon felt he must again return to the United States in order to extend his researches to the north, south, and west, as well as to begin a campaign for subscribers.

Therefore, on 2 August 1831, accompanied by his wife, he set sail for New York, arriving in that metropolis on 3 September. After a brief stay in that city and a stopover in Philadelphia, where he obtained three subscribers, he arrived in Washington, probably late in September. Here, on 4 October he received from the Hon. Thomas L. Smith, Register of the Treasury and Agent of the Joint Library Committee, a payment of $219.11 for 23 numbers of the *Birds of America*.

Audubon's receipt for this payment is now preserved in the National Archives in Washington.[160]

From the letter sent to Gilmor in Baltimore, it is known that the first shipment sent to the Library of Congress consisted of 16 Numbers of 80 engravings. At the time Audubon received his first payment of $219.11, the Library of Congress had received one hundred and fifteen engravings, all the prints for the first volume and fifteen for the second volume. On 31 October 1830, writing from Edinburgh, Audubon had instructed his engraver to deliver to Obadiah Rich, the English agent for the Library of Congress, Numbers 18 and 19.[161] It is possible that Audubon may have brought Numbers 20, 21, 22 and 23 with him from England.

Additional information is obtained from the receipt; namely, that the Chairman of the Joint Committee was now Asher Robbins, a senator from Rhode Island, and that the engravings as well as "silk paper for guards" were deposited in the Library of Congress.

In his prospectus Audubon had stated that the price of one number or five engravings was to be 2 Guineas (£2.2s.). On the receipt the 23 numbers had been totaled according to their value in English currency, £48.6s. To this had been added £1 for "Silk Paper," making a total of £49.6s., which, converted to United States currency, amounted to $219.11.

In tracing the history of the subscriptions to the Double Elephant folio of the *Birds of America*, there is available a source book which is of great value. This is Audubon's bookkeeping record, Ledger "B," now on loan to the Audubon Museum at Audubon State Park, Henderson, Kentucky. This ledger, together with much other Auduboniana, is the property of two daughters of the late Mrs. Leonard Tyler. The husband of Mrs. Tyler was the grandson of Victor Audubon, the elder son of John James Audubon. In this ledger there are recorded the accounts of the individual subscribers, with detailed information as to the numbers of engravings, or, in certain instances, complete volumes sent to subscribers, date these were sent out or billed. In some entries payments are also shown. Both charges and payments are shown in English currency, since Audubon would remit by English drafts for funds collected in the States.

The first entry on the account of the Library of Congress is:

78-1831—January 1, 1831 To first volumes of Birds of
America & No. 21 inclusive   45-2-0.

This is then followed by sixteen additional entries, seventeen in all, with the last entry dated in 1838, which is as follows:

1838– To Nos. 82–87   (151)   12-12-0.

The last entry indicates that the subscription of the Library of Congress was completed, there being 87 numbers or 435 engravings in the complete set. Havell had finished engraving the last plate on 26 June 1838.[162]

The "contra" items, or payments, begin with an entry dated 1832, as follows:

1832– Dec. 10   Audubon   (58)   48-5-0.

There are only two other entries under the "contra" heading. These are:

1834–June—1 Vol.	Cash Pd. on delivery	(58)	50-8-0.
1837	"	(135)	83-5-0.

The ledger was undoubtedly kept in England, probably by Audubon's son Victor who had gone to England in 1832, there to oversee his father's affairs. Audubon, as he received payments from American subscribers, would remit to his son in England. The letters referring to these transactions indicate that the payments were sent in the form of English drafts.

Three additional receipts given by Audubon were also found in the National Archives. One, dated 9 October 1833, in the amount of $84.66 is for Numbers 24–31. $80.00, and the 1st vol. of the *Biography* $4.66. Another, also dated 9 October 1833, in the amount of $30 is for numbers 32, 33, 34. The third, dated 28 March 1834, in the amount of $224, is for

20 Nos. at $10.00	$200.00
Binding same	20.00
Box for the same	4.00
	$224.00

It should be noted that the cost was now being figured on the basis of $10 per number.

As has been stated earlier, the entries in Ledger "B" indicate that all 87 numbers of the folio had been charged to the Library of Congress, to which a complete set of loose prints had been furnished. These were bound later into four volumes. In Ledger "B" it was customary to place the letter "C" at the right margin of the first entry in those instances in which the subscription was completed. Such a symbol appears in the account of the Library of Congress. In an instance when the subscription was not completed, the symbol "X" was used.

On 4 October 1831, when Audubon gave his receipt for a payment of $219.11, this payment covered all the prints for the first volume, which comprised 20 numbers, plus Numbers 21, 22, and 23. However, a check of the entries in ledger "B" shows the following:

1834   June   1 volume   Pd. on delivery   50-8-0.

Furthermore, the receipt given by Audubon on 28 March 1834 called for "one volume first Birds of America, half bound and containing twenty numbers at $10.00 ... $200.00."

From the entry in Ledger "B" and from the receipt given by Audubon, there is evidence that, in addition to the first volume of loose prints sent to the Library of Congress, the library also received a bound copy of Volume 1 (the first 100 prints). It has been possible to find additional evidence that such was the case.

On 7 October 1836 John S. Meehan, the librarian of the Library of Congress, wrote to Audubon as follows: "The Committee do not want a *second* copy of the work, I believe. I recollect that at the time you furnished the duplicate copy of the first volume, it was purchased with the understanding that only the first volume, then in the library and much used, should be publicly exhibited, so that when the whole work was completed, every portion of our copy should be in good condition. It is intended to have the whole work bound to match the half-bound copy of the first volume you mention."[163]

In his letter Meehan also noted that the first volume, publicly exhibited, was much used. Further information regarding this volume is furnished by another source. In the spring of 1838, Captain Frederic Marryat visited Washington. A description of this visit is found in his *Diary in America*. Here he writes: "The best lounge at Washington is the library of the Capitol, but the books are certainly not very well treated. I saw a copy of Audubon's Ornithology, and many other works, in a very dilapidated state; but this must be the case when the library is open to all, and here are so many juvenile visitors. Still it is much better than locking it up, for only the bindings to be looked at. It is not a library for show, but for use and it is a great comfort and amusement."[164]

But still more information concerning this single Volume 1 has been found, again in Ledger "B." Here is to be found an account with a Baltimore subscriber, E. Poultney. The entry is as follows:

80—Poultney, E. Baltimore 1 volume half bound—Returned & went to Library of Congress   49-10-0.

Although this entry is not dated, it is known that Audubon had obtained the Poultney subscription in October 1833. In a letter dated 11 October 1833 to his son Victor in London he included Poultney's name among three subscribers he had obtained in Baltimore.[165] In other letters Audubon wrote can be found the reason for the return of that volume. On Sunday, 6 April 1834, Audubon had written two letters, one to his son Victor and the other to Miss Maria Martin of Charleston, a sister-in-law of John Bachman. In his letter to Maria Martin he stated, "I procured a new subscriber and lost an old one—Mr. Poultney, the President of the fallen bank of Maryland."[166] In his letter to Victor, the story is related as follows: "Mr. Poultney of Baltimore has failed for an enormous amount and I did not choose to deliver the first Volume to him."[167]

Also in the letter of 6 April to Victor, Audubon listed the names of American subscribers from whom he had received payments and included, "Library of Congress, a second copy of *1st Vl* $224.00."[168] It will be recalled that a receipt signed by Audubon for the Library of Congress on 28 March 1834 was for a like amount.

Audubon had arrived in the United States in September of 1831. He was to remain until April 1834. During his visit to Washington in September of 1831 he had received payment of $219.11 for the prints delivered up to that time; these included the first volume of 20 numbers plus Numbers 21, 22, and 23. He visited Washington again in the autumn of 1833, at which time he received payment for Numbers 24 to 34. It was at this time that he left with the Library of Congress the half-bound copy of the first volume. In a letter from Baltimore, dated 11

October 1833, to his son Victor in London, he wrote: "I left *one volume* half bound in the hands of the Librarian of Congress because he told me that he *had* no doubt that Congress would subscribe for a 2d copy of the Work—he will write your Mamma at Charleston respecting this as soon as Congress meets."[169] The matter is again referrred to in a letter to his son written in Baltimore on 9 March 1834: "We have a first Volume ½ bound in the [Con———] Library which if not subscribed for & paid for in course of a week or 10 days I will take & forward to New Orleans for the State's Libra[———] of Louisiana."[170]

At the present time this "first Volume ½ bound" is not in the Library of Congress. Nor was it possible to locate any definite reference to it in the catalogs of the Library. One reference was found which may refer to the volume. On page 59 of the "Alphabetical Catalogue of the Library" (Washington Printing Office, 1864), the following items appear:

> Audubon, John James. Birds of America from Original drawings. 4 V. Great Folio. London 1827–1838
> ——— The Same. Vol 1. Folio. Title Missing.

Mr. Frederick R. Goff, Chief of the Rare Book Division, is of the opinion that the reference "The Same" is to the single volume of the Bien Chromolithograph edition of the prints, published by Roe-Lockwood under the direction of John Woodhouse Audubon between 1858 and 1860. There is such a volume in the library today. In writing about it on 16 November 1961, Mr. Goff advises that it appears to have been in the Library for a great number of years. However, it was not cataloged until 1948, and at that time it was recorded incorrectly as an imperfect third copy of the Double Elephant folio.

Audubon's final visit to Washington on this visit to America was made during the later part of March 1834, when he was paid for the single copy of Volume I delivered to the Library of Congress the previous October. Afterward, on 16 April 1834, together with his wife and son John Woodhouse, he sailed from New York to England.

Meehan's letter of 7 October 1836 provides additional information regarding the delivery of numbers of the engravings to the Library of Congress. Meehan, having been ill with "bilious fever," had asked his assistant "who is very careful" to make inquiry as to the receipt of the numbers of the folio. This assistant was probably E. B. Steele, assistant librarian from 1830 to 1861. The information furnished by his assistant was that "we want plate III, of No. 23, the whole of No. 48, 49, 59, 60. The last numbers which came to hand a few days ago in one parcel are 61 and 62 which bring our collection (wanting what is mentioned above), to plate 310. We have received the 3d volume of your letter-press—the second we have not had."[171]

One final reference to the folio of the *Birds of America* at the Library of Congress. On 23 December 1851 there occurred a disastrous fire in the library, then located in the Capitol. Fortunately, the folio was uninjured as it had been placed in the Library Committee Room, which the fire did not reach. A letter referring to the fire, written to Eli French of New York by Meehan on 29 December 1851, made no mention of the copy of Volume 1 (this letter has been reproduced on p. 74 of the Library of Congress Annual Report for 1964).

LIBRARY OF CONGRESS
War Department copy

Included on the list of final subscribers published by Audubon in Volume 5 of the *Ornithological Biography* is that of the "State Departments, Washington City."[172]

At the present time, none of the libraries of those departments of the United States government in Washington which were in existence at the time the subscription list was published lays claim to a set of the Double Elephant folio of the *Birds of America*. On the other hand, there is located in the Library of Congress a set which is identified as "The War Department Copy." Although many of the individual prints bear a stamp reading "War Department" there is little historical information available other than that the folio was received by the Library of Congress from the Army War College Library on 1 October 1929.

In the September–October 1958 issue of the *Audubon Magazine* there was published an article by this author entitled "The Elephant Hunter." Here was recounted the early stages of the search for extant sets of the Double Elephant folio of Audubon's *Birds of America*. Included was a statement that the Library of Congress had two complete sets, one the result of the original subscription, the other the set given to the Library by the Army War College in 1929.

Shortly after the publication of the article there was received by the author a letter dated 22 October 1958 from William Durward Connor, Major General, United States Army, retired. The General wrote as follows:

> While I was Commandant of the institution now called "The National War College," here in Washington, D.C., I found among the locked up pieces a copy of Audubon's beautifully illustrated books (one or more, I do not recall). I felt that it could never be of any military value and that it was a shame to hold it there in the library like a "pack rat" of evil story out on the plain. I directed that it be turned over to the Library of Congress or some other library where it might be available to the public at large. Whether or not that is the second volume that the Library of Congress now has obtained from the War Department as you describe it, I have no way of knowing, but I thought if it were so, I am the only living person that would have knowledge of it. The above occurred about 1928 but positively in one of the two or three years following, certainly between 1928–1932.

General Connor was named Commandant of the Army War College in 1927, a post which he held until 1932. He died in Washington on 16 June 1960 at the age of 86.

In the spring of 1961 at the Library of the National War College there was shown to the author the record indicating the transfer on 1 October 1929 of the four volumes of the folio, four volumes of the *Ornithological Biography*, and the seven volumes comprising the Octavo edition of the *Birds of America* to the Library of Congress by the Army War College Library. Yes, "Audubon's beautifully illustrated books" referred to by General Connor is the second set of the folio in the Library of Congress.

Of all the government libraries in Washington, how did a set of the Double Elephant folio come into the possession of the Army War College Library? In considering this question it should be explained that in 1914 the Library of the War Department, which was founded in 1795, the second oldest government library, had been transferred to the Army War College whose library had been founded in 1904. The two libraries were combined at that time. The Army War College was suspended in 1940 and its library and personnel were transferred to the National War College.

After Audubon had received a subscription for the *Birds of America* from the Library of Congress in March 1830, he continued his efforts to have other departments of the government subscribe to the work. On 19 October 1836 he received from Washington Irving a letter addressed to Benjamin F. Butler, then Attorney General of the United States. In this letter Irving had written, "Why cannot the departments at Washington furnish themselves with copies (of the Double Elephant folio) to be deposited in their libraries or archives?"[173]

While in Washington on 8 November in the same year, Audubon had presented Irving's letter to Butler. However, Butler gave Audubon little encouragement, saying that the government allowed so little money to departments that he did not think it probable their subscriptions could be obtained without a law to that effect from Congress.

On the same day, prior to presenting the letter to Butler, Audubon had visited Levi Woodbury, then secretary of the Treasury, whom he had first met in 1830 when he had received the subscription of the Library of Congress Woodbury, a senator from New Hampshire, had been on the Joint Committee of the Library of Congress. The matter of a subscription was broached to him but nothing decisive was said. Later while spending the evening at Woodbury's home, Audubon was informed that the Treasury Department had subscribed "for a copy of our work."[174]

In Volume 4 of the *Ornithological Biography*, on page 613, under the heading "Subscribers to 'Birds of America,' Obtained Since the Publication of the Third Volume" is listed: "The Honourable Levi Woodbury, Washington City, for the State Departments."[175]

This volume is dated Edinburgh, 1 November 1838. Audubon had returned to England in July 1837 and immediately set about the writing of this volume of the *Ornithological Biography*.

Another reference to this subscription has also been found in Audubon's Ledger "B," now exhibited at the Audubon Museum in Henderson, Kentucky. Here there appears the following entry:

132—Nov. 1836—Treasury Department delivered   C
I, II, III vol. Hf Bound
(115)   £148-10-0
June 23, 1837   Cash J. J. Audubon (125)   £148-10-0.

Although only three volumes of the folio are mentioned, the fact that there is written the letter "C" at the right of the entry indicates that the subscription was completed, since this was the symbol Audubon used to denote such an occurrence.

Thus there is evidence from two sources that Audubon did obtain a subscription from Levi Woodbury, Secretary of the Treasury, and that he listed the subscription "for the State Departments." The use of the plural would seem to indicate that other departments of the government were involved in the subscription. That this was indeed true, as well as the names of the other departments, was determined from evidence in the National Archives. Here were located several memoranda, or vouchers, from which it has been possible to reconstruct the story.

The first memorandum is dated 9 November 1836 and reads as follows:

> The State, Treasury, War & Navy Departments
> To John J. Audubon
> Each, for their equal proportions of the sum of Six hundred and Sixty Dollars, the Price of Volume First, second and third of one copy of the Birds of America, delivered this day. In another hand is written, "$220 each in consequence of State dept declining to execute agreement." Draft on Charleston sent 3d Dec.[176]

As it was on the evening of 8 November that Audubon had been advised of the subscription, it would appear that Woodbury had wasted no time in obtaining the cooperation of other departments in joining in the subscription. Also, a way had been found to pay for the folio without resorting to a law from Congress, but just how this was done is not clear. An interesting sidelight as to the amount spent by the libraries of the various departments is found on page 544 of Leonard D. White's *The Jacksonians*.[177]

From the additional statement on the aforementioned memorandum, it appears that for some reason the State Department later declined to go along with the original agreement. This seems particularly strange since the evidence indicates that the State Department usually spent several thousand dollars more for books than did the Library of Congress and considerably more than the other departments.

Other memoranda found in the records of the National Archives include "Voucher A," request by the Navy Department of 11 November 1836 to R. Ela, disbursing agent of the Treasury Department, for "one-quarter of the cost of three volumes of Audubon's Birds of America, deposited in the State Department. Whole amount $660. $165"; and "Voucher B," request by the U.S. War Department, dated 3 December 1836, to Richard Ela, disbursing agent, Treasury Department, for "one-third part cost of Audubon's Birds of America. $220." From the latter request it is known that "the whole cost $660.00 [is] being jointly defrayed

Although it is not known who actually pleaded Audubon's cause before the legislature, it is possible that it may have been his brother-in-law, for on 15 February 1834, in a letter written to his son in England from Charleston, Audubon stated: "We expect N. Berthoud here daily, from New Orleans on his way home. —he wrote us that the State of Louisiana had Subscribed to the Work, but we know not any particulars as yet."[183]

It will be recalled that the Act authorizing the purchase of the *Birds of America* by the legislature was not signed by the governor until 6 March, but it often happens that there is considerable delay in between the passage of an act and the signing by the executive.

Just where the four volumes of the folio were housed after the completion of the work is not clear. In 1897 Mary Fluker Bradford, in a biographical sketch of Audubon read before the Quarante Club of New Orleans, stated, "The State Library also boasts of a copy of his greatest ornithological work."[184]

At a later time the volumes were deposited at the Cabildo, a part of the State Museum. In the early 1960s when Charles E. Frampton became business manager of the State Museum, "he found the prints, heaped one on top of the other and deteriorating on the floor of a dusty, hot attic. Their original binding was gone. He made their rescue and rehabilitations one of his main projects at the Museum."[185] The prints have now been lined with acid-resisting paper and special cases for them have been built in one of the Cabildo's air-conditioned storerooms. Many of the prints are being framed.

LOUISIANA STATE UNIVERSITY
Baton Rouge, La.

This folio was originally subscribed for by the Duke of Northumberland (#77 on Audubon's list of subscribers in v. 5 of the O.B.). On 29 May 1836, writing from London to John Bachman in Charleston, S. C., Audubon stated: "Your friend A. McDowall came to see us yesterday morning and handed us yours of the 16th of April last. I was not at home however when he came, but four miles out of Town breakfasting with Lord Ravensworth, whose son had procured me the previous evening the subscription of the Duke of Northumberland."[186] This was entered on the original subscription list as, "His Grace the Duke of Northumberland, by T. Lidell—May 27, 1836."

The Naturalist had hoped to obtain the Duke's subscription from the very beginning of the engraving of the drawings of the *Birds of America*. As early as 22 December 1826, he had written to his wife from Edinburgh, "Mr. Selby will take me to the Duke of Northumberland when I call at his house on my way to New Castle."[187] However, as late as March 1833, Audubon was to tell his son Victor, "The Duke of Northumberland is greatly prejudiced against me through

Waterton[188] who is a crony of the House." This subscription was among the last Audubon was to obtain in England before returning to America.

The Northumberland folio came into the possession of the English bookdealer Lionel Robinson, probably in the 1950s. In 1963 it was offered for sale by Quaritch for £25,000 ($70,000).[189] The University of Louisiana purchased the set in 1964, with the aid of a portion of the Crown Zellerbach Foundation funds, at a price reported to have been $65,000.[190]

Shortly after acquiring the folio, the university also purchased an additional copy of Volume 1 (100 prints). This volume contains earlier states of certain of the prints found in the four-volume set.

H. BRADLEY MARTIN
New York, N.Y.

Item no.177 in the Sotheby (London) auction catalog for 21 and 22 March 1955 reads as follows:

> Audubon, (John James). A selected portion of the Library from Conington Castle, Peterborough. The property of John Heathcote, Esq. The Birds of America from Original Drawings 4 vols. in 5, engraved title pages (that to Vol. II lacking) 435 plates, one detached, numbered I–XI, 12–100, CI–CCCCXXXV engraved, printed and coloured by W. H. Lizars and Robert Havell, father and son, one-eighth inch tear in margin of plate 200 (touching about one inch of plate) and another (3-½ inches) in plate 201 (both repaired), a few insignificant tears in margin, contemporary half morocco, double elephant folio (leaves measure 38-7/16 in. by 25-¾ in.) 1827–1838. Apart from very slight defects mentioned above this is a superb copy of very large size; the edges of Vol. II are uncut by the trimmer's knife. Plate I, III, IV, V & XI are original impressions by Lizars, Plate II is by the Havells, plate VI–X were engraved by Lizars but printed and coloured by R. Havell, Sr.
>
> With the five volumes of plates is a copy of Audubon's text Ornithological Biography, or an account, accompanied by Descriptions of the Objects represented in the work entitled the Birds of America, 5 vols., small tear in one leaf, work engravings, contemporary half morocco, m.e., 8vo. Edinburgh 1831–1849 (sic).

On the original Audubon subscription list is found "John Heathcote, Esq. 41 Charles St. Berkeley Square, (Nov.–March)." And on the list of European subscribers which Audubon included in Volume 5 of the *Ornithological Biography*, the Heathcote subscription is no.32.

The folio was acquired at the Sotheby sale by Lionel and Philip Robinson, of London for £9,200 ($25,760).[191] They, in turn, sold it to Mr. Martin.

Over the years Mr. Martin has built up a very comprehensive ornithological collection which has been described in detail by Mr. G. W. Cottrell, Jr., in *The Book Collector*.[192]

Provenances of Sets in the United States and Canada

MC GILL UNIVERSITY
Montreal, Que., Canada

The presentation of the Audubon folio to McGill University is recorded as follows:

At the Quarterly Meeting of the Corporation of McGill University held on the 23rd day of October 1861–

A letter from Theodore Hart, Esq., was read presenting in the name of several Merchants and Citizens of Montreal, Audubon's Birds of America, to the Library of McGill College–

Whereupon it was Resolved—

"That the cordial thanks of the University are due to the following Gentlemen who have enriched its Library by the presentation of Audubon's magnificent work on American Ornithology, and that in testimony of the gratitude of the University the names of the donors be inserted in the work."–

Names of Subscribers

Theodore Hart	$20	D. Davidson	10
L. H. Holton	20	B. Holmes	10
David Torrance & Co.	20	Thos. Rimmer	10
Wm. Edmonstone	20	Thos. Paton	10
Louis Renaud	20	Taylor Bros	10
Jno. Frothingham	20	Geo. Desbarats	10
J. G. Mackenzie	20	Wm. Stephen & Co.	10
Jas. Logan	20	Elliott & Co.	10
John Redpath	20	Jacques Tracey & Co.	10
Ira Gould	20	John Carter	10
Henry J. Shaw	20	Jas B. Greenshields	10
John Ross (Quebec)	10	David E. McLean & Co.	10
Jas. Gordon	10	Miller Thompson & Co.	10
John Lovell	10	Corse & May	10
R. D. Collis	10	H. L. Routh	10
John & Thos. Caverhill	10	Walter Scott	10
John Dougall	10	O. S. Wood	10
James McDougall	10	Wm. Ross (Toronto)	10
Mulholland & Baker	10	Robert Esdaile	10
James Ferrier Jr.	10	John Esdaile	10
James Hutton	10	Robert Simms	10
George H. Frothingham	10	Thos. Wilson	10
Ogilvy & Co.	10	A. Heward	10
J. H. Joseph	10	David Allan Poe	10
Alfred Savage	10	W. P. McLaren	10
Kerry Bros. & Crathern	10	Henry Chapman	10
Simpson J. Mitchell	10	R. Leckie	10
Thos. Ryan	10	J. H. Winn	10
Henry Thomas	10	Hugh Fraser & Co.	10

Names of Subscribers—*Continued*

Andw. Law	10	Smith & Gardyne	10
Alex. Urquhart	10	James Reekie	10
McDougall & Davidson	10	Thos. J. Fennell (Liverpool)	10
Edwin Atwater	10	Thos. Kay	10
Mitchell & Gear	10	Benning & Barsalou	10
Wm. Cunningham	10	Capt. Raynes	10
John M. Young	10	Henry Lyman	10
A. M. Forbes	10	Wm. Murray	10
John Glennon	10	Grant Hall & Co.	10
Z. Benoit	10	James Mitchell	10
Wm. Workman	10	Wm. Lunn	10
Macdougall & Budden	10	C. Dunkin	10
Henderson Holcomb & Co.	10	Jas. Court	10
Thomas Workman	10	Thos. Kershaw	10
Andrew Allan	10	Jesse Joseph	10
Geo. Moffatt, Jr.	10	Andrew Shaw	
E. A. Prentice & Co.	10	Wm Spiers	10

TOTAL $1030[193]

The foregoing appears as an entry on the fly leaf of the folio. It has not been possible to ascertain from what source the folio was obtained.

The Redpath Library at McGill University collection also includes the five volumes of the *Ornithological Biography*. In the first volume is found the following inscription: "To Baron G. Cuvier with the highest respect of the author, 17th May 1831." The University Library purchased the five volumes from the dealer Friedlander on 9 January, 1931, and the canceled stamps in the five volumes indicate these as having come from the "Muséum d'Histoire Naturelle."[194]

PAUL MELLON
Oak Spring, Upperville, Va.

This set of the folio, together with the five volumes of the *Ornithological Biography*, were obtained from a New York dealer in February 1937 at a cost of $11,000. Both folio and *Biography* are uniformly bound in half-dark blue morocco (spine and all sides) with cloth centers, and leather labels in the center of the front covers of the folio volumes.

The first five prints are from the Lizars plates, not retouched by Havell, with 1826 Whatman watermark. Plates 6 and 7 also have the 1826 watermark, while that of plates 8, 9, and 10 is 1827.

The New York dealer referred to above was Thomas Gannon. In March 1969, William McKinley Gannon, who was associated with the firm when the folio was sold to Mr. Mellon, told the author that he believed that the folio came from David Randall, then associated with the firm of Charles Scribner's Sons of New York.

Provenances of Sets in the United States and Canada

MILWAUKEE PUBLIC LIBRARY
Milwaukee, Wis.

This copy of the folio was presented to Yale University by George Bird Grinnell (1849–1938), and is supposed to have had Audubon's autograph on the title page. Yale sold it to R. J. Barry of Stonehill, Inc., which then resold it to the Weyhe Galleries of New York.[195]

George Bird Grinnell, ethnologist and author, graduated from Yale University in 1880 and received a doctorate degree from that school in 1887. As a boy he had lived in Audubon Park, New York City, the original location of Minnie's Land, the Audubon homestead. He had attended a school conducted by the Naturalist's widow who exerted a benign influence on the boy. Later in life he was to found the first Audubon Society.[196]

In 1945 the folio was purchased from the Weyhe Galleries by the Schlitz Brewing Company of Milwaukee and presented to the public schools of that city.[197] The prints have all been framed so that they can be sent to various schools in the city and loaned to other interested groups for special exhibits.

MINNEAPOLIS ATHENAEUM
Minneapolis, Minn.

The *Minneapolis Journal* of 17 April 1909 carried an article referring to the Athenaeum's purchase of the Double Elephant edition of Audubon's *Birds of America*: ". . . Edmund D. Brooks, authorized to get the books, purchased them through his London agent, Charles J. Sawyer Ltd., 23 Oxford Street and sent through in bond to Minneapolis Customs."

The accession records of the institution indicate that the set was received in June 1909. The price, which included the five-volume *Ornithological Biography*, was $2,725.[198]

Inquiry was made of present members of the Sawyer establishment who advised that although Edmund D. Brooks had been a great personal friend of the founder of the firm, Charles James Sawyer, there were no records available covering the transaction.[199]

MITCHELL WOLFSON FOUNDATION, INC.
Audubon House, Key West, Fla.

The folio was purchased by Duncan H. Read of Middleburg, Virginia, at the sale held 28 February–1 March 1935, (item #53) in the auction galleries of the American Art Association, New York. Item 53 in the catalog reads as follows:

> Audubon, J. J. Birds of America. Pigskin tooled, g.t. in mahogany case (fol. volumes uniform in size) measure 37⅝" x 24⅞"; first ten plates in earliest state, eng. by W.H.L., with full inscriptions and with generous margins on all save a few of the largest plates, and the two Turkey plates are the same large size

as the other, plates almost free from the usual spots; two titles and a few plates creased; slight tears on margins on 4 of these extending into the plates, most of them repaired, a few plate numbers trimmed away or just touched, some offsets; holes in six upper margins-

> American Art Association (53)
> Walter Roesler copy, Feb. 28–March 1, 1935.
> Sold for $5,750.00.

For some years the folio was on loan at the headquarters of the National Audubon Society in New York City. In 1960 it was purchased by the Mitchell Wolfson Foundation, of Miami, and presently is among the treasured exhibits at Audubon House in Key West, Florida, which was originally the home of Captain John H. Geiger where the Naturalist was a guest during his visit to Key West in May 1832.

MUSEUM OF FINE ARTS
Boston, Mass.

Among the subscriptions Audubon obtained during his long visit to Boston in 1832–33, where he had arrived in October 1832, was that of William Sturgis,[200] whose name appears as "Sturges" in the final list of subscribers.[201] Upon the Naturalist's arrival in New York he wrote his son Victor in London listing 18 New England subscribers, among them William Sturgis. He was able to deliver a bound copy of the first volume (first 100 plates), one of seven which had been received from England, for which Sturgis paid him $220.[202] Ledger "B" shows that the subscription was completed in July 1838.

Sturgis (1782–1863), in partnership with John Bryant, was engaged in the foreign trade, principally with the West Coast and China. Shortly after 1832, his daughter Anne (1813–1884) married Samuel Hooper (1808–1875), who became a junior partner of Bryant, Sturgis & Company. Hooper was later to join the importing firm of William Appleton & Company, finally forming his own firm, Samuel Hooper & Company. He served in Congress from 1861 until his death in 1875.[203] His son, William Sturgis Hooper (1833–1863), was an aid on the staff of General Banks of the Department of the Gulf and died in the service on 24 September 1863. His other child, Anne Maria, married Thornton Kirkland Lothrop on 30 April 1866.[204] His wife survived him and lived until 1884.

It appears that the Sturgis folio eventually came into the possession of Robert Chamblett Hooper (1805–1869), a cousin of Samuel. Roger F. Hooper, of Manchester, Massachusetts, and his sister Adeline, of Milton, both recall seeing the folio at the home of their grandmother in Boston before her death in 1902.[205] They further believe that upon her death the folio came into possession of her son William (1855–1932), who in turn presented it to the museum in 1921.

The 435 prints were bound in four volumes when received by the museum. That these might be exhibited individually, the museum's conservator of prints and drawings, Francis Dolloff, some years ago removed the 435 plates, one by one, painstakingly cutting them as close to the bindings as possible. The leather covers were then converted into print portfolios by the James MacDonald Company of New York.

It is now possible to display the prints, singly or in groups, matted (in the museum's standard 40″ by 28″ mats) and framed. Since there has been no trimming other than that done originally when the plates were bound, the prints measure about $38\frac{3}{16}$ inches (in height) by $25\frac{3}{8}$ inches. So close to the bindings were they excised that stitch marks and needle holes remain and are visible on the individual prints.[206]

NATIONAL AUDUBON SOCIETY
New York, N.Y.

The folio of the *Birds of America* was presented to the society by George Hewitt Myers of Washington, D.C., in 1957. He had purchased it at the Anderson Galleries on 9 February 1920 for $4500.[207]

Each volume has, in addition to the title page, a presentation page decorated with a wash drawing by Jacob A. Dallas[208] with the inscription: "Presented by the trustees of the Mercantile Mutual Insurance Company to Joseph Walker late president of that Institution as a memento of his official services and an evidence of their high appreciation of his character and example in public and private life. New York 1853."

The subjects of the presentation pages are: Volume 1, "Navigation."; Volume 2, "Commerce"; Volume 3, "Internal Commerce"; and Volume 4, "Indemnity." The plates in all four volumes have been lined. Included among the first ten prints are some with Whatman watermarks dated as late as 1837, which probably indicates that the set had been assembled near the conclusion of the work.

From a granddaughter of Joseph Walker, Miss Katharine DeB. Parsons, the following information about him was obtained: "Joseph Walker, the son of Joseph and Sarah Walker of Leeds, England, was born in 1798 and died 22 March 1866. He became president of the Security Insurance Company, was a Founder Trustee of the United States Trust Co. of New York, as well as a director to the New York Gas Light Co."[209]

The folio remained continuously in the Walker family's possession until sold at the Anderson Galleries in 1920.

THE NATIONAL GALLERY OF ART
Washington, D.C.

In 1946 this unique set of the Audubon folio of the *Birds of America*, unique in that it consists of 435 loose prints which never have been bound, was presented, together with the five volumes of the *Ornithological Biography*, to the National Gallery of Art, by Mrs. Walter Belknap James of New York, in memory of her husband Dr. Walter B. James (1858–1927) and his brother Norman James, of Baltimore. It was further reported at the time "that it was given in 1836, by Audubon to his friend the naturalist, David Eckley, whose marginal notes add interest to the volumes of the Ornithological Biography which accompanied the set of prints."[210] Although the five volumes of the letterpress were undoubtedly presented to Eckley, the belief that the collection of prints was likewise a present from Audubon is unquestionably in error.

The 435 prints and the five volumes of the *Ornithological Biography* were purchased for $3,200 by a member of the James family at the sale of the Robert H. Sayre Library in November 1907.[211] On the occasion of the auction, certain information concerning the history of the folio and the volumes of letterpress which Sayre had purchased shortly before 1900, was published in the press. Some of this had appeared previously in a magazine story, "Early Days in the Lehigh Valley," written by "Bohemian," a pseudonym for C. S. Boutcher. In his article Boutcher had described many details concerning the Sayre collection, including the Audubon folio.[212]

Mr. Sayre had made his purchase shortly before 1900 from the Cleveland firm of Burrows Brothers. This firm had issued a circular in which certain features of the prints and the letterpress were pointed out, and there was included a transcript of Audubon's inscription in the first volume of the *Biography* as follows:

> To
> My Worthy Friend
> Dr. Eckley Esq. of Boston
> This volume is given with he[art]
> felt sincere [———] and Good Wishes
>   JOHN J. AUDUBON

The inscriptions in the second and third volumes were dated 1836. It should also be pointed out that the first volume of the *Biography* had been published in Philadelphia and the second in Boston.

The supposition that "it (the folio) was given in 1836 by Audubon to his friend the naturalist David Eckley of Boston," was based on the inscriptions in the *Biography*, although it was stated in the circular that the prints had been purchased from the English firm of Messrs. Sotheran & Company.[213] It is evident that Burrows Brothers, the Cleveland dealer, had obtained the loose prints and the *Biography* from different sources.

The circular also stated that the only other presentation copy known was in the Manchester (England) library, to which it had been bequeathed by the Earl of Crawford. There is not now, nor has there ever been, an Audubon folio in the Manchester Public Library.[214]

The facts concerning the folio belonging to the Earl of Crawford are as follows.

When the library at Haigh Hall was dispersed, many of the more important books were taken by the earl to Balcarres. These included the Audubon folio which is cataloged in *Bibliotheca Lindesiana*. It should be added that this copy was not a presentation copy but that of an original subscriber, Joseph John Gurney, who had undoubtedly subscribed on behalf of his son John Henry, a keen ornithologist, whose "arms" are to be found in the four bound volumes.[215]

When the first ten prints of the set were examined by this writer, it was found that the Lizars engravings had not been retouched by Havell, the legends were of the earliest state, and the watermarks were for the years 1826–1827, all evidence that the subscriber to the set had been among the very first, which Gurney had been.

Unfortunately, many of the erroneous statements contained in the circular issued by the Cleveland bookdealer were included by Herrick in his biography of the Naturalist.[216] It is of interest to note that the James collection of loose prints now in possession of the National Gallery was used by the Macmillan Company when that firm published the Audubon reproductions in 1937.

THE NEW-YORK HISTORICAL SOCIETY
New York, N.Y.

Audubon's original drawings of the *Birds of America* were purchased from his widow by the New-York Historical Society in 1863 at a cost of $4,000. However, it was not until 1954, nearly 100 years later, that the 435 prints of the Double Elephant folio became part of the society's treasure. They were presented to the society by Mrs. Harvey Breit and Mrs. Gratia R. Laiser in memory of their mother, Gratia Houghton Rinehart.

The set had been in possession of the seventh Duke of Newcastle and was sold at Sotheby's for £2,400 ($12,000) on 21 June 1937, when the Clumber Library was put up for auction.[217] The fourth Duke of Newcastle (1785–1851) appears to have been the one mainly responsible for the formation of the finest part of the Clumber Library.

The four volumes are full bound in russia, with gilt edges and panelled sides enclosing the arms of the Duke. The five volumes of the *Ornithological Biography*, similarly bound, were included in the auction sale and the gift to the New-York Historical Society.

The Duke of Newcastle is not listed among Audubon's subscribers. However, many of the prints in the first volume are signed in pencil with the name "G. Kirkpatrick" and the final subscription list includes the name "Kirk Patrick, London."[218]

Two references to "Kirk Patrick" have been found in Audubon's correspondence. On 15 September 1835, he wrote to his engraver from Edinburgh, "I am glad that you have harpooned that Tough Fish Kirk Patrick at last."[219] Then, on

1 October 1835,[220] in sending Havell some copies of an American review of his work, the Naturalist asked that one be sent to Kirkpatrick. The Duke of Newcastle presumably acquired the copy of the folio originally subscribed for by "Kirk Patrick."

THE NEW YORK PUBLIC LIBRARY
Astor, Lenox, and Tilden Foundations, New York, N.Y.

In 1895 there was effected in the City of New York a consolidation of a number of libraries including the Astor, Lenox Libraries, the Tilden Trust and other smaller libraries, which became the New York Public Library, Astor, Lenox, and Tilden Foundations.[221]

The personal Library of John Lenox (1800–1880) had been incorporated by an act of the New York legislature on 20 January 1870, and a building was erected on Fifth Avenue between 70th to 71st Streets and opened to the public on Monday, 15 January 1877.

The will of John Jacob Astor, who died on 29 March 1848, provided the sum of $400,000 for the establishment of a public library. Such a library was incorporated by the New York State legislature on 18 January 1849, and a building which was built on the property located on Lafayette Place near Broadway and Astor Place was officially opened to the public on 9 January 1854.[222]

In the will of Samuel Jones Tilden (1814–1886), dated 23 April 1884, it was stated, "I request my said executors and Trustees to obtain as speedily as possible from the Legislature an Act of incorporation of an institution to be known as the 'Tilden Trust' with capacity to establish and maintain a free library and reading room in The City of New York etc. etc." The will was contested by the heirs and the clause relative to the Tilden Trust upset.

Fortunately an agreement had been reached by the executors with certain of the heirs to set aside certain securities estimated to be worth $500,000. But it has been estimated that, had the clause been sustained, something in the neighborhood of $6,000,000 would have been reserved for the great public library Tilden had designed to be his monument, in the spirit of devotion to the popular welfare which distinguished him. No separate library was ever established, though various plans were considered by the trustees, until finally the Tilden Trust combined with the other libraries, as has been related above.

Included on the list of "The Elephant folio edition of Audubon's 'Birds of America' to Whom They Have Belonged and Where They Can Be Found," prepared by Anthony Woodward and dated 1901, are the following references to folios in the New York Public Library.[223] These, with the exception of the Astor Library set, are presently in the New York Public Library.

Astor Library, New York City.
  Copy not complete; have seen it.
Mr. Robert L. Stuart, New York City. Fifth Ave.
  This copy is now at the Lenox Library, 1901, a branch of the New York City Public Library. Have seen it, 1884.
Lenox Library, Fifth Ave., New York City.
  Mr. Lenox's copy.
Samuel J. Tilden, New York City. (now dead.)
  This copy is also in the Lenox Library building.

From the foregoing it would appear that there were at that time three copies of the folio in the Lenox Library and an incomplete set in the Astor Library. The presence of three sets in the Lenox Library was noted also by John Burroughs in his book about Audubon.[224]

At the present time there are in the library four complete sets of the folio and a single volume containing 75 prints (all carry the library symbol $+^{QMO}_{+++}+$).

Folio number one is known as the Tilden set. On the back of the title page of Volume 1 is the seal of the Tilden Library with the date 1895. Examination of the prints disclose that many of them have on the back a notation reading "for Nath'l Potter, Esq. M.D."

The subscription of Dr. Nathaniel Potter (1770-1843) probably was obtained by Audubon in March 1830, just before he returned to England after his first trip to America in 1829-30.[225] The watermarks of the first ten prints, some as early as 1828, are evidence of the fact that they were among the first to be sent to America. Strangely, the subscription is not included in the final list of subscribers.[226] However, there is a reference to the subscription in Audubon's journal entry of 21 February 1840, written after the work was completed.[227] When or how Tilden obtained the set is not known.

Folio number two, known as the "Lenox set," is believed to be the one originally purchased by John Lenox. In one of Audubon's journals, under the date of 12 February 1840, there is the following bookkeeping entry:

        46. Bank of America
        38. J.J.A. & Sons—cash this day
            sold to J. Lenox. $1100.00.[228]

The four volumes of the folio are listed in the Lenox Library catalog (Short Title) dated 1881, on page 2.

Folio number three is called the Stuart set. Very little is known of the provenance of this. From the late watermarks of the first ten prints, it would appear that it had been subscribed for or purchased near the conclusion of the engraving of the plates. The folio is mentioned as being among the books in the library of Stuart by James Wynne in his book, *Private Libraries of New York*,[229] which was published in 1860. Robert Leighton Stuart (1806-1882) was a sugar refiner and philanthropist who, with his wife, was a benefactor to many institutions in New York City.

The source of the fourth folio now in the library is unknown. As for the Astor set, on 24 November 1839, Audubon wrote his son in Charleston that "I called Twice on Jacob Astor, and at last sold him the full bound Copy, and also 5 Vol. of Letter press for $1030 payable early in Jan.y."[230]

Kenneth Wiggins Porter in his book, *J. J. Astor, Business Man*, states that the *Birds of America* was the only work personally purchased by Astor for the projected library. Porter states further that when Audubon visited the merchant and requested payment he "was put off with one excuse or another."

> "Ah, M. Audubon," would the owner of millions observe, "you come at a bad time; money is very scarce; I have nothing in the bank; I have invested all my funds." At length, for the sixth time, Audubon called upon Astor for his thousand dollars. As he was ushered into the presence, he found William B. Astor, the son, conversing with his father. No sooner did the rich man see the man of art, than he began, "Ah, M. Audubon so you have come again after your money. Hard times, M. Audubon—money scarce!" But just then catching an inquiring look from his son, he changed his tone: "However, M. Audubon, I suppose we must contrive to let you have some of your money, if possible. William" he added, calling to his son, who had walked into an adjoining parlour, "have we any money at all, in the bank?"—"Yes, father," replied the son, supposing that he was asked an earnest question, pertinent to what they had been talking about when the ornithologist came in, "we have two hundred and twenty thousand dollars in the Bank of New York, seventy thousand in the City Bank, ninety thousand in the Merchants', ninety-eight thousand four hundred in the Mechanics', eighty-three thousand—" "That'll do," exclaimed John Jacob, interrupting him, "it seems that William can give you a check for your money."[231]

On 14 April 1919, there were offered for sale at the Anderson Galleries, New York, duplicates from The New York Public Library. Item 10 of the sale catalog was the following:

> Audubon, (John J.) Birds of America from Original Drawings (429) beautifully colored plates (should be 435) representing the subjects in life size. 4 vols. elephant folio, russia, (covers worn and loose), backs broken (cover of vol. 2 missing, several of the first and last plates of each vol. creased and frayed, 6 plates missing). London: Published by Author, 1827-38. The original Folio edition. Not returnable.

When the Anderson copy of the catalog for this sale was examined, item 10 was marked "OUT," signifying that it had been passed and not sold. The library's copy of the catalog is not priced for this item, another indication that the folio was not disposed of at the time. What has happened to the folio is a mystery.[232]

The description of the folio listed in the Anderson Gallery catalog to be sold on 14 April 1919 mentions, "(covers worn and loose, backs broken. Cover of volume 2 missing, several of the first and last plates of each creased and frayed, 6 plates missing)." In the list of extant folios recorded by Anthony Woodward is noted that the copy at the Astor Library "was not complete." It is believed that the folio withdrawn from the Anderson sale was in all probability the original Astor set of the *Birds of America*.

THE NEW YORK SOCIETY LIBRARY
New York, N.Y.

It appears that occasionally applications were made to the trustees of this venerable institution for full membership certificates in return for other than the stipulated monetary equivalent. As a rule such requests were declined, but in 1850, when Audubon made a proposition "to sell his work on the Birds of America (Octavo edition) for a free share," it was voted to "pay him fifty dollars and give him certificates for two ordinary Rights."[233] Although the historian states it was John J. Audubon who made the proposition, it should be pointed out that at the time the Naturalist was in very poor health. Even before 1850 signs of decrepitude had appeared, so much so that two years previously, in 1848, his friend John Bachman had written from the Audubon home, Minnie's Land, "Alas my poor friend Audubon, the outlines of his countenance and his form are there but his noble mind is all in ruins."[234] Thus it must have been one of the sons from whom the request came. However, since the society did not publish a list of shareholders between 1813 and 1856, this cannot be definitely determined.[235]

Though the New York Society Library had obtained the Octavo edition of the *Birds of America* in this way, it was not until December 1883 that the Double Elephant folio, through the gift of Charles H. Contoit, came into its possession.[236] Also, at the death of Contoit the library was named residuary legatee and in 1903 received $142,585.68 from the estate.

Comment should be made on certain unique features of this set of the folio. It appears to have been assembled from loose prints which had been brought over from England by Havell after completion of the engraving. First of all, the title page of Volume 1 has a Whatman watermark dated 1836. Also, among the first ten plates are some with watermarks as early as 1830 (*see* Pl. 7, Purple Grakle), while Plates 1 and 6 (the Turkey plates) have 1836 watermarks. Even more interesting are the notations written on many prints, for example, the cryptic remark "Boston needs" which is found on the back of many prints (e.g., Pl. 12, 136, 142, and others).

Finally, the folio contains three of the thirteen composite plates which Audubon had instructed his engravers to prepare after the completion of the original work.[237] These consist of (1) plate 110, male and female "Hooded Warbler" combined with plate 9, "Selby's Flycatcher"; (2) plate 23, male and female "Yellow-breasted Warbler or Maryland Yellow-throat" to which has been added the birds on plate

24, "Roscoe's Yellow-throat"; and (3) plate 373, "Evening Grosbeak," to which two birds from plate 424, the female and the young male "Evening Grosbeak," have been added.

In March 1973 the author was advised by letter that this folio had been stolen.

NORTH CAROLINA STATE LIBRARY
Raleigh, N.C.

The following information concerning the provenance of this folio of the *Birds of America* was furnished by Georgia H. Faison, the reference librarian.

"Strong circumstantial evidence indicates that it was obtained for the State Library around 1848 through the assistance of Mr. Joseph G. Cogswell during one of his book-buying trips for John Jacob Astor.

Prior to 1848 Mr. Cogswell had been connected with a boy's school in Raleigh. It seems a valid conclusion, based upon our records, to assume that he had become one of the Library's advisers and that the purchase of books should have been entrusted to him under certain circumstances."[238]

NORTHWESTERN UNIVERSITY
Evanston, Ill.

The Audubon folio of the *Birds of America* was presented to Northwestern University in 1918 by Charles Deering (1852–1927), for whom the main library, the Charles Deering Library, was named. Deering was a member of a prominent Chicago family which had contributed substantially to Northwestern University.[239]

Inside the front cover of each volume is found the bookplate of the Earl of Hardwicke. On the final list of subscribers Audubon gives "#78 Earl Hardwicke, &c.,&c.,&c., Wimpole, Arrington, Cambridge."[240] It was probably the fourth Earl of Hardwicke (1799–1873), who subscribed.

The Earl of Hardwicke's folio, together with the five volumes of the *Ornithological Biography*, was offered for sale at £300 in Bernard Quaritch's Rough List, Number 134, July 1893. The folio was described therein as follows:

> 79. Audubon, (J.J.) Birds of America, genuine Original Edition, 4 vols. Double Elephant folio, 435 superbly Coloured Plates, the Birds full size of life, an early Subscriber's copy in pale russia, gilt back, sides tooled with broad gold borders, joints inside, for the Earl of Hardwicke, a magnificent copy. London 1827–49 [sic]. The binding must have cost about fifty pounds.

The Hardwicke family left Wimpole Hall about 1890.[241]

Provenances of Sets in the United States and Canada

RICHARD W. NORTON ART GALLERY
Shreveport, La.

The five volumes of this folio of Audubon's *Birds of America* were obtained for the gallery in 1939. For many years the volumes were in the library of Queen's College, Oxford, England, and the library stamp of the college is found in them. The binding was done by Clarke.

The folio was bought for Queen's College on 19 September 1843 from Payne & Foss, presumably a London bookseller, for £135. The money came from the £30,000 bequest of Robert Mason, a former member of the college, which was to be spent in three years on books. Between 1841–1843 Queen's College purchased many of the fine books which had come on the market. The Audubon folio was sold by the college in 1939 to help finance the reconstruction of the library to its original appearance.[242]

The first ten prints of this set are on paper with J. Whatman 1827 watermarks, the first five from unretouched Lizars plates, an indication that the original subscription was an early one.

PEABODY INSTITUTE
Eben Dale Sutton Reference Library, Peabody, Mass.

In October of 1866 Mrs. Eben Sutton, with the approval of George Peabody, gave the sum of $20,000 to establish the Eben Dale Sutton Reference Library in honor of her son who had been killed in a tragic accident in 1862. A memorial room which was furnished in solid black walnut with shelves for books extending around three sides, the upper rows reached by a circular staircase was constructed within the walls of the institute library. This was a replica of a room in Oxford, England, and was opened on 7 June 1869.[243] In 1871, 320 volumes (including the Audubon folio), were given to the library.

The binder of the Audubon folio is not known. Each print was backed with linen and a special stand was built for each of the four volumes. In these stands the volumes are stored vertically, but when the stands are opened they are horizontal, as if on a table. The previous history of the folio is not known, but, as Mrs. Sutton had traveled abroad extensively, it may have been purchased in England.

PEABODY MUSEUM
Salem, Mass.

In Audubon's Ledger "B" there is an entry, dated May 1833, listing a payment from "E. L. Pickman, Miss," of £48-10-0, which indicates that the subscription had been obtained in the spring of that year while the Naturalist was visiting Boston.

Elizabeth Leavitt Pickman was born in Salem on 23 April 1815, the daughter of Dudley Leavitt Pickman. On 17 March 1847 she was married to Richard Saltonstall Rogers. Rogers was a member of the Essex Historical Society which was merged with the Essex County Natural History Society in 1848 to found the Essex Institute. Elizabeth Pickman Rogers died in 1853 and in her will her copy of the *Birds of America* was bequeathed to the Essex Institute.

In the annual report of the Essex Institute of 1 May 1916 there is found the following reference to this folio:

> May 27, 1867: "deposited with the trustees of the Peabody Academy of Science upon a permanent deposit and trust, to be kept by them and their successors forever in the East India Marine Hall. . . ."[244]

CLARA S. PECK

New York, N.Y.

This set of the folio was obtained for Miss Peck in 1932 by Frank Walters, a New York rare book dealer. In a letter dated 8 September 1958 he wrote, "Miss Clara Peck's copy—this was listed in a book catalogue (entire back cover) put out by Samuel Rains, a bookseller in New York, about thirty-five years ago, and sold to someone in Chicago. I never knew the name of the buyer as it was sold by him or estate through an agent in 1932, going to Miss Peck. Sam Rains died many years ago."[245] The sale to Miss Peck had been conducted in partnership with a Mr. Macdonald, another New York dealer.

When the folio was examined, it was discovered that eight of the plates were missing and in their place had been substituted drawings by some unknown person. The missing prints were:

Plate		
178	Orange-crowned Warbler
179	Wood Wren
180	Pine Finch
181	Golden Eagle
182	Ground Dove
183	Golden-crested Wren
184	Mangrove Humming Bird
185	Bachman's Warbler

These were subsequently replaced with the original Audubon prints engraved by Havell.

Miss Peck also has in her possession a complete set of the Octavo edition of the *Birds of America*, in parts. The name of Capt. W. S. Williams appears at the top of many of the parts. In addition, there are included in her collection of Auduboniana twenty-one of the original drawings made for the Octavo edition.

Provenances of Sets in the United States and Canada

ALFRED F. PFLAUMER
Haverford, Pa.

It is believed that this folio of Audubon's *Birds of America* and the *Ornithological Biography* were acquired by the artist Carol S. Tyson at some time in the early 1920s.[246] They remained in the Tyson family until the death of his widow, when both the folio and the Biography were sold to a Philadelphia bookdealer and then resold in 1964 to the present owner. It has not been possible to learn anything regarding the history of either the folio or the five volumes of letterpress prior to their ownership by Mr. Tyson.

RAWLSTON D. PHILLIPS, JR.
Baton Rouge, La.

On Sunday, 13 May 1827, while in Manchester, Audubon wrote in his journal, "My time has been so completely occupied during each day procuring subscribers, and all my evenings at the house of one or another of my friends and acquaintances that my hours have been late, and I have bidden thee good night without writing it down. Manchester has most certainly retrieved its character, for I have had eighteen subscribers in *one week*, which is more than anywhere else."[247]

On the original list of subscribers, those from Manchester are grouped together and included among these is "The Rev. Peter Hordern, M.A. for the Cheetham [sic] Library." The same error in the library's name is found in the listing of the subscription (no. 24 on the final list of European subscribers) in the fifth volume of the *Ornithological Biography*, in which the name of the Reverend Hordern is misspelled as well, appearing therein as "Horden."[248] He was Chetham's librarian from 1821 to 1834.

The library's files contain the record of payments made for the numbers of the *Birds of America* beginning in September 1827 and ending in September 1839. It is of particular interest to note that most of these payments were made to T. Sowler, the publisher of a local newspaper and a bookseller, who had been appointed by Audubon as his agent in Manchester. There is also in the possession of the library a copy of Audubon's prospectus, probably printed in March 1827, after the first five numbers (pl. 1–25) had been engraved.[249]

On 6 January 1972, as this work was being prepared for publication, word came to the author from Miss Hilda Lofthouse, the librarian, that the Board of Governors of Chetham's Library had decided to sell its set of the folio, to raise needed funds. The set, together with the five volumes of the *Ornithological Biography*, was sold on 26 June 1972 by Sotheby's of London to an American bookdealer, J. N. Bartfield, and his associates for £62,000 ($151,280). In July 1973 the folio was sold by one of the associates, Taylor Clark, Baton Rouge, La., to Rawlston D. Phillips, Jr., also of Baton Rouge.

PHILLIPS ACADEMY
Oliver Wendell Holmes Library, Andover, Mass.

This set of the folio was presented to the Oliver Wendell Holmes Library by Thomas Cochran (1871-1936), a trustee of Phillips Academy, in 1929. It had been purchased for him from the Rosenbach Galleries of New York by his friend Thomas S. Gates (1873-1948) for $7,850.[250] It has not been possible to determine where Rosenbach had obtained the folio.

THE PIERPONT MORGAN LIBRARY
New York, N.Y.

Mr. Henry S. Morgan bought the sets of Audubon's *Birds of America* and the *Quadrupeds* which he gave to the library, in December 1928, from Charles E. Lauriat Company, Boston.[251]

These appear as Item 97, page 36, in a catalog, "Choice Books from the Stock of the Lauriat Co., of Boston (ca. 1928?)."

No additional information has been found as to the early provenance of the folio.

PRINCETON UNIVERSITY
Princeton, N.J.

On 15 April 1833 Audubon, writing from New York to his son in London, advised him that he had received the subscription of "Genl Stephen VanRenseller [sic] . . . Albany State of New York."[252] No further details regarding the subscription are given in the letter. However, in Audubon's Ledger "B," an entry indicates that the Naturalist had been paid in cash, £49-10-0, for the first volume in April 1833, when the subscription had been received. On the original subscription list the name is recorded as "Stephen Van Rensselaer by Ch[?]."

Stephen Van Rensselaer was born 1 November 1764. His father's death in 1769 left the five-year-old child heir to a vast landed estate in Rensselaer and Albany counties. His grandfather, Philip Livingston, took charge of young Van Rensselaer's education which was begun at Albany and, after numerous changes due to the disturbances and dislocations of wartime, was completed at Harvard, from which he was graduated in 1782.[253] It is also believed that Van Rensselaer spent some time at Princeton (College of New Jersey).[254] He died in 1839.

The folio was presented to Princeton University in 1929 by Alexander Rensselaer who had graduated from Princeton in 1871. In writing to James Thayer Gerould, Librarian of the university, he stated, "This set of Audubon's Birds of America belonged to my grandfather, General Stephen Van Rensselaer of Albany, and I got them from his son Eugene, fifteen years ago, so they have been in the family ever since my grandfather subscribed for them."[255]

Provenances of Sets in the United States and Canada

THE PROVIDENCE ATHENAEUM
Providence, R.I.

The Providence Athenaeum was incorporated in June of 1831.[256] At a meeting of the Board of Trustees held on 9 January 1832, the matter of subscribing to Audubon's *Birds of America* was brought up for consideration. While the Board approved of the idea it was felt that subscription was not practical unless the cost could be defrayed without drawing upon the funds of the Institution.[257]

To this end the secretary, Dr. Thomas H. Webb, and a member of the committee for selecting books, obtained the support of twelve subscribers and prepared the following report:

> It is deemed highly desirable by the Board of Trustees, that the Providence Athenaeum should be possessed of Audubon's great work on Ornithology, as being admirably calculated for giving a character to, and establishing permanently the reputation of the institution. This is now in course of publication in London, it is to be completed in eighty livraisons or numbers of five Plates each, making in all, four hundred Plates, comprising about two thousand figures accompanied by three volumes of letter press descriptions. The Plates are to be of double elephant folio size (being four feet long and between three and four feet wide) five numbers, at least, to be issued annually. There will have been completed up to June 1832 about one hundred and fifty Plates. The whole is to be executed in the most costly style, every bird represented of the full size, and most exquisitely coloured from Nature. Not only are the general outlines to be accurately delineated, by exact measurements taken of every part, even to the feathers. The habits and peculiarities of each species are also to be illustrated in the most striking manner, either by representation of the fish, insect or reptile on which it feeds, on the tree or plant in which it builds, or a representation presented of the natural scenery of the place that it inhabits. It is unquestionably the most magnificent thing of the kind ever attempted and is pronounced by the best judges of our own Country and in Europe, to stand unrivalled. The manuscript drawings were laid before the French Institute and Baron Cuvier, the Chairman of the Committee appointed to examine, and report upon their merits, declared the work the proudest monument of which science can boast. The numbers already finished, and received by the Boston Athenaeum fully answer the most sanguine anticipations that had been cherished respecting it.
>
> Though American in its origin and its objects, it has received but trifling encouragement in this country and were it not for the timely and munificent aid derived from foreign sources, this grand undertaking, like many that have been heretofore projected among us would have come to naught, and the author's years of exertions, of bodily fatigue, and mental anxiety would have profited him nothing; his youth of labour would have been followed by an age of toil.
>
> Being desirous of patronizing so noble a design, and assisting at the same time in building up an institution that bids fair to prove highly beneficial to the community in which we reside, we the subscribers agree to advance the sum affixed to our respective names, in order to defray the expense attendant on the

purchase of the Plates that will have been issued by the time our order reaches London, and do further agree to transfer, all our right, title and interest in and to said Plates, to the Athenaeum immediately upon their arrival, provided the sum by us expended, with interest thereon from the time of being advanced, are refunded, or to present the same to the Institution, provided the receipts obtained by an exhibition of them (after the manner of a gallery of Painting) should be sufficient to cover our expenses, or if not, provided said Institution shall pay us the difference between the receipts and expenditures, with interest and agree also, in either of the above cases to subscribe for all the subsequent numbers of the work.

(Signed) John Mackie	Twenty-five dollars
Thomas Burgess	" " "
R. W. Greene	" " "
J. Kingsbury	" " "
William T. Grinnell	" " "
Thomas C. Hoppin	" " "
Stephen Tripp	" " "
Samuel Shove	" " "
Amasa Manton	" " "
William Butler	" " "
Robt. Rhodes	" " "
J. R. Bartlett	" " ".258

Much of the description of the plates of the *Birds of America* included in the foregoing is found in Audubon's prospectus for the *Birds of America*. No copy of the prospectus has been found among the Audubon papers in the Athenaeum. It could also have been extracted from one of the reviews which had appeared in the Boston papers after the receipt of the plates at the Boston Athenaeum in the latter half of 1831 and where they had evidently been seen by one of the Providence Athenaeum proprietors.

A further reference to the subscription is found in the minutes of the Board of Trustees of the meeting held on 26 November 1832, as follows:

At the monthly meeting in January (1832) the secretary submitted for consideration the expediency of purchasing Audubon's splendid work on Ornithology provided the sum requisite for procuring the portion which shall have been published previous to June 1832 could be raised without drawing upon the funds of the Institution. The proprietors having received the approbation of the board of the library committee drew up a subscription paper upon the following terms: The work was to have been received previous to the last anniversary of our Independence; in which case it was supposed that the avails of the public exhibition would defray the expense of purchase. It was not received till sometime in the month of September and in consequence of this as of other causes the avails of the exhibition after defraying the incidental expenses are only about $75.00. Nor can we be surprised at the receipt of so small a sum when it was said that out of 74 proprietors of the Athenaeum only about 10 or 12 besides the proprietors of the Plates have taken tickets for the exhibition. Under the circumstances, as the funds of the Institute will not justify, in the opinion of the board, the transference of the plates to the Athenaeum by paying the balance to the proprietors, the subject must be at present deferred."[259]

The subscription for the *Birds of America* had been sent by Dr. Webb to the Boston firm of Marsh Capen & Lyon, who in turn sent it to their New York agent, William Johnson. The latter wished to send the first volume of 100 plates bound but the Athenaeum desired loose prints which could be exhibited. Correspondence in the files of the Athenaeum indicates that this may have been the reason for the delay. The first mention of the subscription is found in a letter written by the Naturalist from New York on 1 April 1833, where it is included in a list of New England subscribers.[260]

Among the papers in the archives of the Athenaeum relating to the Audubon subscription is a document headed, "We the subscribers agree to present to the Providence Athenaeum all our right, title and interest in and to the Plates of Audubon's Ornithology provided that all of the subscribers for said Plates will consent to do the same." This has been signed by eight of the proprietors.[261]

There is a second document in which it is stated that the subscribers agree to present the plates in exchange for shares of the institution. This is signed by nearly all of the subscribers.[262]

It appears likely that this latter procedure was finally adopted for the transfer of the plates to the Athenaeum, since at the annual meeting held on 24 November 1834, the following resolution was adopted: "On motion of Thomas Doyle the Board of Trustees was authorized to receive from the Proprietors, the numbers of Audubon's Birds of America, and pay for the same by 'issuing' certificates of stock in the institution."[263]

Another exhibition of the plates was held by the Athenaeum in the Arcade. On 7 March 1835, the committee appointed to superintend the exhibition of the *Birds of America* reported "a balance from the exhibition of $72.04."[264] At the same time additional numbers were being received. On 4 April 1835, "The Library Committee made a report of the reception of 4 numbers of Audubon's The Birds of America and the treasurer was authorized to pay the bill amounting to $40.00."[265]

In August 1837, after the Athenaeum and the Providence Library had been united, more plates arrived, Numbers 67–71, Plates 331–55, and were recorded in the minutes.

Final references to the Athenaeum subscription is found in one of Audubon's journals. When visiting Providence in 1840 after the completion of the engraving he wrote on Monday, 10 August, "Visited Athenaeum and laid my Claim," and on the 12th he added, "The *Athenaeum* won't pay without an a/c being presented and says that 10 plates are missing in the lot? Nous Verrons!"[266]

The loose plates were bound in four volumes in 1847 by a New York binder at a cost of $60. In 1929 each plate was backed with linen and all were rebound in eight parts.

THE PUBLIC LIBRARY OF CINCINNATI AND HAMILTON COUNTY
Cincinnati, Ohio

On 28 March 1834, Audubon wrote his friend Edward Harris from Baltimore, "I have had a new subscriber in Doc. Edmondson, Jr."[267] He also advised his son Victor regarding the subscription on 6 April 1837, adding that he had received $220 for a bound copy of the first 100 prints.[268]

Dr. Thomas Edmondson (1808–1856) of Baltimore was a man of wealth, having inherited from his father and a childless uncle a considerable fortune. He patronized American painters and indulged his interest in the arts and sciences.[269]

As to his acquisition of the *Birds of America*, it appears that Audubon had learned from his friend J. J. Ducatell of Charleston that Edmondson was interested in subscribing to the work. On 25 October the Naturalist wrote Edmondson a long letter from Charleston, giving him the details as to publication and cost. At that time the first volume of 100 prints was completed and the second volume of an additional 100 prints was expected to be ready by the following August or September. Audubon estimated that completing the work of 400 plates (or possibly more) would probably take another eight years.[270]

After the death of Edmondson his library was sold on 17, 18 and 19 March 1870 at the auction rooms of Gibson & Co., in Baltimore, Md. The four volumes of the *Birds of America*, together with the Synopsis and the five volumes of the *Ornithological Biography*, fetched $750.[271] It is believed that after Edmondson's death and until the auction sale the volumes were kept at the Maryland Historical Society.

The next reference to the Edmondson folio is found in the minutes of the meeting of the Board of Managers of the Public Library of Cincinnati and Hamilton County, held on 24 October 1870, when "Mr. Francis Perry made a motion which was carried unanimously, to the Board of Managers of the Library, that the library purchase from Mr. Joseph Longworth of this city a bound copy of Audubon's *Birds of America* for the sum of $1,000, the books' first selling price."[272] The bookplate of Thomas Edmondson is to be found in each volume.

"How Joseph Longworth, whose claim to fame, is that he is the son of Nicholas Longworth, the millionaire and the father of Nicholas Longworth, the speaker of the House of Representatives, obtained a copy of the *Birds of America* we do not know."[273] It should be noted that only seven months had elapsed between the sale of the folio in Baltimore until its purchase by the library.

JOSEPH VERNER REED
Greenwich, Conn.

This set of the folio was purchased in England in 1948.[274] All four volumes have the bookplate of the Yorkshire Philosophical Society, with accession number

3591 and class symbol "Mi." The latter appears on the top of the spine of each volume.

It has been possible to determine the date when the Naturalist obtained the subscription of the society. He had arrived in York on Sunday, 22 April 1827.[275] Finding it difficult to obtain subscriptions, he wrote in his journal, "It will be strange if York gives me no subscribers, when I had eight at Newcastle."[276] However, in the entry for the 27th he noted, "A long walk early, and then many visitors, Mr. Vernon (president of the Philosophical Society of York) among them who subscribed for my work."[277] Before leaving Leeds on the following day, Audubon had obtained five more subscribers.[278]

The 1826 and 1827 watermarks of the first ten prints is corroborative evidence that this subscription was among the earliest received by Audubon.

There are also in the possession of Mr. Reed the original subscription lists for both the Double Elephant folio of the *Birds of America* and for the Octavo edition. These he obtained from a great-grandson of the Naturalist.

ST. LOUIS MERCANTILE LIBRARY ASSOCIATION
St. Louis, Mo.

In the year 1858 there was purchased by the St. Louis Mercantile Library Association from descendants of Audubon a set of the *Birds of America* for $800.[279] This purchase was recorded in the minutes of the library as follows: "Among the purchases will be found 'Audubon's Birds of America' Elephantine edition, ... This copy is one which comes with a weight of interest which is probably attached to no copy of his great work. It was a copy preserved by him for presentation to a very dear relative and delivered to her volume by volume as issued. Each number contains on the title page an autographic note expressive not only of the Author's affectionate regard for this relative but of the feelings of pride which inspired him to continue it to its completion. The last one is represented to have been peculiarly interesting as exhibiting his gratitude that he had been permitted to complete the work to which he had devoted a life time. Unfortunately for us, the family to whose ancestor it was presented and from whom it was obtained by the library, from a feeling which it is impossible to explain, expunged from the work all those sacred sentiments except the mere signatures of Audubons that still remain and will serve to retain the interest which all must feel in this copy of the work."[280]

Although, as it is stated in the minutes, the inscriptions on the four title pages were for the most part expunged, it is possible to decipher that for Volume 2, which reads as follows:

Now my dear sister Eliza Berthoud I have another pleasure afforded me by presenting to you the second volume of my Birds of America. May it prove acceptable to yourself and your b———.

Your Friend and Brother
JOHN J. AUDUBON

Nicholas Augustus Berthoud married Eliza Bakewell, the sister of Lucy, Audubon's wife, in 1816. As a member of the firm of Forstall Brothers and Berthoud he had acted as Audubon's New York agent during the engraving of the *Birds of America*. It is believed that the Berthouds moved to St. Louis in 1843[281] where Eliza Berthoud died in 1853 (September).[282]

SMITHSONIAN INSTITUTION
Washington, D.C.
on loan from the National Academy of Sciences

The four volumes of the *Birds of America*, with one volume of the Mammals, were sent to the Smithsonian "on loan" by the National Academy in 1946, as "The Council feels that this disposition will insure proper care of the volumes and at the same time make them more available for scholars than they are at present."[283] Given by Dr. John C. Merriam, the volumes had been in his personal library. Dr. Merriam, who had been elected to the academy in 1918 and had served it in numerous capacities, was president of the Carnegie Institute of Washington at the time of the gift. The academy actually received the volumes 25 November 1936.[284]

The late watermarks of certain of the first ten prints (1838) indicate that the set was one which was subscribed for or purchased near the completion of the engraving of the plates.

H. J. LUTCHER STARK FOUNDATION
Orange, Tex.

In 1861 John Woodhouse Audubon, the Naturalist's younger son, undertook the sale of part of the family library. In this connection he sent a letter to John Taylor Johnston (1820–1893), one of the founders and first president of the Metropolitan Museum of Art. In the letter written to Johnston, J. W. Audubon wrote in part, "it is only, the effects of our distracted country that compel me to part with what I do so much value."[285]

Further information as to why the Audubon family disposed of their set of the *Birds of America* is known from a letter written by Maria R. Audubon on 12 March 1896 to J. Herbert Johnston, the son of John Taylor Johnston. Maria was the daughter of Victor Audubon. She wrote,

It is a sad story. . . . In the beginning of 1860 my uncle John, and my mother who took my father's place in the matter, owing to his illness, began a new republication of the "small work," i.e., *The Quadrupeds of North America*, and the 2nd edition of the Birds. A large number of subscribers had been secured; Roe Lockwood & Son were printing and publishing at an immense profit for themselves; when the gun that was fired at Ft. Sumter put a fatal end to their enterprise. Nearly all of the subscribers were at the South. *Fifteen hundred* repudiated their debts, and of course my uncle and mother were ruined as Roe Lockwood had to be paid, though there were not enough subscribers who met their obligations to cover the expense of the bindings. Nearly all our real estate went then, for the price of land then was almost nothing, and in the wreck of so much actual want, for the demands of his two families (for my father had died during the years of preparation) stared him in the face. It was then that your dear, good and noble father bought these books.[286]

John Woodhouse Audubon had written Johnston on 5 November 1861. On 7 December 1861 there were sold to Johnston the following volumes from the Naturalist's personal library:

Complete set of the *Birds of America*	$ 600
Quadrupeds of North America	200
Gould's *Birds of Europe*	
Gould's *Himalayan Mts.*	
Gould's *Monograph of Toucans*	400
	$1,000[sic][287]

John Taylor Johnston, who had been trained for the bar, turned instead to railroading. As the head of the Central Railroad of New Jersey, he had accumulated a large fortune and his private collection of paintings was probably the best in America during the 1870s. Although financial reverses caused him to sell most of the collection in 1876, he remained head of the Metropolitan Museum of Art until 1889.[288]

The Audubon folio remained in the possession of the Johnston family for many years until it was inherited by William W. Appleton, a great-grandson of John Taylor Johnston. Since Appleton had no particular interest in ornithology, he sold the folio to a New York bookdealer in 1939.[289] Soon the folio was again sold, this time to a Philadelphian who, in 1954, sold it to H. J. Lutcher Stark of Orange, Texas.[290]

The 435 prints with an additional 13 have been bound in five volumes and have been arranged systematically (instead of numerically) according to Audubon's *Synopsis of the Birds of North America*.[291] Thus the first print in Volume 1 is not the Turkey but the California Turkey-vulture, plate number 426.

On 28 August 1838, Victor Audubon wrote to Havell, the engraver, "that his father wished him to print those plates which have old or young birds to add on them or females."[292] To comply with this request, the engraver created thirteen composite plates, of which six sets were made. The Stark folio contains one of these sets.[293] The only other folio which has been located wherein these thirteen extra prints are to be found is in the Field Museum of Natural History in Chicago. Other sets of the folio with a lesser number of composite plates are at the Legislative Library, Ottawa, Canada, and the New York Society Library.

When the Stark copy of the folio was examined, it was found that the plates were numbered according to the order in which they were bound. The thirteen composite plates, having been scattered through the four volumes, are identified by numbers signifying their placement in those volumes. Following are listed the composite plates found in the Stark set, together with the birds figured on those plates:

Volume 1

- 43.
  - 9 Selby's Flycatcher, Muscicapa Selbii
  - 110 Hooded Warbler, Sylvia Mitrata
    1. Male 2. Female
- 56.
  - 30 Vigors Vireo, Vireo Vigorsii
    [Male]
  - 140 Pine Creeping Warbler, Sylvia Pinus, Lath.
    1. Male 2. Female
- 65.
  - 135 Blackburnian Warbler, Sylvia Blackburnia
    Male
  - 399 Blackburnian Warbler, Sylvia Blackburnae
    3. Female (Of five birds figured on this plate, only this one used on composite)
- 79.
  - 23 Maryland Yellow Throat, Sylvia Trichas
    1. Male 2. Female
  - 24 Roscoe's Yellow Throat, Sylvia Rosco

Volume 2

- 133.
  - 398 Lazuli Finch, Fringilla Amoena
    1. Male Spring Plumage
    Clay Coloured Finch, Emberiza Pallida, Swain.
    2. Male
    Oregon Snow Finch, Fringilla Oregona, Towns.
    3. Male 4. Female
  - 424 Lazuli Finch
    (Of six birds figured on this plate, only this one used on composite)
- 165.
  - 373 Evening Grosebeak, Fringilla Vespertina, Cooper
    1. Old Male
    Spotted Grosebeak, Fringilla Maculuta
    2,3. Males 4. Female
  - 424 Evening Grosebeak, Fringilla Vespertina, Coop.
    5. Female 6. Young Male (Of the six birds on this plate, only these two used on composite)

Provenances of Sets in the United States and Canada

168. 354 Louisiana Tanager, Tanagra Ludoviciana, Wils.
    1. and 2. Males Spring Plumage
  Scarlet Tanager, Tanagra Rubra, Linn.
    3. Old Male, Spring Plumage 4. Old Female, Spring Plumage
  400 Louisiana Tanager, Tanagra Ludoviciana
    3. Female (Of three birds on this plate, only this one used on composite)

172. 388 Nuttall's Starling, Icterus Tricolor, Aud.
    1. Adult Male
  Yellow-headed Troopial, Icterus Xanthocephalus, Bonap.
    2. Adult Male 3. Adult Female 4. Head of Young Male
  Bullock's Oriole, Icterus Bullocki
    5. Adult Male
  433 Bullock's Oriole, Icterus Bullocki, Swain.
    1. Young Male 2. Old Female (Of seven birds on this plate only these two used on composite)

176. 12 Baltimore Oriole, Icterus Baltimore
    1. and 2. Males 3. Female (all three on composite)
  433 Baltimore Oriole, Icterus Baltimore, Bonap.
    3. Old Female (Of seven birds on this plate, only this one used on composite)

Volume 3

193. 369 Mountain Mocking Bird, Orpheus Montanus, Towns.
    1. Male
  Varied Thrush, Turdus Narvius, Gmel.
    2. Male 3. Female (All three on composite)
  433 Varied Thrush, Turdus Noevius, Lath.
    6. Female (Of seven birds on this plate, only this one on composite)

215. 107 Canada Jay, Corvus Canadensis, Linn.
    1. Male 2. Female
  419 Canada Jay, Corvus Canadensis, Linn.
    3. Young Male (Of three birds on this plate, only this one used on composite)

Volume 4

287. 209 Wilson's Plover, Charadrius Wilsonius
    1. Male 2. Female
  284. [Wilson's Plover] Charadrius Wilsonius (Of three birds on this plate, only this one used on composite)

306. 230 Ruddy Plover, Tringa Arenaria
    1. Male 2. Female (Both birds on composite)
  285 [Ruddy Plover,] Tringa Arenaria
    2. Male Spring Plumage (Of two birds on this plate, only this one used on composite).

All were printed on Whatman paper with an 1838 watermark.

THE STATE LIBRARY
Annapolis, Md.

Audubon obtained the subscription of the State Library, Annapolis, Maryland, in 1833 during the month of April. Negotiations for the subscription had been inaugurated by John B. Morris of Baltimore, Audubon's friend and agent. On 17 April Audubon acknowledged the receipt of a letter from Morris advising him that the State of Maryland had subscribed. In addition, in a letter dated 20 April 1833, the librarian of the library, David Ridgely, wrote Audubon, who at the time was in New York making preparations for his trip to Labrador, "I now request that my name be entered in my official Capacity as a Subscriber in behalf of Md. to that work—a work which I think will meet with the patronage of all our State governments—none of whose public libraries should be without a copy—also that of other public libraries and Institutions friendly to native glories—and the encouragement of the Arts and Sciences." Ridgely further advised the Naturalist that he or his agent Nicholas Berthoud in New York could draw on him (Ridgely) for the amount of the subscription. He also noted that it was John B. Morris of Baltimore who had been so kind as to institute the "inquiry as to the most direct mode of entering my subscription."[294]

When Audubon learned of this subscription he advised Morris to notify Ridgely that, as soon as copies of the first volume of 100 prints bound had arrived in New York, one would be sent to him. Ledger "B" indicates that this was done but that the remaining prints were sent loose. At some later time the title page to Volume 1 was cut from the binding and pasted on cloth. The volumes were rebound in the 1920s and the plates have been somewhat rearranged in the process.

There is in the possession of the library considerable correspondence between Audubon and the librarian, David Ridgely, mostly concerning the subscription to the *Birds of America* but, in addition, it is known from a letter dated 4 July 1837 that most of the American edition of the second volume of the library's *Ornithological Biography*, published in Boston by Brown Hilliard & Co. in 1834, was nearly all destroyed by fire.[295]

There is also a letter dated 9 September 1835 from John B. Morris, Audubon's agent in Baltimore, in which he advised Librarian Ridgely of the destruction of his home by a mob and the plundering of its contents. Destroyed was a box containing sets of a few numbers for six subscribers to Audubon's work, one set of which had been destined for the State of Maryland. Some years later Audubon was reimbursed by the State of Maryland for the loss of these prints.

Strangely enough, although considerable correspondence between Ridgely and the Naturalist had been exchanged, there is no record of their ever having met; if they did it was after the completion of the *Birds of America*, for on 29 June 1837 Audubon wrote Ridgely, "One would think, that some unfriendly spirit had ordered me to pass & repass through Maryland, purposely to tempt me with an augmenting desire to form your personal acquaintance or without affecting my purpose and Wishes." Again, on 4 July 1837, he wrote, "Hope to see you in less than two years."[296]

SYRACUSE UNIVERSITY
Syracuse, N.Y.

In a report of 9 June 1897, made by the University Librarian to Chancellor Day, it is stated:

> The most important gift during the past year is the Hon. Jas. J. Belden's gift of that magnificent work, Audubon's Birds of America with elegant case for housing it, the whole valued at $2120.

The donor, James J. Belden (1825–1904), had been a trustee of the university since its founding in 1870. No additional information concerning the earlier history of the folio has been found.

However, the following reference to an Audubon folio appeared in the *University Herald* of 2 April 1877 (whole no. 54, 5, no. 8):

> The last meeting of the Esthetic Society, composed mostly of the students of the College of Fine Arts of the University, was held last evening at the residence of Hon. N. F. Graves.... After the literary exercises the ... members then returned to the library and devoted an hour to the examination of the large number of works of art and curiosities which Mayor Graves collected in his late trip around the world. The illustrations of Art in India were found to be especially interesting, as also were the magnificent illustrations in Audubon's Birds of America....

The "Hon. N. F. Graves" was Nathan Fitch Graves (1813–1896) who, although educated for the law, became instead a financier and banker in Syracuse. His term as mayor of the city was 1874–1876. Could there be a connection between this folio and the one presently at the university? In "A Brief Record of the Elephant Folio Edition of Audubon's 'Birds of America,' to Whom They Have Belonged and Where They May Be Found," prepared in the latter part of the nineteenth century by Anthony Woodward, the first librarian of the American Museum of Natural History, is listed the name of James Graves of Syracuse.

THE TORONTO PUBLIC LIBRARY
Toronto, Ont., Canada

Information concerning the provenance of this set of the folio was obtained from James L. Baillie of the Royal Ontario Museum, Department of Zoology. It appears that while looking through the Museum's copy of Audubon's *Ornithological Biography*, originally the property of J. H. Fleming, one-time president of the

American Ornithologists Union, he had found, tacked in the front of Volume 1, a note in Mr. Fleming's handwriting which read as follows:

> This copy I bought from the Public Library, Toronto through Dr. James Bain (the librarian at the time) and it is the one formerly at Moss Park, Toronto (the home of the Hon. G. W. Allan before his death). I bought the contents of the natural history museum formed by the late Hon. G. W. Allan of Moss Park from his executors in April 1903 and about the same time the elephant folio copy of Audubon's Birds of America, together with his copy of the "Ornithological Biography" were bought by the Public Library, and as the library already had a copy of the Biography Dr. Bain sold me the Moss Park copy for $25. The library paid $1900 for the "Birds of America." Audubon is said to have, himself, brought the books to Toronto and stayed at Moss Park with the Hon. William Allan (1770–1853).[297]

The purchase by the library was later confirmed by a member of the staff of the library who wrote, "In November of 1902 the executors of the late Hon. George W. Allan made an offer to sell to this library four folio and five octavo volumes of Audubon's *Birds*—the rare first edition. This offer was accepted. We have found records of amounts paid for the books to the estate of G. W. Allan over a five year period, altogether in the neighborhood of $2,000."[298]

No record has been found of any dealings or correspondence between Audubon and William Allan. It is of interest to note that the watermarks of the first ten prints are of a late date, several being J. Whatman 1837 or J. Whatman 1838. It is therefore possible that this folio was one of those bound and brought over to America after the completion of the engraving.

TRINITY COLLEGE
Hartford, Conn.

In the *Hartford Courant* of 11 July 1900 there appeared the following news item: "Dr. Gurdon W. Russell [1815–1909] of this city yesterday gave to the Library of Trinity College the most valuable single work ever received by it in the course of its history." The item also mentioned that Dr. Russell was the oldest graduate of the college.

With the presentation Dr. Russell had sent a letter to the president of the college, the Reverend G. Williamson Smith, D.D., in which he stated:

> I beg to present to Trinity College a copy of the magnificent folio edition of the Birds of America by John J. Audubon, in four volumes, together with the text, Ornithological Biography, in five volumes.
> This copy belonged originally to Havell the engraver of the plates who sold it to Francis & Co. of New York, from whom I purchased it. It is believed to be in perfect condition.

Provenances of Sets in the United States and Canada

The Trinity College set of the folio, every plate of which is said to have been selected by Havell himself, the engraver had brought with him to America. It is undoubtedly one of the finest in existence and passed from the Havell family's possession into the hands of C. S. Francis and Company, 544 Broadway, New York, the publishers and booksellers who in 1856 had charge of the sale of all of Audubon's works. The folio eventually was purchased by Dr. Gurdon W. Russell of Hartford, Conn., benefactor of the Trinity College library. In May 1909, through the bequest of Dr. Russell, the library also received 275 volumes which, with few exceptions, dealt with British and North American flora and ornithology.

An early reference to the purchase of this folio by Dr. Russell is found in the 15 December 1882 issue of the *Ornithologist and Oologist* in which it is stated, "The Doctor (G. W. Russell, 490 Main Street, Hartford, Connecticut) also owns the Robert Havell copy of Audubon's Birds, Double Elephant Folio. The copy cost $1150 and the table and roller drawers in which to keep it $100 new. Some years ago we furnished to the Doctor a letter from Robert Havell to one of Audubon's sons stating that every plate was carefully selected as he was colouring the work, making it one of the best, if not the best, copy known."[299] The present whereabouts of Havell's letter is not known. The four volumes of the folio are in excellent condition and the coloring of the plates is superb, making this example of the Audubon work probably the finest extant.

UNION COLLEGE
Schaffer Library, Schenectady, N.Y.

In a letter to his family from Schenectady, N.Y., Audubon wrote that he had reached "this pretty village" the previous Sunday night (14 July 1844). At the time, the Naturalist was soliciting subscriptions for both the Octavo edition of the *Birds of America* and the *Quadrupeds*. His first call after arrival was on Dr. Eliphalet Nott (1773–1866), President of Union College, who subscribed for one copy of the *Quadrupeds*. The following day Dr. Nott called on Audubon, who was at the home of Professor Jackson, and "talked about the Large Work, and finally told me that he would purchase it, provided I would agree to wait for one half the price of it for 6 months; to which I agreed. He will therefore pay 500$ down on delivery, as well as for a sett of the Quadrupeds and in six months more will pay 500$."[300]

On 13 August the Naturalist returned to Schenectady to find that the folio had not been delivered to the college, but had remained in the office of the express company where it had lain for upwards of two weeks. He ordered it sent at once to the college. On the following morning he called on Doctor Nott and found "his Lady and his son looking over one of the volumes, with all of which they are perfectly delighted." In addition, the president told him "that he would go to the

Bank, and see if he can, in the absence of the treasurer from the College give me 500$ this afternoon before I leave for Troy, and I think he will."[301]

There is evidence that Doctor Nott was able to make the necessary arrangement, for a transcript of the records of the treasurer of the college shows that an additional $250 was paid to Audubon on 18 January 1845, and the final payment of $250 was made on 8 January 1846.[302]

During the night of 13–14 June 1971, the first volume of the Double Elephant folio of Audubon's *Birds of America* was stolen from the Schaffer Library at Union College. The thief smashed a rear window of the library's main reading room, after which he broke open a glass display case to get at the volume. The other three volumes of the set, stored elsewhere, were not touched.[303]

Fortunately, the 100 plates contained in the first volume were recovered with the aid of John H. Jenkins, a dealer in rare books of Austin, Texas, and have been returned to the Schaffer Library at Union College, Schenectady, N.Y.[304]

UNIVERSITY OF ILLINOIS
Urbana, Ill.

The acquisition of the Audubon folio by the University of Illinois is recorded in the *Illinois Alumni News* of July 1949 as follows:

> The Illini Achievement Fund, one of the major projects of the U. of I. Foundation, has made possible the purchase for the University of four huge volumes of Audubon's "The Birds of America."
>
> The purchase of the volumes is a dramatic story in itself. The books were owned by Brooks School, North Andover, Mass., which felt that they would be more generally viewed in a large university. Several universities sought the collection and the U. of I., through the prompt action of Director Downs of the Library, Dean Rexford Newcomb, and W. H. Butterfield, executive director of the Achievement Fund, acquired the works for $10,500.
>
> Several days later an offer of double that amount was made for the books. In 1942 a similar set brought $15,600.
>
> Each of the four books is 38 by 26 inches and all are in perfect condition. Birds of all sizes, from the turkeys down, are shown life size in the books. The 435 full-page pictures are hand colored.
>
> Publication was in London between 1827 and 1838. The U. of I. set was in the possession of the family of the original purchaser, Frank Arnold of New Concord, R. I. (? p.2 ?) for more than 100 years. During most of that time the books were kept sealed in a safe.

Unfortunately the above account does not check with the facts, especially in reference to the provenance.

The folio was given to the Brooks School at North Andover, Mass., by Mrs. Ledyard Cogswell of Albany, N.Y. Information from her son states that the folio was purchased by his "grandfather Benjamin W. Cogswell between 1900 and 1910, in England, at an auction held by some English nobleman." Later Mr. Cogswell wrote that the date of acquisition may have been between 1895 and 1905.[305]

While it is a fact that the maiden name of Mrs. Cogswell was Brown, the confusion as to the original subscriber may have arisen from a letter by George Brown on 21 June 1940, then head of the Acquisitions Department at the University, to Mr. Ashburn of the Brooks School. In this he wrote,

> Through various publications we have determined that the father and grandfather of Mrs. Ledyard Cogswell both had the name of Benjamin Walworth Arnold. We have been trying to trace the relationship between Benjamin Arnold and James Arnold without success. James Arnold of New Bedford, Rhode Island [sic], was listed as one of the original subscribers to the Audubon set. *We have assumed that this set was in the Arnold family from the time of the original subscription* [italics the present author's].

James Arnold of New Bedford, Massachusetts, was an original subscriber, and his set of the prints are presently in the Free Library of New Bedford, given to that institution by Mr. Arnold when the library was organized.

There is, in the University of Illinois folio, internal evidence that the set must have been originally subscribed for in England. When the first ten plates were examined, it was found that the Whatman watermark of one of the prints was 1827. In addition, the title of the first plate is "Great American Cock," not "Wild Turkey." Both facts are evidence of a very early subscription. Audubon had obtained no subscriptions in America until after 1830.

UNIVERSITY OF MICHIGAN
Ann Arbor, Mich.

In the fourth volume of Audubon's *Ornithological Biography* is a list of subscribers to the *Birds of America* obtained since the publication of the third volume. Included is "The State of Michigan, by Governor Mason."[306] The volume is dated "Edinburgh, MDCCCXXXVIII," and the introduction, the first of November of that year. The subscription appears as the "Legislature of Michigan" on the final list of subscribers.[307] Stevens T. Mason, after having been the fourth territorial governor of Michigan, was elected governor of the state in October 1835, almost two years before Michigan was admitted to the Union.

It has not been possible to determine the date nor the manner in which this subscription was obtained by Audubon. Two references to the subscription have been found. The first in a letter written from Edinburgh by Audubon on 30 January 1839, to his engraver in London, as follows: "Let me know when the copy half bound for the *State of Michigan* [is ready] and do not forget to have Locks &c as per memorandum left with you...."[308] The second is found in an Audubon journal, in which, on a page headed "New York—July 9th & 10th, 1840," there is the following entry:

> W. A. Colman To
> J. J. Audubon & Son, Locks on Copy of "Birds of America" for State of Michigan on 29 May 1839.
> $20 & Box for ditto $23.
> Per. M. Berthoud a/c

However, this entry has been crossed with a line and on the left margin has been written "Null."[309]

At the present time there is a set of the folio, bound in eight volumes (though originally bound in four), in the Library of the University of Michigan. The provenance of this set has been recorded in great detail by Dr. Russell E. Bidlack of the Department of Library Science at the university.[310] Dr. Bidlack notes that on 5 February 1838 the Board of Regents of the University of Michigan decided to make its first library purchase which was effected by authorizing the secretary to subscribe for one copy of "Audubon's Ornithology." At this meeting of the board, Governor Mason, as one of the regents, was present.

On 1 March 1839, Dr. Zina Pitcher (1797–1872), another of the Regents, submitted to the Board "a communication from William A. Colman of the City of New York advising the Board that Audubon's Ornithology was ready for delivery, and enclosing a bill for the same." Later, during the same meeting, the "necessary sum" was appropriated for paying Colman, and the president of the Board, Governor Mason, was directed to "take the necessary steps for the transportation and safe deposit of said work in the library of the University." The amount of the "necessary sum" appears to have been $970, which was "rendered to Audubon" on 26 April 1839.

Additional details concerning the provenance of this set have come to light from other sources. Some are found in the following letter, dated 25 May 1838, written by Audubon, while still in London, to the bookdealer Colman in New York:

> Your favor of the 23d Instant [this must have referred to 23 April] came to hand yesterday morning, and I hasten to Answer its contents. I have shown your letter to Mr. Havell My Engraver, and mentioned your anxiety to have Nine Plates forwarded to you for the Purpose of Substituting them to an equal Number in your Set purchased at Baltimore, but not purchased from us. We find that five of the plates you want are not only the largest figs, but some extremely full and difficult to Colour, and he says that our Printers and our Colourers would not undertake to go through them without charging a most extravagant price. I have no extra plates whatever on hand, and in consequence of this must be obliged to decline furnishing you with them.
>
> If at the conclusion of my publication I find any of the plates you want they will be sent to you forthwith, but I wish you not to calculate upon this until you hear again from me, or my Sons on this Subject.
>
> My work will be entirely finished by the end of Next Month, our Engraving

and printing establishments will then be broken up, and few will indeed there be [sic] Copies to be had by any one, who has not subscribed to the "Birds of America!"

Should you see any of my American Subscribers who have not yet received any portion of the Work, please to assure them that as soon as the fourth Volume is quite finished, and *bound* according to their desires, their copies will be forwarded at once to their respective houses, or to whomever they have directed me to send their copies.

I hope that you and the rest of the American Merchants will feel relieved from the problem now felt through out the Union, and I remain My Dear Sir very respectfully

                Your ob*t*. Servant
                JOHN J. AUDUBON[311]

As Dr. Bidlack points out, Audubon had recorded a subscription of "W. A. Coleman [sic] Esq. New York" in the third volume of the *Ornithological Biography*, published in 1835.[312] His name is also recorded in the final list of subscribers, as "W. L. [sic] Colman, Esq."[313]

It has been possible to identify the Baltimore subscriber from whom Colman purchased many numbers of the folio. On 11 October 1833, Audubon wrote his son in London that he had added three names to his subscription list, one of these being Joseph E. Walker.[314] Further information concerning the Walker subscription is found in Audubon's Ledger "B." Here it is recorded that this subscriber received the first volume of 100 plates and numbers 21 to 49, inclusive. It is also possible to obtain details of the Colman subscription from the same source. An entry in the ledger under Colman's name, dated July 1838, records that numbers 50–87, inclusive, had been sent to him. It is possible that with the numbers of the Walker set and his own, Colman had acquired a complete set of 87 numbers or 435 plates. It was in April 1838 that Colman had written to Audubon relative to substituting some plates. Then, in March 1839, he had advised the regents at the University of Michigan that "Audubon's Ornithology" was ready for delivery. Had Colman been able to obtain the desired plates from other sources?

No trace has been found of the subscription listed in the name of the State of Michigan. Available records have been searched by Dr. Bidlack and, although there are some loose prints at the Michigan State Library, it is believed that these were a gift to the library in the 1890s.[315] It occurs to this writer that, inasmuch as Governor Mason was present at the meeting of the regents when the library subscription was authorized, it would seem unlikely, especially considering the cost involved, that he would have approved two subscriptions to the *Birds of America*. On the other hand, is it not reasonable to assume that, prior to the authorization by the regents, some arrangement had been made to replace the subscription of the state by that of the library of the university?

There is evidence that relations between Audubon and Colman were not always cordial. On 18 July 1840 the Naturalist wrote his son Victor from Boston: "I am glad to hear that you will close with Coleman [sic], he is not a good Man, and sooner you have done with him the better."[316] The bookdealer seems not to have enjoyed a very good reputation. George Templeton Strong writes of him in his diary, "went into that rascally citidel of humbug W. A. Colman," and comments elsewhere, "What an inveterate puffer that Colman is."[317]

UNIVERSITY OF MINNESOTA
Minneapolis, Minn.

The folio was purchased by William Overton Winston (1853–1927) of Minneapolis from a Chicago bookdealer for a price reported to have been $10,000. The exact date of purchase is not known but it is believed that it was shortly before Winston's death in 1927.

Winston and Dr. Thomas S. Roberts of the University of Minnesota, author of *The Birds of Minnesota*, had been close friends, so that after Winston's death, the family presented the set to Dr. Roberts for the Museum of Natural History.[318]

Another account of the gift states that "it was given to the Museum in Mr. Winston's will, and we know that Dr. Thomas S. Roberts was personally known to Mr. Winston."[319]

No additional information concerning the provenance of this set of the folio has been obtained.

UNIVERSITY OF PENNSYLVANIA
Philadelphia, Pa.

This set of the Double Elephant folio of Audubon's *Birds of America*, bound in six volumes and accompanied by the five volumes of the *Ornithological Biography* was sold by Sotheby & Co. of London for £500 (approx. $2500) on 24 April 1923, to the Treat Book Shop of Atlanta, Georgia.

The folio was then offered by the purchaser, in his catalog, for $3150, F.O.B. Atlanta, and was eventually bought by George Stuart III., a Philadelphia banker.[320]

George Stuart III was for many years an active member of the Delaware Valley Ornithological Club. His special interest was the collection of bird's nests and eggs which he bequeathed to the Academy of Natural Sciences of Philadelphia.[321] The folio and the *Ornithological Biography* were sold, by the executors of Stuart's estate, to Edwin Vare of Philadelphia who, in 1960, presented them to the University of Pennsylvania.

It was learned that the owner of the folio, when it was sold at Sotheby's in 1923, was H. J. B. Beaufoy.[322] It is possible that he was the son of Mark Hanbury Beaufoy who had died on 10 November 1922, the year prior to the sale of the folio.[323]

Provenances of Sets in the United States and Canada

The name Henry Beaufoy is written on the table of contents page of each volume of the *Ornithological Biography* with the date 24 June 1844 appended.[324] However, the Beaufoy name is not found on the list of original subscribers.

UNIVERSITY OF PITTSBURGH
The Darlington Memorial Library, Pittsburgh, Pa.

The Darlington Library was established in 1837 by William McCullough Darlington (1815-1889). His daughters, Edith Darlington Ammon and Mary O'Hara Darlington, presented the family library to the University of Pittsburgh. Their initial gift of eleven thousand volumes was made in the spring of 1918. Several thousand additional volumes and the bulk of the estate were bequeathed by Miss Mary Darlington, last survivor of the family, in May 1925.[325]

It has been determined that the Audubon folio was purchased by Mr. Darlington from an American dealer between 4 August 1852 and 25 October 1852. The price was $100 per volume. The information came from a "Ledger of Books Ordered—Nov. 30, 1847-January 14, 1867." There are seventeen items on the page including the Audubon entry and each was checked for a dealer's label but none was found. Item 743 is the Audubon folio and refers to the catalog of an unknown dealer.

All entries in the ledger, with the exception of two, are in English money. The exceptions are on the page containing the Audubon purchase and another listing books purchased from Joseph Sabin. The presumption is that this set of the folio may have been purchased from Sabin.[326]

UNIVERSITY OF SOUTH CAROLINA
McKissick Memorial Library, Columbia, S.C.

Audubon, while bound for Charleston, S.C., in October 1831, decided to stop also at Columbia, S.C., where he hoped to obtain the subscription of Columbia College (now the University of South Carolina). He had been encouraged in this effort by his fellow coach passenger, Col. W. C. Preston,[327] a member of the South Carolina legislature and resident of Columbia, who turned out to be the nephew of an old Louisville acquaintance of the Audubons, "the Large Colonel Preston."[328] It is possible that due to high water which impeded coach travel Audubon may have changed his plans and proceeded directly to Charleston.[329] The subscription of the college was not obtained until two months later.

Soon after his arrival in Charleston Audubon wrote his wife, "I have sent my Book[330] to Columbia College care of a Professor Gibbs [sic][331] to whom Ward has sold his English bird skins for 50 dollars. Doc*r* Cooper[332] the President of that

College is the son of Mr. Cooper who came to [from] England with thy Father and Doc*r*. Priestly who knows thee well."³³³

It was to be through the efforts of John Bachman, who not only busied himself obtaining subscribers in Charleston but who even went to Columbia, that the subscription of the college was received. On 23 December 1831 he wrote Audubon, who was then in St. Augustine, "I arrived in Columbia, S.C., almost too late, for the 'House' had just resolved that the State was too poor for Audubon's work. I felt that it would be a disgrace to the State; and, for the first time in my life, I turned to electioneering. And, now behold me among the countrymen, spinning long yarns. The thing, however, took and your book is subscribed for."³³⁴

It is interesting to speculate whether Audubon ever knew how necessary had been Bachman's "electioneering," for when on 17 December 1831 the South Carolina Assembly was called upon to vote "On the question to agree that the clause in the said Bill making an appropriation to purchase Mr. Audubon's work on American Ornithology" the tally was close indeed, with 51 yeas and 50 nays.³³⁵

UNIVERSITY OF SOUTHERN CALIFORNIA

Hancock Library of Biology and Oceanography, Los Angeles, Calif.

The first formal report of the Library of the Boston Natural History Society was given at the annual meeting of 7 May 1834. It was noted at the time that "In the department of Ornithology our poverty is now apparent. An attempt was made some time since to purchase the splendid work of Mr. Audubon, the price is $800."³³⁶

Two years later, on 5 October 1836, a donation of the *Birds of America* was announced which was made possible by the generosity of the following persons: Amos Lawrence, Benjamin D. Greene, Samuel A. Eliot, David Eckley, George B. Emerson, William Ingalls, George Parkman, Charles Amory, George C. Shattuck, George C. Shattuck, Jr., and Mrs. A. A. Shattuck.³³⁷

Audubon referred to this subscription in his journal entry of 27 September 1836:

> In the evening Dr. Shattuck finished the subscription list of the society [the Naturalist had been dining with Dr. B. D. Greene, President of the Natural History Society], by presenting me to his lady, who subscribed for one-tenth, and the Dr. then put down his son George's name for one-twentieth, making in his own family one-fourth of the whole, or two hundred and twenty dollars, for which he gave me his cheque. Without the assistance of this generous man, it is more than probable that the society never would have had a copy of the "Birds of America."³³⁸

On 19 February 1840, Colonel Thomas N. Perkins, one of the early Boston subscribers, presented his set of the folio to the society.³³⁹ Since this set was an early impression and believed to be unsurpassed in the country, it was decided that those members who had subscribed to the original set should be a committee to decide what disposition should be made of that copy. With the three nonmembers of the Society, Parkman, Geo. Shattuck, Jr., and Mrs. Shattuck, in agreement, all the subscribers gave their consent to the exchange of this for other works on natural history. As a result, many important later accessions were labeled "From Audubon Fund" and the library was greatly enriched by the generosity of those farseeing friends.[340]

The Perkins set of the folio remained in the library of the society until 1947 when the library was reorganized, and the folio was among a number of extremely valuable books which were sold to the Allan Hancock Foundation Library, University of Southern California, Los Angeles, California.[341]

UNIVERSITY OF WISCONSIN
The Memorial Library, Madison, Wis.

When, in 1946, the University of Wisconsin purchased from his estate the Chester H. Thordarson library, the Audubon folio was among the books acquired. The details of the acquisition of the folio by Thordarson have been furnished by Dr. Jens Christian Bay, for many years the librarian of the John Crerar Library of Chicago:

> Thordarson obtained the copy from Walter M. Hill. It originally was in a worn half-leather binding and belonged to two (elderly) ladies in Chicago. They had been offered $200 for it about 1920, but somehow called on Mr. Hill for advice. He bought it of them for $2500, and Thordarson paid $3000. The copy for some years rested on shelves in Thordarson's office in his factory and was located above a waste paper basket. About 1922 somebody, some caller, because Thordarson never smoked, seems to have dropped a lighted cigarette into the waste basket and the flames scorched the four Audubon volumes. Thordarson had insured his books and reported the damage, to which I certified. The work was shipped to Rivière in London and rebound. It stayed at Rivière's a long time as there was difficulty in finding skins of adequate size. Years later, when the books were moved to the stone house at Rocky Island, the case was made which I suppose still holds the volumes. I have no knowledge about the earlier history of the copy."[342]

In some instances information helpful in tracing the folio to the original subscriber has been found in the volumes of the *Ornithological Biography* which generally accompany the folio. When such information was requested from the Memorial Library, the following reply was received: "Yes, we do have the five volumes of the Ornithological Biography and to the best of my knowledge they were acquired at the same time as the elephant folio—being part of the Thordarson purchase. Each volume bears a label on the verso of the front cover indicating the previous ownership of Erastus Corning. (There is nothing but his name on the white slip of paper.)"[343]

Erastus Corning (1794–1872) was a prominent manufacturer in Albany, N.Y., of the firm of Corning, Winslow and Company, steel products. In addition, he was active in the development of the railway system in the state of New York. He was not a subscriber to the *Birds of America*.

It is likely that the folio and the volumes of the *Ornithological Biography* were obtained by Thordarson at different times.

VASSAR COLLEGE
Poughkeepsie, N.Y.

On 9 April 1897, Irving Putnam, of G. P. Putnam's Sons of New York, wrote to Mrs. F. A. Wood, the librarian of Vassar College, the following letter:

> A friend of the writer who has been dispersing his collection of fine books, principally by presenting at Columbia University, has a copy of the magnificent Elephant folio Edition of Audubon's Birds of America, worth 1800 to 2000. The Columbia University already possess this work, so that I did not suggest that it be included in his donation for them. Mr. Baker, of the Columbia Library, suggests that your institution may be glad to have it.
>
> Will you kindly let me know whether or not the library already possesses a set, and if not, whether the presentation of the set would be agreeable and appreciated. If so, I think I am in a position to say that my friend would be happy to make this donation.[344]

Although no correspondence between the library and Putnam has been found, it is evident that the "presentation of the set" would be "agreeable" and no doubt "appreciated" for the folio was "acquisitioned" on 5 June 1899. The records of the library state that the donor was Charles H. Senff. Not much is known about the donor. Records at Columbia show that he had made a series of gifts in the 1890s. His first gift in 1891 is described in Columbia's official listing merely as "Books." The second, described as "The Northrop collection for the Library," was made in 1893. Finally, in 1897, the year the Putnam letter was sent to Vassar, he presented a collection of 365 volumes. He is not listed among Columbia's alumni.[345]

When the folio was examined it was observed that on the back of many prints appeared the name "J. Clough".[346] Among the early subscribers was John Clough (1773–1843) of Oxton Hall, near Tadcaster, Yorkshire. On 27 April 1827 Audubon noted in his journal that he had obtained five subscriptions during his stay in York. That of Clough was probably among the five.[347]

John William Clough built and lived in Oxton Hall, near Tadcaster, and is listed in the directories for the period in question. He was also the owner of Newbald Hall and Acomb Hall, as well as Clifton House and Bootham in York, and a house in London. He was a director of York's oldest banking firm, Swann, Clough and Company, which carried on business until taken over in 1879 by Beckett and Company. He was also one of the founders of the York and Ainsty Hunt.[348]

His son, John Clough, was born at Bramham in 1803 and died in 1865. He lived at Newbald Hall and Clifton House, became a partner in Swann, Clough and Company, and was a Justice of the Peace for the North, West, and East Ridings of Yorkshire.[349]

From the foregoing details it seems most probable that John William Clough was the subscriber, but John Clough (1803–1865) cannot be ruled out. Audubon first listed the subscription in Volume 1 of the *Ornithological Biography*,[350] and it appears again in the final list of European subscribers.[351]

WILLIAMS COLLEGE
Chapin Library, Williamstown, Mass.

The Double Elephant folio of Audubon's *Birds of America* is included in the noteworthy collection of rare books, manuscripts, and prints which had been assembled by Alfred Clark Chapin (1848–1936), Williams alumnus, class of 1869, and presented by him to Williams College in 1923.[352] Chapin, a prominent citizen of Brooklyn, where he had been mayor (1888–1891), purchased the folio from James T. Drake, the New York bookdealer, at a cost of $3,000 in August 1915.[353]

It is believed that the folio had been acquired for Drake in England by Lathrop Harper. No additional information concerning the provenance of this folio has been found. The four volumes are three-quarter bound in russia and edged in gilt.

YALE UNIVERSITY
Henry Farnam copy
New Haven, Conn.

This folio was for many years in the possession of Henry Farnam (1803–1883), a canal and railroad builder born in Scipio, Cayuga County, New York. Among his railroad projects was the construction of the Chicago and Rock Island Railroad, of which he later became president.[354]

Upon his retirement in 1863 Farnam moved to New Haven, having lived in Connecticut during his post as chief engineer of the construction of the Farmington Canal. He made notable gifts to Yale, including Farnam Hall. In 1871 the college conferred upon him the honorary degree of Master of Arts.[355]

Upon Farnam's death the folio was bequeathed to Yale.[356] However, it was to remain in the possession of the family until after the death of a son, Henry Walcott Farnam (1853–1933), a member of the Yale class of 1874. It was actually turned over to the University in 1934.[357]

It has not been possible to determine when and from what source Henry Farnam obtained the folio.

YALE UNIVERSITY
Francis P. Garvan copy

The donor of this copy of the folio to the Yale University Art Gallery was Francis Patrick Garvan (1875–1937), class of 1897. Shortly after obtaining a law degree from New York University in 1899, he became an assistant district attorney for the City of New York under William Travis Jerome. In 1917, with the entrance of the United States in World War I, Garvan became associated with the office of the Alien Property Custodian. Two years later he became Alien Property Custodian.[358]

After the conclusion of the war Garvan organized the Chemical Foundation, a nonprofit organization dealing with foreign chemical patents. He was to remain with the foundation until his death.[359]

Garvan made frequent donations to his alma mater from 1930 to 1937 and it is believed that the four volumes of the Audubon folio were included among his gifts. The early provenance of the folio has not been determined, but it is known that it was purchased from Russell W. Thorpe, a dealer in Flushing, N.Y.[360]

This set of the folio is of particular interest for its examples of the early states of certain plates. One, plate 2, bears the incorrect legend, "Black-billed Cuckoo—Coccyzus Erythopthalmus," for the bird thereon figured is actually the "Yellow-billed Cuckoo." Another, plate 230, the "Ruddy Plover" in the Garvan set, was printed on Whatman paper with the watermark dated 1834 and has only two birds figured, whereas in the Farnam set the same plate bears the legend "Sanderling," depicts three birds, and has a J. Whatman watermark dated 1838.

27

PROVENANCES OF SETS IN ENGLAND AND SCOTLAND

BIRMINGHAM PUBLIC LIBRARIES
Reference Library, Birmingham, England

Audubon arrived in Birmingham on 23 June 1830 and the following day arranged an exhibition in "an excellent room in the Society of Arts offered me Gratis and as I charge nothing myself I may have Visitors and Perhaps some Subscribers. I procured one yesterday in the name of John Reeves.—I have issued 400 Notes of Invitation for Town & Country So that if I do not succeed it will not be for lack of Industry."[1] The exhibition remained open until 1 July, on which date Audubon left Birmingham in rather low spirits, for he had not been successful in obtaining any additional subscribers.[2]

However, the Naturalist did find in Birmingham "a Bookseller of the name of Bilby [sic] who is more of a Gentleman to me than any of his caste I have met with heretofore."[3] That gentleman was a member of the firm of Beilby, Knott and Beilby, booksellers, which was shortly to obtain the subscription of the Birmingham Old Library, called "Old Birmingham" to distinguish it from a secondary institution which for a time existed independently as the Birmingham New Library.[4]

The folio remained in the collection of the Birmingham Old Library, a subscription library founded in 1779, until 1934 when it was purchased by Birmingham Public Libraries.[5]

BRITISH MUSEUM
Natural History
Cromwell Road, London

The Natural History Department of the British Museum was moved to South Kensington during the period 1880–1883. There are two sets of the folio at the Museum.

Set number 1 was purchased by the British Museum (Natural History) from Bernard Quaritch, the London bookseller, on 22 June 1885 for £285.[6] Nothing is known of the earlier provenance of this set.

Set number 2 was the gift of the second Baron Rothschild (Lionel Walter, 1868–1937), who bequeathed his museum and library at Tring, Hertfordshire, to the British Museum (Natural History). Included in the library was this set of Audubon's *Birds*. No information as to date of purchase or of former ownership is available.

The Museum had inquired of Hatchards, the booksellers in London with whom Baron Rothschild dealt extensively, but they have no records as the firm had changed hands several times during the past century. The Honourable Miriam Rothschild, however, believes the purchase was made around 1895, but there is no supporting evidence.[7]

When the legends of the first ten plates of the two sets were compared, interesting variations were noted, some of which follow:

Set No. 1. Plate 1. Great American Cock—Vulgo (Wild Turkey)
" 2. " " Wild Turkey

Set No. 1. Plate 2. Yellow-billed Cuckoo, Coccyzus carolinensis,
" 2. Yellow-billed Cuckoo, Coccyzus Americanus, Bonap.

Set No. 1. Plate 3. Purple Finch
Fringilla purpurea.
Plant Pinus pendula
" 2. Purple Finch,
Fringilla purpurea, Gmel.
Male .1.2. Female .3.
Red Larch, Larix americana.

When Audubon returned to England from America in May of 1834 he carried with him a letter of introduction to the famous London banker, Baron Nathan Mayer Rothschild (1777–1836), given to him by the New York banking firm, Prime, Ward and King.[8] On 12 May he visited the baron and presented the letter in the hope that he might obtain a subscription to the *Birds of America*.[9] This visit he described in some detail in a journal entry dated 12 May.[10] From that account it is known that his attempt had proved fruitless.

However, another reference to the Rothschild dealings has been found in his Ledger "B." Here the account with N. M. Rothschild is set down as follows:

1834–July 1 & 2—Birds of America   93–13–0.
Paid Havell—Feby 1836

It is clear from the foregoing that in February of 1836 Havell had been paid for two volumes of the *Birds of America*. Whether this was in payment for those which Audubon's journal states were sent to the baron and supposedly returned or was for others sent at a later date cannot be ascertained. It should be noted that Baron Rothschild died on 28 July 1836, five months after the recorded payment.

Again, whether these volumes remained in his branch of the family and were inherited by his great-grandson, Lionel Walter, or whether a complete set was purchased later appears to be conjecture.

BRITISH MUSEUM
Reading Room

In the fourth volume of the *Ornithological Biography*, published in 1838, Audubon listed the British Museum among the subscriptions he had obtained after the publication of the third volume three years previously.[11] References in his journals to the Museum indicate that from the earliest days after his arrival in England twelve years previously he had hoped to obtain a subscription from that institution.

Audubon's journal for 24 February 1828 notes, "I also learned that it was Sir Thomas Lawrence (1769–1830) who prevented the British Museum from subscribing to my work; he considered the drawing so-so, and the engraving and coloring bad; when I remember how he praised these same drawings *in my presence*, I wonder—that is all."[12] But shortly afterwards, in March of the same year, the Naturalist realized that he must have been misinformed. On 12 March he wrote in his journal, "Mr. David Lyon called to see my work, and said that it had been recommended to him by Sir Thomas Lawrence. This seems strange after what I heard before but like all other men Sir Thomas has probably his enemies, and falsehoods have been told about him."[13] It was at this time that the Naturalist learned from a member of the staff of the Museum, John Edward Gray (1800–1875), that only £200 per annum were allowed for the purchase of natural curiosities.[14]

In May 1827, soon after Audubon had reached London, he became acquainted with John George Children and, on the evening of 23 May, accompanied him to the Linnean Society to exhibit the first number of his engravings.[15] At this time Children was associated with the Zoology Department of the British Museum. In addition, he had been and would again be Secretary of the Royal Society. Audubon and Children became intimate friends, so much so that the Naturalist listed him among the individuals he recalls with "every sense of gratitude" when he returned to Edinburgh in October.[16]

Finally, before sailing to America on 1 April 1829, Audubon arranged with Children to oversee the engraving of the drawings during his absence.[17]

Audubon included Children's name on the first list of subscribers, where it appears thus: "J.G. Children, Esq. British Museum."[18] The subscription is also included on the final list of European subscribers.[19] Audubon recorded the following details of the subscription in his Ledger "B":

J. G. Children

p/37

1830 Jan 31 To 1st Volume and another No. 1.	44– 2– 0
1831 April 21 To No. 21 Journal No. 22	4– 4– 0
	48– 6– 0
1833 Mar. 21 No. 23–31 Inc. f 22.	18–18– 0
Contra—British Museum	
1830 Jan 31 By cash	44– 2– 0
1831 June " " Paid Havell	4– 4– 0
	48– 6– 0
1832 December 11 R. Havell f 10.	18–18– 0

According to the above record, the subscription was not completed beyond plate 155. Also, does "Contra—British Museum" indicate that the payments were made by that institution and that Children was acting on its behalf? No information regarding this could be obtained from the files of the museum. Inquiry of officials brought forth the response, "We have some letters of J. G. Children in our collections ... I am afraid none of them contain any references to Audubon, so the problem remains unsolved."[20]

Sometime between 9 May and 13 June 1835, there was received at the British Museum by a bequest from Major General Thomas Hardwicke, who was an original subscriber, a number of prints of the *Birds of America*. There is, however, no information available at the museum regarding the exact number.[21] Fortunately, there is an entry relating to the Hardwicke subscription in Audubon's Ledger "B," as follows:

> 63 Hardwicke, Major General Thomas, Pall Mall, London
> Vol. I., 21 to 31 Inc. Mar. 21, 1833
> and Biog.

From this we know that General Hardwicke received plates 1 to 155 and the first volume of the *Ornithological Biography*. It would appear, then, that it was these plates which were bequeathed to the museum.

Although there are four volumes in the so-called Hardwicke set, the first two volumes do not contain any date stamp, because from 1834 to 1837 it was not the museum's custom to put any date stamp on its books.[22] However, there is in Volume 3 the museum's receipt stamp, which leads to an entry in the ledgers which reads as follows:

> 1838 April 10. Audubon (John James) "Birds of America"
> vol. III. Ptes. CCXLI–CCCCX, fol. Lond.1834–35
> Purchased of Audubon.[23]

This is evidence that plates 241 to 410 were purchased directly from the Naturalist. That the remaining plates, 411 to 435, were also purchased from him is ascertained from the following entry in his Ledger "B":

Provenances of Sets in England and Scotland

38—British Museum
May 1838   No. 49–82 (241–410)
July 1838   No. 83–87 (411–435)
Paid Victor Audubon Jan. 19, 1839.

The foregoing also provides a confirmation of the 10 April 1838 entry in the ledgers of the museum. It was undoubtedly the purchase of these plates which led Audubon to include the subscription of the British Museum among those listed in the fourth volume of the *Ornithological Biography*.

While it has been possible to determine that in the set of the Audubon folio presently in the Reading Room of the British Museum, plates 1 to 155 were from the original Hardwicke subscription and plates 241 to 435 were purchased from Audubon, the origin of plates 156 to 240 is presently not known.

CAMBRIDGE UNIVERSITY
The Fitzwilliam Museum, Cambridge, England

Early in March 1828 the Naturalist spent a week in Cambridge. Writing his wife about this visit, he listed five subscriptions received while there, among which was that of the Fitzwilliam Museum. In the original European subscription list it is recorded as number 46, "The Fitzwilliam Museum, by M. Davy, Vice Chancellor."[24]

Martin Davy (?–1839) had been appointed vice-chancellor in 1803 and was nearing the end of his chancellorship when Audubon met him.[25] In his journal entry for 5 March 1828, Audubon described him as "a small old man, with hair as white as snow, dressed in a flowing gown, with two little bits of white muslin in lieu of a cravat." He went on to describe the vice-chancellor's visit to his rooms, "He remained with me upwards two hours; admired my work and promised to do all he could. I was delighted with his conversation; he is a man of wide knowledge, and it seemed to me sound judgement."[26]

Before leaving Cambridge Audubon dined with the vice-chancellor, recording this visit as follows: "I dined at the Vice-Chancellor's, and found myself among men of deep research, learning and knowledge, mild in expressions, kind in attentions and under whom I fervently wished it had been my lot to have received such education as they possess."[27]

CAMBRIDGE UNIVERSITY
University Library

Audubon had arrived in Cambridge from London on the afternoon of 3 March 1828. Writing in his journal he commented,

On entering Cambridge I was struck with its cleanliness, the regular shape of the colleges, and the number of students with floating mantles, flat caps, and long tassels of silk, hanging sideways. I had a letter for a lodging house where I expected to stay, but no numbers are affixed to any doors in Cambridge. I do not know if it is so in order to teach the students to better remember things, but I found it very inconvenient; I hunted and searched in vain, and as the students in their gay moods have been in the habit of destroying all the doorbells, I had to knock loudly at any door where I wished to make inquiries, but not finding the good lady to whom my letter was addressed, I am still at the Inn.[28]

The Naturalist promptly set about delivering his letters of introduction and soon was meeting professors and others, leading him to write, "Since I left Edinburgh I have not had a day as brilliant as this in the point of being surrounded by learned men."[29] It was on the third day of his stay that he received the subscription (no.43 on the original list of European subscribers) "of the Librarian for the University."[30] That librarian was John Lodge (1793?–1850).[31] Audubon's receipts for the payment of all the individual numbers of the *Birds of America* are among the records in the archives of Cambridge University.[32]

THE EARL OF CRAWFORD AND BALCARRES
Balcarres, Colinsburgh, Fife, Scotland

It was at Haigh Hall, situated two and one half miles northeast of Wigan in Lancaster County, England, that the Bibliotheca Lindesiana was brought together. Lord Crawford left Haigh Hall in 1946, at which time he deposited at the John Rylands Library, Manchester, the whole of his collection of French Revolutionary pamphlets and journals, his remarkable set of De Bry, his collection of Lutheran tracts, and his collection of English historical tracts. His collection of English broadsides he deposited with Cambridge University. There were also several sales at Sotheby's. Part of the library, including the Audubon folio, was retained and transferred to Balcarres.[33]

In the catalog of the Bibliotheca Lindesiana, the Audubon folio is described as follows:

Vol. 1.
Catalogue of the Printed Books
Preserved at
Haigh Hall, Wigan
Co. Pal. Lancast.
A–D at the Aberdeen University Press 1910.

p. 447 Audubon (John James) The Birds of America from original drawings...................London 1827–38

Folio. 39 in.   in 4 vols.   435 colored prints.
Half gr. morocco with bookplate of John Henry Gurney
and crest on sides.

Included also are the five volumes of the *Ornithological Biography*, with the inscription, "To Abraham Thompson Esq. [from] John J. Audubon."

It is possible that the original subscriber was Joseph John Gurney, Esq., Earlham Hall, Norfolk (no.33 on the final list of European subscribers).[34] Gurney was a banker and a Quaker revivalist. His son, John Henry Gurney, whose bookplate appears in the volumes, was a keen ornithologist.[35]

DUKE OF DEVONSHIRE
Chatsworth, Bakewell, England

The folio in the Devonshire Collections at Chatsworth is a magnificent one, of maximum size, appearing to be a special copy made up of the very best specimens of the engravings. It is believed to have been purchased by and bound up for the sixth Duke of Devonshire (1790-1858), who was mainly responsible for the great library at Chatsworth.[36] The folio is listed on page 94 of the catalog of the library, which was compiled in 1879 under the auspices of his cousin and heir, William Cavendish (1808-1891), seventh Duke of Devonshire.

The first ten prints are all from the early states of the plates, for there is none with a Whatman watermark later than 1828. It has not been possible to identify the original subscriber.

MRS. BARBARA FANE
London

This folio's original subscriber is number 10 on Audubon's final list of European subscribers. On 21 December 1826, Audubon wrote his wife, "The University of Edinburgh having subscribed I look to the rest of them 11 in number to follow."[37] On the original subscription list, the third name below that of the University of Edinburgh is "The Society of Writers to Her Majesty's Signet Edinburgh," evidently one of the "11." Thus it is safe to assume that not many days after the university subscription had been received, so had that of the Society.

The folio remained in the possession of the society until it was sold, with other valuable books from its library, at Sotheby's on 19 October 1959. The purchaser, acting on behalf of Stanley Smith, the father of Mrs. Fane, was Henry Sotheran Ltd., who paid £13,000 ($36,400).

The 435 prints comprising this copy have been linen-backed and are bound in eight volumes.

THE HONOURABLE LORD FITZWILLIAM
Milton, Peterborough, England

In his journal entry for 7 March 1828, Audubon wrote that while he was in the library of the University of Cambridge looking at the three volumes of Le Vaillant's *Birds of Africa*, he

> was called from there to show his work to the son of Lord Fitzwilliam, who came with his tutor Mr. Upton. The latter informed me the young nobleman wished to own the book. I showed my drawings, and he, full of the ardor of youth, asked where he should write his name. I gave him my list; his youth, his good looks, his courtesy, his refinement attracted me much, and made me wish his name should stand by that of some good friend. There was no room by Mrs. Rathbone's, so I asked that he write immediately above the Countess of Morton, and he wrote in a beautiful hand which I wish I could equal, "Hon. W. C. Wentworth Fitzwilliam." He is a charming young man, and I wish him *bon voyage* through life.[38]

The Naturalist's good wishes notwithstanding, the young Fitzwilliam did not live long after this meeting, for he died in November 1835. Two years before his death he became Viscount Milton when his father succeeded to the earldom in February 1833.[39] However, before his death, according to Ledger "B," there were sent him the first volume of the *Birds of America*, as well as additional prints, Numbers 21 to 31, inclusive (pl.101–55) and Volume I of the *Ornithological Biography*.

In July of the same year Audubon was visited at his lodgings in London by Viscount Milton, the father of the "charming young man" who had subscribed at Cambridge. The Naturalist wrote to his friend William Swainson of this visit, stating, "I received a visit on Saturday last of the whole of Lord Milton's family who after complimenting the author of the 'Birds of America' very kindly subscribed for two copies of the work."[40]

For many years there were two copies of the Audubon folio in the Fitzwilliam family. One, belonging to the senior family branch at Wentworth Woodhouse, is still kept there. The other belonged to the junior branch at Milton and was sold some thirty years ago.[41]

Audubon included the names of both son (7. The Honourable W. C. Wentworth Fitzwilliam, London) and father (50. The Right Honourable Viscount Milton, London) in his final list of European subscribers.[42] It is difficult to explain why the name of the younger Fitzwilliam appears on the list, since the subscription had not been completed, his death having occurred on 8 November 1835.

As well as a set of the folio, the library of Lord Fitzwilliam at Milton contains a complete set of *The Viviparous Quadrupeds of North America* by John James Audubon and Reverend John Bachman (New York: John James Audubon, 1845–48), consisting of 150 lithographed color plates. This had been issued in thirty parts of five plates each, without text except for nomenclature on plates. The set of *Quadrupeds* in Lord Fitzwilliam's collection is unusual in that it has never been bound and is the only one in parts ever encountered by this author.

THE COLLEGE OF GLASGOW
(As Trustees of the Hunterian Museum)
Glasgow University Library
Glasgow, Scotland

Audubon had arrived in Glasgow on 4 November 1827. On the last day of his stay, 8 November, he wrote in his journal, "I am off tomorrow morning, and perhaps forever will say farewell to Glasgow. I have been here *four* days and have obtained *one* subscriber. One subscriber in a city of 150,000 souls, rich, handsome, and with much learning. Think of 1400 pupils in one college!"[43] It is most likely that the one subscriber alluded to by Audubon was "The College of Glasgow, as Trustees of the Hunterian Museum" (no. 38 on his final list of European subscribers). Several years were to elapse before Audubon was again to visit Glasgow. Furthermore, no other Glasgow name is to be found on the original subscription list.

Additional evidence that the subscription was obtained within a year after Lizars had begun the engraving of the prints is found in the legends of the first ten plates. In plate 1 is an example of the "Great American Cock." This and plates 2, 3, 4, and 5 were all engraved by Lizars, with the last showing an 1825 watermark. Plate 6 is the "Great American Hen & Young, coloured by R. Havell, Sen*r*" which indicates that it was struck shortly after the work had been transferred to Havell in London. All the watermark dates except that of plate 5 are 1827.

The most important special collection to be given to Glasgow College (it arrived in 1807) is the Hunterian Library. The depositing of the Audubon folio of the *Birds of America* in this collection is an indication of the respect with which the work was regarded.[44]

THE HONOURABLE LORD HESKETH
Easton Neston, Towcester, England

The original subscriber of this folio was Henry Witham, Esq., of Lartington, Durham, number 11 on the final list of European subscribers.[45]

In a journal entry dated Sunday, 3 December 1826, the Naturalist tells in some detail of dining with Witham:

> I had to dine with Mr. Witham of Yorkshire in *No.* 24 Great King Street [Edinburgh], but I did not know him at all. I had mistaken him for Sir Patrick

Walker in the street and addressed him as such a man. He had invited me on [that] occasion, and I am ready to experiment on human propensity to please. Mr. Bridges who goes everywhere and knows everybody led me to his house. Dr. Knox, the daughter of my host, his wife and his wife's sister were all [the company]. I determined in an instant that this gentleman was a gentleman indeed, quite wealthy, polite and versed in all courteous ways. We dined, we drank coffee, we supped at 11. At 12 the ladies bid us good night. I wished and longed to retire, but it was impossible. Mr. Bridges talked much. We all talked much, for I believe the good wine of Mr. Witham had a most direct effect. It was determined by Dr. Knox to propose me as an honorary member of the Wernerian Society. Our host said he would second the motion. It was determined that, to satisfy Mr. B. [Bridges], Miss W. would set for her portrait to Mr. Watson Gordon. And at half past one, after been dubbed a great philosopher and an extraordinary man, my health drank, &c., &c., I retired with Dr. Knox but left Mr. B. [Bridges] and Mr. W. [Witham] at their whiskey toddy.[46]

Witham subscribed to the *Birds of America* on 18 December 1826, shortly before the Naturalist had been elected to the Wernerian Society.[47] The Witham subscription is listed in Ledger "B" as follows:

    134 Witham, Henry, Edinburgh—to July 1838
        Bound with Locks.

This subscriber, Henry Witham, was born Henry Thomas Silvertop (1779–1844), the third son of John Silvertop of Minsteracres, Northumberland. He assumed the name of Witham after his marriage to Eliza Witham, daughter of Thomas Witham of Headlam, Durham (as well as niece and heir of William Witham of Cliff, Co. York).

A son of Henry Witham's was the Rt. Reverend Monsignor Thomas Edward Witham (1806–1897) of Lartington Hall, Durham, Domestic Prelate of Pope Leo XIII. A daughter, Catherine, married Henry Englefield. Their son, Henry Charles Englefield, by royal licence in 1849, assumed the name and arms of Silvertop upon succeeding George Silvertop, his great-uncle, to the Minsteracres property. Henry Charles Silvertop, né Englefield, was succeeded by his eldest son, Henry Thomas Silvertop, whose heir was his eldest son, Francis Somerled Silvertop, who also inherited the estate of his great-granduncle, Monsignor Thomas Witham.[48]

The folio was sold at auction on 3 July 1951 (lot #198), for £7,000, by Christie, Manson & Woods, Ltd., London, who were acting for the estate of the late Charles A. J. O. Silvertop. Furthermore the auctioneers state "the Audubon Bird Books of America belonged to the Trustees of The Will of the late F. S. J. Silvertop, who obtained these by inheritance from his family."[49] Purchaser of the folio was the father of the present Lord Hesketh.

When the four volumes were examined it was found that each one had a lock. Also, in the front of the first volume was written the following inscription, "From Eliza Witham with sincere affection. June the 24th, 1831."

The Field Museum Library's set photographed beside one of its book stacks, showing the imperial size of the Double Elephant folio. Courtesy of the Library, Field Museum of Natural History.

One volume of the Trinity College Library set on display in a glass case. The individual prints have been carefully protected by interleaving. This set was the personal set of Robert Havell, Jr. Courtesy of the Trinity College Library, Hartford, Conn.

One volume of the set belonging to the Public Library of Cincinnati and Hamilton County on display in a specially prepared storage and display case. Courtesy of the Public Library of Cincinnati and Hamilton County.

Two volumes of the Duke University set on display. Courtesy of Duke University, Durham, N.C.

One volume of the Audubon Shrine and Wildlife Sanctuary set on display, again showing contrast in size between the folio and conventionally sized books. Courtesy of the Audubon Shrine and Wildlife Sanctuary, Audubon, Pa.

Volume I of Lord Hesketh's set, showing a specially designed pair of locks. Courtesy of the Honourable Lord Hesketh, Easton Neston, Towcester, England.

Provenances of Sets in England and Scotland

THE JOHN RYLANDS LIBRARY
Manchester, England

It is believed that this folio was purchased by Mrs. Rylands herself from Henry Sotheran & Co. Ltd., the date of the invoice being 2 March 1891, which indicates that it was delivered to her on 17th February of that year.[50]

Inquiry was made of Henry Sotheran Ltd. in the hope that the records of the firm would disclose some information as to previous ownership. A letter from the firm, dated 31 October 1963, stated, "All our records, through two Wars and the constant moving of warehouses, has necessitated, by turning out for salvage, or by damage, anything of the nature being kept."[51]

The Whatman watermarks (1826–1827) and the legends of the first ten plates indicate that this folio is that of an early subscriber.

LIVERPOOL PUBLIC LIBRARIES
The Picton Reference Library

There is written on a plate inside the front cover of Volume 1 of this set of the Audubon folio the following:

> This work was purchased out of the Donation of
> One Thousand Pounds
> Presented to the Liverpool Free Public Library
> by
> Joseph Shipley Esq*re*
> of Brandywine—Delaware—United States.

Joseph Shipley became a partner of William Brown in 1826. He was a bachelor and a Quaker, belonging to one of the old families who had settled in Wilmington, Delaware, who had come over to Liverpool in 1819. In recognition of his services to the firm in the financial crisis of 1837, the name of the firm in England was changed, in 1839, to Brown, Shipley and Co. Due to ill health, Joseph Shipley retired in 1850 and returned to the United States to live in Wilmington.

In 1860, after hearing of William Brown's gift of a public library building in Liverpool, Joseph Shipley sent a donation of £1,000. The money was used for the purchase of rare books, mainly relating to the country of his birth, such as Catlin's *Original Drawings of the American Indians* and Audubon's *Birds of America*.[52]

On the inside of the back cover of the first volume is a sticker reading:

> Liverpool Free Public Library
> Class C.   No. 69   Fol. Vols. 4
> Received 16th Jan. 1861
> From Willis & Sotheran
> Price jit 1-1- nett.
> (Shipley Don.)

335

No further information as to the previous history of the set is known. In World War II, during a bombing raid which occurred on 3 May 1941, the folio was saved by R. Bioletti, the reference librarian, who carried the water-soaked volumes out of the building to safety.

MITCHELL LIBRARY
Glasgow Corporation Public Libraries, Glasgow, Scotland

The set of the folio was obtained by the Mitchell Library in 1902 when the Jeffrey Library was bequeathed to the Mitchell Library. The folio formed a part of the ornithological collection acquired by Robert Jeffrey (1827–1902) of Crosslee House, Renfrewshire. Formerly, it had been in the library of John Wingfield Larking (1801–1891), which library was sold by Sotheby's on 4 April 1892. The Larking folio was purchased for £345, and included the five volumes of the *Ornithological Biography*. The first volume of the *Birds of America* has a pasted-in catalog entry for all nine volumes at £420, the price which Jeffrey probably paid for them. This volume also includes the bookplate of John Wingfield Larking.[53]

It is interesting to note that in addition to the bookplate of John Wingfield Larking in each of the five volumes of the *Ornithological Biography*, there is also a written note on the flyleaf stating that it was presented by Audubon to Professor Robert Jameson (1774–1854), professor of natural history at Edinburgh University from 1804 to 1854. There is, however, no evidence that Larking obtained this set directly from Professor Jameson.[54] It should also be recorded that neither Larking nor Jameson were original subscribers to the *Birds of America*.

However, the original subscriber was surely among the early ones, for the first ten prints are from the early states of the plates, struck on paper with Whatman watermarks no later than 1828.

According to a letter written 8 March 1972 to the author by C. W. Black, City Librarian, The Mitchell Library, Glasgow, it was discovered some years ago, when the folio was removed from storage, that four prints were missing. It has been possible to replace two of these, but still missing, as of March 1972, are plate 150, "Black-capped Titmouse, Parus Atricapillus, Lin., 1. Male, 2. Female. Supplejack. 1833," and plate 163, "Palm Warbler, Sylvia Palmarum, 1. Male. 2. Young. Wild Orange. 1833."

OXFORD UNIVERSITY
Christ Church Library, Oxford, England

The Christ Church Library's folio is number 47 on the original list of European subscribers. On 25 March 1828, Audubon wrote in his journal, "My feet are practically sore battering the pavement; I have walked from one house and College to another all day, but have a new subscriber, and one not likely to die soon, the

Anatomical School, through Dr. Kidd."[55] He was referring to Dr. John Kidd (1775–1851), who was at the time professor of Chemistry and Medicine at Oxford.

Complete details of the payments made on this subscription were found in the Christ Church archives as follows:

			Amount £	d	d
11 July 1829	Mr. Audubon for plates of American Birds		10	10	0
14 June 1832	Havell Birds of America 22–25		8	8	0
6 June 1833	Havell Audubon's Birds		14	14	0
29 May 1834	Havell Print seller		14	14	0
4 June 1835	Havell (Audubon's birds)		22	1	0
18 June 1836	Havell (Audubon's Birds)		19	19	0
5 June 1837	Havell (Audubon's Birds)		31	10	0
30 May 1839	Havell Audubon's Birds (completed)		30	9	0
		[Total £	152	5	0][56]

For a better understanding of the foregoing, it should be recalled that the English price for each number of 5 plates was two guineas, or 2 pounds and 2 shillings. Thus the first entry on 11 July 1829 was the payment for five numbers, and the payment on 14 June 1832 was for the four numbers, 22, 23, 24, 25.

After the payment made on 29 May 1834, Dr. Kidd sent a most interesting letter (dated 30 May 1834) to the engraver, Havell:

> As an admirer of Mr. Audubon's enterprising spirit, Dr. Kidd is desirous that the present work on the Birds of America should answer expectations that have been formed of it—he therefore takes the liberty of requesting Mr. Havell to let him know, as far as it is in his power, what will be the plan on which the remaining 105 plates will be published [Audubon's original plan had been to publish only 400 plates]: for if the present plan be continued Dr. Kidd will be desirous of parting with the work at the best price he can obtain for it. The forgoing observation is not made from any dissatisfaction with the price of the individual numbers, for certainly that is moderate; but with the general character of the subjects selected & he thinks that the following statement will show that there is ground for that dissatisfaction, as it will be seen by the statement that, out of the six orders into which birds are commonly distributed, there has not yet been produced a single individual of the 5th & 6th orders; while of the 195 [194?] species that have been represented nearly three-fourths consist of small birds, such as larks & sparrows, which contribute but little to the beauty of the work and scarcely anything to its physiological utility.

Accipitres	Passeers	Scansores	Gallina	Grallae	Palmipeds
27	142	11	14		

[57]

Audubon, who was at the time in London, having returned early in May from a visit to America, answered the letter on 31 May, according to a notation to this effect on the original Kidd letter. The reply has not been located in the Christ Church archives. It is evident that Dr. Kidd must have been satisfied by Audubon's explanations, for the subscription was completed.

The 435 prints comprising this set are bound in eight volumes, not in numerical order but according to families, as set forth in Audubon's *Synopsis*.

OXFORD UNIVERSITY
Radcliffe Science Library

On the second day of his visit to Oxford in March 1828, Audubon had lunch with Dr. George Williams who subscribed to the *Birds of America* on behalf of the Radcliffe Science Library.[58] Dr. Williams (1762?-1834) was a graduate of Corpus Christi College, Oxford (1781). In 1788, after studying medicine at St. Bartholomew's Hospital, he received his medical degree. He returned to Oxford and, in 1789, was appointed Regius and Sherardian Professor of Botany. However, in 1810 he was appointed as the fourth Librarian of the Radcliffe Library, a position he held until his death in 1834. He was the first physician to hold the office, and under him the library's holdings were devoted mainly to medical books. He was succeeded by Dr. John Kidd.[59]

After lunching with Dr. Williams, Audubon went with him to the Radcliffe Library to inspect the first number of the *Birds of America*, which the Naturalist had brought. The inspection was not a happy one. "When I saw it [the first five plates]," Audubon stated in his journal, "it drew a sigh from my heart. Ah! Mr. Lizars! was this the way to use a man who paid so amply and so punctually? I rolled it up and took it away with me, for it was hardly coloured at all, and have sent a fair new set of five numbers."[60] The prints are bound according to families as represented in Audubon's *Synopsis*, the first volume beginning with plate 426, the "California Vulture."

PAISLEY PUBLIC LIBRARY
Corporation of Paisley, Scotland

The Paisley Library was built in 1871 with funds supplied by Sir Peter Coats (1808-1890) of the Cotton Thread Mills of Paisley. It was he who gave to the Reference Library, among other gifts, the Double Elephant folio set of the *Birds of America* and the five volumes of the *Ornithological Biography* along with it.[61]

Andrew Coats (1814-1900), a brother of Sir Peter, went to America in 1839 where he later became the American agent for the thread business which his brothers James, Peter, and Thomas were building up in Paisley. It was during his stay in America that he changed the spelling of his name from "Coats" to "Coates." He left America in 1860 and spent five years in Glasgow before moving to Pitcullen House in Perth and, until 1878, he continued as an agent for Messrs. J. and P. Coats. He died in 1900.[62]

While in America Andrew Coates had visited Audubon at his home and later wrote an account of this visit, entitled "Personal Reminiscences of Audubon," which was printed in the *Proceedings* of the Perthshire Society of Natural Science.[63] Coates wrote that in the spring of 1843 he paid a visit "to the family of Mr. Audubon, whose country residence was in New York State, not far from New York City." He went on to say that "it was only after reaching the house that I learned we had chosen a very trying time for the family, because on the following morning, Mr. Audubon was to take his departure for the Rocky Mountains, on his last excursion in pursuit of his favorite study."

After a description of the house surrounded by "grassy parks and natural wooding" and of the family circle of three generations, he mentioned that, "In the course of conversation with different members of the family I got many interesting particulars bearing on the preparation of Audubon's great work, The Birds of America." Coates was told by the Naturalist's sons, who, he observed, had taken charge of the publication, that there "now only remained three copies unsold. One copy they kept for themselves, but that, they told me was an expensive luxury which they meant to part with. I afterwards purchased the whole three copies, one for myself and the others for my two brothers in Paisley. One of these was afterwards presented to the Paisley Free Library where it now is."[64] Coates made the additional interesting observation regarding one of the folios purchased by him, "My own copy possesses two advantages over the other copies. First, it is engraved on very much thicker paper; and, second, Mr. Victor Audubon informed me that it was the only copy of which the colouring had been touched up by his own hand."[65]

The visit to the Audubon family recorded by Coates was made early in March 1843, for on the 11th of that month the Naturalist left New York en route to the West.[66]

To return to the alleged statement of the sons, made on the day of the Coates visit, that, in addition to the family copy, there were but three sets left, *all* of which were subsequently purchased by Coates: from an entry in Ledger "B," it would appear that there were fifteen bound sets brought to America upon the completion of the engraving, as well as a quantity of loose prints.

The purchasers of many of these fifteen sets have been ascertained in the process of tracking down the extant sets of the folio. The evidence is clear that these include the following, sold after the visit of Coates to the Audubon home: Union College, July 1844 (*see* p. 313); the City of New York, 1850 (*see* p. 243); and the State Department, for Japan, 1852 (*see* p. 189).

When the first ten prints of the folio in the Paisley Library were examined, it was found that the legends were of an early state, the prints having been struck on paper with Whatman watermarks of 1827. It is difficult to understand how a set of the folio purchased from the Audubon family as late as 1843 would have prints of the first ten plates with an 1827 watermark.

Finally, additional information concerning the Coates Audubon sets has come to light. The last set of an Audubon folio purchased by Dr. A. S. W. Rosenbach, the rare-book dealer, was from the Coates family of Scotland in about 1931. This was a magnificent copy in contemporary binding and one of the three copies printed on heavy paper. The folio was sold to a Boston architect, then resold to a New York bookdealer who broke it up.[67] It is not known from what member of the Coates family Rosenbach purchased the folio, but the reference to the "thick" paper would indicate that it was the copy which Andrew had retained for himself.

DUKE OF PORTLAND
Welbeck Abbey, Workshop, Nottingham, England

It is believed by Francis Needham, formerly librarian at Welbeck Abbey, that the folio of Audubon prints was probably acquired by the fourth, William Henry (1768–1854), or fifth, William John (1800–1879), Duke of Portland, but certainly bound for the latter, as he had a great liking for good bindings and a taste for floral and bird prints.[68]

The prints have been beautifully bound in red morocco with considerable gold tooling, gold-edged all around. There are, in addition, green leather patches for titles.

The first ten prints are from the very earliest state of the plates, with Whatman watermarks of 1826 and 1827. Plate 2, the "Yellow-billed Cuckoo" shows the erasure for correction.

THE ROYAL LIBRARY
Windsor Castle, Windsor, England

The 435 plates of Audubon's *Birds of America* in the Royal Library at Windsor Castle are assembled in four volumes, each bound in half-leather, the back tooled in gold and blind, with Queen Victoria's cipher stamped in gold on the top panel.

The style of tooling is in the Georgian tradition, and the inference is that the plates were acquired for the Royal Library on publication and then bound up early in Queen Victoria's reign, although, in the absence of documentary evidence, no certain statement can be made.[69] The four volumes of the folio as well as the accompanying five volumes of the *Ornithological Biography* were bound by J. Mackensie, believed to have been a London bookbinder.[70] An indication of the date of binding is obtained from the flyleaf, in all four volumes, which consists of J. Whatman Turkey Mill paper watermarked 1843.

There is also in the Royal Library a copy of the Octavo edition of the *Birds of America* as well as a copy of *The Quadrupeds of America*. These were both sent by the British Foreign Office to J. H. Glover, Deputy Librarian at Windsor, accompanied by a letter, dated 16 May 1857, which reads as follows:

> The President of the United States [James Buchanan] having presented to Her Majesty's Government two copies of a work recently published under the auspices of the American Government, viz "The Birds of America" and "The Quadrupeds of America", I am directed by the Earl of Clarendon to forward to you one of these copies, to be deposited in the Library of Buckingham Palace.

Although the details are lacking, it has been determined that in 1856 the Congress of the United States of America was prevailed upon to purchase 100 copies of the Octavo edition of the *Birds of America* and 100 copies of the *Quadrupeds of North America*. The pertinent provision of the act reads as follows:

> To enable the Secretary of State [Lewis Cass] to purchase one hundred copies, each, of Audubon's "Birds of America" and "Quadrupeds of North America," for presentation to Foreign Governments, in return for valuable works sent by them to the government of the United States, sixteen thousand dollars.[71]

It was on 23 August 1856 that Victor Gifford Audubon was requested by J. A. Thomas, Assistant Secretary of State, to furnish these copies for which Congress had made the above appropriation.[72]

In June 1937, while the author was checking the Auduboniana at the Österreichische National-Bibliotek in Vienna, the copy of the Octavo edition sent to the Austrian government was seen.

UNIVERSITY OF EDINBURGH
Old College

Audubon, in a letter written in Edinburgh on 21 December 1826 to his wife in America, reported that, "It is now a month since my work has been begun by Mr. W. H. Lizars of this city. . . . Two of my plates were finished last week—some of the engravings colored and now put up in my Exhibition Rooms and are truly beautiful. I think that by the middle of January the first number will be completed and under way to each subscriber."[73] In this letter also was the optimistic comment, "The University of Edinburgh having subscribed I look to the rest of them 11 in number to follow."[74] The subscription of the University of Edinburgh is shown as number 9 on Audubon's final list of European subscribers.[75]

The 435 plates in the four volumes of this folio are bound, not in numerical order but by families, in accordance with Audubon's *Synopsis of the Birds of North America*, published by him in 1839 upon completion of the engraving of the "Large Work." Hence, the first plate in Volume 1 of this set is the "California Vulture, Cathartes Californianus," plate 426.

VICTORIA AND ALBERT MUSEUM
South Kensington, London

This set of Audubon's *Birds of America* is bound in eight parts, as follows:

Volume	Part	Plates
1	1	1–50
1	2	51–100
2	1	101–150
2	2	151–200
3	1	201–250
3	2	251–300
4	1	301–365
4	2	366–435.

The prints were received in 1868 as part of the bequest from the estate of the Reverend Chauncey Hare Townshend.[76] It is believed that the prints were bound about 1950.

When this set was examined, it was found that the first ten prints were struck from the original Lizars engravings and that nine have Whatman watermarks of 1827, the tenth that of 1826. When and how Townshend obtained the set could not be ascertained, for he is not included by Audubon among the European subscribers, nor is his name on the original subscription list. However, the evidence of the early states of the first ten plates indicates that the Naturalist must have obtained the subscription in the early days of the engraving of the work.

Chauncey Hare Townshend, born on 20 April 1798, was the only son of Henry Hare Townsend (the son changed the spelling of his name in 1835). The family estates were at Downhills, Tottenham, Bushbridge Hall, Godalming and at Walpole, Norfolk. He was educated at Eton, and at Trinity Hall, Cambridge, which granted him the Bachelor of Arts degree in 1821 and the Master of Arts degree in 1824. Townshend also took holy orders, but shortly thereafter illness disabled him, preventing active pursuit of his profession. He married Eliza Frances Norcott in May 1826, but left no issue.

A man of many talents and interests, Townshend wrote and had published some volumes of poetry, as well as a book about travel in Scotland and two on mesmerism. His religious writings were published posthumously by Charles Dickens, his friend and literary executor.[77] Townshend spent much of his time in travel and in collecting gems, cameos, coins, and pictures. Also, he was himself adept at drawing and painting. He died on 25 February 1868, bequeathing "his collections of precious stones, coins, and cameos, and such of his pictures, watercolours, and drawings as might be selected, to the South Kensington Museum [now the Victoria and Albert Museum]."[78]

28

PROVENANCES OF SETS IN OTHER COUNTRIES

AUSTRALIA
STATE LIBRARY OF VICTORIA
Melbourne, Victoria

This set of the folio was purchased by the library from one William Stallard, a schoolmaster of Geelong, Victoria. Stallard had come to Geelong in 1867 from the mining town of Ballarat, Victoria, where he had been principal of a grammar school, or "commercial academy" in Doveton Street, in 1857.[1]

Upon his arrival in Geelong, Stallard opened a commercial academy at the corner of Victoria Terrace and La Trobe Terrace. In 1869 he moved the school to Fairfield Hall, at the corner of Myer Street and Bourke Crescent, Geelong, renaming it "The Western College." This was his address when he offered the folio to the trustees of the Public Library of Victoria for £200.[2] The trustees offered him £100, which he accepted in February 1871.[3]

Nothing further is known of Stallard, who disappeared from Victoria directories shortly after that date. Since his name does not appear in the directories of other Australian states, it is possible that he left Australia about this time.[4]

The library also has the first four of the five volumes of the *Ornithological Biography* which were presented to it by William Stallard on 10 June 1872. This is obviously the same William Stallard from whom the *Birds of America* was purchased, which suggests that he may still have been residing somewhere in Victoria.[5]

DENMARK
UNIVERSITY OF COPENHAGEN
Scientific Library, Copenhagen

Johan Frederick Classen (1725–1792), titular Major-General, was born in Kristiania (now Oslo), Norway, and graduated from the University of Copenhagen in 1744 as a parson. Parsonage life held no attraction for young Classen, who turned to business and amassed a great fortune in the large-scale manufacture of gunpowder and cannons.[6]

A bequest in his will founded the Classen Foundation, Det Classenske Fideikommis, which had at its disposal an interest-bearing capital of several million kroner and other assets, including real estate. In addition, the will stipulated that the public should be admitted to and have the use of the testator's library. In 1867 the Classen library, which possessed this set of the folio, was united with the library at the University of Copenhagen.[7]

Inquiry was made at the University Library and by them at the offices of Det Classenske Fideikommis, but no information was available as to the purchase date of the folio.[8]

When the folio was examined, there was discovered on the back of plate 315 the notation "for P. Jackson, Esq. Boston." Also on the back of this print was the name "James Brown," which was crossed out.

Patrick Tracy Jackson (1780–1847) was one of the Boston merchants whose subscriptions Audubon had obtained during his stay in that city in the winter and spring of 1832–1833. The subscription was incorrectly listed as "P. J. Jackson" in the final list of American subscribers.[9] The Naturalist received $250 in payment for the first volume when delivery, which had been delayed for some unaccountable reason, was finally made.[10] Jackson had at one time been a man of considerable wealth, but due to losses resulting from a severe fire in Boston and a financial panic, his own financial situation became desperate, at which time the folio probably was sold.[11]

James Brown, whose name was crossed out, was another of the Boston subscribers. It has not been possible to determine why his name had been written on the back of the print and crossed off.

DEUTSCHE DEMOKRATISCHE REPUBLIK (EAST GERMANY) STAATLICHE MUSEEN
Meiningen

The story of this folio is to be found in an article included in the *Südthüringer Forschungen*, Heft 2/66, hrsg. Staatliche Museen Meiningen (Meiningen, 1967), Ludwig Baege of Erfurt, East Germany, brought to the attention of the author by Dr. Claus Nissen of Mainz.

From information contained in the article by Dr. Baege, it appears that the folio was originally obtained by Bernhard Ehrich Freund-Herzog von Sachsen-Meiningen (Duke Bernhard II), who was born in 1800 and died in 1882. The Meiningen ducal library, either during or after World War II, was packed up by the invading army of some foreign power and has not been located since. Only a few books, including the Audubon folio, remained and have been integrated into the Meiningen Museum Library.

The folio has one defect, namely that 11 of the 435 plates of the collection are missing. These are plates 106, 131 to 135, and 166 to 170. The first ten plates bear the early legends and are printed on Whatman paper with watermarks of 1826 or 1827.

FRANCE
BIBLIOTHÈQUE DE L'INSTITUT DE FRANCE
Paris

No information was available as to the provenance of this set. The first ten prints, all examples of an early state of the legends, have the Whatman Turkey Mill watermark of 1827.

The first four hundred prints of this folio have been bound as follows:

> Plates 1 to 200 in Volumes 1 and 2, both bound together
> Plates 201 to 400 in Volumes 3 and 4, again bound together
> The final thirty-five prints, Plates 401 to 435, are loose in a portfolio.

MUSÉUM NATIONAL D'HISTOIRE NATURELLE
Bibliothèque Centrale, Paris

The prints of this folio, all of which are in excellent condition, are bound in four volumes. The first ten plates have a Whatman Turkey Mill watermark of 1834. No definite information was located regarding the provenance of the set. However, it is believed the folio may have been acquired at the time of publication, but whether at the expense of the museum or under the subscription of the Minister of the Interior is not known.[12]

IRELAND (EIRE)
JOHN GALVIN
Loughlinstown House, County Dublin

This folio was sold at auction at Sotheby's on 12 June 1935, when the description of the set was given as follows:

> Audubon, Birds of America. 4 Volumes in 5, engraved titles and 435 plts. eng. printed and coloured by R. Havell and W. H. Lizars. plts 1–5 original imp. by Lizars, Nos. 6–10, retouched by Havell with his & Lizars imprints.

51 of the small plts. in Vol. 1 inlaid, imprints cut into on plate 68 & 79 and cut from pl. 3, bottom line of imprint on pl. 6. (Great American Hen) shaved, pl. 21 torn and mended, hf. Russia, rubbed, joints weak, gt. (25 5/8" × 22 1/16") f. 1827–38.

Sotheby June 12, 1935 (472) F. F. Fox Esq. Edwards. £3,700.

To obtain the page-size of 25⅝ inches by 22 1/16 inches, the large double elephant-size paper (39½" × 26½"), in the instance of the large plates, was folded and pasted on stubs. The small plates were cut down and inlaid with about a three-inch margin. All five volumes carry the bookplate of Francis Frederick Fox.

Audubon listed two subscribers by the name of Fox. These were "Charles Fox, Esq., Perair, near Truro, England," and "George Lane Fox, Esq., Yorkshire" (numbers 67 and 68, respectively, in the final list of European subscribers).[13] It has not been possible to find a link between Francis Frederick Fox of Yate House, Gloucestershire, whose books were sold at Sotheby's in 1935, and either of the two subscribers with the same surname listed by Audubon.

The folio was purchased by Galvin in 1966.

ITALY

BIBLIOTECA NAZIONALE CENTRALE
Florence

On 23 December 1828 Audubon wrote his wife from London that on the following Saturday he was to dine with an envoy of the Grand Duke of Tuscany and that he hoped to procure his name for the list of subscribers.[14] However, it was not until 22 July 1834 that a subscription materialized.[15] Judging from the Audubon-Bonaparte correspondence, it is possible that the latter may have exerted his influence toward the procurement of this subscription.[16] With the subscription (in the final list of European subscribers published by Audubon in Volume 5 of the *Ornithological Biography:* "71. His Royal and Imperial Highness the Duke of Tuscany, &c, &c, &c.") the Naturalist received a payment of £95 for the first two volumes which had been shipped to the duke.[17]

The folio had been kept for many years in the lower recesses of the Biblioteca Nazionale Centrale in Florence (Firenze).[18] In the flood which ravaged Florence in November 1966, the storage area in which the folio was located was inundated. As of early April 1967, the volumes which were ruined had not as yet been returned from restoration, nor was the date foreseen when they would again be available to the public.[19]

Provenances of Sets in Other Countries

THE NETHERLANDS
BIBLIOTHEEK VAN TEYLER'S STICHTING
Haarlem

Early in October 1832, the Naturalist's older son, Victor Gifford Audubon, had gone to England where he was to supervise the engraving of the *Birds of America* while his father remained in America to solicit subscriptions and to draw additional birds.[20]

During the summer of 1833 Victor visited the Continent and obtained the subscription of Teyler's Stichting Bibliotheek,[21] which appears in the final list of European subscribers as "65. Haarlem Library, Holland."[22] The subscription was obtained by Victor on 25 August 1833, according to the receipt he gave to the librarian, Martinus van Marum, for the first volume.[23] An entry in Audubon's Ledger "B" records this payment as £42-0-0.

Martinus van Marum (1750–1837) was both the first director of the museum as well as the first librarian of the Teyler's Stichting, from its inception in 1784 until his death in 1837. He was a member of Teyler's Tweede Genootschap (Second Learned Society), and was, from 1790 to 1837, Secretary of the Dutch Society of Sciences at Haarlem.[24]

The prints comprising this folio have been bound in five volumes, with a hundred plates in each of the first four, the remaining thirty-five in the fifth.

NORTHERN IRELAND
LORD CALEDON
Sixth Earl, Caledon Castle, Caledon, Tyrone

In a letter written on 7 November 1842 from New York to Dr. Benjamin Phillips in London, Audubon recounted that he had been on a trip to Canada and that while "At Quebec I sold a copy of our large Work to the Earl of Caledon who also subscribed to the Quadrupeds."[25] Dr. Phillips had been the Audubon family physician and had treated Lucy during her illness in the last year of the stay in England. The families had been neighbors on Wimpole Street in London and the doctor had been one of Audubon's subscribers.

A record of the sale of the Caledon folio is also found in the journal the Naturalist kept during his Canadian trip. Entries dated Quebec, 26 and 27 September 1842, noted both the details of the delivery of the "Large Work" and the purchase of a draft for $1,000 in payment for the Caledon folio which was sent to Victor Audubon in New York.[26]

Lord Caledon (1812–1851) had succeeded to the title in 1839 and, as the third Earl, was a captain in the Coldstream Guards. He died in 1855.

When inquiry was made in 1960 regarding the folio, the fifth Earl of Caledon, a grandson of the original owner of the folio, wrote that at the time there was no folio at Caledon Castle and that he had never seen any among the family possessions.[27]

However, some years later an American bookdealer[28] learned that the folio was still in the possession of the family, namely the sixth Earl of Caledon (1920–   ), who had succeeded his uncle to the title in 1968. The folio was seen in July 1969 by Walter Armytage. Upon examination, it was found that the first ten plates have late watermarks, namely 1836 and 1838, and also that the binding is "½ drab boards," both facts evidence that the folio was one which had been sent to America after the completion of the engraving.[29]

PORTUGAL
BIBLIOTECA NAÇIONAL DE LISBÕA
Lisbon

This is another set of the folio in which the first ten plates have the early state of the legends and watermarks. The prints are bound in four volumes, with the binding in poor condition. All 435 prints are on linen hinges at the back. The binding appears to have been done in Portugal, for the broken top panel in Volume 4 shows Portuguese printing underneath.

No information was available as to how and when the folio was obtained. It is well to point out that King Carlos I (1863–1908) had been a student of ornithology and published *Catalgo ilustrado das aves de Portugal*. It is highly probable that the folio was purchased during his reign.[30]

In Volume 2, plates 102, 130, and 193 are missing.

UNION OF SOVIET SOCIALIST REPUBLICS
DARWIN MUSEUM
Moscow

The 435 prints of this set of the Audubon folio have never been bound. All are double-elephant size, 39 1/2 inches by 26 1/2 inches, untrimmed. They are kept in four portfolios, all the same, each with a brown leather spine, leather corners, and fastened with four leather strips and buckles.

When the first ten plates were examined it was found that plate 2 bore the legend, "Black-billed Cuckoo—Coccyzus Erythropthalmus." This then is the uncorrected version of a very early printing, since the species is actually the "Yellow-billed Cuckoo."

The director of the Museum, Madam Ignatieva Vera, was unable to furnish any history of the set, although it is believed the folio may have been obtained by Professor A. Kohts, a former head of the museum. In connection with this folio and the one at the Institute of Zoology, Leningrad, the following is of interest:

Provenances of Sets in Other Countries

The Audubon folio at Amherst College, Amherst, Mass., (*see* in chap. 26) was presented to that institution by Mr. Herbert L. Pratt who had obtained it from the English dealer, Bernard Quaritch.

The transaction is referred to in a letter dated 20 November 1915, written to Mr. Pratt by Quaritch.[31] In this letter Mr. Pratt is informed that, "I had another uncut copy, now in Russia, but its condition is not so good as yours, but with title pages and some six or eight plates with repaired margins." To which of the Russian sets Quaritch is referring is not known.

STATE LIBRARY

(Saltykov-Schedrin State Public Library)

Leningrad

On a page (p. 87) torn from an Audubon ledger or daybook, in possession of the Audubon Museum at Henderson, Kentucky, there was recorded the following:

July 7, 1840—set per Handry—Car.—for Boston
        1. Copy of the LARGE WORK
        1. Set of Biography
        1. Synopsis
       12. Nos. Little work.
in a box marked à *Sa Majésté Impériale* au départment des relations interieure du Ministère des Affaires Étrangères St. Petersbourg pr/ La Barque Razan—care of C. E. Hatitch, Esq. Swedish Consul 70 State Street, Boston.[32]

In 1840, when the shipment of the folio of the *Birds of America* and other Auduboniana was sent to St. Petersburg, Nicholas I (1796–1855) was Emperor of Russia. It is possible that he may have seen and examined a set of the folio when he visited England at some time during Audubon's stay.[33]

A reference to the shipment of the folio to the emperor has been found in a letter written by Audubon from New York to his son Victor on 25 January 1841: "Not a word from Russia, and I will write Mr. Poinsett on the subject as I have no faith in the consul here."[34]

The prints of the folio are bound in four volumes. A small blue spot on the spine of each volume, on which there is a call number, indicates that the folio belonged to the emperor's foreign collection in the Hermitage library. There is also in each volume an elongated octagonal stamp, the English translation of which further identifies the folio as "No. 11./The Emperor's Hermitage/Foreign Library/Case No. 5/Shelf 1." The 1836 watermarks of the first ten prints and of the title page of Volume 3 indicate that this folio was among those on hand which were taken to America when the engraving of the plates was completed in 1838.

While visiting Washington, D.C., in March 1830 Audubon had met Baron Krudener, the Russian Envoy to the United States (from 1827–1838), but the subscription did not materialize at that time.[35]

ZOOLOGICAL INSTITUTE
Academy of Sciences, Leningrad

This folio is composed of individual loose prints which are untrimmed and of the full double-elephant size, 39 1/2 inches by 26 1/2 inches. Two of the 435 plates are missing, plate 12, the "Baltimore Oriole," and plate 204, the "Salt Water Marsh Hen."[36] The prints are stored in four portfolios. The legends of the first ten plates are of the earliest state and their Whatman watermarks are dated 1827.

Professor A. I. Ivanov, Curator of Birds, Zoological Institute, Academy of Sciences, Leningrad, who kindly arranged for the author and his wife to examine the prints, believes that they came into the possession of the institute in approximately 1860.

APPENDIXES

A

THE OCTAVO EDITION

In September 1839, with his return to America, Audubon immediately plunged into the work of publishing the "Small Work," or Octavo edition of the *Birds of America*. It was published in Philadelphia under the names of John J. Audubon and J. B. Chevalier. The lithographing and coloring of the prints was done by J. T. Bowen, and the printing of the letterpress was the work of E. G. Dorsey, also of Philadelphia.

That the work progressed rapidly we know, for as early as October 1839 payments were made to Chevalier, and in November to J. & J. Burke of Philadelphia for 20 reams of paper. By 13 December 100 copies of the first number had been delivered to Victor Audubon.[1] On 16 December the printer, Dorsey, was paid $30.27 for printing 1200 copies of Number 1.[2]

The work was issued in 100 parts, in paper covers (blue or gray, 11 by 7 inches), each with 5 lithographed, colored plates. The parts sold for $1 each. A total of 500 plates represented a complete set. It is believed that the work of reducing the size of the plates was accomplished by means of a camera lucida. In the letterpress which accompanied the reproduction of the birds, the nomenclature is made to conform to the Synopsis which Audubon completed in early 1839 before leaving England. When the work was completed in 1844, the parts were bound in 7 volumes, as follows:

Volume	Parts	Plates	Pages	Year of Publication
1	1–14	1–70	i–viii, 9–256	1840
2	15–28	71–140	" 9–206	1841
3	29–42	141–210	" 9–236	1841
4	43–56	211–280	" 9–324	1842
5	57–70	281–350	" 9–348	1842
6	71–84	351–420	" 9–460	1843
7	85–100	421–500	i–x, 9(11)–474	1844

APPENDIX A

The number of complete sets of all 500 plates published is not known. Some idea of the popularity of the work is obtained from the list of subscribers whose names were listed at intervals on the inside covers of some of the parts. When the seven volumes were published, these names appeared either in the front or in the back of each volume. A total of 1199 subscribers has been found by checking these names. Complete sets of the Octavo edition in parts are now exceedingly rare; the author knows of only two. The seven volumes are seldom offered by rare book dealers and then at a price in excess of $5,000.

B

THE BIEN
CHROMOLITHOGRAPH
EDITION

In 1858 or 1859 John Woodhouse Audubon entered upon an ambitious project, that of reproducing the *Birds of America* at one-half the original price, from the copper plates transferred to stone. Every plate was to be colored from the original drawings. The work was to be issued in forty-five numbers, forty-four of plates and one of text. Printed on seven double-elephant sheets, of the best quality for the purpose, 27 by 40 inches, each number was to contain two large plates, each occupying a whole sheet; two of medium size, each also occupying an entire sheet; and six of the smaller size, two on a sheet.

The text was to be properly and scientifically classified so that, when the work was completed, the plates could be placed and bound corresponding with the order of text, in either three or four volumes.[1]

However the work was never completed, and only one volume containing 15 numbers of 105 double-elephant plates with 150 species was issued. The outbreak of the Civil War, aided, it is believed, by unscrupulous dealings of business partners, resulted in disaster. The publication had been attempted in association with Messrs Roe Lockwood & Son, New York, and the lithographers J. Bien & Company also of New York.[2]

The lithographer, Julius Bien (1826–1909), was born at Naumberg (near Cassell), Germany. He took part in the Revolution of 1848, one of the group of notable men brought to the United States by that cataclysm. He will be remembered also as the first great scientific cartographer in the United States. During the presidency of Pierce he produced maps of the new surveys of the West. His engravings and lithographs were of the highest quality.[3]

No copy of a prospectus prepared for American subscribers has been located. The one issued for English subscribers stated that the price of each number was to be £ 2 8s., or roughly $11. The forty-five numbers were to be issued for approximately $500, a price which was, as stated in the prospectus, half of $1,000, the price of the original work. The paper used for the publication does not have a watermark.

APPENDIX B

The personal fortunes of Mrs. Audubon were seriously affected by the failure of her son's attempt to reproduce the *Birds of America*. Her older son died in 1859 and the younger died in 1862, within two years after the failure of the publication. It became necessary for the mother to raise funds in the only way left open to her, namely to try to dispose of the original drawings and the copper plates of the *Birds of America*. The original drawings she was able to sell to the New-York Historical Society in 1863 for $4,000.

On 19 October 1864, when she was in her 76th year, she wrote to Professor Joseph Henry, the first director of the Smithsonian Institution in Washington, in the hope that he might be able to help her sell the copper plates. In the letter the sale of the drawings is touched upon:

> The sale was a sacrifice both of the Drawings and my feelings, and cruelly to state nearly the whole of the proceeds past from me soon, for the claims on notes I had indorsed for my unfortunate sons. Now I have the *Copper Plates* entire of the "Birds of America" which I chiefly depend on for the support of myself and orphan grand daughter.[4]

She was not able to sell the copper plates and most of them were melted. (See Appendix G, "The Copper Plates.")

There is no way of knowing how many copies of the one-volume Bien Chromolithograph edition were published. During the Audubon research 49 copies were located. (See list below.[6])

In 1963 a Massachusetts public library sold a copy for $2,100,[5] and this writer knows of a copy sold to a collector about the same time for $3,000. Individual prints when offered, which is rare, are priced from $30 to $500, the latter price being that asked for the "Wild Turkey."

CHROMOLITHOGRAPH PLATES

Page	No.	Plate	
1	1–	1	Wild Turkey
2	1–	2	Virginia Partridge
3	1–	3	Dusky Duck
4	1–	4	Purple Grakle or Common Crow Blackbird
5	1–	5	Towhe Bunting
	1–	6	Song Sparrow
6	1–	7	Kentucky Warbler
	1–	8	Children's Warbler
7	1–	9	Sea-side Finch
	1–	10	Grass Finch or Bay-winged Bunting
8	2–	1	Mallard Duck
9	2–	2	White headed Eagle
10	2–	3	Yellow-billed Cuckoo
11	2–	4	Blue Jay

The Bien Chromolithograph Edition

Page 12	No. 2– Plate 5	Crested Purple Finch
	2– 6	Pine Grosbeak
13	2– 7	Wood Thrush
	2– 8	Hermit Thrush
14	2– 9	Ruby crowned Wren
	2– 10	American Golden-crested Wren
15	3– 1	American Crow
16	3– 2	Mocking Bird
17	3– 3	Rose-breasted Grosbeak
18	3– 4	Blue Grosbeak
19	3– 5	Bohemian Chatterer
	3– 6	Cedar Bird
20	3– 7	Carolina Titmouse
	3– 8	Hudson's Bay Titmouse
21	3– 9	Marsh Wren
	3– 10	Nuttall's lesser-marsh Wren
22	4– 1	Pinnated Grouse
23	4– 2	Black-Winged Hawk
24	4– 3	Boat-tailed Grackle
25	4– 4	Orchard Oriole
26	4– 5	Arctic Tern
	4– 6	Sandwich Tern
27	4– 7	Bachman's Warbler
	4– 8	Swainson's Warbler
28	4– 9	Azure Warbler
	4– 10	Nashville Warbler
29	5– 1	Summer or Wood Duck
30	5– 2	Reddish Egret
31	5– 3	Belted Kingfisher
32	5– 4	Purple Martin
33	5– 5	Red backed Sandpiper
	5– 6	Pectoral Sandpiper
34	5– 7	Least Water-hen
	5– 8	Yellow-breasted Rail
35	5– 9	Yellow poll Warbler
	5– 10	Rathbone Warbler
36	6– 1	Great White Heron
37	6– 2	Eider Duck
38	6– 3	Green Heron
39	6– 4	Crested Grebe
40	6– 5	Buff breasted Sandpiper
	6– 6	Little Sandpiper
41	6– 7	Barn Swallow
	6– 8	Republican or Cliff Swallow
42	6– 9	Canada Warbler
	6– 10	Bonaparte's Flycatcher
43	7– 1	Carolina Parrot
44	7– 2	Pileated Woodpecker

APPENDIX B

Page 45	No. 7–	Plate 3	Night Hawk
46	7–	4	Rusty Grakle
47	7–	5	White-bellied Swallow
	7–	5*	American Swift
48	7–	6	Carbonated Warbler
	7–	6	Yellow red poll Warbler
49	7–	7	Wood Wren
	7–	7	Winter Wren Rock Wren
50	8–	1	American Flamingo
51	8–	2	Great Auk
52	8–	3	Red-headed Duck
53	8–	4	White Headed Pigeon
54	8–	5	Columbian Humming Bird
	8–	6	Mango Humming Bird
55	8–	7	Black-throated Blue Warbler
	8–	7*	Blue-grey Flycatcher
56	8–	7	Forked-tailed Flycatcher
	8–	8	Tyrant Fly-catcher
57	9–	1	Night Heron or Qua bird
58	9–	2	Red-tailed Hawk
59	9–	3	Gadwall Duck
60	9–	4	Smew or White Nun
61	9–	5	Lincoln Finch
	9–	6	Henslow's Bunting
62	9–	7	Yellow Shank
	9–	8	Greenshank
63	9–	9	Razor billed Auk
	9–	10	Puffin
64	10–	1	Fish Hawk or Osprey
65	10–	2	Fish Crow
66	10–	3	Black Skimmer or Shearwater
67	10–	4	Yellow-breasted chat
68	10–	5	White-crowned Sparrow
	10–	6	White throated Sparrow
69	10–	7	Olive sided Flycatcher
	10–	8	Great Crested Flycatcher
70	10–	9	Semipalmated Sandpiper
	10–	10	Curlew Sandpiper
71	11–	1	Barn Owl
72	11–	2	Ferruginous Thrush
73	11–	3	Pigeon Hawk
74	11–	4	Common Crossbill
75	11–	5	Small Green Crested Flycatcher
	11–	6	Wood Pewee
76	11–	7	Black & Yellow Warbler
	11–	8	Bay-breasted Warbler

* Plates 6–10 in Number 7 and Plates 7–10 in Number 8 have been misnumbered in the Bien edition.

358

The Bien Chromolithograph Edition

Page	No.	Plate	
77	11–	9	Crested Titmouse
	11–	10	Black & White Creeper
78	12–	1	Brown Pelican
79	12–	2	Great-footed Hawk
80	12–	3	Golden-winged Woodpecker
81	12–	4	American Sparrow Hawk
82	12–	5	Spotted Sandpiper
	12–	6	Solitary Sandpiper
83	12–	7	Wilson's Fly Catcher
	12–	8	Yellow-throated Vireo
84	12–	9	Prairie Titlark
	12–	10	Brown Titlark
85	13–	1	Black Vulture or Carrion Crow
86	13–	2	Iceland or Jer Falcon
87	13–	3	Glossy Ibis
88	13–	4	Blue Crane or Heron
89	13–	5	Hooded Warbler
	13–	6	Green Black-capt Flycatcher
90	13–	7	Esquimaux Curlew
	13–	8	Great Marbled Godwit
91	13–	9	Sharp-tailed Finch
	13–	10	Mac Gillivray's Finch
92	14–	1	White-fronted Goose
93	14–	2	Ruffed Grouse
94	14–	3	Red winged Starling or Marsh blackbird
95	14–	4	Baltimore Oriole
96	14–	5	Pipiry Flycatcher
	14–	6	Arkansaw Flycatcher Swallow Tailed Flycatcher Says Flycatcher
97	14–	7	Bewick's Wren
	14–	8	House Wren
98	14–	9	Chipping Sparrow
	14–	10	Field Sparrow
99	15–	1	Canvas-backed Duck
100	15–	2	Yellow-crowned Heron
101	15–	3	Swallow-tailed Hawk
102	15–	4	Ruby-throated Humming Bird
103	15–	5	White-eyed Flycatcher or Vireo
	15–	6	Red-eyed Vireo
104	15–	7	Pine Creeping Warbler
	15–	8	Solitary Flycatcher or Vireo
105	15–	9	Ring-necked Duck
	15–	10	Scaup Duck

C

JOSEPH BARTHOLOMEW KIDD AND THE OIL PAINTINGS OF AUDUBON'S *BIRDS OF AMERICA*

According to the biography of John J. Audubon included by Maria R. Audubon in the first volume of *Audubon and His Journals*, an arrangement between Audubon and Kidd had been made during the winter of 1831 whereby Kidd was to copy some of the *Birds of America*, paint in backgrounds, sell them, and divide the proceeds. Eight were finished and sold immediately, but on 1 May 1831 the agreement was discontinued because Audubon became annoyed by Kidd's seeming lack of industry. It was Maria Audubon's belief that many of the paintings which had been ascribed to Audubon were those copies made by Kidd. According to her, the paintings all had been done on millboard, a material, however, which Audubon himself used, so that, as he rarely signed an oil painting, such millboard is no proof of identity one way or the other.[1] At the time the *Journals* were published, the Audubon family possessed only one oil painting signed by Audubon.[2]

It was in 1827, while Audubon was living in Edinburgh where Lizars was engraving the first number of the *Birds of America*, that he met Joseph Bartholomew Kidd. He first mentioned Kidd in his journal entry for 1 March 1827:

> Mr. Kidd the landscape artist breakfasted with me, and we talked painting for a long time. I admired him for his talents at so early a period of his life, he being only nineteen. What would I have been now if equally gifted by nature at that age? But sad reflection, I have been forced constantly to hammer and stammer as if in opposition to God's will, and so therefore am now but poor Audubon. I asked him to come to me daily to eat, drink and give me the pleasure of his company and advice. I told him my wish

---

The text of Appendix C is an adaptation of an earlier article written by Waldemar H. Fries, "Joseph Bartholomew Kidd and the Oil Paintings of Audubon's Birds of America," published in *Art Quarterly* 26, no.3:339–49 (Autumn 1963), and his letter to the editors of *Art Quarterly* 27, no.4:549–51 (Winter 1964).

was so intense to improve the delightful art of painting that I should begin a new picture to-morrow, and took down my portfolio to look for one of my drawings to copy in oil. He had never seen my work, and soon his bright eyes gazed eagerly on what he saw with admiration.[3]

Biographical information about Kidd is all too sparse. A painter of Scottish descent, he was born in 1808, probably in Edinburgh, and is thought to have been a pupil of the Rev. John Thomson of Duddingston. When the Royal Scottish Academy was founded in 1826, Kidd was elected one of the original associates, becoming an academician of that institution in 1829. He was engaged in painting and drawing in Edinburgh until about 1836, when he removed to London. There Kidd settled at Greenwich and established himself as a teacher of drawing, resigning from the Royal Scottish Academy in 1838. Greenwich was to be his residence until May 1889, when he died at the age of 81. His artistic endeavors consisted chiefly of paintings of the scenery of his native Scotland and a few etchings of highland views. Some of his works were engraved. Not long before his death he painted a portrait of Queen Victoria for the Royal Hospital Schools in Greenwich.[4] Since Kidd seems to have been an intimate friend of Sir Walter Scott, it is possible that Audubon first may have made his acquaintance when he visited Scott in Edinburgh during the winter of 1826–27.

Other references to Kidd appeared in the Naturalist's journal during the month of March, one of particular interest being that of the 22d, in which Audubon stated, "I paid young Kidd three guineas for his picture."[5] The next day's entry notes that "Young Kidd breakfasted with me."[6]

Audubon left Edinburgh shortly after this, but on 1 June 1827, while in London, he again met Kidd, quite unexpectedly.[7] Audubon mentioned him again in his journal entries for the 2d[8] and the 18th.[9] No other references to Kidd have been found in the published journals.

There are, however, references by other writers to the arrangement with Kidd. Francis H. Herrick in *Audubon the Naturalist* mentioned it in some detail, indicating that Audubon had entered into an agreement with Kidd to copy some of his drawings in oil on 31 March 1831, and quoted Audubon as saying: "It was our intention to send them to an exhibition for sale and divide the amount between us. He painted eight, and then I proposed, if he would paint one hundred engravings which composed my first volume of the Birds of America, I would pay him one hundred pounds."[10]

On 31 July 1831 Audubon, accompanied by his wife, sailed from Portsmouth, England, to America on the packet *Columbia*. In the month of July prior to his departure there had been sent to Kidd the following original drawings:

> July 15, 1831. Sent to Mr. J. B. Kidd of Edinburgh the following *ten* drawings to be painted in oil by him for one pound each: 1. Chuck wills Widow, Turtle Doves, Red headed Woodpeckers, Black billed Cuckoo, Pigeon Hawk, Golden

APPENDIX C

winged Woodpecker, Kings fisher, Orchard Oriole, purple Martin, Humming Birds and flowers.

July 29th, 1831. Sent the following drawings to Mr. Kidd, Edinburgh: 97 Mottled Owl, 87 florida Jay, 82 Whip poor Will, 72 Swallow tailed Hawk, 67 Red winged Starling, 62 Passenger pigeon, 57 Logger headed Shrike, 3 Prothonotary Warbler, 18 Bewicks Wren, 19 Louisiana Water thrush, 23 Maryland yellow throat, 24 Roscoes yellow throat, 25 Song Sparrow, 28 Solitary flycatcher, 29 Towee Bunting, 30 Vigors vireo, 33 American gold finch, 34 Worm eating Warbler, 35 Childrens Warbler, 38 Kentucky Warbler, 39 Crested titmouse, 40 American Red Start, 43 Cedar Bird, 44 Summer Red bird, 45 Traills flycatcher, 48 Cerulean Warbler, 49 blue green warbler, 50 Swainsons Warbler, 53 Painted bunting, 54 Rice Bunting 55 Cuviers wren, 58 Hermit thrush, 59 Chestnut sided Warbler, 60 Carbonated Warbler, 61 Great Horned Owl, 63 White eyed Flycatcher, 64 Swamp Sparrow, 65 Rathbones Warbler, 68 Republican Swallow, 69 Bay breasted warbler, 70 Henslows Bunting, 73 Wood thrush, 74 Indigo Bird, 75 Petite Corporal, 78 Great Carolina Wren, 79 Tyrant flycatcher, 80 Anthus pipiens, 83 house Wren, 84 Blue grey flycatcher, 85 yellow throated Warbler, 89 Nashville Warbler, 90 Black and White creeper, 93 Seaside finch, 94 Bay winged Bunting, 98 Marsh Wren, 99 Cowpen Bunting, 100 White Bellied green swallow, Autumnal Warbler, Blue eyed Warbler.[11]

The following article, written by Captain Thomas Brown (1785–1862), which appeared in the *Caledonian Mercury* in 1832, provides evidence that the agreement between Audubon and Kidd had not been discontinued on 1 May 1831:

About a year ago Audubon conceived the grand idea of a Natural History Gallery of Paintings, and entered into an agreement with Mr. Kidd to copy all his drawings of the same size, and in oil, leaving to the taste of that excellent artist to add such backgrounds as might give them a more pictorial effect. In the execution of such of these as Mr. Kidd has finished, he has not only preserved all the vivacious character of the originals, but he has greatly heightened their beauty, by the general tone and appropriate feeling which he has preserved and carried throughout his pictures.[12]

Again, in *Blackwood's Magazine* for 1831, John Wilson, in a review of Audubon's work, said: "It is expected that there will be completed by Audubon, Kidd and others,—Four Hundred Subjects . . . of which may the proceeds prove a moderate fortune!"[13] But the plans referred to by Captain Brown and Wilson either were deferred or circumvented, and a misunderstanding with Kidd finally terminated them in 1833. To fill in the additional details of this story of the relationship between Audubon and Kidd it is necessary to refer to Audubon's correspondence with his son Victor.

On 5 February 1833, while Audubon was in Boston, he wrote to Victor, then in London supervising the work of engraving the *Birds of America*, as follows: "Push Jos. B. Kidd of Edinburgh if he *can* be pushed to paint copies of our drawings. I look on that series as of great importance to all of us."[14] As Audubon had then been in America since September 1831, it would appear that Kidd may have been engaged in copying the Audubon drawings for a considerable time, perhaps since the agreement was entered into on 31 March 1831 (as related by Herrick). From that letter it is also evident that Audubon was finding the "Lack of industry" in Kidd's work, which Maria Audubon mentioned.

During the year there were other references to Kidd. On 15 April 1833, the Naturalist, again writing to Victor, commented, "As much as I would like to have J. B. Kidd with me for the purpose of painting backgrounds for the Water Birds (a thing which must be accomplished by someone) I cannot decide at present but will be guided by your complete answer to this, when I expect to be able to judge and know the actual number of our subscribers and standing of your cash account, including money due in England and in America—when this is the case, Mama will write you about Kidd."[15] (Mrs. Audubon had accompanied her husband to America. It should also be remembered that some years previously Audubon had received the help of George Lehman in the painting of some of the backgrounds of his land birds.)

On 9 September the Naturalist again mentioned Kidd in a letter written from New York: "Keep Kidd at work as much as possible and take away the paintings & Drawings whenever good opportunity offers—these would be better in your possession at any time."[16] That Audubon had really placed great store on the benefits which were to accrue from Kidd's work is known from another letter written to Victor, this time from Charleston, on 24 November 1833, "I long to hear that Kidd goes on with his task, for I truly believe that an exhibition of these Pictures in this Country would pay *Monstrously* well!"[17]

Early in December 1833, while Audubon was living with his friend John Bachman in Charleston, S.C., and painting the watercolors for the volume of waterbirds, he received two letters from Victor, one written on 18 October, the other on 28 October. These were referred to by Audubon in a long letter to Victor dated 24 December 1833. In a postscript to this letter, also dated 24 December, the Naturalist advised his son, "Respecting Kidd, and his prospectus, depend on it, nothing is to be feared from that quarter: that work *is dead at the moment I write*, and as to his publishing the intention of the pictures, it signifies nothing. All you have to do is to *take all* the pictures from him, by *goodwill or otherwise*, and *give him no more* originals to copy."[18]

The foregoing had seemed to be all the information available concerning the Audubon-Kidd relationship. However, the author, while engaged in the research leading to this present work, found additional interesting and pertinent facts related to the Kidd matter. There is on loan to the Audubon Museum at Henderson, Kentucky, Ledger "B" which had been used by Audubon to set down his transactions with the subscribers to the Double Elephant folio. On page 72 of this ledger is found the following entry:

APPENDIX C

1832—December	17—Cash of A. Hill per V. G. Audubon's order	f 14	£10–0–0
1833—February	9—A. Black. V. G. Audubon's order	f 9	50–0–0
	11—A. Hill per V. G. A.	f 20	10–0–0
	18—J. J. Audubon	f 21	33–0–0
April	9—My order on Hill	f 21	10–0–0
			£113–0–0

14—Henderson Row-Edinburgh

Contra

1833—February	18—33 Paintings delivered to John J. Audubon 1831 (11 April)		33–0–0
December	61 Paintings delivered to J. J. A.		61–0–0
1835—January	19—Exp. Paintings delivered J. J. A.		19–0–0
			£113–0–0

The information obtained from Audubon's own records is that there were received from Kidd 94 oil paintings for which Audubon paid £113, or approximately $565, at the rate of $5 per painting. Also, it is evident that the final delivery of paintings by Kidd was made in December 1833.

In the file of the Houghton Library at Harvard University there was located correspondence between Robert Havell, Audubon's engraver, and Victor G. Audubon, the son who was acting as agent in England while the Naturalist was absent on a trip to America.

On 24 January 1832, evidently in reply to a letter inquiring what progress he was making with the oil paintings of the *Birds of America*, Kidd wrote to Havell telling him that he had been busy with the approaching exhibition of Scottish artists in Edinburgh which had, "kept me back a good deal with Mr. Audubon's pictures but I will soon set to again with ten fold vigor." He also set down a list of those drawings "I am done with," and states further, "if they are those you require you can have them immediately." Following are the paintings listed, with plate numbers referring to the *Birds of America*:

Red-headed Woodpecker	*Plate* 27
Pigeon Hawk	92
Belted Kingfisher	77
Golden-winged Woodpecker	37
Chuck-Will's-Widow	52
Cuckoo	2 or 32
Orchard Oriole	42
Ruby-throated Humming Bird	47
Prothonotary Warbler	3
Swallows (Republican-Cliff)	68
Marsh Wren	98
Henslow's Bunting	70.[19]

Joseph Bartholomew Kidd

On 22 November 1832, Kidd wrote to Audubon, who was in America, "I completed the first series of your Pictures a considerable time ago and am busy with the second."[20] The first series of pictures here mentioned is undoubtedly the one referred to by Kidd in the letter written to Havell the previous January. That additional paintings were being sent to Kidd is known from the instructions included in a letter written by Victor Audubon to Havell on 19 February 1833: "I will thank you to send him as many of the drawings belonging to the second volume which he has not already painted."[21]

However, Kidd was unable to proceed actively with the work for reasons set forth at length in a letter, dated 4 April 1833, to Victor Audubon, in which he advised Victor that on 16 March, while he was attending the sale of Lord Elgin's pictures, "the floor gave way and about one hundred fifty individuals were precipitated into the flat below, many of them head first, for at least ten minutes after did material of which the floor was composed, together with furniture continue to fall, burying and suffocating in their ruins the unfortunate victims."[22] In all, three persons died as a result of the accident and Kidd was severely injured. He wrote further that he had finished ten paintings when the accident occurred and that now he hoped to set to work again as hard as ever. In addition, Kidd stated that "in my present dilemma I will require 15 or 16 pounds to pay my rent and other little expenses for which I am altogether unprepared. I must therefore ask you if you will have the kindness to me the very particular favor of sending 12 or 14 pounds." The bookkeeping entries already referred to show that on 9 April 1833, five days after the date of Kidd's letter, a payment of £10 was made to Kidd. Perhaps this was in answer to Kidd's request for assistance.

In the letter which Audubon had written to his son Victor on 24 December 1833, he had alluded to a prospectus of Kidd's, adding, "depend on it, nothing is to be feared from that quarter." This reference to a prospectus has been puzzling. However, definite information concerning the prospectus has been found in a letter to Victor Audubon which was written by Kidd on 4 October 1833.[23] The contents of that letter also explain why Audubon, some months later, instructed his son to "take all the pictures from him by *goodwill* or *otherwise*, and *give him no more* originals to copy." In this lengthy letter Kidd advised Victor:

> I am engaged in a work along with Sir Thomas Dick Lauder & Capt. T. Brown, author of "Anecdotes of Dogs & Horse." This work is entitled "*The Miscellany of Natural History.*"[24] The first volume will appear in a *fortnight*, the plates are all finished and the letter press is printing as hard as possible—the first volume treats of Parrots and contains 36 specimens—accompanied with a *portrait* of your Father's (beautifully engraved) and Memoir chiefly taken from your Father's own "Autobiography"—the portrait is from Syme's picture—but for further particulars see prospectus & specimens at Smith Elder & Co. publishers, London. The portrait will be finished in 2 or 3 days & I will have the proof sheets of the Memoir and letterpress by that time, which I will not fail to send you along with an impression of the portrait for your correction. I do not know what you will say to all this—but it, I must confess, was chiefly done by me. I

proposed that a portrait of your father in place of any defunct naturalist should embellish our work—it was agreed & here we are—my opinion is that it will add much to the fame of the American Ornithologist & we expect that the work will have a circulation of many thousands.

Since Victor's reply to Kidd's letter seems not to have been preserved, it is not known what he had "to say," but it may be assumed he was not pleased. That he wrote his father regarding Kidd's activities is known, for Audubon, in his letter written at Charleston on 24 December, noted the receipt of letters written by Victor on 18 and 28 October. The Naturalist was correct in his observation that "nothing is to be feared from that quarter, the work is dead at the moment I write," for *The Miscellany of Natural History, Vol. I—Parrots*, met with little success and no additional volumes of the *Miscellany* were published.

Over the years, oil paintings of the *Birds of America* have appeared in Audubon exhibitions and examples are known to be located in the National Gallery in Washington and the American Museum of Natural History, New York City. Edward H. Dwight, Director of the Museum of Art, Munson-Williams-Proctor Institute, Utica, New York, has located fifty-eight oil paintings of the *Birds of America*.

At the exhibition of Auduboniana, "The World of John James Audubon," held at Princeton University from 15 May to 30 September 1959, two oil paintings were shown, items 62, "Song Sparrow," and 63, "Nuthatches."[25] The song sparrow painting is an oil on cardboard, unsigned and undated. However, on the back of the board is written, "Painted by J. J. Audubon, certified by his elder granddaughter Lucy Audubon Williams." Howard C. Rice, Jr., then Assistant Librarian for Rare Books and Special Collections at Princeton University, under whose guidance this outstanding Audubon exhibition was organized, comments on the painting in part as follows: "A variant version in oils of Plate No. 25, Birds of America, with added landscape backgrounds showing distant mountains." After citing the "certification" by Audubon's granddaughter, Mr. Rice then raises the question of the Kidd copies.

The National Gallery of Art in Washington has four oil paintings which are variants of plates of the *Birds of America*. These are Plate 42, "Orchard Oriole"; Plate 65, "Rathbone Warbler"; Plate 132, "Three-toed Woodpecker"; and Plate 149, "Sharp-tailed Finch." These were presented to the gallery in 1951 by E. J. L. Hallstrom of Australia. Sir Edward Hallstrom had obtained these and other paintings from a member of the Audubon family. In the oils of Plates 42 and 132 again are depicted the "landscape backgrounds showing distant mountains." Moreover, it is stated in Victor Audubon's letter to Havell of 24 January 1832 that Kidd had painted an oil of Plate 42, the "Orchard Oriole."

When Audubon entered into the arrangement with Kidd, he mentioned reproductions of only those plates included among the first hundred. However, it is known from the letter of Victor Audubon, written on 19 February 1833, to Havell that Kidd had been provided with drawings of the birds which appear in

Volume 2. In the collection at the National Gallery of Art are found reproductions of Plates 132 and 149 of the second volume, the "Three-toed Woodpecker" and the "Sharp-tailed Finch." Included among the oils at the American Museum of Natural History in New York are reproductions of Plates 3 and 47, the "Prothonotary Warbler" and the "Ruby-throated Humming Bird." In his correspondence with Havell, Kidd had advised that he had completed the painting of these birds.

The foregoing has been set down in an endeavor to relate the story of the arrangement between John James Audubon and Joseph Bartholomew Kidd to reproduce the *Birds of America* in oil. When the evidence indicates that a painting was the work of Kidd, this should not disparage it as a copy nor exaggerate the importance of an original. Audubon, when he was arranging with Kidd for the reproductions, was not practicing a form of deception. The copies in oils were both authorized and encouraged by him, for he envisaged them to be a legitimate means of multiplying his work, as were the engravings executed by Havell and others, particularly since the bird itself was still his concept and his composition, no matter who might copy it.[26]

D

REPRODUCTIONS OF AUDUBON'S *BIRDS OF AMERICA*

PRINTS

Forest and Stream

The first reproductions[1] of the Audubon prints made in the United States seem to have been those announced by *Forest and Stream* in the 5 September 1896 issue.[2] Here it was stated that a series of halftone reproductions of selected Audubon bird plates were to be included in forthcoming issues, the plates having been photographed especially for this purpose from a copy of the original Double Elephant folio of the work (erroneously dated 1827–1835 in the announcement) in possession of a member of the Forest and Stream Publishing Company.

The first one published appeared on page 243 in the 26 September 1896 issue,[3] a reproduction of plate 302, depicting the "Black Duck" (Audubon's Dusky Duck). The size of the print was 15¾ by 11 inches. It was stated then, "The copies of Audubon now in existence are confined to a few libraries and fewer individual possessions; and when the work falls on the market, as it does now and then, it sells at prices ranging from $2,500 to $3,000." The reproductions were included as pages of the magazine.

In the 24 October 1896 issue of the magazine, Maria R. Audubon, the Naturalist's granddaughter, was quoted as saying, "The reproductions to me are most satisfactory; they lack color, of course, but in every other respect are the best we have ever seen, and I think I may say that those of the Audubon family still remaining are much gratified with the first of the series." Miss Audubon seemed here to intimate that other reproductions had been made. However, none prior to 1896 have been located by the present author.

Reproductions of the following plates (Audubon's nomenclature in parentheses) were published in *Forest and Stream*. It has not been possible to determine the date of issue in every instance:

Reproductions

Plate			
302	Black Duck (Dusky Duck)	*Reproduced*	26 Sept. 1896
186	Prairie Chicken (Pinnated Grous)		24 Oct. 1896
301	Canvasback (Canvass-backed Duck)		21 Nov. 1896
191	Willow Ptarmigan (Willow Grous or Large Ptarmigan)		19 Dec. 1896
300	American Golden Plover (Golden Plover)		27 Feb. 1897
322	Redhead (Red-headed Duck)		10 July 1897
327	Shoveller (Shoveller Duck)		9 Oct. 1897
286	White-fronted Goose (same)		[?]
284	Purple Sandpiper (same)		25 June 1898

The Macmillan Company

In 1937 the Macmillan Company published in one volume not only the reproductions of the 435 prints of the Double Elephant folio edition of the *Birds of America* but an additional 65 prints from the Octavo edition. The loose prints used for the 435 are at present at the National Gallery in Washington, to which institution they were presented in 1946 by Mrs. Walter B. James.

The work of reproducing the prints was entrusted to the Duenewald Printing Corporation. A regular edition of 50,000 copies which would sell for $12.50 was projected. For this edition a binding of green Bancroft buckram, stamped in gold foil on the front cover and spine, was selected. At the same time trade interest indicated there would be a demand for a limited issue. Accordingly, a special edition of 500 copies, later increased to 2500, to sell at $25, was announced. This latter edition (in a slip case with label) was bound in "Cockerell marble paper of a feather design, with harmonizing buckram spine, gold leaf stamped with gold top." The pages in both editions are 9 by 12½ inches.[4]

The volume was reprinted in 1941, 1942, 1944, and at intervals since, but with the number of prints reduced to 435.

It appears that the Macmillan Company also has sold the prints separately from the bound volume. There was presented to the author by Howard C. Rice, formerly assistant librarian at Princeton University, an envelope containing the following reproductions (each 12″ × 9″) which are identical to those found in the Macmillan bound volume:

18 Best Loved Bird Paintings by Audubon
Suitable for framing—
Includes all the Audubon favorites

Summer Tanager	Mockingbird
Cardinal	Purple Finch
Blue Jay	Bobolink
Meadowlark	Field Sparrow
Wild Turkey	Warblers and Bluebirds
American Redstart	Ruby Throated Hummingbird
Great Blue Heron	Robin
Belted Kingfisher	Baltimore Oriole
Goldfinch	Mourning Dove

Handsome   Full Color   Prints

APPENDIX D

It is possible that Macmillan used the sets as a promotion or premium item and later "remaindered" them.

Northwestern Mutual Life Insurance Company

In 1946, R. R. Donnelley & Sons Company (The Lakeside Press) of Chicago began, by a process known as "Deeptone Offset," the reproduction of the prints of the *Birds of America* for the Northwestern Mutual Life Insurance Company of Milwaukee. These reproductions, measuring approximately 21 by 16 inches, were used on large wall calendars. In 1960 the large-size calendar was discontinued and replaced by a smaller one, with the prints measuring 11 by 16 inches.[5]

The insurance company estimated that between 1946 (when the calendars were first issued) and 1968 over 10,000,000 Audubon prints had been distributed. The larger prints without the calendar were still being offered to the public in 1968, but the supply of many of the individual species had been depleted and would not be restocked.[6] Thus far, 185 of the 435 original prints of the Double Elephant folio have been reproduced by Northwestern Mutual.

History Institute of America

In 1950 there was offered the so-called "The History Edition of Audubon Prints," reproduced by special permission of the American Museum of Natural History, New York City, and published by The History Institute of America, Inc., New York City. These reproductions were described as follows: "Each of the twelve Audubon prints, now available, is standard size: Over-all dimensions of paper, 27⅞ by 22¼ inches; this gives pleasing wide margins of 3 to 4 inches." These prints were priced at $15 each. How many sets were published has not been determined.

The twelve plates reproduced were:

	Plate			
	1	Wild Turkey Cock	159	Cardinal
	26	Carolina Paroquet	206	Wood Duck
	41	Ruffed Grous	221	Mallard Duck
	43	Cedar Waxwing	231	Long-billed Curlew
	62	Passenger Pigeon	242	Snowy Egret
	66	Ivory-billed Woodpecker	431	American Flamingo.

New York Graphic Society

It was probably in the early 1950s that there was published by the New York Graphic Society, Fine Art Publishers, New York City, the following reproductions:

	Plate			
	1	Wild Turkey	167	Key-West Dove
	26	Carolina Parrot	327	Shoveller Duck
	61	Pileated Woodpecker	401	Red-breasted Merganser.

Reproductions

These reproductions are the size of the original Double Elephant prints, 39½ inches by 26½ inches. All six were displayed in the lobby at the former Princeton Inn, Princeton, N.J.

AMERICAN PRINT CRAFT GUILD

The author has seen two reproductions, Plate 79, "Tyrant Flycatcher," and Plate 249, "Snowy Heron or White Egret," published in 1951 by the American Print Craft Guild, 44 Archer Drive, Bronxville, N.Y. (endorsed by the National Association of Audubon Societies).

Reader's Digest

In 1959 *Reader's Digest*, with the sale of *Our Amazing World of Nature*, accompanied this book with certain reproductions of the *Birds of America* which the company states were made from photographs of prints that are part of the Double Elephant folio Collection at the New York Public Library.

HARRY N. ABRAMS, INC.

In 1964 the New York publishers, Harry N. Abrams, Inc., New York, N.Y., published reproductions of 30 prints of the Double Elephant folio of the *Birds of America*, size 17 by 14 inches, which were sold for $25. A brochure containing the story of the Naturalist and the folio, written by George Dock, Jr., accompanied the set of prints. These reproductions were also offered in England by Heron Books of London. Following is a list of the prints reproduced.

Plate				
1	Wild Turkey		136	Meadowlark
12	Baltimore Oriole		137	Yellow-breasted Chat
17	Carolina Pigeon		159	Cardinal Grosbeak
26	Carolina Parrot		206	Summer or Wood Duck
53	Painted Finch		211	Great Blue Heron
62	Passenger Pigeon		217	Louisiana Heron
77	Belted Kingfisher		221	Mallard Duck
82	Whip-poor-will		250	Arctic Tern
87	Florida Jay		251	Brown Pelican
91	Broad-winged Hawk		313	Blue-winged Teal
97	Little Screech Owl		357	American Magpie
102	Blue Jay		366	Iceland or Jer Falcon
107	Canada Jay		367	Band-tailed Pigeon
111	Pileated Woodpecker		406	Trumpeter Swan
128	Cat Bird		431	American Flamingo.

On one occasion the Book-of-the-Month Club offered these prints as a "Book-Dividend," obtainable for two Book-Dividend Certificates plus $4.50.

APPENDIX D

KIMBERLY-CLARK CORPORATION

In the 1960s a product promotion campaign of the Kimberly-Clark Corporation of Neenah, Wis., used a selection of twenty-four 8- by 6-inch lithographed reproductions of Audubon's *Birds of America*, produced "especially for Kleenex Man Size Tissues with the cooperation of the National Audubon Society." Each package of the tissues contained a single reproduction and on the back of each was printed an offer of the entire set of twenty-four reproductions which included "Audubon's American Eagle, garden and game birds from all sections of the United States" for $1 and the premium seal from a box containing the product. The offer was withdrawn when the supply of reproductions was exhausted.

Woman's Day

In the 1960s *Woman's Day* magazine, at that time published for the Atlantic & Pacific Stores, offered to the public the following reproductions of the *Birds of America*, the size of which were 11¼ inches by 8¼ inches:

Plate			
44	Summer Red-bird	202	Red-throated Diver
87	Florida Jay	327	Shoveller Duck
53	Painted Bunting	354	Louisiana Tanager and Scarlet Tanager.
159	Cardinal Grosbeak		
188	Boat-tailed Grackle		

ARIEL PRESS

In 1971 there was offered for subscription a full-sized (98 × 68 cm) facsimile edition of twenty selected plates reproduced from the original folio edition of Audubon's *Birds of America* limited to 250 copies for the United States, numbered and signed by J. A. C. Roberts, Director, The Ariel Press Ltd., Covent Garden, London, England. The first volume was published in 1972, the price of which was $350.

The twenty subjects selected for the first volume were:

White Throated Sparrow	Rose-breasted Grosbeak
Baltimore Oriole	White-crowned Sparrow
Blue Winged Yellow Warbler	Pigeon Hawk
Carolina Parrot	Summer or Wood Duck
Yellow Bird or American Goldfinch	Louisiana and Scarlet Tanager
Painted Bunting	White-winged Crossbill
Red-shouldered Hawk	Hairy, Red-bellied, Red-shafted, Lewis', Red-breasted Woodpeckers
Passenger Pigeon	
Snow Owl	Band-tailed Pigeon
Florida Jay	American Sparrow Hawk.
Pileated Woodpecker	

A second volume of twenty "horizontal or landscape" plates has been scheduled for publication at a yet-to-be-determined date in 1973. The selection of plates for the second volume had not been completed at the time of this writing nor had a price been set.

Reproductions

The set of the folio from which the reproductions in this two-volume edition of facsimiles are made is that in the collection of the Meiningen State Museum.

Johnson Reprint Corporation

In 1971 the Johnson Reprint Corporation of New York and Theatrum Orbis Terrarum of Amsterdam undertook a full-sized, full-color facsimile edition of Audubon's *Birds of America* from the prints of the folio at the Teyler's Museum of Haarlem in the Netherlands, one of the original subscribers. This edition was limited to 250 numbered sets of 435 full-color plates (each measuring 38½ inches high and 26½ inches wide), obtainable either in boxed sets of six portfolios, each portfolio comprising six parts (36 parts in all) of loose plates, or in four hand-bound, half-leather volumes. The price of a boxed set of portfolios was $5940; of a hand-bound set of four volumes, $6960.

The individual parts of the boxed set of six parts, as well as the individual volumes of the bound set, were issued as each became available. The facsimile edition was completed early in 1973.

Herbert Lang et Cie. AG

A limited edition of 20 selected full-sized (98 × 67 cm), full-color (printed in 7 to 9 colors by the collotype process) facsimile plates, reproduced from Audubon's *Birds of America*, was issued in 1972 by Herbert Lang et Cie. AG, the antiquarian bookdealers and publishers, of Bern, Switzerland. Each 90-page, half linen, slipcased volume was numbered and specially bound to permit removal of the individual plates. Included, in addition to the 20 reproductions, were 4 pages of titles, 6 pages of introduction, and 40 interleaved pages of explanatory text, in German and English. The price per copy was $385.

Miscellaneous

Other reproductions in the author's possession include the following prints:

Ruffed Grouse, Tetrao umbellus, Linn. This print is erroneously identified in the upper right corner as "Plate XII" (but actually should be pl.41) and in the upper left corner is labeled "Deluxe Edition." The drawing is 13½ by 18½ inches, printed on a sheet $18\frac{9}{16}$ by 23⅞ inches. The credit line indicates that it was published by J. B. Fisher Co., New York, N.Y., "A Genuine Craft Print."

Three prints, each $19\frac{7}{16}$ by 16 inches, as follows: Plate 12, Baltimore Oriole; Plate 67, Florida Jay; and Plate 205, Summer or Wood Duck. At the bottom of each print is the statement, "Original, courtesy of Harry Shaw Newman, The Old Print Shop, New York, N.Y."

Boat-tailed Grackle, Quiscalus major, Vieill. Plate 187. This 21⅞ by 18-inch reproduction was issued "By A. Inc. 1937, Engraved, Printed and Colored by A.P.P. Co., Inc., N.Y. Endorsed by the National Association of Audubon Societies," according to the statement on the print.

APPENDIX D

Red-shouldered Hawk, plate 56. This reproduction is 23½ by 16⅞ inches and, according to the statement on the verso, was "Printed in Switzerland. Edita Lausanne."

Summer Red-bird. The size of this reproduction is 20 by 15⅞ inches. The credit line in the lower left corner attributes this to "Penn Prints, New York." In the upper left corner, the plate is incorrectly identified as No. 42 and in the upper right corner as Plate 208 (should be No. 9, pl.42). No additional information is available.

COLOR SLIDES
NATIONAL AUDUBON SOCIETY

In 1961 the National Audubon Society, with the cooperation of the National Gallery of Art, offered five sets of ten slides each of the *Birds of America*. Each 2-by-2-inch slide was from an original photograph taken with a special camera produced by Eastman Kodak Company for the National Gallery of Art, Washington, D.C. The gallery had permitted the National Audubon Society to make 400 copies each of 50 selected prints of Audubon's Double Elephant folio edition of the *Birds of America*, of which the gallery possesses the only original, unbound copy in the United States. The cost of the sets to purchasers was: 1 set, $5; 3 sets, $14.50; 5 sets, $23.50. The sets consisted of the following prints:

Set 1
1. Hooping Crane   *Original plate*   226
2. Yellow-breasted Chat   137
3. Mallard Duck   221
4. Great Horned Owl   61
5. Passenger Pigeon   62
6. Carolina Pigeon or Turtle Dove   17
7. Meadow Lark   136
8. Black Skimmer or Shearwater   323
9. Belted Kingfisher   77
10. American Magpie   357

Set 2
1. Roseate Spoonbill   321
2. Summer Red Bird   44
3. Canvas-backed Duck   301
4. Fish Hawk   81
5. Carolina Parrot   26
6. Cedar Bird   43
7. Cat Bird   128
8. Yellow Shank (Lesser Yellowlegs)   288
9. Florida Jay   87
10. Barn Swallow   173

Reproductions

Set 3
1. American Flamingo *Original plate* 431
2. Blue Jay 102
3. Summer Duck 206
4. Swallow-tailed Hawk (Kite) 72
5. Ivory-billed Woodpecker 66
6. Gold-winged Woodpecker (Flicker) 37
7. Black Yellow Warbler (Magnolia Warbler) 123
8. Roseate Tern 240
9. Fish Crow 146
10. American White Pelican 311

Set 4
1. Snowy Heron or White Egret 242
2. Rose-breasted Grosbeak 127
3. Hooded Merganser 232
4. Mottled Owl (Screech Owl) 97
5. Trumpeter Swan 406
6. House Wren 83
7. White-breasted Black-capped Nuthatch 152
8. Great Northern Diver or Loon 306
9. Pileated Woodpecker 111
10. Great American Cock (Wild Turkey) 1

Set 5
1. Louisiana Heron 217
2. Baltimore Oriole 12
3. Goosander (American Merganser) 331
4. Broad-winged Hawk 91
5. Long-billed Curlew 231
6. Yellow-billed Cuckoo 2
7. White-crowned Sparrow 114
8. Black-bellied Darter (Water Turkey) 316
9. Whip-poor-will 82
10. Glossy Ibis 387

After the original issue of slides was sold the project was discontinued.[7]

SILVER IN COMBINATION WITH BRONZE AND COPPER

REED & BARTON, SILVERSMITHS

In the autumn of 1970 Reed & Barton, Silversmiths, of Taunton, Mass., offered for sale an 11-inch plate with the reproduction of an Audubon Double Elephant folio bird on it, the Pine Siskin from Plate 180, the first in a series, handcrafted in the firm's patented "Damascene" process. The second of the series, the Red-shouldered Hawk, reproduced from Audubon's Plate 56, was issued in 1971 and the third, that of the Stilt Sandpiper, from Audubon's Plate 344, in 1972. The Red Cardinal from his Plate 159 is the 1973 reproduction. It is planned to issue the following Audubon plates in future editions:

    Plate 168   Fork-tailed Flycatcher   382   Sharp-tailed Grouse
             336   Yellow-crowned Night Heron   69   Bay Breasted Warbler.

The edition of each plate is limited to 5,000.

SILVER-INGOT COLLECTION

The Rare and Endangered Birds Silver-Ingot Series

In September of 1973 the National Audubon Society offered to its members a Limited Edition collector's item, the Rare and Endangered Birds Silver-Ingot Series. The designer of the series, D. George Andrew Woloch, began with Audubon's depiction of the twelve birds chosen and then fashioned each into an example of the sculptor's art. Each one-ounce, pure .999 fine silver ingot will be mounted with an authorized reproduction of the original John James Audubon painting on which the sculpture was based. The unit price of each framed reproduction with ingot was $29.50 (unframed $15.50), and the society stated that only 10,000 first edition sets would be minted.

The following Audubon prints were selected for reproduction:

Plate	16.	Peregrine Falcon	Great-footed Hawk
	66.	Ivory-Billed Woodpecker	Ivory-billed Woodpecker
	81.	Osprey	Fish Hawk
	126.	Bald Eagle	White-headed Eagle
	185.	Bachman's Warbler	Bachman's Warbler
	186.	Greater Prairie Chicken	Pinnated Grous
	208.	Eskimo Curlew	Esquimaux Curlew
	226.	Whooping Crane	Hooping Crane
	251.	Brown Pelican	Brown Pelican
	261.	Sandhill Crane	Hooping Crane
	281.	Great White Heron	Great White Heron
	426.	California Condor	Californian Vulture

REPRODUCTIONS ON CHINA

Original Audubon Paintings

Among the historic landmarks in Natchez, Miss., is Green Leaves, the home of Mrs. Melchior Beltzhoover, which was built prior to the War of 1812. One of

Reproductions

the treasures of the home is a set of china with a different bird or flower on each plate, reputed to have been painted by Audubon.[8]

Audubon had visited Natchez the last week of 1820 while en route to New Orleans and again for a longer period in the late spring and summer of 1823. On the latter occasion both he and his son were seriously ill. It has not been possible to find a reference to Audubon's having painted any china while in Natchez. That at Green Leaves has been examined by the present author who found the style of the painted birds and flowers to be radically different from that employed in the drawings of the Birds of America.

In 1959 the author was advised by the curator of Villa Louis, at Prairie du Chien, Wis., that in the museum there were, in addition to the Octavo edition of Audubon's Birds of America, ten plates painted by the Naturalist.[9] These have not been examined by the author.

DOUBLE ELEPHANT FOLIO

Reproductions from the prints of the Double Elephant folio on china have been produced in England by the firm of William Adams & Sons, Potters Ltd., Tunstall.[10]

In the mid-1930s the Royal Worcester Porcelain Company was commissioned to produce a set of twenty-four service plates, each bearing a subject selected from Audubon's *Birds of America* "in observance of the centenary of this great work," the 87 numbers of which had been issued as completed between 1826 and 1838. The idea for this "collector's set" of commemorative plates originated with the English publishing house of A. C. & H. W. Dickins. Each subject portrayed on the individual plates was painted by hand "within a border of two tones of celadon green enriched with gold, the Worcester factory having revived for this purpose the long disused process of 'honey gilding,' in which the powdered gold is mixed with beeswax and honey." Only a small number of sets were produced, for each plate required 11 firings and took 30 days to complete. When the stipulated number of sets had been made, the Worcester factory destroyed the original design models to ensure that no more would be produced.[11]

The author has in his possession eight cups and saucers and eight plates on which there are reproductions of the following Audubon birds:

Plate				
	17	Columba carolinensis Carolina Turtle Dove	79	Tyrannus tyrannus Kingbird
	18	Thryomanes Bewicki Bewick's Wren	114	Zonotrichia leucophrys White Crowned Sparrow
	43	Bombycilla carolinensis Cedar Bird	168	Muscivora tyranus Forked-tailed Flycatcher
	62	Columba migratoria Passenger Pigeon	367	Columba fasciata Band-tailed Pigeon.

On each cup and saucer is found a seal in the form of a crown, the letter "A," and the name, Alfred Meakin England, followed by the Audubon plate number

APPENDIX D

and Latin name of bird, and the statement, "Reproduced from the Elephant Folio Edition of Audubon's Birds of America endorsed by National Audubon Society, New York," followed by Audubon's name of the bird figured.

Inquiry at the National Audubon Society regarding these brought the following information:

> All I can find out here is that our Service Department at one time, about five or so years ago, sold some Meakin dinnerware of the type you describe. Subsequently Meakin discontinued that line. We never did have their address as this dinnerware was purchased for us through Mr. Donald Miller of Maddock & Miller, 129 Fifth Avenue, New York City.[12]

TEXTILES

There is to be found in the Archives of the Calico Printers' Association of Manchester, England, a Lancashire pattern book containing hundreds of different designs, among which are six designs after Audubon's plates of the *Birds of America*. The first known dated textile printed with Audubon reproductions appears in 1830.

Detailed information, with photographs of the chintzes on which reproductions of the *Birds of America* appear, is to be found in "English Printed Textiles: VIII. Designs Based on Audubon's *Birds of America*," by Barbara J. Morris, which appeared in the December 1957 issue of *Antiques*.[13]

Also, in *English Printed Textiles*, a publication of the Victoria & Albert Museum published in London in 1960 by Her Majesty's Stationery Office, are two plates with reproductions of roller-printed cotton fabrics on which are depicted some of Audubon's *Birds of America*.

It is believed that John Potts of New Mills, Derbyshire, an early subscriber to the *Birds of America*, engraved the Audubon designs. This subscription does not appear to have been completed, the entry in Ledger "B" indicating that Potts had received only the first volume of 100 plates and Numbers 21 and 22 (pl. 101–10) in addition, though it is possible that he may have received additional prints.

On 10 October 1972 four examples of these textiles (the size of each being 27½" × 21½") were sold by Sotheby Parke Bernet, Inc., New York, for a total of $1,400, as follows:

Plate		
97	Mottled Owl (Little Screech Owl)	$400
107	Canada Jay	300
147	Night Hawk	300
187	Boat-tailed Grackle	400.

The Sotheby Parke Bernet catalog for this sale lists these as items 346, 347, 348, and 349 and contains a photograph of the reproduction of the Canada Jay (item 348).

Reproductions

John C. Annesi

In April 1971 the author and his wife visited the shop of Las Olas Tailors in Fort Lauderdale, Fla., where, it had been reported to them, were reproductions of some of Audubon's *Birds of America*, purportedly printed on silk. There indeed were four framed reproductions of Audubon's *Birds*.[14]

Each frame, the size of which measures 31 inches (height) by 24¾ inches (width), encloses a black mat ⅞ inch wide at the sides and 1 inch at top and bottom, which makes the size of the exposed print 25 inches by 19¼ inches. Fortunately it was possible to remove the backing of one of the frames to reveal that the material on which the print had been made was either linen or calico, not silk. Further, it is evident that the reproductions had been made by means of copper rollers.

The four prints had been purchased some years ago from a Fort Lauderdale resident by John C. Annesi, the owner of the shop. The plates represented, as well as the legend which appears on each reproduction, are as follows:

No. 20   PLATE XCVII

Little Screech Owl, Strix Asio. Linn.
Adult, 1. Young, 2,3. Jersey Pine Pinus inops.

Drawn from Nature by J. J. Audubon F.R.S. F.L.S.
                                        Engraved Printed & Coloured by R. Havell.

No. 22   PLATE CVII

Canada Jay, Corvus Canadensis, Linn.
Male 1. Female 2.
White Oak. Quercus alba.

Drawn from Nature by J. J. Audubon F.R.S. F.L.S.
                                      Engraved, Printed & Coloured by R. Havell 1831

No. 30   PLATE CXLVII

Night Hawk
Caprimulgus Virginianus, Brisson
Male 1. Female 2.

Drawn from Nature by J. J. Audubon F.R.S. F.L.S.
                                      Engraved, Printed & Coloured by R. Havell 1832

No. 38   PLATE CLXXXVII

Boat-tailed Grackle
Quiscallus Major. Vieill
Male 1. Female 2.
Live Oak. Quercus virens.

Engraved Printed & Coloured by R. Havell 1834
                              Drawn from Nature by J. J. Audubon F.R.S. F.L.S.

[*In this reproduction the name of the artist and engraver have been transposed by the copper-roller engraver.*]

These were the textiles sold by Sotheby Parke Bernet on 10 October 1972.

APPENDIX D

STAMPS

A five-cent stamp (7 Dec. 1963, *Perf.11*, Unwmkd., *1241 A673*, 5¢, dark blue and multicolored)[15] and a twenty-cent stamp (Giori Press Printing, 26 Apr. 1967, Lumin., *Perf.11*, *C71 AP48*, 20¢, multicolored),[16] both reproductions of plate 96, which Audubon had mistakenly named the "Columbia Jay," were issued by the U.S. Post Office to honor the "ornithologist and artist." This bird, actually Collier's magpie jay, is a species native to Mexico and was never seen alive by the Naturalist. He had figured the birds, both males, from a specimen sent him by a friend who said it had come from the Columbia River.[17]

REPRODUCTIONS FROM ORIGINAL COPPER PLATES

THE NEW YORK BOTANICAL GARDEN

Shortly before his death in 1911, a Staten Island naturalist, John J. Crooke (1824–1911), presented to Dr. Nathaniel Lord Britten (1859–1934), the first director of the New York Botanical Garden, two of the copper plates of Audubon's *Birds of America*: Plate 64, "Swamp Sparrow, Fringilla Palustris, Wils."; and Plate 194, "Hudson's Bay Titmouse, Parus Hudsonicus."

It is of interest to note that in each instance the plate bears the second state of the legend. On Plate 64 the legend originally read, "Swamp Sparrow, Male., Spiza Palustris," while the common name of the bird on Plate 194 was "Canadian Titmouse."

In 1959 the society authorized the Andersen-Lamb Photo Gravure Corp., of Brooklyn, N.Y., to strike off 50 prints of each plate. These were then colored by the Walter Fischer Company of New York and the prints sold to the membership of the society at $75 per print, unframed, and $100, framed.[18] Due to a most enthusiastic response of the members the first 100 prints were quickly sold and another 50 copies of each ordered.

The size of each print is 26 by 16⅞ inches. Nowhere on these prints is there to be found any indication to identify them as later reproductions, and not original strike-offs. However, the paper used shows neither Whatman nor any other watermark.

ALONZO BOARDMAN

Some years ago Alonzo Boardman, of Augusta, Ga., who at the time was the owner of the original copper plate for Plate 102, the "Blue Jay," which in 1962 he presented to the Metropolitan Museum of Art, New York, sent his friends a black-and-white print of this plate.

Reproductions

American Museum of Natural History

At the 75th anniversary dinner of the American Ornithologists Union, held in New York on 17 October 1958, the American Museum of Natural History, New York, distributed black-and-white prints of their copper plate no.277, "Hutchins's Barnacle Goose," to members of that organization. This reproduction, as well as that of the Boardman plate, was printed by the Andersen-Lamb firm of Brooklyn, N.Y.

Providence Athenaeum

In the autumn of 1972 the Providence (R.I.) Athenaeum arranged with the Meriden Gravure Company, Meriden, Conn., to reproduce a limited edition of 500 prints from the print of Audubon's "Florida Jay" (pl.87) which is owned by the Athenaeum. These reproductions, the exact size and color of the originals made by Havell, were struck on paper 22 inches by 34 inches. The prints went on sale 4 December 1972 for $20 each to members of the Providence Athenaeum, to non-members for $25.

REPRODUCTIONS OF AUDUBON'S ORIGINAL PAINTINGS

Metropolitan Museum of Art

In addition to the reproductions of the Double Elephant folio prints, in 1957 there was published by the Metropolitan Museum of Art, New York, a set of 24 colored reproductions (5"×4"), the "Art Miniatures" series, of the following original watercolor paintings of Audubon's *Birds of America*:

1. Carolina Wren
2. Wild Turkey
3. Sharp-tailed Grouse
4. Gyrfalcon
5. Collie's Magpie
6. Blackburnian Warbler
7. Fork-tailed Flycatcher
8. Great Blue Heron
9. Great Black-backed Gull
10. Snowy Egret
11. Roseate Spoonbill
12. Ivory-billed Woodpecker
13. Great Auk
14. Long-billed Curlew
15. Canvasback
16. Swallow-tailed Kite
17. Osprey
18. White-crowned Sparrow
19. Yellow-billed Cuckoo
20. Bohemian Waxwing
21. Great Gray Owl
22. Passenger Pigeon
23. Lesser Yellow-legs
24. Brown Pelican

These reproductions were accompanied by a booklet (10"×6½") in which they could be attached.

This set of colored miniatures, engraved and printed by the Beck Engraving Company, were reproduced from Audubon's original watercolor portraits of the

Birds of America located at the New-York Historical Society. The Book-of-the-Month Club was the distributor.

The booklet accompanying the miniatures contains, in addition to the spaces on which to attach them, interesting and instructive comments concerning each bird prepared by Dr. Robert Cushman Murphy, Lamont Curator Emeritus of Birds, the American Museum of Natural History. In the text Dr. Murphy analyzes the drawings, pointing out for example the skill with which Audubon obtained certain effects, as in the way the Naturalist drew feathers. He explains that a bird's feathers "do not grow evenly all over the body. Rather, their insertions lie only in special tracts, with bare spaces between. The shingling, or lay, of the feathers, nevertheless, covers and insulates the whole skin. The planes produced by the many feather tracts are functional, but they have as a by-product a rare and subtle beauty." In conclusion, Dr. Murphy states that "only an artist who had faithfully and minutely studied the plumage could utilize it in the perfection of detail that helps to create distinction" in Audubon's paintings. Also, included in the text are many incidents concerning the particular birds Dr. Murphy found in the *Ornithological Biography*.

Early in 1971 Mrs. Margaret S. Kelley, General Supervisor of the Art and Book Shop at the Metropolitan Museum of Art, advised the author that the "Art Miniatures" series is no longer being published by either the museum or the book club.

American Heritage Publishing Company

There was published in 1966 by American Heritage, New York, and distributed by Houghton Mifflin Company, Boston, *The Original Water-Colour Paintings for the Birds of America*, a two-volume work with an introduction by Marshall Davidson. In these two volumes were presented for the first time reproductions in color of virtually the entire series of original paintings which Audubon had created for the *Birds of America* (actually 431 paintings were reproduced). The color plates for the reproductions were made by Chanticleer Press; the printing and binding were done at the R. R. Donnelley & Company's Lakeside Press in Chicago. The price for the two volumes was $55 to October 1966 and $75 thereafter. The publisher advises that 45,000 copies were printed and that no reprints are projected at this time.

Edward H. Dwight, Director of the Museum of Art, Munson-Williams-Proctor Institute, provided the editors with historical and critical information on each of Audubon's paintings.

E

UNCOLORED PRINTS OF THE *BIRDS OF AMERICA*

In June 1838, when the engraving of the *Birds of America* had been completed and the subscribers furnished with the final numbers, there evidently were a large number of leftover prints in the uncolored state in the possession of the engraver. That many of these had been brought to the United States is evident from the fact that around 1925 the Misses Florence and Maria Audubon presented nearly two hundred uncolored prints to the American Museum of Natural History.[1]

While on a visit to Germany in 1936, a San Francisco print dealer, Roy Vernon Sowers, purchased 96 prints in the uncolored state. Around 1940 this dealer published a list of 72 prints remaining in his possession, which he offered at an inclusive price of $1750, with individual prices varying from $15 for such plates as no.5, "Bonaparte's Fly-catcher," and no.8, the "White-throated Sparrow," to $75 for no.91, the "Broad-winged Hawk," and $100 for no.62, the "Passenger Pigeon."[2]

At the Parke-Bernet Galleries, Sale no.146, held in New York on 25 and 26 October 1939, the following framed, uncolored plates were offered for sale, with the lot bringing $187.50:

Plate				
208	Esquimaux Curlew	274	Semipalmated Snipe or Willet
209	Wilson's Plover	308	Tell-tale Godwit or Snipe
223	Pied Oyster-catcher	327	Shoveller Duck
225	Kildeer Plover	334	Black-bellied Plover
227	Pin-tailed Duck	335	Red-breasted Snipe
228	Green-winged Teal	343	Ruddy Duck.
229	Scaup Duck		

The sale catalog specified that there were "14 uncoloured plates" in the lot. The purchaser, Mr. Albert E. Lownes, of Providence, R.I., however states that there were only 13.

APPENDIX E

In January 1960 there was offered to H. J. Lutcher Stark, the Texas collector, by Mrs. Margaret McCormick, of Staten Island, a descendent of the Naturalist, the following 25 uncolored prints at a price of $10,000. They were not purchased by Mr. Stark, and it is not known whether Mrs. McCormick found another buyer.[3]

Plate 17 Carolina Pigeon
23 Maryland Yellow Throat
41 Ruffed Grous
57 Loggerhead Shrike
66 Ivory-billed Woodpecker
67 Red-winged Starling
75 Le Petit Caporal
83 House Wren
95 Blue-eyed Yellow Warbler
107 Canada Jay
120 Pewit Flycatcher
122 Blue Grosbeak
129 Great Crested Flycatcher
140 Pine Creeping Warbler
149 Sharp-tailed Finch
177 White-crowned Pigeon
182 Ground Dove
191 Willow Grous
199 Little Owl
220 Piping Plover
303 Bartram Sandpiper
304 Turn-stone
319 Lesser Tern
320 Little Sandpiper
373 Evening Grosbeak.

The following uncolored plates are in the collection of the New-York Historical Society:

Plate 31 White-headed Eagle (Bald Eagle)
54 Rice Bunting (Bobolink)
61 Great Horned Owl
71 Winter Hawk (Red-shouldered Hawk)
109 Savannah Finch (Savannah Sparrow).

F

EDITIONS OF AUDUBON'S PROSPECTUS

Shortly after his arrival in England, where he went to seek an engraver, Audubon began to give consideration to the preparation of a prospectus to announce and describe the engravings of the *Birds of America*. On 28 September 1826, the Naturalist noted in his journal, "Mr. Rathbone and Mr. Roscoe will both aid me in the drawing up of a prospectus for my work."[1] The following day, in a discussion about his work with the London bookdealer, Henry J. Bohn, the Naturalist was again advised to issue a prospectus.[2] However, after a later conversation with Mr. Roscoe, it was decided that "nothing could be done about the prospectus without more definite knowledge of what the cost of the publication would be."[3]

It was in October 1826 that the arrangements for the engraving of the drawings with William Lizars of Edinburgh were completed. By the end of January 1827 the first number of five plates had been engraved. On 17 March 1827 the Naturalist noted in his journal, "Issued my 'Prospectus' this morning for the publication of my great work," the details of which he set forth as follows:

The Prospectus

To those who have not seen any portion of the author's collection of original drawings, it may be proper to state, that their superiority consists in the accuracy as to proportion and outline, and the variety and truth of the attitudes and positions of the figures, resulting from the peculiar means discovered and employed by the author, and his attentive examination of the objects portrayed during a long series of years. The author has not contented himself, as others have done, with single profile views, but in very many instances has grouped his figures so as to represent the originals at their natural avocations, and has placed them on branches of trees, decorated with foliage, blossoms, and fruits, or amidst plants of numerous species. Some are seen pursuing their prey through the air, searching for food amongst the leaves and herbage sitting in their nests, or feeding their young; whilst others, of a different nature, swim, wade, or glide in or over their allotted element.

The insects, reptiles, and fishes that form the food of these birds have now and then been introduced into the drawings. In every instance where a difference of plumage exists between the sexes, both the male and the female have been represented; and the extraordinary changes which some species undergo in their progress from youth to maturity have been depicted. The plants are all copied from nature, and, as many of the originals are remarkable for their beauty, their usefulness, or their rarity, the botanist cannot fail to look upon them with delight.

The particulars of the plans of the work may be reduced to the following heads:

I. The size of the work is double elephant folio, the paper being of the finest quality.

II. The engravings are, in every instance, of the exact dimensions of the drawings, which without any exception, represent the birds and other objects of their natural size.

III. The plates are colored in the most careful manner from the original drawings.

IV. The work appears in numbers, of which five are published annually, each number consisting of five plates.

V. The price of each number is two guineas, payable on delivery.[4]

On 24 March 1827, within a week of the journal entry, Audubon sent "a copy of the first number of the Birds of America and some Prospectus" to his wife Lucy at Bayou Sara, La.[5] A copy of this prospectus is in the library of the American Philosophical Society in Philadelphia. It was addressed to "Thomas Sully, Esq. Artist—Philadelphia favored by The Prince of Musignano (Charles Lucien Bonaparte)." The date of receipt by the society of this copy is not known. However, in a letter Audubon wrote to Sully on 21 September 1827, he stated that he was sending Sully a copy of his prospectus.[6]

That the published prospectus closely followed the outline set forth in the journal is evident by a comparison with the printed copy at the American Philosophical Society. In the introductory statement after the sentence beginning with "The Plants are all copies . . . ," there has been added, "The Eggs of most of the species will appear in the course of publication." Unfortunately, Audubon never included his paintings of eggs in the *Birds of America*. He also had hoped to show both the male and female on each plate, but this had not always been possible. Often the two sexes of a species, as well as the immature bird, are to be found on separate plates.

There were also added some remarks concerning the exhibition of the original paintings and excerpts from published encomiums bestowed upon these which had induced Audubon to publish the engravings. Finally, he expressed his appreciation for the encouragement received from naturalists both in America and Great Britain and his hope for the support from the public to enable him to complete "One of the most splendid publications which has ever appeared."

Editions of Audubon's Prospectus

In the printed prospectus, "The particulars of the Plan of the Work" have been rearranged and additions made.

Item IV was amplified to include, "one Plate from the largest Drawings, one from one of the second size, and three from the smaller Drawings. In every number there will be a Non-descript Bird, or one not generally understood to be a native of the United States." This arrangement was carried out throughout the entire work. However, as the work proceeded, he found it was not possible to include a new species in every number.

There was also added a new item, "V," "There are upwards of four hundred Drawings, and it is proposed that they shall comprise Three Volumes, each containing about 130 Plates, to which an Index will be given at the end of each, to be bound with the Volume." The final number of plates was 435. No index was ever published but a title page was prepared for each of the four volumes in which the prints were bound, the first three comprising 100 prints and the fourth 135. Following "The particulars of the Plan of the Work," there was added a paragraph stating, "The First Number being now completed, will give an exact idea of the nature and style of the Work. All the other Numbers will at least equal the present in interest and execution. They will be delivered in Tin-cases, to preserve them from injury; and it would be advisable for the Subscribers to procure a portfolio in which to keep the Numbers till a Volume is completed. These Portfolios may be had at the shop of D. Lizars, Bookseller, 5, St. David Street, or W. H. Lizars, Engraver, 3, St. James Square, Edinburgh."

The "finest Drawing paper" referred to by Audubon was a quality known as "J. Whatman" or "J. Whatman Turkey Mill." The watermark on each sheet includes a date, beginning with 1825 and ending with 1838, below the name of the maker.

During the period the folio was being published, the British guinea was valued at approximately $5 and the pound sterling at $4.50. The original price per number amounted to $10, or $2 for each print. As the work progressed, a complete volume of 100 prints (20 numbers) was usually sold at the following prices:

	England	United States
Loose prints	£42–0–0	$189
Half-bound	49–10–0	225
Full bound	52–0–0	234.

The fourth volume of 135 prints, half-bound, usually sold in England for £65–5–0 and in America for $292.50, although some slight variation in price did occur. The complete sets of the folio which were sent to the United States in 1838, upon completion of the engraving, were sold at a price of $1,000.

Not long after the first copy of the prospectus was printed, an enlarged copy must have been prepared, for on 6 August 1827 Audubon wrote to his wife: "I enclose in this one of my Prospectus because I am anxious thou should see the names of my Subscribers."[7] No copy of this prospectus has been located, but other editions have been found.

APPENDIX F

At the Academy of Natural Sciences of Philadelphia there is a copy dated May 1828, issued after six numbers had been engraved. In this issue Audubon included the review of the *Birds of America* by Swainson published in the *Natural History Magazine* of May 1828, as well as the names of 124 subscribers. Since Audubon had by this time received the subscription of King George IV of England, the title page bears the following notation: "Under the Particular Patronage & Approbation of His Most Gracious Majesty."

Another copy, presently at the American Philosophical Society, was issued after ten numbers had been engraved and probably was published early in 1829. This contains the Swainson review as well as the "Rapport Verbal fait à L'Académie Royale des Sciences—Par M. Cuvier," wherein it is stated that the *Birds of America* is the greatest monument ever erected to ornithology. In addition, 131 subscribers are listed.

Finally, at Union College, Schenectady, N.Y., is a copy dated 1831 which was published upon completion of the first 100 plates. In addition to the Swainson and Cuvier critiques, it contains a list of the first 100 plates as well as the names of 180 subscribers. Also, with the death of King George IV in 1830, the wording on the cover was changed to, "Under the Special Patronage of her Most Excellent Majesty, Queen Adelaide." The publisher of this edition was Neill & Co., Printer, Edinburgh.

There are sixteen copies of the six extant editions of the prospectus to Audubon's *Birds of America*. These are to be found in the following locations:

Edition

1. AMERICAN PHILOSOPHICAL SOCIETY, Philadelphia, Pa.   A
   This copy, sent to Thomas Sully, was Published after the first number (5 engravings) had been completed, probably in March 1827.

2. MASSACHUSETTS HISTORICAL SOCIETY, Boston, Mass.   B
   Dated 1 April 1828, published when six numbers (30 plates) had been completed, and includes names of 119 subscribers. (Found in the Adams papers with a letter, dated 10 Apr. 1828, addressed to Gen. Andrew Jackson, then President of the United States.)

3. ACADEMY OF NATURAL SCIENCES OF PHILADELPHIA.   C
   Also published after six numbers had been completed, but dated May 1828. Smaller format than #2, but also includes the names of five additional subscribers, as well as the Swainson review, "Extracted from the Natural History Magazine, May 1828."

4. AMERICAN PHILOSOPHICAL SOCIETY, Philadelphia.   D
   Published after ten Numbers had been completed. Not dated, but probably printed in early 1829 since the copy reached America in April of that year. Includes the Swainson review, the "Rapport Verbal fait à L'Académie Royale des Sciences—Par M. Cuvier—sur L'Histoire Naturelle des Oiseaux de L'Amérique Septentrionale de M. Audubon," and the names of 131 subscribers.

Editions of Audubon's Prospectus

		Edition
5.	UNION COLLEGE, Schenectady, N.Y.	E

Published after the first volume had been completed (100 plates), dated 1831. Includes a list of plates engraved in 1827–1828–1829–1830, extracts from both the Swainson and Cuvier reviews, and lists names of 180 subscribers.

6.	UNIVERSITY OF LONDON, England.	F

Published in March 1835, prospective subscribers were therein advised that the third volume was in progress, that the fourth would end the series, and that the second volume of letterpress had been published. Includes extracts of the Cuvier and Swainson reviews, among others, and concludes with a list of 250 subscribers.

7.	AMERICAN MUSEUM OF NATURAL HISTORY, New York.	C

This copy in v.5, "Zoological Tracts," N.Y. Lyceum of Natural History; it was probably sent to the latter institution by Audubon.

8.	AUDUBON MUSEUM, Audubon State Park, Henderson, Ky.	E
9.	BOSTON PUBLIC LIBRARY.	D

Presented to the library by William Everett, 7 Aug. 1867. Similar to the copy described in #4, above.

10.	CHETHAM'S LIBRARY, Manchester, England.	D
11.	HARVARD UNIVERSITY, Cambridge, Mass.	E

Originally in the possession of Edward Harris, a subscriber.

12.	LILLY LIBRARY, Indiana University, Bloomington, Ind.	E
13.	MCGILL UNIVERSITY, Blacker-Wood Library, Montreal, Canada.	(?)

This has not been examined by the author.

14.	NATIONAL AUDUBON SOCIETY, New York, N.Y.	C

This copy is believed to have belonged to Henry Clay.

15.	ERIC H. L. SEXTON, Camden, Me.	D
16.	YALE UNIVERSITY, New Haven, Conn.	C

This copy of the prospectus is no.13 in a collection of scientific pamphlets, circulars, and the like, which had been bound together by Prof. Benjamin Silliman (1779–1864) of that university.

G

THE COPPER PLATES

Early in 1839 Audubon instructed his engraver, Robert Havell, to prepare the copper plates of the *Birds of America* for shipment to America. At the same time he asked that these be insured for $5,000.[1] It is likely that the vessel carrying this shipment was the *Wellington*, which sailed from London on 31 March and reached New York harbor on 4 May.[2]

Along with copper plate 391, the "Brant Goose," given to the Pleasant Valley Bird and Wildlife Sanctuary at Lenox, Mass., there was sent by the donor, Mrs. William Church Osborne, a memorandum relating the story which had been told to her by Mrs. Shelton E. Martin concerning the shipment of the plates from England. Mrs. Martin wrote a similar account to the author in 1959.

According to Mrs. Martin, the vessel on which the coppers were shipped sank soon after its arrival in New York harbor. Several months later, the firm of Phelps, Dodge and Company financed the raising of the ship. The plates, covered with verdigris and almost unrecognizable, were then taken to the office of that firm, there to be scrapped for copper. The account continues that at the time, "John S. Barnes, a personal friend of the firm, happened in and saw the plates. Recognizing their value, he asked whether he might have a few and was told to take as many as he wished. He went out to get a four-wheeler on which to load the plates. By the time Barnes returned, members of the firm, aroused by his enthusiasm, had decided they would take their pick first, giving him four."[3] It has not been possible to verify the sinking of any vessel at that particular time by inquiry either of Lloyds of London or the Special Services Administration at Washington.

When an officer of Phelps, Dodge and Company was asked about the matter, he replied that he had discussed it with Mr. Cleveland E. Dodge, a grandson of one of the founders of the firm, who said that he had never heard the story and was very skeptical of it.[4] Mr. Dodge has stated further that his grandfather,

Adapted from *Audubon*, the magazine of the National Audubon Society; copyright © 1966.

William E. Dodge, was a partner in the firm of Phelps, Dodge and Company, which owned the copper and brass plant at Ansonia, Conn.; at the time the Audubon plates were sent to Ansonia, he believes that the plant superintendent notified his grandfather, who immediately went to the plant and was instrumental in saving them.[5]

The plates which Mrs. Martin said had been obtained by her father, John S. Barnes, are the "Baltimore Oriole" (pl.12), the "Mocking Bird" (pl.21), the "Golden-winged Woodpecker" (pl.37), and the "Key West Dove" (pl.167). In 1959 the latter two were still in Mrs. Martin's possession. However, with her recent death, their ownership has passed to her son, Richard S. Martin. The plate of the "Mocking Bird" had been given earlier to the Groton School, while that of the "Baltimore Oriole" had been presented many years before to Mayor Ferdinand Latrobe of Baltimore and no trace of its present whereabouts has been found.

That the plates had arrived safely from England has been established from a letter Audubon wrote from New York to Daniel Webster, wherein it is stated:

> I have here the whole of the Copper Plates from which have been printed the Illustrations of the Birds of America, and as they are valuable to me and my children, I am anxious to place them in full security from the danger of fire. Could I be allowed to have them deposited in the new fireproof Building of the New York Custom house? Free of Charge.[6]

The date of Audubon's letter is missing. However, it is known that the customhouse was built in 1839, but it is doubtful that the permission he requested was ever granted.

In a letter written by Audubon to his son Victor on 6 April 1842, he advised Victor that the plates were sent to "Mr. Hall's Store, and the policy has been regulated accordingly by paying a few dollars extra."[7] In July 1845, a destructive fire devastated a large section of the city of New York, including the warehouse (probably Hall's) in which the copper plates had been stored.[8] When Audubon's friend Spencer Fullerton Baird of the Smithsonian Institution in Washington learned about the fire and the possible destruction of the copper plates, he wrote Audubon expressing his regret.[9] To this letter Audubon immediately responded stating: "You have been sadly too well informed about the plates of our large work. They have indeed passed through the great fire of the 19th ulto but we are now engaged in trying to restore to their wonted former existence; although a few of them will have to be reingraved for use, if ever the work is republished in its original size at all."[10]

During the period between 1852 and 1853, after the death of their father, Audubon's sons built houses for their growing families on their mother's estate. On the land behind John Woodhouse Audubon's house a small building, later known as the "cave," was especially constructed for the safekeeping of the famous plates.[11]

A letter written by Mrs. Audubon to Prof. Joseph Henry of the Smithsonian in 1863 confirms that the plates were still in her possession and also that a "kind of proposition concerning the placing of the Copper Plates of the 'Birds of America' in one of the National libraries at Washington was under consideration."[12] However, that nothing came of that "proposition" is evident from another letter she wrote to Prof. Henry in 1864.[13]

In the *American Literary Gazette and Publishers' Circular* for July 1870 there appeared the following advertisement:

> Audubon's Birds of America. On behalf of the widow of the great Ornithologist, Messrs. Putnam & Sons offer for sale the whole of the large copper plates of this magnificent work. There are altogether 350, and they are to be sold to the highest bidder before the first of September next.[14]

It should be noted that the advertisement specifies 350 plates; originally, of course, there had been 435 plates.

Less than a year after the appearance of the advertisement, in March 1871, there was printed in the *New York Times*, an article headed, "The Audubon Plates Sold for Old Copper." The article reads in part as follows:

> There is something almost sad in the statement that the original plates of that magnificent work, Audubon's "Birds of America", were recently sold in this city for their value as old copper, after having vainly sought a purchaser upon their artistic merits. But the new owners, who are well known merchants, have agreed to wait a reasonable time for any proposition to redeem the plates from the destruction which otherwise awaits them.[15]

That some thought was given to using the original copper plates for publishing another edition of the *Birds of America* is known from a reference to the plates in the magazine *Forest and Stream*. In the issue of 12 September 1896 there appeared a letter to the editor in which it is stated that around 1870–1871 a few of the plates were sent to Boston in the hope that some publisher in that city might be interested in reproducing the work. Among the publishers approached was James R. Osgood (1836–1892), but nothing came of it and the sample plates were returned to New York.[16] However, while the plates were in Boston, a hand-rubbed print of plate 11, the bald eagle, was made.[17]

In the 26 September issue of *Forest and Stream* another letter referring to the plates appeared. A Mr. Jno. H. Sage wrote that there had been given to him by Thomas R. Pickering, president of the Pickering Governor Company of Portland, Conn., two plates, no. 47, the "Ruby-throated Humming Bird," and no. 267, the "Arctic Yeager." Pickering had purchased a number of plates for old metal in a junk shop in New York City, all of which were scratched and bent. Those given to Mr. Sage were the only ones in the lot that could be put into reasonably good condition. It is possible that these were some of the plates which Audubon had felt could not be restored to "their wonted former existence." Mr. Sage bequeathed his plates to the Children's Museum of Hartford, Conn. The plates are no longer in the possession of that institution, however, and it is believed that they may have been contributed to one of the World War II scrap drives.[18]

In 1908 there was published in *The Auk* an article by Ruthven Deane concerning the copper plates, including a list of 37 which he had been able to locate.[19] In this article it is stated: "Under date of February 10, 1908, Miss Grace H. Dodge writes me that the plates were stored in the warehouse of Phelps, Dodge and Company, New York, about 1865, and at that time her father, the late William F. Dodge, had them sorted and presented a number of those that were in the best state of preservation to several colleges, museums, friends and members of his family." Mr. Dodge did indeed present plates to the American Museum of Natural History, Metropolitan Museum of Art, Smithsonian Institution, and Princeton University. However, this must have been done long after 1865, for it is evident from the Putnam advertisement that the plates were still in the possession of Mrs. Audubon in 1870.

In the article Deane continues:

> The probabilities are that the majority of the plates were shipped from the New York warehouse to the Ansonia Brass and Copper Company, Ansonia, Conn., of which company Mr. Dodge was president, and I am indebted to Charles A. Cowles of Ansonia for a most interesting account of how he was the means of saving several of these plates from being thrown into the smelting furnace and converted into copper bars. I quote from Mr. Cowles' letter of March 7, 1907: "The story of saving these plates from a smelting furnace will probably interest you. Some time about the year 1873, there were found a number of Audubon copper plates among the scrap copper sent to the refinery of the Ansonia Brass & Copper Company at Ansonia, Conn., to be converted into copper bars. I am of the opinion that the number included the complete set of the plates engraved by Robert Havell for the Birds of America.
>
> "At that time I was about fourteen years old. I was beginning the study of taxidermy, and was naturally deeply interested in birds. I happened to be at the refinery watching the process of loading one of the furnaces, and noted on one of the sheets of copper that a man was throwing into the furnace, what appeared to me to be a picture of a bird's foot. I took the plate from him, cleaned it with acid, and thereupon discovered the engraving, or as I termed it, the picture of a bird [Plate 106, Black Vulture]. I made an immediate but unsuccessful request to the foreman of the furnace not to melt the plates; and then I appealed to the superintendent, but without avail. I next brought the matter to the general manager of the concern, my father, from whom I received no encouragement. This sort of treatment was evidently what I needed, for I hastened back to the works in a state of mind so determined that I succeeded in having all of the plates that had not been melted removed to a place of safety. This occurred in the spring of the year; and the plates remained undisturbed until the annual inventory was taken the first of the following year. At that time the question of the disposition of the plates was brought up. I appealed to my mother and interested her to such an extent that she drove to the factory and looked at one of the plates. She of course recognized that they were Audubon plates; and in-

structions were given to my father to keep them intact. The plates were subsequently submitted to a treatment which removed all oxidation and then taken to the main office of the company, and to the best of my recollection, distributed as follows: Mr. W. E. Dodge, president of the company had a few plates sent to the American Museum of Natural History, New York City, and a few plates to the Smithsonian Institution, Washington, D.C., and I think retained one or two for himself. The remainder of them, with the exception of two, my father kept; and they have since come into my possession by purchase from the estate. The two plates just excepted were Nos. 22 [Purple Martin] and 82 [Whip-Poor-Will] and they particularly struck my fancy, so much so that when the plates were first discovered I managed to secure them on the quiet, cleaned them myself and hid them, and when the plates were distributed no one knew of the existence of these two and they later became my property.

"I have sent two plates to Miss M. R. Audubon and there are two others that I think I could locate. This will make nine plates that I know of besides the plates in the museums previously mentioned and those that may be in the possession of the heirs of Mr. Wm. E. Dodge."[20]

In his account Deane also related that John H. Sage of Portland, Conn., had obtained two plates, and that Pickering from whom Sage had obtained his plates had presented two plates to Wesleyan University at Middletown, Conn. These were Plate 309, the "Great Tern," and Plate 409, "Havell's and Trudeau's Terns,"[21] which remain in the possession of the university.

As to the copper plates which Cowles wrote he had sent to Miss Audubon, these are alluded to in a letter written by her to *Forest and Stream* in 1896, wherein she states: "Two, the Snow Goose [pl. 381], and the Great White Heron [pl. 281], are in my possession, having been given to me by an utter stranger, who most liberally sent them to me, hearing I regretted owning none. This gentleman (whose name I shall withhold at his request) has a number set in the walls of his dining-room. He wrote to me that his father bought them at a sale of the old copper plates some years ago."[22]

While all the details do not agree, the two plates mentioned by Miss Audubon as having been given to her by an "utter stranger" were probably the ones mentioned by Mr. Cowles as having been sent to Miss M. R. Audubon. At a later date these were presented by her to the American Museum of Natural History.

In 1934 another article concerning the plates was prepared by Phoebe Knappen of the Biological Survey, Washington, D.C., and published in *The Auk*.[23] Not only was she able to bring up to date the locations of the extant plates for which changes had taken place, but she also located additional ones, with the result that, in all, 59 were recorded.

The Deane and Knappen articles and lists provided the starting point for the current list of extant copper plates and their ownership or location. Listed are 78 plates, as well as their most recent location or ownership, of which all but three have been verified. Examination of some plates has revealed that Havell had more than one source of the copper he used to make the engravings of Audubon's drawings. The names and addresses of two of his suppliers—namely A. Hian, 9 Ratcliff Road, Bath Street, City Rd. and Pontifex & Stiles, 23 Lisle Street, Soho, London—have been found on the plates. Some of the plates examined by the author also were steel faced, but when this had been done is not known.

EXTANT COPPER PLATES

Plate		Location
1.	Wild Turkey	Cleveland E. Dodge, New York, N.Y.
2.	Yellow-billed Cuckoo	Metropolitan Museum of Art, New York, N.Y.
6.	Great American Hen and Young (Wild Turkey)	American Museum of Natural History, New York, N.Y.
11.	Bird of Washington (Bald Eagle)	Metropolitan Museum of Art, New York, N.Y.
12.	Baltimore Oriole	Not located.[24]
21.	Mocking Bird	Groton School, Groton, Mass.
22.	Purple Martin	Philip B. Schnering, Stevenson, Md.
37.	Gold-winged Woodpecker (Flicker)	Estate of Richard S. Martin, Berkeley Heights, N.J.
47.	Ruby-throated Hummingbird	Edward Ballentine, Santa Barbara, Calif.
52.	Chuck-will's Widow	Smithsonian Institution, Washington, D.C.
56.	Red-shouldered Hawk	Princeton University, Princeton, N.J.
64.	Swamp Sparrow	New York Botanical Garden, New York, N.Y.
71.	Winter Hawk (Red-shouldered Hawk)	Metropolitan Museum of Art, New York, N.Y.
72.	Swallow-tailed Hawk (Swallowtailed Kite)	Pratt Memorial Library, Cohasset, Mass.
76.	Virginian Partridge (Bob-White)	Smithsonian Institution, Washington, D.C.
82.	Whip-poor-will	Estate of Frederic E. Church, Near Hudson, N.Y.
83.	House Wren	New-York Historical Society, New York, N.Y.
99.	Cow Bunting (Cowbird)	New York Zoological Society, Bronx Park, N.Y.
101.	Raven	Princeton University, Princeton, N.J.
102.	Blue Jay	Metropolitan Museum of Art, New York, N.Y.
106.	Black Vulture or Carrion Crow	Yale University, New Haven, Conn.
107.	Canada Jay	Metropolitan Museum of Art, New York, N.Y.
112.	Downy Woodpecker	New York Zoological Society, Bronx Park, N.Y.
113.	Blue Bird	Not located.[25]
121.	Snowy Owl	American Museum of Natural History, New York, N.Y.
131.	American Robin	Smithsonian Institution, Washington, D.C.
138.	Connecticut Warbler	New-York Historical Society, New York, N.Y.

APPENDIX G

Plate		Location
144.	Small Green-crested Flycatcher (Acadian Flycatcher)	Howard A. Van Vleck, Montclair, N.J.
150.	Red-eyed Vireo	Robert D. Johnson, Houston, Texas.
157.	Rusty Grakle	Donald Rowell, Coconut Grove, Fla.
161.	Brazilian Caracara Eagle (Audubon's Caracara)	Metropolitan Museum of Art, New York, N.Y.
167.	Key West Dove (Key West Quail-Dove)	Estate of Richard S. Martin, Berkeley Heights, N.J.
177.	White Headed Pigeon	J. Stewart Kellogg, New York, N.Y.
190.	Yellow-bellied Woodpecker (Yellow-bellied Sapsucker)	Rosedown Plantation, St. Francisville, La.
194.	Canadian or Hudson Bay Titmouse (Hudsonian Chickadee)	New York Botanical Garden, Bronx Park, N.Y.
196.	Labrador Falcon (Gyrfalcon)	Audubon Shrine and Wildlife Sanctuary, Audubon, Pa.
201.	Canada Goose	Audubon Museum, Henderson, Ky. (on loan from American Museum of Natural History)
211.	Great Blue Heron	Not located.[26]
217.	Louisiana Heron	Robert D. Johnson, Houston, Texas.
221.	Mallard Duck	American Museum of Natural History, New York, N.Y.
226.	Hooping Crane (Whooping Crane)	Smithsonian Institution, Washington, D.C.
236.	Night Heron (Black-crowned Night Heron)	Cleveland E. Dodge, Jr.
253.	Jaeger (Pomarine Jaeger)	Bayard Dodge.
257.	Double-crested Cormorant	A. Douglas Dodge.
259.	Horned Grebe	Smithsonian Institution, Washington, D.C.
261.	Hooping Crane (Sandhill Crane)	Smithsonian Institution, Washington, D.C.
267.	Arctic Jaeger (Long-tailed Jaeger)	Edward Ballentine, Santa Barbara, Calif.
271.	Frigate Pelican (Man-o'-War-Bird)	Carnegie Institute Library, Pittsburgh, Pa.
277.	Hutchins's Barnacle Goose	American Museum of Natural History, New York, N.Y.
278.	Schinz's Sandpiper (White-rumped Sandpiper)	Albert E. Lownes, Providence, R.I.
281.	Great White Heron	American Museum of Natural History, New York, N.Y.
291.	Herring Gull	Yale University, New Haven, Conn.

The Copper Plates

Plate		Location
297.	Harlequin Duck	Johns Hopkins University, Evergreen House, Baltimore, Md.
306.	Great Northern Diver or Loon (Common Loon)	American Museum of Natural History, New York, N.Y.
308.	Tell-tale Godwit (Greater Yellow-Legs)	George F. Havell, Fayetteville, N.Y.
309.	Great Tern (Common Tern)	Wesleyan College, Middletown, Conn.
322.	Red-headed Duck	Mrs. W. B. Marvin, Ansonia, Conn.
323.	Black Skimmer or Shearwater	Yale University, New Haven, Conn.
338.	Bemaculated Duck	Paul Mellon, Upperville, Va.
356.	Marsh Hawk	Yale University, New Haven, Conn.
358.	Pine Grosbeak	Rosedown Plantation, St. Francisville, La.
362.	Yellow-billed Magpie, Steller's Jay, California Jay, and Clark's Nutcracker	John E. Parsons, Harrison, N.Y.
372.	Common Buzzard (Swainson's Hawk)	Metropolitan Museum of Art, New York, N.Y.
378.	Hawk Owl	American Museum of Natural History, New York, N.Y.
381.	Snow Goose (Blue and Snow Goose)	American Museum of Natural History, New York, N.Y.
391.	Brant Goose (American Brant)	Pleasant Valley Bird & Wildlife Sanctuary, Lenox, Mass.
392.	Louisiana Hawk (Harris's Hawk)	American Museum of Natural History, New York, N.Y.
397.	Scarlet Ibis	Smithsonian Institution, Washington, D.C.
407.	Dusky Albatros (American Sooty Albatros)	American Museum of Natural History, New York, N.Y.
408.	American Scoter Duck	Yale University, New Haven, Conn.
409.	Havell's and Trudeau's Terns (Forster's and Trudeau's Terns)	Wesleyan College, Middletown, Conn.
410.	Marsh Tern	Mrs. Belton A. Copp, Smith Neck, Old Lyme, Conn.
415.	Brown Creeper, California Nuthatch (Pygmy Nuthatch)	Mrs. Kirk Fourcher, Ridgefield, Conn.
417.	Maria's, Three-toed, Phillips's, Canadian, Harris's, and Audubon's Woodpeckers	Princeton University, Princeton, N.J.
421.	Brown Pelican	Metropolitan Museum of Art, New York, N.Y.

APPENDIX G

Plate		Location
422.	Rough-legged Falcon (Rough-legged Hawk)	Princeton University, Princeton, N.J.
432.	Burrowing Owl, Large-headed Burrowing Owl, Little Night Owl, Shorteared Owl	New-York Historical Society, New York, N.Y.
434.	Flycatchers (Flycatchers and Vireo)	Mrs. James Rea, Pittsburgh, Pa.

H

CHRONOLOGY OF THE ENGRAVING OF THE PLATES

1826

Lizars undertook the engraving on 10 November 1826. By 31 December 1826 it is likely that two plates of Number 1 were completed (pl.1, Great American Cock; pl.2, Yellow-billed Cuckoo).

1827

By 1 May 1827, plates 3, 4, and 5 (Prothonotary Warbler, Purple Finch, and Bonaparte Flycatcher) had been engraved. On 1 August 1827 the work was transferred to London, by which time Lizars had completed the engraving of plates 6, 7, 8, 9, and 10 (Great American Hen and Young, Purple Grakle, White-throated Sparrow, Selby's Flycatcher, and Brown Lark), which comprised Number 2. Havell, during the remainder of the year, engraved Numbers 3, 4, and 5, plates 11 to 25, inclusive.

1828

Havell engraved Numbers 6 to 10, comprising plates 26 to 50, inclusive.

1829

Numbers 11 to 15, inclusive, comprising plates 51 to 75 were engraved by Havell.

1830

Havell engraved Numbers 16 to 20, comprising plates 76 to 100, inclusive, completing Volume I, probably in October or November 1830.

1831

Havell engraved Numbers 21 to 25, plates 101 to 125, inclusive.

APPENDIX H

1832

Havell engraved Numbers 26 to 31, plates 126 to 155, inclusive.

1833

Havell engraved Numbers 32 to 37, plates 156 to 185, inclusive. On 24 November 1833, JJA wrote his son Victor in London, asking "Could we not manage to publish 8 or 10 numbers per annum of that third volume?" Havell appears to have complied with the Naturalist's request in the following year.

1834

Havell engraved Numbers 38 to 47, plates 186 to 235, inclusive. Volume 2 was completed in February 1834.

1835

Havell engraved Numbers 48 to 58, plates 236 to 290, inclusive.

1836

Havell engraved Numbers 59 to 68, plates 291 to 340, inclusive. Volume 3 was completed in January 1836, although this actually may have occurred in December 1835.

1837

Havell engraved Numbers 69 to 80, plates 341 to 400, inclusive.

1838

Havell engraved Numbers 81 to 85, plates 401 to 435, inclusive, the engraving of the plates having been completed on 16 June 1838.

SUMMARY

Engraving of plates began	10 Nov. 1826
Volume 1 (plates 1–100) completed	Oct.–Nov. 1830
Volume 2 (plates 101–200) completed	Feb. 1834
Volume 3 (plates 201–300) completed	Jan. 1836 (possibly Dec. 1835)
Volume 4 (plates 301–435) completed	16 June 1838

I

BAY'S ALPHABETICAL INDEX TO THE *BIRDS OF AMERICA*

KEY TO THE ABBREVIATIONS
ad.—adult ad.m.—adult male ad.f.—adult female f.—female m.—male
m.f.—male and female m.f.y.—male, female and young
y.—young

Alauda alpestris Z. m.f.y. 200
Albatross, dusky. 407
Alca impenna 341
    ″ torda m. & f. 214
Alcedo alcyon L. m.f. 77
American avocet ad. 318
    ″ bittern m.f. 337
    ″ coot 239
    ″ crossbill m.f.y. 197
    ″ crow m. 156
    ″ flamingo m. 431
    ″ golden crested wren m.f. 183
    ″ goldfinch m.f. 33
    ″ gull, common ad., y. 212
    ″ magpie m.f. 357
    ″ oyster catcher 223
    ″ piedbill dobchick 248
    ″ ptarmigan m. 418
    ″ redstart m.f. 40
    ″ robin m.f.y. 131
    ″ scoter duck m.f. 408
    ″ snipe m.f. 243
    ″ sparrow hawk m.f. 142

[American] swift m.f. 158
    ″ water ouzel m.f. 370
    ″ white pelican m.ad. 311
    ″ widgeon m.f. 345
    ″ woodcock m.f.y. 268
Anas americana Gm. m.f. 345
    ″ Boschas m.f. 221
    ″ clypeata L. m.f. 327
    ″ crecea Lath. m.f. 228
    ″ discors m.f. 313
    ″ glocitans m.y. 338
    ″ obscura m.f. 302
    ″ sponsa L. m.f. 206
    ″ strepera L. m.f. 348
Anser albifrons m.f. 286
    ″ bernicla m.f. 391
    ″ Hutchinsii Richd. & Swain. 277
    ″ hyperboreus Pallas m.f. 381
    ″ leucopsis m.f. 296
Anthus pipiens m. 80
    ″ spinoletta Bonap. m.f. 10
Aramus scolopaceus Vieill. 377
Arctic bluebird m.f. 393

This list, which provides the common and scientific names of the birds appearing on the plates comprising the set of the folio of Audubon's *Birds of America* in the collection of the John Crerar Library, was compiled in 1911 by Jens Christian Bay. Dr. Bay at the time was the Crerar Library's reference librarian. The list was typed and reproduced on the hectograph in 1932 and distributed as "The John Crerar Reference List no.17." It is now out of print, but the hand-written Bay manuscript itself remains in the library's collection.

APPENDIX I

[Arctic] ground finch m.f. 394
    ″ tern 250
    ″ water ouzel m. 435
    ″ yager 267
Ardea alba L. m. 386
    ″ candidissima Gmel. ad.m. 242
    ″ coerulea ad.m. & y. 307
    ″ exilis m.f.y. 210
    ″ herodias 216
    ″ ludoviciana Wils. m.ad. 217
    ″ minor m.f. 337
    ″ nycticorax L. ad.,y. 236
    ″ occidentalis m.ad. 281
    ″ rufescens Buff. ad.,y. 256
    ″ violacea L. ad.m.,y. 336
    ″ virescens ad.m.,y. 333
Arkansaw flycatcher m.f. 359
    ″ siskin m. 400
Audubon's warbler m.f. 395
    ″ woodpecker m. 417
Auk, curled-crested 402
    ″ , great 341
    ″ , little m.f. 339
    ″ , nobbed billed 402
    ″ , razor billed m.f. 214
Autumnal warbler m.f. 88
Avocet, American ad. 318
    ″ , long legged m. 328
Azure warbler m.f. 48

Bachman's finch m. 165
    ″ warbler m.f. 185
Baltimore oriole f. 433
    ″ ″ m.f. 12
Band tailed pigeon m.f. 367
Bank swallow m.f.y. 385
Barn owl m.f. 171
    ″ swallow m.f. 173
Barnacle goose m.f. 296
    ″ ″ Hutchins's 277
Barred owl m. 46
Bartram sandpiper m.f. 303
Bartram's vireo m. 434
Bay-breasted warbler m.f. 69
    ″ winged bunting m. 94
Belted kingfisher m.f. 77
Bemaculated duck m.y. 338
Bewick's wren m. 18
Bird of Washington 11
Bird, tropic m. 262
Bittern, American m.f. 337
    ″ least m.f.y. 210
Black and white creeper m. 90
    ″ ″ yellow warbler m.f. 123
    ″ ″ ″ ″ m.(y.) 50
    ″ backed gull 241

[Black] bellied darter 316
    ″ ″ plover ad.m.,y. 334
Black billed cuckoo m.f. 32
Blackbird, common crow m.f. 7
    ″ , marsh m.f.y. 67
Blackburnian warbler f. 399
    ″ ″ m. 135
Black-capt titmouse m.f. 353
Black Crown bunting ad.m. 394
    ″ duck m.f. 317
    ″ guillemot ad. & y. 219
    ″ headed gull ad.m. & y. 314
    ″ ″ siskin m. 394
    ″ poll warbler m.f. 133
    ″ skimmer m. 323
    ″ tern ad. & y. 280
    ″ -throated blue warbler m. 155
    ″ ″ bunting m. 384
    ″ ″ diver m.f.y. 346
    ″ ″ green warbler m.f. 399
    ″ ″ grey warbler m. 395
    ″ ″ guillemot ad. & y. 402
Black vulture m.f. 106
    ″ warrior m.f. 86
    ″ winged hawk m.f. 352
Blue crane ad.m. & y. 307
Blue-green warbler m. 49
    ″ -grey flycatcher m.f. 84
Blue grosbeak m.f.y. 122
    ″ headed pigeon m.f. 172
Blue heron ad.m. & y. 307
    ″ jay m.f. 102
    ″ mountain warbler m. 434
    ″ winged teal m.f. 313
    ″ ″ yellow warbler m.f. 20
Blue yellow-backed warbler m.f. 15
Bluebird m.f.y. 113
    ″ , arctic m.f. 393
    ″ , Western m.f. 393
Boat tailed grackle m.f. 187
Bohemian chatterer m.f. 363
Bombycilia carolinensis Briss. m.f. 43
    ″ garrula m.f. 363
Bonaparte's flycatcher m. 5
    ″ gull m.f.y. 324
Booby gannet 207
Brant goose m.f. 391
Brasilian Caracara eagle 161
Broad winged hawk m.f. 91
Brown creeper m.f. 415
    ″ -headed nuthatch m.f. 125
    ″ ″ worm-eating warbler 198
    ″ longspur f. 424
    ″ pelican m.ad. 251
    ″ ″ y. 421
Brown songsparrow m. 390
    ″ titlark m.f. 10

Alphabetical Index to the *Birds of America*

Buff-breasted finch m. 400
" " sandpiper m.f. 265
Buffel-headed duck m.f. 325
Bullfinch, crimson-necked m. 424
Bullock's oriole m.f. 388, 433
Bunting, bay-winged 94
" , black crown ad.m. 394
" , " -throated m. 384
" , Henslow's m. 70
" , snow ad. & y. 189
" , Towhe 29
Burgomaster gull m. & y. 396
Burrowing owl m. 432
" " , large-headed m. 432
Butcher-bird m.f.y. 192
Buteo Harrisi Aud. ad.f. 392
" lagopus m. & y. 422
" vulgaris f. 372
Buzzard, common f. 372
" , Turkey m. & y. 151

Californian nuthatch 415
" partridge m.f. 413
" vulture m. 426
Canada goose m.f. 201
" grouse m.f. 176
" jay m.f. 107
" " m. & y. 419
" warbler m.f. 103
Canadian titmouse m.f.y. 194
" woodpecker m. 417
Canvas back duck m.f. 301
Cape May warbler m.f. 414
Caprimulgus carolinensis Briss. m.f. 52
" virginianus Briss. m.f. 147
" vociferus Wils. m.f. 82
Caracara eagle, Brasilian 161
Carbonated warbler m. 70
Cardinal grosbeak m.f. 159
Carduelis mexicanus Swains. m.f. 433
Carolina parrot m.f. 26
" titmouse m.f. 160
" turtle-dove m.f. 17
" wren m.f. 78
Carrion crow m.f. 106
Cat bird 128
Cathartes atratus m.f. 106
" aura m. & y. 151
" californianus Illiger m. 426
Cayenne tern m.ad. 273
Cedar bird m.f. 43
Ceratorrhinca occidentalis Bonap. 402
Certhia familiaris L. m.f. 415
" varia Wils. m. 90
Charadrius helveticus ad.m. & y. 334
" melodus m.f. 220
" montanus Townsend ad.f. 350

[Charadrius] pluvialis L. 300
" semipalmatus ad.m. & y. 330
" Wilsonius 284
" " m.f. 209
Chat, yellow breasted m.f. 137
Chatterer, Bohemian m.f. 363
Chestnut-backed titmouse m.f. 353
" -colored finch m. 394
" -crowned titmouse m.f. & nest 353
" -sided warbler m.f. 59
Children's warbler m.f. 35
Chipping sparrow m. 104
Chuck-will's widow m.f. 52
Cinclus americanus m.f. 370
" Mortoni Townsend m. 435
" Townsendi Aud. f. 435
Clangula vulgaris 403
Clark's crow 362
Clay colored finch m. 398
Cliff swallow m.f. & egg. 69
Coccyzus americanus Bonap. m.f. 2
" erythrophthalmus Bonap. m.f. 32
" seniculus m. 159
Cock of the plains m.f. 371
Columba carolinensis L. m.f. 17
" cyanocephala m.f. 172
" fasciata m.f. 367
" leucocephala m.f. 177
" migratoria L. m.f. 62
" montana m.f. 167
" passerina m.f.y. 182
" zenaida m.f. 162
Columbia jay m.f. 96
Columbian humming bird m.f. 425
" owl m. 432
" water-ouzel f. 435
Colymbus arcticus L. m.f.y. 346
" glacialis ad. & y. 306
" septentrionalis m.f.y. 202
Common crow blackbird m.f. 7
" gallinule ad.m. 244
" water-thrush m. 433
Connecticut warbler m.f. 138
Coot, American 239
Cormorant, common m.f.y. 266
" , double crested ad.m. 257
" , Florida ad.m. 252
" , Townsend's m. 412
" , violet-green f. 412
Corvus americanus m. 156
" bullockii m.f. 96
" canadensis m. & y. 419
" " m.f. 107
" columbianus Wils. 362
" corax m. 101
" cristatus m.f. 102
" floridanus Bartram m.f. 87

APPENDIX I

[Corvus] Nuttallii Aud. 362
"   ossifragus Wils. m.f. 146
"   pica m.f. 357
"   Stelleri 362
"   ultramarinus 362
Courlan, scolopaceous 377
Cow-pen bird m.f. 99
"   "   m.y. 424
Crane, blue ad.m.& y. 307
" , hooping ad.m. 226
" ,   "   y. 261
Creeper, black and white m. 90
" , brown m.f. 415
Crested flycatcher m. 129
"   grebe ad.m.& y. 292
"   titmouse m.f. 39
Crimson-necked bullfinch m. 424
Crow, American m. 156
Crow, blackbird m.f. 7
" , Clark's 362
" , fish m.f. 146
Crossbill, American m.f.y. 197
" , white-winged m.f.y. 197
Cuckoo, black-billed 32
" , mangrove m. 159
" , yellow-billed m.f. 2
Curled-crested auk 402
Curlew, Esquimaux m.f. 208
" , great Esquimaux 237
" , long tailed m.f. 231
" , sandpiper ad.m.& y. 263
Cuvier's regulus m. 55
Cygnus americanus Sharpless 411
"   buccinator Rich. y. 376
"   "   ad. 406
Cypselus pelasgius Temm. m.f. 158

Darter, black bellied 316
Diomedea fusca 407
Diver, black throated m.f.y. 346
" , red throated m.f.y. 202
Dobchick, American pied-bill 248
Double-crested cormorant m.ad. 257
Dove, ground m.f.y. 182
" , Zeneida [zenaida/WHF] m.f. 162
Downy woodpecker m.f. 112
Duck, American scoter m.f. 408
" , Bemaculated m.y. 338
" , black m.f. 317
" , buffel headed m.f. 325
" , canvas backed m.f. 301
" , dusky m.f. 302
" , Eider m.f. 246
" , Gadwall m.f. 348
" , golden-eye 403
" ,   "   "   m.f. 342
" , Harlequin m.f.y. 297

[Duck], king m.f. 276
" , long tailed m.f.y. 312
" , mallard m.f. 221
" , pied m.ad.& f. 332
" , pin-tailed m.f. 227
" , red headed m.f. 322
" , ring necked m.f. 234
" , ruddy m.f.y. 343
" , scaup m.f. 229
" , shoveler m.f. 327
" , summer m.f. 206
" , surf m.f. 317
" , velvet m.f. 247
" , Western 429
" , wood m.f. 206
Dusky albatross 407
"   duck m.f. 302
"   grouse m.f. 361
"   petrel m. 299

Eagle, Brasilian Caracara 161
" , golden f. 181
" , white-headed m. 31
" ,   "   "   y. 126
Eared grebe ad.& y. 404
Egret, reddish ad.& y. 256
" , white ad.m. 242
Eider duck m.f. 246
Emberiza atricapilla Gmel. ad.m. 394
"   Henslowii m. 70
"   nivalis ad.& y. 189
"   pallida swains m. 398
"   picta m. 400
"   Townsendi m. 400
Esquimaux curlew m.f. 208
"   "   , great 237
Evening grosbeak m. 373
"   "   m.f. 424

Falco borealis Gmel. m.f. 51
"   chrysaetos f. 181
"   columbarius L. m.f. 92
"   cyaneus m.f.y. 356
"   dispar m.f. 352
"   furcatus m. 72
"   haliaetus m. 81
"   harlani m.f. 86
"   hyemalis Gmel. m. 71
"   labradora m.f. 196
"   lagopus m. 166
"   leucocephalus L. m. 31
"   "   y. 126
"   lineatus Gmel. m.f. 56
"   palumbarius L. m.& y. 141
"   pennsylvanicus Wils. m.f. 91
"   peregrinus Gmel. m.f. 16
"   plumbeus Gmel. m.f. 117

Alphabetical Index to the *Birds of America*

[Falco] sparverius m.f. 142
" Stanleii Aud. ad. 141
" " [Stanleyi] m.f. 36
" temerarius m. 75
" velox Wils. m.f. 374
" Washingtonii Aud. m. 11
Falcon, Iceland f. 366
" , Jer. f. 366
" , Labrador m.f. 196
" , rough-legged m. 166
" , " " m.& y. 422
Ferrugineous thrush m.f. 116
Field sparrow m. 139
Finch, arctic ground m.f. 394
" , Bachman's m. 165
" , buff breasted m. 400
" , chestnut colored m. 394
" , clay colored m. 398
" , grass m. 94
" , lark m. 390
" , Lazuli f. 424
" , Lincoln m.f. 193
" , McGillivray's m.f. 355
" , Oregon snow m.f. 398
" , painted m.f. 53
" , pine m.f. 180
" , prairie m.f. 390
" , purple m.f. 4
" , Savanna m.t. 109
" , sharp tailed m.f. 149
" , Townsend's m. 400
Fish crow m.f. 146
" hawk m. 81
Flamingo, American m. 431
Florida cormorant ad.m. 252
" jay m.f. 87
Flycatcher, Arkansaw m.f. 359
" , blue grey m.f. 84
" , Bonaparte's m. 5
" , fork-tailed m. 168
" , green black-capt m.f. 124
" , little tyrant 434
" , olive-sided m.f. 174
" , Pewee m.f. 120
" , pipiry 170
" , Rocky Mountain m. 434
" , Say's m.f. 359
" , Selby's m. 9
" , small green-crested m.f. 144
" , small-headed m. 434
" , solitary m.f. 28
" , swallow-tailed m. 359
" , Traill's m. 45
" , tyrant m.f. 79
" , warbling m.f. 118
" , white eyed m. 63
Foolish guillemot. m.f. 218

Forked-tailed flycatcher m. 168
" " gull m. 285
" " petrel m.f. 260
Fox-coloured sparrow m.f. 108
Fresh water marsh-hen m.& y. 203
Frigate pelican m.ad. 271
Fringilla americana m.f. 384
" amoena Say m. 398
" " f. 424
" Bachmani m. 165
" bicolor Townsend m.f. 390
" canadensis Lath. m.f. 188
" cardinalis Bonap. m.f. 159
" caudacuta Wils. m.f. 149
" cinerea Gmel. m. 390
" ciris Temm. m.f. 53
" corulea Bonap. [sic!] m.f.y. 122
" cyanea Wils. m.f. 74
" erythrophthalma L. m.f. 29
" graminea Gmel. m. 94
" grammaca Say m. 390
" hyemalis L. m.f. 13
" iliaca m.f. 108
" laponica m.f. 365
" leucophrys m.f. 114
" linaria L. m.f. 375
" Lincolnii m.f. 193
" ludoviciana Bonap. m.f.y. 127
" Macgillivrayii m.f. 355
" maculata m.f. 373
" magellanica Vieill. m. 394
" melodia Wils. m.f. 25
" oregona Townd. m.f. 398
" palustris Wils. m. 64
" passerini Wils. m. 130
" pennsylvanica Lath. m.f. 8
" pinus m.f. 180
" purpurea Gmel. m.f. 4
" pusilla Wils. m. 139
" savanna m.f. 109
" socialis m. 104
" spaltria m. 400
" tristis L. m.f. 33
" vespertina Cooper m. 373
" " m.f. 424
Fulica americana Gmel. 239
Fuligula albeola m.f. 325
" americana m.f. 408
" clangula m.f. 342
" ferina Steph. m.f. 322
" fusca m.f. 247
" glacialis m.f.y. 312
" histrionica m.f.y. 297
" labradora m.ad.& f. 332
" marila m.f. 229
" mollissima m.f. 246
" perspicillata m.f. 317

APPENDIX I

[Fuligula] rubida m.f.y. 343
" rufitorques Bonap. m.f. 234
" spectabilis Lath. m.f. 276
" Stelleri Bonap. 429
" vallisneriana Steph. m.f. 301
Fulmar petrel ad.m. 264

Gadwall 16
" duck m.f. 348
Gallinula chloropus ad.m. 244
" martinica ad.m. 305
Gallinule, purple ad.m. 305
Gannet ad.m. & y. 326
" , Booby 207
Glossy ibis ad.m. 387
Godwit, great marbled m.f. 238
" , Hudsonian m.f. 258
" , telltale m.f. 308
Golden-crested wren, American m.f. 183
" -crowned thrush m.f. 143
Golden eagle f. 181
Golden-eye duck m. 403
" " " m.f. 342
Golden plover 300
Golden-winged woodpecker m.f. 37
Goldfinch, American m.f. 33
" , Mexican m.f. 433
Goosander m.f. 331
Goose, barnacle m.f. 296
" , Brant m.f. 391
" , Canada m.f. 201
" , Hutchins's barnacle 277
" , snow m.f. 381
" , white-fronted m.f. 286
Goshawk m. & y. 141
Grackle, boat-tailed m.f. 187
" , purple m.f. 7
" , rusty m.f.y. 157
Grass finch m. 94
Gray-crowned linnet m. 424
Great auk 341
" blue heron m. 216
" Carolina wren m.f. 78
" cinereous owl ad.f. 351
" crested flycatcher m. 129
" Esquimaux curlew 237
" horned owl m.f. 61
" marbled godwit m.f. 238
" northern diver ad. & y. 306
" tern m. 309
Great-footed hawk m.f. 16
Grebe, crested ad.m. & y. 292
" , eared ad. & y. 404
" , horned m.f. 259
" , red necked ad.m. 298
Green black-capt flycatcher m.f. 124
" heron ad.m. & y. 333

Green-crested flycatcher, small m.f. 144
Green-winged teal m.f. 228
Greenshank 269
Grosbeak [blue/WHF] m.f.y. 122
" , cardinal m.f. 159
" , evening m. 373
" , " m.f. 424
" , pine m.f.y. 358
" , rose-breasted m.f.y. 127
" , spotted m.f. 373
Ground dove m.f.y. 182
" finch, arctic m.f. 394
Grouse, Canada m.f. 176
" , dusky m.f. 361
" , long tailed m.f. 361
" , pinnated m.f. 186
" , rock m.f.y. 368
" , ruffed m.f. 41
" , sharp tailed m.f. 382
" , spotted m.f. 176
Grus americana ad.m. 226
" " y. 261
Guillemot, black ad. & y. 219
" , foolish m.f. 218
" , horned-billed 402
" , large-billed 245
" , red-throated ad. & y. 402
" , slender-billed m.f. 430
Gull, black-headed ad.m. & y. 314
" , Bonapartian m.f.y. 324
" , burgomaster m. & y. 396
" , common American ad. & y. 212
" , forked-tailed m. 285
" , herring ad.m. & y. 291
" , ivory ad.m. & y. 287
" , Kittiwake ad. & y. 224
" , white-winged silvery m. & y. 282

Haematopus Bachmani Aud. m. 427
" palliatus 223
" Townsendi Aud. f. 427
Hairy woodpecker m.f. 416
Harlequin duck m.f.y. 297
Harris's woodpecker m.f. 417
Havell's tern 409
Hawk, black-winged m.f. 352
" , broad-winged m.f. 91
" , fish m. 81
" , great-footed m.f. 16
" , Louisiana ad.f. 392
" , marsh m.f.y. 356
" , pigeon m.f. 92
" , red-shouldered m.f. 56
" , red-tailed m.f. 51
" , sharp-shinned m.f. 374
" , sparrow (American) m.f. 142
" , Stanley m.f. 36

Alphabetical Index to the *Birds of America*

[Hawk], winter m. 71
Hawk owl m.f. 378
Hemlock warbler m.f. 134
Henslow's bunting m. 70
Hermit thrush m.f. 58
    ″ warbler m.f. 395
Heron, great blue m. 216
  ″ , green ad.m.& y. 333
  ″ , night ad.& y. 236
  ″ , snowy ad.m. 242
  ″ , white m. 281, 386
  ″ , yellow-crowned ad.m.& y. 336
Herring gull ad.m.& y. 291
Himantopus nigricollis Vieill. m. 328
Hirundo bicolor Vieill. m.f. 98
  ″ fulva Vieill. m.f.& egg 68
  ″ purpurea L. m.f. 22
  ″ riparia m.f.y. 385
  ″ rustica m.f. 173
  ″ thalassina Swain. m.f. 385
Hooded merganser m.f. 232
  ″ warbler m.f. 110
Hooping crane ad.m. 226
  ″   ″ y. 261
Horned-billed guillemot 402
Horned grebe m.f. 259
  ″ owl m.f. 61
House wren m.f.y. 83
Hudsonian godwit m.f. 258
Humming-bird, Columbian m.f. 425
  ″   ″ , Mango m.f. 184
  ″   ″ , ruff-necked m.f. 379
  ″   ″ , yellow-throated m.f. 47
Hutchins's barnacle goose 277
Hyperborean phalarope m.f.y. 215

Ibis alba ad.& y. 222
 ″ falcinellus ad.m. 387
Ibis, glossy ad.m. 387
 ″ , rubra ad.m.& y. 397
Ibis, white ad.& y. 222
Iceland falcon f. 366
Icteria viridis Bonap. m.f. 137
Icterus agripennis Ch. Bonap. m.f. 54
   ″ Baltimore Bonap. f. 433
   ″   ″ m.f. 12
   ″ Bullockii Swains. m.f. 388, 433
   ″ gubernator Aud. m.f. 420
   ″ pecoris Bonap. m.f. 99
   ″   ″ m.& y. 424
   ″ phoeniceus Daud. m.f.y. 67
   ″ spurius Bonap. m.f. 42
   ″ tricolor Aud. ad.m. 388
   ″ xanthocephalus Bonap. m.f. 388
Indigo bird m. 74

Ivory-billed woodpecker m.f. 66
  ″ gull ad.m.& y. 287

Jager, pomarine 253
  ″ , Richardson's ad.m.& y. 272
Jay, Canada m.f. 107
  ″ ,   ″ m.& y. 419
  ″ , Columbia m.f. 96
  ″ , Florida m.f. 87
  ″ , Steller's 362
  ″ , ultramarine 362
Jer falcon f. 366

Kentucky warbler m.f. 38
Key West pigeon m. 166
Kildeer plover m.f. 225
King duck m.f. 276
Kingfisher, belted m.f. 77
Kite, Mississippi m.f. 117
Kittiwake gull ad.& y. 224

Labrador falcon m.f. 196
Lanius excubitor m.f.y. 192
  ″ ludovicianus L. m.f. 57
Lapland longspur m.f. 365
Large-billed guillemot 245
  ″   ″ puffin m.f. 293
  ″ -headed burrowing owl m. 432
Lark finch m. 390
  ″ , meadow m.f. 136
  ″ , shore m.f.y. 200
Larus argentatus Brunn. ad.m.& y. 291
  ″ atricilla ad.m.& y. 314
  ″ Bonapartii m.f.y. 324
  ″ canus ad.& y. 212
  ″ eburneus Gmel. ad.m.& y. 287
  ″ glaucus Brunn. m.& y. 396
  ″ leucopterus Bonap. m.& y. 282
  ″ marinus 241
  ″ Sabini Swain. & Richards. m. 285
  ″ tridactylus ad.& y. 224
Lazuli finch f. 424
Least bittern m.f.y. 210
  ″ stormy petrel m.f. 340
  ″ water hen m.& y. 349
Le petit caporal m. 75
Lesser red-poll m.f. 375
  ″ tern ad.& y. 319
Lestris parasitica 267
  ″ pomarinus 253
  ″ Richardsonii ad.m.& y. 272
Lewis' woodpecker m.f. 416
Limosa fedoa m.f. 238
  ″ hudsonica Swain. & Richards. m.f. 258
Linaria tephrocotis Swains. m. 424
Lincoln finch m.f. 193

APPENDIX I

Linnet, gray-crowned m. 424
Linota borealis m. 400
Little auk m.f. 339
    " night owl f. 432
    " owl m.f. 199
    " sandpiper f. 320
    " screech owl ad.& y. 97
    " tawny thrush m. 419
    " tyrant flycatcher 434
Loggerhead shrike m.f. 57
Long-eared owl m. 383
    " -legged avocet m. 328
    " - " sandpiper 344
Longspur, brown f. 424
    ", Lapland m.f. 365
Long-tailed curlew m.f. 231
    " " duck m.f.y. 312
    " " grouse m.f. 361
Loon ad.& y. 306
Louisiana Hawk ad.f. 392
    " heron ad.m. 217
    " tanager f. 400
    " " m. 354
    " water thrush m. 19
Loxia curvirostra L. m.f.y. 197
    " leucoptera m.f.y. 364
Luzuli finch [Lazuli/WHF] m. 398

MacGillivray's finch m.f. 355
Magpie, American m.f. 357
    ", yellow billed 362
Mallard duck m.f. 221
Mango humming-bird m.f. 184
Mangrove cuckoo m. 159
Manks [Manx/WHF] shearwater m. 295
Maria's woodpecker m.f. 417
Marsh blackbird m.f.y. 67
    " hawk m.f.y. 356
    " hen, fresh water m.& y. 203
    " ", salt water m.f. 204
    " tern m. 410
    " wren m.f. 100
Martin, purple m.f. 22
Meadow lark m.f. 136
Mealy red-poll m. 400
Meleagris gallopavo L. f.& y. 6
    " " m. 1
Merganser, hooded m.f. 232
    ", red breasted m.f. 401
Mergulus antiquus Bonap. ad.& y. 402
Mergus albellus L. m.f. 347
    " cucullatus m.f. 232
    " merganser m.f. 331
    " serrator m.f. 401
Mexican goldfinch m.f. 433
Mississippi kite m.f. 117

Mocking bird m.f. 21
    " ", mountain m. 369
Mormon arcticus m.f. 213
    " cirrhatus Lath. m.f. 249
    " glacialis Lesch. m.f. 293
Mountain mocking bird m. 369
Mourning warbler m.f. 399
Muscicapa acadica m.f. 144
    " Bonapartii Aud. m. 5
    " coerulea Wils. m.f. 84
    " Cooperi m.f. 174
    " crinata L. m. 129
    " dominicensis 170
    " forficata Gm. 359
    " fusca Gm. m.f. 120
    " phoebe Lath. m. 434
    " ruticilla L. m.f. 40
    " savanna m. 168
    " Saya m.f. 359
    " Selbii Aud. m. 9
    " Traillii m. 45
    " tyrannus Briss. m.f. 79
    " verticalis Bonap. m.f. 359
    " virens m. 115
    " Wilsonii m.f. 124

Nashville warbler m.f. 89
Night hawk m.f. 147
    " heron ad.& y. 236
Nobbed-billed auk. 402
Noddy tern ad.m. 275
Numenius borealis Lath. m.f. 208
    " hudsonicus Lath. 237
    " longirostris m.f. 231
Nun, white m.f. 347
Nuthatch, brown-headed m.f. 125
    ", Californian 415
    ", red-breasted m.f. 105
    ", white-breasted black-capped m.f. 152
Nuttall's lesser marsh-wren m.f. 175
    " starling ad.m. 388

Olive-sided flycatcher m.f. 174
Orange crowned warbler m.f. 178
Orchard oriole m.f. 42
Oregon snow finch m.f. 398
Oriole, Baltimore f. 433
    ", " m.f. 12
    ", Bullock's m.f. 388
    ", " m.f. 433
    ", orchard m.f. 42
Orpheus montanus Tonsend [Townsend/WHF] m. 369
Osprey m. 81
Ouzel, arctic water m. 81

Alphabetical Index to the *Birds of America*

[Ouzel], Columbian water f. 435
    ″ , water m.f. 370
Owl, barn m.f. 171
    ″ , barred m. 46
    ″ , burrowing m. 432
    ″ , Columbian m. 432
    ″ , great cinereous ad.f. 351
    ″ , ″ horned m.f. 61
    ″ , hawk m.f. 378
    ″ , large-headed burrowing m. 432
    ″ , little m.f. 199
    ″ , ″ night f. 432
    ″ , ″ screech ad.& y. 97
    ″ , long eared m. 383
    ″ , short-eared m. 432
    ″ , Tengmalm's m.f. 380
Oyster catcher, American 223
    ″   ″ , slender-billed f. 427
    ″   ″ , white-legged m. 427

Painted finch m.f. 53
Parrot, Carolina m.f. 26
Partridge, Californian m.f. 413
    ″ , plumed m.f. 423
    ″ , thick-legged m.& y. 423
    ″ , Virginian m.f.y. 76
Parus atricapillus Wils. m.f. 353
    ″ bicolor L. m.f. 39
    ″ carolinensis m.f. 160
    ″ hudsonicus m.f.y. 194
    ″ minimus Townsend m.f.& nest 353
    ″ rufescans Townsend m.f. 353
Passenger pigeon m.f. 62
Pectoral sandpiper m.f. 294
Pelican, American white ad.m. 311
    ″ , brown ad.m. 251
    ″ , ″ y. 421
    ″ , frigate ad.m. 271
Pelecanus fuscus ad.m. 251
    ″   ″ y. 421
Perdix neoxenus Aud. m.y. 423
    ″ plumifera Gould m.f. 423
    ″ virginiana Lath. m.f.y. 76
Petrel, dusky m. 299
    ″ , fork tailed m.f. 260
    ″ , Fulmar ad.m. 264
    ″ , least stormy m.f. 340
    ″ , Wilson's m.f. 270
Pewee flycatcher m.f. 120
    ″ , short-legged m. 434
Phaeton aethereus m.f. 262
Phalacrocorax carbo Dumont m.ad.,f.,y. 266
    ″ dilophus Swain & Richards. ad.m. 257
    ″ floridanus ad.m. 252

Phalarope, red. m.f. 255
    ″ , Wilson's ad.m.,& f. 254
Phalaropus fulicarius m.f. 255
    ″ hyperboreus m.f.y. 215
    ″ Wilsonii Sab. ad.m.& f. 254
Phaleris nodirostris Bonap. 402
    ″ superciliata Bonap. 402
Phillips' woodpecker m.f. 417
Phoenicopterus ruber L. m. 431
Picus Auduboni Trudeau m. 417
    ″ auratus L. m.f. 37
    ″ canadensis Buff. m. 417
    ″ carolinus L. m.f. 416
    ″ erythrocephalus L. m.f.y. 27
    ″ Harrisi m.f. 417
    ″ hirsitus Vieill. m.f. 417
    ″ Martini Aud. m.f. 417
    ″ mexicanus Aud. m.f. 416
    ″ Phillipsi Aud. m.f. 417
    ″ pileatus L. m.f.y. 111
    ″ principalis L. m.f. 66
    ″ pubescens m.f. 112
    ″ querulus Wils. m.f. 389
    ″ ruber Lath. m.f. 46
    ″ torquatus Wils. m.f. 416
    ″ tridactylus m.f. 132
    ″ varius L. m.f. 190
    ″ villosus m.f. 416
Pied duck ad.m.,& f. 332
Pigeon, band tailed m.f. 367
    ″ , blue headed m.f. 172
    ″ , hawk m.f. 92
    ″ , Key West m.f. 166
    ″ , passenger m.f. 62
    ″ , white-crowned m.f. 177
Pileated woodpecker m.f.y. 111
Pine creeping warbler m.f. 140
    ″ finch m.f. 180
    ″ grosbeak m.f.y. 358
    ″ swamp warbler m.f. 148
Pinnated grouse m.f. 186
Pin-tailed duck m.f. 227
Pipilo arctica Swain m.f. 394
Piping plover m.f. 220
Pipiry flycatcher 170
Plains, cock of the m.f. 371
Platalea ajaja L. ad.m. 321
Plectrophanes ornata Townsend m. 394
    ″ Townsendi Aud. f. 424
Plotus anhinga L. 316
Plover, Black bellied ad.m.,& y. 334
    ″ , golden 300
    ″ , killdeer m.f. 225
    ″ , piping m.f. 220
    ″ , ring ad.m.,& y. 330
    ″ , Rocky Mountain ad.f. 350

APPENDIX I

[Plover], Wilson's m.f. 209
Plumed partridge m.f. 423
Podiceps auritus ad. & y. 404
        " cornutus m.f. 259
        " cristatus Lath. ad.m. & y. 292
        " rubricollis ad.m. 298
Podiceus carolinensis 248
Polyborus vulgaris 161
Pomarine jager 253
Prairie finch m.f. 390
    " starling m.f. 420
    " titlark m. 80
    " warbler m.f. 14
Procellaria glacialis L. ad.m. 264
Prothonotary warbler m.f. 3
Psittacus carolinensis L. m.f. 26
Ptarmigan, American m. 418
Ptiliogonys Townsendi Aud. f. 419
Puffin, m.f. 213
    ", large-billed m.f. 293
    ", tufted m.f. 249
Puffinus anglorum Ray m. 295
    " cinereus Bonap. m. & y. 283
    " obscurus Cuv. m. 299
Purple finch m.f. 4
    " gallinule ad.m. 305
    " grakle m.f. 7
    " martin m.f. 22
    " sandpiper m.f. 284
Pyrrhula enucleator m.f.y. 358
    " frontalis Bonap. m. 424

Qua bird (night heron) ad. & y. 236
Quisqualus ferrugineus Bonap. m.f.y. 157
    " major Vieill. m.f. 187
    " versicolor Vieill. m.f. 7

Rail, sora m.f.y. 233
    ", yellow breasted ad.m. 329
Rallus carolinus m.f.y. 233
    " crepitans m.f. 204
    " elegans m.y. 203
    " jamaicensis Gmel. m. & y. 349
    " noveboracensis Bonap. ad.m. 329
    " virginianus L. m.f.y. 205
Rathbone warbler m.f. 65
Raven m. 101
Razor-billed auk m.f. 214
Recurvirostra americana ad. 318
Red phalarope m.f. 255
Red-backed sandpiper 290
" -bellied woodpecker m.f. 416
Redbird, summer m.f. 44
Red-breasted merganser m.f. 401
" - " nuthatch m.f. 105
" - " sandpiper 315

[Red-breasted] snipe 335
" - " woodpecker m.f. 416
" -cockaded woodpecker m.f. 389
" -eyed vireo m. 150
" -headed duck m.f. 322
" - " woodpecker m.f.y. 27
" -necked grebe ad.m. 298
" -poll, lesser m.f. 375
" - ", mealy m. 400
" - " warbler, yellow m.f. 145
" -shafted woodpecker m.f. 416
" -shouldered hawk m.f. 56
" -tailed hawk m.f. 51
" -throated diver m.f.y. 202
" -winged starling m.f.y. 67
Reddish egret ad. & y. 256
Redstart, American m.f. 40
Regulus calendula Stephens m.f. 195
    " Cuvierii m. 55
    " tricolor m.f. 183
Republican swallow m.f. & egg. 68
Rhincops nigra L. m. 323
Rice bird m.f. 54
Richardson's jager ad.m. & y. 272
Ring necked duck m.f. 234
    " plover ad.m. & y. 330
Robin, American m.f.y. 131
Rock grouse m.f.y. 368
  " wren f. 360
Rocky Mountain flycatcher m. 434
  " " plover ad.f. 350
Roscoe's yellow-throat m. 24
Rose breasted grosbeak m.f.y. 127
Roseate spoonbill ad.m. 321
    " tern 240
Rough-legged falcon m. 166
  " " m. & y. 422
Ruby-crowned wren m.f. 195
  " -throated humming bird m.f.y. 47
Ruddy duck m.f.y. 343
Ruffed grouse m.f. 41
Ruff-necked humming bird m.f. 379
Rusty grakle m.f.y. 157

Salt water marsh-hen m.f. 204
Sanderling m.f. 230
Sandpiper, Bartram m.f. 303
    ", buff breasted m.f. 265
    ", Curlew ad.m. & f. 263
    ", little m.f. 320
    ", long legged 344
    ", pectoral m.f. 294
    ", purple m.f. 284
    ", red-backed 290
    ", red-breasted 315
    ", Schinz's 278

Alphabetical Index to the *Birds of America*

[Sandpiper], semipalmated 405
″ , solitary m.f. 289
″ , spotted ad.m. & f. 310
″ , Townsend's f. 428
Sandwich tern 279
Savanna finch m.f. 109
Say's flycatcher m.f. 359
Scarlet ibis ad.m. & y. 397
″ tanager m.f. 354
Scaup duck m.f. 229
Schinz's sandpiper 278
Scolopaceous courlan 377
Scolopax grisea Gmel. 335
″ minor Gmel. m.f.y. 268
″ Wilsonii m.f. 243
Scoter duck, American m.f. 408
Screech owl, little ad. & y. 97
Selby's flycatcher m. 9
Semipalmated sandpiper 405
″ snipe ad.m., ad.f. 274
Shank, yellow m. 288
Sharp-shinned hawk. m.f. 374
Sharp-tailed finch m.f. 149
″ ″ grouse m.f. 382
Shearwater m. 323
″ , wandering m. 283
Shore lark m.f.y. 200
Short-eared owl m. 432
Short-legged pewee m. 434
Shoveller duck m.f. 327
Shrike, loggerhead m.f. 57
Sialia arctica Swain. m.f. 393
″ occidentalis Townsend m.f. 393
Silvery gull, white-winged m. & y. 282
Siskin, Arkansaw m. 400
″ , black-headed m. 394
Sitta canadensis m.f. 105
Sitta carolinensis Briss. m.f. 152
″ pusilla Lath. m.f. 125
″ pygmea Vig. 415
Skimmer, black m. 323
Slender-billed guillemot m.f. 430
″ ″ oyster-catcher f. 430
Small green-crested flycatcher m.f. 144
Small-headed flycatcher m. 434
Smew m.f. 347
Snipe m.f. 308
″ , American m.f. 243
″ , red-breasted 335
″ , semipalmated ad.m. & ad.f. 274
Snow bird m.f. 13
″ bunting ad. & y. 189
″ finch, Oregon m.f. 398
″ goose m.f. 381
Snowy heron ad.m. 242
″ owl m.f. 121

Solitary flycatcher m.f. 28
″ sandpiper m.f. 289
″ vireo m.f. 28
Song sparrow m.f. 25
″ ″ , brown m. 390
Sooty tern 235
Sora rail m.f.y. 233
Sparrow, chipping m. 104
″ , field m. 139
″ , fox colored 108
″ , swamp m. 64
″ , tree m.f. 188
″ , white throated m.f. 8
″ , yellow-winged m. 130
Sparrow hawk, American m.f. 142
Spoonbill, roseate ad.m. 321
Spotted grosbeak m.f. 373
″ grouse m.f. 176
″ sandpiper ad.m. & f. 310
Stanley hawk ad. 141
″ ″ m.f. 36
Starling, Nuttall's ad.m. 388
″ , prairie m.f. 420
″ , red winged m.f.y. 67
Steller's jay 362
Sterna anglica Montagn. m. 410
″ arctica 250
″ Boyssii Lath. 279
″ cayana Lath. ad.m. 273
″ Dougallii 240
″ Havelli Aud. 409
″ hirundo L. m. 309
″ minuta ad. & y. 319
″ nigra ad. & y. 280
″ stolida ad.m. 275
″ Trudeaui Aud. 409
Stormy petrel, least m.f. 340
Strepsilas interpres 304
Strix acadica Gmel. m.f. 199
″ asio ad. & y. 97
″ brachyotus Wils. 432
″ californica m. 432
″ cinerea Gmel. ad.f. 351
″ cunicularia m. 432
″ flammea m.f. 171
″ funerea m.f. 378
″ nebulosa L. 46
″ nyctea L. m.f. 121
″ otus m. 383
″ passerinoides Temm. m. 432
″ Tengmalmi m.f. 380
″ virginiana Gmel. m.f. 61
Sturnus ludovicianus L. m.f. 136
Sula bassana Lacep. ad.m., & f. 326
″ fusca 207

APPENDIX I

Summer duck m.f. 206
    ″ redbird m.f. 44
Surf duck m.f. 317
Swallow, barn m.f. 173
    ″ , cliff m.f. & egg 68
    ″ , republican m.f. & egg 68
    ″ , violet-green m.f. 385
    ″ , white-bellied m.f. 98
Swallow-tailed flycatcher m. 359
    ″   ″   hawk m. 72
Swamp sparrow m. 64
Swan, common American 411
    ″ , trumpeter ad. 406
    ″ ,   ″   y. 376
Swift, American m.f. 158
Sylvia aestiva m. 95
    ″ agilis Wils. m.f. 138
    ″ americana Lath. m.f. 15
    ″ Auduboni Townsend m.f. 395
    ″ autumnalis m.f. 88
    ″ azurea Steph. m.f. 48
    ″ Bachmanni Aud. m.f. 185
    ″ Blackburniae Lath. f. 399
    ″   ″   m. 135
    ″ canadensis Lath. m. 155
    ″ carbonata m. 60
    ″ castanea m.f. 69
    ″ celata m.f. 178
    ″ Childrenii Aud. m.f. 35
    ″ chrysoptera Lath. m.f. 414
    ″ coronata Lath. m.& y. 153
    ″ discolor Vieill. m.f. 14
    ″ formosa Wils. m.f. 38
    ″ icterocephala Lath. m.f. 59
    ″ maculosa Lath. m.(y.) 50
    ″   ″   ″   m.f. 123
    ″ maritima Wils. m.f. 414
    ″ mitrata m.f. 110
    ″ montana Wils. m. 434
    ″ nigrescens Townsend m. 395
    ″ occidentalis Townsend m.f. 395
    ″ pardalina m.f. 103
    ″ parus m.f. 134
    ″ pensilis Lath. m. 85
    ″ peregrinata Wils. m. 154
    ″ petechia Lath. m.f. 145
    ″   ″   m.& y. 163
    ″ philadelphia m.f. 399
    ″ pinus Lath. m.f. 140
    ″ prothonotarius Lath. m.f. 3
    ″ rara Wils. m. 49
    ″ rathbonia m.f. 65
    ″ Roscoe Aud. m. 24
    ″ rubricapilla Wils. m.f. 89
    ″ sialis m.f.y. 113
    ″ solitaria Wils. m.f. 20

[Sylvia] sphagnosa Bonap. m.f. 148
    ″ striata Lath. m.f. 133
    ″ Swainsonii 198
    ″ Townsendi Nutt. m. 393
    ″ trichas Lath. m.f. 23
    ″ troglodytes m.f.y. 360
    ″ vermivora Lath. m.f. 34
    ″ vigorsii Aud. m. 30
    ″ virens m.f. 399

Tachypetes aquilinus Vieill. ad.m. 271
Tanager, Louisiana f. 400
    ″ ,   ″   m. 354
    ″ , scarlet m.f. 354
Tanagra aestiva Gmel. m.f. 44
    ″ ludoviciana Wils. f. 400
    ″   ″   m. 354
    ″ rubra m.f. 354
Tantalus loculator 216
Tawney thrush m. 164
Teal, blue-winged m.f. 313
    ″ , green-winged 16
    ″ ,   ″   ″   m.f. 228
Tell-tale godwit m.f. 308
Tengmalm's owl m.f. 380
Tennessee warbler m. 154
Tern, arctic 250
    ″ , black ad. & y. 280
    ″ , cayenne ad.m. 273
    ″ , great m. 309
    ″ , Havell's 409
    ″ , lesser ad. & y. 319
    ″ , marsh m. 410
    ″ , noddy ad.m. 275
    ″ , roseate 240
    ″ , sandwich 279
    ″ , sooty 235
    ″ , Trudeau's 409
Tetrao canadensis m.f. 176
    ″ cupido L. m.f. 186
    ″ leucurus Swains. m. 418
    ″ mutus Leach m. 418
    ″ obscurus m.f. 361
    ″ phasianellus 382
    ″ rupestris Leach m.f.y. 368
    ″ saliceti m.f.y. 191
    ″ umbellus L. m.f. 41
    ″ urophasianus m.f. 371
Thalassidroma Leachii m.f. 260
    ″ pelagica m.f. 340
    ″ Wilsonius m.f. 270
Thick-legged partridge m. & y. 423
Three-toed woodpecker m.f. 132
    ″   ″   ″   m.f. 417
Thrush, ferrugineous m.f. 116
    ″ , golden-crowned m.f. 143

Alphabetical Index to the *Birds of America*

[Thrush], hermit m.f. 58
 ″ , little tawny m. 419
 ″ , tawny m. 164
 ″ , varied f. 433
 ″ , ″   m.f. 369
 ″ , water m. 433
 ″ , wood m. 73
Titlark, brown m.f. 10
 ″ , prairie m. 80
Titmouse, black-capt m.f. 353
 ″ , canadian m.f.y. 194
 ″ , Carolina m.f. 160
 ″ , chestnut-backed m.f. 353
 ″ , ″ -crowned m.f.& nest 353
 ″ , crested m.f. 39
Totanus bartramius m.f. 303
 ″ chloropygius Vieill. m.f. 289
 ″ flaviceps Vieill. m. 288
 ″ glottis Temm. 269
 ″ melanoleucus Vieill m.f. 308
 ″ mercularius [macularius/WHF]
         ad.m.& f. 310
 ″ semipalmatus Temm. ad.m.& ad.f. 274
Towhe bunting m.f. 29
Townsend's cormorant m. 412
 ″   finch m. 400
 ″   sandpiper f. 428
 ″   warbler m. 393
Traill's flycatcher m. 45
Tree sparrow m.f. 188
Tringa alpina 290
 ″ arenaria m. 285
 ″   ″   m.f. 230
 ″ himantopus 344
 ″ islandica L. 315
 ″ maritima Bonap. m.f. 284
 ″ pectoralis m.f. 294
 ″ pusilla Wils. m.f. 320
 ″ rufescens Vieill. m.f. 265
 ″ semipalmata 405
 ″ Schinzii Brehm 278
 ″ subarquata Temm. ad.m.,& y. 263
 ″ Townsendi f. 428
Trochilus anna Less. m.f. 425
 ″ colubris L. m.f.y. 47
 ″ mango m.f. 184
 ″ rufus Lath. m.f. 379
Troglodytes aedon Vieill. m.f.y. 83
 ″   americana m. 179
 ″   Bewickii Aud. m. 18
 ″   brevirostris m.f. 175
 ″   ludovicianus Bonap. m.f. 78
 ″   obsoletus Say f. 360
 ″   palustris Bonap. m.f. 100
Troopial, yellow-headed m.f. 388
Tropic bird m.f. 262

Trudeau's tern 409
Trumpeter swan ad. 406
 ″   ″   y. 376
Tufted puffin m.f. 249
Turdus aquaticus Wils. m. 433
 ″ aurocapillus Wils. m.f. 143
 ″ felivox Vieill. m.f. 128
 ″ ludovicianus Aud. m. 19
 ″ migratorius m.f.y. 131
 ″ minor Gm. m. 419
 ″   ″   m.f. 58
 ″ mustellinus Gmel. m.f. 73
 ″ naevius Lath. f. 433
 ″   ″   m.f. 369
 ″ polyglottus L. m.f. 21
 ″ rufus m.f. 116
 ″ Wilsonii m. 164
Turkey buzzard m.& y. 151
 ″ , wild f.& y. 6
 ″ , ″   m. 1
Turn-stone 304
Turtle-dove, Carolina m.f. 17
Tyrannula nigricans Swains. m. 434
 ″   pusilla Swains 434
Tyrant flycatcher m.f. 79

Ultramarine jay 362
Uria alle Temm. m.f. 339
 ″ Brunnichii 245
 ″ grylle ad.& y. 219
 ″ Townsendi Aud. m.f. 430
 ″ troile Lath. m.f. 218

Varied thrush f. 433
 ″   ″   m.f. 369
Velvet duck m.f. 247
Vigors's warbler m. 30
Violet-green cormorant f. 412
 ″   ″   swallow m.f. 385
Vireo Bartrami Swains. m. 434
 ″ flavifrons m. 119
 ″ gilvus m.f. 118
 ″ noveboracensis Ch. Bonap. m. 63
 ″ olivaceus Bonap. m. 150
 ″ solitarius Vieill. m.f. 28
 ″ yellow-throated m. 119
Virginia rail m.f.y. 205
 ″ partridge m.f.y. 76
Vulture, Black m.f. 106
 ″ , californian m. 426

Wandering shearwater m. 283
Warbler, Audubon's m.f. 395
 ″ , Autumnal m.f. 88
 ″ , azure m.f. 48
 ″ , Bachman's m.f. 185

APPENDIX I

[Warbler], bay breasted m.f. 69
" , black and yellow m.(y.) 50
" , " " " m.f. 123
" , Blackburnian f. 399
" , " m. 135
" , black poll m.f. 133
" , black-throated blue m. 155
" , " " green m.f. 399
" , " " grey m. 395
" , blue-green m. 49
" , blue mountain m. 434
" , blue-winged yellow m.f. 20
" , blue yellow-backed m.f. 15
" , brown-headed worm-eating [Swainson's/WHF] 198
" , Canada m.f. 103
" , Cape May m.f. 414
" , carbonated m. 60
" , chestnut-sided m.f. 59
" , Children's m.f. 35
" , Connecticut m.f. 138
" , golden-winged m.f. 414
" , hemlock m.f. 134
" , hermit m.f. 395
" , hooded 110
" , Kentucky m.f. 38
" , mourning m.f. 399
" , Nashville m.f. 89
" , orange-crowned m.f. 178
" , pine-creeping m.f. 140
" , pine-swamp m.f. 148
" , prairie m.f. 14
" , prothonotary m.f. 3
" , Rathbone m.f. 65
" , Tennessee m. 154
" , Townsend's m.f. 393
" , Vigors's m. 30
" , worm-eating m.f. 34
" , yellow-breasted m.f. 23
" , yellow poll m. 95
" , yellow red poll m.f. 145
" , " " " m.y. 163
" , " rump m.y. 153
" , " throated m. 85
Warbling flycatcher m.f. 118
Warrior, black m.f. 86
Washington's bird 11
Water hen, least m.& y. 349
" ouzel, American m.f. 370
" " , arctic m. 435
" " , columbian f. 435
" thrush, common m. 433
" " , Louisiana m. 19
Western blue-bird m.f. 393
" duck 429
Whip-poor-will m.f. 82

White-bellied swallow m.f. 98
" -breasted black-capped nuthatch m.f. 152
" -crowned pigeon m.f. 177
" - " sparrow m.f. 114
White egret ad.m. 242
" -eyed flycatcher m. 63
" -fronted goose m.f. 286
" -headed eagle m. 31
" - " " y. 126
White heron ad.m. 281
" " m. 386
" ibis ad.& y. 222
" -legged oyster-catcher m. 427
White nun m.f. 347
" pelican ad.m. 311
" -tailed grouse 418
" -throated sparrow m.f. 8
" -winged crossbill m.f.y. 364
" -winged silvery gull m.y. 282
Widgeon, American m.f. 345
Widow, chuck-will's m.f. 52
Wild turkey f.& y. 6
" " m. 1
Willet ad.m.& ad.f. 274
Willow grouse m.f.y. 191
Wilson's petrel m.f. 270
" phalarope ad.m.,& f. 254 (Misnumb. 256)
" plover m.f. 209
Winter hawk m. 71
" wren m.f.y. 360
Woodcock, American m.f.y. 268
Wood duck m.f. 206
" ibis 216
Woodpecker, Audubon's m. 417
" , Canadian m. 417
" , downy m.f. 112
" , golden-winged m.f. 37
" , hairy m.f. 416
" , Harris's m.f. 417
" , ivory-billed m.f. 66
" , Maria's m.f. 417
" , pileated m.f.y. 111
" , red-bellied m.f. 416
" , red-breasted m.f. 416
" , red-cockaded m.f. 389
" , red-headed m.f.y. 27
" , red-shafted m.f. 416
" , three-toed m.f. 132
" , " " m.f. 417
" , yellow-bellied m.f. 190
Wood pewee m. 115
" thrush m.f. 73
" wren m. 179
Worm-eating warbler m.f. 34
Wren, American golden-crested m.f. 183
" , Bewick's m. 18

Alphabetical Index to the *Birds of America*

[Wren], great Carolina m.f. 78
" , marsh m.f. 100
" , Nuttall's lesser marsh 175
" , rock f. 360
" , winter m.f.y. 360
" , wood m. 179

Yager, arctic 267
Yellow shank m. 288
" warbler, blue-winged m.f. 20
" -backed warbler, blue m.f. 18
" -bellied woodpecker m.f. 190
" -billed cuckoo m.f. 2
" - " magpie 362
" -breasted chat m.f. 137

[Yellow-breasted] rail ad.m. 329
" - " warbler m.f. 23
" -crowned heron ad.m.,& y. 336
" -headed troopical [troopial/WHF] m.f. 388
" -poll warbler m. 95
" red-poll warbler m.f. 145
" " - " " m.y. 163
" rump warbler m.& y. 153
" throat, Roscoe's 24
" throated vireo m. 119
" " warbler m. 85
" -winged sparrow m. 130

Zenaida dove m.f. 162

J

WOODWARD'S LIST

A Brief Record of the Elephant Folio Edition of Audubon's "Birds of America,"
to Whom They Have Belonged and Where They Can Be Found.
ANTHONY WOODWARD, Ph.D.
23 March 1901.[1]

ROBERT B. WOODWARD, Napa Valley, San Francisco, California.
Said to have a copy. [Believed to have been a chromolithograph edition. (WHF)]

W. A. WOODWARD, Alta, California.
Said to have a copy. [Probably confused with Robert Woodward. (WHF)]

DR. GURDON W. RUSSELL, Hartford, Connecticut.
This copy belonged to the engraver Havell. [Presently in possession of Trinity College, Hartford, Conn. (WHF)]

DR. STEARNS, at the Hartford Retreat for the Insane, Connecticut.
[Unable to find any trace. (WHF)]

LIBRARY OF YALE UNIVERSITY, New Haven, Connecticut.
[In situ. (WHF)]

MR. AYRE, Rookery Building, Chicago, Illinois.
Values his copy at $2,000. [Folio presented to the Field Museum of Natural History, Chicago. See chapter 21, under Field Museum of Natural History. (WHF)]

IOWA STATE LIBRARY, Des Moines, Iowa.
This information was given to me March 14th, 1901, by a young man who was formerly employed in said Library. [Advised that this was a Bien chromolithograph edition. (WHF)]

MRS. PHIL. S. JOHNSON, of Owensboro, Kentucky.
Offered to sell a copy to our Museum; no price stated, January 28th, 1898. [Unable to obtain any information concerning this folio. (WHF)]

A. H. MERRILL, of Brownville, Maine.
1886. His heirs wished to sell it. [Informed by great-granddaughter of Merrill that set of loose prints was sold to a Boston bookdealer in 1910. Prints in the possession of her great-grandfather had originally belonged to Joseph Lamson who had purchased them in Boston around 1848. The sale of the prints was made by a granddaughter of A. H. Merrill; see chapter 22, under the name of Adams Huss Merrill. (WHF)]

J. B. MORRIS, M.D., Baltimore, Maryland.
Said to have a copy. [Not located. (WHF)]

ROBERT GILMOR, Baltimore, Maryland.
Said to have a copy. [Now in the collection of the Enoch Pratt Library, Peabody Library Branch, Baltimore, Md. (WHF)]

THE BOSTON ATHENAEUM, Boston, Massachusetts.
[In situ. (WHF)]

BOSTON SOCIETY OF NATURAL HISTORY, Mass.
The copy was presented by a Mr. Perry. I have seen it. [Boston Society of Natural History in 1947 sold the folio acquired from Thos. N. Perkins to the University of Southern California. (WHF)]

PUBLIC LIBRARY, Boston, Mass.
[In situ. (WHF)]

HARVARD COLLEGE, Cambridge, Mass.
[In situ. (WHF)]

ATHENAEUM LIBRARY, Salem, Mass.
Presented by Nath. Bowditch, J. I. Bowditch, Wm. Pickman, D. L. Pickman, Joseph Peabody, N. Silsbee, Dan. A. White, Miss Susan Burly and S. C. Phillips. Have seen it. 1885 [Sold to Boston book dealer and broken up. (WHF)]

MISS SUSAN BURLY, Salem, Mass.
Also had a copy of her own. 1885. [*See* chapter 26, under Groton School, Groton, Mass. (WHF)]

ESSEX INSTITUTE, Salem, Mass.
The gift of the late Mrs. Eliza L. Rogers of Salem, Mass. Have seen the copy. 1885. [On loan to Peabody Museum, Salem. (WHF)]

WILLIAM OAKES, Ipswich, Massachusetts.
Said to have a copy, 1885. [Not located. (WHF)]

LIBRARY OF THE UNIVERSITY OF MICHIGAN, Ann-Arbor, Mich.
Informed March 14th, 1901. [In situ. (WHF)]

MERCANTILE LIBRARY, St. Louis, Mo.
Informed March 14th, 1901. [In situ (WHF)]

PRINCETON COLLEGE, Princeton, New Jersey.
[In situ. (WHF)]

WM. P. WRIGHT, Union Hill, New Jersey.
Said to have a copy. 1876. [Not located. (WHF)]

NEW YORK STATE LIBRARY, Albany, N.Y.
From the Catalogue of the Library, 1856. [Partially destroyed by fire but not presently in library. See in chapter 21 under "Sets Destroyed by Fire." (WHF)]

CHARLES H. WILLIAMS, Buffalo, New York, 1901.
[In the collection of the Buffalo and Erie County Public Library, Buffalo, N.Y. (WHF)]

LONG ISLAND HISTORICAL SOCIETY, Brooklyn, N.Y.
[*See* chapter 26, under Mrs. Frederick Beinecke. (WHF)]

WILLET'S FAMILY, Jamaica, Long Island, N.Y.
Had a fine copy which they offered for $2,000. 1897. [No trace. (WHF)]

EASTBURN HASTINGS of Sing Sing, N.Y.
Had a copy; at his death it was sold to a book dealer in New York City. [No trace. (WHF)]

JOHN BELL, Sparkill, Rockland Co., N.Y.
The great taxidermist and a friend of Audubon. Died 1890. [No trace. (WHF)]

THE AUDUBON FAMILY.
Had a copy which they sold recently. [John Taylor Johnston purchased the folio from John Woodhouse Audubon around 5 November 1861; now in the possession of the H. J. Lutcher Stark Foundation, Orange, Texas. (WHF)]

ASTOR LIBRARY, New York City.
Copy not complete; have seen it. [*See* chapter 26 under New York Public Library. (WHF)]

THE CITY HALL LIBRARY, New York City.
[*See* chapter 26, under The City College of the City University of New York. (WHF)]

COLUMBIA UNIVERSITY, New York City, West 116th St.

The copy belonged to J. Whitney Phoenix, left by will to the University. Have seen the copy. [The university has a set of the folio, having been among the original subscribers. M. Halsy Thomas, at one time archivist of Columbia, advised that the Phoenix collection did not include an edition of the Double Elephant folio. It did include an edition of the Octavo edition which Woodward must have confused with the Elephant edition. (WHF)]

MERCANTILE LIBRARY, New York City.

From their Catalogue, 1850. Have seen it. [Set broken up after being sold to New York dealer. (WHF)]

NEW YORK SOCIETY LIBRARY, New York City.

Presented to them about 3 years ago by Contoit, the man who was poisoned by ice cream. [Reported stolen in 1973; exact date unknown. Some prints recovered. (WHF)]

MR. ROBERT L. STUART, New York City. Fifth Ave.

This copy is now at the Lenox Library, 1901, a branch of the New York City Public Library. Have seen it, 1884. [In the collection of the New York Public Library. (WHF)]

SAMUEL J. TILDEN, New York City. (now dead.)

This copy is also in the Lenox Library building. [Also in the collection of the New York Public Library. (WHF)]

CORNELIUS VANDERBILT, New York City. (now dead.)

This copy was destroyed by fire. [Unable to verify destruction of set by fire. (WHF)]

LENOX LIBRARY, Fifth Ave., New York City.

Mr. Lenox's copy. [In the collection of the New York Public Library. (WHF)]

LIBRARY PHILADELPHIA ACADEMY OF NATURAL SCIENCES, Pa.

Have seen the copy. [In situ. (WHF)]

PROVIDENCE ATHENAEUM, Providence, R.I.

Information received from the Librarian of Brown University, 1901. [In situ. (WHF)]

CALLET. Charleston, S.C.

His copy was destroyed by Sherman during the War, 1863. [In John B. Irving's *A Day on the Cooper River*, enl. and ed. by Louisa Cheves Stoney, publ. under the auspices of St. John's Hunt Club (1st ed.; Charleston, S.C.: pr. by A. E. Miller, ca. 1931; 2d ed.; Columbia, S.C.: pr. by Press of R. L. Bryan Co., 1932) is to be found an account of the destruction of a set of the folio. (WHF)]

LIBRARY OF CONGRESS, Washington, D.C.

From the Catalogue of the Library, 1861. [In situ. (WHF)]

AARON RAYMOND.

A copy of the *first edition* of *Audubon's* "Birds and Quadrupeds" consisting of the folio plates of the Birds, the smaller volumes of the plates of the Quadrupeds and eight volumes of text, were sold last week at auction in New York for $1,100. The work belonged to the estate of Aaron Raymond, May, 1898. [Not located. (WHF)]

GEORGE H. RIGBY

A few years ago I noticed the following in a book-list from George H. Rigby, 1113 Arch Street, Philadelphia, Pa.: A copy of Audubon's Birds with the Biography 1827-38, the 9 volumes he valued at $2,000. He also says, a few years ago a set sold at auction for $2,500, and would not be surprised in time $3,000. should be asked. [Not located. (WHF)]

The following said to have copies:

EX. GOV. SEYMORE
[No record. (WHF)]

WM. C. JOHNS, Utica, New York, 1898.
[No record. (WHF)]

DR. EGBERT BAGG, Utica, New York, 1898.
[No record. (WHF)]

J. V. L. PRIME, Albany, New York, 1898.
[No record. (WHF)]

J. ALEX. JOHNSON
[No record. (WHF)]

ALEXANDER T. STEWART, New York City. (now dead)
[No trace. (WHF)]

J. PIERPONT MORGAN, New York City.
[There is presently a set in the Pierpont Morgan Library, New York City. (WHF)]

MORRIS K. JESUP, New York City.
[No trace. (WHF)]

NAT. POTTER, M.D., Baltimore, Maryland.
[This set presently in the New York Public Library. (WHF)]

MISS HARRIET DOUGLASS [sic], New York City?
[Mrs. Douglas Cruger. Have not been able to locate. (WHF)]

JAMES GRAVES, Syracuse, N.Y.
[*See* chapter 26 under Syracuse University. (WHF)]

W. E. DODGE, New York City.
[In 1966 Mr. Cleveland E. Dodge wrote: "our family has no copies of the Audubon folio. If my great-grandfather or grandfather ever had a copy it must have been given away to some library a long time ago." (WHF)]

[CHAMBERLAIN?] 1890.
At an auction sale at the rooms of George A. Leavitt and Company, a copy was bid on by Mr. Chamberlain (grandson of Daniel Drew and nephew of Washington Irving), $2,430; this included the 5 volumes of the Biography. It remained in a storage room for some time, then resold to Dodd, Mead and Co., (New York City), for $1,600. They sold it for $2,250. [Have not been able to locate. (WHF)]

LIBRARY OF THE BRITISH MUSEUM, London, Eng.
[In situ. (WHF)]

WM. JARDINE, England.
Had a copy which was sold with his library. [No trace. (WHF)]

THE PAISLEY FREE LIBRARY, Scotland.
Presented by Sir Peter Coats. [In situ. (WHF)]

THE EARL OF KINNOULL, Dublin Castle, Perth, Scotland.
[At an auction sale by Sotheby, Wilkinson & Hodge, held 7 and 8 November 1911 (item 498, p.30) there were sold to B. F. Stevens for £23 plates 1–25 of the *Birds of America* which had been the property of the Earl of Kinnoull. (see *Book Prices Current*, London, 1912. WHF)]

MRS. THOMAS COATS, Ferguslie House, Paisley, Scotland.
[Not located. (WHF)]

ANDREW COATS, Pitcullen House, Perth, Scotland.
[Not located. (WHF)]

ROYAL LIBRARY AT BERLIN, Germany.
[On 28 Oct. 1958 Dr. Claus Nissen wrote: "As far as I know there is only one set, and a very incomplete one of 7 plates only of Audubon's elephants in Germany. It is listed in the 'Gesamtkatalog der preussischen Bibliotheken,' Vol. 8, 1935, No. 2442 as in the possession of the Preuss. Staatsbibliotek at Berlin." On 31 Mar. 1959 Deutsche Staatsbibliothek advised that the Audubon work belonged to the stored sections of the German Staatsbibliothek of which location nothing definite is known. (WHF)]

IMPERIAL LIBRARY AT VIENNA, Germany (sic).
[No trace. (WHF)]

UNIVERSITY LIBRARY AT GÖTTINGEN, Germany.
[A letter dated 1 Nov. 1966 from the Niedersächsische Staats- und Universitäts-bibliothek, Göttingen, states: "Die Eintragung in der Liste von Herrn Anthony Woodward muss auf einem Irrtum beruhen, wir besitzen das Werk von J. J. Audubon: The Birds of America nicht" (We do not have it). (WHF)]

[QUARITCH] Aug. 7, 1893.
See Bernard Quaritch's Catalogue, No. 134, p. 7. Audubon's Birds of America with Biography 9 volumes. Copy belonging to *Earl of Hardwicke*. Valued at £300 An early subscriber's copy. [Now in the possession of Northwestern University, Evanston, Ill. (WHF)]

For sale a copy of Audubon's Birds of America 4 vols., with the Ornithological Biography, 5 volumes Phila. & Edinburgh, 1827–49, £250. From Capt. Pinwell's Library. A similar copy brought at the Larking sale, May 1892. £345. [Author not certain about this second reference. (WHF)]

JOHN TAYLOR JOHNSTON, New York City., No. 8 Fifth Avenue.

Now the property of J. Herbert Johnston, his son, 18 Washington Square, who kindly gave me the following information March 18, 1901: Elephant edition J. J. Audubon, purchased about 1863 from the Audubon family. The set was the one presented to his brother by J. J. Audubon. [Now in possession of the H. J. Lutcher Stark Foundation, Orange, Texas. (WHF)]

PETER A. B. WIDENER, Philadelphia, Pa.

Informed March 22, 1901. [Set now at the Widener Library, Harvard University. (WHF)]

K

ADDITIONAL VARIANTS FOUND IN PLATE LEGENDS AND WATERMARKS

Number 3
Plate 11 (2 variants found)

PLATE .II.   No. 3.

The Bird of Washington
or
Great American Sea Eagle.
Falco Washingtoniensis—Male.

Drawn from Nature by John J. Audubon, F.R.S.E. M.W.S.
Engraved by R. Havell Jun*r*.
Printed and Coloured by R. Havell Sen*r*.
[Legend on rock]

Yale University, Garvan set   J. W. T. M. 1827

No. 3   PLATE .XI.

Bird of Washington Falco Washingtonii.Aud, Male.

Drawn from Nature by J. J. Audubon F.R.S. F.L.S.
Engraved Printed & Coloured by R. Havell
[Legend centered on bottom of plate]

Yale University, Farnam set   J. Whatman 1833

Plate 13 (2 variants found)

No. 3   PLATE 13.

Snow Bird,   1.Male.   2.Female
Fringilla Nivalis,
Plant Vulgo. Great Swamp Ash.

Brown University   J.W.T.M.   1827
Yale University, Garvan set   J.W.T.M.   (date bound in)

421

APPENDIX K

No. 3.   PLATE XIII.
Snow Bird.
Fringilla Hyemalis. Linn,
Male .1.   Female .2.
Large Tupelo.   Nyssa tomentosa.

    Providence Athenaeum   J. Whatman 1831
    Yale University, Farnam set   J.W.T.M.   1833

NUMBER 4
Plate 17 (2 variants found)
No. 4   PLATE 17.
Carolina Pigeon, or *Turtle Dove.* Male 1. F.2.
Columba Carolinensis.
Plant, Steuartia. Malacodendron.

    Brown University   J.W.T.M. (date bound in)
    Yale University, Garvan set   J.W.T.M. (date bound in)

No. 4   PLATE, XVII.
Carolina Turtle Dove, Columba Carolinensis. Linn,
Males, .1.   Females, 2.
White flowered Stuartia. Stuartia Malacodendron.

[Audubon's credit and that of Havell are not at bottom of plate, but the former is to the left and the latter to the right, both slightly above legend]

    Providence Athenaeum   J. Whatman 1831
    Yale University, Farnam set   J. Whatman 1833

Plate 20 (2 variants found)
No. 4   PLATE 20.
Blue Winged Yellow Warbler, Male 1,F.2.
Dacnis Solitaria.
Plant Vulgo. Wild Althea.

[Audubon's credit line and that of Havell are not at bottom of plate, but the former is to the left and the latter to the right, both slightly above legend]

    Brown University   J.W.T.M.   1827
    Yale University, Garvan set   J.W.T.M.   1827

No. 4 [4 is engraved backwards]   PLATE, XX.
Blue-winged Yellow Warbler,
Sylvia Solitaria. Wils,
Male,1.   Female,2.
Cotton Rose. Hibiscus grandiflorus.

    Providence Athenaeum   J. Whatman 1831
    Yale University, Farnam set   J.W.T.M.   (date not discernible)

Additional Variants Found in Plate Legends and Watermarks

NUMBER 5
Plate 23 (2 variants found)

No. 5.   PLATE 23.

Maryland Yellow Throat, M.1. F.2.
Sylvia Trichas,

    Brown University   J.W.T.M.   1827
    Yale University, Garvan set   J.W.T.M.   (date bound in)

No. 5.   PLATE, XXIII.

Yellow-breasted Warbler,
Sylvia trichas. Lath,

    Yale University, Farnam set   J. Whatman 1833
    John Crerar Library   (Not discernible)

NUMBER 6
Plate 28 (2 variants found)

No. 6   PLATE. 28.

Vireo Solitarius. Male.1. F.2.
Solitary Flycatcher

    Brown University   J.W.T.M.   1827
    Yale University, Garvan set   J.W.T.M.   1827

No. 6   PLATE, XXVIII.

Solitary Flycatcher or Vireo,
Vireo Solitarius. Vieill,

    Providence Athenaeum   J. Whatman 1831
    Yale University, Farnam set   J.W.T.M.   1833

Plate 29 (2 variants found)

No. 6   PLATE 29.

Towee Bunting, Male .1. F.2.
Fringilla Erythrophthalma

    Brown University   J.W.T.M.   1827
    Yale University, Garvan set   J.W.T.M.   1827

No. 6   PLATE XXIX.

Towhe bunting,
Fringilla erythrophthalma. Linn,

    Providence Athenaeum   J. Whatman 1831
    Yale University, Farnam set   J. Whatman 1833
    John Crerar Library   (Not discernible)

APPENDIX K

NUMBER 7
Plate 31 (2 variants found)

No. 7   PLATE. 31.

White-headed Eagle, Male.
Falco Leucocephalus.
Fish Vulgo—Yellow mud Cat.

[Three-line legend in lower right on print]

  Brown University   J.W.T.M. 1827
  Yale University, Garvan set J.W.T.M. 1827

No. 7.   PLATE, XXXI.

White-headed Eagle, Falco Leucocephalus. Linn, Male. Yellow Cat-fish.

[Legend all on one line; also Audubon's credit line and that of Havell are not at bottom of plate, but the former is to the left and the latter to the right, both slightly above legend]

  Providence Athenaeum   J. Whatman 183?
  Yale University, Farnam set J. Whatman 1833

NUMBER 7
Plate 35 (2 variants found)

No. 7   PLATE. 35.

Children's Warbler, Male 1. F.2.
Silvia Childreni.
Plant Cassia occidentalis.
Vulgo Spanish Coffee.

  Brown University   J.W.T.M. (date bound in)
  Yale University, Garvan set J.W.T.M. 182? (probably 1827)

No. 7.   PLATE, XXXV.

Children's Warbler,
Sylvia Childrenii. Aud,
Male, 1. Female, 2.
Wild Spanish Coffee Cassia occidentalis.

[Both credits on same line as "Children's Warbler," rather than at bottom of plate, Audubon's to the left and Havell's to the right]

  Providence Athenaeum   J. Whatman 1831
  Yale University, Farnam set J. Whatman 1833

424

Additional Variants Found in Plate Legends and Watermarks

Number 10

Plate 47 (2 variants found)

No. 10   PLATE 47

Ruby-throated Humming Bird, Male .1. F.2. Young 3.
Trochilus Columbris.
Plant, Bignonia radicans
Vulgo, Trumpet Flower.

| Yale University, Garvan set | J.W.T.M. | 1828 |
| Brown University | J.W.T.M. | (date bound in) |

No. 10   PLATE .XLVII.

Ruby-throated Humming Bird,
Trochilus Columbris. Linn,
Male,1. Female,2. Young,3.
Trumpet-flower   Bignonia Radicans.

| Providence Athenaeum | J. Whatman 1831 |
| Yale University, Farnam set | J. Whatman 1833 |

Plate 48 (2 variants found)

No. 10   PLATE 48

Cerulean Warbler, Male 1. F.2
Sylvia Azurea.

| Yale University, Garvan set | J.W.T.M. | 1828 |
| Brown University | J. Whatman (date bound in) |

No. 10.   PLATE, XLVIII.

Azure Warbler,
Sylvia Azurea. Steph,

| Providence Athenaeum | J. Whatman 1831 |
| Yale University, Farnam set | J.W.T.M. 1833 |

Plate 50 (2 variants found)

No. 10   PLATE 50

Swainson's Warbler, Male.
Sylvicola Swainsonia.

| Yale University, Garvan set | J.W.T.M. 1828 |
| Brown University | J.W.T.M. (date bound in) |

No. 10   PLATE L.

Black & Yellow Warbler,
Sylvia Maculosa. Lath,

| Providence Athenaeum | J. Whatman 1831 |
| Yale University, Farnam set | J. Whatman 1833 |

APPENDIX K

NUMBER 11
Plate 53 (2 variants found)
No. 11   PLATE 53
Painted Bunting,
1 & 2. Old Males; 3.M. of 1st Year; 4. 2nd Year; 5.Female.
Fringilla Ciris.
Plant, Prunus Chicasa.

    Brown University   J.W.T.M.   1828
    Yale University, Garvan set   J.W.T.M.   1828
    Providence Athenaeum   J. Whatman 1830

No. 11   PLATE .LIII.
Painted Finch,
Fringilla Ciris. Temm.
1,2, Old Males, 3,M of 1st Year, 4, 2nd Year, 5, Female.
Chickasaw Plum. Prunus Chicasa.

    Yale University, Farnam set   J. Whatman 1833
    John Crerar Library   J. Whatman, 1834

Plate 54 (2 variants found)
No. 11.   PLATE 54.
Rice Bunting

    Brown University   J.W.T.M.   (date bound in)

No. 11   PLATE. LIV.
Rice Bird

    Providence Athenaeum   J. Whatman 1831

NUMBER 13
Plate 64 (2 variants found)
No. 13   PLATE 64
Swamp Sparrow Male.
Spiza Palustris,
Plant Vulgo May Apple.
Podophyllum peltatum.

[Drawing of bird credited to Lucy Audubon]

    Brown University   J.W.T.M.   1828
    Yale University, Garvan set   J.W.T.M.   1828

Additional Variants Found in Plate Legends and Watermarks

No. 13.   PLATE, LXIV.

Swamp Sparrow,
Fringilla Palustris. Wils,
Male.
May-apple.   Podophyllum peltatum.

[Drawing of bird credited to Lucy Audubon]

Providence Athenaeum	J. Whatman	1831
Yale University, Farnam set	J.W.T M.	1833

NUMBER 16
Plate 80 (2 variants found)

No. 16   PLATE 80

Anthus Hypogaeus,
[No common name]

Brown University	J.W.T.M.	(date bound in)
Yale University, Garvan set	J.W.T.M.	(date bound in)

No. 16   PLATE .LXXX.

Prairie Titlark
Anthus Pipiens, Male.

Providence Athenaeum	J. Whatman	1831
Yale University, Farnam set	J. Whatman	1833

NUMBER 17
Plate 84 (2 variants found)

No. 17   PLATE 84

Blue-Grey Flycatcher, Male 1.F.2.
Sylvia Coerula,

Brown University	J. Whatman	1830
Yale University, Garvan set	J. Whatman	1830

No. 17   PLATE.LXXXIV.

Blue-grey Fly-catcher
Muscicapa coerulea, Wils.

Yale University, Farnam set	J.W.T.M.	1833

Plate 85 (2 variants found)

No. 17   PLATE 85

Yellow Throat Warbler Male.
Sylvia Pensilis,

[Legend in lower left corner of plate]

Brown University	J. Whatman	1830
Yale University, Garvan set	J. Whatman	1830

APPENDIX K

No. 17   PLATE .LXXXV.

Yellow Throated Warbler
Sylvia Pensilis, Lath. Male.

    Yale University, Farnam set   J. Whatman 1833

NUMBER 18
Plate 87 (2 variants found)
No. 18   PLATE 87

Florida Jay. Male 1.F.2
Garrulus Floridanus,
Biospyros Virginiana
Vulgo persimon

    Brown University   J. Whatman 1831

No. 18   PLATE LXXXVII

Florida Jay Corvus Floridanus, Bartram, Male,1.Female,2.
Persimon Tree
Biospyros virginiana

    John Crerar Library   (Not discernible)
    Providence Athenaeum   J. Whatman 1831

NUMBER 19
Plate 95 (2 variants found)
No. 19   PLATE 95

Blue-eyed yellow Warbler,
Sylvia Aestiva,

    Brown University   J. Whatman 1830
    Yale University, Garvan set   J. Whatman 1830

No. 19   PLATE .XCV.

Yellow-poll Warbler,
Sylvia Aestiva, Gmel,

    Providence Athenaeum   J. Whatman 1831
    Yale University, Farnam set   J. Whatman 1833

NUMBER 20
Plate 96 (2 variants found)
No. 20   PLATE 96

Columbia Jay, Male.F.2.
Garrulus Ultramarinus.

[Very poor, dull blue birds]

    Yale University, Garvan set   J. Whatman 1830

Additional Variants Found in Plate Legends and Watermarks

No. 20   PLATE .XCVI.

Columbia Jay,
Corvus Bullockii.
Male, 1. Female, 2,

[Birds a good blue color]

Yale University, Farnam set   J. Whatman 1833

Plate 97 (2 variants found)
No. 20   PLATE 97

Mottled Owl, Adult 1. Young 2 & 3.
Strix Asio,
Plant Pinus inops.
Vulgo Jersey Pine.

Brown University   J. Whatman 1830
Yale University, Garvan set   J. Whatman 1830
National Gallery, Washington   (Not discernible)

No. 20   PLATE .XCVII.

Little Screech Owl, Strix Asio. Linn, Adult, 1. Young,2,3.
Jersey Pine Pinus inops.

[Audubon's and Havell's credits on same line, not at bottom of plate]

Providence Athenaeum   J. Whatman 1831(?)
Yale University, Farnam set   J. Whatman 1833
John Crerar Library   J. Whatman (date not discernible)

NUMBER 20
Plate 99 (2 variants found)
No. 20   PLATE 99

Cow Bunting, Male 1,F.2.
Icterus Pecoris.

Brown University   J. Whatman 1830
Yale University, Garvan set   J. Whatman 1830

No. 20   PLATE .XCIX.

Cow-pen Bird,
Icterus Pecoris.

Providence Athenaeum   J. Whatman 1831
Yale University, Farnam set   J. Whatman 1833

APPENDIX K

NUMBER 24
Plate 120 (2 variants found)
No. 24   PLATE CXX

Pewit Flycatcher.
Muscicapa Fusca. Gmel,
Male, 1 Female, 2
Cotton Plant Gossypium.

Brown University	J. Whatman 1831
Yale University, Garvan set	J. Whatman 1831
Yale University, Farnam set	J. Whatman 1834

No. 24   PLATE .CXX.

Pewee Flycatcher
Muscicapa fusca Gm,

John Crerar Library	J. Whatman (date not discernible)

NUMBER 31
Plate 151 (2 variants found)
No. 31   PLATE CLI

Turkey Buzzard,
Cathartes Atratus.
Male,1. Young,2.

Brown University	J. Whatman 1832
Providence Athenaeum	J.W.T.M. 1832(?)
Yale University, Garvan set	J.W.T.M. 1832
Yale University, Farnam set	J. Whatman 1833

No. 31.   PLATE .CLI.

Turkey Buzzard
Cathartes Aura
Male,1. Young,2.

John Crerar Library	J. Whatman (date not discernible)

Plate 153 (2 variants found)
No. 31   PLATE CLIII

Yellow-Crown Warbler,
Sylvia Coronata. Lath.

Brown University	J.W.T.M. (date bound in)
Providence Athenaeum	J.W.T.M. (date bound in)
Yale University, Garvan set	J.W.T.M. (date bound in)
Yale University, Farnam set	J. Whatman 1832

Additional Variants Found in Plate Legends and Watermarks

No. 31   PLATE CLIII

Yellow-rump Warbler
Sylvia coronata Lath.

John Crerar Library   J. Whatman (date not discernible)

NUMBER 32
Plate 160 (2 variants found)

No. 32   PLATE CLX

Black-capped Titmouse,
Parus Atricapillus. Linn,
Male .1. Female .2.
Supple-jack

Brown University   J.W.T.M.   1832
Providence Athenaeum   J. Whatman 1833
Yale University, Garvan set   J. Whatman 1833
Yale University, Farnam set   J. Whatman 1834

No. 32   PLATE .CLX

Carolina Titmouse
Parus Carolinensis
Male .1. Female .2.
Supple-jack

John Crerar Library   J. Whatman 1833

NUMBER 33
Plate 163 (2 variants found)

No. 33   PLATE CLXIII

Palm Warbler,
Sylvia Palmarum.

Providence Athenaeum   J. Whatman 1833
Yale University, Farnam set   J. Whatman 1833
Yale University, Garvan set   J. Whatman 1833
Brown University   J.W.T.M.   (date bound in)

No. 33   PLATE .CLXIII.

Yellow-red Poll Warbler
Sylvia petechia

John Crerar Library   (Not discernible)

431

APPENDIX K

NUMBER 33
Plate 165 (2 variants found)

No. 33   PLATE CLXV.

Bachman's Finch,
Fringilla Bachmani.
Male,
Pinckneya pubens.

Providence Athenaeum   J. Whatman 1833

No. 33   PLATE .CLXV.

Bachmans Finch,
Fringilla Bachmani.
Male,
Pinckneya pubens.

[Lacking apostrophe in "Bachman's"]

Brown University   J. Whatman 1833
Yale University, Garvan set   J. Whatman 1833
Yale University, Farnam set   J. Whatman 1834

NUMBER 34
Plate 170 (2 variants found)

No. 34   PLATE CLXX

Gray Tyrant.
Tyrannus Grisens.
Agati grandiflora.

Yale University, Garvan set   J. Whatman 1833
Brown University   J.W.T.M.   1833
Yale University, Farnam set   J.W.T.M.   1833
Providence Athenaeum   J.W.T.M.   1831(?)

No. 34   PLATE .CLXX

Pipiry Flycatcher
Muscicapa Dominiscensis
Agati grandiflora.

John Crerar Library   J. Whatman 1833

Additional Variants Found in Plate Legends and Watermarks

NUMBER 35
Plate 174 (2 variants found)

No. 35   PLATE CLXXIV

Olive-sided Flycatcher.
Muscicapa Inornata.
Male .1. Female, .2.
Pinus Balsamea Fir Balsam.

Providence Athenaeum	J.W.T.M.	1833
Yale University, Garvan set	J.W.T.M.	1833
Yale University, Farnam set	J.W.T.M.	1834
Brown University	J.W.T.M.	(date bound in)

No. 35   PLATE .CLXXIV.

Olive sided Flycatcher
Muscicapa Cooperi
Male ,1. Female ,2.
Pinus Balsama Fir Balsam.

John Crerar Library   (Not discernible)

NUMBER 36
Plate 177 (3 variants found)

No. 36   PLATE CLXXVII

White-crowned Pigeon
Columba Leucocephala

Brown University	J. Whatman 1833
Providence Athenaeum	J. Whatman 1833

No. 36   PLATE, CLXXVII

White-Headed Pigeon
Columba Leucocephala

Union College   J. Whatman 1836

No. 36   PLATE. CLXXVII

White-Headed Pigeon
Columba Leucocephala, Linn.

H. J. Lutcher Stark Foundation   J. Whatman 1838

APPENDIX K

NUMBER 37
Plate 183 (3 variants found)
No. 37   PLATE CLXXXIII
Golden-Crester-Wren Regulus Cristatus. Vieill. Male .1. Female.2. Thalia dealbota

        Brown University   J. Whatman 1833
        Yale University, Garvan set   J. Whatman 1833

No. 37   PLATE. CLXXXIII.
Golden crested-Wren Regulus cristatus. Vieill, Male,1. Female,2. Thalia dealbota.

        Yale University, Farnam set   J. Whatman 1834

No. 37   PLATE CLXXXIII
                                American golden crested wren
                                     Regulus tricolor

        John Crerar Library   (Not discernible)

Plate 184 (2 variants found)
No. 37   PLATE CLXXXIV
                                 Mangrove Humming Bird
                                  Trochilus Mango.

        Brown University   J. Whatman 1833
        Providence Athenaeum   J. Whatman 1833
        Yale University, Garvan set   J. Whatman 1833
        Yale University, Farnam set   J. Whatman 1834

No. 37   PLATE CLXXXIV
                                 Mango Humming-bird
                                  Trochilus mango

        John Crerar Library   (Not discernible)

NUMBER 39
Plate 194 (2 variants found)
No. 39   PLATE CXCIV.
                                 Canadian Titmouse,
                                 Parus Hudsonicus.

        Brown University   (Not discernible)
        Yale University, Farnam set   J. Whatman 1834
        Yale University, Garvan set   J. Whatman 1834

Additional Variants Found in Plate Legends and Watermarks

No. 39   PLATE CXCIV

Hudson's Bay Titmouse
Parus Hudsonicus

Windsor Castle, Berkshire, England   J. Whatman 1836

NUMBER 40
Plate 197 (2 variants found)

No. 40   PLATE CXCVII.

American Crossbill,
Loxia Curvirostra. Linn

Brown University	J. Whatman 1834
Yale University, Farnam set	J. Whatman 1834
Yale University, Garvan set	J.W.T.M. 1834

No. 40   PLATE CXCVII

Common Crossbill
Loxia Curvirostra. Linn

Windsor Castle, Berkshire, England   J. Whatman 1836

Plate 198 (2 variants found)

No. 40   PLATE, CXCVIII.

Brownheaded Worm eating Warbler,
Sylvia Swainsonii.

Brown University	J.W.T.M. 1834
Yale University, Farnam set	J. Whatman 1834
Yale University, Garvan set	J.W.T.M. 1834

No. 40   PLATE CXCVIII

Swainson's Warbler
Sylvia Swainsoni

Windsor Castle, Berkshire, England   J. Whatman 1836

NUMBER 41
Plate 203 (2 variants found)

No. 41   PLATE CCIII

Fresh-Water Marsh Hen,
Rallus Elegans. Aud.

Brown University	J.W.T.M. 1832
Yale University, Garvan set	J.W.T.M. 1834
Yale University, Farnam set	J. Whatman 1836

APPENDIX K

No. 41   PLATE CCIII

Great Red breasted Rail or
Fresh-water Marsh hen
Rallus Elegans. Aud.

Windsor Castle, Berkshire, England   J. Whatman 1836

NUMBER 45
Plate 223 (2 variants found)
No. 45   PLATE CCXXIII

Pied oyster-catcher
Haematopus Ostralegus. L.

    Brown University   J.W.T.M.   1834
    Yale University, Farnam set   J.W.T.M.   1834
    Yale University, Garvan set   J.W.T.M.   1834

No. 45   PLATE CCXXIII

American Oyster catcher
Haematopus palliatus

John Crerar Library   J. Whatman 1836

NUMBER 46
Plate 230 (2 variants found)
No. 46   PLATE CCXXX

Ruddy Plover
Tringa Arenaria

[Two birds depicted]

    Brown University   J.W.T.M.   1834
    Yale University, Garvan set   J.W.T.M.   1834

No. 46   PLATE CCXXX

Sanderling
Tringa arenaria

[Three birds depicted]

    Yale University, Farnam set   J. Whatman 1838
    John Crerar Library   (Not discernible)

NUMBER 47
Plate 233 (2 variants found)
No. 47   PLATE CCXXXIII

Sora Rail. Rullus Carolinus L, 1.Male.2.Female.3.Young.

    Brown University   J. Whatman 1834

Oil painting of Audubon's "Song Sparrow," unsigned and undated. This oil rendering of Plate 25 is probably by J. B. Kidd. Courtesy of Princeton University Library.

Audubon's "Red-shouldered Hawk" reproduced in a limited edition series of Audubon plates in handcrafted Damascene by Reed & Barton. Courtesy of Reed-Barton Silversmiths.

Audubon's "Stilt Sandpiper" reproduced in a limited edition series of Audubon plates in hand-crafted Damascene by Reed & Barton. Courtesy of Reed-Barton Silversmiths.

BIRDS OF AMERICA,

FROM

DRAWINGS

MADE

DURING A RESIDENCE OF UPWARDS OF TWENTY-FIVE YEARS

IN

THE UNITED STATES AND ITS TERRITORIES,

BY

JOHN JAMES AUDUBON,

CITIZEN OF THE UNITED STATES;

MEMBER OF THE LYCEUM OF NEW YORK; FELLOW OF THE ROYAL SOCIETY OF EDINBURGH; MEMBER OF THE WERNERIAN NATURAL HISTORY SOCIETY; FELLOW OF THE SOCIETY OF SCOTTISH ANTIQUARIES AND NEW CASTLE TYNE; MEMBER OF THE SOCIETY FOR PROMOTING THE USEFUL ARTS IN SCOTLAND; OF THE LITERARY AND PHILOSOPHICAL SOCIETY OF LIVERPOOL, &c. &c.

Prospectus.

To those who have not seen any portion of the Author's splendid collection of original Drawings, it may be proper to explain, that their superiority consists in every specimen being of the full size of life, pourtrayed with a degree of accuracy as to proportion and outline, the result of peculiar means discovered and employed by the Author, and lately exhibited to a meeting of the Wernerian Society. Besides, in every instance where a difference of plumage exists between the sexes, both the Male and the Female Birds have been represented. The Author has not contented himself with single profile views of the originals, but in very many instances he has grouped them, as it were, at their natural avocations, in all sorts of attitudes, either on branches of trees, or amidst plants or flowers: some are seen pursuing with avidity their prey through the air, or searching diligently their food amongst the fragrant foliage; whilst others of an aquatic nature swim, wade, or glide over their allotted element. The Insects, Reptiles, or Fishes, that form the food of the birds, have been introduced into the drawings; and the Nests of the Birds have been frequently represented. The Plants are all copied from nature, and the Botanist, it is hoped, will look upon them with delight. The Eggs of most of the species will appear in the course of publication.

First sheet of the prospectus to *Birds of America* which was probably sent out in May of 1827.

2

The great interest which has been excited by the exhibition of these Drawings, and the flattering praise which has been bestowed upon them in Edinburgh and Liverpool, induce the Author to propose to publish Engravings from them, upon a scale of elegance never before attempted in this or any other country. He has been encouraged to commence such an arduous undertaking, at the suggestions of some of the most eminent Naturalists both in America and Great Britain; and he is proud to acknowledge, that their patronage has been extended to him towards the encouragement of the Work; and he trusts to their support, and that of the Public, enabling him to complete one of the most splendid publications which has ever appeared.

The particulars of the Plan of the Work will be found detailed below:

1. The Engravings in every instance to be the exact dimensions of the Drawings, which, without any exception, represent the Birds of their natural size; and the Work will appear in Numbers, at moderate intervals.
2. The Plates will be coloured in the most careful manner from the original Drawings.
3. The size of the Work will be double Elephant Folio, and printed on the finest Drawing paper.
4. Five Plates will constitute a Number; one Plate from one of the largest Drawings, one from one of the second size, and three from the smaller Drawings. In every Number there will be a Non-descript Bird, or one not generally understood to be a native of the United States.
5. There are upwards of 400 Drawings, and it is proposed that they shall comprize Three Volumes, each containing about 130 Plates, to which an Index will be given at the end of each, to be bound up with the Volume.
6. The price of each Number will be Two Guineas, payable on delivery.

The First Number being now completed, will give an exact idea of the nature and style of the Work. All the other Numbers will at least equal the present in interest and execution. They will be delivered in Tin-cases, to preserve them from injury; and it would be advisable for the Subscribers to procure a Portfolio, to keep the Numbers till a Volume is completed. These Portfolios may be had at the shop of D. LIZARS, Bookseller, 5, St. David Street, or W. H. LIZARS, Engraver, 3, St. James's Square, Edinburgh.

Second sheet of the prospectus to *Birds of America*. Both sheets courtesy of the American Philosophical Society, Philadelphia, Pa.

Plate 34, "Worm-eating Warbler," as found in the set owned by the Library of Parliament, showing Audubon's critical instructions to Havell. Reproduced by permission of The Parliamentary Librarian, Ottawa, Canada. Reproduit avec la permission du Bibliothécaire Parlementaire, Ottawa, Canada.

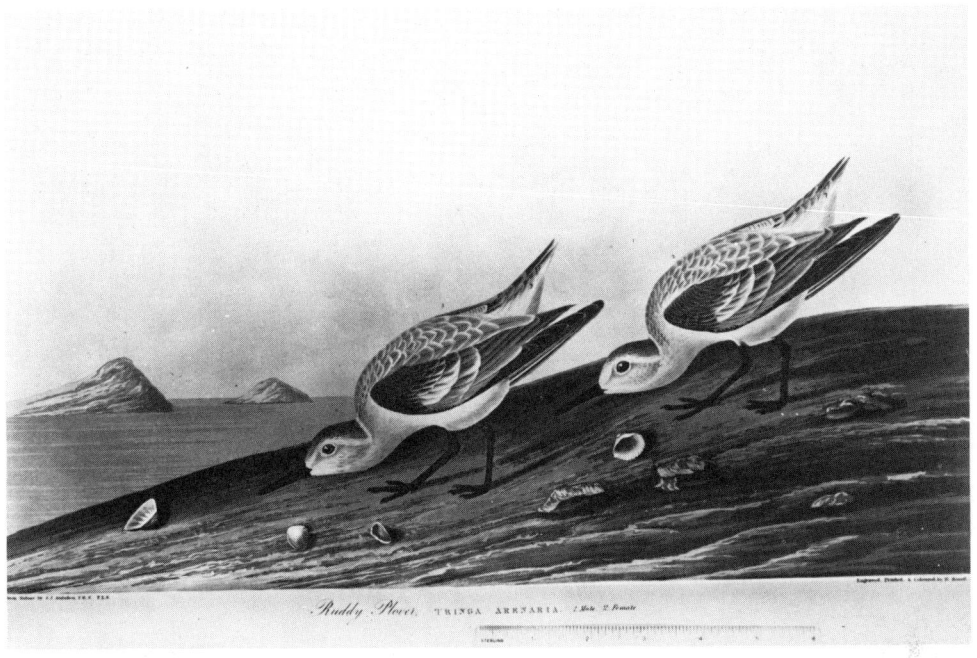

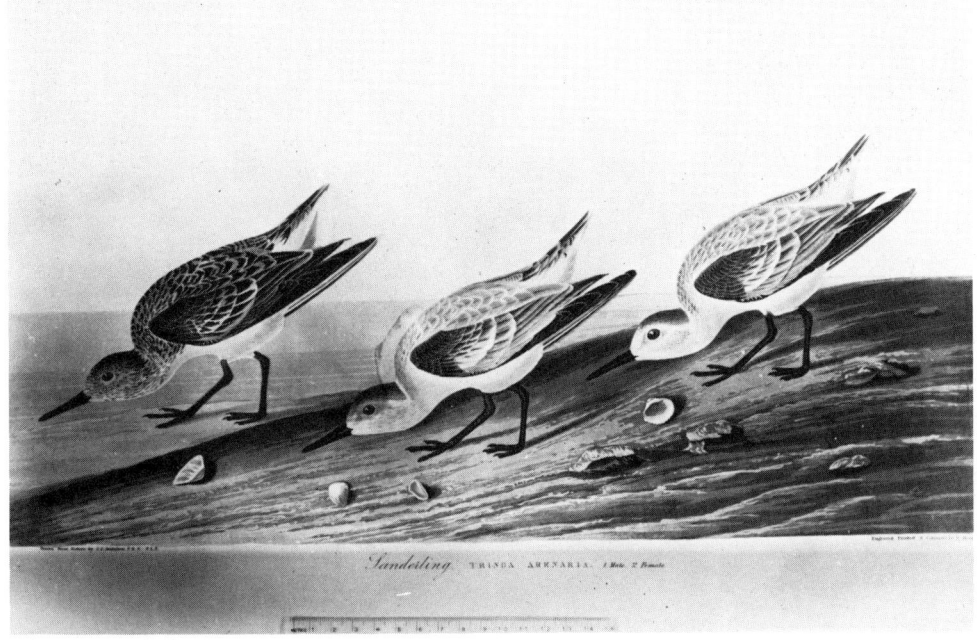

Plate 230 as found in the Yale University sets of the folio. The Farnam set, above, is the original state of the print. The Garvan set, below, is the second state of the print, showing the addition of a male bird figure which had been omitted by Havell during Audubon's absence from London. The Naturalist explained the circumstances in his *Ornithological Biography*, v. 3, p. 230. Courtesy of Yale University Library, New Haven, Connecticut.

Above, a section of Plate 6 in the first state of the print. The section of Plate 6 in the second state, below, shows the addition of a snail. For names of individuals and institutions owning sets with these variants, see page 220.

Additional Variants Found in Plate Legends and Watermarks

No. 47 PLATE CCXXXIII

Sora or *Rail*, Rallus Carolinus. L, 1.Male.2.Female.3.Young.

Providence Athenaeum J.W.T.M. 1834

NUMBER 48
Plate 237 (2 variants found)

No. 48 PLATE CCXXXVII

Great Esquimaux Curlew,
Numenius Hudsonicus, Lath.

Brown University J. Whatman 1834
Yale University, Garvan set J.W.T.M. (date bound in)

No. 48 PLATE CCXXXVII

Hudsonian Curlew
Numenius Hudsonicus, Lath.

Yale University, Farnam set J. Whatman 1836

NUMBER 49
Plate 245 (2 variants found)

No. 49 PLATE CCXLV

Uria Brunnichii.
[no common name given]

Brown University J. Whatman 1834
Yale University, Farnam set J. Whatman 1834
Yale University, Garvan set J. Whatman 1834

No. 49 PLATE CCXLV

Large-billed Guillemot
Uria Brunnichii

John Crerar Library (Not discernible)

NUMBER 50
Plate 249 (2 variants found)

No. 50 PLATE CCXLIX

Tufted Auk,
Mormon Cirrhatus, Lath. Male,1. Female,2.

Brown University J.W.T.M. 1835
Yale University, Farnam set J. Whatman 1836
Yale University, Garvan set J.W.T.M. 1836

437

APPENDIX K

No. 50   PLATE CCXLIX

Tufted Puffin
Mormon cirrhatus Lath.

    John Crerar Library   J. Whatman 1836

NUMBER 51
Plate 253 (2 variants found)

No. 51   PLATE CCLIII

Jager.
Lestris Pomarina, Temm.

    Brown University   J.W.T.M.   1835
    Yale University, Garvan set   J.W.T.M.   1835
    Yale University, Farnam set   J. Whatman 1836

No. 51   PLATE CCLIII.

Pomarine Jager,
Lestris pomarinus.

    John Crerar Library   J. Whatman 1836

NUMBER 52
Plate 256 (2 variants found)

No. 52   PLATE CCLVI

Purple Heron,
Ardea Rufescens, Buff.

    Brown University   J. Whatman 1835
    Yale University, Farnam set   J. Whatman 1835
    Yale University, Garvan set   J. Whatman 1835

No. 52   PLATE CCLVI

Reddish Egret
Ardea rufescens Buff.

    John Crerar Library   J. Whatman 1836

NUMBER 53
Plate 263 (2 variants found)

No. 53   PLATE CCLXIII

Pigmy Curlew,
Tringa Subarquata, Temm,

    Yale University, Garvan set   J. Whatman 1834
    Brown University   J. Whatman 1835
    Yale University, Farnam set   J. Whatman 1835

Additional Variants Found in Plate Legends and Watermarks

No. 53   PLATE CCLXIII

Curlew Sandpiper
Tringa subarquata Temm.

John Crerar Library   J. Whatman 1836

NUMBER 54
Plate 270 (2 variants found)

No. 54   PLATE CCLXX

Stormy Petrel,
Thalassidroma Wilsonii,

Brown University   J. Whatman 1835
Yale University, Farnam set   J. Whatman 1835
Yale University, Garvan set   J. Whatman 1835

No. 54   PLATE, CCLXX.

Wilson's Petrel
Thalassidroma Wilsonius

John Crerar Library   (Not discernible)

L

SUBSCRIBERS WHOSE NAMES AUDUBON PUBLISHED

SUBSCRIBER	PROSPECTUS*	V.1 MAR. 1831	V.2 DEC. 1834	V.3 DEC. 1835	V.4 NOV. 1838	V.5 MAY 1839
Academy of Natural Sciences, Philadelphia. Richard Harlan, Esq., M.D.			x			x
Her Most Excellent Majesty, Queen Adelaide			x			x
Mrs. P. Ainsworth, Hall, near Bolton	x	x				
American Philosophical Society, Philadelphia. John Vaughan, Esq., Sec'ry.			x			x
R. O. Anderson, Esq., Georgetown, S.C.			x			x
Samuel Appleton, Esq., Boston			x			x
James Arnold, Esq., New Bedford, R.I. (sic)			x			x
S. P. Atkins, Esq., Walbrook, London	x	x				x
Mrs. Bailey, New York			x			x
A. J. Cresswell Baker, Esq., of Brown Park	x	x				x
L. Baldwin, Esq., Civil Engineer, Boston					x	x
George Banks, Esq., Leeds	x	x				
Mr. Alexander Barclay, Bookseller, York		x				
Robert Barclay, Esq., Bury Hill, Dorking, Surrey	x	x				
Thomas Barker, Esq., Oldham, Manchester		x				
John Barton, Esq., Swinton, Manchester	x	x				
Dr. Bickersteth, Liverpool	x	x				x

* Received at the American Philosophical Society in Philadelphia on 17 April 1829.

Subscribers Whose Names Audubon Published

SUBSCRIBER	PROSPECTUS	V.1 MAR. 1831	V.2 DEC. 1834	V.3 DEC. 1835	V.4 NOV. 1838	V.5 MAY 1839
IN ORNITHOLOGICAL BIOGRAPHY PUBLISHED IN EDINBURGH						
W. Birch, Esq., St. John's Street, Manchester	x	x				
The Birmingham Old Library by Beilby, Knott, and Beilby		x				x
Daniel Blake, Esq., Savannah, Ga.			x			x
John Backhouse, Esq., Darlington, Newcastle-upon-Tyne	x	x				
John Blackwall, Esq., F. L. S., Manchester	x	x				x
Henry G. Bohn, Esq., London					x	x
Charles L. Bonaparte, Prince de Musignano, Rome	x	x				
The Boston Atheneum. By the Honourable T. H. Perkins		x				x
Boston Society of Natural History			x			x
The Right Honourable the Earl of Bradford, Pall Mall, London		x				x
The British Museum, London [in part]					x	x
John Broadley, Esq., South Ella, near Hull, Yorkshire	x	x				
Wm. Brodrick, Esq., Gower Street, London		x				
S. R. Brooks, Esq., Manchester, Deputy Consul of the United States of America, and Agent of Commercial Relations of the Republic of Columbia	x	x				
James Brown, Esq., Boston			x			x
His Grace the Duke of Buccleuch, Dalkeith Palace, Scotland			x			x
John Buddle, Esq., Wallsend, Newcastle-upon-Tyne	x	x				x
John Bulman, Esq., Percy Street, Newcastle-upon-Tyne	x	x				
Miss Susan Burley, Salem, Mass.			x			x
Matthew Burrell, Esq., Broom Park Castle, Alnwick	x	x				
James Burton, Esq., Regent's Park, London	x	x				
The Right Honourable the Earl of Caernarvon, Grosvenor Square, London	x	x				x
The Cambridge Philosophical Society, Cambridge	x	x				x

APPENDIX L

SUBSCRIBER	PROSPECTUS	IN ORNITHOLOGICAL BIOGRAPHY PUBLISHED IN EDINBURGH				
		V.1 MAR. 1831	V.2 DEC. 1834	V.3 DEC. 1835	V.4 NOV. 1838	V.5 MAY 1839
Cambridge University						
Fitzwilliam Museum, M. Davy, Vice-chancellor	x	x				x
George Thackeray, D. D., Provost, King's College	x	x				x
University Library, Dr. Lodge	x	x				x
Richard F. Carman, Esq., New York			x			x
Mrs. Case, Liverpool		x				
His Most Christian Majesty, Charles X	x	x				x
Charleston Citizens' Library, S.C.			x			x
Charleston Library, S.C.			x			x
Charleston Natural History Society, S.C.			x			x
Lieut-Colonel Charlewood, York Terrace, Regent's Park, London		x				
The Cheetham [Chetham] Library, Manchester, per the Rev. Peter Hordern, M.A.		x				x
J. G. Children, Esq., British Museum	x	x				x
Colonel Cholmley, Howshaw, York	x	x				
Her Royal Highness The Duchess of Clarence	x					
James Graham Clarke, Esq., Fenham Hall, Newcastle-upon-Tyne	x	x				
Henry Clay, junior, Esq., Ashland, Ky.					x	x
John Clayton, Esq., Newcastle-upon-Tyne	x	x				
John Clough, Esq., Oxton Hall, Tadcaster, Yorkshire	x	x				x
The Rev. J. Clowes, Manchester	x	x				
W. A. Colman, Esq., New York				x		x
Columbia College of New York, Rev. W. A. Duer, President			x			x
The Rev. E. Craig, Edinburgh, Great King Street	x	x				x
Thomas Crawhall, Esq., Newcastle-upon-Tyne	x	x				
William Cririe, Esq., Manchester	x	x				
Josiah S. Crompton, Jun., Esq., Esholt Hall, Bradford, Yorkshire	x	x				x
John Croghan, Esq., Louisville, Ky.			x			x

Subscribers Whose Names Audubon Published

SUBSCRIBER	PROSPECTUS	IN ORNITHOLOGICAL BIOGRAPHY PUBLISHED IN EDINBURGH				
		V.1 MAR. 1831	V.2 DEC. 1834	V.3 DEC. 1835	V.4 NOV. 1838	V.5 MAY 1839
Mrs. Douglas Cruger, New York	x	x				x
Matthew Culley, Esq., Coupland Castle, Northumberland	x	x				
J. P. Cushing, Esq., Watertown, near Boston, Mass.			x			x
Baron G. Cuvier, Paris	x	x				
James Darbyshire, Esq., Manchester	x	x				x
The Right Honourable Earl of Darnley, Berkeley Square, London	x	x				
Mr. Rees Davies, Bookseller, Hull (2 copies)	x					
H. C. DeRham, junior, Esq., New York					x	x
James Dickson, Esq., Philadelphia				x		
Armorer Donkin, Esq., Newcastle-upon-Tyne	x	x				x
John S. Donnel, Esq., Baltimore, Md.			x			
The Reverend Mr. Dunbar, Applegarth		x				
Garnett Duncan, Esq., Louisville, Ky.			x			x
Joseph C. Dyer, Esq., Manchester		x				x
The University of Edinburgh	x	x				x
Thomas Edmondston, Jr., Esq., Baltimore, Md.			x			x
Joseph Elgin, Esq., Coltingham, Yorkshire		x				
Patterson Ellames, Esq., Allerton Hall, near Liverpool	x	x				
Charles Elley, Esq., Hampstead, near London	x	x				
Henry Ellisan, Esq., Beverly, Yorkshire		x				x
Thomas H. Faile, Esq., New York					x	x
Mrs. Hamilton Nisbit Ferguson, Edinburgh		x				x
The Honourable W. C. Wentworth Fitzwilliam, Grosvenor Place, London	x	x				x
Mrs. Ford						x
Thomas Forster, Esq., Adderstone House, Belford, Northumberland	x	x				
Lawrence Fort, Esq., Birch Hill, near Manchester	x	x				
Mrs. John Foster, Liverpool	x	x				
Mrs. Foulis, York		x				

APPENDIX L

SUBSCRIBER	PROSPECTUS	IN ORNITHOLOGICAL BIOGRAPHY PUBLISHED IN EDINBURGH				
		V.1 MAR. 1831	V.2 DEC. 1834	V.3 DEC. 1835	V.4 NOV. 1838	V.5 MAY 1839
M. Foulis, Esq., Heslerton Malton, Yorkshire		x				
Charles Fox, Esq., Perrair, near Truro, England			x			x
George Lane Fox, Esq., Yorkshire			x			x
The Private Library of the King of France	x					
Thomas Frost, Esq., Gorton Hall, near Manchester			x			x
William Gambier, Esq., Sacombe Park, near Ware	x	x				
Robert Garnett, Esq., Oakhill, near Manchester	x	x				
William Gaston, Esq., Savannah, Ga.			x			x
E. Geddings, Esq., M.D. Baltimore, Md. and Charleston, S.C.			x			x
Robert Gee, Esq., Hollywood, near Stockport		x				
His Most Gracious Majesty, George IV	x	x				
The Reverend Mr. Gibson, Lochmaben		x				
Mrs. Euphemia Gifford, Duffield Bank, Derby			x			x
Robert Gilmor, Esq., Baltimore, Md.		x				x
The College of Glasgow, as Trustees of the Hunterian Museum	x	x				x
Benjamin Gott, Esq., Armley House, Leeds		x				
John Gott, Esq., Leeds	x	x				
John Gould, Esq., F.L.S., &c. London					x	
Lieutenant-General Graham, Stirling Castle		x				
D. Grant, Esq., Mosley Street, Manchester	x	x				
Ethan A. Greenwood, Esq., Museum, Boston			x			x
Samuel Greg, Esq., Quarry Bank, near Manchester	x	x				x
The Honourable and Reverend J. G. Grenville, Cambridge	x	x				
James Grimshaw, Esq., New Orleans, La.				x		x
Joseph Gurney, Esq., Lackenham Grove, Norwich	x	x				

Subscribers Whose Names Audubon Published

SUBSCRIBER	PROSPECTUS	IN ORNITHOLOGICAL BIOGRAPHY PUBLISHED IN EDINBURGH				
		V.1 MAR. 1831	V.2 DEC. 1834	V.3 DEC. 1835	V.4 NOV. 1838	V.5 MAY 1839
Joseph John Gurney, Esq., Earlham Hall, Norwich	x	x				x
Haarlem Library, Holland			x			x
Ogden Haggerty, Esq., New York				x		x
Thomas Haigh, Esq., Cheetham Hill, near Manchester	x	x				
Stephen A. Halsey, Hallet's Cove, Long Island, N.Y.					x	x
Thomas Hardman, Esq., Manchester	x	x				
Earl Hardwicke, &c. &c. &c. Wimpole, Arrington, Cambridge					x	x
Major-General Hardwicke, London		x				
Thomas Hardwicke, Esq., 46, Pall Mall, London	x					
Richard Harlan, Esq., M.D., Philadelphia			x			x
Edward Harris, Esq., Moorestown, N.J.			x			x
Joseph Harris, Esq., Liverpool		x				
Harvard University, Cambridge, Mass., Josiah Quincy, President			x			x
S. H. Haslam, Esq., Green Bank, near Bury, Lancashire	x	x				
Sir Jacob Hastley, Bart., &c. &c. &c. 7 Cavendish Square, London					x	x
R. H. Hay, Esq., Colonial Office, Downing Street	x	x				
George H. Head, Esq., Banker, Carlisle		x				
Mr. Hearne, Bookseller, Strand, London		x				x
John Heathcote, Esq., 41, Charles Street, Berkeley Square	x	x				x
The Right Honourable the Countess of Hertford		x				
B. A. Heywood, Esq., Claremont, near Manchester	x	x				
Thomas Heywood, Esq., Manchester	x	x				
George Hibbert, Esq., 38, Portland Place, London	x	x				
Robert Hindley, Esq., Manchester	x	x				
Henry Hitchcock, Mobile, Ala.					x	x
Edward Holme, M.D., Manchester		x				

445

APPENDIX L

SUBSCRIBER	PROSPECTUS	IN ORNITHOLOGICAL BIOGRAPHY PUBLISHED IN EDINBURGH				
		V.1 MAR. 1831	V.2 DEC. 1834	V.3 DEC. 1835	V.4 NOV. 1838	V.5 MAY 1839
Thomas Hoyle, Esq., Manchester	x	x				
J. J. Hughes, Esq., Manchester, Miss.					x	x
George Humphreys, Esq., Oxford Road, Manchester		x				
John Hunt, Esq., Mobile, Ala.					x	x
P. Hussey, Esq., Wyeslely Grove, near Walsall, Staffordshire		x				
Messrs. Daniel and Peter Jackson, 83, Market Street	x					
P. T. Jackson, Esq., Boston			x			x
Sir William Jardine, Bart., of Jardine Hall	x	x				
J. L. Joseph, Esq., New York			x			x
John Kennedy, Esq., Manchester		x				
James G. King, Esq., Banker, New York			x			x
Thomas Butler King, Esq., St. Simon's Island, Ga.			x			x
The Right Honourable Viscount Kingsborough, London		x				
The Right Honourable the Earl of Kinnoul		x				
James Knight, Esq., Rhual, Flintshire	x	x				
Baron Krudener, Envoy Extraordinary from Russia		x				
Mansfeldt de C. Lawson, Esq., Cromlington, Newcastle	x	x				
The Leeds Philosophical & Literary Society, Philosophical Hall, Leeds	x	x				x
Legislature of Louisiana			x			x
Legislature of Maryland, T. D. Teakle, Librarian			x			x
A. H. Everett, for the Library of the General Court of Massachusetts			x			x
Legislature of New York, John A. Dix, Secretary			x			x
Legislature of South Carolina, for the Columbia College			x			x
E. Everett, Esq., for the Library of Congress of the United States of America		x				x
Edwd. Lloyd, Esq., Greenhill, near Manchester	x	x				x

Subscribers Whose Names Audubon Published

SUBSCRIBER	PROSPECTUS	IN ORNITHOLOGICAL BIOGRAPHY PUBLISHED IN EDINBURGH				
		V.1 MAR. 1831	V.2 DEC. 1834	V.3 DEC. 1835	V.4 NOV. 1838	V.5 MAY 1839
London Institution, by Mr. Brayley, Librarian				x		x
The Right Honourable the Marquis of Londonderry	x	x				
Messrs Longman & Company, Booksellers, London			x			
Cornelius C. Low, Esq., New York			x			x
David Lyon, Esq., New Norfolk Street		x				
The Manchester Society for the Promotion of Natural History	x	x				x
John Marshall, Jun. Esq., Headingly, Leeds	x	x				x
Prince Massena, Paris	x	x				x
Thomas Metcalf, Esq., Augusta, Ga.					x	x
The State of Michigan, by Governor Mason					x	x
Philip John Miles, Esq., Little Court, near Bristol	x	x				
Viscount Milton, Grosvenor Place, London	x	x				x
John David Mongin, Esq., Savannah, Ga.			x			x
John B. Morris, M.D., Baltimore, Md.		x				x
The Right Honourable the Countess of Morton, Dalmahoy		x				
John Neal, Esq., Portland, Me			x			
Major Norcliffe, York		x				
His Grace the Duke of Northumberland &c. &c. &c.					x	x
The Reverend Henry Pearson Norton, Derby	x					
William Oakes, Esq., Ipswich			x			x
W. Ogilvie, Esq., Glasgow	x	x				
James Pickering Ord. Esq., Edge Hill, near Derby	x	x				x
H. R. H. The Duke of Orleans	x					
H. R. H. Mademoiselle D'Orleans	x	x				x
Oxford University						
Dr. King, for Anatomical School, Christ College	x	x				x
Christ Church, T. BL. L. Baker, Esq.	x	x				x
Dr. Williams, for Radcliffe College	x	x				x

APPENDIX L

SUBSCRIBER	PROSPECTUS	IN ORNITHOLOGICAL BIOGRAPHY PUBLISHED IN EDINBURGH				
		V.1 MAR. 1831	V.2 DEC. 1834	V.3 DEC. 1835	V.4 NOV. 1838	V.5 MAY 1839
Francis Charles Parry, Esq., 4, Onslow Terrace, Brompton	x	x				
Kirk Patrick, Esq., London	x	x				x
The Reverend Henry Pearson, Norton Vicarage, near Derby		x				
Charles Peers, Esq., Chislihampton Lodge, Oxfordshire	x	x				
Thomas H. Perkins, Esq., Boston, Mass.			x			x
His Majesty Philippe I, King of the French		x				x
Benjamin Phillips, Esq., F.R.S.L., &c. &c. &c. 17 Wimpole Street, London					x	x
Miss Elizabeth L. Pickman, Salem, Mass.					x	x
M. Pitois, Paris	x	x				x
The Honourable William S. Ponsonby, 19, St. James's Square, London	x	x				
Tho. Ponton, Esq., Hill Street, Berkeley Square, London		x				
ames Potter, Esq., Savannah, Ga.			x			x
Nat. Potter, M.D., Professor of Medicine, Baltimore, Md.		x				
John Potts, Esq., New Mills, near Manchester		x				
George W. Pratt, Esq., Boston			x			x
Edward Prime, Esq., Banker, New York			x			x
Providence Athenaeum, R.I.			x			x
Mrs. Rathbone, Green Bank, Liverpool	x	x				x
The Right Honourable the Countess of Ravensworth, Ravensworth Castle		x				x
Robert Ray, Esq., New York			x			x
P. J. Redouté, Esq., Paris	x	x				
William J. Rees, Esq., Stateburgh, S.C.			x			x
John G. Reeves, Esq., Birmingham		x				x
Miss Rhodes, Park Place, Leeds, Yorkshire		x				
Joseph Ridgway, Esq., Ridgemont, near Manchester	x	x				
Thomas Ridgway, Esq., Wallsuchess, Bolton	x	x				

Subscribers Whose Names Audubon Published

SUBSCRIBER	PROSPECTUS	IN ORNITHOLOGICAL BIOGRAPHY PUBLISHED IN EDINBURGH				
		V.1 MAR. 1831	V.2 DEC. 1834	V.3 DEC. 1835	V.4 NOV. 1838	V.5 MAY 1839
Cuthbert Rippon, Esq., Stanhope Castle, Durham	x	x				
Lewis Rogers, Esq., New York					x	x
William Roscoe, Esq., Foxteth Park, near Liverpool	x	x				
Baron N. M. Rothschild, Banker, London			x			
M. Feuillet, for the Library of the Royal Institute of France	x	x				x
His Grace the Duke of Rutland, London	x	x				x
John Rutter, Esq., M.D., Liverpool	x	x				x
The Salem Atheneum, Salem, Mass.					x	x
Gustavus Schmidt, Esq., New Orleans, La.			x			x
P. J. Selby, Esq., of Twizel, Northumberland	x	x				
E. W. Sergeant, Esq.	x	x				
The Rev. A. Sharpe, Bamburgh, Belford, Northumberland	x	x				
John Sharpe, Esq., Northwick Terrace, Edgeware Road		x				
George C. Shattuck, Esq., M.D., Boston			x			x
Vicomte Simeon for the Ministry of the Interior of France, 6 copies		x				x
.... Smith, Esq., Baltimore						x
Benjamin Smith, Esq., M.P., London		x				x
George Smith, Esq., Liverpool	x	x				
Maria Woodroof Smith, Aire Lane, Clapham	x	x				
The Society of Writers to her Majesty's Signet, Edinburgh	x	x				x
The Right Honourable Earl Spencer, St. James' Place, London	x	x				x
The Right Honourable Lord Stanley, Knowseley, Lancashire	x	x				x
The Honourable Levi Woodbury, Washington City, for the State Department					x	x
Dr. Stephenson, Newcastle-upon-Tyne	x	x				
William Stuart, Esq., Alderston	x	x				

APPENDIX L

SUBSCRIBER	PROSPECTUS	IN ORNITHOLOGICAL BIOGRAPHY PUBLISHED IN EDINBURGH				
		V.1 MAR. 1831	V.2 DEC. 1834	V.3 DEC. 1835	V.4 NOV. 1838	V.5 MAY 1839
William Sturges, Esq., Boston			x			x
P. J. Stuyvesant, Esq., M.D., New York			x			x
Samuel Swartout, Esq., New York					x	x
Sir John Swinburne, Bart. Cupheaton, near Newcastle	x	x				
Alexander Telfair, Esq., Savannah, Ga.			x			x
The Reverend John Thomson, Duddingston	x	x				
Augustus Thorndike, Esq., Boston, Mass.					x	x
Sir John Tobin, Liverpool			x			x
Thomas Joseph Trafford, Trafford Park	x	x				
Messrs Treuttel and Wurtz, Booksellers, London		x				
Frederic Tudor, Esq., Boston			x			x
His Imperial and Royal Highness the Grand Duke of Tuscany &c. &c. &c.			x			x
Jer Van Rensselaer, Esq., M.D., New York					x	x
Stephen Van Rensselaer, Esq., Albany, N.Y.			x			x
N. A. Vigors, Esq., Bruton Street, London	x	x				
John Walker, Esq., Benwell House, Newcastle-upon-Tyne	x	x				
Joseph E. Walker, Esq., Baltimore, Md.			x			
Thomas Walker, Esq., Killinbeck, near Leeds	x	x				x
Thomas Walker, Esq., Ravenfield, near Doncaster		x				x
Sir Wathen Waller, Bart K. C. H., Pope's Villa, Twickenham	x	x				
Charles J. Warde, Esq., Welcomb, near Stratford-on-Avon					x	x
Mrs. Warden, King Street, Portman Square	x	x				x
James Watson Webb, Esq., New York					x	x
The Honourable Daniel Webster, Boston, Mass.					x	x
The Wernerian Natural History Society of Edinburgh	x	x				

Subscribers Whose Names Audubon Published

SUBSCRIBER	PROSPECTUS	V.1 MAR. 1831	V.2 DEC. 1834	V.3 DEC. 1835	V.4 NOV. 1838	V.5 MAY 1839
John P. Wetherell, Esq., Philadelphia			x			x
Mrs. Wilson, Ledston Hall, near Ferrybridge, Yorkshire			x			
James Wilson, Esq., Edinburgh			x			
Captain Windowe, York		x	x			
Joseph Winter, Esq., Strand, near Manchester		x	x			
Henry Witham, Esq., of Lartington, Durham			x			x
George William Wood, Esq., Manchester		x	x			x
N. E. Yarburgh, Esq., Heslington Hall, near York			x			
The York Subscription Library, York		x	x			x
The Yorkshire Philosophical Society, York		x	x			x
Thomas Young, Esq., Savannah, Ga.				x		x

M

SUBSCRIBERS WHO DISCONTINUED AND AMOUNTS PAID

George IV, King of England	£37–10–0	S. R. Brook of Manchester	21– 0–0
Countess of Morton	14–14–0	Joseph Winter of Manchester	43– 1–0
University of Edinburgh	21– 0–0	Benjamin A. Heywood of Manchester	21– 0–0
Wernerian Society of Edinburgh	18–18–0	James Darbyshire of Manchester	43– 0–0
James Wilson of Edinburgh	12–12–0	Thomas Joseph Trafford of Manchester	21– 0–0
John Lizars M.D. of Edinburgh	6– 6–0		
W. H. Williams Artist of Edinburgh	2– 2–0	Thomas Haigh	21– 0–0
Henry Witham of Edinburgh recommened (recommenced ?)	8– 8–0	Joseph Ridgeway	21– 0–0
		Patterson Ellams	21– 0–0
Lieut Genl Graham of Sterling Castle	2– 2–0	Mr. P. Ainsworth has never paid 21– 0–0	
Matthew Burrel of Brown Park	8– 8–0	Wam Broderick	14–14–0
Lieut Coll Charlewood	8– 8–0	John Hibbert	27– 6–0
Thomas Ponton	8– 8–0	Charles Peers	14–14–0
Lady Ellen Hall	2– 2–0	Robert Barclay	39–19–0
Wam Tyler Work	2– 2–0	James Burton	18–18–0
Rev. d. John Thomson of Edinston	31–10–0	Guerney	42– 0–0
Major Norclife	21– 1–6	Mathew Culley	10–10–0
Col. Cholmley	16–16–0	A. J. Creswell, Banker	21– 0–0
M. Foulis	23– 2–0	Wam Burrell never paid 14–14–0	
Mr. Wilson numbers returned	———	Earl of Kinnoul	12–12–0
Capn Windome [?]	8– 8–0	George Smith of Liverpool	21– 0–0
Mr. Foulis	12–12–0	Doc. Stephenson of New Castle Tyne	21– 0–0
Robt Hindley of Manchester	42– 0–0	R. H. Hay, Col. Office London	42– 0–0
D. & P. Jackson of Manchester	30– 0–0	David Lyon	18– 0–0
E. W. Sergeant of Manchester	43– 1–0	Rev. d. Henry Pearson	38–18–0
Thos. Hardman of Manchester	43– 1–0	John Sharpe	33–12–0
Thomas Ridgeway of Manchester	21– 0–0	The Marchioness of Hertford	40–11–6
John Barton of Manchester	43– 1–0	John Eglin	35–14–0

List of 54 names taken from p.140 of Audubon's Ledger "B," now at the Audubon Museum, Henderson, Ky. The subscriptions of the University of Edinburgh and of Henry Witham, Edinburgh, were completed, however.

ABBREVIATIONS OF WORKS CITED

PUBLISHED WORKS

Audubon and His Journals, Maria R. Audubon. With zoological and other notes by Elliott Coues. 2v.; New York: C. Scribner's Sons, 1897.
   Cited as *Journals*

The 1826 Journal of John James Audubon. Transcribed with an introduction and notes by Alice Ford; from the original in the collection of Henry Bradley Martin. Norman, Okla.: Univ. of Oklahoma Pr., 1967.
   Cited as *1826 Journal*

Letters of John James Audubon, 1826–1840, ed. by Howard Corning. 2v.; Boston: The Club of Odd Volumes, 1930.
   Cited as *Letters*

The Life of John James Audubon, the Naturalist, ed. by his widow. With an introduction by Jas. Grant Wilson. New York: G. P. Putnam & Son, 1869.
   Cited as *Life*

Ornithological Biography, or *An Account of the Habits of the Birds of the United States of America;* Accompanied by Descriptions of the Objects Represented in the Work Entitled The Birds of America, and Interspersed with Delineations of American Scenery and Manners. 5v.; Edinburgh: A. Black [etc., etc.], 1831–1849 [i.e., 1839].
   Cited as *OB*

Audubon the Naturalist; A History of His Life and Time, Francis Hobart Herrick. 2v.; New York, London: D. Appleton and Co., 1917.
   Cited as *Herrick*

ABBREVIATIONS OF WORKS CITED

Journal of John James Audubon 1840–1843, ed. by Howard Corning. Foreword by Francis H. Herrick. Boston: Club of Odd Volumes, 1929.
    Cited as *Journal 1840–1843*

Dictionary of American Biography, publ. under the auspices of the American Council of Learned Societies. 20v. and index; New York: Scribner, 1928–37.
    Cited as *DAB*

Dictionary of National Biography, ed. by Leslie Stephen and Sydney Lee. 22v. (reissue of 63v.); London: Smith, Elder, 1908–9. Suppl. 2–6, 5v.; Oxford: Oxford Univ. Pr., 1912–59.
    Cited as *DNB*

UNPUBLISHED PRIMARY SOURCES

John James Audubon papers located in the Library of the American Philosophical Society, Philadelphia, Pa.
    Cited as APS Phila. BAu 25

Joseph Y. Jeanes bequest to Harvard University. Included in these papers are sixty-eight letters written by John James Audubon to Edward Harris; in the Houghton Library, Harvard University.
    Cited as Houghton pfMS Am 21

Collections of letters written by and to John James Audubon, given to the Museum of Comparative Zoology, Harvard University, by Col. John E. Thayer; deposited in the Houghton Library, Harvard University.
    Cited as Houghton bMS Am 1482

Collection of eight copy books, variously used by John James Audubon as ledgers, day books, and the like, given by Col. John E. Thayer to the Museum of Comparative Zoology, Harvard University; deposited in the Houghton Library.
    Cited as Houghton MCZ 118

NOTES

PART I

CHAPTER 1

1. *Journals*, v.1, p.81–82.
2. *Life*, p.93–94.
3. Ibid., p.94.
4. Ibid., p.101.
5. *Journals*, v.1, p.56.
6. *Life*, p.101.
7. Ibid., p.117.
8. Ibid., p.119.
9. Ibid., p.119.
10. Vincent Nolte, *Fifty Years in Both Hemispheres* (New York: Redfield, 1854), p.177.
11. *Journals*, v.1, p.98.
12. Ibid., v.1, p.102–3.
13. Ibid., v.1, p.115 and 120.
14. Ibid., v.1, p.107.
15. Ibid.
16. *1826 Journal*, p.328–30.
17. *Letters*, v.1, p.3 (JJA to Mrs. A, Bayou Sara, 1 Sept. 1826 [Original, APS Phila. BAu 25]).
18. Ibid., v.1, p.5.
19. *Journals*, v.1, p.120.
20. Ibid., v.1, p.120.
21. Ibid., v.1, p.109.
22. Ibid., v.1, p.111.
23. *Letters*, v.1, p.3–4 (JJA to VGA, Louisville, Ky., 1 Sept. 1826, APS Phila. BAu 25).
24. *Journals*, v.1, p.119.
25. Ibid., v.1, p.123.
26. Ibid., v.1, p.123.
27. Ibid., v.1, p.117.
28. Ibid., v.1, p.123–24.
29. Ibid., v.1, p.124. In the 1826 *Journal*, Ford records, "I concluded to-day to have a book of subscriptions, open to receive the names of all persons inclined to have the *best American Illustrations of birds that country ever yet transmitted to posterity*," p.161.
30. Ibid., v.1, p.127.
31. *1826 Journal*, p.226, 355.
32. *Journals*, v.1, p.127. In the Ford transcription there is no reference to Rathbone and Roscoe aiding him with prospectus, p.172–74.
33. *Life*, p.145.
34. *Journals*, v.1, p.128–29. "This I will not do, etc. etc.," not found in Ford transcription, p.176–77.
35. Ibid., v.1, p.135.
36. Ibid., v.1, p.141.
37. Ibid., v.1, p.150–51.
38. Ibid., v.1, p.157.
39. Ibid., v.1, p.152.
40. Ibid., v.1, p.159.
41. *1826 Journal*, p.304–5.
42. *Journals*, v.1, p.159.
43. Ibid., v.1, p.144.
44. Ibid., v.1, p.146.
45. *The Journal of Sir Walter Scott 1825–32*, new ed. (Edinburgh: David Douglas, 1891), p.343–45.
46. *Journals*, v.1, p.177, 207, 217.
47. *1826 Journal*, p.293. The Wernerian Natural History Society, founded in 1808, was named

NOTES

in honor of Abraham Gottlob Werner, the geologist, of whom Prof. Robert Jameson of the Chair of Natural History of Edinburgh University was an ardent admirer. There are extant two minute books covering the existence of the society from 1808 to 1858, when it came to an end. Audubon's attendance at the meetings of 16 Dec. 1826, 13 Jan. 1827, 27 Jan. 1827, and 10 Feb. 1827 is recorded.
48. Ibid., p.292–93.
49. Ibid., p.298.
50. *Journals*, v.1, p.153.
51. Ibid., v.1, p.155.
52. Ibid., v.1, p.156.
53. Ibid., v.1, p.160.
54. Ibid., v.1, p.165.
55. Ibid., v.1, p.166.
56. Ibid., v.1, p.175.
57. Ibid., v.1, p.179–80.

Chapter 2

1. *Letters*, v.1, p.7.
2. *Journals*, v.1, p.167.
3. *The Auk* 25:412–13 (Oct. 1908).
4. *Journals*, v.1, p.177.
5. Ibid., v.1, p.196.
6. Ibid., v.1, p.199.
7. Angus Davidson, *Miss Douglas of New York.* (New York: Viking, 1953), p.64.
8. *Journals*, v.1, p.222.
9. *Life*, p.135.
10. Ibid., v.1, p.209.
11. Ibid., v.1, p.210.
12. *Journals*, v.1, p.225.
13. *Letters*, v.1, p.9.
14. Ibid., v.1, p.18 (APS Phila. BAu 25).
15. *Journals*, v.1, p.225.
16. *Letters*, v.1, p.22 (APS Phila. BAu 25, 16 May 1827).
17. *Journals*, v.1, p.234.
18. Ibid.
19. *O.B.*, v.3, p.300–304.
20. *Journals*, v.1, p.239.
21. Ibid., v.1, p.242.
22. Ibid., v.1, p.243.
23. Ibid., v.1, p.244.
24. Ibid., v.1, p.243.
25. Ibid., v.1, p.248.
26. *Letters*, v.1, p.23.
27. Ibid., v.1, p.23 (APS Phila. BAu 25).
28. Ibid., v.1, p.22–25.

Chapter 3

1. *Journals*, v.1, p.249.
2. Ibid., v.1, p.252.
3. Ibid.
4. *Letters*, v.1, p.37–38 (APS Phila. BAu 25).
5. *Life*, p.154.
6. Ibid., p.153.
7. Ibid., p.152.
8. *Journals*, v.1, p.258.
9. *Letters*, v.1, p.31 (APS Phila. BAu 25).
10. Ibid., v.1, p.22–23 (APS Phila. BAu 25).
11. Ibid., v.1, p.39 (APS Phila. BAu 25).
12. *Journals*, v.1, p.259.
13. Ibid., v.1, p.260.
14. Ibid., v.1, p.261.
15. Ibid.
16. Ibid., v.1, p.263–64.
17. Ibid., v.1, p.265.
18. Ibid., v.1, p.266.
19. Ibid., v.1, p.267.
20. Ibid., v.1, p.270.
21. *Letters*, v.1, p.48 (APS Phila. BAu 25).
22. *Journals*, v.1, p.272.
23. Ibid., v.1, p.273.

Chapter 4

1. *Journals*, v.1, p.255.
2. Ibid., v.1, p.257.
3. *Life*, p.158.
4. *Letters*, v.1, p.29–30 (APS Phila. BAu 25, 6 Aug. 1827).
5. *1826 Journal*, p.286, 12 Dec. 1826.
6. George Alfred Williams, "An English Engraver of American Nature," *The Antiquarian* 17:26–30, 62, 64 (July 1931), p.28.
7. Ibid.
8. Ibid., p.29. See also the earlier account by Williams, "Robert Havell, Junior, Engraver of Audubon's 'The Birds of America'," which appeared in *Print Collector's Quarterly* 6:227–56 (Oct. 1916).
9. *Letters*, v.1, p.30 (APS Phila. BAu 25).
10. Ibid., v.1, p.36 (APS Phila. BAu 25).

Notes

Chapter 5

1. *Journals*, v.1, p.275.
2. Ibid.
3. *Letters*, v.1, p.58 (APS Phila. BAu 25, 6 Feb. 1828).
4. *Journals*, v.1, p.255.
5. Ibid., v.1, p.303.
6. Ibid., v.1, p.282.
7. Alexander Wilson, *American Ornithology* v.3, 1811, p.25, pl.19, fig.4.
8. *OB*, v.1, p.153.
9. *Journals*, v.1, p.291.
10. Ibid., v.1, p.279.
11. Ibid.
12. *Letters*, v.1, p.62–63, 17 Mar. 1828.
13. *Journals*, v.1, p.289.
14. *Letters*, v.1, p.63.
15. *Journals*, v.1, p.291.
16. Ibid., v.1, p.292.
17. Ibid.
18. Ibid., v.1, p.293–94.
19. Ibid., v.1, p.282.
20. Ibid., v.1, p.278.
21. *Herrick*, v.1, p.406–7, Audubon to Swainson, "Thursday July 1828."
22. *Journals*, v.1, p.299.
23. Ibid.
24. Ibid., p.282.
25. Ibid., v.1, p.303. Little is known about Parker. The usual sources give neither date of birth nor death. His portrait of Audubon presently is in the home of Morris Tyler, New Haven, Conn.
26. Ibid., p.276.
27. Ibid., p.295.
28. Ibid., p.296.
29. *Letters*, v.1, p.63, 17 March 1828.
30. *Journals*, v.1, p.297.
31. *Letters*, v.1, p.66 (APS Phila. BAu 25).
32. *Journals*, v.1, p.299.
33. *Herrick*, v.1, p.405–6.
34. Ibid., p.401 and 403.
35. *Journals*, v.1, p.298–99.
36. Ibid., v.1, p.300.
37. Ibid., v.1, p.304–6.
38. Ibid., v.1, p.307–8.
39. Ibid., v.1, p.308–9.
40. Ibid., v.1, p.312.
41. Ibid., v.1, p.313.
42. Ibid., v.1, p.314.
43. Ibid.
44. Ibid., v.1, p.315.
45. Archives des France, o 3 2214, dossier 617, lettre de Audubon au Baron de la Bouillerie, 13 Sept. 1828.
46. Ibid., o 3 2216.
47. *Journals*, v.1, p.327–30.
48. Ibid., v.1, p.330.
49. Ibid., v.1, p.338.
50. Ibid., v.1, p.326.
51. Ibid., v.1, p.317.
52. Ibid., v.1, p.331.
53. Ibid., v.1, p.338.
54. Ibid., v.1, p.339.
55. *Letters*, v.1, p.70 (APS Phila. BAu 25, 10 Nov. 1828).
56. *OB*, v.1, p.xii.
57. *Journals*, v.1, p.340.
58. Richard Harlan to JJA, 19 Nov. 1828; original in possession of the New-York Historical Society.
59. Cooper-Bonaparte correspondence, 24 Sept. 1827 (APS Phila., film 542).

Chapter 6

1. *Letters*, v.1, p.9–10; Edinburgh, 21 Dec. 1826.
2. Ibid., v.1, p.17; Edinburgh, 24 Mar. 1827.
3. Ibid., v.1, p.24–25 (APS Phila. BAu 25; Liverpool, 16 May 1827).
4. Ibid., v.1, p.54–56 (APS Phila. BAu 25; Liverpool, 26 Dec. 1827).
5. Ibid., v.1, p.57–59 (APS Phila. BAu 25; London, 6 Feb. 1828).
6. Ibid., v.1, p.77; London, 20 Jan. 1828.
7. Ibid., v.1, p.79.
8. Ibid., v.1, p.79–80 (APS Phila. BAu 25; London, 1 Feb. 1829).
9. *Journals*, v.1, p.342.
10. Bibliothèque Centrale du Muséum National d'Histoire, Paris (APS Phila., film 542).
11. *Life*, p.183–84, 5 May 1829 (Houghton bMS Am 1482 #6).
12. *Letters*, v.1, p.81–86 (APS Phila. BAu 25; New York, 10 May 1829).
13. Stanley Clisby Arthur, *Audubon: An Intimate*

457

NOTES

Life of the American Woodsman (New Orleans: J. S. W. Harmonson, 1937), p.291.
14. *Letters*, v.1, p.81 (APS Phila. BAu 25; to Lucy, New York, 10 May 1829).
15. *Life*, p.188-96.
16. *Letters*, v.1, p.96-98; to Lucy, Philadelphia, 11 Oct. 1829.
17. Ibid.
18. Ibid., v.1, p.93-94 (APS Phila. BAu 25; Great Pine Swamp, 25 Aug. 1829).
19. Ibid., v.1, p.96-98, 11 Oct. 1829.
20. Herrick, v.1, p.426, 431.
21. *Life*, p.202-3.
22. Ibid., p.203.
23. *OB*, v.5, p.650; see also *Life*, p.183.
24. F. C. Haber, "Notes on the Peabody Copy of Audubon's Birds of America, Elephant Folio Edition." Maryland Historical Society, n.d.
25. *Life*, p.203.
26. Haber, "Notes on the Peabody Copy of Audubon's Birds of America," referred to in note 24.
27. *Letters*, v.1, p.103-5; to Victor Audubon, Louisville, 2 Mar. 1830.
28. Ibid., v.1, p.100-2, 27 Oct. 1829.

Chapter 7

1. *Letters*, v.1, p.106-7 (Houghton bMS Am 1482 #17).
2. Ibid.
3. Letter of 10 June 1830, JJA to Havell; in the possession of Mrs. Grace Phillips Johnson, New Castle, Pa.
4. *Letters*, v.1, p.108-11, 23 June 1830.
5. Ibid., v.1, p.109.
6. Ibid., v.1, p.111-13, 29 June 1830.
7. *Life*, p.204.
8. *Letters*, v.1, p.114-16 (Houghton bMS Am 1482 #23, 8 Sept. 1830).
9. G. E. C(okayne), *The Complete Peerage* (London: St. Catharines Press, 1926).
10. *Letters*, v.2, p.46 (APS Phila. BAu 25, 22 Sept. 1834).
11. Letter, JJA to Havell, 28 Aug. 1830 (Houghton bMS Am 1482 #21).
12. *Letters*, v.1, p.116-17 (Houghton bMS Am 1482 #25, 13 Sept. 1830).
13. Ibid., v.1 p.117-19 (30 Sept. 1830, Houghton bMS Am 1482 #26).
14. Ibid.
15. Houghton bMS Am 1482 #349, 20 Nov. 1829.
16. *Letters*, v.1, p.102-3 (Houghton bMS Am 1482 #13).
17. Ibid., v.1, p.113-14 (Houghton bMS Am 1482 #19, 1 July 1830).
18. Ibid., v.1, p.117-19 (Houghton bMS Am 1482 #26, 30 Sept. 1830).

Chapter 8

1. *Journals*, v.1, p.163.
2. Herrick, v.2, p.101-3.
3. *The Auk* 22:21-34 (Jan. 1905).
4. JJA to Charles Lucien Bonaparte; in the Bibliothèque Centrale du Muséum National d'Histoire, Paris (APS Phila., film 542).
5. *Journals*, v.1, p.157. James Wilson was the brother of Prof. John Wilson, a naturalist and well-known scientific writer whose articles often appeared in *Blackwood's Magazine* under the pen name "Christopher North."
6. *Life*, p.205.
7. Herrick, v.1, p.442-45. The three editions of Wilson's *Ornithology* are listed, described, and discussed at length herein.
8. *Life*, p. 205-6.
9. JJA to Charles Lucien Bonaparte; Bibliothèque Centrale du Muséum National d'Histoire, Paris (APS Phila., film 542).
10. Ibid.
11. Ibid.
12. *OB*, v.1, p.xvii-xix.
13. Ibid., v.5, p.xi-xii.
14. Houghton bMS Am 1482 #33, 8 Jan. 1831.
15. JJA to Havell, 29 Mar. 1831. Original in the possession of Mrs. Grace Phillips Johnson, New Castle, Pa.; see also *Letters*, v.1, p.126, 21 Feb. 1831.
16. *Letters*, v.1, p.132-33, 23 Mar. 1831.
17. JJA to Havell, Houghton bMS Am 1482 #40, 13 April 1831.
18. *Letters*, v.1, p.127-30 (APS Phila. BAu 25, 21 Feb. 1831).
19. *Life*, p.207.

Notes

20. JJA to Havell, 28 Dec. 1830; original in possession of Mrs. Grace Phillips Johnson, New Castle, Pa.
21. *Letters*, v.1, p.132 (Houghton bMS Am 1482 #38, 23 Mar. 1831).
22. Ibid., v.1, p.120 (Houghton bMS Am 1482 #28, 31 Oct. 1830).
23. Ibid., v.1, p.125-26 (Houghton bMS Am 1482 #31, 18 Nov. 1830).
24. Houghton bMS Am 1482 #34, 16 Jan. 1831.
25. Havell to JJA, 20 Jan. 1831. Original in the New York Public Library, Ford Collection.
26. Houghton bMS Am 1482 #18, 29 June 1830.
27. Ibid., #188, 27 Feb. 1831.
28. Ibid., #186, 3 Dec. 1830.
29. Ibid., #353, 29 Nov. 1830.
30. Ibid., #36, 17 Feb. 1831.
31. Ibid., #34, 16 Jan. 1831.
32. Ibid., #40, 13 Apr. 1831.
33. *OB*, v.5, p.291.
34. JJA to Euphemia Gifford, dated London, 27 April 1831; in the collection of the H. J. Lutcher Stark Foundation, Orange, Texas.
35. JJA to Euphemia Gifford, 19 July 1831; original in the H. J. Lutcher Stark Foundation collection.
36. *Life*, p.207-8.

Chapter 9

1. *OB*, v.3, p.434-46.
2. *Herrick*, v.2, p.2.
3. *Letters*, v.1, p.136 (Houghton bMS Am 1482 #42, 20 Sept. 1831).
4. Ibid., v.1, p.137.
5. Ibid.
6. Houghton bMS Am 1482 #43.
7. *Letters*, v.1, p.139 (APS Phila. BAu 25, 9 Oct. 1831).
8. Ibid., v.1, p.140.
9. *Herrick*, v.2, p.35-36.
10. *Letters*, v.1, p.143; Charleston, S.C., 23 Oct. 1831.
11. Ibid.
12. C. L. Bachman, *John Bachman* (Charleston: Walker, Evans & Cogswell, 1888), p.94.
13. *Letters*, v.1, p.143.
14. *John Bachman*, p.99-102.
15. Ibid.
16. *Letters*, v.1, p.146 (APS Phila. BAu 25, 30 Oct. 1831).
17. Ibid., v.1, p.148 (APS Phila., 7 Nov. 1831).
18. Ibid., v.1, p.151-55, 23 Nov. 1831.
19. Ibid., v.1, p.155-59, 29 Nov. 1831.
20. Ibid., v.1, p.161, 5 Dec. 1831.
21. *OB*, v.2, p.550.
22. *Letters*, v.1, p.184-87, 13 Mar. 1832.
23. Ibid.
24. Ibid., v.1, p.152, 23 Nov. 1831.
25. Ibid., v.1, p.192, 29 Mar. 1832.
26. Ibid., v.1, p.186, 13 Mar. 1832.
27. Ibid., v.1, p.187.
28. Ibid., v.1, p.177-80, 1 Feb. 1832.
29. Original letter in the Howland Collection, Buffalo Museum of Science, Buffalo Society of Natural Science.
30. *Letters*, v.1, p.193, 15 Apr. 1832.
31. Houghton bMS Am 1482 #49, Charleston, 28 Mar. 1832.
32. *Letters*, v.1, p.193-95, 15 Apr. 1832.
33. *OB*, v.2, p.312.
34. *Letters*, v.1, p.170, 4 Jan. 1832.
35. Ibid., v.1, p.157, 29 Nov. 1831.
36. Houghton bMS Am 1482 #190, 2 Oct. 1831.
37. Ibid., #191, 11 Oct. 1831.
38. Ibid., #198, 26 Dec. 1831.
39. Ibid., #193.
40. Ibid., #200, 16 Jan. 1832.
41. Ibid., #204, 22 Mar. 1832.
42. Ibid., #224, 29 Apr. 1832.
43. *OB*, v.3, p.483.
44. Houghton bMS Am 1482 #225, 21 July 1832.

Chapter 10

1. Houghton bMS Am 1482 #52.
2. *OB*, v.2, p.xvii-xviii.
3. Rhoda Truax, *The Doctors Warren of Boston* (Boston: Houghton, 1968), p.204-10.
4. Houghton bMS Am 21 #6, 14 Aug. 1832.
5. Thomas Nuttal, *A Manual of the Ornithology of the United States and of Canada, The Land Birds* (Cambridge: Hilliard and Brown, 1832).
6. Houghton bMS Am 21 #6, 15 Aug. 1832.
7. *OB*, v.2, p.459-63, 97-101.
8. *Letters*, v.2, p.17-21. See also Irving T. Richards, "Audubon, Joseph R. Mason, and John Neal," *American Literature* 6:122-40 (May 1934); also made available as a reprint at one time.
9. *OB*, v.2, p.437.

NOTES

10. Letter of 10 Oct. 1832; original in the possession of Mrs. Grace Phillips Johnson, New Castle, Pa.
11. *Letters*, v.1, p.207-11 (APS Phila. BAu 25).
12. Ibid., v.1, p.209.
13. Ibid., v.1, p.205.
14. Ibid., v.1, p.202-7.
15. Ibid., v.1, p.203.
16. Ibid., v.1, p.208.
17. George Bird Grinnell, "Some Audubon Letters," *The Auk* 33:120-23 (Apr. 1916).
18. *The Auk* 33:122 (Apr. 1916).
19. OB, v.2, p.464-68.
20. *Letters*, v.1, p.202-7, 1 April 1833.
21. Ibid., v.1, p.207-11, 15 April 1833.
22. *The Auk* 33:120-23 (Apr. 1916).
23. For details of Audubon's trip to Labrador, see OB, v.3, p.82-86, "The Eggers of Labrador"; refer also to *Journals*, v.1, p.349-445; and Charles Wendell Townsend, *In Audubon's Labrador* (Boston: Houghton, 1918), p.1-17. Also among the references listed in the Herrick bibliography, v.2, p.441-42, no.166-67 pertain to the Labrador expedition.
24. *Letters*, v.1, p.247-50, 15 Sept. 1833.
25. Ibid., v.1, p.251-55, 20 Sept. 1833.

Chapter 11

1. *Letters*, v.1, p.213 (Houghton bMS Am 1482 #54, 20 Apr. 1833).
2. Ibid., v.1, p.243 (APS Phila. BAu 25, 9 Sept. 1833).
3. Ibid., v.1, p.250 (APS Phila. BAu 25, 15 Sept. 1833).
4. *Life*, p.378.
5. *Letters*, v.1, p.261-63 (APS Phila. BAu 25, 11 Oct. 1833).
6. Ibid., v.1, p.262.
7. *Life*, p.378-79.
8. *Letters*, v.1, p.261 (APS Phila. BAu 25, 11 Oct. 1833).
9. *Life*, p.379.
10. Ibid., p.380.
11. Ibid.
12. *Letters*, v.1, p.252 (APS Phila. BAu 25, 20 Sept. 1833).
13. Ibid., v.1, p.264-65 (APS Phila. BAu 25, 4 Nov. 1833).
14. Ibid., v.1, p.274 (APS Phila. BAu 25, 21 Dec. 1833).
15. Ibid., v.2, p.6 (APS Phila. BAu 25, 14 Jan. 1834).
16. Ibid., v.2, p.9 (APS Phila. BAu 25, 15 Feb. 1834).
17. Ibid., v.1, p.270, 24 Nov. 1833.
18. Annie Roulhac Coffin, "Maria Martin (1796-1863)," *Art Quarterly* 23, no.3:281-300 (Autumn 1960).
19. *Letters*, v.1, p.272-77.
20. *Boston Journal of Natural History* 1:15-25 (Boston: Hilliard, Gray & Co., 1837).
21. See *Herrick*, v.1, p.227, 231-32, 328-29, 333, 339, 422; v.2, p.4, 27, 55, 61, 72, 80, and 83 for Ord's attacks. For references to Waterton and his criticisms of Audubon, see v.1, p.12, 224, 232, 415; v.2, p.55, 61, 73, 79, and 82.
22. Loudon's *Magazine of Natural History* 6:215-16 (1833) and 7:66-74 (1834).
23. Loudon's *Magazine* 6:369 (1833).
24. *Letters*, v.1, p.263 (APS Phila. BAu 25, 4 Nov. 1833).
25. Ibid., v.1, p.272 (APS Phila. BAu 25, 21 Dec. 1833).
26. Ibid., v.1, p.263-64 (APS Phila. BAu 25, 4 Nov. 1833).
27. J.J. Audubon-Bonaparte correspondence, 14 July 1830, Bibliothèque Centrale du Muséum National d'Histoire, Paris (APS Phila., film 542).
28. Houghton bMS Am 21 #68, 1 Dec. 1833.
29. *Letters*, v.1, p.274 (APS Phila. BAu 25, 21 Sept. 1833).
30. Ibid., v.1, p.265 (APS Phila. BAu 25, 4 Nov. 1833).
31. Ibid., v.2, p.4 (APS Phila. BAu 25, 14 Jan. 1834).
32. Ibid., v.2, p.6.
33. Ibid., v.1, p.276 (APS Phila. BAu 25, 21 Dec. 1833).
34. Ibid., v.2, p.3-7 (APS Phila. BAu 25, 14 Jan. 1834).
35. Ibid.
36. Ibid., v.2, p.8 (APS Phila. BAu 25, 15 Feb. 1834).
37. Bayard Tuckerman, ed., *The Diary of Philip Hone, 1828-1851* (New York: Dodd, 1889), p.82, 86.
38. *Letters*, v.2, p.11 (APS Phila. BAu 25, 9 Mar. 1834).
39. Ibid., v.2, p.8 (APS Phila. BAu 25, 15 Feb. 1834).
40. Ibid., v.2, p.6 (APS Phila. BAu 25, 14 Jan. 1834).

Notes

41. Ibid., p.10-13 (APS Phila. BAu 25, 9 Mar. 1834).
42. JJA to Bachman, 13 Mar. 1834; the original is in the Princeton Univ. Library's collection.
43. Ibid.
44. Ibid.
45. Ibid.
46. Houghton bMS Am 21 #12, 28 Mar. 1834.
47. *Letters*, v.2, p.15-17 (APS Phila. BAu 25, 5 Apr. 1834).
48. Ibid., v.2, p.25-27 (APS Phila. BAu 25, 15 Apr. 1834).
49. Ibid., v.1, p.267-68 (Houghton bMS Am 1482 #55, 24 Nov. 1833).
50. Ibid., v.2, p.25-27 (APS Phila. BAu 25, 15 Apr. 1834).

Chapter 12

1. *Letters*, v.2, p.27 (Houghton bMS Am 1482 #60, 8 May 1834).
2. Lucy Audubon to Miss Gifford, 21 May 1834. Original is now in the H. J. Lutcher Stark Foundation collection, Orange, Texas.
3. This refers to the miniature painted on ivory by Frederick Cruikshank, probably in London, sometime before Audubon's return to America on 2 Aug. 1831. The portrait became well known through the excellent engraving of it by C. Turner, A.R.A., and was first published in London "Jany. 12, 1835, for the Proprietor, by Robert Havell, Print-seller, 77, Oxford Street" with Audubon's characteristic autograph.
4. *Letters*, v.2, p.30-31 (Houghton bMS Am 1482 #61, 25 Aug. 1834).
5. Ibid., v.2, p.104-5 (Houghton bMS Am 1482 #87, 1 Dec. 1835).
6. Ibid., v.2, p.109-14 (Houghton bMS Am 1482 #90, 22 Jan. 1836).
7. JJA to Miss Gifford, 27 July 1834; original in the collection of the H. J. Lutcher Stark Foundation, Orange, Texas.
8. Lucy Audubon to Miss Gifford, 8 Aug. 1834; in the H. J. Lutcher Stark Foundation collection.
9. *Letters*, v.2, p.9 (APS Phila. BAu 25, 15 Feb. 1834).
10. MacGillivray to JJA, 28 May 1834; first published in the *Bulletin of the Nuttall Ornithological Club* 5, no.4:204 (Oct. 1880). The first eight volumes of *The Auk* were originally published as the *Bulletin of the Nuttall Ornithological Club* of Cambridge, Mass.
11. Letter of 18 July 1834, MacGillivray to JJA, *The Auk* 18:243 (July 1901).
12. *Letters*, v.2, p.29 (Houghton bMS Am 1482 #61, 25 Aug. 1834).
13. Ibid.
14. Ibid., v.2, p.69 (Houghton bMS Am 1482 #70, 20 Apr. 1835).
15. Ibid., v.2, p.50 (Houghton bMS Am 1482 #65, 19 Nov. 1834).
16. Ibid., v.2, p.60-62 (Houghton bMS Am 1482 #69, 16 Jan. 1835).
17. Ibid., v.2, p.65 (Houghton bMS Am 1482 #70, 20 Apr. 1835).
18. Ibid., v.2, p.102 (Houghton bMS Am 1482 #86, 1 Dec. 1835).
19. Ibid., v.2, p.26 (APS Phila. BAu 25, 15 Apr. 1834).
20. Houghton pfMS Am 21 #14, 1 June 1834.
21. *Life*, p.381-83.
22. JJA to Charles Lucien Bonaparte, 20 Aug. 1834; original in Bibliothèque Centrale du Muséum National d'Histoire, Paris (APS Phila., film 542).
23. Houghton pfMS Am 21 #22, 21 July 1835.
24. JJA to Bachman, 13 Mar. 1834; original in the Princeton Univ. Library's collection.
25. *Letters*, v.1, p.252 (APS Phila. BAu 25, 20 Sept. 1833).
26. J. G. Children to JJA, 21 June 1834; original in the Research Library, Howland Collection, Buffalo Museum of Science, Buffalo Society of Natural Sciences.
27. *Letters*, v.2, p.30 (Houghton bMS Am 1482 #61, 25 Aug. 1834).
28. Ibid.
29. Ibid., v.2, p.33-38 (APS Phila. BAu 25, 5 Sept. 1834).
30. Ibid., v.2, p.38-47 (APS Phila. BAu 25, 22 Sept. 1834).
31. Ibid., v.2, p.109 (Houghton bMS Am 1482 #90, 22 Jan. 1836).
32. Ibid., v.2, p.125 (Houghton bMS Am 1482 #95, 9 July 1836).
33. Ibid., v.2, p.93-94 (Houghton bMS Am 1482 #81, 26 Sept. 1835).
34. Ibid., v.2, p.100 (Houghton bMS Am 1482 #84, 1 Nov. 1835).
35. Ibid.
36. Ibid., v.2, p.107 (Houghton bMS Am 1482 #87, 12 Dec. 1835).
37. Ibid., v.2, p.87 (Houghton bMS Am 1482 #78, 15 Sept. 1835).

38. Ibid., v.2, p.109–14 (Houghton bMS Am 1482 #90).
39. Ibid., v.2, p.84–90 (Houghton bMS Am 1482 #78).
40. Ibid., v.1, p.98 (APS Phila. BAu 25, 11 Oct. 1829).
41. Houghton pfMS Am 21 #48.
42. *Letters*, v.2, p.109–14 (Houghton bMS Am 1482 #90).

Chapter 13

1. *Letters*, v.2, p.127 (APS Phila. BAu 25, 7 Sept. 1836).
2. Bachman to JJA, 14 Sept. 1836, in C. L. Bachman, *John Bachman, D.D., L.L.D., Ph.D.* (Charleston: Walker, Evans & Cogswell, 1888), p.137.
3. *Letters*, v.2, p.128 (APS Phila. BAu 25, 7 Sept. 1836).
4. Ibid., v.2, p.127.
5. Ibid., v.2, p.129.
6. JJA to VGA, 17 Sept. 1836. The original letter is in the Howland Collection, Buffalo Museum of Science, Buffalo Society of Natural Sciences.
7. *Letters*, v.2, p.130 (Houghton bMS Am 1482 #96, 10 Sept. 1836).
8. JJA to Havell, 26 Oct. 1836. Original in the possession of Mrs. Grace Phillips Johnson, New Castle, Pa.
9. *Life*, p.391.
10. Shattuck papers, Mass. Historical Society.
11. *Letters*, v.2, p.133–35 (Houghton bMS Am 1482 #98, 2 Oct. 1836).
12. Ibid., v.2, p.127 (APS Phila. BAu 25, 7 Sept. 1836).
13. Ibid., v.2, p.130 (Houghton bMS Am 1482 #96, 10 Sept. 1836).
14. *Life*, p.387.
15. Ibid.
16. Ibid., p.388.
17. *Letters*, v.2, p.135–36 (Houghton bMS Am 1482 #101, 23 Oct. 1836).
18. Jeanette E. Graustein, "Audubon and Nuttall," *Scientific Monthly* 74, no.2:84–90 (Feb. 1952).
19. Ibid.
20. JJA to Havell, 18 Dec. 1836. The original is in possession of R. Gwynne Stout, Ardmore, Pa.; a copy is in the Princeton Univ. Library.
21. *Letters*, v.2, p.137 (Houghton bMS Am 1482 #103, 6 Nov. 1836).
22. *Life*, p.396.
23. Ibid.
24. Ibid.
25. Ibid., p.397.
26. Ibid., p.398.
27. *OB*, v.4, p.xiii.
28. Ibid., p.xiv.
29. *Letters*, v.2, p.142 (APS Phila. BAu 25, 13 Feb. 1837).
30. Ibid., v.2, p.140.
31. Ibid., v.2, p.145–46 (Houghton bMS Am 1482 #103, 24 Feb. 1837).
32. Ibid., v.2, p.153–54 (APS Phila. BAu 25, 23 Mar. 1837).
33. Ibid., v.2, p.151 (Houghton bMS Am 1482 #109, 22 Mar. 1837).
34. Ibid., v.2, p.157–60 (Houghton bMS Am 1482 #111, 6 Apr. 1837).
35. *Herrick*, v.2, p.158–63.
36. *Letters*, v.2, p.160 (Houghton bMS Am 1482 #112, 18 Apr. 1837).
37. Texas became a Spanish province in 1691, a Mexican state in 1821. American settlers revolted in 1835. After suffering defeat at the Alamo 6 Mar. 1836, they defeated the Mexicans at San Jacinto on 21 Apr. 1836 and the Republic of Texas was formed. In 1845 the Texans voted annexation to the United States.
38. *Life*, p.411–14.
39. Ibid., p.414.
40. *OB*, v.4, p.xix.
41. Ibid., v.2, p.xix–xx.
42. *Letters*, v.2, p.164 (Houghton bMS Am 1482 #114, 2 July 1837).
43. John Crosby Brown, *Years of Merchant Banking* (New York: Privately printed, 1909), p.77–93. A history of and for Brown Brothers and Company, Shipley & Company, and allied firms.
44. JJA to S. G. Morton, 12 June 1837 (APS Phila., Morton papers).
45. *OB*, v.4, p.xx.
46. Ibid., v.4, p.xx–xxi.
47. *Letters*, v.2, p.161 (Houghton bMS Am 1482 #114, 2 July 1837).
48. Ibid.
49. Ibid.
50. JJA to Shattuck, 5 July 1837 (Mass. Hist. Soc., Shattuck papers).
51. *Letters*, v.2, p.163 (Houghton bMS Am 1482 #114, 2 July 1837).

Notes

Chapter 14

1. *Letters*, v.2, p.179 (Houghton bMS Am 1482 #119, 14, 18 Aug. 1837).
2. *OB*, v.4, p.xxi–xxii.
3. *Letters*, v.2, p.96–97 (Houghton bMS Am 1482 #83).
4. Ibid., v.2, p.187–89 (Houghton bMS Am 1482 #121, 31 Oct. 1837).
5. Ibid., v.2, p.182 (Houghton bMS Am 1482 #120, 4 Oct. 1837). The Naturalist or his amanuensis may have meant to say in this letter that the four volumes would include a total of 83 numbers, since 115 plates comprise only 23 numbers. It should be remembered that when the work finally was completed, the fourth volume actually contained 135 plates in 27 numbers.
6. *The Auk* 20:377–80 (Oct. 1903).
7. Ibid.
8. Houghton bMS Am 21 #42, 19 Jan. 1838.
9. *Letters*, v.2, p.196–97 (Houghton bMS Am 1482 #125, 6 Feb. 1838).
10. Ibid., v.2, p.187–88 (Houghton bMS Am 1482 #121, 31 Oct. 1837).
11. Ibid., v.2, p.200 (Houghton bMS Am 1482 #126, 14 Apr. 1838).
12. Ibid., v.2, p.202.
13. Ibid., v.2, p.189 (Houghton bMS Am 1482 #121, 31 Oct. 1837).
14. Ibid., p.227 (Houghton bMS Am 1482 #148, 8 Dec. 1839).
15. JJA to S. G. Morton, 25 June 1838, APS Phila., Morton papers.
16. *The Auk* 11:309–13 (Oct. 1894). The original letter is in the library of Princeton University.
17. *Letters*, v.2, p.203 (Houghton bMS Am 1482 #130, 29 Sept. 1838).
18. Ibid., v.2, p.205 (Houghton bMS Am 1482 #131, 20, Oct. 1838).
19. Ibid., v.2, p.208 (Houghton bMS Am 1482 #132, 27 Oct. 1838).
20. Ibid., v.2, p.209 (Houghton bMS Am 1482 #134, 6 Nov. 1838).
21. Ibid., v.2, p.210 (Houghton bMS Am 1482 #135, 30 Jan. 1839).
22. Ibid., v.2, p.209–10 (Houghton bMS Am 1482 #135).
23. Ibid., v.2, p.213–14 (Houghton bMS Am 1482 #139, 13 Mar. 1839).
24. Ibid., v.2, p.187 (Houghton bMS Am 1482 #120, 4 and 8 Oct. 1837).
25. Ibid., v.2, p.212 (Houghton bMS Am 1482 #139, 13 Mar. 1839).
26. Ibid., v.2, p.215 (Houghton bMS Am 1482 #140, 21 Mar. 1839).
27. Ibid., v.2, p.219 (Houghton bMS Am 1482 #142, 4 May 1839).
28. Ibid., v.2, p.213 (Houghton bMS Am 1482 #139, 13 Mar. 1839).
29. Ibid., v.2, p.219 (Houghton bMS Am 1482 #142, 4 May 1839).
30. Ibid.
31. Houghton bMS Am 1482 #243, 20 Aug. 1838.
32. Ibid., Houghton bMS Am 1482 #252, 14 Dec. 1838.
33. Ibid., Houghton bMS Am 1482 #253, 22 Dec. 1838.
34. *Letters*, v.2, p.222 (Houghton bMS Am 1482 #144, 30 June 1839).
35. Ibid., v.2, p.220–21 (Houghton bMS Am 1482 #143, 15 May 1839).
36. *Herrick*, v.2, p.191.
37. Houghton pfMS Am 21 #48, 7 July 1839.
38. National Archives and Records, Serial roll 39, list 631.

Chapter 15

1. Houghton MCZ 118, v.2, p.14: Amounts due from subscribers.

T. B. King, St. Simons Island 3 & 4th Vols. Large Work & 4th Vol. Biog.	$	475.50
J. P. Wetherill Bal. of a/c Large Work $160. Vol. 4 Biog. 5.50		165.50
Acady. of Nat. Sciences Phila. Balance of a/c for Large Work	[$]	302.57
Philos Society. Bal. Large Work		90.00
Citizens Private Library Charleston, S.C.		750.00

463

E. Geddings, M.D. Bal. Large Work and Biog.	[$] 427.50
Charleston Nat. His. Society. Balance	70.00
Columbia College S.C. Balance on Large Work for a/c Rev. R. W. Barnwell President	505.50
State of Maryland 5th Vol. Biog.	5.50
J. B. Morris Bal. on Large Work	90.00
N. Potter " " " "	210.00
I. R. Peters (Bal. for Large Work)	430.00
State of Louisiana (ditto)	730.00
J. P. Grimshaw (ditto)	989.12
Garnett Duncan (ditto)	470.37
John Croghan (ditto)	150.00
John Hunt (4th Volume Full bound)	320.00
Mrs. Kruger (Balance on Large Work)	270.00
J. L. Joseph (4th Vol. hf. bound)	290.00
J. W. Webb Vol. 1 to 4 full bound	1070.00
Greenwood (note & a/c)	700.00
Boston Nat. Histy Socy	75.50
F. Tudor	325.50
P. J. (T) Jackson	30.00
D. L. Pickman [Miss Elizabeth L.]	22.00
Hilliard Gray & Co. (Note)	180.00
J. Arnold	220.00
Daniel Webster	950.00
Wm Sturgis	295.50
	$10,610.06

2. Houghton bMS Am 1482 #251, 8 Dec. 1838.
3. *Letters*, v.2, p.211 (Houghton bMS 1482 #136, 23 Feb. 1839).
4. *Herrick*, v.2, p.190.
5. American Museum of Natural History, 57th Annual Report, 1925.
6. *Letters*, v.2, p.223 (APS Phila. BAu 25, 24 Nov. 1839).
7. Ibid., v.2, p.128 (APS Phila. BAu 25, 7 Sept. 1836).
8. *OB*, v.5, p.648.
9. *DAB*, v.18, p.238-39.
10. Houghton MCZ 118, v.2, p.14.
11. *Letters*, v.2, p.223 (APS Phila. BAu 25, 24 Nov. 1839).
12. La Monnier papers, Tulane Univ. Library, New Orleans, La.
13. Houghton MCZ 118, v.2, p.29-30.
14. Ibid., v.3, p.80.
15. Ibid., v.3, p.83.
16. Ibid.
17. Ibid., v.3, p.85.
18. *Letters*, v.2, p.258 (APS Phila. BAu 25, 15 Apr. 1840).
19. John James Audubon, F. R. SS. L. & E.(&c. &c.), *The Birds of America* from Drawings Made in the United States and Its Territories. 7v. of text and plates, roy. 8vo. Published by the Author and J. B. Chevalier (New York and Philadelphia, 1840-1844).
20. *The Auk* 52:159-61 (April 1935), JJA to family, 9 Aug. 1840. Original letter in possession of A. E. Lownes, Providence, R.I.
21. *Journal 1840-1843*, p.5 (Houghton MCZ 118, v.1).
22. *New Bedford Directory 1839, 1846*. The Pardon G. Seabury papers, p.16, Free Public Library, New Bedford, Mass.
23. On 31 March 1831, Audubon made an agreement with Joseph Bartholomew Kidd, a young artist whom he had met in Edinburgh the previous March, to copy some of his drawings in oils and put in appropriate backgrounds (*see* Appendix C).
24. JJA to family, 9 Aug. 1840, *The Auk* 52:159-61 (April 1935).
25. *Journal 1840-1843*, p.19 (Houghton MCZ 118, v.1, 15 Sept. 1840).
26. Ibid., p.33 (Houghton MCZ 118, v.1, 16 Nov. 1840).
27. Ibid., p.56-58 (Houghton MCZ 118, v.1, 12 Dec. 1840). Davis did, however, subscribe to the Octavo edition.
28. *The Auk* 25:168-69 (April 1906).
29. *Letters*, v.2, p.268-69 (APS Phila. BAu 25, 4 May 1840).
30. *The Auk* 52:161-65 (April 1935).
31. Broadside in possession of the Lilly Library, Univ. of Indiana.
32. *Journal 1840-1843*, p.82 (Houghton MCZ 118, v.2, p.256).
33. John James Audubon and Rev. John Bachman, *The Vivparous Quadrupeds of North America*. 2v. of 150 lithographic colored plates; imp. folio (New York: John J. Audubon, 1845-46).
34. *Journal 1840-1843*, p.105 (Houghton MCZ 118, v.1, 16 Sept. 1842).
35. Ibid., p.106.
36. Ibid., p.117 (Houghton MCZ 118, v.1, 21 Sept. 1842).
37. Ibid., p.121 (Houghton MCZ 118, v.1, 23 Sept. 1842).
38. Ibid., p.125 (Houghton MCZ 118, v.1, 26 Sept. 1842).
39. Ibid., p.127 (Houghton MCZ 118, v.1, 27 Sept. 1842).

Notes

40. Ibid., p.137-38 (Houghton MCZ 118, v.1, 3 Oct. 1842).
41. Ibid., p.139.
42. Houghton MCZ 118, v.2, p.290.
43. N. E. Dionne, "Historique de la Bibliothèque du Parliament à Quebec 1792–1892," *Transactions, Royal Society of Canada*, 1902, Section 1, p.8.
44. *Journal 1840–1843*, p.147 (Houghton MCZ 118, v.1, 10 Oct. 1842).
45. Proceedings, Perthshire Society of Natural Science 1893-1898, v.2. This information from the letter of 4 July 1967 to the author from A. J. Tait, City Librarian, Sandeman Library, Perth, Scotland.
46. JJA to family, 16 July 1844. Original letter in possession of the Historical Society of Schenectady, N.Y.
47. Isaac Newton Phelps Stokes, *Iconography of Manhattan Island 1498–1909* (6v., New York: R. H. Dodd, 1915–28), v.5, p.1826 (26 Feb. 1850).
48. Houghton bMS Am 1482 #309.
49. Francis L. Hawks, D.D. LL.D., comp., *Narrative of the Expedition of the American Squadron to the China Seas and Japan, Performed in the Years 1852, 1853, and 1854 under the Command of Commodore M. C. Perry, United States Navy . . .* (3v.; Washington, D.C.: A. O. P. Nicholson, Printer, 1856), v.1, p.414 (footnote).
50. Houghton bMS Am 1482 #311.
51. See provenance of the folio of the Library of Parliament, Ottawa, Canada, in chap. 26.
52. Writers Program, Kentucky, *Henderson: Home of Audubon* (American series; Northport, N.Y.: Bacon, Perry & Daggett, 1941), p.84.
53. *Herrick*, v.2, p.300.
54. *The Birds of America;* from Original Drawings by John James Audubon, Fellow of the Royal Societies of London & Edinburgh, &c., &c., Reissued by J. W. Audubon. IV. of 105 double elephant folio plates, in chromolithography, by J. Bien, 180 Broadway, representing 150 of the original copper plates, Roe Lockwood & Son, Publishers, New York, 1859–60.
55. *Herrick*, v.2, p.296.
56. Lucy Audubon to Professor Henry, 18 Oct. 1864, from Washington Heights, N.Y.; original in the Archives of the Smithsonian Institution.

Chapter 16

1. John Bachman to Edward Harris, 24 Dec. 1845, in *Herrick*, v.2, p.269.
2. C. L. Bachman, *John Bachman* (Charleston, S.C.: Walker, Evans & Cogswell, 1880), p.205–6.
3. Audubon was actually 61 years old at this time.
4. Thomas M. Brewer, "Reminiscences of John James Audubon," *Harper's New Monthly Magazine* 61, no.365:675 (Oct. 1880).
5. Original letter in the possession of John Page-Phillips, London, Eng.
6. Brewer, "Reminiscences," cited in note 4.
7. *National Intelligencer* (Washington, D.C.) 52, no.7:3 (1 Feb. 1851).
8. *Boston Daily Advertiser*, Monday morning, 3 Feb. 1851.
9. *Boston Daily Atlas*, Monday morning, 3 Feb. 1851.
10. *Diary of Philip Hone 1828–1851*, ed. by Allan Nevins (2v.; New York: Dodd, 1927), v.2, p.911.
11. *Gallery of Illustrious Americans*, ed. by C. Edward Lester (New York: M. B. Brady, C. E. Lester, and F. D'Avignon, 1850).
12. *Boston Evening Transcript*, Friday, 31 Jan. 1851.
13. *Illustrated London News*, Saturday, 15 Feb. 1851.
14. Among the scientific and honorary societies of which Audubon was a member:
    Wernerian Society of Edinburgh
    Linnaean Society of London
    Royal Society of Edinburgh
    Royal Society of London
    American Philosophical Society
    Academy of Natural Sciences of Philadelphia
    Lyceum of Natural History of New York
    Societé d'Histoire Naturelle de Paris
    American Academy of Arts and Science.
15. *Proceedings of the Academy of Natural Sciences of Philadelphia*, v.5, 1850–1851. Printed for the Academy by Merihew & Thompson, 1852.
16. Lloyd Goodrich, *American Watercolor and Winslow Homer—An Exhibition Monograph*, published by the Walker Art Center, Minneapolis, in collaboration with the Detroit Institute of Arts and the Brooklyn Museum. The exhibition was held in Minneapolis (27 Feb.–23 Mar. 1945), Detroit (3 Apr.–1 May, 1945), and Brooklyn (15 May–12 June 1945).

For other discussions of Audubon, the artist, the following may be consulted:
- a. Elliott Coues, *Key to North American Birds* (2d ed.; London: Macmillan, 1884; Boston: Estes and Lauriat, 1884).
- b. Helen McColgin, "The Audubon Prints," *Antiques* 8, no.6:361-63 (6 Nov. 1925).
- c. Herman J. Wechsler, "Audubon's 'Birds of America,'" *Parnassus* 4, no.1:18-19 (Jan. 1932).
- d. Charles D. Childs, "Audubon's 'Birds of America,'" *Antiques* 26:226-28 (Dec. 1934).
- e. Donald Culross Peattie, *A Gathering of Birds* (New York: Dodd, 1939), p.341-47.
- f. Donald A. Shelley, "Audubon's Technique as Shown in His Drawing of Birds," *Antiques* 49:354-57 (Jan. 1946).
- g. ——— "John James Audubon, Artist," *Magazine of Art* 39, no.5:171-75 (May 1946).
- h. "A Review of American Bird Prints," by an American Correspondent, *Connoisseur* 121:47-52 (Mar. 1948).
- i. Robert Henry Welker, *Birds and Men* (Cambridge, Mass.: Belknap Pr. of Harvard Univ. Pr., 1955), p.71-90.
- j. Don Richard Eckelberry, "Bird in Art and Illustration," in *The Living Bird* (2d annual, Cornell Laboratory of Ornithology, 1963).
- k. R. L. Scheffel, *Bird Art in Science* (Educ. Leaflet no.16, Albany: Univ. of the State of New York, State Education Dept., New York State Museum and Science Service, 1964), p.16-20.
- l. Wilfred Blunt, "The Original Watercolor Paintings by John James Audubon for the 'Birds of America,'" *Burlington Magazine* 109:373 (June 1967).
- m. D. Kirkpatrick, "National Wildlife Visits Arthur Singer," *National Wildlife* 8:58-63 (Dec. 1969).

17. Robert Cushman Murphy, "John James Audubon (1785-1851): An Evaluation of the Man and His Work," reprinted from *The New-York Historical Society Quarterly* (Oct. 1958), p.340-43.
18. *Graphis* 17:68-73 (Jan. 1961).
19. Sacheverell Sitwell, Handasyde Buchanan, and James Fisher, *Fine Bird Books* (London and New York: Collins and Van Nostrand, 1953). Also see Sacheverell Sitwell, *Audubon's American Birds* (Batsford Colour Books; London: Batsford, 1949).
20. Mary F. Boynton, *Louis Agassiz Fuertes* (New York: Oxford Univ. Pr., 1956).
21. Ibid.
22. Audubon-Bonaparte correspondence, Bibliothèque du Muséum Nationale d'Histoire Naturelle, Paris (APS Phila., Film 542).
23. *OB*, v.1, p.xvii-xix.
24. Robert Cushman Murphy, "John James Audubon (1785-1851): An Evaluation of the Man and His Work."

PART II

Chapter 17

1. *Journals*, v.1, p.123.
2. Ibid., v.1, p.124.
3. Ibid., v.1, p.127.
4. Catalogue of the Exhibition, item #102.
5. *Journals*, v.1, p.199.
6. Ibid., v.1, p.289.
7. *Letters*, v.1, p.246 (APS Phila. BAu 25, 9 Sept. 1833).
8. *OB*, v.1 (Edinburgh: Adam Black, 1831), back matter, p.12-15. The copy of the American edition owned by the present writer (Waldemar H. Fries), published in Philadelphia in the same year, does not contain such a list of subscribers.
9. Ibid., v.2, (Edinburgh, 1834), p.581-82.
10. Ibid., v.3 (Edinburgh, 1835), p.633.
11. Ibid., v.4 (Edinburgh, 1838), p.613.
12. Ibid., v.5 (Edinburgh, 1839 [a typographical error gives the publication date as MDCCCXXXXIX]), p.647-51.
13. Ibid., v.5, p.xxiv.
14. *Journals*, v.1, p.71.

Notes

Chapter 19

1. *Letters*, v.1, p.148 (APS Phila. BAu 25, 7 Nov. 1831).
2. Houghton MCZ 118, v.2, p.14.
3. *Letters*, v.2, p.270 (APS Phila. BAu 25, 7 May 1840).
4. *National Cyclopaedia of American Biography* (New York: James T. White and Co., 1898), v.1.
5. Bayard Tuckerman, ed., *The Diary of Philip Hone, 1828-1851* (2v.; New York: Dodd, 1889), v.2, p.259.
6. This catalog is in the Widener Library, Harvard University.
7. *Letters*, v.2, p.128 (APS Phila. BAu 25).
8. *DAB*, v.18, p.238-39.
9. *Letters*, v.2, p.128 (APS Phila. BAu 25).
10. Houghton MCZ 118, v.2, p.15.
11. James L. Crouthamel, *James Watson Webb: A Biography* (Middletown, Conn.: Wesleyan Univ. Pr., 1969), p.86-87.
12. *Letters*, v.1, p.203 (APS Phila. BAu 25).
13. Herrick, v.2, p.185; see also *The Auk* 20:382 (Oct. 1903).
14. A typescript of the original letter was made by Howard Corning in the preparation of his two-volume work of JJA's letters, published by the Club of Odd Volumes in 1930. This is letter no.34 in a copy of the typescript now at Princeton University.
15. *The Auk* 22:170 (April 1905).
16. J. Thomas Scharf, *Chronicles of Baltimore* (Baltimore: Turnbull Brothers, 1874), p.467 ff.
17. *Letters*, v.2, p.13 (Houghton bMS Am 1482 #90).
18. Ibid., v.2, p.128.
19. Ibid., v.2, p.246-50. In this letter of 7 Mar. 1840 Audubon set down in detail his arrangements with Gideon B. Smith.
20. Ibid., v.2, p.11.
21. JJA to William Gaston. This letter is now in the possession of John Henry Dix, Meggett, S.C.
22. *Letters*, v.1, p.187.
23. *Letters*, v.1, p.152.
24. Houghton MCZ 118, v.2, p.61.
25. *Trans. Amer. Medical Assn.* 30:823 (1879).
26. *Letters*, v.2, p.142.
27. *A Short History of the Winyah Indigo Society of Georgetown, South Carolina, 1755-1958* (Georgetown, S.C.: The Society, 1958).
28. Alberta Morel Lachicotte, *Georgetown Rice Plantations* (Columbia, S.C.: State Printing Co., 1955).
29. See in Zadock Thompson, *History of Vermont; Natural, Civil, and Statistical* (Burlington, Vt.: Chauncey Goodrich, 1853). The account of the death of Oakes is to be found on p.36 of the Appendix. See also Thompson's *Natural History of Vermont* (Tokyo, Japan, and Rutland, Vt.: Charles E. Tuttle, 1972), p.256, a paperback reissue of this work, originally published in 1853.
30. *Letters*, v.2, p.127-28 (APS Phila., 7 Sept. 1836).
31. *Letters*, v.2, p.161 (Houghton bMS 1482 #114, 2 July 1837).
32. *Journals*, v.1, p.338.
33. Ibid., v.1, p.329.
34. Ibid., v.1, p.338.
35. Ibid., v.1, p.314.
36. Letter of 28 Apr. 1958 to Joseph Verner Reed from Abel Doysié, 32 Rue Saint-Paul, Paris, France.
37. *Journals*, v.1, p.289, 7 Mar. 1828.
38. Ibid., v.1, p.244.
39. Letters to the author from Major Osbert M. Greg, 15 Sept. 1971, and Sylvia M. England, 24 July 1971.
40. *Letters*, v.1, p.119-20 (Houghton bMS 1482 #28).
41. Ibid., v.2, p.84 (Houghton bMS 1482 #77).

Chapter 20

1. An interesting account of the Audubon-Webster relationship is to be found in the *Dartmouth College Library Bulletin* 10, no.1:2-9 (Nov. 1969), in which Richard W. Morin, former librarian of Dartmouth College, has retold in detail the association of the two men in their occasional and, at times, uneasy encounters.
2. *Book-Auction Records*, v.1, part 1.
3. Letter of 28 July 1964 to the author from Charles W. Traylen, 49-50, Quarry St., Guilford, Eng.

NOTES

4. C. L. Bachman, *John Bachman . . .* (Charleston, S.C.: Walker, Evans & Cogswell Co., 1888), p.101.
5. *Letters*, v.1, p.119–22 (JJA to Havell, Houghton bMS 1482 #28, 31 Oct. 1830).
6. *Journals*, v.1, p.338 and 258.
7. *Letters*, v.1, p.137 (JJA to Havell, Houghton bMS 1482 #42, 20 Sept. 1831).
8. Ibid.
9. Ibid., v.1, p.151 (APS Phila. BAu 25; Charleston, S.C., 13 Nov. 1831), JJA to Mrs. Audubon.
10. Ibid., v.2, p.16 (Houghton bMS Am 1482 #57, 5 April 1834).
11. Letter of 16 July 1958 to the author from Mrs. Walter Oakman (a granddaughter of Robert J. Hubbard).
12. Letter of 16 June 1958 to the author from Virginia A. Conklin, Librarian, Cazenovia Public Library.
13. Letter of 17 Sept. 1973 to the author from I. H. J. Lyster, Assistant Curator of Ornithology, Royal Scottish Museum. The author is indebted to Mrs. J. Bunting and W. M. E. Cooke, of the Public Archives of Canada, for bringing this collection to his attention.
14. Letter to the author of 25 July 1970 from Mrs. Joseph Rutledge Young of Charleston, S.C.

Chapter 21

1. Card of 7 Aug. 1958 to the author from Mrs. Thomas Barrett.
2. Letter of 15 Dec. 1958 to the author from Miss Jean D. Cochran, Director, Augusta (Ga.) Library.
3. Letter of 22 May 1965 to author from Mrs. G. Dawson Coleman, Bryn Mawr, Pa.
4. *OB*, v.2, p.581.
5. Ledger "B," Audubon Museum, Henderson, Ky.
6. Ibid.
7. Letters of 16 Sept. 1959 and 23 Feb. 1960 to the author from J. Donnell Tilghman.
8. *Catalogue of the Edward E. Ayre Ornithological Library*, Part 1, by John Todd Zimmer and Wilfred H. Osgood (Field Museum of Natural History, Publication 239, Zoological Series, v.16; Chicago: The Museum, 1926), p.v–vi.
9. Letter of 10 Sept. 1968 to the author from Bertha W. Gibbs, Reference Librarian, Field Museum.
10. *Ayre Catalogue*, note 1, p.18–19.
11. Letter of 10 Jan. 1958 to the author from Mrs. Meta P. Howell, Librarian, Chicago Natural History (Field) Museum.
12. From the March 1956 issue of "Portfolio," issued from time to time by the Old Print Shop, New York.
13. Letter of 8 July 1959 to the author from Miss Margaret R. McKinlay, the buyer for Macy's Art Dept. at the time the folios were purchased.
14. Information provided by David Randall, Librarian, Lilly Library, Indiana University.
15. *OB*, v.5, p.647.
16. Ibid., v.5, p.648.
17. Edith Benham Helm, *The Captains and the Kings* (New York: Putnam's, 1954), p.7.
18. Letter of 17 Oct. 1960 to the author from Mrs. J. M. Helm (Edith B. Helm). Mrs. Helm for 25 years was the White House Social Secretary.
19. The purchase of the two sets of the folio is recorded in *The Journal of John James Audubon 1840–1843*, the original of which is in the Houghton Library at Harvard University (MCZ 118, v.1–5). The information about the burning of the Parliament building in Montreal was sent to the author on 3 Sept. 1957 by William Kaye Lamb, National Library, Ottawa, Can. Reference to the fire is to be found in N. E. Dionne, "Historique de la Bibliothèque du Parliament à Quebec, 1792–1892," *Transactions, Royal Society of Canada*, 1902, sec. 1, p.8.
20. *See* John B. Irving, M.D., *A Day on the Cooper River*, enlarged and ed. by Louise Chever Stoney (2d ed., Charleston, S.C.: R. L. Bryon Co., 1932), p.179.

Chapter 22

1. Mary Cobb, "Early Days in the Library," *Bulletin of the Boston Society of Natural History* no.55:33–34 (Apr. 1930).
2. *Life*, p.389–90.
3. Cobb, "Early Days in the Library."
4. *OB*, v.5, p.647–51 (also in *Herrick*, v.2, p.380–85).
5. Audubon Museum, Henderson, Ky.

Notes

6. *Herrick*, v.1, p.394.
7. Alice Ford, *John James Audubon* (Norman, Okla.: University of Oklahoma Pr., 1964), p.347.
8. JJA to Benjamin Phillips, FRS, 17 Wimpole St., London; dated Sheffield, 21 July 1839 (copy in possession of author).
9. See book auction records of 1890 in chap.24.
10. *National Cyclopaedia of Biography*, v.30, p.538-39.
11. Houghton bMS Am 1482 #309.
12. Ibid., #311.
13. Francis L. Hawks, comp., *Narrative of the Expedition of the American Squadron . . . under the Command of Commodore M. C. Perry, United States Navy* (3.v.; Washington, D.C.: A. O. P. Nicholson, Printer, 1856), v.1, p.414 (footnote).
14. Letter of 27 Mar. 1960 to the author from Dr. Nagahisa Kuroda, Yamashina Museum of Birds, Tokyo, Japan.
15. Letter of 28 May 1960 to the author from Miss Kuniko Aoki, Librarian, Library Imperial Household, Tokyo, Japan.
16. Ibid.
17. Ibid.
18. Letter of 21 Mar. 1963 to the author.
19. Ibid.
20. *OB*, v.5, p.34.
21. Letter of 19 Nov. 1965 to the author from Howell J. Heaney, Bibliographer, The Free Library of Philadelphia.
22. Letters of 4, 8, and 19 Sept. 1958 to the author from Nathaniel C. Nash, Jr.
23. Letter of 23 Nov. 1922 to Frank M. Chapman, Curator of Birds, Amer. Museum of Natural History, New York, from Ruthven Deane, Chicago, Ill.
24. Letter of 27 Mar. 1971 to the author from Prof. Joseph Ewan, Tulane Univ.
25. Letters of 19 and 26 Apr. 1971 to the author from James Bond, Curator of Birds, Academy of Natural Sciences, Philadelphia.
26. Letter of 23 Apr. 1971 to the author from Howell J. Heaney, Rare Book Librarian, The Free Library of Philadelphia.

Chapter 24

1. *Letters*, v.1, p.185 (APS Phila. BAu 25; Charleston 13 Mar. 1832).
2. Ibid.
3. *Letters*, v.1, p.202-7 (APS Phila. BAu 25, New York, 1 Apr. 1832).
4. From one of the pages torn from Audubon's Day Book, now in the Audubon Museum at Henderson, Ky.
5. Catalog, Widener Library at Harvard University, Items 2115, 2564.
6. *Letters*, v.2, p.4 (APS Phila. BAu 25, 14 Jan. 1834, from Charleston).
7. Luther S. Livingston, ed., *Auction Prices of Books* (4v.; New York: Dodd, 1905).
8. Frank Karslake, ed., *Book-Auction Records*.
9. *Oölogist* 10, no.9 (Sept. 1893).
10. Goodspeed's catalogs nos.34 (May 1904) and 43 (June 1906).
11. The Franklin Bookshop, Philadelphia, Pa., catalog no.39, "Auduboniana & Other Nature Books," comp. by Samuel Rhoades, the proprietor. (The author is indebted to Prof. Joseph Ewan of Tulane University for a Xerox copy of the catalog.)
12. Goodspeed's Catalog of series 4, 1 Oct. 1929 (2d ed.) no.3.
13. Letter to the author of 20 Mar. 1957 from David A. Randall.
14. See "Portfolio" 16, no.9 (May 1957), issued by the Old Print Shop.
15. Letter to the author of 1 Dec. 1959 from Edward J. Snyder, Milwaukee.
16. Letter to the author of 2 Aug. 1959 from Margaret R. McKinlay.
17. Ibid., 28 July 1959.
18. Ibid., 28 Aug. 1959.
19. Ibid.
20. Column A, *from* Old Print Shop, "Portfolio" 6, no.5 (Jan. 1947).
21. Column B, *from* the 1968 catalog of a print dealer in Baton Rouge, La.
22. See "Portfolio" 31, no.1 (1971), issued by the Old Print Shop.

NOTES

PART III

Chapter 25

1. *The Auk* 23:298–312 (July 1906).
2. Ibid., p.300.
3. *Herrick*, v.2, p.197–98.
4. E. F. Hanaburgh, *Audubon's "Birds of America": A Check List of First Issue of the Plates of the First Folio Edition 1828–1838* (Buchanan, N.Y.: Published by the Author, 1941).
5. *Herrick*, v.2, p.197.
6. Houghton bMS Am 1482 #225.
7. *Letters*, v.1, p.202–7.
8. Ibid., v.2, p.6.
9. Ibid., v.2, p.93 (Houghton bMS Am 1482 #81).
10. Ibid., v.1, p.111–113 (Houghton bMS Am 1482 #18).
11. The original is in the collection of Princeton University Library.
12. JJA to Havell, 20 April 1833, *Letters*, v.1, p.212 (Houghton bMS Am 1482 #54).

Chapter 26

1. *Herrick*, v.1, p.424.
2. Dr. Harlan to Swainson, Linnaean Society, London, Eng.
3. *Letters*, v.1, p.184–85 (APS Phila. BAu 25).
4. Letter to JJA from Richard Harlan, dated Philadelphia, 19 Nov. 1828. Original at the New-York Historical Society. See also Bonaparte-Cooper correspondence 1825–57, letter to Cooper of 24 Sept. 1827 from Charles Lucien Bonaparte (APS Phila.).
5. *Letters*, v.1, p.136 (Houghton bMS Am 1482 #42).
6. Minute Book of the Academy of Natural Sciences (ANS Minute Book) of Philadelphia, v.5 (Oct. 1827–26 Mar. 1833).
7. *Letters*, v.1, p.148. Isaac Lea was a member of the firm of Carey & Lea, Philadelphia, publishers of Charles L. Bonaparte's *American Ornithology*, which was issued in 4 volumes from 1825 to 1833. It was thought that the prejudice Lea manifested toward Audubon was traceable to his desire to maintain sales for Bonaparte's work.
8. ANS Minute Book, v.6 (2 Apr. 1833–26 Mar. 1839).
9. See memorandum in Audubon's unpublished journals, Houghton MCZ 118, v.3, p.80.
10. Princeton Univ. Library.
11. ANS Minute Book, v.6.
12. Dr. Samuel G. Morton correspondence (APS Phila.).
13. Ibid.
14. Houghton pfMS Am 21 #76.
15. *American Museum Journal* 4, no.2 (Apr. 1904).
16. *Natural History* 26, no.2 (Mar./Apr. 1926).
17. Letter to JJA from Richard Harlan, dated Philadelphia, 19 Nov. 1828. The original is in the New-York Historical Society. See also the William Cooper correspondence (1825–27): letter of 24 Sept. 1827 to Cooper from Charles Lucien Bonaparte (APS Phila.).
18. Now at the Eleutherian Mills Historical Library, Greenville, Wilmington, Dela.
19. Letter of V. G. Audubon to John Vaughan, 30 June 1831 (APS Phila.).
20. Correspondence; Amherst College Library.
21. *Letters*, v.1, p.125–26 (Houghton bMS Am 1482 #31).
22. Ibid., v.1, p.132–33 (Houghton bMS Am 1482 #38).
23. Letter to the author of 25 Sept. 1962 from John Preston, Librarian, University Club of New York.
24. Letter of 13 Jan. 1965 to the author from Willman Spawn, American Philosophical Society.
25. Letter of 25 Aug. 1958 to the author from Dr. Robert Cushman Murphy stating that v.1 of the *Ornithological Biography* accompanying folio has signature of Thomas Walker, Killingbeck (Audubon spells name Killinbeck).
26. *Journals*, v.1, p.244–46.
27. Ibid., v.1, p.246.
28. Ibid., v.1, p.247.
29. *OB*, v.2, p.vii, viii.
30. Letter of 12 July 1957 to the author from Dr. Robert Cushman Murphy.
31. Item 101, "The Nineteenth Catalogue: English books, Manuscripts, Incunabula,

Notes

Voyages, Americana, Geography, Bindings, Natural History" (New York: H. P. Krause, 1959). In this catalog, the Audubon folio is offered for $45,000.

32. Letter of 13 Apr. 1957 to the author from Mrs. K. Stryker-Rodda, Assistant to the Librarian, The Long Island Historical Society.
33. Letter of 11 June 1968 to the author from John H. Lindenbusch, Executive Director, The Long Island Historical Society.
34. Letter of 19 April 1969 to the author from John H. Lindenbusch.
35. In the 13 Apr. 1957 letter from Mrs. Stryker-Rodda (*see* note 32).
36. *OB*, v.5, p.380–82.
37. *Letters*, v.2, p.260 (APS Phila. BAu 25).
38. Edward Biddle and Mantle Fielding, *The Life and Works of Thomas Sully (1783–1872)* (Philadelphia [Lancaster, Pa.]: Wickersham Press, 1921). The author is indebted to Miss Sally M. Moffitt, Assistant in Reference, Alderman Library, Univ. of Virginia, for bringing to his attention the Sully material, a privately printed, limited edition.
39. Obituary in the *Public Ledger* (Philadelphia) of 16 Feb. 1928.
40. *Herrick*, v.2, p.68–69.
41. Trustee's Report, Boston Athenaeum.
42. Letter of 20 Jan. 1831 from Havell to JJA. Original in the N.Y. Public Library, Ford Collection.
43. *Herrick*, v.1, p.449.
44. John Perkins Cushing, "Diary, 1834–56"; manuscript at the Boston Athenaeum.
45. Thomas Gold Appleton (1812–84) was the son of Nathan Appleton (1770–1861), the younger brother of Samuel Appleton (1766–1853), who had been an original subscriber to the *Birds of America*. The subscription is listed in a letter written on 1 April 1832, from New York, to which the Naturalist had returned after spending the winter and spring of that year in Boston and where many other subscriptions had been obtained.
46. Letter shown to the author on 6 Jan. 1967 by George Goodspeed of Boston.
47. *National Cyclopaedia of American Biography*, v.10, p.302.
48. All information, genealogical and other, concerning the Baldwin family was supplied the author on 18 Nov. 1958, 12 Dec. 1958, and 19 Feb. 1959 by Mrs. Lila W. Baldwin (Mrs. James R. Baldwin). Her husband's father was Loammi F. Baldwin, the benefactor under the will of Dame Catherine Rumford Griffith.
49. Information concerning the Park family was received by the author from Julian Park of Buffalo, 19 Sept. 1961.
50. William Carey Jones, Jr., *The Illustrated History of the University of Southern California* (San Francisco: Frank H. Dukesmith, 1895), p.218 ff.
51. *The Cardinal* 1, no.5:22–23 (Jan. 1925).
52. *OB*, v.5, p.651.
53. Burke's *Peerage* (1956 ed.), p.105-53.
54. *DAB*, v.6, p.161–63.
55. *Letters*, v.1, p.189–92.
56. *Letters*, v.1, p.148 (APS Phila.).
57. Houghton MCZ 118, v.3 (Audubon's unpublished journals 1839–55).
58. Ibid.
59. The author is indebted to Eugene J. Bockman, Principal Librarian of the Municipal Reference Library, City of New York, who on 16 Dec. 1959 sent him copies of the Aldermanic proceedings of Jan.–May 1850 and the Sturtevant resolution.
60. Proceedings of the Boards of Aldermen and Assistant Aldermen Approved by the Mayor, v.16. New York, 1849. The reference is to M. Alexander Vattermore, a Frenchman well known at the time for his efforts of some twenty years to establish

> ... an international exchange of all that is valuable in science, literature, natural history and the fine arts—and the establishment in every nation and state of an *institution* (under the fostering care of its government), to receive these exchanges, forming not only a *museum* illustrative as well of the powers of nature, as of the state of perfection to which the productions of the human mind and hand have arrived, or are tending to in every corner of the globe, but a kind of *patent office*, where the creations of the industry, the achievement of the intellect, of the inventive faculties, and of governments of each country, may at once and always be assigned to their true origin, and always verified without doubt or difficulty.

The foregoing is from an address Vattermore gave before the two houses of the New York state legislature, 20 Oct. 1847. In 1848 Vattermore had obtained for New York City "a splendid case of valuable medals commemorative of interesting events during the administration of" Pope Pius IX, which in January 1849 led to the establishment of the City Hall Library in City Hall. See Austin Baxter Keep, "The Library in Colonial New York," in *History of the New York Society Library* (New York: De Vinne Press [Printed for the Trustees], 1908), footnote, p.55.

NOTES

61. Letter of 6 Jan. 1970 to the author from Eugene J. Bockman, Principal Librarian, Municipal Reference Library, New York, N.Y.
62. Letter of 27 Feb. 1971 to the author from Miss Carolyn E. Jakeman, Houghton Library, Harvard Univ.
63. *The Diary of George Templeton Strong*, ed. by Allan Nevins and Milton Halsey Thomas (4v.; New York: Macmillan, 1952). See v.1 (*Young Man in New York, 1835–1849*), p.174 (10 Jan. 1842).
64. Ibid., p.27.
65. Letter of JJA to A. H. Everett. This was listed as item 41 in the American Art Assn. sale of the W. F. Gable collection, which took place on 13–14 Feb. 1924 (it has not been possible to ascertain the purchaser of this letter and its present location is not known).
66. *Letters*, v.1, p.200.
67. Journal of the Senate and House, v.54, Jan.–Apr. 1833.
68. *Columbia Centennial* (Boston), Sat., 23 Mar. 1833.
69. Letter of 26 Dec. 1957 to the author from Marguerite Pettet, formerly secretary to William R. Cole.
70. *Journal 1840–1843*, p.82.
71. *Book-Auction Records*, v.9 (1911–1912), p.327.
72. Item 267, the library of Louisa, Lady Ashburton (deceased), removed from Melchet Court, Monday, 15 Apr. 1912.
73. Shattuck Papers, Massachusetts Historical Society, Boston, Mass.
74. Letter of 3 Oct. 1836 to I. P. Davis, Boston; the original is now in the collection of the Library, State of Connecticut, Hartford, Conn.
75. Claude Moore Fuess, *Daniel Webster* (2v.; Boston: Little, 1930), v.2, p.384.
76. Houghton MCZ 118, v.2, p.14.
77. *Journal 1840–1843*, p.7–8. Journal entry made while obtaining subscriptions to his *Birds of America*. An interesting historical account of the Audubon-Webster relationship is to be found in the Dartmouth College *Library Bulletin* for November 1969 (10, no.1:2–9). Here Richard W. Morin, former librarian of Dartmouth College, has retold in detail the association of the two men in their occasional and at times uneasy encounters.
78. Ibid., p.40–41.
79. Corning copies of JJA letters in the Houghton Library, Harvard University (fm Am 1265): Letter #27, 5 July 1842; #28, 17 July 1842; #29, 19 July 1842; #31, 23 July 1842 and 25 July 1842; #71, 12 May 1844.
80. *The Auk* 52:166 (Apr. 1935); original letter is now in the possession of A. E. Lownes, Providence, R.I.
81. In the Boston Public Library is a copy of the catalog for the sale which was held by Leonard, Auctioneers of Boston, 8 June 1875; item #68.
82. *Bulletin of the Haverhill Public Library* 7, no.3 (Mar. 1921).
83. Letter of 14 Feb. 1966 to the author from Charles M. Fleischner, Librarian, Haverhill Public Library.
84. Letters to the author, dated 17 June 1970 from Bruce St. John, Director, The Wilmington Society of the Fine Arts, and 30 June 1970 from Elizabeth Handy, Curatorial Assistant, Delaware Art Museum, Wilmington, Del.
85. Letter of 18 Aug. 1959 to the author from Mabel Zahn (of Charles Sessler, Inc.), Philadelphia, Pa.
86. *Book-Auction Records* 1950–51, v.48, p.28. The rate of exchange for the British pound at the time was $2.79.
87. *Journals*, v.1, p.263.
88. Walford's *Men of Mark 'Twixt Tyne & Tweed* (Newcastle, 1895), p.574. (Courtesy of Lionel Robinson, London, Eng., 4 Sept. 1959.)
89. *OB*, v.5, p.649–51 (European subscribers); see "Names of Subscribers" in v.1, with "Prospectus" at back of volume, p.13.
90. Ibid., v.5, p.649.
91. *Journals*, v.1, p.246.
92. Letter of 27 Mar. 1968 to the author from Christopher Gilbert, Temple Newsam House, Leeds, Eng.
93. *Letters*, v.1, p.159 (Letter of 5 Dec. 1831 to Mrs. Audubon, APS Phila. BAu 25).
94. Ibid., v.2, p.164 (Houghton bMS Am 1482 #114).
95. Graduate of Columbia College of Physicians and Surgeons, 1895 (see *Journal of the American Medical Assn.* 158:134 (14 May 1955), (with appreciation to Miss Maria Patrucco, Asst. Librarian, Rhode Island Medical Society Library).
96. Sale no.1631, held 6–7 Dec. 1955 by Parke-Bernet Galleries, Inc., New York, N.Y.
97. Letter of 21 July 1958 to author from Frank Walters, Hollis, N.H.
98. Letter in the possession of H. J. Lutcher Stark Foundation, Orange, Texas.
99. Ibid.
100. Letter in possession of Princeton University Library, Princeton, N.J.

Notes

101. *American Literary Gazette and Publishers' Circular* 15:7 (2 May 1870).
102. *Book-Auction Records 1921–22*, v.19, p.406.
103. Letter of 19 Dec. 1969 to the author from Henry Sotheran Ltd.
104. *The Complete Peerage* 2:240 (London: St. Catherine Press, 1912); Chambers's *Biographical Dictionary* (new ed.; New York: St. Martin's Pr., 1968), p.195–96.
105. Houghton, bMS Am 1482 #244.
106. Sotheby & Co., London: Audubon's *Birds of America*, sale, Monday, 24 Nov. 1969.
107. *Letters*, v.2, p.219.
108. Letter of 3 Mar. 1840 from George Parkman to JJA. Now in the Ford Collection of the New York Public Library.
109. *Letters*, v.1, p.203.
110. Letters of 27 Oct. 1960, 11 Nov. 1960, and 7 Mar. 1961 to the author from Mrs. Henry A. Murray.
111. Letter of 2 Apr. 1968 to the author from Richard R. Pleasants, Business Mgr., The Groton School.
112. *Letters*, v.1, p.185 (APS Phila. BAu 25); *OB*, v.2, p.549–51.
113. *Letters*, v.1, p.192 (APS Phila. BAu 25, 29 Mar. 1832 to his wife Lucy).
114. Letters of 8 June 1960 and 24 June 1960 to the author from Mrs. Oscar Torian, Archivist, Sewanee University. Her grandfather was the original subscriber.
115. Letter of 29 Sept. 1960 to the author from Mrs. Frank L. Polk (Elizabeth Potter Polk).
116. Anthony Woodward, "A Brief Record of the Elephant Folio . . . " at the Buffalo & Erie County Public Library, Buffalo, N.Y.
117. Letter of Ralph Bixby to the author, October 1959.
118. Letter of 28 Dec. 1959 to the author from Caroline Dunn, Librarian of the William Henry Smith Memorial Library, Indiana Historical Society, Indianapolis.
119. For details of the life of William Wesley Borden and the Borden Institute, *see*: "And Thereby Hangs a Tale: Or How a Hoosier Became a Collector," by Nellie M. Coats of the Catalogue Division in the Indiana State Library and Librarian of the Indiana Academy of Science. Published by the Indiana University Library for the *Bookman of Indiana* and for Friends of the University. A digest of this article was published in the *Indiana Quarterly for Bookmen* 5, nos. 2 & 3 (July 1949).
120. *See* Note 118.
121. Letter of 22 Jan. 1960 to the author from O. S. Tomlinson F.L.A., City Librarian, York, England.
122. *The Yorkshire Gazette* of 17 Oct. 1889 (provided by Mr. Tomlinson).
123. Ibid., Annual Meeting, Jan. 1896.
124. Letter of 17 July 1958 to the author from Mabel Zahn, Charles Sessler, Inc.
125. Letter of 11 July 1958 to the author from F. B. Adams, Jr., Director, The Pierpont Morgan Library, New York.
126. Letter of 20 Mar. 1957 to the author from David A. Randall, Rare Book Librarian, The Lilly Library, Indiana University.
127. Letter of 28 Sept. 1964 to the author from Russell F. Barnes, Librarian, James Jerome Hill Reference Library.
128. Letter of 24 Jan. 1958 to the author from Mrs. Michael Gavin (Gertrude Hill).
129. Letter of 14 Mar. 1960 to the author from Yeatman Anderson III, Curator of Books, Public Library of Cincinnati and Hamilton County, Ohio.
130. Ibid.
131. Letter of 27 Jan. 1960 to the author from Ben C. Bowman, Asst. Librarian, the Newberry Library, Chicago, Ill.
132. *See* Appendix I.
133. For the history of the Garrett Library, consult *John Work Garrett and His Library at Evergreen House* (Baltimore: Privately printed, 1944).
134. Audubon had appended a story of the Mangrove to his description of the brown pelican (*OB*, v.2, p.386).
135. *Journals*, v.2, p.522–27.
136. Letter of Howard M. Nixon, Dept. of Printed Books, British Museum, 16 Dec. 1957, to Howell J. Heaney, Free Library of Philadelphia.
137. Maurice P. Boone and Daniel Gammon, "The Audubon Mystery," *The Atlantic Advocate* (Canada) 49, no.7:64–70 (Mar. 1959).
138. Ibid., p.69.
139. Ibid., p.70.
140. Letter of 8 July 1970 to the author from James D. Mack, Director, Lehigh University Libraries.
141. Letter of 12 Apr. 1968 to the author from James D. Mack.
142. Letter of 10 Feb. 1958 to the author from James H. Burghardt, Head, Social Science and Science, The Library Association of Portland (Ore.).
143. Letter of 5 Apr. 1968 to the author from Elizabeth Anne Johnson, Head, Literature and History Dept., The Library Association of Portland.

144. *OB*, v.5, p.647.
145. *Journals*, v.1, p.272.
146. *Life*, p.119.
147. *Journals*, v.1, p.253.
148. Ibid., v.1, p.275.
149. *Life*, p.114.
150. Microfilm of the Adams papers, beginning 3 Mar. 1828, #485.
151. *Memoirs of John Quincy Adams, Comprising Portions of His Diary from 1795–1848*, ed. by Charles Francis Adams (3v.; Philadelphia: J. B. Lippincott, 1876), v.3, p.435.
152. *Life*, p.203.
153. *OB*, v.1, back matter, "Names, of Subscribers," p.25.
154. Original in the possession of Mr. Albert Lownes, Providence, R.I.
155. *Herrick*, v.1, p.436.
156. *Life*, p.203.
157. Goodspeed's Catalogue #101, Boston, Dec. 1913.
158. *Letters*, v.1, p.117.
159. *Herrick*, v.1, p.448–50.
160. Photostat from the Department of Archives, Washington, D.C.
161. *Letters*, v.1, p.121.
162. Letter from JJA, dated Edinburgh, 25 June 1838, to Samuel George Morton, Library, American Philosophical Society, Philadelphia.
163. Ford Collection, New York Public Library.
164. Captain Frederick Marryat, *Diary in America*, ed. with a foreword by Jules Zanger (Bloomington, Ind.: Univ. of Indiana Pr., 1960)
165. *Letters*, v.1, p.262.
166. Ibid., v.2, p.23.
167. Ibid., v.2, p.20.
168. Ibid., v.2, p.19.
169. Ibid., v.1, p.261.
170. Ibid., v.2, p.11.
171. Ford Collection, New York Public Library.
172. *OB*, v.5, p.647.
173. *Life*, p.394.
174. Ibid., p.396.
175. *OB*, v.4, p.613.
176. National Archives, Washington, D.C., Record group 217 M.T. 72175.
177. *The Jacksonians; A Study in Administrative History, 1829–1861* (New York: Macmillan, 1954)

> Meanwhile the departmental libraries, already well established, continued to use their special appropriations or contingency funds to maintain their collections. The State Department library, fostered earlier by Secretary John Quincy Adams, was the most extensive. Annual expenditures from 1830 to 1834 inclusive averaged about $9,000—a figure that may be compared with the annual appropriation to the Library of Congress at that time of $5,000. Treasury spent less than $2,000 in an average year for its library, War a little over $1,000, and Navy and Post Office negligible amounts.

A footnote to the foregoing quotation gives the source of this information as "Senate Doc. 11, 24th Cong., 1st sess., p.16–74 (Dec. 10, 1835)."

178. National Archives. Washington, D.C., Record group 217, M.T. 71466 and M.T. 72172.
179. Library of Congress, *Information Bulletin* 29, no.43:567 (29 Oct. 1970), and supplemental information sent to the author by F. R. Goff, Chief, Rare Books Division, Library of Congress in Jan. 1971. The author is grateful to James D. Mack, Director of University Libraries, Lehigh Univ., and to Russell E. Bidlack, Dean, School of Library Science, Univ. of Michigan, for alerting him to this matter.
180. JJA to Victor Gifford Audubon, dated New York, 6 Oct. 1842 (Corning copy #44, Houghton Library, Harvard Univ.); original in the collection of the Princeton Univ. Library.
181. N. E. Dionne, "Histoire de la Bibliothèque du Parliament à Quebec, 1792–1892," *Transactions, Royal Society of Canada, 1902*, sec.1, p.8. (Letter of 3 Sept. 1957 to the author from William Kaye Lamb, National Librarian of Canada).
182. *Letters*, v.1, p.18 (APS Phila. BAu 25; Edinburgh, 24 Mar. 1827).
183. Ibid., v.2, p.9 (APS Phila. BAu 25).
184. Mary Fluker Bradford, *Audubon* (New Orleans: L. Graham & Son, Ltd., 1897), p.41.
185. The *Times-Picayune*, New Orleans, La., 17 Jan. 1963.
186. *Letters*, v.1, p.119 (Houghton bMS Am 1482 #9).
187. Ibid., v.2, p.15 (APS Phila. BAu 25).
188. Charles Waterton (1782–1865) of Walton Hall, an eccentric Briton who wrote about natural science, was the most pertinacious of Audubon's critics. He wrote 19 polemics in all against the "foreigner" and "stranger," as he called the Naturalist, publishing 14 bitter attacks on Audubon in the period between 1833–34.
189. Quaritch catalog no.842, 1963.
190. Press release issued by the Univ. of Louisiana, 25 Nov. 1964; New Orleans *Times-Picayune*, 25 Nov. 1964.

191. *London Evening Standard*, 21 Mar. 1955.
192. *The Book Collector* 12, no.3:316–32 (Autumn 1963).
193. Letter of 30 Apr. 1957 to the author from Margaret E. Hibbard, Wood Library of Ornithology, Redpath Library, McGill Univ., Montreal.
194. Letter of 24 July 1961 to the author from Miss K. Hanson, for the Secretary of the University Library, McGill Univ., Montreal.
195. Letter of 22 July 1957 to author from Marjorie G. Wynne, Rare Book Room, Yale Univ.
196. *National Cyclopaedia of American Biography*, v.30, p.278–79.
197. Letters of 7 Aug. 1957 and 23 Jan. 1958 to author from Schlitz Brewing Co., Milwaukee, Wis.
198. Letter of 27 Jan. 1958 from Betty L. Engebretson, Athenaeum Librarian, to the author.
199. Letter of 12 Oct. 1967 from Charles J. Sawyer to the author.
200. *Letters*, v.1, p.203 (APS Phila. BAu 25, 1 Apr. 1833).
201. OB, v.5, p.648.
202. *Letters*, v.1, p.203 (APS Phila. BAu 25, 1 Apr. 1833).
203. *DAB*, v.9, p.203–4.
204. Charles Henry Pope and Thomas Hooper, comp., *Hooper Genealogy* (Boston: Charles H. Pope, 1908).
205. Letters to the author of 9 Aug. 1951 from Adeline D. Hooper and of Aug. 1959 from Roger F. Hooper.
206. Letter of 1 Oct. 1968 to the author from Mrs. John S. Reed, Assistant, Dept. of Prints & Drawings, Museum of Fine Arts, Boston, Mass.
207. *Book Prices Current*, v.36, p.34: item 34. Anderson Galleries.
208. New-York Historical Society, *Dictionary of Artists in America, 1564–1860*, George C. Groce and David H. Wallace, eds. (New Haven: Yale Univ. Pr., 1957), p.162.
209. Letter of 16 May 1959 to the author.
210. Press release of 26 May 1946, National Gallery of Art, Washington, D.C.
211. Catalog, Stan V. Henkels. Item 395, sale of the library of Robert H. Sayre, held 6, 7, 8 Nov. 1907 in the auction rooms of Davis & Harvey, Walnut St., Philadelphia, Pa.
212. *Public Ledger* (Philadelphia), Sat. morning, 9 Nov. 1907, p.8; *Black Diamond Express* 4, no.5 (May 1900). The latter publication, later retitled *Transportation*, was the house organ of the Lehigh Valley Railroad.
213. *Black Diamond Express*.
214. Letter of 7 July 1967 to the author from Ronald Hall, M.A., Librarian, John Rylands Library, Manchester, England; *also* letter of 23 Mar. 1959 to the author from Hilda M. McGill, Reference Librarian, Central Library, Manchester, England.
215. Letter of 7 July 1967 to the author from the Earl of Crawford.
216. *Herrick*, v.2, p.7–8.
217. *Book-Auction Records* (English), v.34, p.353.
218. OB, v.5, p.647–51.
219. *Letters*, v.2, p.90.
220. Ibid., v.2, p.96.
221. Harry Miller Lydenberg, *A History of the New York Public Library* (New York: The Library, 1923), p.129–50, 337, 99–101.
222. Annual Report of the Trustees of the Astor Library for the year 1853, dated 25 Jan. 1854.
223. List obtained at the Buffalo and Erie County Public Library.
224. John Burroughs, *John James Audubon* (Boston: Small Maynard & Co., 1902), p.117–23.
225. *Life*, p.203.
226. OB, v.5, p.647–51.
227. Houghton MCZ 118, v.3 (Baltimore, 21 Feb. 1840).
228. Ibid., v.2, p.30.
229. James Wynne, M.D., *Private Libraries of New York* (New York: E. French, 1860).
230. *Letters*, v.2, p.223 (APS Phila.; New York, 24 Nov. 1839).
231. Kenneth Wiggins Porter, *John Jacob Astor, Business Man* (2v.; Cambridge, Mass.: Harvard Univ. Pr., 1931), v.2, p.1057.
232. Letter of 15 May 1968 to the author from David Lasell, Parke-Bernet Galleries, successors to the Anderson Galleries.
233. Austin Baxter Keep, A.M., *History of the New York Society Library* (New York: De Vinne Press [For the Trustees], 1908), p.409.
234. *Herrick*, v.2, p.289, 11 May 1848.
235. Keep, p.403.
236. Ibid., p.510.
237. Letters of 28 Aug. 1838 and 26 Sept. 1838 from Victor Audubon to Havell, instructing the engraver as to the composite plates (Houghton bMS Am 1482 #244–45).
238. Letter of 5 Mar. 1958 to the author from Georgia H. Faison, Reference Librarian, North Carolina State Library.
239. Letter of 1 Oct. 1959 to the author from Jens Nyholm, Northwestern University Librarian.
240. OB, v.5, p.651.
241. Letter to the author from Mrs. Elsie Bambridge, present owner of Wimpole Hall, Cambridgeshire.

242. Letter of 8 Apr. 1959 to the author from Robin Drummond-Hay, Queen's College, Oxford, England.
243. Letter of 18 Oct. 1966 to the author from David R. Proper, Librarian, Essex Institute, Salem, Mass.
244. Letter of 2 Apr. 1968 to the author from Miss Dorothy Snyder, East India Marine Hall, Peabody Museum, Salem, Mass.
245. Letter of 8 Sept. 1958 to the author from Frank Walters, Hollis, N.H.
246. Letter of 13 Dec. 1962 to the author from Louis C. Madeira, Gladwyne, Pa.
247. *Journals*, v.1, p.247-48. Nearly every entry in all the journals begins with a morning greeting and ends with an affectionate good night.
248. OB, v.5, p.650. This subscription is no.24 on the final list of European subscribers.
249. Letter of 8 Aug. 1968 to the author from Miss Hilda Lofthouse, Librarian, Chetham's Library.
250. Letter of 14 May 1957 to the author from Dorothy Bloom, Oliver Wendell Holmes Library, with a copy of letter dated 12 Dec. 1928 from Thomas Gates to Thomas Cochran.
251. Letter of 8 Mar. 1957 to the author from F. B. Adams, Jr., Director, The Pierpont Morgan Library.
252. *Letters*, v.1, p.210.
253. *DAB*, v.19, p.211.
254. Letter of 27 Mar. 1903 to Princeton Univ. from Mrs. Justine Van Rensselaer Townsend.
255. Letter of 6 June 1929 to James Thayer Gerould, Librarian, Princeton University.
256. For a detailed history of the Providence Athenaeum, the merger with the Providence Library, and subsequent history see (1) Sixty-sixth Annual Report of the Board of Directors submitted 21 September 1911, p.23-55; and (2) "The Providence Athenaeum: A Brief History 1753-1929," Grace F. Leonard and W. Chesley Worthington (1940).
257. Papers relating to the subscription of the *Birds of America* have been assembled by the librarian of the Providence Athenaeum.
258. Ibid.
259. Ibid.
260. *Letters*, v.1, p.204 (APS Phila. BAu 25).
261. Providence Athenaeum, papers relating to the subscription to the *Birds of America*.
262. Ibid.
263. Minutes of the Athenaeum.
264. Ibid.
265. Ibid.
266. *Journal 1840–1843*, p.4 (Houghton MCZ 118, v.1).
267. Houghton bMS Am 21.
268. *Letters*, v.2, p.19 (APS Phila. BAu 25).
269. Thomas Edmondson, "Man in the Street," *Baltimore Sun*, 12 June 1949.
270. Letter dated Charleston, 25 Oct. 1833, from JJA to Edmondson; original in the possession of the Maryland Historical Society.
271. Copy of auction catalog in the collection of the Maryland Historical Society.
272. *The Guide Post* (publication of the Public Library of Cincinnati and Hamilton County) 20, no.6 (June–July 1955).
273. Ibid.
274. Letter of 30 Jan. 1959 to the author from Walter Schatzki.
275. *Journals*, v.1, p.238-243 (22-27 Apr. 1827).
276. Ibid., v.1, p.241, 24 Apr. 1827.
277. Ibid., v.1, p.242, 27 and 28 Apr. 1827.
278. Ibid.
279. St. Louis Mercantile Library Association Annual Report for 1858 (St. Louis, 1859).
280. St. Louis Mercantile Library Association, Minutes, dated 8 Jan. 1859.
281. Letter of 20 June 1958 to the author from Professor John Francis McDermott.
282. Letter, dated New York, 17 Sept. 1853, to John Bachman from Victor G. Audubon (Houghton bMS Am 1482 #312).
283. Letter of 17 Aug. 1946 from Frank B. Jewett, President, National Academy of Sciences, to Dr. Alexander Wetmore, Secy., Smithsonian Institution.
284. Letter of 2 Feb. 1971 to the author from Paul K. McClure, Archivist, National Academy of Sciences.
285. Letter of 5 Nov. 1861 from John W. Audubon to J. T. Johnston, the original of which is in the collection of the H. J. Lutcher Stark Foundation, Orange, Texas.
286. Letter of 12 Mar. 1896 from Maria Audubon to Herbert Johnston; original in the collection of the H. J. Lutcher Stark Foundation.
287. Receipt for payment; original in the collection of the H. J. Lutcher Stark Foundation (note explains Gould).
288. The *Diary of George Templeton Strong*, ed. by Allan Nevins and Milton Halsey Thomas (4v.; New York: Macmillan, 1952). See v.4 (*Post-war Years, 1865–1875*), p.417.
289. *New York Times Book Review* for 26 Nov. 1939 has a full account of the sale.
290. *Boston Sunday Post* of 19 Sept. 1954.
291. John James Audubon, *Synopsis of the Birds of North America* (Edinburgh and London: Adam and Charles Black; Longman, Rees, Brown, Green, and Longman, 1839).
292. Houghton bMS Am 1482 #243.

Notes

293. Ibid., #244.
294. Letters in the State Library's collection: copy of letter, dated Philadelphia, 17 Apr. 1833, from JJA to J. B. Morris; J. B. Morris to D. Ridgely, dated Philadelphia, 17 Apr. 1833; D. Ridgely to JJA, dated Annapolis, 20 Apr. 1833.
295. Letter, dated New York, 4 July 1837, from JJA to Ridgely.
296. Letters, JJA to Ridgely, dated Baltimore, 29 June 1837, and New York, 4 July 1837.
297. Letter of 2 Feb. 1959 to the author from James L. Baillie.
298. Letter of 25 Mar. 1959 to the author from Jean MacMillan, Head, Reference Division, The Toronto Public Library, Toronto, Canada.
299. *Ornithologist and Oölogist* 7, no.24 (15 Dec. 1882).
300. JJA to family, dated Schenectady, Tuesday, 16 July 1844. The letter is in the possession of the Historical Society of Schenectady. It had been sent to Dr. James R. Truax by Maria Audubon, a granddaughter of the Naturalist.
301. JJA to family, dated Schenectady, 14 Aug. 1844. The original is in the collection of the American Philosophical Society, Philadelphia.
302. Union College Treasurer's records of 18 Jan. 1845 and 8 Jan. 1846.
303. *Union College Chronicle* 61, no.9 (June 1971). See also the full page advertisement in *AB Bookman's Weekly* 48, no.1-2:5 (5-12 July 1971).
304. See newsletter, *Friends of the Union College Library* (9 Sept. 1971); also *AB Bookman's Weekly* 48, no.7-9:370-72 (16-30 Aug. 1971).
305. Letters of 1 July 1957 and 8 Dec. 1958 to the author from Arnold Cogswell.
306. *OB*, v.4, p.613.
307. Ibid., v.5, p.647.
308. *Letters*, v.2, p.210 (Houghton bMS Am 1482 #134).
309. Houghton MCZ 118, v.2 (1839), p.87.
310. Russell E. Bidlack, "The University of Michigan General Library: A History of Its Beginnings, 1837-1852" (Ph.D. diss., Univ. of Michigan, 1954). The author is indebted to Dr. Bidlack's history for the story of the library subscription to Audubon's *Birds of America*.
311. The New York Public Library, Ford Collection.
312. *OB*, v.3, p.633.
313. Ibid., v.5, p.648.
314. *Letters*, v.1, p.262.
315. Letter of 17 Apr. 1959 from Dr. Russell E. Bidlack to the author.
316. *Letters*, v.2, p.273.
317. *The Diary of George Templeton Strong*, ed. by Allan Nevins and Milton Halsey Thomas (New York: Macmillan, 1952), v.1, p.15 (2 Apr. 1836) and p.49 (7 Jan. 1837).
318. Letter of 26 July 1957 to the author from Dr. Gustave A. Swanson.
319. Letter of 17 May 1968 to the author from Carol Urness, Assistant Curator, Univ. of Minnesota Libraries.
320. Scrapbook of Ruthven Deane, in the possession of Albert E. Lownes, Providence, R.I.
321. Letter of 13 Mar. 1958 to the author from Julian K. Potter.
322. Letter of 6 May 1960 to the author from Sotheby & Co.
323. *Who Was Who*, v.11 (1916-1928) (London: Adam & Charles Black).
324. Letter of 3 Mar. 1960 to the author from Edwin Vare.
325. Agnes Starret, *The Darlington Memorial Library, University of Pittsburgh* (Pittsburgh: Univ. of Pittsburgh Pr., 1938).
326. Letter of 16 July 1968 to the author from George McM. Jones, First Assistant Librarian, Univ. of Pittsburgh Libraries.
327. William Campbell Preston (1794-1860), member of the legislature of South Carolina 1828-34. He voted in favor of the appropriation to purchase Audubon's work.
328. *Letters*, v.1, p.142 (APS Phila. BAu 25, 13 Oct. 1831, to Mrs. Audubon).
329. Ibid., v.1, p.143.
330. Reference is to the first volume of the *Birds of America* (100 plates), several copies of which Audubon had brought with him to America.
331. Robert W. Gibbes (1809-1866).
332. Thomas Cooper (1759-1840), President of Columbia College.
333. *Letters*, v.1, p.151 (APS Phila. BAu 25, 13 Nov. 1831, to Mrs. Audubon).
334. C. L. Backman, *John Bachman* ... (Charleston, S.C.: Walker, Evans & Cogswell Co., 1888), p.99-102.
335. Journal of the Assembly, South Carolina, 17 Dec. 1831, p.189.
336. Mary Cobb, "Early Days in the Library," *Bulletin of the Boston Museum of Natural History* no.55:33-34 (Apr. 1930).
337. Ibid.
338. *Life*, p.391.
339. Cobb, "Early Days ...," p.33-34.
340. Ibid.
341. Letter of 25 April 1957 to the author from

Bradford Washburn, Director, Society of Natural History (Museum of Science), Boston, Mass.
342. Undated letter in the files of the Memorial Library from Dr. J. Christian Bay, 210 Elm St., Elmhurst, Ill.
343. Letter of 29 June 1960 to the author from Felix Pollak, Curator of Rare Books, The Memorial Library, Univ. of Wisconsin, Madison, Wis.
344. Vassar College files.
345. Letter of 29 Oct. 1962 to the author from Roland Baughman, Butler Library, Columbia Univ.
346. See prints 255, 295, 300, 420, and 435 of this set of the folio.
347. *Journals*, v.1, p.242.
348. Letter of 10 Oct. 1962 to the author from O. S. Tomlinson, F.L.A., City Library, York, England.
349. Ibid.
350. *OB*, v.1, Names of Subscribers, back matter, p.13.
351. Ibid., v.5, p.649, no.16 on the list of European subscribers.
352. H. Richard Archer, ed., "Chapin Library— An Introduction to the Collections (Williamstown, Mass.: Chapin Library, 1970), p.[8–9]. Also, letter of 22 Nov. 1968 to the author from H. Richard Archer, Custodian, Chapin Library.
353. Letter of 4 Aug. 1959 to the author from James Drake, Inc.
354. *DAB*, v.4, p.281–82.
355. Yale Obituary Record, p.24.
356. Letter of 11 Oct. 1961 to the author from Henry W. Farnam, Jr.
357. Letter of 18 Oct. 1968 to the author from William D. Farnam, Library Assistant for the Yale Archives.
358. *National Cyclopaedia of American Biography*, suppl. C, p.156–57; *see also* Yale Obituary Record, p.84–85.
359. Ibid.
360. Letters of 22 July 1957 and 24 Oct. 1968 to the author from Marjorie G. Wynne, Research Librarian, Beinecke Rare Book Room, Yale Univ. Library.

Chapter 27

1. *Letters*, v.1, p.109 (APS Phila. BAu 25, to Mrs. Audubon, 23 June 1830).
2. Ibid., v.1, p.114 (to Havell, 1 July 1830).
3. Ibid., v.1, p.109.
4. Letter of 26 Mar. 1958 to the author from V. H. Woods, City Librarian, Birmingham (England) Public Libraries.
5. Ibid.
6. Letter of 18 Feb. 1966 to the author from M. J. Rowlands, Librarian, British Museum (Nat. History).
7. Ibid.
8. *Life*, p.381–83.
9. Ibid.
10. Ibid.
11. *OB*, v.4, p.613 and v.5, p.651.
12. *Journals*, v.1, p.284.
13. Ibid., v.1, p.291.
14. Ibid., v.1, p.301.
15. Ibid., v.1, p.252.
16. Ibid., v.1, p.264.
17. Ibid., v.1, p.342.
18. *OB*, v.1, p.12–15 (back matter).
19. Ibid., v.5, p.650.
20. Letter of 14 June 1966 to the author from T. C. Skeat, Keeper of Manuscripts, Dept. of Manuscripts, British Museum. Letters of Children are in *Catalogues of Additions to the Manuscripts in the British Museum* for 1894–1899 and 1900–1905.
21. Letter of 9 Apr. 1958 to the author from A. G. Cumbers, The Reading Room, British Museum.
22. Letter of 25 May 1966 to the author from J. Marks, The Reading Room, British Museum.
23. Ibid.
24. *Letters*, v.1, p.65 (22 Mar. 1828); *OB*, v.5, p.650.
25. John A. Venn, *Alumni Cantabrigienses* (6v.; London: Cambridge Univ. Press, 1954).
26. *Journals*, v.1, p.287.
27. Ibid., v.1, p.289.
28. Ibid., v.1, p.285–86.
29. Ibid., v.1, p.287, 5 Mar. 1828.
30. Ibid., v.1, p.287–88, 5 Mar. 1828.
31. Letter of 30 Aug. 1968 to the author from J. C. T. Oates, Under-Librarian, Cambridge University, who writes, "He [Lodge] was of a strange, nervous hypochondriacal disposition, and deserves a memoir which someday I hope to give him."
32. Letter of 21 Aug. 1959 to the author from Miss E. Raven, University Archives, Old Schools, Cambridge, England.

33. Letters of 7 July 1967 and 7 Aug. 1968 to the author from Ronald Hall, M.A., Librarian, The John Rylands Library, Manchester, England.
34. *OB*, v.5, p.650; also *Herrick*, v.2, p.383.
35. Letter of 18 Nov. 1954 to Miss Katherine Tousey from C. R. Gurney.
36. Letter of 22 Feb. 1960 to the author from Thomas S. Wragg, Keeper, Devonshire Collections, Chatsworth, Bakewell.
37. *Letters*, v.1, p.8.
38. *Journals*, v.1, p.289.
39. Details of the Fitzwilliam descent from the fourth Earl were provided in the letter of 24 Feb. 1967 to the author from Earl Fitzwilliam, Milton, Peterborough, Eng.
40. *Proceedings of the Linnaean Society of London*, 112th Session, 1900; Bibliography, no.204.
41. Letter of 23 Nov. 1966 to the author from Earl Fitzwilliam.
42. *OB*, v.5, p.649 and 650; also *Herrick*, v.2, p.382 and 384.
43. *Journals*, v.2, p.267.
44. "Special Collections in the Glasgow University Library," *The Book Collector* 16, no.2:161–68 (Summer 1967).
45. *OB*, v.5, p.649.
46. *1826 Journal*, p.272.
47. Ibid., p.297.
48. Letters of 24 Aug. 1967 and 8 Jan. 1973 to the author from H. Horton, Sub-librarian, Social Sciences Library, Manchester Public Libraries. See also Sir John Bernard Burke, *A Genealogical and Heraldic History of the Landed Gentry of Great Britain*, ed. by Ashworth P. Burke (10th ed.; London: Harrison and Sons, 1900).
49. Letter of 3 Aug. 1959 to the author from Christie, Manson & Woods, Ltd.
50. Letter of 26 Sept. 1967 to the author from Ronald Hall, Librarian, The John Rylands Library, Manchester.
51. Letter of 31 Oct. 1967 to the author from L. G. Simpson, Henry Sotheran Ltd.
52. Letter of 13 Feb. 1968 to the author from R. Bioletti, Reference Librarian, City of Liverpool Libraries Department. See also John Crosby Brown, *A History of Brown Brothers and Company, Brown, Shipley and the Allied Firms* (New York: Privately printed, 1909), p.305–12. Also, Aytoun Ellis, *Heir of Adventure: The Story of Brown, Shipley and Co., Merchant Bankers 1810–1960* (London: Privately published, 1960), p.36–56.
53. Letter of 1 July 1958 to the author from C. W. Black, City Librarian, Libraries Department, Corporation of Glasgow.
54. Letter of 14 Mar. 1960 to the author from C. W. Black, City Librarian, Corporation of Glasgow.
55. *Journals*, v.1, p.292.
56. Letter of 1 Apr. 1968 to the author from Dr. J. F. A. Mason, Librarian, Christ Church, Oxford.
57. The original letter is now in the possession of Morris Tyler, New Haven, Conn.
58. *Journals*, v.1, p.292, 25 Mar. 1828.
59. Letter of 10 Sept. 1968 to the author from Miss M. A. Haddon, Radcliffe College Science Library.
60. *Journals*, v.1, p.292.
61. Letter of 20 Mar. 1958 to the author from C. R. McEwan, Librarian, Public Library, Corporation of Paisley, Scotland.
62. Letter of 18 Nov. 1966 to the author from A. J. Tait, A.L.A., City Librarian, Sandeman Public Library, Perth, Scotland.
63. *Proceedings*, Perthshire Society of Natural Science, v.2, p.*xxiv–xxvi* (1893–98). These "Personal Reminiscences" were written by Andrew Coates in October 1893, in Perth. He was unable to read it in person to the society, so it was read by his son, Henry Coates, to the members at their meeting of 8 Mar. 1894 (letter of 29 Oct. 1968 to the author from A. J. Tait, City Librarian, Sandeman Library, Perth).
64. *Proceedings*, Perthshire Society of Natural Science, v.2.
65. Ibid.
66. *Life*, p.417.
67. Letter of 6 Oct. 1958 to the author from John F. Fleming. See Edwin Wolf II with John F. Fleming, *Rosenbach: A Biography* (Cleveland and New York: World, 1960), p.338.
68. Letter of 2 May 1967 to the author from Her Grace, Duchess of Portland, Langwell, Berriedale, Caithness.
69. Letter of 11 April 1961 to the author from Robert Mackworth Young, Librarian of the Royal Library.
70. Letter of 31 May 1961 to the author from Robert Mackworth Young.
71. U.S. Statutes-at-Large, v.2, p.90.
72. Letter of 14 Dec. 1965 to the author from W. Neil Franklin, Chief, Diplomatic, Legal, and Fiscal Branch, General Services Administration, National Archives and Records Service. See also letter of 23 Aug. 1856 to V. G. Audubon from J. A. Thomas, Asst. Secy. of State, requesting that Audubon furnish 100 copies each of the Octavo edition of the *Birds of America* and the *Quadrupeds of North America*, for which Congress had made an appropriation

(In the records of the Bureau of Accounts: "Press Copies of Letters Sent," v.27, p.40).
73. *Letters*, v.1, p.8.
74. Yale University has a copy of the aforementioned letter, dated 21 Dec. 1826, transcribed by an amanuensis. In a journal entry of the same date Audubon noted, "I have engaged Mr. D. Lizar's brother-in-law to copy letters for me and he also sat in my room at work." See p.301, *1826 Journal*.
75. *OB*, v.5, p.649; also *Herrick*, v.2, p.383.
76. Letter of 20 Mar. 1958 to the author from A. Wheen, Keeper of the Library, Victoria and Albert Museum, London.
77. *DNB*, v.19, p.1048.
78. Ibid.

Chapter 28

1. Letter of 5 Aug. 1958 to the author from C. A. McCallum, Chief Librarian, Public Library of Victoria, Melbourne, Victoria.
2. Ibid., 10 Sept. 1957.
3. Ibid., 27 Feb. 1958.
4. Ibid., 10 Sept. 1957.
5. Ibid., 26 Jan. 1960.
6. "About Major-General Johan Frederick Classen and The Classen Foundation," prepared by the University Library, Copenhagen, 1960.
7. Ibid.
8. Letter of 2 Dec. 1967 to the author from B. Loppenthan, Librarian, University Library, Copenhagen.
9. *OB*, v.5, p.648; also *Letters*, v.1, p.203-4.
10. *Letters*, v.1, p.214 (JJA to Lucy, 4 May 1833).
11. Letter of 22 Jan. 1964 to the author from Mrs. William N. Stevenson, Kittery Point, Me.
12. Letter of 1 April 1964 to the author from Yves Laissus, Archivist, Paléographe, Bibliothécaire au Muséum National d'Histoire Naturelle.
13. *OB*, v.5, p.651.
14. JJA to Lucy, dated London, 23 Dec. 1828. Original in the collection of the American Philosophical Society, Philadelphia.
15. Letter of 24 July 1834, JJA to Edward Harris (Houghton pfMS Am 21).
16. Bonaparte-Cooper correspondence (APS Phila. Film 669, frame 43).
17. From p.87, Ledger "B," in the Audubon Museum, Henderson, Ky.: "July 1834. 1st and 2d Volumes 93–5–0. Cash July 1834 from Molini of Paternoster Row."
18. The author is indebted to Prof. Antonio Pace, formerly of Syracuse Univ., and to his then associate, Frederick H. Jackson. The latter examined the folio in 1960.
19. Letter of 2 April 1968 to the author from Prof. Emanuale Casamassima, Il Direttore, Biblioteca Nazionale Centrale.
20. *Herrick*, v.2, p.31.
21. *Letters*, v.1, p.262 (JJA to Victor, 11 Oct. 1833).
22. *OB*, v.5, p.651.
23. Copy of receipt sent to the author on 14 Sept. 1968 by J. G. de Bruijn, Librarian, Bibliotheek van Teyler's Stichting, Haarlem, Netherlands.
24. Letter of Aug. 1968 to the author from J. G. de Bruijn, Librarian, Bibliotheek van Teyler's Stichting, Haarlem, Netherlands.
25. *Herrick*, v.2, p.245.
26. *Journal 1840–1843*, p.125-27; original in the Houghton Library, Harvard Univ.
27. Letters of 13 Dec. 1959 and 15 Jan. 1960 to the author from the Earl of Caledon.
28. Letter of 27 Nov. 1968 to the author from Warren R. Howell.
29. Letter of 12 July 1969 to Warren R. Howell from Walter Armytage, Halston, Moyvore, County Westmeath, Eire.
30. Claus Nissen, *Die Illustrierten Vogel Bücher* (Stuttgart: Hiersemann Verlag, 1953), p.99, no.171.
31. Letter in possession of the Amherst College Library.
32. Among the exhibits at the Audubon Museum at the State Park at Henderson, Ky., are several loose pages, evidently torn from a ledger or daybook of Audubon's; these are numbered 5, 6, 87–104, etc. The entry quoted is on the page numbered 87.
33. *Life*, p.202.
34. Letter, dated "New York, Jany. 25th (Sunday) 1841," the original of which is in the possession of Albert E. Lownes, Providence, R.I. It was published in *The Auk* 52:154-68 (Apr. 1935).
35. *Herrick*, v.1, p.436; v.2, p.38.
36. Letter of 4 May 1960 to David Jonah, Librarian, Brown Univ. from V. Ia. Khvatov, Director, Section of International Exchanges, Library of the Academy of Sciences, Leningrad, USSR.

Notes

Appendix A

1. Houghton MCZ 118, v.2.
2. Ibid., v.5.

Appendix B

1. Prospectus found in *Ibis* 1, no.3 (July 1859), in the collection of the John Crerar Library, Chicago, Ill.
2. *Herrick*, v.2, p.296.
3. Harry T. Peters, *America on Stone* (New York: Doubleday, 1931).
4. Smithsonian Institution, Washington, D.C., "Letters received," v.58.
5. *Worcester* (Mass.) *Telegram*, 23 Aug. 1963.
6. The author is indebted to the Walpole (Mass.) Public Library and Mary E. Locke, Librarian, for making available to him the library's copy of the Bien edition to compile the chronological list of plates comprising that edition for inclusion in the present work.

Appendix C

1. *Journals*, v.1, p.65.
2. Ibid., v.1, p.66, footnote.
3. Ibid., v.1, p.214.
4. *DAB*, v.11, p.92; *see also* Thieme and Becker, *Kunstler Lexicon*, v.20, p.255.
5. *Journals*, v.1, p.224.
6. Ibid., v.1, p.224.
7. Ibid., v.1, p.254.
8. Ibid., v.1, p.255.
9. Ibid., v.1, p.256.
10. *Herrick*, v.1, p.446-47.
11. From a memorandum, on large folio pages, 17 × 10 inches, sent to Robert Havell, the engraver. The original is in the possession of the Richard W. Norton Art Gallery, Shreveport, La.
12. *Herrick*, v.1, p.446.
13. Ibid., v.1, p.447.
14. Ibid., v.2, p.35.
15. *Letters*, v.1, p.210.
16. Ibid., v.1, p.246.
17. Ibid., v.1, p.270.
18. *Herrick*, v.2, p.55-62, with references to Kidd on p.57, 61, and 62. The same letter is also found in *Letters*, v.1, p.272-77. However, in the latter work, this letter is dated 21 Dec. 1833. The letter used by Herrick had been transcribed from a letter shown him by Maria R. Audubon, while that in the Corning compilation had been loaned to the compiler by Victor Morris Tyler, a great-grandson of Audubon's. The Tyler copy of the letter is not complete.
19. Houghton bMS 1482 #358.
20. Ibid., #359.
21. Ibid., #231.
22. Ibid., #360.
23. Ibid., #361.
24. The title page for this work reads, "The Miscellany of Natural History/Vol. 1/Parrots/By/Sir Thomas Dick Lauder, Bart. F.R.S.E./and Capt. Thomas Brown, F.L.S./The Engravings/By Joseph B. Kidd, Esq./Member of the Scottish Academy of Painting, Sculpture and Architecture/Edinburgh:/Published by Fraser & Co. 54, North Bridge;/Smith, Elder & Co. Cornhill, London;/and W. F. Wakeman, Dublin/MDCCCXXXIII."
25. *Princeton University Library Chronicle* 21, nos.1 and 2:9-88 (combined Autumn 1959-Winter 1960 issue). Specific reference to the paintings is to be found on p.45.
26. For additional information regarding Kidd's renderings in oil of Audubon's original watercolor paintings, *see also* Alice Ford, *John James Audubon* (Norman, Okla.: Univ. of Oklahoma Pr., 1964), p.430-45.

NOTES

Appendix D

1. It had been brought to the author's attention by Howard C. Rice, formerly Asst. Librarian in charge of rare books and manuscripts at Princeton Univ., that ten or more wood engravings after the plates of Audubon's *Birds of America* are included in *Voyages dans les Deux Océans Atlantique et Pacifique, 1844 à 1847....*, by M. Eugene Delessert (Paris: A. Franck, Libraire, 1848). Several of the engravings include the engraver's signature (Cordier, Meunier,...). It is not known whether a member of the Delessert family, possibly Benjamin Delessert, a well-known nineteenth century French industrialist interested in natural history, might have possessed a set of the folio. The name does not appear in either Ledger "B" or in any of the subscription lists.
2. *Forest and Stream* 47, no.10:182.
3. Ibid., 47, no.11:243.
4. Arthur Brentano, Jr., "Macmillan's New Audubon," *Publisher's Weekly* 132, no.16: 1567–68 (16 Oct. 1937).
5. Letter of 2 Nov. 1967 to the author from Mrs. Ruth Karras, Advertising Correspondent, Northwestern Mutual Life Insurance Co., Milwaukee, Wis.
6. Ibid.
7. Letter of 8 Sept. 1972 to the author from Katharine Shepard, Asst. Curator of Graphic Arts, National Gallery of Art.
8. "Meet the Beltzhoovers of Natchez, Mississippi," *Ladies Home Journal* 64, no.1:129–34, 160–61 (Jan. 1947). See also "History Repeats in Old Natchez," *National Geographic Magazine* 94, no.2:187, 188, 201 (Feb. 1949).
9. Letter of 30 Aug. 1959 to the author from Florence Bittner, Curator, Villa Louis, Prairie du Chien, Wis.
10. The American Philosophical Society, Philadelphia, Pa., has in its collection plates with Audubon *Birds* manufactured by William Adams & Sons.
11. H. Comstock, "An Audubon Centenary Recorded in Porcelain," *The Connoisseur* 96:164–65 (Sept. 1935).
12. Letter of 2 Sept. 1970 to the author from Helen Smindak, secy. to Roland C. Clement, National Audubon Society, New York.
13. *Antiques* 72:560–63 (Dec. 1957).
14. The author is indebted to Mr. and Mrs. Joseph Amore of Palm Beach, Fla., for bringing these reproductions to his attention and to Mr. John C. Annesi of Ft. Lauderdale, Fla., for the privilege of examining them.
15. Scott's *Standard Postage Stamp Catalogue* (New York: Scott Publ. Co., 1972), v.1, p.34.
16. Ibid., v.1, p.46.
17. *OB*, v.1, p.483–85.
18. New York Botanical Garden, *Newsletter* 3, no.2 (Feb. 1969).

Appendix E

1. The American Museum of Natural History Endowment, 57th Annual Report of the Trustees for the year 1925, p.116.
2. Folder, "Audubon's 'Birds of America' 1827–1831 [sic] in the Excessively Rare Uncoloured States," of Roy Vernon Sowers, 518 Powell Street, San Francisco, Calif.; sent to the author in 1958.
3. Copy of letter of 21 Jan. 1960 to H. J. Lutcher Stark, Orange, Texas, from Margaret McCormick, Staten Island, N.Y., in letter of 27 Jan. 1960 to the author from H. J. Lutcher Stark.

Appendix F

1. *Journals*, v.1, p.127.
2. Ibid., v.1, p.128.
3. Ibid., v.1, p.127.
4. *Life*, p.145–47.
5. *Letters*, v.1, p.18 (APS Phila BAu 25, JJA to Lucy, 24 Mar. 1827).
6. Houghton bMS Am 1482 #370.
7. *Letters*, v.1, p.33 (APS Phila. BAu 25, dated London, 6 Aug. 1827).

Notes

Appendix G

1. *Letters*, v.2, p.212 (Houghton bMS Am 1482 #139, Edinburgh, 13 Mar. 1839).
2. Ibid., v.2, p.216 (Houghton bMS Am 1482 #141, Edinburgh, 29 Mar. 1839).
3. Memorandum to Pleasant Valley Bird and Wildlife Sanctuary, Lenox, Mass., from Mrs. William Church Osborne; also letter of 17 Feb. 1959 to the author from Mrs. Shelton E. Martin. Mrs. Martin was the daughter of John S. Barnes.
4. Letter of 15 June 1959 to the author from John E. Mastin, Secy., Phelps, Dodge Corp.
5. Letter of 8 Dec. 1959 to the author from Cleveland E. Dodge.
6. Houghton bMS Am 1482 #89.
7. Princeton Univ. Library, Howard Corning typescripts, no.24, p.2.
8. Isaac Newton Phelps Stokes, *Iconography of Manhattan Island* (6v.; New York: Robt. H. Dodd, 1915–28), v.5, p.1792. The fire broke out on 19 July 1845.
9. William R. Dall, *Spencer Fullerton Baird: A Biography* (Philadelphia and London: Lippincott, 1915), p.124.
10. Ibid.
11. *Herrick*, v.2, p.294–95.
12. Smithsonian Institution Archives, Lucy Audubon to Joseph Henry, 29 Dec. 1863.
13. Ibid., 19 Oct. 1864.
14. *American Literary Gazette and Publisher's Circular* 15:131; reference found by Mrs. Norman V. Ballou.
15. Quoted in the *Peninsular Courier*, 10 Mar. 1871. Sent to the author by Mr. R. S. Bidlack, Univ. of Michigan Library.
16. *Forest and Stream* 47, no.11:203 (12 Sept. 1896).
17. Ibid.
18. Reported to author in Oct. 1964 by Mrs. Jane B. Cheney, Executive Director, Children's Museum, West Hartford, Conn.
19. *The Auk* 25, no.4:401–5 (Oct. 1908).
20. Ibid.
21. Ibid.
22. *Forest and Stream* 47, no.25:481 (19 Dec. 1896).
23. *The Auk* 51:343–49 (July 1934).
24. *The Auk* 48:284 (Apr. 1931). John B. May reported the plate at the time had been in the possession of Mayor Ferdinand Latrobe of Baltimore. Has not been located.
25. *The Auk* 51:343–49 (July 1934). Phoebe Knappen states that the copper plate of the "Blue Bird" had been in the possession of Miss Grace H. Dodge of New York City.
26. The "Great Blue Heron" had been reported by Ruthven Deane to be in the possession of the Smithsonian Institution in *The Auk* 25, no.4: 401–5 (Oct. 1908), but Phoebe Knappen claimed that this was a case of mistaken identity in *The Auk* 51:343–49 (July 1934).

Appendix J

1. Anthony Woodward was librarian at the American Museum of Natural History from 1881 until 1909. Miss Hazel Gay, the librarian in 1959, wrote the author, "In checking I find an item in the annual report of 1881, 'a librarian is now employed' and in the 1886–87 Report, the Library Section is signed by Anthony Woodward. Dr. Tower came in December 1902, but Dr. Woodward was kept on as a Curator of Maps and Charts."

INDEX

Abercrombie & Fitch Co., 181
Aberdeen, University of, 178
Abert, John James, 100
Harry N. Abrams, Inc., 371
Academies, sets in, 193, 195
Academy of Natural Sciences, Philadelphia, 3, 34, 56, 65, 98, 105, 110, 129–130, 142, 152, 172, 193, 217, 222, 225–227, 388, 418, 440
Academy of Sciences, Zoological Institute, Leningrad, 170, 176, 195, 215
Act to Alter and Amend the Several Acts Imposing Duties on Imports (1832), 58
Adams, John Quincy, 269–270
Adelaide, Queen, 19, 162, 197, 388, 440
Advocates Library of Edinburgh, 142
Ainsworth, Mrs. P., 440, 452
Albatross, 397
Alden, F. L., 123
Allen, Robert, 50
Alphabetical index to *Birds of America*, 401–415
American Academy of Arts and Letters, 181
American avocet, 95
American bittern, 89, 95
American brant, 397
American crossbill, 75, 76
American flamingo, 63
American Harbor, 74
American Heritage Publishing Company, 382
American Museum of Natural History, 116, 172, 188, 194, 217, 219, 227, 366, 381, 389, 393, 395, 396, 397
American Ornithology (Wilson), 3, 4, 10, 79, 81, 280
American Philosophical Society, 3, 34, 56, 142, 152, 172, 193, 221, 227–228, 270, 388, 440
American Print Craft Guild, 371
American robin, 5, 202, 395

American scoter duck, 397
American sooty albatross, 397
Amherst College, 52, 172, 193, 215, 229
Anas strepera, 81
Anderson, R. O., 159, 440
Anthus aquaticus, 223–224
Anthus spinoletta, 224
Appleton, Samuel, 67, 155, 235, 440
Arctic jaeger, 396
Ardea occidentalis, 93
Ardia herodias, 89
Ariel Press, 372–373
Arnold, James, 70, 98, 112, 159–160, 259, 315, 440
Art galleries, sets in, 193
Ashburton, Lord, 120, 123, 248–249
Astley, Sir Jacob, 171, 199, 241, 443
Astor, John Jacob, 116, 123, 292, 294–295
Athenaeums, sets in, 193
Atkins, S. P., 166, 440
Auctions, 164, 183, 198–199, 262, 419
Audubon, Florence, 116, 383
Audubon, Georgiana Richards Mallory, 114
Audubon, John James, 177, 197–198, 385–386
  articles about, 14
  articles by, 13–14, 30, 79, 266
  as artist, 129, 130–133, 382
  attitudes toward scientific publication, 30
  and coloring of plates, 29, 34
  death, 127
  drawings, *see* Drawings, Audubon's
  exhibitions, *see* Exhibitions, Audubon's
  expeditions, *see* Expeditions, Audubon's
  family life, 86–87
  finances, 4, 26, 62, 83–85, 106
  honesty, 8

INDEX

Audubon, John James—*Continued*
  journal, 3, 5, 6, 8, 9, 10, 11–15, 17, 20, 21–22, 23, 28, 29, 30, 31, 33, 34, 37, 39, 45, 50, 51, 54–55, 98, 101–103, 116–119, 137, 226, 242, 250, 251–252, 253, 269, 303, 316, 327, 329–330, 332, 333–334, 338, 360–361
  journeys, *see* Journeys, Audubon's
  letters to Bachman, 86–87, 88–90, 93–95, 97–98, 99, 103–104, 106, 107, 110–111, 112, 123, 157, 283
  letters to Havell, 41, 42–43, 45, 46, 53, 56, 57, 67, 68–69, 77, 85, 93, 111–112, 169–170, 212–214, 226, 229, 271, 291–292, 315, 390
  letters to Lucy Audubon, 14, 24, 35–39, 43, 62, 63, 92, 154, 157, 158, 161, 225, 241, 282, 283, 319–320, 341, 346, 387
  letters to others, 5, 7, 10, 16, 18, 19, 22, 23–24, 35–43, 44, 47–48, 51–54, 56–59, 67–71, 75–77, 79–81, 84–90, 93–99, 101–106, 108–112, 116, 152–154, 159, 162, 169, 188, 226, 249, 256, 257–258, 269, 271, 274, 303, 304, 310–311, 316–317, 336–337, 347, 391
  letters to Victor Audubon, 33, 38, 39, 40–41, 75–76, 79, 82–84, 85, 101–102, 119, 138, 152–153, 156, 157, 212, 225, 233, 235, 247, 248, 270, 274, 283–284, 288, 304, 317–318, 349, 362–363, 391, 400
  methods and techniques, description, 34
  methods of travel, 15
  obituaries and eulogies, 127–130
  old age, 126–127, 295
  paintings, *see* Paintings
  portraits of, 30, 257
  reaction to criticism, 79–80
  reference books used by, 80–81
  relations with Kidd, 13, 119, 360–367
  as scientist, 49–50, 133
  will, 40–41
  See also Birds of America (Double Elephant folio)
Audubon, John Woodhouse (son), 39, 73, 74, 77, 78, 79, 84, 86–87, 96, 97, 102, 103, 104, 105, 113, 124, 275, 306–307, 355, 391, 417
Audubon, Lucy (wife), 4, 15, 23, 46, 56, 77, 78, 80, 84, 86, 87, 107, 113, 114, 124–125, 138, 160, 258, 287, 356, 391–392
  letters from Audubon to, 14, 24, 35–39, 43, 62, 63, 92, 157, 158, 161, 225, 241, 282, 283, 319–320, 341, 346
  letters to Havell, 53, 63–66
Audubon, Maria R. (granddaughter), 37, 116, 266, 306–307, 360, 368, 383, 394
Audubon, Maria Rebecca (daughter-in-law), 104, 105
Audubon, Victor Gifford (son), 35, 37, 56, 62, 86, 87, 91, 107, 111, 113, 114, 123, 140, 161, 189, 227, 228, 243, 244, 273, 274, 306, 339, 341, 347
  correspondence with Kidd, 365–366
  J. J. Audubon's letters to, 33, 38, 39, 40–41, 75–76, 79, 82–84, 85, 101–102, 119, 138, 152–153, 156, 157, 212, 225, 235, 247, 248, 270, 274, 283–284, 288, 317–318, 349, 362–363, 391, 400
  letters to Havell, 53, 63–66, 113, 258–259, 307, 365, 366
  sent to London, 62, 65, 68–70
Audubon House, Key West, Fla., 173, 287–288
Audubon Museum, 115, 117, 137, 272, 349, 363, 389, 396, 452
Audubon Sanctuary, Key West, 218, 221
Audubon Shrine and Wildlife Sanctuary, Mill Grove, Audubon, Pa., 30, 125, 172, 193, 218, 220, 222, 230–231, 396
Audubon societies, sets in, 193
Audubon State Park, Henderson, Ky., 114, 115, 117, 137, 172, 179, 193, 231–232, 272, 349, 363, 389, 452
Audubon's caracara, 59, 396
Audubon's woodpecker, 397
Australia, sets in, 195
  complete, 175, 196, 343
  incomplete, 178, 196
Autographs, 255–256
Avocet, 95
Ayre, Edward E., 182, 416

Bachman, John, 78, 82, 84–87, 101, 126, 295, 320, 363
  Audubon gift to, 177–178
  Audubon's first meeting with, 58
  help to Audubon, 58–59, 79, 159, 241, 242
  letters to, 86–87, 88–90, 93–95, 97–98, 99, 103–104, 106, 107, 110–111, 112, 123, 157, 189, 283
Bachman, Maria, 86
Bachman, Mrs., 256
Bachman's warbler, 71
Backhouse, John, 441
Bagg, Dr. Egbert, 418
Bai de Portage, 74
Bailey, Mrs., 153, 440
Baker, T.B.L.L., 112, 447
Bakewell, William G., 39, 41
Bald eagle, 395
Baldwin, Loammi, 105, 156, 238–239, 440
Ballentine, Edward, 395, 396
Baltimore, 39, 40, 57, 77, 78, 85, 253–256
Baltimore oriole, 43, 202, 203, 270, 309, 395
Band-tailed pigeon, 99
Bank swallow, 94
Banks, George, 231, 440
Barataria Island, 103
Barclay, Alexander, 45, 440
Barclay, M. A., 20

486

Index

Barclay, Robert, 440, 452
Baring, Alexander, 120, 123, 248–249
Barker, Thomas, 45, 440
Barret, Alexander Buchanan, 230
Barret, Cecil, 124, 230
Barrett, Mrs. Thomas, 181
Bartfield, J. N., 194, 219, 232
Barton, John, 440, 452
Bartram sandpiper, 95
Bay, Jens Christian, 210, 265, 401
Bayou Sara, Louisiana, 4, 35, 39
Beech Grove, 39
Beinecke, Mrs. Frederick W., 194, 223, 232–234, 417
Bell, John, 417
Bemaculated duck, 397
Benham, Commander Timothy Green, 184–185
Bentley, Robert, 17, 27, 28
Berlin, Royal Library at, 419
Berthoud, Eliza, 5, 117, 306
Berthoud, Nicholas, 5, 39, 41, 80, 85, 97, 106, 116–117, 154, 157, 161, 162, 283, 306, 310
Bewick, Thomas, 14, 21, 252, 280
Biblioteca Naçional de Lisbõa, 176, 195, 348
Biblioteca Nazionale Centrale, Florence, 176, 195, 347
Bibliotheca Lindesiana, 330–331
Bibliotheek van Teyler's Stichting, Haarlem, Netherlands, 91, 148, 169, 176, 195, 347
Bibliothèque de l'Institut Royal de France, 146, 168, 176, 195, 345
Bibliothèque du Muséum National d'Histoire Naturelle, 176, 195
Bibliothèque Nationale, 179, 215
Bickersteth, Dr., 164, 440
Bien, Julius, 355
Birch, W., 92, 441
"Bird of Washington," 202, 252, 395
Bird skins, 92, 99, 101–102
Birds, see Drawings, Audubon's; Paintings; specific names
Birds of America (Bien Chromolithograph edition), 124, 185, 188, 275, 307, 355–359
Birds of America (Double Elephant folio), 16, 21, 22, 45, 53, 70, 71, 75, 76, 82, 92–93, 96, 108
  additional prints of early numbers, 140
  alphabetical index to, 401–415
  auctions sold at, 164, 183, 198–199, 419
  Audubon's instructions on legends, 52–53, 213–214
  bookkeeping for, see Ledger "B"
  chronology, 399–400
  classes of drawings by size, 38
  coloring, see Coloring
  complete sets, 139–140, 172–176
  composite plates, 295–296, 307–309
  conclusion, 110

  copper plates, 112, 153, 380–381, 390–395
  cost of each number, 26
  cost of publishing, 114
  criticism of, 30, 32, 79–80, 127, 129, 130–133
  difficulties with shipment of numbers, 82
  difficulty caused by new species, 107–109
  engraving, see Engraving operations
  extra prints, 113
  first number, 15, 16
  import duty imposed on, 57–58, 271
  incomplete sets, 177–180
  letterpress, see *Ornithological Biography*
  loose prints, 116, 179–180, 196, 198, 200–205, 383–384
  made up of loose sheets, 124
  mistakes in packing and shipping prints, 111–112
  mode of delivery to subscribers, 69
  number of plates, 100, 107–108
  oil paintings, 13, 119, 360–367
  original cost, 197–198, 387
  prices asked for, 199–200, 262
  procuring of subscribers, see Promotional activity
  prospectus, 7, 19, 32, 138, 197, 227, 385–389
  provenances of sets, 225–350
  reproductions of plates, 368–382
  sale of remaining folios, 115–125
  sets broken up, 181–184, 196, 201–203
  sets destroyed, 184–186, 196
  sets, ultimate disposition of, 151–171
  sets whose whereabouts are not known, 187–192, 196
  subscribers, see Subscribers
  subscription book decided on, 7
  variations in legends and watermarks, 209–224, 230, 234–235, 263, 265, 286, 295, 315, 324, 326, 348, 421–439
  Woodward's list of folios, 416–420
Birds of America (Octavo edition), 13, 70–71, 118, 119, 122, 295, 298, 313–314, 340–341, 353–354
Birmingham, 1830 visit to, 43, 325
Birmingham Old Library, 147, 168, 325, 441
Birmingham Public Libraries, Reference Library, 175, 195, 215, 325
Bittern, 89, 95
Black-bellied plover, 95
Black-billed cuckoo, 131, 211–212, 216, 263, 265, 324, 348
Blackbird, 205
Blackburnian warbler, 308
Black-capped chickadee, 81
Black-capped titmouse, 75, 94
"Black Cocks," 13, 30
Black-crowned night heron, 396
Black-headed titmouse, 81, 82, 212
Black skimmer, 95, 397
Black-throated bunting, 95
Black vulture, 39, 395

INDEX

"Black Vulture Attacking the Head of Deer," 39
Blackwall, John, 20, 166, 441
Black-winged hawk, 94
Blackwood's Magazine, 51
Blake, Daniel, 61, 157, 158, 441
Bluebird, 64, 202, 395
Blue crane, 202
Blue grosbeak, 66
Blue-headed pigeon, 205
Blue heron, 95
Bluejay, 395
Blue mountain warbler, 81, 94
Blue-winged yellow warbler, 94
Board of Assistant Aldermen of the City of New York, 122, 123
Boat-tailed grackle, 71
Bobwhite, 395
Bohn, Henry G., 8, 170, 441
Bonaparte, Charles Lucien, 3, 4, 19, 37, 48, 80, 81, 91, 110, 226, 227, 280, 441
    Audubon's letters to quoted, 7, 49, 133
    and new species, 109
Bonaparte's flycatcher, 187, 201, 219
Booby gannet, 63
Book-of-the-Month Club, 371
Boston, 67, 98
Boston Athenaeum, 52, 72, 147, 152, 172, 193, 217, 219, 220, 234-235, 417, 441
Boston Museum of Fine Arts, 155, 173, 193, 288-289
Boston Natural History Society, 70, 79, 98, 148, 152, 187, 320-321, 417, 441
Boston Public Library, 155, 172, 177, 194, 235, 389, 417
Bowdoin College, 172, 193, 224, 235-236
Bradford, Earl of, 168, 441
Bradore Bay, 74
Brant goose, 205, 397
Brazilian caracara eagle, 59, 396
Brewer, Thomas Mayo, 101, 126, 127-128
Brewster, David, 13
British Copyright Act of 1709, 47, 51
British Museum, 150, 170, 175, 195, 325, 327-329, 419, 441
Broadley, John, 441
Brodrick, Wm., 441, 452
Brontë, Patrick, 246
Brookes, F. S., 7
Brooks, Joshua S., 137
Brooks, S. R., 441, 452
Brown, Captain Thomas, 48
Brown, James, 70, 71, 155, 156, 344, 441
Brown, John, 98
Brown creeper, 397
Brown-headed worm-eating warbler, 76
Brown lark, 223-224
Brown pelican, 131, 397

Brown titlark, 224
Brown University, 172, 179, 193, 215, 216, 217, 218, 219, 220, 221, 223, 236
Buccleuch, Duke of, 91, 169, 181, 202, 441
Buddle, John, 166, 441
Buffalo and Erie County Public Library, 172, 177, 194, 237-238, 417
Buffalo Museum of Natural History, 156
Buffalo Society of Natural Sciences, Buffalo Museum of Science, 172, 194, 220, 238-239
Buffle-head duck, 81
Bullock's oriole, 309
Bulman, John, 441
Buntings, 71, 95, 116
Burley, Susan, 68, 159, 259, 417, 441
Burrell, Matthew, 441, 452
Burrell, William, 452
Burrowing owl, 398
Burton, James, 441, 452
Butler, Benjamin F., 100-101, 277

Caernarvon, Earl of, 166, 441
Caledon, Lord, 120, 123, 195, 347-348
California Academy of Sciences, 172, 193, 239-240
California jay, 397
California nuthatch, 397
California State Library, 172, 195, 217, 221, 222, 240
California turkey-vulture, 307, 338
Callet, 186, 418
Cambridge, 1828 visit to, 28-29, 329-330
Cambridge Philosophical Society, 28, 146, 167, 441
Cambridge University, Fitzwilliam Museum and University Library, 28, 146, 167, 175, 219, 329-330, 442
Camden, N. J., 38
Camera lucida, 13, 353
Canada
    Audubon's journeys to, 68, 120-122
    complete sets in, 173, 174, 196
    distribution of sets in, 193-194
    House of Assembly, 121
    Legislative Library, New Brunswick, 173, 194, 209, 221, 267-268
    Library of Parliament, 113, 121, 123, 173, 185, 194, 216, 281-282
    loose prints in, 196
    Public Archives, 180
Canada goose, 204, 396
Canada jay, 205, 309, 395
Canadian titmouse, 75, 396
Canadian woodpecker, 397
Canvas-backed duck, 203
Cape May warbler, 81, 94
Carman, Richard F., 73, 153, 442
Carnegie Institute, 171, 172, 194, 240-241, 396
Carolina paroquet, 29

Index

Carolina parrot, 202
Carolina turtle dove, 52, 53, 203, 214
Carrion crow, 395
Amon Carter Museum of Western Art, 179
Case, Mrs., 442
Case-Western Reserve University, 179
Catbird, 133
Cathartes aura, 212
Cathartes californianus, 341
Cayenne tern, 93
Centenary College of Louisiana, 187
Cerulean warbler, 201
Chamberlain, Mr., 419
Charadrius wilsonius, 309
Charles X of France, 32, 33, 45, 162, 268, 442, 444
Charleston citizens' Library, 148, 152-153, 442
Charleston Library Society, 148, 152, 172, 194, 218, 241, 442
Charleston Museum, 152, 172, 194, 242-243
Charleston Natural History Society, 148, 152, 242-243, 442
Charleston, S. C., 58-59, 62, 65, 78-79
Charlewood, Lieutenant Colonel, 442, 452
Chetham's Library, 144, 165, 299, 389, 442
Chickadees, 81, 396
Children, John George, 17, 18, 19, 27, 30, 37, 41, 45, 50, 165, 327-328, 442
Children's warbler, 27
China, reproductions on, 376-378
Chipping sparrow, 200, 201
Cholmley, Colonel, 442, 452
Chorley, John, 22, 50
Chromolithograph plates, 124, 185, 188, 275, 307, 355-359
Chuck-will's-widow, 395
Church, Frederic E., 395
Cincinnati and Hamilton County, Public Library of, 157, 174, 194, 222, 304
City College, City University of New York, 122, 172, 193, 217, 219, 220, 222, 243-245, 417
Clarence, Duchess of, 19, 442
Clark, General William, 4, 7
Clarke, James Graham, 442
Clark's nutcracker, 397
Clay, Henry, 4, 7, 269
Clay, Henry, Jr., 160, 442
Clay-colored finch, 308
Clayton, John, 251-252, 442
Cleveland Museum of Natural History, 172, 194, 222, 245-246
Clinton, DeWitt, 4, 7
Clough, John, 15, 164, 322-323, 442
Clowes, Rev. J., 442
Coates, Andrew, 122, 123, 124, 183, 338-339, 419
Coats, Mrs. Thomas, 419
Coccyzus americanus, 211, 217
Coccyzus caroliniensis, 216-217, 268
Coccyzus erythropthalmus, 211, 212, 216, 263, 324, 348
Coleman, George Dawson, 181
College of Physicians, Philadelphia, 109
Colleges, sets in, 193-194
Collie's magpie-jay, 131
Colman, W. A., 154, 316-318, 442
Color slides, 368-374
Colorado Springs Fine Arts Center Taylor Museum, 179
Coloring
  Audubon's supervision of, 29, 34
  cost of, 26
  faults in, 42-43, 64, 66
  at Lizars establishment, difficulties, 23
  and storage of volumes, 43-44, 209-210
Columba carolinensis, 53, 214
Columbia College (now University), 73, 82, 138, 152, 172, 193, 246, 418, 442
Columbia jay, 200, 201, 202
Common buzzard, 397
Common crow blackbird, 221
Common loon, 397
Common tern, 397
Composite plates, 295-296, 307-309
Congress, U.S., 341
Connecticut warbler, 201, 395
Coolidge, Joseph A., 73
Cooper, Thomas, 78
Cooper Union Museum, 194, 232
Coot, 89
Copenhagen, University of, 155, 175, 195, 216, 220, 221, 343-344
Copp, Mrs. Belton A., 397
Copper plates, 112, 153, 390-394
  locations, 395
  reproductions from, 380-381
Cormorants, 63, 103, 396
Cornell University, 173, 183, 193, 216, 248-249
Cornus nuttalli Aud., 99
Corvus canadensis, 309
Cow bunting (cowbird), 395
Craig, Rev. Edward, 166, 442
Cranes, 89, 200, 201, 202, 203, 396
Crawford, Earl of, 195, 290-291, 330-331
Crawhall, Thomas, 442
John Crerar Library, 173, 194, 264-265, 401
Cresswell Baker, A. J., 166, 440, 452
Cririe, William, 442
Croghan, John, 160, 442
Crompton, Joshua S., 15, 164
Crossbill, 75, 76, 95
Crows, 395
Cruger, Mrs. Douglas, 13, 153, 419, 443
Cuckoos, 11, 63, 131, 201, 203, 211-212, 216-217, 263, 268, 324, 326, 340, 395
Culley, Matthew, 443, 452

489

INDEX

Curlews, 59, 89, 103, 200, 201, 203, 204
Currier Gallery of Art, 179
Cushing, J. G., 67, 155, 443
Cuvier, Baron, 27, 31–32, 33, 286, 388–389, 443
Cuvier's regulus, 27
Czar Nicholas I of Russia, 118, 123, 349

Dacnis protonotarius, 211, 217
Darbyshire, James, 20, 166, 443, 452
Darnley, Right Hon. Earl of, 443
Dartmouth College Library, 156, 177, 249–251
Darwin Museum, Moscow, 176, 195, 216, 349
Davies, Jacob, 45
Davies, Rees, 45, 443
Delacour, Jean, 186
Delaware Art Museum, 173, 193, 251
Dendroica pinus, 28, 308
Denmark, complete set in, 175, 195, 196, 343–344
Dennis, George, 199
Dennisville, Me., 68, 73, 75
Derby, Lord Stanley, Earl of, 5, 19, 166, 182
deRham, H. C., Jr., 154–155, 443
Deutsche Demokratische Republik, complete set in, 176, 195, 196, 344–345
Devonshire, Duke of, 195, 331
Dick, John Henry, 194, 251–252
Dickson, James, 443
Dodge, A. Douglas, 396
Dodge, Bayard, 396
Dodge, Cleveland E., 395, 396
Dodge, W. E., 419
Donkin, Armorer, 15, 164, 197, 443
Donnell, John S., 78, 182, 443
Double-crested cormorant, 396
Douglas, Harriet, 13, 61, 153, 419
Doves, 52, 53, 59, 63, 71, 119, 203, 396
Dowitcher, 81
Downy woodpecker, 395
Drawings, Audubon's, 59, 261
  for benefactors, 5
  classes, by size, 38
  of eggs, 95–96, 386
  exhibitions, *see* Exhibitions, Audubon's
  positions of birds in, 34, 132, 133
  sent to Kidd, 361–362
  size of, 8
  of water birds, 78–79
  See also specific names of birds
Ducks, 19, 74, 81, 89, 95, 131, 200, 201, 202, 203, 205, 396, 397
Duer, W. D., 138
Duke University, 193, 215, 252–253
Dunbar, Rev. Mr., 28, 443
Duncan, Garnett, 64, 160, 443
Dusky albatross, 397
Dyer, Joseph C., 45, 168–169, 443

Eagles, 30, 71–72, 119, 205, 395
Eastport, Me., 73
Eckley, David, 290, 320
Edgeworth, Maria, 6
Edinburgh
  1826 visit to, 8–14
  1827 visit to, 21
Edinburgh, University of, 12, 142, 164, 175, 195, 218, 341, 443, 452
Edmondson, Thomas, 157, 304, 443
Eggs, drawings of, 95–96, 386
Eglin, John, 452
Egret, 204
Eider duck, 200, 201, 202, 203, 205
Eire, set in, 195, 345–346
Elgin, Joseph, 443
Ellames, Patterson, 443, 452
Elley, Charles, 443
Ellison, Henry, 168, 443
Emberiza pallida, 308
England, 195
  Audubon journeys in and to, *see* Journeys, Audubon's
  complete sets in, 175, 196
  incomplete set in, 178, 196
  prices of folios in, 198–200
  See also London
"English Pheasants Surprised by a Spanish Dog," 18, 188
Engraving operations
  Audubon's anxiety about, 63
  begun by Lizars, 11, 16
  chronology, 399–400
  costs of, 26, 93
  English engraver suggested, 4
  engravers, *see* Havell, Robert, Jr.; Lizars, William Home
  Mrs. Audubon's and Victor's letters about, 63–65
  payment for, 112
  transfer from Lizars to Havell, 23–26
Engravings
  alphabetical index to, 210, 265, 401–415
  composite, 295–296, 307–309
  copper plates, 112, 153, 380–381, 390–395
  cost of publishing, 26
  faults in, 64, 82
  instructions on, 52–53, 213–214
  letter, faults in, 52
  loose prints, *see* Loose prints
  number of, and work schedule, 53
  numbering, variations in, 210, 265–266
  reproductions, *see* Reproductions
  size of, 7, 8, 71, 210
  variations in legends and water-marks, 209–224, 230, 234–235, 263, 265, 286, 295, 315, 324, 326, 348, 421–439
Essex Institute, 417

Index

European robin, 5, 261
Evans, Daniel W., 218, 220, 221
Evans, Mrs. Daniel W., 194, 256–257
Evening grosbeak, 296
Everett, A. H., 138, 247, 248
Everett, Edward, 39, 41, 52, 57–58, 62, 235, 270, 271
Exhibitions, Audubon's
  1826, in Edinburgh, 9
  1826, in Liverpool, 5–6
  1826, in Manchester, 6, 8
  1827, in Liverpool, 19, 22
  1827, in London, 17
  1827, in Manchester, 15
  1828, in Paris, 32
  1829, in New York, 37
  1830, in Baltimore, 39, 40, 255
  1830, in Birmingham, 43
  1830, in Manchester, 43
  1830, in York, 45
  1832 or 1833, at Boston Athenaeum, 72
  1832 and 1835, at Providence Athenaeum, 302–303
Expeditions, Audubon's
  to Florida, 56–60, 62–63
  to Labrador, 73–75
  to Louisiana and Texas, 102–103
  to New Brunswick and Maine, 68
  to New Jersey, 38

Faile, Thomas H., 97, 154, 443
Fairman, Gideon, 4
Falco dispar, 94
Falco Harrisii, 189–190
Falcon, 75, 76, 119, 396, 398
Fane, Mrs. Barbara, 195, 331
Feathers, drawing of, 382
Female wild turkey, 130–131, 203, 220
Ferguson, Mrs. Hamilton Nisbit, 443
Ferruginous thrush, 66, 203, 205
Field Museum of Natural History, 113, 169, 173, 182, 194, 416
Finches, 73–74, 75, 218–219, 308, 326
Fire, sets destroyed by, 184–185, 196, 281
Fitzwilliam, Hon. W. C. Wentworth, 28, 138, 163, 175, 195, 332–333, 443
Flamingo, 63, 95
Flicker, 133, 203, 395
Florida, expeditions to, 56–60, 62–63
Florida cormorant, 63
Flycatchers, 27, 52, 54, 68, 82, 187, 201, 205, 212, 213, 223, 396, 398
Ford, Mrs., 153, 233–234, 443
Forest and Stream, 368–369, 392, 394
Forked-tailed petrel, 56, 265–266
Forster, Thomas, 443
Forster's tern, 397

Fort, Lawrence, 20, 443
Foster, Mrs. John, 443
Foulis, M., 444, 452
Foulis, Mrs., 443
Foundations, sets at, 194
Fourcher, Mrs. Kirk, 397
Fowls, 19
Fox, Charles, 91, 169, 346, 444
Fox, George Lane, 169, 199, 346, 444
France, 195
  complete sets in, 176, 196, 345
  incomplete set in, 179, 196
  journey to, 1828, 31–34
  Minister of the Interior, 33, 139, 146, 168
Frigate pelican, 63, 89, 396
Fringilla amoena, 308
Fringilla coerulea, 66
Fringilla lincolnii, 73
Fringilla maculata, 308
Fringilla oregona, 308
Fringilla pensylvanica, 222
Fringilla purpurea, 218–219, 326
Fringilla vespertina, 308
Frost, Thomas, 168, 444
Fuertes, Louis Agassiz, 132–133
Fuligula albola, 81
Fulmar petrels, 56

Gadwall duck, 81
Gallatin, Albert, 18, 269
Gallery of Illustrious Americans, 128
Gallinule, 95
Galveston Bay, 103
Galvin, John, 195, 345–346
Gambier, William, 444
Gannet, 201
Garnett, Robert H., 20, 92, 444
Gaston, William, 83, 84, 105, 138, 157, 197, 261–262, 444
  first meeting with Audubon, 60–61
  help given to Audubon, 62
Gates, Thomas, 182
Geddings, E., 78, 85, 158, 444
Gee, Robert, 444
Geese, 204, 205, 396, 397
"Gentleman of Boston," 70, 138
George IV, 18, 19, 177, 178, 188, 388, 444, 452
Georgia Museum of Art, 180
Germany
  complete set in, 176, 195, 196, 344–345
  Woodward's list of sets in, 419
Gibson, Rev. Mr., 444
Gifford, Euphemia, 54, 87, 169, 182, 197, 257–259, 444
Gilman, Samuel, 58
Gilmor, Robert, 40, 57, 61, 156, 253–256, 270, 272, 417, 444

INDEX

Glasgow, College of, 21, 145, 166, 175, 195, 219, 333, 444
Glasgow, 1827 visit to, 21–22
Glasgow, Royal Faculty of Physicians and Surgeons, 178
Glasgow, University of, 21
Glasgow Corporation Public Libraries, 175, 195
Glossy ibis, 95
Godwits, 63, 95, 397
Golden-crested wren, 71
Golden eagle, 71–72
Golden-eye duck, 205
Golden-winged warbler, 94
Golden-winged woodpecker, 133, 203, 395
Goodrich, Lloyd, 130
Gordon, Alexander, 5, 16
Gordon, Anne, 5, 46
Gott, Benjamin, 44, 147, 444
Gott, John, 231, 444
Göttingen, University Library, 419
Gould, John, 88, 444
Grackles, 71, 119, 221–222, 295, 396
Graham, Lieutenant-General, 444, 452
Grand Manan Island, 73
Grant, D., 20, 92, 444
Graves, J. K., 187-188
Graves, James, 419
Gray tyrant, 63, 82, 212
"Great American Cock" legend, 210, 215, 234–235, 315, 326, 333
"Great American Hen and Young" legend, 203, 220, 235, 333, 395
Great American shrike, 75, 76
Great black-backed gull, 131
Great blue heron, 201, 204, 396
Great Egg Harbor, N.J., 38
Great-footed hawk, 119
Great marbled godwit, 63
Great northern diver, 397
Great Pine Swamp, N.J., 38
Great tern, 95, 397
Great white heron, 63, 93, 200, 396
"Great Work," see Birds of America (Double Elephant folio)
Greater yellowlegs, 397
Grebes, 396
Green heron, 95
Greenshank, 200, 201, 205
Greenwood, E. A., 98, 156, 444
Greg, Samuel, 164–165, 444
Grenville, J. G., 444
Grimshaw, James, 97, 116–117, 160–161, 444
Grosbeaks, 66, 95, 296, 308, 397
Groton School, 159, 173, 195, 259–260, 395, 417
Ground doves, 59, 71
Grouse, 68, 71, 75, 76, 119
Gulls, 95, 103

Gurney, John Henry, 291, 331
Gurney, Joseph John, 166, 291, 331, 444, 452
Gyrfalcon, 396

Haarlem Library, Holland, 91, 148, 169, 176, 195, 347, 445
Haggerty, Ogden, 154, 445
Haigh, Thomas, 20, 445, 452
Hairy woodpecker, 94
Hall, Captain Basil, 9, 254
Hall, Lady Ellen, 21, 452
Halsey, Stephen A., 155, 445
Hanaburgh, E. F., 211
Hancock, Mr., 61, 64
Hardman, Thomas, 445, 452
Hardwicke, Earl of, 171, 296, 445
Hardwicke, Major General Thomas, 171, 328–329, 445
Hare Harbor, 74
Harlan, Richard, 3, 34, 39, 56, 61, 98, 101, 153, 225, 228, 445
Harlequin duck, 200, 201, 397
Harris, Edward, 56–57, 61, 73, 80–81, 85, 91, 94, 99, 102, 103, 104, 108–109, 122, 155, 156, 201, 227, 261, 304, 445
Harris, Joseph, 445
Harris's hawk, 397
Harris's woodpecker, 397
Harvard College (now University), 13, 68, 70, 98, 113, 138, 148, 152, 173, 177, 182, 193, 211, 223, 260-262, 389, 417, 420, 445
Haslam, S. H., 445
Hastings, Baron, 199, 241
Hastings, Eastburn, 417
Havell, George F., 397
Havell, Luke, 24
Havell, Robert, Jr., 18, 22, 38, 39, 41, 45, 46, 47, 52, 61, 75, 82, 84, 115, 125, 188, 209, 210–211, 234, 248, 257, 312–313, 337, 364, 399–400, 416
and coloring, see Coloring
departure for America, 112, 113
first meeting with Audubon, 24–25
letters from Audubon to, 41, 42–43, 45, 46, 53, 56, 57, 67, 68–69, 77, 85, 93, 111–112, 169–170, 212–214, 226, 229, 271, 291–292, 315, 390
letters from Lucy and Victor Audubon to, 53, 63–66, 113, 258–259, 307, 365, 366
Havell, Robert, Sr., 25
Havell's tern, 397
Hawk owl, 397
Hawks, 64, 94, 119, 189–190, 395, 397, 398
Hay, R. H., 445, 452
Head, George H., 50, 51–52, 229, 445
Hearne, Mr., 168, 445
Heathcote, John, 166, 284, 445
Heppenstall, John, 188, 199
Herons, 34, 63, 93, 95, 131, 200, 201, 202–205, 396

492

Index

Herrick, Francis H., 132–133, 211, 291, 361
Herring gull, 396
Hertford, Countess of, 445, 452
Hesketh, Lord, 164, 195, 333–334
Hesse Homburg, Landgravine, 54
Heywood, Benjamin A., 452
Heywood, Thomas, 20, 445
Hibbert, George, 445
Hibbert, John, 452
James J. Hill Reference Library, 173, 194, 264
Hindley, Robert, 445, 452
Historical societies, 194
History Institute of America, 370
Hitchcock, Henry, 102, 162, 445
Hodgsons, 5
Holme, Edward, 20, 445
Hone, Philip, 83, 128, 153
Hooded merganser, 89
Hooded warbler, 203, 295, 308
Hopkins, Major Robert E., 188–189
Hornblower, Ralph, 183
Horned grebe, 396
House of Representatives, 39, 40
House wren, 395
Houston, Samuel, 103
Howland, George, Jr., 119
Hoyle, Thomas, 446
Hudson Bay titmouse, 396
Hughes, J. J., 97, 161, 446
Humboldt, Baron, 6
Hummingbirds, 64, 71, 202, 203, 395
Humphrey, George, 92, 446
Hunt, John, 105, 161, 446
Hunterian Museum, 21
Henry E. Huntington Library and Art Gallery, 173, 193, 241, 262
Hussey, P., 446
Hutchins's barnacle goose, 396

Ibis, 89, 95, 200, 201, 202, 397
Icterus baltimore, 309
Icterus tricolor, 309
Illinois, University of, 174, 193, 216, 314–315
Index, alphabetical, to *Birds of America*, 401–415
Indiana Historical Society, 166, 173, 194, 215, 216, 223, 262–263
Indiana, University of, 173, 190, 193, 202, 224, 263–264, 389
Indigo bird, 64
Ingalls, William, 73, 320
Institut de France, 33, 146, 168, 176, 195
Institute of Zoology, Academy of Science, Warsaw, 179
Institutions, 194
Iowa State Library, 416
Ireland, complete sets in, 176, 196, 345–348
Irving, Washington, 78, 100–101, 277

Italy, complete set in, 176, 196, 346
Ithaca Public Library, 183

Jackson, Andrew, 4, 7, 39, 83, 100, 101, 104, 269, 270, 388
Jackson, Daniel and Peter, 446, 452
Jackson, P. T., 67, 155, 344, 446, 452
Jaeger, 396
Jameson, Robert, 8, 9, 12, 13, 48, 87, 336
Japan, possible folio in, 123, 189, 339
Jardine, Sir William, 10, 22, 24, 28, 48, 65, 88, 419, 446
Jays, 200, 201, 202, 205, 309, 395, 397
Jenkins, John Carmichael, 189–190
Jesup, Morris K., 419
Jim Thorpe, Pa., 38
Johns, Wm. C., 418
Johns Hopkins University, 173, 193, 216, 265, 397
Johnson, Grace Phillips, estate, 194, 217, 218, 265–266
Johnson, J. Alex., 418
Johnson, Mrs. Phil. S., 416
Johnson, Robert D., 396
Johnson, William Garret, 39
Johnson Reprint Corporation, 373
Johnston, John Taylor, 125, 306–307, 417, 420
Joint Committee of the Library of Congress, 40
Joseph, J. L., 73, 153, 446
Journeys, Audubon's
  1826, Edinburgh to London, 14–17
  1826, to England, 3–5
  1826, Liverpool to Edinburgh, 6–8
  1827, to northern England, 14–16, 231–232
  1827, "Grand Tour" to collect funds, 19–22
  1828, to Oxford and Cambridge, 28–29
  1828, to Paris, 31–34
  1829, to America, 36–37, 225–226
  1830, to Edinburgh, 44–46
  1831, Edinburgh to London, 54–55
  1831, to America, 56, 271
  1833, from New York to Charleston, 77–78
  1834, to England, 84–86
  1835, to Manchester, 92
  1836, to America, 96–97
  1836, to Charleston, 100–101
  1837, to England, 105
  1839, to America, 113–114
  1840, to New England, 118–119
  1842, to Canada, 120–122
  1843, to West, 122
Junco, 205

Kellogg, J. Stewart, 396
Kemble, William H., 190, 199
Kennedy, John, 45, 446
Kent, Edward G., 190
Kentucky warbler, 201

INDEX

Key West dove, 63, 396
Kidd, Joseph Bartholomew, 13, 119, 360–367
Kildeer plover, 89
Kimberly-Clark Corporation, 372
King, James G., 73, 153, 183, 446
King, Thomas Butler, 61, 84, 158, 446
Kingsborough, Right Hon. Viscount, 38, 446
Kingston, Canada, 121
Kinnoul, Lord, 112, 419, 446, 452
Kirkpatrick, G. ("Kirk Patrick"), 167, 291–292, 448
Kluckauf, Dr. Walter Z., 190
Knight, James, 446
Krudener, Baron, 39, 40, 349, 446

Labrador, expedition to, 73–75
Labrador duck, 74
Labrador falcon, 75, 76, 396
Lafayette, General, 6
Lake Sabine, Texas, 103
Herbert Lang et Cie. AG, 373
Large-headed burrowing owl, 398
"Large Work," *see Birds of America* (Double Elephant folio)
Lark, 75, 76, 223–224
Lark-bunting, 255
Larking, John Winfield, 199
Laval Université, 173, 193, 219, 266–267
Lawrence, Sir Thomas, 6, 18, 327
Lawson, Mansfeldt de C., 446
Lawson, Thomas, 4
Lazuli finch, 308
Leach's petrels, 56
Least bittern, 89
Least tern, 95
Ledger "B," 20, 31, 32, 33, 38, 40, 52, 73, 115, 123, 139, 151–171, 188, 197–198, 229, 233, 249, 268, 272–273, 274, 277–278, 288, 297, 310, 317, 326, 327–329, 334, 363–364, 452
Leeds, 15, 20, 92, 231–232, 253
Leeds Philosophical and Literary Society, 15, 143, 164, 231, 446
Legends
　Audubon's instructions on, 52–53, 213–214
　variations in, 209–224, 234–235, 263, 265, 324, 326, 348, 421–439
Lehigh University, 173, 193, 268
Lehman, George, 38, 56, 59, 65
Leibold, Mrs. Carl Peter, 183
Leningrad Academy of Sciences, 170, 176, 195, 215
Lenox, J., 117, 123
Lenox Library Associates, 180
Lenox set, 173, 292–293, 418
Lesser black-headed titmouse, 82, 212
Lesser redpoll, 75
Lestris richardsonii, 212
Libraries, sets in, 194–195

Library Company of Baltimore, 40
Library of Congress, 61, 62, 85, 101, 105, 141, 151, 173, 194, 216, 269–281, 418, 446
Limerick House, 186
Lincoln, Thomas, 73, 74, 75
Lincoln's finch, 73–74, 75
Linnaean Society, 17, 30
Literary and Philosophical Society of Newcastle on Tyne, 14–15, 143
Little beautiful owl, 108
Little Maccatina Harbor, 74
Little night owl, 398
Little owl, 75, 76
Liverpool
　1826 visit to, 5–6
　1827 visits to, 16, 22
Liverpool Public Libraries, 175, 195, 216, 335–336
Liverpool Royal Institution, exhibition at, 5–6
Lizars, Daniel, 21, 28
Lizars, John, 452
Lizars, William Home, 4, 12, 16, 29, 35, 209, 210–211, 399
　Audubon's difficulties with, 23–24
　concludes work with Audubon, 21
　meets Audubon, 10–11
Lloyd, Edward, 165, 446
Lockwood, Amelia Jane Havell, 24, 25
Loggerhead shrikes, 131, 205
London, 54
　1827 visit to, 17–19
　1828 visit to, 27–31
　1834 visit, 86–88
　Victor Audubon sent to, 62, 65, 68–70
London, University of, 170, 389
Londonderry, Charles William Stewart, 3d marquis of, 20–21, 447
London Institution, 91, 149, 169–170, 447
Long-billed curlew, 89, 200, 201, 203, 204
Long Island Historical Society, 417
Long-legged avocet, 95
Longman & Company, 447
Long-tailed jaeger, 396
Loon, 397
Loose prints, 116, 235, 251
　collections of, 179–180, 196
　original cost, 198
　prices asked for, 200–205, 261
　uncolored, 383–384
Loudon's *Magazine of Natural History*, 30, 79, 131
Louisiana, legislature of, 61, 147, 152, 282–283, 446
Louisiana hawk, 189–190, 397
Louisiana heron, 202, 396
Louisiana State Museum, 152, 173, 195, 282–283
Louisiana State University, 171, 177, 193, 220, 283–284
Louisiana tanager, 309

Index

Louis Philippe I, 33, 44, 162–163, 267, 268
Low, Cornelius, 73, 153, 447
Lowell, Amy, 245–246
Lownes, Albert E., 236, 396
Lyon, Daniel, 28, 447, 452

McCullough, Thomas, 74, 101
McGill University, 173, 193, 285–286, 389
MacGillivray, William, collaborator on *Ornithological Biography*, 48–49, 87–88, 102, 110, 133
McKinlay, Margaret A., 203, 204
McLane, Louis, 62
Macmillan Company, 368–370
McMurtry, Dr., 39, 50
Macy, R. H., 183, 203–204
Magazine of Natural History, 30, 79, 131
Magdalen Islands, 73
Magpie, 99, 397
Maine, 68, 73, 75
Mallard duck, 396
Manchester, 92
  1826 visit to, 6–7
  1827 visits to, 15–16, 20, 299
  1830 visit to, 42, 45
Manchester Society for the Promotion of Natural History, 144, 165, 447
Mangrove cuckoo, 63
Mangrove hummingbird, 71
Man-o'-war bird, 396
Maria's woodpecker, 397
Marryat, Frederic, 274
Marshall, John, 15, 164, 231, 253, 447
Marsh hawk, 397
Marsh hens, 89
Marsh tern, 95
Marsh wren, 68, 397
Martin, H. Bradley, 166, 194, 218, 221, 284
Martin, Maria, 79, 101, 177, 274
Martin, Richard S., 395, 396
Martins, 395
Marvin, Mrs. W. B., 397
Maryland, Legislature of, 152, 446
Maryland, state of, 73, 105, 148
Maryland State Library, 152, 174, 195, 310–311
Maryland yellow-throat, 295, 308
Massachusetts, General Court, Library of, 70, 138, 148, 151, 446
Massachusetts Historical Society, 70–71, 138, 388
Massachusetts State House Library, 173, 195, 209, 247–248
Massena, Prince of, 32, 33, 163, 447
Mauch Chunk, Pa., 38
Mayor, A. Hyatt, 131
Mechanics Mercantile Institute of San Francisco, 185
Meikleham, Dr., 12
Meleagris gallopavo, 52, 215–216, 220

Mellon, Paul, 194, 216, 218, 221, 286, 397
Melospiza lincolnii, 73–74
Mercantile Library Association, New York, 119–120, 123, 183, 418
Merrill, Adams Huse, 190–191, 416
Metcalf, Thomas, 111, 158, 447
Metropolitan Museum of Art, 381–382, 393, 395, 396, 397
Meyers brothers, 88
Michigan, legislature of, 152
Michigan, state of, 111, 150, 315–316, 317, 447
Michigan, University of, Library, 152, 174, 193, 315–318, 417
Miles, Philip John, 447
Milton, Right Hon. Viscount, 31, 168, 332, 447
Milwaukee Public Library, 173, 194, 287
Minister of the Interior, France, 33, 139, 146, 168
Minneapolis Athenaeum, 173, 193, 287
Minnesota, University of, 194, 218, 224, 318
Mitchell Library, 175, 195, 336
Mobile, Ala., 102
Mockingbird, 203, 309, 395
Mongin, John David, 62, 157, 158, 447
Moore, Hannah, 6
Morgan, Charles, 119
Morgan, J. Pierpont, 419
Pierpont Morgan Library, 174, 194, 215, 219, 300
Morris, John B., 40, 57, 61, 156–157, 198, 255, 310, 416, 447
Morton, Countess of, 12, 138, 447, 452
Morton, Samuel G., 105, 110, 226–227
Morton Arboretum, 180
Mountain mocking bird, 309
Mourning doves, 119
Mourning warbler, 81
Murphy, Robert Cushman, 50, 130–131, 133, 382
Muscicapa bonapartii, 219
Muscicapa cooperi, 82, 212
Muscicapa matinatus, 82, 212
Muscicapa selbii, 223, 308
Musée National d'Histoire Naturelle, 33, 286, 345
Museum of Fine Arts, Boston, 173, 193, 288–289
Museums, sets in, 194, 195

Nashville warbler, 201
Natashquan River, 73, 74
National Academy of Sciences, 194, 216, 306
National Audubon Society, 173, 193, 289, 374–375, 376, 378, 389
National Gallery of Art, 173, 193, 224, 289–291, 366–367, 369, 374
Natural History, British Museum of, 175, 325–327
Neal, John, 68, 70, 447
Neill, Patrick, 10
Netherlands, complete set in, 176, 195, 196, 347
New Bedford, Free Library, 173, 194, 209, 259
New Brunswick, Canada, 68, 173, 194, 209, 221

INDEX

Newcastle upon Tyne, 14–15, 20–21, 143, 251–252
New Jersey, 38
New Orleans, 102
New York, state of, 73, 148, 446
New York Botanical Garden, 380, 395, 396
New York City, 72, 85, 97, 115, 339
New York City Hall Library, 417
New York Graphic Society, 370–371
New-York Historical Society, 30, 173, 194, 215, 291–292, 395
New York Public Library, 40, 173–174, 180, 194, 218, 292–295, 417, 418
New York Society Library, 113, 174, 194, 223, 224, 295–296, 418
New York State Library, 152, 185, 417
New York Zoological Society, 395
Nicholas I of Russia, 118, 123, 349
Night hawk, 131
Night heron, 204, 396
Noddy tern, 63
Nolte, Vincent, 4
Norcliffe, Major, 447, 452
North Carolina State Library, 174, 195, 296
Northern Ireland, set in, 347–348
Northumberland, Duke of, 91, 170–171, 283–284, 447
Northumberland, visits to, 14–15
Northwestern Mutual Life Insurance Company, 370
Northwestern University, 171, 174, 193, 224, 296, 419
Norton Art Gallery, 174, 193, 297
Nuthatch, 397
Nutt, Haller, 123–124
Nuttall, Thomas, 68, 96, 98–99, 100
Nuttall's lesser marsh wren, 68
Nuttall's starling, 309

Oakes, William, 70, 98, 159, 417, 447
Oberlin College, 180
Ogilvie, W., 447
Olive-sided flycatcher, 68
Ord, George, 3, 4, 79, 228
Ord, James Pickering, 167, 447
Oregon snow finch, 308
Orioles, 43, 202, 203, 270, 309, 395
Orléans, Duc d', 32, 33, 138, 162–163, 447
Orléans, Duchesse d', 32, 33, 163
Orléans, Mademoiselle d', 163, 268, 447
Ornithological Biography, 20, 21, 28, 32, 34, 46, 47, 60, 62–63, 65, 67, 70, 88–90, 94, 100, 101, 107, 110, 111, 113, 123, 139, 151, 179, 189, 199, 241, 261, 264, 271, 279, 286, 290, 310, 318–319, 321, 343
American edition, 50–51, 88
anatomical studies in, 94, 108
collaboration with MacGillivray, 48–49, 87–88, 102, 110, 133
critical reception, 51
manuscript in Johnson collection, 266
price, 50
Ornithology (Bonaparte), 3, 4, 280
Ornithology (Wilson), 48
Orpheus montanus, 309
"Otter in a Trap," 6
Otters, 6, 19
Owls, 75, 76, 108, 395, 397, 398
Oxford, 1828 visit to, 28, 29
Oxford University, 29, 146, 167, 175, 195, 220, 221, 336–338, 447
Oystercatcher, 89

Painted bunting, 116
Paintings, 17, 19
  "Black Cocks," 13, 30
  "Black Vulture Attacking the Head of Deer," 39
  cuckoos on pawpaws, 11
  "English Pheasants Surprised by a Spanish Dog," 18, 188
  Kidd reproductions, 13, 119, 360–367
  original, reproductions of, 381–382
  "Otter in a Trap," 6
  "Pheasants Attacked by Fox," 13
  "Turkey Cock with Hen and Nine Young," 6, 9
  western birds, 99, 100, 101
  "Wild Pigeons," 13
Paisley, Corporation of, Public Library, 175, 195, 215, 338–340, 419
Panic of 1837, 103–104
Paris, Audubon visit to, 1828, 178
Parker, C. R., 30, 31
Parkman, George, 67–68, 72, 83, 84, 155, 159, 187, 260, 320
Parrots, 202
Parry, Francis Charles, 448
Parsons, John E., 397
Partridge, 19, 64
Parus caroliniensis, 212
Passenger pigeon, 64, 201, 203
Paul, John Jay, 191–192
Peabody Institute Library, Peabody, Mass., 174, 194, 297
Peabody Institute of the City of Baltimore, 40, 156
Peabody Museum, Salem Mass., 159, 174, 194, 297–298
Peale, Robert Rembrandt, 3
Peale, Titian, 3
Pearson, Rev. Henry, 447, 448, 452
Peck, Clara S., 194, 298
Peers, Charles, 448, 452
Pelicans, 63, 89, 103, 131, 396, 397
Pennsylvania, University of, 174, 194, 318–319

Index

Peregrine falcon, 119
Perkins, Thomas, 61, 67, 68, 152, 155, 234, 320, 448
Perry, William, 183
Perry expedition to Japan, 123, 189, 339
Peters, Samuel J., 116–117, 123
Petrels, 56, 265–266
Pflaumer, Alfred F., 194, 299
Pheasants, 13, 18, 188
"Pheasants Attacked by Fox," 13
Philadelphia, 3, 39, 56, 65, 77–78, 85, 98–99, 225–226, 227
Philippe I of France, 33, 44, 162–163, 267, 268, 448
Phillips, Benjamin, 170, 448
Phillips, Colonel Lloyd, 91
Phillips, Rawlston D., Jr., 215, 216, 220, 221, 299
Phillips Academy, 174, 195, 300
Phillips's woodpecker, 397
Philosophical Society, Philadelphia, 61
Pica nuttalli, 99
Pickman, Elizabeth L., 98, 159, 297–298, 448
Picton Reference Library, Liverpool, 222, 223, 335–336
Pictou, Nova Scotia, 74
Pied oystercatcher, 89
Pigeons, 13, 19, 34, 63, 64, 99, 201, 203, 205, 396
Pine grosbeak, 95, 397
Pine warbler, 28, 308
Pinnated grouse, 71
Pipiry flycatcher, 82, 212
Pitois, Monsieur, 33, 168, 448
Pittsburgh, University of, 174, 194, 319
Plates, *see* Copper plates; Engravings
Plectrophanes smithii, 255
Plovers, 89, 95, 204, 309, 324
Poland, incomplete set in, 179, 196
Pomarine jaeger, 396
Ponsonby, Hon. William S., 448
Ponton, Thomas, 452
Portland, Duke of, 195, 340
Portland (Ore.), Library Association of, 173, 194, 268
Portugal, complete set in, 176, 195, 196, 348
Potter, James, 61, 157, 262, 448
Potter, Nathaniel, 40, 57, 61, 85, 140, 255, 293, 419, 448
Potts, John, 448
Poultney, Evan, 78, 84, 274
Pratt, G. W., 67, 156, 448
Enoch Pratt Free Library, 40, 156, 173, 194, 253–256
Pratt Memorial Library, Cohasset, Mass., 395
Prime, Edward, 73, 153, 448
Prime, J. V. L., 418
Princeton University, 52, 154, 174, 193, 220, 300, 393, 395, 417
Prints, reproductions, 368–374

Promotional activity, 7, 13–16, 17, 19, 22, 28–29, 30–33, 37, 44–45, 59, 77–78, 90–92, 97, 197
Prospectus, 7, 19, 32, 138, 197, 227, 385–389
Prothonotary warbler, 25–26, 201, 203, 211, 217–218
Providence Athenaeum, 70, 148, 152, 174, 193, 219, 223, 224, 301–303, 381, 418, 448
Ptarmigan, 76
Purple finch, 218, 326
Purple gallinule, 95
Purple grackle, 119, 221–222, 295
Purple heron, 204, 205
Purple martin, 395
Pygmy nuthatch, 397

Quadrupeds, see *Viviparous Quadrupeds of North America*
Quaritch, 419–420
Quebec, 120
Quincy, Josiah, 138, 261
Quiscalus versicolor, 221

Rabbits, painting of, 19
Raeburn, Sir Henry, 87
Rails, 89, 95, 103
Rathbone, Mrs., 165, 448
Rathbone, Richard, 4, 5
Rathbone, William, 5, 16, 17
Rathbone family, 5, 6, 22, 41, 60, 261
Rattlesnakes, 78, 79
Raven, 53, 395
Ravensworth, Right Hon. Countess of, 163, 448
Ray, Robert, 73, 153, 264, 448
Raymond, Aaron, 418
Rea, Mrs. James, 398
Reader's Digest, 371
Red-bellied woodpecker, 75, 76, 94
Red-breasted snipe, 81
Red-cockaded woodpecker, 94
Reddish egret, 204
Red-eyed vireo, 396
Red-headed duck, 205, 397
Red-headed woodpecker, 201
Redouté, Pierre Joseph, 32, 33, 448
Red-shouldered hawk, 119, 395
Red-tailed hawk, 64
Red-winged blackbird, 205
Reed, Joseph Verner, 137, 164, 194, 231, 304–305
Reed, L., 73
Rees, William J., 84, 158–159, 448
Reeves, John G., 43, 168, 325, 448
Reproductions
 china, 376–378
 chromolithograph plates, 124, 185, 188. 275, 307, 355–359
 color slides, 374–375
 Kidd paintings, 13, 119, 360–367

INDEX

Reproductions—*Continued*
   of original paintings, 381–382
   prints, 368–374
   silver ingot collection, 376
   silver plate, 375–376
   stamps, 380
   textiles, 378–379
Rhodes, Miss, 448
Richardson's yeager, 212
Richmond, Va., 57
Ridgely, David, 310–311
Ridgway, Joseph, 448, 452
Ridgway, Thomas, 448, 452
Rigby, George H., 418
Ring plover, 95
Rippon, Cuthbert, 449
Robins, 5, 202, 261, 395
Rodman, Samuel, 119
Rogers, Lewis, 154, 449
Roman, André Bienvenue, 102
Roscoe, Edward, 8
Roscoe, William S., 5, 6, 7, 8, 137, 449
Roscoe family, 17
Roscoe's yellow-throat, 296, 308
Roseate spoonbill, 50, 95, 201, 202, 203
Rosedown Plantation, 192, 396, 397
Rothschild, Baron Nathan Mayer, 61, 90–91, 326–327, 449
Rothschild, Lionel Walter, 91, 326
Rough-legged falcon (hawk), 398
Rowell, Donald, 396
Royal Academy of Sciences, Paris, 31–32
Royal Faculty of Physicians and Surgeons, Glasgow, 178
Royal Institut of France, 33, 146, 168, 176, 195
Royal Library, Windsor, 175, 195, 216, 220, 222, 224, 340–341
Royal tern, 93
Royal Worcester Porcelain Company, 377–378
Ruby-crowned wren, 75
Ruby-throated hummingbird, 202, 203, 395
Ruddy plover, 309, 324
Ruffed grouse, 119
Russell, Gurdon W., 312–313, 416
Russia, *see* Union of Soviet Socialist Republics
Rusty grackle, 396
Rutland, Duke of, 163, 449
Rutter, John, 164, 449
John Rylands Library, 175, 195, 216, 223, 335

St. Augustine, Florida, 59–60
St. John's River, 60
St. Louis Mercantile Library Association, 174, 194, 305–306, 417
Salem Athenaeum, 98, 152, 183, 417, 449
Sanderling, 324
Sandhill crane, 396

Sandpipers, 89, 95, 103, 396
Sandwich tern, 63
Savannah, Ga., 60–61, 62
Say, Thomas, 3
Scarlet ibis, 95, 201, 202, 397
Scarlet tanager, 94–95, 309
Schinz's sandpiper, 396
Schmidt, Gustavus, 67, 161, 449
Schnering, Philip B., 395
Schools, sets at, 195
Scolopax courlan, 95
Scolopax grisea, 81
Scolopax novaboracensis, 81
Scotland
   Audubon in, 8–14, 21
   complete sets in, 175, 196
   incomplete sets in, 178, 196
Scott, Anne, 9
Scott, Sir Walter, 6, 9, 87
Seabury, Joseph, 118–119, 123
Selby, Prideaux John, 8, 9, 10, 14, 21, 22, 24, 28, 65, 88, 449
Selby's flycatcher, 52, 201, 223, 295, 308
Sergeant, E. W., 27, 449, 452
Sexton, Eric H. L., 389
Seymore, Ex-Gov., 418
Sharpe, John, 449, 452
Sharpe, Rev. A., 449
Shattuck, George C., 67, 72, 98, 155, 184, 187, 249, 320, 449
Shattuck, George C., Jr., 73, 187, 320, 321
Shearwater, 397
Shelburne Museum, 180
Shepard, Mrs. Helen Gould, 184
Shore lark, 75, 76
Shorteared owl, 398
Shrike, 75, 76, 131, 205
Silver ingot collection, 376
Silver plate, 375–376
Simeon, Viscount, 139, 146, 168, 449
Simon, S., 199
Sitwell, Sacheverell, 132
Small green-crested flycatcher, 396
Small-headed flycatcher, 54
"Small Work," *see* Birds of America (Octavo edition)
Smith (Baltimore), 449
Smith, Benjamin, 39, 168, 449
Smith, George, 449, 452
Smith, Gideon B., 157, 255
Smith, Maria Woodruff, 51, 449
Smith's lark-bunting, 255
Smithsonian Institution, 174, 194, 216, 306, 393, 395, 396, 397
Snow bird, 205
Snow bunting, 71
Snow goose, 397

498

Index

Snowy heron, 131, 200, 201, 203,
Snowy owl, 395
Society of Natural History, Charleston, 61
Society of Natural Sciences, Philadelphia, 59, 61
Society of Writers to His Majesty's Signet, 13, 142, 164, 331, 449
Solitary flycatcher, 205
Solitary sandpiper, 89
Sooty tern, 63
South Carolina, legislature, 58–59, 61, 76, 147, 151, 446
South Carolina, University of, 152, 174, 194, 212, 319–320
Southern California, University of, 152, 155, 174, 194, 219, 320–321
Sowler, Thomas, 113, 299
Sparrows, 71, 200–203, 222, 395
Spencer, Earl, 166, 449
Spoonbill, 50, 95, 201, 202, 203
Spotted grosbeak, 308
Spotted or Canada grouse, 68
Spotted sandpiper, 89
Spruce grouse, 68
Staatliches Museum, Germany, 176, 195, 196, 344
Stamps, 380
Stanley, Lord, 449
H. J. Lutcher Stark Foundation, 113, 125, 174, 177, 194, 215, 224, 306–309, 417, 420
Starling, 309
State Departments, 150, 151, 270
  folio sent to Japan, 123, 189, 339
  War Department copy, 101, 216, 276–281, 449
State libraries, sets at, 195
State Library, Leningrad, 118, 195, 349
Stearns, Dr., 416
Steller's jay, 397
Stephenson, Dr., 449, 452
Stewart, Alexander T., 419
Stuart, Robert L., 418
Stuart, William, 449
Stuart set, 174, 293
Sturgis, William, 70, 156, 288, 450
Stuyvesant, P. J., 72, 153, 450
Subscribers, 5, 12–16, 18–22, 28–29, 31–33, 38, 39, 44–45, 54, 56–57, 67, 68, 70–73, 78, 84, 91, 97, 98, 104–105, 111
  American, 139, 151–162
  collecting payment from, 19–20
  complaints, dealing with, 51–52
  discontinued, list of, 139
  engraved list, 52
  European, 139, 162–171
  final lists of, 151–171
  list in Ledger "B," 452
  list published by Audubon, 440–451
  mode of delivery to, 69
  original list, 20, 69, 137–139, 141–150, 305

solicitation, *see* Promotional activity
  to Octavo edition, 70–71, 118, 119, 305
  withdrawal of, 21, 28, 42, 51, 54, 55, 70, 84, 107, 108, 113
Subscription book, decision in favor of, 7, 137
Sully, Thomas, 3, 18, 39, 233–234, 386, 388
Swainson, William, 30, 31, 47–48, 130–131, 225, 332, 388, 389
Swainson's hawk, 397
Swallow, 94
Swallow-tailed hawk, 395
Swamp sparrow, 202, 203, 395
Swan, 34
Swartout, Samuel, 97, 100, 116, 154, 450
Swinburne, Sir John, 450
Sycamore, 99
Sylvia blackburniae, 308
Sylvia maritima, 81
Sylvia philadelphia, 81
Sylvia pinus, 28, 308
Sylvia protonotarius, 218
Sylvia rosco, 308
Sylvia tigrina, 81
Sylvia trichas, 308
Sylvia vigorsii, 28
Synopsis of the Birds of North America, 108, 110, 111, 113, 353
Syracuse University, 174, 193, 311

Tanagers, 309
Tanagra ludoviciana, 309
Tanagra rubra, 309
Taney, Roger B., 78
Telfair, Alexander, 61, 157–158, 450
Tell-tale godwit, 95, 397
Temminck, Coenraad Jacob, 6, 27, 88
Terns, 63, 89, 93, 95, 397
Tetrao umbellus, 119
Texas, 103
Textiles, reproductions on, 378–379
Thackeray, George, 28, 146, 167
Thayer, Col. John Eliot, 184
Thayer, Mrs. Brooks, 204
Theological Seminary, New Brunswick, N.J., 184
Thomason, John, 452
Thomson, Rev. John, 450
Thorndike, Augustus, 98, 156, 450
Thorne, Colonel, 97
Three-toed woodpecker, 397
Thrushes, 66, 68, 203, 205, 309
Tilden, Samuel J., 418
Tilden set, 173, 292–293
Titmice, 75, 81, 82, 94, 212, 396
Tobin, John, 91, 169, 450
Took, Dr., 51
Toronto, University of, 185
Toronto Public Library, 174, 194, 217, 311–312

INDEX

Townsend, John Kirk, 95, 98, 100, 107, 108
Trafford, Thomas Joseph, 20, 450, 452
Traill, Thomas S., 6, 8, 17, 22, 31, 87, 137
Traills, 5
Traill's flycatcher, 27, 205
Tree sparrow, 71
Treuttel and Wurtz, 450
Tringa arenaria, 309
Trinity College Library, Hartford, Conn., 125, 174, 193, 209, 218, 312-313, 416
Troopial, 309
Tropic bird, 63
Trudeau's tern, 397
Tudor, Frederic, 70, 72, 156, 450
Tulane University, 178, 217
Turdus narvius, 309
Turdus noevius, 309
Turkey buzzard, 79, 212
"Turkey Cock with Hen and Nine Young," 9, 11
Turkeys, 6, 9, 11, 101, 130-131, 181, 202, 203, 210, 215-216, 220, 295, 326, 395
Turnstone, 95
Turtle doves, 119
Tuscany, Grand Duke of, 91, 169, 347, 450
Tyler, Delia Tallman, 114
Tyler, Victor H., 137
Tylerian Library, Haarlem, Holland, 91, 148, 169, 176, 195, 347

Union College, Schenectady, N.Y., 122, 123, 174, 193, 214, 313-314, 339, 389
Union of Soviet Socialist Republics, 195
  complete sets in, 176, 196, 348-350
  collection of loose prints in, 180, 196
United States
  complete sets in, 172-174, 196
  distribution of sets in, 193-195
  government, help given to Audubon by, 57, 60, 62, 78, 100-101
  incomplete sets in, 177-178, 196
  loose prints in, 196
Universities, sets in, 193-194

Van Buren, Martin, 104, 105
Vanderbilt, Cornelius, 185, 418
Van Rensselaer, J., 97, 154, 450
Van Rensselaer, Stephen, 72, 153-154, 300, 450
Van Vleck, Howard A., 396
Varied thrush, 309
Vassar College, 164, 174, 194, 215, 322-323
Victoria, National Museum of, 178
Victoria, State Library of, 175, 195, 219, 343
Victoria and Albert Museum, 175, 223, 342
Vienna, Imperial Library at, 419
Vigors, Nicholas Aylward, 27-28, 108, 450
Vigor's vireo, 27, 28, 308
Vireos, 27, 28, 308, 396, 398

Virginian partridge, 395
Virginian rail, 89
Viviparous Quadrupeds of North America, 120, 121, 122, 123, 126, 189, 190, 191, 238, 243-244, 246, 300, 307, 313, 332-333, 340, 341

Walker, John, 450
Walker, Joseph E., 78, 289, 317, 450
Walker, Thomas, 15, 52, 164, 231-232, 450
Walker, Thomas (Ravenfield), 169, 450
Waller, Sir Walthen, 18, 19, 450
Wapitagun, 74
Warblers, *see* specific names
Ward, Henry, 56, 59, 65
Warde, Charles J., 170, 450
Warden, Mrs., 168, 450
War Department copy, 101, 216, 276-281, 449
Warren, John C., 72
Warren, William, 91
Wars, sets destroyed or lost in, 186, 196
Washington, D.C., 78, 100-101, 270, 271
Water bird specimens, search for, 56-60, 62-63
Watermarks, variations in, 209-224, 230, 265, 286, 295, 315, 324, 421-439
Waterton, Charles, 79-80
Webb, James Watson, 97, 116, 123, 450
Webster, Daniel, 98, 139-140, 156, 248, 249-251, 391, 450
Wernerian Society, Edinburgh, 9-10, 13, 142, 334, 450, 452
Wesleyan College, Middleton, Conn., 397
Western birds, paintings of, 99, 100, 101
Wetherell, John P., 56, 61, 153, 228, 451
Whippoorwill, 57, 131, 395
White-crowned pigeon, 63
White egret, 131
White-headed eagle, 119, 205
White-headed pigeon, 396
White heron, 95, 202
White ibis, 200, 201
White-rumped sandpiper, 396
White-throated sparrow, 222
White-winged crossbill, 75, 76, 95
Whooping crane, 11, 89, 200, 201, 203, 396
Widener, Peter A. B., 420
"Wild Pigeons," 13
"Wild Turkey Cock," 6, 11
"Wild Turkey" legend, 210
Wilks, Langdon, 186
Willet's family, 417
William IV, 19
Williams, Charles H., 237, 417
Williams, George Alfred, 24-25
Williams, W. H., 21, 452
Williams College, 174, 194, 217, 221, 223, 323
Willow grouse, 75, 76
Wilson, Alexander, 3, 4, 28, 48, 79, 81, 90, 280

Index

Wilson, James, 48, 87, 451, 452
Wilson, John, 51
Wilson, Mr., 452
Wilson's plover, 89, 204, 309
Windowe, Captain, 451, 452
Windsor Castle, set at, 175, 195, 216, 220, 222, 224, 340–341
Winter, Joseph, 451, 452
Winter hawk, 395
Winterthur Museum, 180, 204
Winter wren, 75, 76, 95
Winthrop, Thomas Lindell, 70–71, 138, 184
Wisconsin, University of, 174, 194, 321–322
Witham, Henry, 13, 164, 197, 333–334, 451, 452
Mitchell Wolfson Foundation, Inc., 173, 194, 287–288
Woman's Day, 372
Wood, G.W., 92, 165, 451
Woodbury, Levi, 62, 100, 101, 270, 277, 278, 280, 449
Woodcock, 89
Wood duck, 131
Wood ibis, 89, 200, 201
Woodpeckers, 71, 75, 76, 94, 201, 203, 395, 397
Woodward, Anthony, 416
Woodward, Robert B., 416
Woodward, W. A., 416
Work, William Tyler, 452

Wrens, 68, 71, 75, 76, 95, 395
Wright, Wm. P., 417

Yale University, 174, 194, 215, 216, 217, 218, 219, 220, 221, 222, 223, 224, 323–324, 389, 395, 396, 397, 416
Yarburgh, N. E., 451
Yarrel, Mr., 88
Yellow-bellied sapsucker, 396
Yellow-bellied woodpecker, 71, 396
Yellow-billed cuckoo, 201, 203, 211–212, 216–217, 268, 324, 326, 340, 348, 395
Yellow-billed magpie, 397
Yellow-breasted rail, 89
Yellow-breasted warbler, 295
Yellow-headed troopial, 309
Yellow red-poll warbler, 200, 201
Yellow warbler, 203
York, 15, 20, 45, 305
Yorkshire, 15, 20, 45
Yorkshire Philosophical Society, 15, 143, 164, 304–305, 451
York Subscription Library, 146, 166–167, 263, 451
Young, Thomas, 62, 157, 158, 451

Zenaida dove, 63
Zoological Institute, Academy of Sciences, Leningrad, 170, 176, 195, 215, 350
Zoological Society of London, 30

THE DOUBLE ELEPHANT FOLIO

Designed by Vladimir Reichl
Composed by the Printing Department
of the University of Chicago
in Monotype Bembo with display lines
in Monotype Centaur
Printed on Finch cream white Textbook Vellum
Cover design, suggested by Pauline A. Cianciolo,
printed by Superior Silkscreen Industries
on Joanna Buckram Natural Finish
Hand bound by DeLuxe Bindery
with spine in Whitman Bucksyn Levant